A THUNDERING WIND

An HISTORICAL NOVEL by
Gregory Barnes Watson

A Thundering Wind is an account of market hunting at the turn of the 20th century. Real people from history are depicted, but their stories have been fictionalized for this novel.

Cover design by: Gregory Barnes Watson
Cover art by: Doug Real
Book design by: Gregory Barnes Watson
Interior art by: Marilyn Posluszny
Layout by: Paula Dana

Inquiries can be made to:
Gregory Barnes Watson
194 Summerside Drive
Centralia, WA 98531
Phone: 360.736.1082
Fax: 360.807.6387
Email: jobyrn@comcast.net

And e'en while fashion's brightest arts decoy,
The heart distrusting asks if this be joy.

Oliver Goldsmith
(1730–1774)

Acknowledgments

Placing words onto a blank page is an agonizingly lonely process that can only be accomplished by the author, but it is never done in a vacuum. There is always inspiration which comes from many sources: one's surroundings, friends, family, personal experiences, spiritual beliefs, study, research, and history. As this is a work of fiction based upon historical events, people, and places, it has been my privilege to learn about extraordinary men and women, who, if they could speak for themselves, would modestly say, "I was only doing my job," "It's just a living," "I'm no one special," and "It's a gift from God." History gives us a better perspective in which to marvel at those who bravely came before us.

I may be responsible for the order of the words, but without the unwavering support and encouragement from my family and friends, this novel would not have been conceived, let alone finished. From the bottom of my heart to the tip of my pen-indented fingers, I want to acknowledge and thank each of you who spent mind-numbing hours online, or who scoured dusty bookshelves for the research that was required to accurately fill these pages. Your efforts were invaluable as I delved into a fascinating way of life that has passed into history.

With Extra Special Thanks to:

JoAnne Watson—Your many times unselfish and thankless job as gofer, typist, editor, and copy person, taking care of items that needed to be done, did not go unnoticed. I dearly cherish you.

Bill Einsig—Your willingness and courage to read an early draft, and then to gently suggest ways to improve the story was both insightful and appreciated.

Jane Currier, Currier House Bed and Breakfast—Your wonderful hospitality and sharing your rich heritage, specifically in regards to James A. Currier, was fascinating.

Ellsworth and Madelyn Shank—As kinsmen to Madison Mitchell, your memories of the world-class carver and the lives of wildfowl hunters has truly been a treasure.

Linda Wills—Your contribution of documentation of many of the historical figures: Bessie Coleman, Harriet Quinby, and Sir Ernest Shackleton to name a few, immeasurably helped to ensure authenticity. I am happily indebted for your generosity and always willing spirit.

Doug Real—Your artwork for the cover brings in vibrant detail which is the carver/hunter's craft. In this case, I hope the book is judged by the cover.

Marilyn Posluszny—Your lifelike sketches for the interior of the book will certainly hold the reader to the marsh where each can delight in the wildfowl at rest or on the wing.

Paula Dana—Your mastery of the computer and ability to decipher my chicken scratch so as to turn my vision into reality has been a godsend.

Judy Miller—You are a wordsmith extraordinaire. I deeply appreciate your time and skills in reviewing the book.

My gratitude for each of your contributions is without end.

Gregory Barnes Watson

Dedication

For my father,
Byrn A. Watson,
whose wisdom, guidance,
and love never
cease to amaze me.

Contents

Note: Chapter titles don't necessarily follow chronological order.

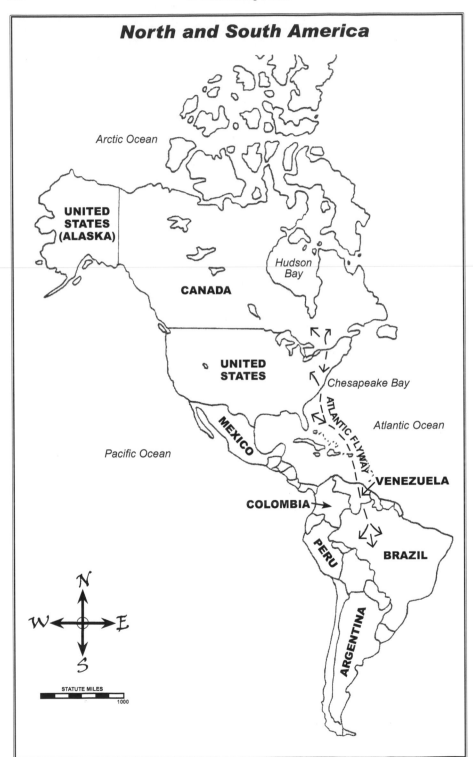

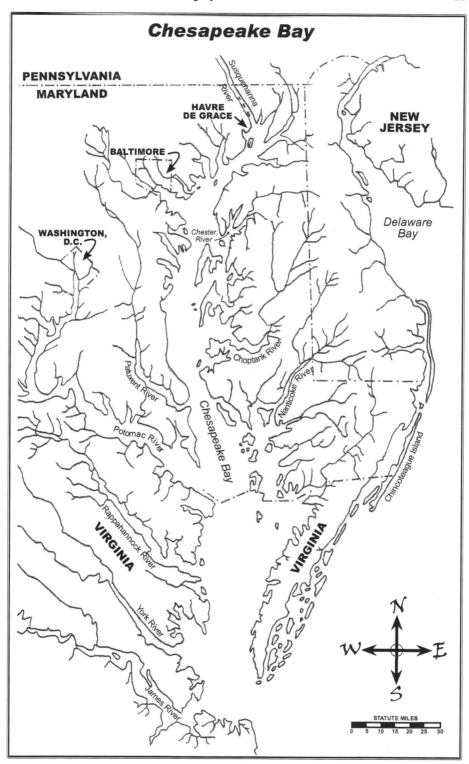

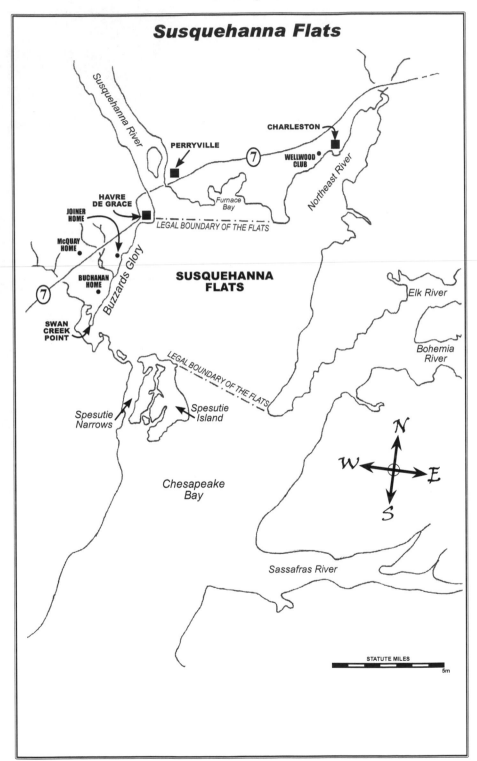

Susquehanna Flats

Susquehanna River

PERRYVILLE

CHARLESTON

⑦

WELLWOOD CLUB

Northeast River

HAVRE DE GRACE

JOINER HOME

Furnace Bay

LEGAL BOUNDARY OF THE FLATS

McQUAY HOME

⑦

BUCHANAN HOME

Buzzards Glory

SUSQUEHANNA FLATS

Elk River

SWAN CREEK POINT

Bohemia River

LEGAL BOUNDARY OF THE FLATS

Spesutie Narrows

Spesutie Island

N

W   E

S

Chesapeake Bay

Sassafras River

STATUTE MILES

5m

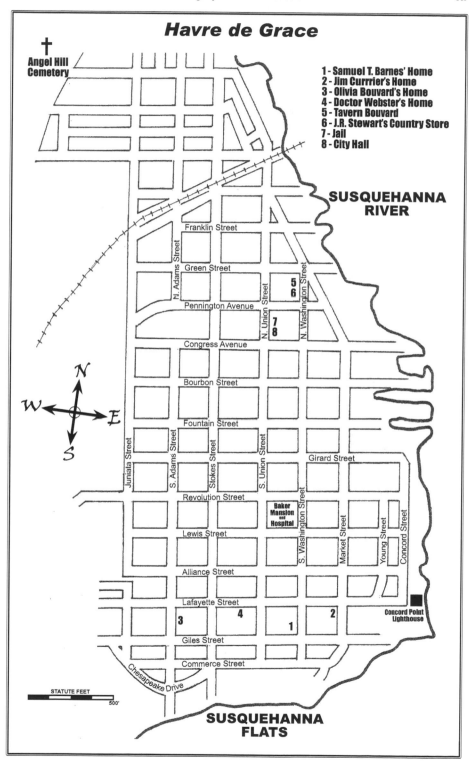

Havre de Grace

1 - Samuel T. Barnes' Home
2 - Jim Currrier's Home
3 - Olivia Bouvard's Home
4 - Doctor Webster's Home
5 - Tavern Bouvard
6 - J.R. Stewart's Country Store
7 - Jail
8 - City Hall

Angel Hill Cemetery

SUSQUEHANNA RIVER

SUSQUEHANNA FLATS

Concord Point Lighthouse

Baker Mansion and Hospital

Chesapeake Drive

STATUTE FEET
500'

Disclaimer

A THUNDERING WIND is a novel. Its characters, the Buchanans, Joiners, McQuays, Bouvard, LeCompte, etc., are inventions of the author's imagination and not based on real persons. The author has attempted to show the historical figures depicted in this book, many widely known, others known only to aficionados of specific fields of study, in the light and with the character for which they are uniquely remembered and for their contributions to the community of man on either a large or small scale. For factual information and images regarding these men and women, as well as images specific to the wildlife, locations, and types of implements used by market hunters in this novel, the author encourages the reader to visit www. *athunderingwind.com*.

The locations identified in the book, Chesapeake Bay, Susquehanna Flats, Buzzards Glory, Spesutie Island, Havre de Grace, etc., are real and accurately described insofar as any human can describe the creations of The Almighty. The author has attempted such folly in the hope that the reader will want to visit the wonderland that is this matchless area, as well as open a window on a lost way of life lived by hardy families, the incredible migrations of wildfowl, and the creatures that to this day struggle to survive in an ever-changing and modernizing world.

– 1492 –

"All night we heard birds passing." These are the words Christopher Columbus inscribed in his diary on October 9, 1492. Most of his crew, swinging in hammocks below deck, stared into the darkness, unable to sleep, believing that at any moment they would fall off the face of the earth. The soon-to-be Admiral of the Sea waited expectantly on deck for the excited shouts of "Land!" from the lookout perched high in the riggings. Columbus knew the Indies were surely near for the night's moon had been blotted out by millions of winged creatures.

Only a sizable land mass could sustain such infinite flocks, he repeated again to himself with confidence as the beat of wings, and the birds' calls shattered the night.

How incredibly wrong and how insightfully right was this Genoese as the Santa Maria sailed westerly beneath the Atlantic flyway toward a continent that held an abundance of natural riches; an immeasurable wealth that could not be fathomed by either its discoverer or his doubting benefactors back in the Old World.

- 1899 -

Clay Herschell Buchanan lays the Davenport into the wooden chock of his sneak skiff. His silhouette is blurred against the snow-covered ground that is Buzzards Glory and the ice floes bumping and grinding on the Chesapeake Bay. Wrinkles crease the corners of his gray eyes as he studies the bloated, low-hanging clouds that foretell of additional snow flurries soon to fall across his stalking grounds.

"The kill will be spectacular tonight," Clay states to Rebel, his disinterested Chesapeake retriever. This statement is not so much one of bravado, but more due to the vast numbers of waterfowl rafting, crowded together within the open waters of the Susquehanna Flats. Some are only resting during their north to south Atlantic migration, others wintering residents. Although, if an acquaintance had been within earshot, he would not deny Clay's mastery of his vocation, even for a 20-something-year-old, for which Clay would simply reply, "It's a living. No duck, no dinner."

Before motioning Rebel into the skiff, Clay lights his ever-present, hand-rolled cigarette. He draws deeply, savoring the smoky burn as it quells the annoying tickle in his throat. "In ya go, Reb," sputters Clay between irritating coughs, then he and his bird dog partake in their nightly ritual of hesitancy and debasement.

As if it were the first time, and feigning a need to conserve strength, Rebel steps slowly, precisely, one leg at a time over the rail, and into the sneak skiff. Methodically, this red veteran of the hunt lies down under the Davenport's well-oiled barrel, near the bow in an attempt to shield himself from the brisk wind blowing across the bay, and into their faces. However, before resting his head, Rebel's questioning gaze seeks Clay's and his colorful response.

"You lazy S.O.B.," Clay chastises. "I'd be done and back, stuffed with duck and snug by the stove if it weren't for the time I waste wait'n' on you." With that said, Rebel places his furred muzzle upon his paws for a contented nap.

With muscles straining, Clay shoves against the skiff. The snow crunches under his worn leather lace-up boots as the sneak skiff and its load of the Davenport and Rebel break free of the bank to glide into the bay's black water. The thick, shore-lined ice is nudged aside as Clay, lying prone in the 18-foot skiff, uses shortened hand paddles to slowly maneuver out toward his waiting prey hiding far offshore.

Winter on the Chesapeake Bay, especially at night, would be a silent time except for the wind skipping across the ice; the throaty sneezes of diving ducks clearing water from their nostrils; the cat-like meowing of contented redheads; and the guttural croaking of canvasbacks; all rafting together for company and security.

Clay, like all consummate predators, is cautious, patient, deliberate, and at all times focused on the task at hand. His cheek, resting against the over-sized, rough, walnut gunstock becomes familiarly chilled numb. His lean arms propel the skiff further from the safety of the shore and toward a confrontation with nature.

"At all times, concentrate," Clay whispers, being slightly distracted by thoughts other than those at hand. Rebel, annoyed by Clay for breaking the hunter's code of silence, opens one lazy eye to stare with disgust. Feeling the rebuke, Clay seeks to justify a violation that is normally made by only the greenest of seeds.

"You self-righteous, over-fed, indolent, red dog from Hades, you're just as anxious as I for the New Year. Hell-fire and indeed a new century, the twentieth century, wherein my Jennifer will bestow upon me a son," Clay hisses through clenched teeth that mash his hand-rolled cigarette.

Rebel's eye continues to reproach Clay for his misplaced priorities. Clay continues his defense while ignoring the increasing ache in his fingers from the icy water as each practiced paddle stroke dips gently, several inches, beneath the water's surface.

"A son, mind you. 'That's the position it's taken in the womb,' according to the mid-wife. And be sure of this, you flea-bitten blanket of carpet fur," Clay sneers, "my son's belly will be filled before yours. That's my priority."

Not showing the slightest of concern over Clay's threats of starvation, Rebel closes his eye, and then in a show of boredom with Clay's dialogue, he shifts his position to face away from his distracted hunting partner.

"Hmmpf," is Clay's final word.

Now, as it should be, only the meowing, sneezing, and croaks float across the vast expanse of water. This strange mouth-watering chorus cautions Clay, and stimulates Rebel's senses to the nearness of their desire. Within a quarter of a mile, the targets come into view. Waterfowl, ducks from America's Midwest; geese and swan from Canada's tundra—all gifts from God to feed families, and supply hungry eastern markets.

Clay, the Davenport, and Rebel—each having a specific duty; each carrying his own obligation to the other.

Clay exercising patience so agonizing that it nullifies the pain in his back from arching it and the throb in his neck from holding his head just above the gunwale. His body remains prone, stomach down, against the flat-bottomed, three-and-one-half foot beam of the narrow skiff. With the slightest of hand movements, Clay must navigate his expertly crafted, but highly unstable vessel to within range of the rafting, always-on-guard waterfowl.

The Davenport, a 12-foot punt gun with a two-inch bore, its O gauge barrel rammed home with half a pound of black powder and two-and-one-half pounds of bird shot, is a massive shotgun. It was originally named for the family Davenport, who first commissioned its creation from the forges of England, nearly 75 years ago. It was then lost in a poker game to Percy Buchanan, Clay's grandfather. Sacredly, Percy passed down a way of life, and secretly the instrument to accomplish it from father to son to grandson. Meticulously maintained and highly respected for its killing ability; all that is required of the Davenport is to fire on command, never to hang or misfire, which would result in the long, uncomfortable, chilly winter's night of maneuvering being wasted. No duck—no dinner.

Then there is Rebel. As with all bird dogs, his idiosyncrasies are excused so long as he retrieves the downed and crippled birds without hesitation or complaint. Because, in the end, if a hunter's family goes too long without meat, there will be no tears shed over a steaming bowl of spiced canine stew. Bird dogs are born with the instinct to retrieve, but there's nothing wrong with an incentive.

More than a mile from shore, Clay eases the sneak skiff without so much as a ripple closer to the large raft of mixed birds. The fat canvasbacks, or cans, on the outer edge swim away from the approaching menace. Something is there; the cans sense it, but what? They are unsure as it is impossible to distinguish the outline of the off-white vessel which carries the deadly punt gun from the gray sky and surrounding ice floes. Survival depends on discretion, rather than valor. The canvasbacks paddle away.

Clay has ceased breathing and now wills his heart to refrain from its irritatingly loud beating. Rebel, still curled in the bow, could be viewed, as

Clay does, as a lumpy throw rug, except for the tension rippling through his taut muscles. Rebel now stares, as if by magic, through the skiff's solid wood slats at the Davenport's intended victims. He waits impatiently for the starting gun, *Get 'er done and get on home!*

From above comes a blessing and a curse. The clouds drop a silent curtain of snow that further obscures the bobbing birds' perception of the sneak skiff as it glides ever closer, moving to within 25 yards of the main body of the raft. However, this curtain of white can easily become a burial shroud, disorienting a lone hunter in a small craft as he tries to make his way off this wide bay. Stories are told of men who unknowingly paddle in circles to exhaustion, exhaustion to desperation, desperation to recklessness, recklessness to death.

Instinctively knowing the moment has arrived, no closer does Clay dare advance on this nervous flock of several thousand. The hand paddles, now useless, float tethered to the sneak skiff by cord because to raise them into the craft would result in unnatural water droplets upon the surface, alerting the cans, redheads, mallards, teal, swan and geese to alien infiltration.

Clay sights down the Davenport's long barrel. His frozen cheek is forgotten for the moment. His right arm embraces the stock as his index finger curls around the steel of the Davenport's immense trigger.

Rebel's keen sense of timing perceives the exact moment prior to the culmination of the evening's stalking. Clay slowly inhales, fortifying his body against the blast and jerk of the recoil.

Thwack!

Clay slaps his left hand against the gunwale. Divers by the dozen disappear into the black depths. The water under the remaining flock erupts as hundreds of pairs of powerful wings frantically slap the surface, raising feathered bodies into the air. The fowl attempt escape through flight, but finding instead—pellets of death.

Balloom! The Davenport's muzzle spews flame and lead as a swath 15-feet wide is cut through the flock, killing and crippling dozens. "Rebel, back," Clay shouts above his ringing ears, but Rebel is already splashing through the frigid water, swimming strongly, and pushing chunks of ice out of his path to reach the carnage.

The birds that escaped the blast fly in blind confusion through the cascading snow. They are dangerous winged projectiles without direction, streaking wildly, passing over and around the skiff, as they attempt to flee the scene of the massacre.

Being pleased with his success, Clay allows himself another lapse of concentration as his mind wanders to thoughts of his young wife heavy with child. "Thanks be to God, she's safe at home and waiting for my triumphant return." As Clay envisions Jennifer sitting comfortably in her wooden rocking chair, he rises from his prone position—something a concentrating, experienced predator would never do; should never do.

In that instant of predatory superiority, the predator-prey relationship changed. From a mental picture of Jennifer to Rebel returning with the first dead redhead, Clay's vision fills with the hurtling body of a large male snow goose, its all white body nearly invisible within the swirling ice crystals. Its feathered body, appearing velvety soft, crashes against Clay's skull with the weight and force of a cannon ball. The goose flops heavily, broken-winged, within the skiff, as Clay lies unconscious next to the Davenport with a gash across his forehead.

The Buchanan home, described by the rare passerby as "That old shack," rests at the end of a wagon wheel rutted road just above the high tide marker. And though a man with long strides will require a third of a day to journey north to reach the outskirts of Havre de Grace, many a patron warming his hands by the fire and his gullet with spirits at Tavern Bouvard, knows of Clay's self-berating by heart.

"What a fool I was," Umbrella George would mimic, starting the cajoling around the sweetly acrid, smoke-filled room. "And likely drunk. Not to mention young, very young, so as to be swindled into mortgaging land so close to town, that when I sit on my porch during a nor'eastern blow, I swear I can hear Henry O'Neill striking a match to light the beacon in the Concord Point lighthouse." Then laughter, but all done with respect because everyone knows those 93 acres within Buzzards Glory, backed by stately oaks, pine, birch, and maple trees, are a combination of the finest forest and wetlands in Harford County.

To Jennifer Darling Buchanan, regardless of the age of its two-room construction or proximity to anything, this is her adored home. Its recently paned window allows for protective viewing as she waits anxiously for the boy, now a man, who two years ago carried her across the threshold of their only door. Over this planked and nailed barrier to the outside are dried flowers tacked with care—flowers that Jennifer wore in her onyx-colored, shoulder-length hair the day the two vowed to become one.

The child within her kicked, agitated by its mother's worry. Jennifer had been watching the falling snow for over an hour as it coated, clouded, and then finally obscured her vision of the world that her beloved labored in.

"Shush, child. I don't mean to worry us," Jennifer cooed to her bloated belly. "I'm sure your father is right now edging his skiff, piled high with fowl, up onto safe ground. Can you feel his closeness?" With a mother's caress, Jennifer tickles the thin material of her button-front cotton dress, transferring the loving sensation into the womb through the stretched skin around her navel to soothe the restless fetus. As mother and child relax, some natural mechanism triggers the secretion of milk from Jennifer's breasts. Swollen, due to late-term pregnancy, her normally ample bosoms have prevented her from wearing a supportive brassiere, and to purchase an adequate one for use for only a couple months were viewed as an unreasonable and unnecessary expense. So on the occasion of spontaneous lactation, Jennifer would blush embarrassed, though at the same time receiving a perverse thrill at the wetting of her dress. If by chance this leaking occurs in public, Jennifer will cover herself with a knitted shawl that she always carries of late. If at home, a simple change of apparel is required.

The Great Room, as Jennifer likes to call it, takes only eight steps for her to cross, six for Clay. Contained within its pine tar pitch walls, standing squarely in the center along the longest wall, is a black cast iron potbelly stove for cooking. Its two-section stovepipe leaks puffs of smoke as it breaks through at the ceiling that does double duty as the roof. Two simple wooden chairs of Quaker design sit at opposite ends of a rough board table across from the stove and next to the only interior door that leads into the bedroom. A triple-duck stone counter contains a second-hand iron sink. It has the added luxury of a bronze pump handle for water attached to the back wall. Lastly, there's Jennifer's rocking chair where she holds vigil beneath the window when Clay is absent.

Two velvet cushions of robin's egg blue have been intricately sewn with the design of hearts and wildflowers, one for the rocking chair's seat, and the other for the back. These cushions are cherished presents from Olivia Bouvard, Jennifer's friend and confidant, the daughter of the owner of Tavern Bouvard. These cushions were Jennifer's only gift to commemorate her pregnancy announcement, but a more appropriate, thoughtful gift could not have been given. The softness of goose down cushions, combined with the gentle rocking has always helped to ease the dull throb in her lower back that now seems a constant ache, a dull throb that no amount of shifting positions or gentle massaging can ease. The source of Jennifer's discomfort is the extra 28 pounds that Clay calls his progeny carried around her middle while she sees to the daily tasks of a working household. A child on the way does not relieve a woman of her daily chores.

Jennifer squats next to the stove. She has long since given up bending, as her distended belly would throw her off-balance. Hinging open the stove's door, Jennifer pokes the graying embers with a discarded ramrod, while at the same time noting the absence of logs next to the stove. "If your father doesn't come home soon, we'll have to collect logs from the shed ourselves, but first, don't you think I should put on something more presentable?" From the table, Jennifer picks up and carries a brass ship's lantern into the bedroom. This relic from some shipwreck is the household's only source of light. She sets the lantern upon a mahogany chest of drawers. Each time Jennifer gazes upon the six-drawer chest with its meticulously carved designs of cherubim with their playful impish smiles, she pauses to finger their chubby faces, so alive with mischief that giggles always well up and fill her with delight. "What a treasure you are," Jennifer whispers. "What a blessing from God."

This chest, found floating half submerged, by Clay during one of his nightly sojourns onto the bay, was likely lost during a squall, fallen overboard from a side-wheeler plying the bay, or a square-rigger crossing the Atlantic. More than once, Jennifer has considered its true owners and their grief at its loss. When she questioned Clay on finding its owner, Clay was pragmatic. "Of all the gunners, oystermen, and fishermen, it was me who it found. It was me who for two hours dragged it like an anchor ashore. And it was me who worked for days to slow dry it to prevent warping, cracking, and ruin. There is no question of ownership." Finally, Jennifer gave up, accepting it for what it was—a gift.

Jennifer struggles to open the middle drawer, the one that fights her each winter, and contains her only other housedress that is large enough to cover her at this delicate time. "I should either change drawers or have Clay fix this." With a strong tug, the chest lets loose of its hold on the drawer. The sudden release sends Jennifer stumbling backward, fortunately landing on the double bed; its quilted cover softening her awkward sprawl. Laughing at her clumsiness, Jennifer stands to remove her milk-stained dress.

Standing naked, Jennifer's hanging belly, swollen breasts, and pushed back buttocks form a grotesque shadow on the bedroom wall from the lantern's mocking illumination. She frowns while examining the black creature, an unfortunate true silhouette of her deformed figure.

"Clay, look what you've done to me," Jennifer's frown quickly changes to a conspiratorial smile as she remembers her mother's plaintive words: With marriage comes the marriage bed. It is rarely pleasant, but if your need for food and shelter are to be met, then your husband's rutting must be endured. Just keep your mind on the coming sunrise. For with the morning light you'll be able to scrub it all away.

Jennifer clearly remembers her first sunrise as a newlywed and her tears that woke her husband. Clay was so concerned with her feelings; his gentle caring words, and tender caresses finally broke through her hesitancy to speak. Jennifer sobbed, "How can I face my mother after what we've...what I've done?"

"We are man and wife. You've done nothing improper," was Clay's reasoned response.

Burying her face in Clay's curly brown chest hair, she whispered, "You don't understand. Last night after you finished the first time, I asked you to do it again, and now, this morning in the light of day, visible to God and the angels, I want the same."

Clay roared with such infectious laughter, that even today, Jennifer cannot help hugging herself when remembering the tingles that shivered up and down her body as she endured his delicious rutting. Now admiring her ill-proportioned figure, she states with pride, "Clay, look what you've done to me."

A draft sweeps in from under the shack's door to spill into the bedroom chilling Jennifer out of her moment of mesmerism, making her all too aware of the rapid drop in temperature within the room. Quickly stepping into her clean, dry dress, Jennifer looks through the doorway at the dying embers cooling in the potbelly stove. Carrying the lantern into the Great Room, she sets it back on the table. Wrapping her shawl around her shoulders, Jennifer slips her invisible feet into her lace-up boots but makes no attempt to thread the calf-high, cat gut cords through their numerous eyelets. As it has been several weeks since Jennifer last saw her feet, of late she would teasingly ask her husband, while they lie in bed, to describe them so that after the child is born, and she has lost the bulge, she will recognize her feet, and know they are hers to wash.

Built against the shack is a small shed wherein Clay stores his tools, carves hunting decoys, and keeps a stack of seasoned wood for cooking and heating. To save trips during inclement weather, Clay has plans to build a small portal with either a hinged or sliding door to access the wood stack but, to date, other projects have taken priority, besides, "What's a little rain or snow?" Clay teases. "It saves taking a bath."

Jennifer steps out onto the porch. She shivers as the night's snap penetrates the weaves of her dress and shawl, attacking her flesh. Clay has attempted to keep ice from forming on the wooden planks by scattering rock salt, but only so much can be done when the thermometer plummets into the teens. Taking great care with each footstep, Jennifer pauses before stepping off the partly sheltered porch. She tries to stare through the silent falling snow, willing Clay to appear, but her strain is futile.

"At least the wind has stopped," she says to her tummy. Cupping her ears, Jennifer listens for the soft splashes of paddling. "Clay? Are you there?" A woman's hope is without end when her heart desires something, but the only reply is from ice floes bumping and crunching lightly against each other, and piling up onto the shore.

Stepping off the raised porch and into the snow that covers her boots to her ankles, Jennifer uses her mind's eye to visualize the uneven path that leads around the side of her home to the shed. The complete whiteness of the falling snow betrays the darkness of the night. Jennifer places her left hand against the rough, unpainted wall, sliding it around the thick trunk of the barren maple tree to guide and steady her. Reaching the shed's handle, Jennifer tugs. The crooked door's rusty, frozen hinges complain with cracking ice and agonizing creaks. Resistance from the snow that has built up against the bottom of the door adds to her difficulty. Tugging again, yanking with both hands, Jennifer's breathing turns to pants, heavy and steaming, as the door sticks, refusing to open but 12 inches, if not a mere 10. Grunting, sweat beads form across Jennifer's overheated brow, contrasting with her fingers that begin to lose feeling, becoming numb in the frigid air.

"Damn it," groans Jennifer as she yanks again on the frozen knob, but the door is hopelessly wedged at the bottom. The snow, which is wet and heavy, refuses to be pushed aside.

A sideshow contortionist would be amazed watching Jennifer as she wiggles, turns, pushes, twists, and pulls her body through the too-narrow opening. For her reward for squeezing through, the fetus bestows several sharp kicks to voice its annoyance at the unwelcome pressure against the womb, its heavenly home. A place warm, wet, perfect, and not to be disturbed.

"Oh, baby!" gasps Jennifer as she reaches for Clay's workbench to brace herself. "Mama's sorry, but we need the wood for the stove. Please, little one, don't kick. I'm not enjoying this either."

Enjoying his task, and unconcerned with the icy water, Rebel collects the floating carcasses. He has made 36 trips between the drifting sneak skiff and the bobbing dead. With only a six-inch freeboard, Rebel is able to place one paw up on the railing, then lift and drop the fowl into the skiff.

Rebel's pleasure in doing what nature has breed into him, and which added training and incentive has made compulsory, begins to wane. His hunting partner has remained prone far too long, way beyond the need for safety. It is Clay's responsibility to keep the sneak skiff in close proximity, arrange the retrieved in a manner so their vessel does not become unbalanced, and with hand signals, show the line in which a crippled bird has paddled.

Who's the lazy S.O.B now? Rebel thinks while coughing up a feather that has been swallowed with a gulp of bay water after dropping back in to retrieve number 37.

Reminiscent of a Viking burial at sea, Clay lies still within his pyre of cascading snow. The oozing blood from his wound congeals on his forehead with several drops freezing to the Davenport's barrel. The wrong-way goose, an unintended victim of its accidental assault on Clay, quivers in the bow, taking over Rebel's position. Its broken wing useless; its splintered breastplate piercing its erratic heart. Death arrives with a falling flake; unnoticed among the many.

Rebel releases number 37 from his practiced jaw. The limp redhead lands on Clay. Rebel paddles off to collect number 38, unaware of his hunting partner's grave condition. Clay, a fallen predator, surrounded by his prey, is a bouquet of the macabre, on a bay that offers much, but cares not a lick. Clay is correct; the kill is spectacular tonight.

Blinded by the veil of snowflakes; exhausted by her fight both in and out of the shed's door, and already carrying 28 pounds of precious cargo, Jennifer is only able to cradle four logs in her arms. She would readily admit that these would not be called logs by any woodsman, as they are only five-inch round limbs that have been cleaned of shoots and leaves. Despite their size, they will provide sufficient warmth until Clay's return. At least that is Jennifer's silent prayer.

"This will be your chore as soon as your waddle becomes a walk," Jennifer mumbles as she feels the cold touch of heavy flakes upon her oval face. Her tongue darts out to capture their faint teasing moisture. Her feet continue to shuffle through the snow as she rounds the corner of the shed. Jennifer brushes past the sleeping tree as her pace quickens toward the shelter of the porch.

The roots of this strangely hollow, yet healthy mature maple tree stretch wide, then deep into Maryland's nutrient-rich soil, providing a sturdy foundation against the elements. Closer to the trunk the exposed roots have been the cause of several painful stubbed toes, followed by an ungodly curse or two, and the threat of putting it under the axe. Jennifer once remarked with tender teases while Clay hopped teary-eyed into the house, "It's only seeking revenge for all its relatives that we've incinerated." Clay found no humor in her analysis of cause and effect. Though for several days his practical mind pondered this mystical possibility. The end result of the altercation was a permanently cracked toenail that he showed the tree. Clay also renewed their previous agreement for mutual assistance including the vow to never cut it down. Clay did this while Jennifer was in town because even though he believed that all living things had a spirit of sorts, he was not willing to openly admit that a tree would take revenge against him.

Two more shuffled steps to the porch; three carefully placed paces to the door, four to the stove, and then she would have heat. That is Jennifer's plan. Focusing her mind and body on the soothing warmth of a cracking fire is why it took her an eternity of seconds to realize she is falling. Her right boot wedges under a hidden root as Jennifer slides it forward. The logs fly outward, as Jennifer's hands search the air for a firm hold, something, anything to grasp to stop her fall, but she finds only flakes that disappear within her grip.

As a young girl, Jennifer had once been dared to leap from the roof of her one-story home in Baltimore. It didn't look that high, even while dangling her legs off the edge, the distance to the stone walkway seemed only a short drop. This is the vision that played in her mind. There is the same blindness. Then it was caused by her dress being blown up into her face to expose her undergarments, which had been the true purpose of the gathered boys' dare. Now it is the absence of a winter moon and her envelopment by falling snow. Jennifer falls and falls, though the ground is only a few feet away; her hands searching, reaching, as her lungs fill with air to scream her panic.

Snap!

At age 11, it was a bone in her wrist. Now it was either her foot or the tree's root. The searing pain racing up her leg identifies the source. The pain reaches her lungs to wrench away Jennifer's cry.

Silence, though Jennifer's mind shrieks with the knowledge of the absence of one element of her childhood memory. *Where is the impact?!*

The breaking bone was somehow comforting. Years ago her hands had been the first to impact the uneven bricks in front of her home. Now she flails in darkness. It is Jennifer's reliance upon her senses that is the cause of this illusion. Her frozen palms strike the icy porch, but she doesn't feel them as they slide outward. Any mother-to-be would readily sacrifice her face, even if she were blessed with delicate features, to protect her unborn. This surely is Jennifer's sentiment, if given the choice, as her chin is cut open by a tumbling log, but along with the slice to her face comes the kick to the stomach. Jennifer's belly, so vulnerable, so ripe with child, takes the brunt of her fall, the full impact.

The origin of Jennifer's fall could not have been worse. Being four feet from the raised porch, the uneven ends of the planks dig in; jamming and twisting the fetus back against Jennifer's spine, and then forcing it up against her lungs. The sound from her gaping mouth is a rabbit's cry as it is dunked alive into scalding water prior to skinning.

Jennifer's body convulses as she rolls off the porch, slumping in the mounding snow where the shack's wall and porch form a corner. Her dress is awash in liquid. Her frozen hands feebly explore between her legs where they are warmed by fluid spilling from her broken womb. Jennifer's fear and confusion intensifies as the first birthing contraction balls her into the fetal position.

Seconds pass into minutes as Jennifer remains motionless. A sheer sheet of snow slowly covers her. The cold has been replaced by pain. She stares at a crumpled body. It is hers but at the same time foreign. Her pupils send warning signals to a brain scrambled by the unthinkable.

Red!

Red!

Red!

The fluid leading from between Jennifer's legs is swirling with strawberry jam, preservatives. *Strawberry? No. That's not right. Cherry? Yes. Crushed cherries for a birthday pie,* Jennifer's thoughts run in a circle with panic being the only stop. Her conscious mind seeks refuge from the lightning exploding within her. *Oh God! The juice is staining my fingers and I've ruined my dress. Mama, don't be angry with me.*

Muscles contract, breaking her mind game of hide-and-seek with reality. There is no mama. There is no scolding for a ruined dress. There is a baby. Jennifer whimpers as reality sneaks in, grabbing hold, and then slips away again.

"Clay?" calls Jennifer, but the vision before her is just another mind game as flakes form false shadows of her rescuer. "Clay, carry me. I'm hurt."

Minutes return to seconds as time speeds up. Jennifer's need, her longing for a savior turns inward to a memory of a preacher and his understanding of God's greatness: He helps those who help themselves. Jennifer's fingers claw at the icy porch. Her breath, pants of steam, a locomotive straining to gain a grade. She pulls her damaged body up onto the porch and toward the front door.

Desperation.

Panic.

The unimaginable is happening.

Jennifer's eyes gaze across a field of snow, the porch, which seems a mile long, covered in mountains and topped with jagged peaks, sharp ice crystals which threaten to cut and tear at her skin. Inch by inch she pulls her way to what Jennifer hopes is sanctuary. Straining with every muscle, she plows through the frozen obstacles, scratching her face and arms. Her exposed legs drag behind as a crippled dog. Reaching the door, Jennifer lifts her hand to find the latch, her other returns to between her legs. Her fingers are warmed as blood, the fluid of life, hers and the fetus' trickles out of her to cover her wedding band.

Click.

The latch opens, allowing the door to swing wide with a screech as Jennifer leans against it. The door bangs against the inner wall, shuddering with impact. Crawling forward, her vision blurs with the loss of blood as she searches for the doorway to her bedroom.

Jennifer searches for the room of comfort;

For the room of playful adventures;

For the room of slippery, sweaty love;

For the safe room;

This room Jennifer cannot find.

What Jennifer finds is a dark place.

The ship's lantern sits alone on the dining table in the Great Room. It is too far to reach; too impotent for warmth; it is not a crackling fire designed for comfort. Jennifer is alone with Clay's hope for the future. Tears moisten Jennifer's cheeks as she summons her remaining strength to drag herself to the foot of the bed. Burying her face in the quilt which hangs over the bed's edge, she smells its wonderful memories, wondering with tremors of fear whether there will be any more made within its caressing fabric.

Muscles contract, pull, and twist as the progeny bangs from within. Its home is wrecked and it demands to be let out. Jennifer's hand, wet and slippery with flowing blood, is nudged away from the birthing canal.

The child's head is crowning.

"It's too soon. Too fast!" Jennifer screams as her flesh tears.

Outside the shack, the sky, gray and menacing, pauses to take in a breath before casting down another flurry. A puff of wind brushes flakes across the threshold of the shack's open doorway. A passing cottontail stops some 10 feet from the porch. He is distracted. His carefree night of foraging is interrupted by the lantern's erratic flame. The cottontail's whiskers wiggle. His brown eyes are fixed. Ears at attention.

Caution...

The lantern's flame dies, leaving the cottontail with the night's reassuring darkness. He continues on his way without concern.

Rebel's paws splash powerfully through the icy water. His strong jaw gently holds the last victim, number 52, a mallard hen. He paddles after the drifting sneak skiff. Each trip to and from the killing field is becoming more distant making his work more arduous.

Something is not right, Rebel worries. No shouts directing him to where the birds bob. No harassment for slow retrievals, just what seems to be an untimely nap by his partner.

Once again, Rebel places his paw on the gunwale, and flicks the mallard onto the uneven pile of ducks and geese. The bird tumbles overboard to be deftly caught by Rebel before it hits the water. With a snap of his muscled neck, Rebel tosses it higher on the pile where it remains. Both front paws now clasp the edge of the gunwale. Rebel's hind legs kick furiously at the water as he barks for assistance. He considers himself more than adequate to any task set before him, but without his partner's scruff-of-the-neck tug up and into the skiff, well, that thought brings a chill that Rebel does not want to consider.

Rebel drops back into the frigid water to paddle around to the other side of the skiff. He barks irritably, and not wanting to admit it yet, with a pitch that carries worry and urgency.

Still nothing from his partner.

The birds have fled.

Silence has spread across the wide bay.

The pile of feathers with Clay as foundation neither stirs nor emits a sound.

Rebel paddles in small circles to survey his immediate surroundings.

Water...cold...cold...bone cold water everywhere.

Ice ...cold...cold...FLOATING ICE!

Rebel looks at the sneak skiff, forlorn, as it drifts without direction or control. He is hesitant to leave his silent partner but a decision has to be made to save his own life. Even with his extra thick coat of fur to protect him, Rebel will succumb to the cold. He cannot remain in the water indefinitely. Jerking his head away, his decision being made, he paddles to a nearby ice floe. Clawing, scratching grooves into the smooth surface, Rebel pulls himself up onto the ice. Stiff from his numbing task of retrieving birds, then having to find a solid, dry place to stand, Rebel is slow to shake off the black water. Turning back toward the vessel, he searches for the man who brought him to this empty, wind-blown place, but fresh snow flakes, swirling silently down, further camouflages the craft as the distance between the partners increases with the confused tide. The sneak skiff and the ice covered bay become one with the night's bleached sky.

Rebel howls mournfully. His keen eyes blink with fear as the skiff disappears. *Was Charon[1] at the helm?*

Two miles north of the Buchanan's shack, nestled within a birch tree swamp, sleeps the Joiners. This self-sufficient family of five; two adults, two children, and a nursing infant, rest snug under the same oversized quilt; a colorful, if not perpetually dirty, hand sewn, and repeatedly patched collage of rags that the mother tries to keep clean. This once stout, but neglected structure was built in 1862 by Nathaniel Joiner for his bride. The shelter is saving its present occupants from exposure, they being Nathaniel's children and grandchildren.

---

1 Charon. Greek myth. The ferryman that transports souls across the river Styx.

– 1864 –

Nathaniel's bride was comely and of mixed repute. She was a dance hall bride; a bride claiming to carry the child of a patron who felt he had more luck than the next man. Nathaniel's belief was a fact. He did have more luck, but it was invariably bad. He just did not understand it.

The happy newlyweds moved into their 20x20 foot sod floor structure and immediately devised creative ways to avoid each other. Visitors, if there had been any, would have sworn a pious vow of silence had been taken; that was unless they happened to pass by during coupling. Their lovemaking was a violent time of shrieks, howls, scratches, bruising, and bloodletting. If there had been laws against spousal abuse, both would have seen the inside of cells, but because these acts satisfied the needs of both combatants for physical release and revenge for unstated slights, there was not an officer of the court capable of prying a word of malice out of one toward the other.

In 1863, a son he named August was born.

In 1864, a daughter she named Claire was born.

Nathaniel Joiner's bride named their daughter because Nathaniel had left without notice to join the Union army eight months earlier. Nathaniel held no strong Union loyalty; could know less about economics, and concerning the issue of slavery, he had not given it much thought, but if pressed, he would respond, "Everyone is a slave to some master." Nathaniel enlisted in the Union army for one important reason. The North paid more than the South did to fight. The dandy uniform with silver buttons and cap with a golden bugle on top were an added delight to a man who wore secondhand clothing pilfered from unattended clotheslines. Standing by himself and fully outfitted in military garb, Nathaniel cut a visage of a fine military man. It was only when he marched in formation did his five-foot, four-inch frame mislead loose-of-tongue Yanks to remark, "Toy soldier." Rarely was the last syllable allowed to form in its owner's throat before a fist filled the mouth of the unwary speaker, shattering teeth on its violent journey. Bellicose with Viking stamina, Nathaniel quickly became the man to befriend. He fought hard, drank hard, and survived untouched every battle when others to the right and left dropped like flies to moist dung from metal shot fired by men and boys born south of the Mason-Dixon line. To a man in Nathaniel's platoon it was openly said, "Nat Joiner? Yep, he got the most luck. Stick close to him."

None of the farmers, hunters, watermen, or merchants battling alongside Nathaniel gave much thought that all the flying balls zipping past had Nathaniel's name stenciled on them. The only reason Nathaniel survived was due to the inaccuracy of the out-of-round lead balls. Instead of finding its appointed mark, Nathaniel would be spared, and the wobbling ball would spin into the nearest object, another farmer, hunter, waterman, or merchant who was praying for a pinch of Nathaniel's luck. While dying, lying in the mud of a bog or on the needles of pines or among meadow flowers, and gazing up toward heaven, he would not know his prayers had been granted.

Intrusions, skirmishes, and full-fledged battles came and went. The outcome was always the same. Nathaniel still stood, untouched by bullet or bayonet. It was time that Luck changed tactics. For some inexplicable reason, Luck had it in for this colorful, yet innocuous man from the swamp south of Havre de Grace.

It was midday of an unseasonably hot and humid May 1864. Uniforms clung sweaty to the soldiers during the battle of Dalton in Georgia six rugged miles from Camp Sumter and its prisoner of war camp. Gun smoke choked the air from platoons repeatedly close-firing. As if it rose from hell, the sulfur cloud obscured the battlefield. Americans separated by gray and blue played hide-and-seek as the hand-to-hand combat wound down. Abandoned by his retreating men, Nathaniel was found in the enemy's vengeful grasp. As the burnt powder, black and acrid, cleared from the air, 13 surviving Confederate soldiers surrounded Nathaniel. His blue clad body was kneeling on the chest of a grizzled Gray. Nathaniel screamed victory while smashing the Gray's skull with a granite rock. This moment was sexual. No, it was more precious than sex because it occurred only once with each partner. The hearts of the participants pumped, and their juices flowed with passion at the knowledge that this coupling would quickly end, a decisive termination. Unavoidably, one partner surrendered everything to the relationship, and the other accepted nothing less in the climax that was death.

Nothing and no one would dare interrupt Nathaniel's ecstasy; his newfound love; his taking and his partner's giving; perfect intimacy.

Click...fizzle.

A 15-year-old Gray; a lanky farm boy from South Carolina presses the barrel of his army-issue flintlock rifle to Nathaniel's head. Nathaniel's own .57 caliber Enfield musket lies some distance away. Out of powder, and the 18-inch bayonet broken off in the ribs of an enemy, its usefulness is at an end.

Misfire.

The flintlock's powder, damp and ruined by mist that had been carried on the dawn breeze, frustrated the youth's revenge.

A sergeant sporting a mangy mustache shoved the impotent boy out of the way, thinking, *Killing is a man's job.* Grasping the long barrel of his own spent weapon, he swung it, intending to crush Nathaniel's skull, wanting to pop it like a club to a ripe melon. Success, a pulpy mess, was certain had Nathaniel not tired of his intercourse, and slumped forward, exhausted. The sergeant's rifle butt gave a glancing blow to Nathaniel's crown. He lay unconscious but breathing, gurgling, bent forward in the mashed remains of the grizzled Gray's face; two lovers in a final good-bye kiss.

Unaware of when or why he had closed his eyes, Nathaniel struggled to climb up through the wires of the electrical storm in his head. His eyelids fluttered in an attempt to squeeze away the stinging drops of sweat from the high noon sun. He rested for another minute on what felt like barren ground. There were no leaves or pine needles to cushion the hard-packed dirt and sharp rocks digging into his back.

Voices, close by and distant were heard; some in weary conversation, others angry and combative. The words mixed on languid drifts of air. Nathaniel sighed with relief. There were no rifle volleys. No stink of sulfur. No death cries. The battle had passed him.

I'm safe, he assumed.

Nathaniel opened his eyes. A gasp choked from his parched throat. The scene was of hell. The tormented, once jovial comrades in arms, now with unattended wounds ravaged by gangrene, distended bellies filled only with the gas of starvation, bowels sputtered with dysentery, their minds turned primal. The men resembled beasts that must be shot.

"Welcome to Andersonville," a man of 40 hard years held out his four-fingered hand, his thumb blown off when his flintlock exploded. "Tom Riley of Pennsylvania—Harrisburg proper to be exact." A pleasant introduction belied the meanness Nathaniel saw in Tom's eyes. Nathaniel reached to clasp the offered right hand, at the same time noticed that Tom's left was hidden. Fast as a brant bolting from a gunner's shot, Nathaniel jerked Tom to the ground. When the hot dust settled, Nathaniel was in possession of the concealed, makeshift knife, and was pressing his knee against Tom's sunburned neck.

"Tell me quick while you still got breath in you," threatened Nathaniel through his clenched teeth. "My cap and silver buttons; they'd be the finest apparel I ever had. Who's the thief?"

"Johnny Reb," choked Tom. "The Grays cut 'em off before you were brought in. I swear."

"Damn stinkin' bastards!" Nathaniel released Tom but kept the knife, stuffing it in his trousers. "I'll make 'em pay."

"I've already thought of that, but we have to stay alive, and the North got to win," Tom rubbed his bruising neck.

"We'll survive. Ask anyone. I got the most luck around," Nathaniel smiled as he offered his hand to a kindred spirit.

Tom escorted Nathaniel around the interior boundaries of the 27-acre stockade that made up Andersonville, keeping well away from the dead-man line. This line indicated the edge of no-man's land, a buffer between the inmates and the stout pine logs making up the 20-foot-high walls. Union prisoners were daily shot dead for encroaching or appearing to approach this area.

"Need to get the lay of the land," Nathaniel's sharp eye took in every detail he could see. That which he couldn't, Tom filled in. Outside this first stockade were two additional walls, one 16 feet high and the other 12. These were for offensive and defensive positions. Confederate cannon and rifle fire could be quickly brought to bear, sweeping the prisoners if they attempted to break out, or used to repel Union cavalry or infantry if troops attempted to liberate their comrades. Built to house 10,000 prisoners of war, the stockade was overwhelmed with 28,000 sorry souls.

The northern and southern sides of the stockade included two opposing hills with a limp stream running west to east between them. This stream was intended to provide drinking water, washing for body and clothing, and to carry away urine and fecal matter, but the unimpressive flow, the trickle that could only hope to grow into a stream during winter, combined with the excessive quantities of human waste to form a boggy mass of liquid excrement. Union hands dug water wells, but these quickly became contaminated, as the soil was alive with vermin, insects, lizards, worms measuring up to five inches, fleas, and maggots. Every direction Nathaniel turned, he saw the same horrific sight; haggard, distressed, miserable, dejected, living skeletons, crying for food and medical attention, lying beside the stinking corpses of men and boys who died with each passing minute. Flowing in waves over every creature, living and dead, were the flies, millions of them. Men, whose flesh was originally white were coated black from the oily smoke of burned pine pitch. The pine trees and scrub brush within the walls were the soldiers' only source of cooking fuel and shade. Now many days gone, the sea of men groaned in black face at the memory of those precious trees, a necessity not supplied by their southern hosts.

"Can't tell a Negro from a white," opined Nathaniel.

"That's one of the reasons we're here, isn't it?" reflected Tom. "I mean someone said, 'We're all created equal.'"

"That's plain ignorant," Nathaniel stepped over a pungent body, a head wound alive with happy maggots. "You're taller'n me, right?"

"Yeah?"

"Well there you go. We ain't equal," Nathaniel grinned at his own fine logic.

"There's the red devil himself, the Flying Dutchman," Tom pointed to the top of the stockade.

Captain Wirtz, commander, could be tall, but stood stooped, like a buzzard over his carrion. His skin pale, a white, livered look with thin lips, and a face scrunched in a perpetual sneer of an angry old man, but surprisingly, he had only seen 30 odd years.

Nathaniel squinted, looking up at the giver or taker of life as Captain Wirtz spoke to three sentries who snapped to attention.

"Don't tell me those are Union men guarding us?" asked Nathaniel.

"Naw, just wretched Grays. Their own army can't supply 'em so they're wearing our uniforms, taken from the living and dead," Tom began chuckling. "Look, one of them is wearing your precious cap."

"I'll twist off his head along with my cap if I catch him unawares."

"There's not a man here who wouldn't lend you his own hands for the task, but Cap'n Wirtz, well, his retaliation would be..." Tom paused in mid-step, as thinking took up all available energy. The swarming flies landed in droves on his skin and tattered clothes. "A while back Cap'n Wirtz's dog came up missing. She was a fine shepherd. Admittedly a little tough, but filled several of our bellies. Wirtz couldn't prove a thing, but he denied us our rations for three days." Tom walked on. The resting flies exploded off him in all directions, "And that was only for a damn dog."

Clang! Clang! Clang!

What rang out as an alarm was the jarring notice for chow. The entrance gate, massive and imposing, logs lashed together vertically, slowly swung open. All eyes, even the dead ones stared hopefully at the ration wagon moving through the gate. It was pulled into the stockade by two mules, and though their protruding ribs held nary an ounce of meat, they had to be whipped forward, as even dumb asses could see the desperation in the prisoners' eyes, and were terrified that they would be today's meal. The nervous twitch of the Confederate soldier at the reins revealed his own fear as the inmates moved forward to surround the wagon. Angry shouts and fisticuffs broke out among the men due to a lack of discipline, starvation, and perceived acts of disrespect. On the wall of the stockade, safe and commanding, Captain Wirtz pointed toward three Union men climbing onto the wagon. Three muzzle reports sounded as a death knell over the melee. Two heads and a chest were violated as the lead balls penetrated, rattled around to scramble the two brains and exploded one heart. Two bodies dropped to the ground. One collapsed over the mound of coarse corn bread and sacks of peas. Blood and brain matter added nutrients to the sour and musty pile. Order was restored. Each man received his due; a pint of peas full of bugs, and one half pound of hard-baked, rank bread. As each man returned to his place in the dirt to eat his meal, each dreamed of home where hot meals of fresh meat, fish caught from sparkling streams, birds shot on the wing, or critters snared along trails, would be served with a huge helping of love.

Tom and Nathaniel received their share, and then found the group of men whom Tom had spoken of to Nathaniel. The group of ten nodded to the two as Tom and Nathaniel squatted among them. Nathaniel took compass of these men. They seemed better fed, and with the same countenance toward cruelty as Tom. Caution was the watchword.

"Peas with bugs," Tom shook his tin cup, and then let loose with an empty belly laugh. "We must be in good favor with the Red Devil today if he's giving out extra meat."

The group, all except Nathaniel, laughed.

"I've had slim pickin's before, but this isn't enough to sustain a gnat," Nathaniel shook his head, dismayed.

"If Tom has brought you to join us, you needn't fear a belly ache," this spoken by the assumed leader, who introduced himself as Captain Moseby. Nathaniel later learned he took this name after the rebel guerrilla who was the bane of the south. His real name was kept close to his breast, "Tonight we consume the Astor House Mess."

As the afternoon sun waned into dusk, the Federal prisoners settled down in anticipation of the night, and a cooling breeze. None came. Even the southern wind conspired with Captain Wirtz to punish these northerners before their exchange or victory. The setting sun did bring a modicum of relief from the flies, but their swarm was quickly replaced by the torture of mosquitoes. Sufferers of these pestiferous insect attacks resembled measles victims. Night moans did diminish, as many numbers of the living pulled over their shrouds like a curtain on a pitiful play. In the morning, the dead, numbering in the many dozens, would be carried to the gate or left where they lay, their eyeballs staring up into vacant space. The returning flies swarmed down their open and grinning mouths to deposit their offspring in the black and swollen mass of drying pus. Scurvy was a painfully slow, merciless, and always fatal ailment when untreated. Crossing the dead-man line, was to some, preferable, quick and painless if the shot was dead on, but the remaining grin of the scurvy victim was that joyous sign of absolute relief. Exchange or victory no longer mattered. These soldiers had been discharged from further duty and have gone home.

The silver moon, having traveled two-thirds of its journey across the black sky, made it to be two or three in the morning, Nathaniel reckoned. Captain Moseby led his band of raiders with Nathaniel and Tom in tow. Each man carried a club, a knife, or some makeshift instrument for inflicting pain, and to subdue the opposition. Like cockroaches on their way to feast, these nocturnal scavengers scampered over and around their sleeping comrades on a path toward the front gate.

"Are there enough of us to overtake them?" Nathaniel whispered to Tom as he looked at the gate and sentries atop it.

"Not a problem. The Astor House Mess may have once been formidable, but they have weakened from a lack of proper rations," Tom's remaining four brown teeth were visible between grinning lips and blackened gums. "Just do what comes natural."

The raiders' pace quickened. They were now within 40 feet of the reinforced stockade gate. Nathaniel gritted his teeth for the charge up the wall. Captain Moseby shrieked a battle cry. The men took up the call. Nathaniel watched the Confederate soldiers manning the wall. He readied himself to dodge musket fire, but the sentries only glanced at the charge with disinterest. Nathaniel suddenly realized why. The Astor House Mess was not the confederate storehouse on the other side of the gate, but the name of a group of five Union soldiers who were sleeping under a worn coverlet. Captain Moseby, Tom and the rest of the raiders clubbed the five battling victims unconscious, and then stripped them of all food and any personal articles of value; hats without holes, jackets with holes, three blankets, four canteens that had been cut in half and used as plates, and six Union dollars worth 60 Confederate.

During the scuffle, while the occupants of the Astor House Mess put up a respectable fight, not a single raider observed that Nathaniel simply stood by with knife in hand and mouth agape...stunned.

These are our boys, Nathaniel's mind shouted.

When the raiders ran off carrying their booty, Nathaniel turned and walked away, his feet dragging, his ears filled with the moans of beaten men, his heart filled with sadness. "These are our boys," whispered Nathaniel. All around Nathaniel, the accusing eyes of skeletonized men and boys, some alive, some dead, stared at Nathaniel as he passed. He felt so low. Being ashamed was a new experience.

In the morning, Tom found Nathaniel sitting quietly near one of the foul wells, throwing rocks at rats that were affectionately called graybacks. As Tom walked up to Nathaniel, he tossed two small gold finger rings, "Here's your share. We ate all the grub last night so Cap'n Moseby said to give you these. He believes all who work to acquire shall partake equally."

Nathaniel caught the rings. They burned in his hand, "I ain't taking 'em." Nathaniel stood to confront Tom, "You're worse than the grayback vermin skittering around dung. Beating and stealing from our own boys; what kind of men are you?"

"But we would starve," was Tom's reply, not meant as a defense, just a statement.

Nathaniel shook his head, "Didn't I tell you I got the most luck? Even if we have to eat these rats we'll live to reap revenge on these Johnnies. Now whose rings are these?"

Though Tom physically towered over Nathaniel, and meanness was a way of life, he felt smaller than a worm. To look at Tom, even with his imposing size, he appeared as a scolded child shuffling his feet while the schoolmaster inflicted a corrective lecture. Tom was in reality a giant, muscle-bound willow to be bent in any direction the wind blew. He only wanted better for himself, and would look to anyone with a stronger personality than his own to follow into good or evil. "Well? Who do these rings belong to?" demanded Nathaniel. Tom looked around in the direction of the gate to where the Astor House Mess once stood. Mustered, prepared to march, hobble, or be carried out of the stockade, were 150 men.

"There," Tom pointed toward one of the many emaciated men standing in line. "John is his name. Yeah. John something or another."

Two events occurred almost at once. The first was the stockade gate slowly opened for the prisoners to be marched out and transferred south. The rumors were that they were going to Florida, and away from the advancing Union troops. John Ramson was among them. He used to be a handsome, virile man of 24, at one time a strapping 165 pounds, but now a gaunt 115. Being a horseman and hailing from Michigan, John had joined Company "A", 9th Calvary. John loved his mount and would give anything to have her here with him. If he had any saliva he would be salivating at the thought of eating her. John's year as a P.O.W. was horrendous, but he fared better than most. John Ramson was still alive. After Moseby's attack last night, the only belongings left to John were a pair of mismatched boots and hemp pants with only one leg, their previous owner having had his leg amputated by a Confederate surgeon trying to stem a gangrenous leg wound. The gangrene was stopped, but the application of used bandages created an infection that killed the patient. John scrounged a lice-infested shirt from a deceased friend, which no amount of washing could sanitize. There was no soap. He carried several notebooks wherein he journaled daily events. John's hope was that if he did not survive, the world would know what took his life, and as these notes were of no value, they could not be eaten, Moseby's raiders ignored them.

Tom and Nathaniel watched as John Ramson marched out the gate. What they could not see was John rubbing his swollen finger that had until last night bore two gold rings given him by his wife and daughter. They were tangible items that gave him strength daily. The loss of them was immeasurable to his spirit that pined for home.

'"Looks like they're yours now," Tom shrugged his shoulders.

"They're not, and by God, one day I'll see them back to their rightful owner."

The second event secured Tom as Nathaniel's companion. From the open gate, three dozen Union prisoners rushed in. These men had been deputized by Captain Wirtz to act as a prisoner police force. Carrying oak clubs, their attack was upon Captain Moseby and his band of raiders. The fighting was a sight to behold. The outcome would determine the future peace and safety within the stockade, and the life expectancy of the raiders. Clubs swung, men and beasts shrieked and cried out, as bodies were broken. The jumble who were engaged, trampled and tripped over the barely living and the dozens of dead lying stinking and swelling in the sizzling sun. Those who had passed on were rotting fodder for flies and graybacks. This was a charnel house without the comfort of a roof, a gladiator arena where the dispatched were left where they fell.

It is man's eternal prayer that good shall conquer evil, and in this case, prayers were answered. Captain Moseby and the worst of his raiders were arrested and turned over to Captain Wirtz, as cheers of joy and relief echoed off the hills. A military court made up of Union men tried each raider. At the conclusion, a proper sentence was prescribed. On the morning of July 11, 1864, Captain Moseby, now known by his Christian name, William Collins of "D" Company, 88th Pennsylvania, and five others, were hung on gallows erected inside the gate. Nathaniel and Tom looked on from a distance. Tom involuntary rubbed his neck, knowing rightfully, that he, too, should be standing next to Captain Moseby. When Moseby's plank was kicked from under him, Tom flinched, as he watched his leader drop. The rope yanked taut, and then snapped with a twang, dropping the condemned man to the dirt. Whimpering, the terror of comrades, begged for his life, and swore repentance. Among a few Union prisoners who saw blood running from Moseby's nose, mouth, and ears, there were murmurs of clemency, but his victims, both alive and dead, won out, and a sturdier rope was found to make Moseby dance from. He died hard. All who witnessed the hanging declared it a thing of beauty.

That evening, Tom spoke softly to Nathaniel, "It be a dang lucky thing that I was with you when they came for Moseby. You're sure a lucky man to be around. I'm stick'n close, even as you say we got to eat maggots and rats."

And that is what they ate, vermin, along with corn bread that tasted of sand, and a few peas that they could trade for. Day in and day out, Nathaniel and Tom, along with thousands of others tried to conserve energy and wait. Wait to be exchanged or for the Union army to prevail. Unknown to the sufferers, General Grant had ended the gentleman's agreement to trade off prisoners, as he believed this policy would only advantage the South. But the men held out hope, weak hope, and weakening as their bodies crumbled from within from a lack of food and sanitary conditions. Captain Wirtz knew this and took full psychological advantage. Standing stooped and looking like death warmed over with sunken cheeks and hair falling out in clumps, the prisoners took bets on who would pass into eternity first, them or Captain Wirtz. Still, each morning, the red devil stood on the stockade's catwalk. He would hold prominently in each hand so that all could see, two mouth-watering wood ducks, or some other passing fowl that were shot that day, and then offered a pardon to any man who would take an oath of allegiance to the Confederacy. The temptation of food, coupled with the fear of death was strong, but a traitor was still a traitor.

"I'm going to do it," cried Tom. "I've got the scurvy. My vision is blurred. My teeth are falling out and my legs are cramping." Tom was indeed a sorry sight, but not worse than many, and still better than most, including Nathaniel, who simply smiled. "You needn't disgrace yourself like that 'cause I've hatched a plan and I suppose it's time."

The morning of September 5, 1864 began as usual. Some men awoke to a bright fall day while many of their companions did not. Andersonville was culling the human herd by 300 a day. The living, if strength remained, would carry their departed brothers to the gate, to be lined in rows and stacked like cord wood. Each day at four in the afternoon, a six-mule wagon was driven inside to be loaded, and then the bodies carted away as so much refuse, to be indignantly dumped, a hundred in each trench, in a cemetery, a hundred or so rods away. Weary men dug the trenches and covered the dead with a layer of soil. Rarely did the diggers keep up with the body count, and the stack of soulless vessels remained exposed throughout the night. Nathaniel counted on this and was rewarded.

After being roughly tossed onto the wagon, rolled off with a thump onto bodies from the day before, he waited among the empty vessels, but not under dirt. Hours passed. The sun faded from the sky. He was not dead, but the bugs that infested the pile did not know or care. They nibbled and chewed. It was all Nathaniel could do not to scream. He worried that Tom would not be able to remain silent under the torture, and betray them with a cry. Hearing only crickets, Nathaniel wriggled out from under to drink in his first breath of free air in four months...so sweet. It had felt like four years.

Five feet away, the pile of corpses heaved as Tom clawed to the surface. He retched; dry heaves racked his body, tearing at this empty stomach. Tom wiped his parched mouth. Nothing had come up.

"Now that's a birthing. From death we arise. From nothing we will become something," Nathaniel clasped Tom's hand to assist him to his wobbly feet.

"Now the revenge?" Tom asked.

"Now the spoils," Nathaniel's grin was infectious, the good kind.

Tom winked at Nathaniel, "There are those silver buttons of yours to be replaced."

"My price rose with each pound of flesh that has fallen away," Nathaniel's ragged uniform hung on his bony frame like an unfurled sail flapping on the boom of a Chesapeake skipjack.

"I once heard a banker speak of compound interest. I'm thinking that's what we're after," Tom teases Nathaniel with high speak, his idea of fancy, educated man's dialogue. Nathaniel is not only not impressed, but becomes angry, gruffly pushing up against Tom, coming chin to chest with him, and growled, "I ain't interested in interest. I want recompense. You heard of that? I'm owed. Gold and silver for flesh." Nathaniel turned away, his face red, then snorted, "You coming?" Tom followed. Nathaniel's greed for riches and malice for the South was apparent in his determined, purposeful steps, as this dwarfish man led the giant on a treasure hunt.

Their first task was to acquire weapons, transportation and grub. Confederate swords were unearthed from fresh graves. They were used, but not used up, as the two unfortunate Grays, now ex-owners of side arms and quarter horses learned as they tended a bean stew over a secluded campfire. The Grays never tasted the concoction, but Tom did comment that it needed salt.

In the beginning, Tom and Nathaniel's adventure for spoils of war was frustrated. Each plantation the men came upon had already come under plunder, and burned by Union troops; many were abandoned. The few owners who remained to stir the ashes could offer the two fortune seekers only half of what they desired. However, half being better than nothing at all, Tom and Nathaniel took full advantage. Southern gentlemen were beaten until they sang the greatness of the North with gusto, even if it was through swollen and bloodied lips. Frightened ladies were coaxed into offering their feminine ways. The two men would indulge at the same time, or one followed the other depending on the resolve of the gentleman defending the honor of his wife or daughters, or the degree of persuasion required of the ladies. Though to a man, in stories to be told with wild embellishments, in some tavern, where the drinks poured from bottomless casks, each would swear no girl child or woman was violated without prior permission.

"Remember," Nathaniel would say, "most Johnny Rebs been kilt, and well, a woman can go only so long before the urge to have her bed and body warmed overwhelms 'em." Then while laughing, he would add, "And what lady could refuse the likes of us?"

– 1865 –

Months passed since Nathaniel and Tom's last spoil and each was itching for more. The tricky part was avoiding Confederate patrols, but the men had caught two gunners unaware. The feeble husband was digging up their cache of heirlooms; a pair of four-inch silver candle holders. Tom's face took some slicing in the exchange. The deep cut across his chin gave him the appearance of having two mouths, "The old biddy had a knife!" Surprised more than hurt, Tom had kicked the headless body of the woman into the shallow hole. Her husband lay nearby, swearing his last breaths through tears while holding his entrails with one hand, and his wife's head with the other. "You'd think they were protecting the crown jewels."

The direction the men rode, though meandering, was generally westward. Daily quarrels between the two grew to the point that separation or a fight to the death had been imminent. Only Luck prevented the partnership from dissolving, for as the horses crested a rise, there, spread out before the riders was the Mother-lode, a pristine Mississippi plantation. Valley acreage, which the discomforts of war, the violence, and the depravities had miraculously bypassed, leaving a fine, pillared mansion surrounded by productive fields of tobacco. It was apparent to the two salivating men that until recently, this property had been meticulously maintained. Once perfect rows of tobacco were overgrown at the edges, and a light film of brown dirt and gray dust dimmed the white washed house and windowpanes.

A puzzle.

Nathaniel wondered, *where was the benevolent master wearing white, sitting fat on the wide porch, and drinking mint juleps? Where were all the slaves to tend the crop?*

"It's a virgin without no chastity belt," softly whistled by Tom as he licked his lips.

"Not even a black buck to stand in our way," Nathaniel added happily. "Still, let's approach from the back," he said pointing to a stand of elms. "We can come up unseen from there just in case anyone is looking out from a window."

Inside the grand home, Abigail busied herself with the work of three housemaids. She continued to lag behind the gathered dirt. It did not matter to her because her only thought was to prepare the perfect bed chamber for her husband, Captain Henry Parker, the third generation Parker to command this house and its vast holdings. Abigail was 25, and every inch of her scrubbed and perfumed body shouted a passion, a lust built on love that had been held in check for five years. She had waited patiently, counting each long, lonely day, for her Captain to return home from war. The reunion last evening had not gone well. Defeated in battle and relieved of duty, Captain Parker returned home in disgrace. He had stood on the steps of the wide veranda and surveyed another defeat in the making—empty fields and silent slave quarters. The life's work of his grandfather and father of acquiring, trading, and breeding of 215 slaves was gone—vanished with the drying pen stroke of a damn fool President who did not understand, or obviously care about the livelihoods of Southerners.

"If it were up to me I'd cram that Emancipation Proclamation so far up Lincoln's backside..."

"Henry!" Abigail gently shushed her husband as she stepped up behind him. "You shouldn't speak ill of the dead."

"What?" Captain Parker turned to look into the softest eyes he had seen in years, a face so tender, so lovely, with a head full of chestnut hair flowing to her corseted waist. Her ample bosoms discreetly covered in daylight, but all he saw, what drew his thoughts and desires were her two nipples standing at military attention. They called for his caresses. Captain Parker shook away his conflicted thoughts.

Anger or laughter?
Despair or joy?
Hatred or love?
Slaves or Abigail?

"President Lincoln was shot by a Mr. Booth during a play. I believe it was April 14th. He died the next day," Abigail spoke with tenderness as she searched her husband's worried eyes for the answer to the question her heart longed to ask. *Will we make love tonight?* She had missed him so—missed his patient but passionate touch. Although he was only five years her senior, he seemed far more experienced than she when it came to the pleasures found within the marriage bed. Abigail would never dare ask where he had gained this intimate knowledge. She was happy, content to be the one who received the benefits of his bedtime abilities.

"Well they ought to make Mr. Booth the President," Captain Parker turned back to face the darkening fields as the orange sun slipped behind the distant hills. His calloused hands felt Abigail's silky ones. He gave them a comforting, reassuring squeeze, "I have to find some field hands or we'll be ruined. Please don't wait up. I'll return tomorrow, and then we can...celebrate." Captain Parker left the meaning of the word to Abigail's interpretation as he strode off to saddle his horse. Abigail stood as a silhouette. Her mind raced ahead to what tomorrow would bring. So much to do to properly welcome her husband home in that special way only a wife can do.

Nathaniel and Tom walked their horses over spring clover, silent, stealth preceded an attack. The men had prearranged assignments. Nathaniel would race to the second floor while Tom scoured the first for occupants and spoils.

The horses were tied to posts extending from a sweet-water well, 15-feet from the rear door. The horses' heads jerked against their reins, startled by Abigail's scream that pierced the serenity of the peaceful valley. Nathaniel had caught Abigail in the master bedroom. She had finished fluffing and turning down the bed in anticipation of the celebration to come, and was sponging her body afresh when the door burst open.

Downstairs, Tom dragged a tablecloth filled with silver and gold: goblets, plates, utensils, candle holders, ashtrays, snuffboxes, and items he could not identify, but oh God, how they shined, and they were his. Tom would live as a king from that day forward. Abigail's screams were of little interest.

"A king can have all the ladies in the world," mused Tom.

In Havre de Grace, in Tavern Bouvard, the men shouted, slapped one another on the back, and toasted victory, as the newspaper headline was read aloud.

"LEE SURRENDERS TO GRANT"

The date was April 9, 1865.

The five-year war had ended. The States of America remained united. The Union was victorious, but at what cost? The human toll was 364,511 dead, 281,881 wounded. These grisly numbers only took into account those killed and wounded on official battlefields, and those who perished in prisoner of war camps. Not included were those killed and injured by the many hands of the victorious and the vanquished, seeking personal justice on unofficial fields of battle.

The gates of Andersonville opened. Of the 40,611 Union soldiers who entered into this hell, only 31,132 escaped the reaper. Many miles from loved ones, 9,479 died from neglect, and though surrounded by thousands, who would do what they could to ease the passing, each was essentially alone. The men's last thoughts, their only wish had been to return home to their families and to the life-giving victuals awaiting them.

Abigail's lovely body, kept pure, to be offered freely to her husband lay face down on soiled sheets. The skin of her back scratched by the claws of a mistreated animal, whose thoughts were simply to punish Captain Wirtz. Tuffs of Abigail's scented hair lay where they were tossed, ripped, from her bleeding scalp. The sheets Abigail could clean, but she could never scrub hard or deep enough to remove the violation that invaded her, and would begin to grow. Abigail was silent, not so much as a whimper. Her mind as well as her vow of fidelity had been broken. Nathaniel sat in a high back leather desk chair with his trousers scrunched around his ankles, allowing his manhood to cool, and catching his breath, thinking, *She's a hot one indeed.* He struck a match to light his new gold-banded pipe. Mentally contented and physically spent, he exhaled sweet tobacco smoke as he surveyed his room and the woman he had finished loving. "I could live like this," Nathaniel spoke to no one, as he was essentially alone in the room. Abigail's body remained, but her mind had departed. "Yes. I certainly could make of go of a place like this."

"Riders approaching!" Tom called a warning from below.

Yanking up his trousers as he jumped to his feet, Nathaniel stripped a pillow of its case and stuffed everything of value into it: silver bed table trays, brushes and combs with handles edged in gold, and his lady's jewelry, exotic strings of pearls, ruby earrings, and three jade bracelets. Before darting out of the bedroom, Nathaniel caressed Abigail's delicate fingers one last time, and then pulled her diamond wedding ring off. She remained as before, still, unmoving, as if dead. Her mind wanted death, but the muscle that pumped blood would not cooperate.

This is how Captain Henry Parker discovered his wife.

Eight months and 22 days later, a healthy child was born.

One hour after the birth, Abigail Parker threw herself into the well. The mistress of the mansion broke her neck and drowned. Captain Parker named the child Dorothy.

During their hasty departure from the Mother lode, Nathaniel and Tom whipped their mounts without mercy until one, and then the other collapsed from under them. The escape was made without detection. Upon reaching the border of Tennessee, the two men appropriated an unattended buckboard and the harnessed mule to carry them to Memphis. The pace was slow but neither man minded. Their future was set before them, bright and comfortable, because the fortune, their spoils, their recompense, was nestled safely in a gunnysack behind them, always within arm's reach. Justice, at least for Tom and Nathaniel had been meted out to their satisfaction.

The port of Memphis was a confusion of men, women, and children. There were merchants, pickpockets, ex-soldiers, and prostitutes, whites and Negroes—all jostling, all free, but not equal in their minds or under the law. Lined against this Tennessee quay were side-wheelers and stern-wheelers, Mississippi river paddle boats, some sparkling but many worn. Their captains pulled whistle cords, hooted and toot-tooted for attention and commerce.

This was a cacophony of life.

This was a celebration for the living.

These people had survived.

This was a new beginning for all.

They were the lucky ones.

Nathaniel and Tom exchanged enough of their spoil to purchase tailored suits, stiff polished shoes, top hats, and canes. To men who have stood on the bottom rung of the social and economic ladder their entire lives, possessing these symbols of culture and marks of good breeding were necessities and proof that they were gentlemen. There was only one crack in the fine armor.

Neither felt the expenditure of a nickel for a hot and soapy bath was within their budget. Frugality was their new word. Just because one has the means does not mean one has to be extravagant. Three pennies for a shave was sufficient.

The 15-year old deckhand of the *Sultana* bowed deeply as the two gentlemen crossed the gangplank from the quay to board the side-wheeler. This act, which he had learned early on, usually garnered him a penny from the well-heeled, a nickel if they were generous or drunk. It was not until the two passed by, curling the youth's nose, did he recognize them for what they were—wolves in sheep's clothing. The lad would keep clear of these poseurs.

Twilight settled on Memphis as the first cool breeze watched the *Sultana's* paddles churn the chocolate water of the Mississippi as its mooring lines, forward and aft, were tossed aboard—bon voyage. A crew of 12, haggard men and boys, looked after the 2400 Union soldiers who had recently been released from P.O.W. camps, and the 100 civilians; men, women, and children who occupied the first class cabins. Including themselves in this last group, the upper and elite class, were Nathaniel and Tom. This vessel of the great Mississippi also carried horses, mules, hogs, and surprisingly a curiosity, a live ten-foot alligator that was kept in a wooden crate. For a penny, the deckhand would allow the brave to stick their hand through a cut out in the side of the crate to feel the hissing monster's scaled skin. To touch a living dinosaur raised goose bumps large enough to honk. It was worth a penny to prove one's bravery. The captain was hugely pleased with his manifest. He was not concerned that his vessel had a maximum capacity of 376 passengers and crew. "If they have the price of a ticket, I'll give them passage," the captain declared as he slapped his pilot on the back while coins jangled heavy in his purse.

Luck struck again.

In Havre de Grace, in Tavern Bouvard, the men silently toasted the memory of comrades in arms as the news clipping from the local paper, the *Republican* was read aloud.

SULTANA SINKS

One thousand, five hundred and forty-seven lost. On April 27, 1865, eight miles out of Memphis, Tennessee, the boiler of the Mississippi side-wheeler *Sultana* exploded, and the ship burst into flames. Eyewitness accounts report that during the night, the *Sultana* burned to the waterline while its survivors clung to floating debris. Many passengers were trapped aboard the flaming ship and died in the inferno. During the shipboard fire, one desperate individual managed to kill an alligator with a knife, and then used its crate to float to safety. An on-scene reporter attempted to interview this lucky, though waterlogged gentleman as he stomped away, but all he said was, 'It's all gone—all my spoils.' Clearly, this poor man was in a state of shock, as were all the lucky survivors of this tragedy.

– 1866 –

Frustrated by the lack of success, Luck decided to bide its time, figuring Nathaniel Joiner would place himself in a position where Luck could strike with finality. Fifteen months, 1200 mean miles, and many an ill-planned scheme found Nathaniel walking through the front door of his wooden hovel. Two unfamiliar children looked up at the stranger from the corner where they sat, and then returned to their occupation, poking an oyster toadfish that they held hostage in a rusty tin can. His bride was surprisingly welcoming, pleased to see him. She planted an affectionate kiss on his whiskered cheek, while picking his pocket of a dollar and some change, and then departed, never to be seen again.

If Nathaniel had been more direct in his route home, he may have been offered a refreshing mug of beer in Tavern Bouvard, as the daily *Republican* was read aloud, the 23rd of June 1866 by the proprietor. The article was not prominently featured, but it gave a measure of comfort to those personally touched.

CAPTAIN WIRTZ HUNG

The commander of the infamous Confederate prisoner of war camp in Andersonville, Georgia, was found guilty of war crimes during his trial in Washington D.C. Captain Wirtz's conviction was based on numerous eyewitness testimonies including a doctor, Joseph Jones, Surgeon P.A.C.S., and Professor of Medical Chemistry in the Medical College of Georgia, at Augusta, Georgia. Captain Wirtz was dispatched for hanging without ceremony, and then buried in an unmarked potter's grave. This reporter acknowledges that war is hell, but it is a moral imperative that defenseless prisoners be treated with dignity and respect. It is hoped, nay, prayed for that Captain Wirtz's example will be a lesson in what not to do, God forbidding, the good citizens of this nation are unable to resolve their differences over a friendly game of cards at their local watering hole.

Nathaniel allowed the children, August and Claire, to raise themselves, he being absent for days on end until he departed, only to return for a meal every few years.

August and Claire found comfort in each other's company, and managed quite well without formal education or adults for supervision. Their teachers were the swamp, field, forest, stream, marsh, and bay where each received a Master's degree in living off the land.

On a rare sighting of Nathaniel in Havre de Grace, a concerned townie carrying a parasol with the newest decorations, asked of his offspring and their close relationship. Nathaniel snapped, "They happy? Then let 'em find love where they can."

– 1899 –

Claws scratching at the door, and muffled barks, rouse August from the warmth of the family nest. Wearing his too short in the arms and legs long underwear, he rubs his bearded face with massive hands to wake himself as he strides to the door. These hands are rough as sand paper, scarred and calloused from years of work without protective gloves. Sliding the door's bolt, August opens it.

"Dog, what you fussing about?"

Sitting on her haunches in the packed snow, Dog, August's black Labrador retriever excitedly wags her tail, sweeping the entrance mat clean. Dog looks up into August's brown eyes, while offering him the mallard from her mouth. Flakes float in, landing on August's six-foot two-inch, 220-pound frame that spans the entrance, but the sight before him is so surprising, too amazing for him to be bothered by the chill. Dog sits surrounded by seven, no make it eight dead waterfowl.

"Claire. Claire! Get yourself up. You're not going to believe this." August accepts the mallard from Dog, as Claire steps to the door to peer through the crack left between the door's frame and her man. At her breast is her infant, Delbert, who peacefully drinks his first meal of the day.

"Where in the world?" Claire stares at the fowl, and then up at August, just as amazed, and dumbfounded by what appears to be a heavenly gift. Dog jumps in circles, yapping, anxious to run off.

"Wake the boys and start 'em cleaning these birds. I'm going to get to the bottom of this," August pulls on his pants and shirt, drags on his insulated coveralls, his boots, and as he steps outside, he snatches his jacket off a peg by the door, "Go, Dog." Dog shoots off through the snow, circling back every 20 yards to bark to ensure that her boss is still following, despite the darkness, and the obscuring snowfall.

Upon reaching the ice-lined shore of the bay, August follows his bounding dog a hundred yards north to an unfamiliar snow-covered mound. Dog sits proudly, facing and barking at this white heap.

"Hush," August steps forward to better examine Dog's find, and then jumps back, startled, as the mound moves. A groan is heard from within, as August recognizes the mystery object for what it is.

"Clay!"

August urgently brushes off the covering snow, tossing the birds onto shore. Dog, believing this to be a game, tries to catch each one, and then places them neatly in a row as August has taught her. Seeing Clay lying semi-conscious next to the Davenport, August's first thoughts are that the breech has exploded. August shudders at the thought of finding a friend with part of his skull blown away. At that moment, Clay rolls onto his side, exposing an intact face. Relief washes over August.

"Clay, where you hurt?" August checks Clay's arms, legs, torso, and head for obvious injuries, but finds only slight frost bite in the fingers, and a small cut on the side of his head.

"Stupid," Clay mutters.

"What's that?"

"Stupid. I got whomped by a honker right on the head. Stupid!" Clay coughs, and then slowly sits up with August's help.

"Yeah, maybe stupid, but you're damn lucky you weren't knocked overboard," shaking his head, August closely examines the dried blood, and the knot on Clay's forehead. "It doesn't look as if any permanent damage has been done. Let's get you under cover. I'll have my boys collect the birds and stow your gear."

"Hold up. Reb? Where's Rebel?" Clay scans the crooked shore. Fear swims in his eyes as he turns to stare at the bay. The expansive water is quiet, calm, and peaceful. Snow lazily falls and ice drifts as it may from the unseen current below. Clay's gut tightens as he is gripped with sadness and guilt as he realizes he betrayed a partner's, a friend's trust, "Oh, Reb! Damn." With stoic resolve, Clay keeps the emotion from his face, rolling a cigarette for distraction.

August rubs Dog's head.

"Ouch," Claire winces as Delbert bites her nipple. It's his way of letting his mother know that this breast is out of milk. "You're going to be a fat man if this is your attitude toward food now," Claire readjusts Delbert in her arms to give him her full one. With her free hand, she rinses two tin cups in a metal basin. He-man coffee had been the liquor to warm August and Clay. Claire was neutral on the point that Clay was not dead, and very disappointed that the birds were not hers for the keeping.

Refreshed, the men and boys, with Dog tagging along, return to the sneak skiff to retrieve the Davenport. Though August's sons are dependable, kept always in check by the threat of a thrashing, or a handy switch, Clay prefers to carry the Davenport home where he can be assured of its safety. With the boys' practiced help, August ties the fowl in pairs, hen to drake, and then loops them over a long pole to be carried on the boys' shoulders. The skiff will be retrieved in the morning. Clay, August, the boys, and Dog, crunch the crystalline snow as they tramp south along the shore. The snow-laden clouds have scattered with the breeze to reveal a brilliant half moon that casts reflected rays to light their trek.

"If only they were diamonds," the oldest son remarks, pointing to the countless sparkles in the snow. "I'd scoop 'em up and be the richest man in the world."

"Not if I scooped more than you, Chet," the younger challenges, never wanting to be outdone by the firstborn.

"Lloyd, that's a laugh, as it'll never happen. I'm stronger, bigger, and faster. You'd never carry more than me. You're second fiddle and will always be."

"I'm not second fiddle," Lloyd kicks snow at his brother, "Take it back."

"Hush!" orders August. "Let the night be as it is...quiet."

Nighttime in the marsh next to the Chesapeake Bay is anything but quiet, regardless of the season. What August wants, and if asked, Clay would concur, is the silence of humans to allow the critters, creatures, and birds to create their inspiring, sometimes eerie chorus of life: dabbling and diving ducks splashing in the shallows, geese honking as they cross the silvery moon, river otters cracking stream ice as they playfully chase white perch out of their deep holes, beavers snapping branches or felling trees for their lodges, and unbelievable as it sounds, both August and Clay claim to be able to hear the silent flight of the tree owl, an oxymoron to be sure, though no one but an innocent child would challenge these hunters' assertions.

Moving steadily through this dark night that is lit up by the moon, and within the noisy quiet, it is understandable that the group becomes uneasy approaching Clay's shack. There is an unnatural, true silence, a stillness that raises the hair on the back of their necks as they sight the dwelling. A black eye and gaping mouth stare back. Dog leaps ahead, but abruptly stops at the foot of the porch.

Dog barks off key.

Dog has stopped wagging her tail.

Clay's pace quickens.

Striding up next to Dog, the group looks at the peculiar human-size snail trail of discolored ice stretching along the porch. It points through the open doorway as if it were a frozen arrow.

"Jennifer," Clay rushes inside, followed by all, including Dog. The Davenport thuds as it is dropped carelessly to the wood floor. "Jesus Christ Almighty. Keep the boys out," Clay shields the shadowed figure lying on the bed. His boot nudges an unseen object on the floor.

"What's wrong?" August enters the bedroom carrying the lantern from the table. Adjusting and lighting the wick, he holds it above his head. The bright flame illuminates the tragedy before them. At the same instant, the eyes of the boys peering around their father's jacket are burned forever with the horror. They had seen blood in their young lives, but not this kind, and not from this source. Dog sits next to the rocking chair, acting the sentinel, a guardian of the entrance. She knows when to keep quiet.

Tiny puffs of steam rise from Jennifer's mouth, as shallow breaths signal life.

"She's breathing." Clay's body surges with adrenaline, as his mind cries out with relief, *She's alive!*

Jennifer is lying on her back, her flesh blued from the cold. Her soiled housedress is knotted around her waist. Her splayed legs are bloodied, surrounding gelatin afterbirth. Running from the jellyfish glob between her legs to the floor by Clay's boot is a lifeline. Clinging to it with tiny clenched fingers, as a drowning man lost overboard, is Clay's progeny, his future, his hope...his daughter.

"Boys, run fetch your mother, and then to town for Doctor Webster," August's instructions fall on deaf ears as his sons stare, eyes transfixed. "Now!" "Move it!" August shoves the boys toward the front door. They tumble across the icy porch, landing only for an instant in a heap in the snow before each is up and running. The boys will continue to run through the night and into the morning until their mission is complete, because there is nothing more severe than a father's wrath for disobedience...their backsides having felt the sting of August's sand paper hands.

Dog's eyes, black as coals, study the intensity of her boss and Clay. Their movements are economical, serious and deliberate, as each tends to a body whose spirit is deciding which side of the River Jordan to abide on. Dog then twists her powerful neck in time to see the heels of the boys, running enthusiastically, playfully pushing and shoving each other into drifts of snow in a spirited race to somewhere. Dog's decision is easy. Out the door she sprints, kicking up snow and barking her entry into the contest.

Doctor Webster's chestnut mare stamps her feet, snorts steam from flared nostrils, and rattles her buggy harness, as she shakes off the remnants of an errant snowball. The mare, Gracie, patiently waits outside the Buchanan residence. Gracie's large frame is being used as a defensive shield in the battle for world domination. The combatants are older brother versus younger brother. The ferocity and intensity matches the classic Romulus versus Remus conflict, but it is not quite the same due to the canine arbitrator preventing either side from taking any unfair advantage. Dog barks at both sides, and then joins in with the victor's dance, a comic jig eliciting a renewed camaraderie between the antagonists.

Claire Joiner steps out onto the porch of the Buchanan shack, as the first golden rays of the sun streak over the eastern horizon. The light is magnified, as it skips, and reflects off the ice floes on the bay and the snow covering the ground. The brightness hurts Claire's eyes but the rays bring only false warmth. The day is clear of clouds and calm of wind, but all exposed flesh prickle from the chill that causes all in attendance to wither at the cold's nobility.

"Knock it off," Claire's annoyance is not so much with the boys and their antics, but with the child now suckling her nipple. Her precious milk is being drawn off by one not her own. *Del needs every drop,* Claire argues with herself. *If this child's mother can't feed it, then it should die.*

August appears at the threshold, "Please come inside, Claire. The child will catch cold."

Claire obeys. She always obeys. Love and devotion will make a person do that which is detestable, and do it with a smile.

Clay carries a soup bowl containing a light duck broth into the bedroom. He needs an excuse, a reason, and a purpose to return to the scene of the crime.

He is the criminal.

It is his fault.

Guilty as charged.

Neglect in the first degree.

Oh how the innocent suffer. His child was forced to enter a cold world without caring arms to embrace it. His wife, alone, ruptured, body torn, no husband for protection and comfort, is barely clinging to life.

"Stupid...stupid...stupid," Clay mutters, angry with himself. Doctor Webster pulls a clean quilt up to cover Jennifer's inert body. Clay's heart lurches as terror punches with a balled fist. An unthinkable grief drains Clay's soul. His gray eyes moisten as his strong body struggles to remain standing under the weight of despair. Doctor Webster tucks the quilt snugly, tenderly, grandfatherly, under Jennifer's pale chin, and then turns to face Clay.

"She may sleep through the day," whispers Doctor Webster in his gentle, sick room voice, "but wake her this evening, and make her take liquids, but don't force solids if she doesn't want any."

"She'll be all right?" stammers Clay, as the frightening question crosses his tongue. His cigarette smolders, hanging loosely at his lips. Clay cannot remember when he lit it or last inhaled. All his attention, his worry, and his concern have been over Jennifer, his wife, his joy, and his treasure. She is his life.

"Clay, it's a miracle she's still alive," Doctor Webster pauses, measuring his next words. Frankness is the course best taken with a direct man like Clay, "I've done what I can. She almost bled out and there is still some hemorrhaging that I can't stop. It may heal by itself, but that's out of my hands."

Clay's hands tremble, as his hold on the bowl is tentative. Doctor Webster places his soft and pudgy hand on Clay's slumped shoulder, hoping to impart strength to endure the likely, unstated outcome. Clay's gaze never leaves his wife's pallid face. Doctor Webster feels Clay's pain through his touch, though as men do, they never speak of feelings or emotions, so instead, Doctor Webster offers a platitude, "It's in God's hands now." Clay slowly nods in understanding, as if hearing the words from deep under water.

"Thanks for coming so quickly, Doc. I appreciate your efforts. Let me know the charge."

Doctor Webster pulls on his jacket, buttoning the brass buttons to cover his sausage paunch, "I wouldn't think of it. We're like family." Doctor Webster accepts his hat and scarf from August, as he passes Claire, who sits in Jennifer's rocking chair.

The child continues to suckle.

Claire is not rocking.

"It's very neighborly of you, Claire," Doctor Webster smiles at Claire, conveying natural warmth that is freely given.

"It is, isn't it," Claire replies, her tone flat.

Outside, the boys hold Gracie's reins as Doctor Webster hoists himself up onto the seat of the buggy, "Don't hesitate to send for me if need be." Tipping his hat, Doctor Webster snaps the reins to start Gracie on her way. Clay and August wave from the porch. The boys chase behind, and will continue to do so for the better part of a mile...all that energy. Doctor Webster knows two things. If he is sent for again, it will be to pronounce death, and that under his seat are a dozen fowl, the fattest and choicest, picked and cleaned—payment in full.

Hours before Doctor Webster climbed into the seat to drive Gracie home to where his goose-down bed would carry his 54-year-old body to dreamland, his wife, Martha, had sounded the alarm. Martha Marie Webster, a witness to 52 years, plump as a pumpkin, and sweet as fudge with blue-gray hair perfectly coiffed. Her only vice is her best asset. Martha cannot stop talking. There are no secrets in Havre de Grace. No reporter, however clever he may be, can scoop Martha. So depending on the news, she is loved or hated, but hated only momentarily, because Martha Marie Webster believes that no secrets should be kept in a family. The people of Havre de Grace and Harford County are her extended family, and she loves each and every individual, even the hard to love ones.

Olivia Bouvard whips the hindquarters of her father's gelding. Foam flies from its lathered mouth. Steam swirls in the animal's wake as they race past Gracie and Doctor Webster, the doctor attempting to control his startled mare. He is returning from the scene of a crime, and she answering the alarm for assistance. Briefly, Olivia contemplates reining around to consult with the doctor, but she does not want to hear that her dearest friend is dead. Doctor Webster begins to tip his hat in greeting, and to speak, but all he has time to do is look over his shoulder to see the tail of a distressed animal and the flying dress pleats of a fire-headed vixen.

Dog's ears are the first ones to hear the gelding as it stampedes ever closer, but all hear the shod hooves as they slide and then skid to a stop on the packed snow in front of the shack. Dog, his boss August, and the two boys have begun their walk home to begin the day's chores. Claire is left behind with instructions from August to see to the needs of the newborn, to Delbert, who is asleep in the corner, and to Clay and Jennifer. These are tasks that carry a mixed interest for Claire, as she is interested in only pleasing her man.

Upon entering the shack, Olivia takes quick measure of the situation. Clay, for once in his life, cannot figure out what to do. He paces back and forth between the Great Room and the bedroom, but accomplishes nothing except filling the air with tobacco smoke and intermittent coughs. Claire, most sour of disposition, remains seated on cushions handmade for another's comfort. For an instant, Olivia wonders if Claire's milk tastes more like a she-wolf's than a human, but the newborn appears content. And, thank God, the Almighty, Jennifer is alive.

Olivia immediately checks Jennifer from head to toe. She has no formal medical training, but being the daughter of a barkeep, one of curiosity, and with the innate perceptions of a woman, Olivia possesses a natural instinct for what needs to be done to cure, soothe, or ease the apprehension of one crossing over. For Jennifer, nothing can be done, but to wait. From the doorway, Clay watches as Olivia double-checks the wrap around Jennifer's ankle. This night has aged Clay considerably. His eyes, heavy with bags beg for the answer that none could give him.

"She's finished," is Claire's terse statement from behind Clay. He whirls around, shocked by her cruel statement, then realizing Claire means the newborn is finished feeding. Claire places the tiny infant into Clay's arms, scoops Delbert up, and is heading out the door when Olivia grabs her arm from behind.

With another woman present, Claire feels no compunction to remain.

"The child's belly is full. I need to tend to my own family," Claire states, as she pastes a look of pleading onto her face.

Olivia does not know Claire well, but she can read her, so she chooses her words carefully, "Miss Joiner, our good Lord will surely bless you for your unselfish acts. It's just that Mrs. Buchanan may not be strong, or well enough, to nourish the child for a couple days. Will you be returning soon?"

Put the child in a burlap sack and drop it into the bay for all I care is what Claire's eyes say, and she knows Olivia got the message. To Clay, Claire wears a mask of sweet apple pie, and with a toothy smile, answers, "I'll see what I can arrange." Claire jerks her arm free of Olivia's hold, and then exits with the intent of never darkening this doorway where death hovers ever again. Claire's world is her home, and her only desire is to stay sheltered within the birch swamp, raise her pack, and please August.

Five hours later, Claire appears on the Buchanan porch. She carries with her an otter stew and a bruised cheek. The stew was by order of August, as his traps had procured two large males, plenty to go around. And though Olivia silently believes the bruise was a corrective swat, and well deserved, by August, in reality it was self-inflicted when Claire tripped and fell against the center roof support pole. She was attempting to erase August's displeasure with her by coaxing him into their nest for delights of the flesh.

She pulled.

He pulled away.

She fell.

He nurtured, and then spoke in a low tone that allowed for only obedience.

Claire's stew was placed on the table among the many offerings brought by concerned friends. Martha Marie Webster's call reached far and would remain strong until the need passes.

For two weeks the good people of Harford County brought victuals so Clay could remain near Jennifer as she convalesced. Claire made an appearance every five or six hours, sometimes with Delbert crying at one breast, as if to remind Clay and Jennifer just what a sacrifice was being made to sustain the life of their child. Olivia knew better. She watched Claire closely when their paths crossed in the Buchanan home. Olivia made the trip once a day to encourage Clay, chat with Jennifer, and to play with the baby. Olivia saw that Claire suffered no ill effects. Her weight and complexion remained the same. Delbert put on more weight and the Buchanan baby was plump and happy.

Olivia is a great blessing to Clay. Though he can take perfect care of himself, cook, clean, and mend clothes, the sight of his ailing wife unhinges him. Olivia brings a sense of order, friendship, and lifts Jennifer's spirits when she is awake, which is still only a few hours each day. Her hemorrhaging, though slight, continues unabated, as the fall and then the too rapid birth tore her insides beyond repair.

In the evenings, Clay would watch Olivia with amusement. She is the complete opposite of Jennifer. Where Jennifer is ample of figure, Olivia is lean. Where Jennifer's hair is flowing and black, Olivia's is cut short and red. Where Jennifer is demure in her playfulness, Olivia possesses a startling sassiness that many times places a man back on his heels. She is a barkeep's daughter. Olivia is definitely not Clay's type, but she is invaluable to both Clay and Jennifer's positive mental well being, especially as the days turn into weeks, and the weeks turn into months.

Olivia never despaired...at least not publicly.

– 1900 –

Clay holds his daughter over the white marble baptismal while Pastor Isaac Davies sprinkles holy water onto the child's forehead from a silver chalice.

"Who gives this child to God's care and keeping?" asks Pastor Davies.

"I do. Her father," Clay replies.

Ninety days have passed since that long dark night when the Buchanan family almost ceased to exist. Christmas and New Year's came and went without much notice. Olivia continues to make her daily appearance, and on Christmas, she prepared a succulent goose with current jam in an attempt to lift the spirits and health of the household. Jennifer remains bedridden, and though some days are better than others, basic housework is out of the question.

Many men who spend their hours in the harsh elements to bring home food would find incapacitation of a wife a severe diminishment of the woman's worth, "If she can't clean, cook, or take care of my needs, what good is she?" This is a common retort by a disgruntled husband about his ailing wife though this is usually said as an excuse for a dalliance with another that is anything but frivolous.

Clay is just thankful that his child is healthy, and that his wife is alive. Their value to him is intrinsic...though a daughter is not what he expected. Clay rose early to travel to town this morning. The night before, he had argued with Jennifer, between coughs and cigarettes that the baptism could wait until she is well enough to accompany them. Clay could not argue long against tears.

"We must give her back to God," sobbed Jennifer. "She is only given to us in stewardship." Weakened further by exertion and emotion, Jennifer laid back, her face paled, as she appeared to shrink before Clay's eyes.

Olivia met Clay outside St. John's Episcopal Church. This building, the oldest structure in Havre de Grace is remarkable for its Flemish bond brick walls. Clay always admires its well executed round arched windows and its simple early 19th century appearance. Built in 1809 with funds raised by lottery, the British later damaged the building during the war of 1812, and then in 1832, it was gutted by fire. After the Lord's house was rebuilt, the only structural modifications have been a slate roof that was added in 1863 and a belfry in 1884, to call the faithful to worship.

Waiting inside the candle-lit church, and bathed in the glowing rays of the multi-colored stained glass windows is Martha Webster. Doctor Webster was to be in attendance, but was called away at the last minute by a medical emergency. Martha had brought with her a hand-sewn, white flannel cap and gown with lace, for the infant to wear. It was her gift to welcome a new member to the Havre de Grace family. Martha's grin stretched from ear to ear. She was so proud.

Pastor Davies gazes toward the heavens as if able to peer through the thick open beam ceiling and states, "I baptize this child of God, Anastasia Nicole Buchanan, in the Name of our Lord and Savior Jesus Christ."

Curling under the quilt, in a shack next to the great Chesapeake Bay, a mother cries.

– 1903 –

In Tavern Bouvard, tall mugs of chilled beer are passed around by Olivia, and then raised in a toast as Clay reads aloud from the local newspaper, the *Republican*:

MAN TAKES TO THE AIR!!!

Bicycle mechanics Orville and Wilbur Wright successfully flew their home-built air machine called *Flyer I* at Kill Devil Hills, North Carolina. From this day forward, men will no longer be bound by the weight of gravity, though as mortals, it is this reporter's opinion that we should take heed the lesson of poor Icarus.[2]

The year is 1903, the 17th of December.

"'Stick a candle in your pocket; I can't rest, Jim, till we give her a rummaging. Do you reckon Tom Sawyer would ever go by this thing? Not for a pie, he wouldn't. He'd call it an adventure—that's what he'd call it; and he'd land on that wreck if it was his last act. And wouldn't he throw style

---

2 Icarus. Greek myth. A youth, who with his father, Daedalus, built wings of wax and feathers in their attempt to escape from the island of Crete. Daedalus succeeded, but against his father's warnings, Icarus flew too high and the sun melted his wings. Icarus fell to his death.

into it? Wouldn't he spread himself, nor nothing? Why, you'd think it was Christopher Columbus discovering Kingdom Come. I wish Tom Sawyer was here.'" Jennifer reads from *Huckleberry Finn* as Anna snuggles under her arm while playing with the little gold cross on its chain around her mother's neck.

Sitting up in bed and reading to her bright-eyed, three-year-old daughter is the extent of Jennifer's strength, but it is a tender joy for both.

"Is Huck's Mississippi bigger'n my creek?" asks Anna, her eyes aglow, all questioning.

"Sweetheart, from what I know, in some ways the Mississippi is larger than our bay."

Astonished, Anna defends her known world, "No mama. That can't be right. Papa says the Ches-ee-peek is the greatest in the whole wide world."

Hugging Anna, Jennifer replies, "Your father is right, but it's not the biggest, and actually, the bay itself is a drowned river. It was carved thousands of years ago by ice, and then when the ice melted, the river overflowed."

Smiling with pride by her daughter's deductive powers, Jennifer turns their mother-daughter reading nest into a squirming, screeching, caterwaul, as she tickles, kisses, hugs, and nibbles her precious child.

"What's the ruckus?!" demands Clay at the bedroom doorway. "Anna, you've been told not to excite your mother."

"It's all right, Clay," responds Jennifer, winded and overworked, perspiration shining on her face.

"You have a guest. Are you feeling up for company?" asks Clay.

Umbrella George is standing off to the side behind Clay. His old face carries deep crevices of a man whose smile cannot be turned off. His curly black head of hair, which has broken the will of many a barber's comb, mysteriously transforms itself into an elegantly groomed beard, as it migrates down the sides of his V-shaped face.

Scooting Anna off the bed while straightening the coverlet, Jennifer's expression turns somber. It is as if a cloud's shadow stripped the brilliant hues from a monarch butterfly's wing. "Anna, darling, go outside with your father and ask him about the origins of our bay."

Anna bounces off the bed and run-waddles out the door.

I'll leave the two of you to your business," Clay nods to Umbrella George and then strides out after Anna.

Jennifer's tired eyes reveal the truth, the seriousness of her condition, as her gaze is drawn to that which Umbrella George cradles in his arthritic hands. They are old man's hands with wrinkles, swollen joints, and crooked fingers. Jennifer thinks, *I'd surely suffer all forms of maladies that old age can produce if only old age were guaranteed me.* To Umbrella George, Jennifer says, "Please come in. Is that it?"

"Yes, Mrs. Buchanan. It's my Bible sampler."

Outside the shed, Anna sits cross-legged in the dirt. Her yellow gingham dress is fanned out in a fashion to collect all the dirt, twigs, leaves, and crawling bugs as is possible for an inquisitive child. But instead of examining every object under foot, Anna's attention is glued to the mystery unfolding in her father's words. The only interruption to his lesson is his occasional cough, or his pause to roll another handmade cigarette.

Store-bought cigarettes are fine and dandy. They're like a meal in a diner, full of flavor, but lacking the essence of having done it just how you like it, is Clay's sentiment.

Clay, sitting on an upturned oak log, his practiced hands whittling effortlessly on a shapeless block of wood, his mind already picturing a mallard head, a decoy, one of many lures for a sinkbox gunner, he recites the creation of the Chesapeake Bay, "Many thousands of years ago, a block of ice called a glacier..."

"Was it bigger'n our house?" Anna interrupts.

"Much bigger. People call it the Ice Age, though there were no people around, except Indians, who are now gone."

"If no people were around then, except Indians...but aren't Indians people? And if they're gone, how do we really know?"

Clay smiles. A thinker she is, "People who call themselves geologists study the land, the rivers, the bay, and then figure all this stuff out. So as the glacier moved forward, it pushed and scraped at the earth, carving valleys as it went."

"Where are they now?"

"The valleys?"

"The valleys. The block of ice."

"Right there," Clay points toward the bay with his knife. "The whole of the Chesapeake is a wide valley with a river at the bottom. The water is the ice after it melted, flooded the river, and filled up the valley."

That night, Anna lies in her bed next to the stove in the Great Room. Her eyes fixed upon the undulating glow of dying embers, but seeing a far distant past. The glacier in her mind's eye is made of millions of rectangular blocks of ice similar to those she has seen being off-loaded from paddle wheelers at Havre de Grace wharfs. She is unable to imagine ice moving across the land on its own, so she seats Mr. McQuay on top with his plow horses hitched to the front. The horses are lathered, snorting, and whinnying under the crack of McQuay's merciless leather whip. Anna doesn't much like Mr. McQuay. She reasons that if her father doesn't like him, that is good enough for her.

"Always plowing new fields," Clay says with disdain. "How much money does one man need?"

Giggling to herself, Anna's imagination distorts McQuay's features to resemble a toad with many warts. Croaking and cracking his whip, Mr. Toad plows the ground until the glacier melts, the horses run away, and then, a passing fish swallows Mr. Toad. For amusement, Anna has the fish resemble herself, *Take that, Mr. McQuay.* Anna hugs herself while snuggling deeper into her quilt bed. Her eyes close in slumber, as the last of the embers wink good night.

Anna's eyelids snap open, wide with fear. Her little body shudders with fright. The voice in her head shouts, making her ears ring with alarm.

What was that?!

It wasn't the screech of an owl.

It wasn't a thump-bump of a beaver's tail.

Whatever It was, It was close...is close...but how close? The voice reels off her options:

Scream for help—It might attack.

Play dead—It may drag you away.

Peek out—It may not notice.

Slowly, cautiously, using one finger, Anna moves the quilt enough to peer out. The Great Room is dark. It is not hovering over her. In fact all is quiet. Anna looks toward the curtained doorway to her parents' bedroom. A faint light glows around its edges.

They're awake! Cries the scared voice in Anna's head. There is safety beyond the veil.

Squeak...thump.

It's back, but not as close. Run now, shouts the panicking voice. Quick as a lightning bolt, Anna's up, and almost through the curtain, when she stops in her tracks. Her cry for help swallowed by confusion. She stares at her mother. Her mother stares back. The dim flame from the ship's lantern glints off the gold cross lying moist in pooling sweat between Jennifer's bare breasts.

It is in here.

Squeak...thump.

Anna runs back to her quilt bed with echoes of It chasing her.

What was father doing? The voice in Anna's head demands. *Why was he kneeling across mother's neck and shivering so? Shivering as if cold, but he was wet with sweat. Why didn't he put on long underwear? He was grimacing with pain. Was mother biting him?*

A deep guttural groan crawls out from behind the curtain, then silence. Murmurs, and then silence again. A faint, rusty squeak of the lantern's wick being turned down is heard.

Lights out.

Silence.

Anna is alone with her confusing and disturbing vision. She does not remember falling into a troubled dream. This time the fish is her mother, and the toad she swallows is her father.

In the hours before dawn, Anna wakes to find herself in her parents' bed. Her mother's arm is holding her lovingly. The room is lit with warmth by the lantern. Her father is outside, cheerfully whistling.

"Anna, darling, I don't want you to be frightened by what you saw last night," Jennifer's complexion is pale, as she tries to comfort her perplexed child. "In a marriage bed there are certain things," Jennifer's eyes moisten, as she struggles for the right words. "Wonderful things that two people in love do for each other. Never be frightened or ashamed of love. Don't ever hold back anything because love is worth sacrificing the whole world for." Tears flow freely from Jennifer's eyes. Anna's pixie face scrunches with mixed emotions; relief, concern, confusion. Relief, in that the picture of her father sweating and jerking over her mother was not out of anger or from pain. Concern, for her mother's health, as her alabaster complexion turns translucent. Only the streaks of her tears reflect substance. Confusion, because Anna does not have the vocabulary to put into words the questions that would answer, if not calm her complicated fears, so she innocently asks, "Could you breathe through it?"

As one would goose an unsuspecting bottom, Jennifer's face flushes red. The ebony of her eyes explodes with micro stars at the memory of giving and receiving physical oneness, even if it wasn't in the traditional Christian way. Jennifer squeezes Anna so tightly that her joints feel as if they will pop out of their sockets. "At moments like that you don't think about breathing. Love takes your breath away anyway," sighs Jennifer, relaxing her grip on Anna. Anna gasps for air, filling her little lungs. "I see," is all Anna can say, now more curious than concerned.

"Now back to bed. Your father is taking the Davenport out this morning while it's still dark so there will be many ducks to help clean," Jennifer kisses her daughter on her forehead, then Anna tumbles across the bed, and onto the rough plank floor. Lying back, Jennifer closes her eyes, and then listens to her daughter's feet patter away into the distance.

"So far away is the Great Room," Jennifer whispers, as her mind wanders, pondering. "How does that little stove keep my baby warm in such a huge and elegant hall?" She breathes deeply. The walls of the shack, though many years old, still retain the fragrance of fresh hewn wood; maple, birch, probably even some elm. It is a forest of aromas to tickle and entice the senses. "Why am I so lucky?" Jennifer whispers, softer still, as she pictures her daughter's cherubic face. Her fingers, out of habit, gently stroke the angelic face before her...the carvings on the chest...Anna's...or another's? Jennifer's breath is so light it would not flicker the flame of a candle if it were placed an inch from her lips.

The amber beam of light blazing through the windowpane cooks Anna within her cocoon. She awakens startled and hot with perspiration coating her skin. Anna kicks back her quilt, and as she does, the muffled hacking cough of her father is heard beyond the curtain. On the three-duck counter, piled six to eight high, mallards, goldeneyes, and ruddy ducks, all fat with succulent meat, await cleaning. The Davenport lies on the floor. It too, must be cleaned and oiled before secreting away, safe from the game warden's grasp. *How many arms did the little Frenchman LeCompte say he'd give to get it?* Anna giggles at the recent memory of Warden LeCompte raving at her father in front of Tavern Bouvard. His arms waving, his feet stomping, his pencil-thin mustache twisted to a point at the ends, twitching as if infested with fleas. This was the scene Anna witnessed one Sunday when Olivia was returning with her from church.

"Look, Olivia, a dancing puppet," pointing toward LeCompte.

"Anna, LeCompte is the official game warden, dear. He is only doing what the law requires. You should respect him for that," Olivia stated, trying not to laugh at the spectacle before her.

Anna pushes back the bedroom curtain, as she wipes the sleep from the corner of her eyes, "Father?"

Clay is kneeling on the floor next to the bed. His body is racked, not with coughing fits, but something else. He turns slowly toward Anna. His face is drawn, eyes red, though not from tobacco smoke. His cheeks are moist, but not from washing in the bedside basin. The dead stub of a hand-rolled is crushed between yellowed teeth that grind it without conscious thought. Clay turns away from Anna to bury his face in the quilt. Anna's gaze rises to her mother's face. Such a strange expression she wears.

Joy and sorrow.

Peace and unease.

Restful, yet anxious.

These uncertainties, contradictions, are for Anna to ponder out later. For now, her mother is simply too still. Her father is crying. Anna stands in the doorway with one hand clinging to the open curtain, as if to a lifeline, the other without a thing to clasp. She cries quietly, afraid to disturb her sleeping mother.

– 1906 –

Delbert "Cigar" Joiner, Del for short, is the youngest and plumpest of the Joiner rabble. Now six and independent, the only limitation to his travels in the swamp and forest is his cigar foot. Several months after his birth, and while Claire, his mother was alternating between nursing him and Anna; she had left Delbert at home with instructions for the elder boys to look after their baby brother. On her return trip, Claire smelled and then saw smoke rising from the direction of her home. Running possessed, as only a mother can, she came upon their clearing to see August shoveling dirt onto the spreading flames, trying to smother them, while Dog barked and whimpered under a nearby tree.

Hearing Delbert's smoke-choked cries, Claire ran past August without hesitation, catching clumps of dirt in the face. Sputtering and screaming Delbert's name, she flung herself through the doorway to disappear into the black rolling smoke. August tried to follow, but a dragon's belch of flame barred his way. August shouted and paced, "Claire! Claire, come out of there! God in heaven, come out!" Rolling smoke from the doorway was the only answer. August shouted again, and shoveled on the dirt, as worried sweat ran from his pores in rivers. From behind August came the two boys carrying buckets of water. Screaming in pain and on fire, Claire is spewed from the doorway, clutching a blackened bundle in her arms. She fell to the ground as August and the boys tossed dirt and splashed water to douse the flames eating their mother's dress and hair and biting at her flesh.

Their nest was abandoned to the hungry flames. Everything of value was outside. Mother, father, children, dog, and the gun were all safe. The house could be rebuilt.

August carried Claire and Delbert to the bay to rinse off the mud and to cleanse their burns. A replacement dress could be sewn and her hair would grow back. Mother and son were alive, though Delbert's right foot was permanently disfigured. "Burned to the bone it was. Cauterized in the fire. Probably prevented infection," was Doctor Webster's opinion.

The only things hotter that day than the Joiner's fire-eaten house were the seats of the elder boys' backsides for leaving Delbert unattended.

By age six, only Claire and Anna called Delbert by his given name. If town folk were asked who that gimpy boy was, they sincerely replied without malice or offense, "That's little Cigar. Nice boy. Just needs a bath."

Only one other six-year-old living in Harford County could challenge Delbert for the Rhodes[3] scholarship in nature. That six-year-old is Anna Buchanan. Clay may have wanted a son, but since Anna was like a duck to water when it came to learning the ways of a hunter and waterman, he never had a complaint about her lacking a certain appendage, though he never felt the need to tell Anna this. However, an outside observer might accuse Clay of not seeing to the needs of a girl who would one day be a woman of striking natural beauty...not the all dolled up and painted type. In this area, Olivia Bouvard tries to sand down Anna's boyish edges, instructing her on hygiene, apparel, curbing of the sharp tongue, but never wanting to douse the spirit of independence that Olivia herself cultivates against societal objections. "A dependent woman is a slave. Her chains are ignorance and inability. Her master is fear and need," preaches Olivia to any docile woman she can corner.

This fall night, between serving mugs of cask-chilled beer, scalding plates of baked blue-winged teal, and sautéed menhaden, Olivia encourages Anna with her spelling and reading. As Clay sees it, formal schooling should not interrupt Anna's chores, so whenever in Tavern Bouvard, Olivia quizzes and instructs. Again, education is another word for freedom and independence. Anna is torn between acquiring the knowledge books possess, which opens her to a world beyond what she can see, and the knowledge

3 Rhodes, Cecil (1853-1902). Financier, statesman, and empire builder of British South Africa. He was prime minister of Cape Colony (1890-1896) and organizer of the diamond mining company De Beers Consolidated Mines, Ltd. His will established the Rhodes scholarships at Oxford.

her father possesses, which is relevant, immediate, and seems to please her father. Tonight, Anna's desire for the first is more from a never-before-felt fear of going home, despite knowing her father's need for the small brown bottle in her pocket.

Early that afternoon, Clay was carving a Canada goose decoy. Its long slender neck stuck proud atop a pump body. Clay's mouth was watering at the delicious memory of thick slabs of juicy meat dissolving on his hungry tongue. "Anna," Clay called out hearing the whoosh of a broom on the front porch.

"Yes, father?" Anna entered the shed.

"It's past time you learned to carve. Earn your keep so to speak," Clay handed Anna a sharpened wood carving knife. The knife's four-inch blade had been responsible for hundreds of full stomachs after deceiving migrating fowl that friends rest below, bobbing contented on the water's surface.

"Start with the head," Clay instructed, while giving Anna a small block of pine cut from a discarded ship's mast, and a completed goose head as an example. "Get a comfortable grip on the handle, pointing the cutting edge away from you," Clay turned the knife over in Anna's small hand. Anna's eyes beamed with honor. To be let into another room of the hunter's private club where mysteries are revealed was better, far better, than watching the first eagle chicks of winter take to their maiden voyage across the sun-washed, cloudless blue sky. *Now I'll really contribute to...* Anna's thoughts were cut short as Clay suddenly coughed, his hand-rolled cigarette spit from his lips. It landed dangerously on the wood-chip covered workbench. Sparks from the cigarette's cherry danced across the surface, and then exploded, a fiery star blossom in miniature. Anna quickly pounded the scattering sparklers to extinguish their fire as Clay composed himself, wiping the phlegm from the corners of his chapped lips.

Breathing deeply to replenish his depleted lungs with air, Clay resumed his lesson, "Look at the grain of the wood. These lines here," Clay ran his finger along the growth rings of Anna's goose head in the making. "Carve with them. Don't fight nature. See in your mind the finished bird's head. It's already there just waiting for you to remove the extra wood."

Anna puts blade to block. The shiny edge cut deeply. A large sliver flew away. Anna looked up hopefully, searching for approval. Clay was busy rasping the body of his goose, another hand-rolled tight between his teeth raised a cloud of smoke, though pungent to the nose, softened his intense features. This was work, not leisure. This was done out of necessity, not for pleasure. If Clay did not finish the order for 40 geese decoys by the end of the week, three days hence, someone else would, and payment would go there. Shot and powder for the Davenport were not free. Nine more decoys to go.

Anna's goose head began to take shape, even if oddly. She found a rhythm, following the grain, but she had difficulty holding the block of wood securely with one hand while whittling away from her. The blade either dug in too deeply, pulling the block out of her fingers, or didn't take enough off, making the progress amounting to nil...too slow.

Clay busily doweled together the slender neck and head of his goose to its hollow body. A carver learns early on to dig out excess wood, as there is no sense in lugging around three or four pounds of unseen wood per decoy. He holds up the specimen, turns it right, then to the left, and then back to the right. With a grunt of approval at his craftsmanship, he tossed the wooden goose outside where it landed upright, next to its brothers and sisters. Eight more decoys to go.

A coughing spasm doubled Clay over as he choked on his own fluids. He stumbled out of the shed, weaving like a drunk toward the porch and the shack's door. Inside, where he left it on the table, his savior waited, his medication. Doctor Webster's prescribed elixir, laudanum; opium mixed in heavy syrup.

"Modern medicine. That Bayer Company. What will they discover next? It's guaranteed to cure all sorts of ailments," was Doctor Webster's sincere applause for this liquid.

Clay upended the small bottle to gulp down the last ounce. Clay's body savored the opiate as it deadened, but did not completely kill the hack. Leaning against the table, Clay digs deep in his coverall pockets for a couple coins. He pictured Anna knocking on Doctor Webster's door, and then trading coin for a full bottle. The dark, sweet, thick liquid is then carried safely home in his daughter's hands to an appreciative father.

"Ouch!" Anna's cry sliced through the slats of the wall. Clay raced to the shed. Before him, Anna is seated on the wood stack. The carving knife and goose head lie in the dirt at her feet. Tears welled up in her eyes as she tightly held the thumb and first finger of her left hand with her right. Thick blood oozed between her clenched fingers onto her dress.

"Don't you cry. Not one tear. Not one whimper," Clay harshly admonished Anna, seeing exactly the cause. "I told you to cut away from you. Didn't I?"

"I was trying to get a better grip," sniffled Anna.

"Well, how's your grip now?" demanded Clay. "Maybe I was wrong, maybe you're not old enough, or maybe cooking and sweeping is all you'll be good for." More coughing interrupted Clay's reprimand. He throws the coins out of the shed, "Get out and get to town. I need some medicine. Get!"

Anna quickly slid off the wood stack, as the rough wood scratched her thighs, imbedding several splinters to add more pain to her throbbing fingers, but she was more shaken, and frightened by her father's caustic words. She trotted to where the coins landed, and with bloody hands, picked them out of the dirt. Anna turned to watch her father coughing himself to his knees inside the shed, and then she ran down the trail toward town.

Resembling a wild dog with a bone in its throat, Clay coughed himself blind. After what seemed an eternity, the racking spasm subsided. The first objects Clay saw when his vision returned were the blood-spotted carving knife and the malformed goose head. Clay picked them up. He laid the knife on the workbench, and then examined Anna's specimen closely, turning it right to left, and then back to the right. With an approving grunt, and a snort for a chuckle, he placed the goose head, front and center, on a shelf above the workbench. It sat, roughly formed, tilting to the left, and bloody, among Clay's finer works.

Olivia glances at the cracked face of the oak clock hanging on the wall. Its tireless hands brashly point to 11:00 p.m. At this hour, the tavern bustles with laughter. Colorful men of many trades, some honorable, some dubious, all finding camaraderie in drink, stories, cards, and the few hours reprieve from the heavy burdens of life on and along the Chesapeake. At the end of the counter, with bandaged fingers, Anna sits with an expression of concentration. Her focus appears to be the study book before her, but her pencil has not moved in tens of minutes. The vision of her father's fury fills her thoughts. Her only distraction is the smells. Each whiff of man or meal has before been catalogued so she need not turn her head for identification or acknowledgment.

Deep breath, an inhalation of spicy, earthen, oily...it's possum stew.

"Hello, Anna," salty, with a trail of pipe smoke.

"Evening, Mr. O'Neill," Anna replies to the lighthouse keeper.

"Burning the midnight oil?" Henry O'Neill asks.

"No more than you, sir," teases Anna.

Henry chuckles at their ongoing joke while he considers, measuring, estimating, how much longer he can remain in the game before the whale oil lighting the flame to safe entrance to the Susquehanna River will run dry. "A few more hands to break even, and then back to Concord Point. An Irishman never departs a deck of cards when he's down," but at the same time, shivering at the chastisement awaiting him by Mrs. O'Neill for his malingering.

"Hmmpf," too much starch in clothing that crinkles when passing by. Too sweet tobacco smoke puffed from an expensive cigar, and heavy cologne to cover the sour sweat from sitting astride an over-heated Arabian stallion in a sun-baked field.

"Evening, Mr. McQuay," Anna almost manages a polite greeting, but the hint of sarcasm as *McQuay* rolls off the side of her tongue raises Frank McQuay's ire, stopping him in his passage to the gentleman's room.

From midway down the bar's counter, Olivia hears and observes everything and foreseeing the unpleasant and uneven battle to come, quickly places herself between Anna and Frank McQuay.

"Anna, it's getting quite late. Shouldn't you be taking that medicine home to your father?"

Frank McQuay's jowls flush red with anger, readying to lash out at the insolent child. Though before his tongue gets in gear, Anna makes a hasty retreat around the counter and out through the kitchen, knowing she has bitten off more than she can chew. She may have escaped Frank McQuay's full wrath, but snippets of foul words still sting at her backside like a summer wasp.

On her walk out of town, Anna passes the wharves where oyster skipjacks are moored by the dozen, Stockham's Cannery, Havre de Grace's fish and oyster packing house, ice plants, and the feed mill. These buildings of industry, hulking structures of timber and corrugated steel, are sleeping, with only the rare wandering lights of watchmen prowling about. Leaving the road, Anna follows the winding paths along the edge of the bay. Walking alone late at night and early into the morning, it never dawns on her to be frightened by the sounds of the night, as each snap of a twig, whoosh of wing, or splash of fin are friends; neighbors heard often, but only seen when trapped. Anna's flesh prickles with goose bumps, though not from fear, but from a slight chill dancing off the bay, while up in the heavens a full moon blazes down with the light of midday. "Mr. O'Neill needn't worry about the nine wicks winking at incoming watermen. If they can't see the shoals by the glow of tonight's moon, they have no business being captain, do they Mr. Luna?" shouts Anna to the orbiting rock that is pitted with craters.

Laughing, skipping, and leaping along the path as it turns inland among a marsh of cordgrass, Anna believes if she could jump only a little higher, she could touch the moon. The stars, well, that is another matter. Anna's heart warms by the memory of her mother's encouragement.

"Shoot for the stars, darling, but if you only reach the moon, that's well and good, because you're still out of this world."

Ahead on the rising trail are two juvenile muskrats. They both sit upright on their hind legs, impatient like, as if in preamble to the reception waiting for her at home.

"Did father send out scouts in search of me?" Anna wonders aloud. "No. That's crazy thinking."

Like practiced dance steps, these two-pound, 12-inch, furry, rusty red-brown rodents bob and twist their whiskered heads in unison, and then dart down the path in loping gallops toward the shore.

"Wait," Anna calls, but these nocturnal critters have other things in mind. Anna, not wanting to miss the game, races after them. The little brown bottle in her pocket bumps and jiggles, as she leaps over rocks and fallen limbs that lie across the path. Anna cannot quite catch her quarry, though quick of feet as she is, they stay just out of reach. Anna's joy-filled shouts and laughter, echo across the salt marsh, startling a resting pair of loons. Their haunting, spectral call, which would scare a city child out of its wits, does nothing to rattle Anna or dampen her merriment.

Down the winding path the three racers run. The leaders do have an extra pair of legs each, but Anna's lengthy stride should be the equalizer. The soft, forever damp, marsh soil turns to sand, as the path takes the contestants to the bay, signaling what should be the finish line. The front-runners feigned left, as if heading back toward town, and then scampered right. Their jig, the scattering sand, and the unsure footing trips up their pursuer as Anna tries to follow them south.

Anna finds herself flopped face down, sputtering, with a mouthful of sand. Laughing, Anna's thoughts are, *No harm. No foul*, until she sees the precious medicine, her father's bottle flying from her pocket. It is a projectile in search of a target.

The target is a rock.

Before Anna can reach out to grab for, or deflect the bottle, it thuds against the rock, to then slide without damage to the sand. Two things congealed in Anna's mind, bringing her to the realization that this mound in the sand is not a rock. The thud of the bottle being one, and the other is the slow raising of an enormous oblong head. This head is something Anna has never seen before, at least not on this mammoth scale, and certainly not black with white blotches and...dripping blood.

"Holy smokes, Almighty," whispers Anna, a she stares eye-to-eye in awe at this great beast of the sea.

– 1894 –

Clawing with tiny flippers up through a suffocating tar pit of wet sand, a prehistoric dinosaur, *Dermochelys coriacea*, broke its bonds, and gasped for a chilled breath of ocean air.

The nearby water sparkled from moonbeams, guiding what may become the world's largest living reptile, along with its brothers and sisters, from their hiding place, their sandy nest, out into a watery world of constant danger. Maybe one in a thousand will survive to reproduce. The race was on for the Atlantic leatherback turtle.

On that full moon night, on the undeveloped barrier island, off Virginia's eastern shore, hundreds of one and one-half inch leatherbacks flopped frantically across the rough sand. Determined, they paddled straight into waves that seemed to be of tsunami proportions. These breakers flung the leatherbacks back upon the exposed beach. Each turtle must surmount this first obstacle to reach the outgoing swells, because to be caught on the sand at dawn's light was certain death within the beaks of gulls, or within the jaws of foraging raccoons.

The little female leatherback instinctively hugged the ribbed sand, as each rolling whitewater tugged against her small scales. Her half-inch flippers snapped frantically at the swirling water to make progress against the uncaring current. Forward a few inches, then a few feet of progress until there was a lull between wave sets. Just the break she needed to make a dash for calmer, deeper waters. Her muscles were fatigued, and lungs in need of air, as she spied some flotsam; kelp torn from its bed, pieces of driftwood, and a rusty bent can with a faded label. She paddled in and among the debris to rest and to survey her surroundings.

Did any others conquer the shoreline? She wondered, as the first rays of dawn streaked in shafts through her hiding place. Off to her left she saw movement, *Is that one of my brothers, or is he from another nest?*

Exhausted, but determined, the tiny male paddled closer.

He is from my nest. My brother, swim here! She urged with anxious concern for his safety.

From deep below, swift and sure, a hungry grouper with a mouth large enough to swallow a dozen newborns, gulped down the little male, and then with a flick of its tail, disappeared back into the deep from where it came.

Sad and fearful, seeing no others of her kind, the vulnerable female wiggled deeper into the debris for camouflage. *Others must have survived. I can't be the only one?* She questioned while remaining still. She was perceived by passing predators as another piece of flotsam adrift on the current...she was safe for now.

For several months, our little maiden hunkered within the shelter of cast off seaweed, wood, and garbage thrown overboard from passing vessels. The Atlantic current took her far to the north in Canada's icy waters, and then down into the warm tropics of the Caribbean Sea. This current, driven by variations in water temperature and wind, also brought the taste treats to sustain her—jellyfish. Blown in on air sacks above the waterline, the one to three-inch Portuguese man-of-war were delicious. Even their stinging tentacles tasted wonderful going down her gullet. There was only one concern, and that was jellyfish came in many sizes. While off the coast of Nova Scotia, she encountered a school of gigantic jellyfish. The entire parade pulsated in cadence, responding to the beat of some drum only they could hear. Three feet in diameter at the translucent head, they possessed thick tentacles hanging down 70 feet. But alas, her immunity to their poison was limited, so she remained within her carriage of debris, biding her time.

Next time around I'll remember this place. Next time when I'm stronger, bigger, and without fear of your defenses, our little maiden vowed as the innumerable school of lion's mane pulsed out of sight.

- 1906 -

Twelve-years, tens of thousands of nautical miles, and 950 pounds heavier, our little maiden had become the titanic of the deep. Massive but sleek, her six-foot span of flippers rocketed her along with ease. She was the one in a thousand who had survived to reproduce. She had beaten a million possible deaths from every hungry predator in the sea. She remembered her vow and returned each year to decimate the lion's mane off Canada's frigid coast. She was now Queen of the Atlantic, her maidenhead gone, along with the king she chose to give it to.

While summering in the warm, sun-reflective waters off St. Lucia and St. Vincent, she ran into her suitor as she rounded a sunken galleon. She knew immediately that he would father her offspring. He was 35 years if a day, 1,050 pounds and still growing. Like her, to have survived this long and to flourish, bequeaths an inherent wisdom. This is what needed to be passed on, to be preserved. Only wisdom can overcome the odds death placed against life in the depths of the Atlantic Ocean.

Even with her decision made, she remained a lady to be pursued. *If he wants me, he can prove it,* she mused as the chase began. North they sped. She twisted, turned, rose and dived. He followed close in her underwater wake. Past the island of Martinique, the pursuit continued to the lapping shores of Dominica. There in the tranquil shallows, where the water changed from turquoise to tawny to a tessellated green-gold, as ripples on the surface reflected the setting sun, our queen allowed him to overtake her. She could have swum for days, but her desire for coupling overcame her pride for dominance. The languid hours passed in his firm embrace. Their mouths gasped for air with each rise above the water. Their clenched bodies were pressed together as one. He gave and she received. From ancient times before time was measured it was done this way. Two became one to create the magical spark of a third, or in this case, to become dozens. By the red dawn's glow, they had finished. He was done with her and she with him. Exhausted, the king lumbered away on the tide in search of nourishment. For our queen, she was grateful for his gift, but his face was quickly forgotten, as she felt the next generation growing within her. It was time to return to the place of her birth, a quiet, sandy beach some 2,500 miles to the north.

The swim to Virginia was uneventful. The current favored her, as it carried her along the coasts of Florida, Georgia, and the Carolinas. Jellyfish were in ample supply, nurturing both our queen and the eggs filling her womb. Her only concern was swimming close to shore with all the ship traffic. Her preference was deep, open water, just she and the jellyfish, far from man, and his menacing machines.

Several weeks passed. It was now fall as our queen neared her destination, the place of her birth, the barrier island off Virginia's eastern shore. She was tired, her strength diverted to grow the life inside her. It had not helped that for the past few days, a constant offshore breeze blew her meals far out to sea. The queen was hungry.

At the mouth of the Chesapeake Bay, an unusual eddy had formed. As it swirled, the current collected everything not strong enough to fight it, including jellyfish. There were jellyfish from the open ocean and the bay's own stinging nettle. This banquet was worth the detour. *Poseidon does look after his creatures. Well, at least this queen leatherback.* She thought giddily, while tearing heads from tentacles.

Sound is amplified in water, giving those who dwell within a warning if danger is approaching. However, changes in temperature, differences in salinity, and the ever-varying current, have an effect that can distort and disguise the source of any sound. The bay is a unique mixture with cold, salty water flowing north, up the bay near its bottom, and warmer, fresh water flowing south, down the bay near the surface. Adding surface wind, rain, and tides, further complicates and confuses the acoustic equation. Therefore, blame should not lie with our experienced queen for not accurately hearing, and then identifying the chopping-churning-thumping sound for what it was, and for remaining near the surface.

The hit was not direct, because if the metal bolts and stout boards had not glanced off her shell, she would have been sliced in two, to be killed instantly. Our queen, survivor of the sand pit, gulls, raccoons, tsunamis, groupers, drifting nets, and all manner of predators, did not receive a crushing blow from the immense blades of the passing side-wheeler steaming up the bay to Norfolk. She did, however receive a gash in her soft shell, stunning, and disorienting her. Our queen tumbled without purchase in the side-wheeler's frothy wake. The pain, exploding throughout her body was of second concern. The unborn within her were her only thought. They must survive. Her obligation to the species demanded it.

Instead of struggling against the incoming tide, out to the coastal islands of her birth, our queen allowed herself to be swept down near the bottom where the current pushed her up the Chesapeake toward Maryland and the Susquehanna Flats. With any luck there would be a quiet place, a sandy shore, a nest hole to safely deposit the next generation.

The rest of the night, through the following day, and into night again, the northerly push of the current dragged our queen along. She stayed as deep as the shallow bay would allow, coming to the surface only for air, and a bearing check. The ship traffic increased, raising the danger, but she was pleased to see shoreline fit for incubation. The pain from her sliced shell did not abate. Small fish nibbled relentlessly at the wound, tearing bits of flesh, bits of life from her body. Our queen was afraid to close her eyes and rest on the bottom for fear she would fade into unconsciousness, drown, and fail in her mission. Poking her head above the water she again checked the sky where a full moon blazed above. Our queen remembered her first night as a tiny frightened turtle scratching across the sand toward the water. Now she had to heave herself, almost a thousand pounds heavier, out of her liquid world, a buoyant place where she flies uninhibited on powerful wings.

Her purpose would defeat gravity.

Our queen inched forward.

Sand scraped her smooth undercarriage.

Foot by agonizing foot she lumbered, coming to rest above the high tide line. She shook her head and squinted one eye, as something warm and thick burned, as it dripped in. The liquid was from her wound. Upward, a few more feet she struggled. She was undeterred. A labored breath, a heavy sigh from within rumbled the ground. *No time to rest*, our queen chastised herself. The first pains of labor instinctively began, as our queen's hind flippers scooped sand to form a bassinet that would be the nest for her offspring.

The next generation, one by one, of shelled turtles, tiny dinosaurs, passed from our queen into the perfectly carved hole. Our queen was weak, extremely exhausted, but she had to cover the evidence of her presence, and then return to the water.

With the last flipper of sand tossed over her sleeping children, our queen struggled to pull herself back to her watery realm. *Find the strength,* she encouraged herself. *I have to get off this beach.*

Laughter, then the muffled thumping of running feet was heard. A startled gasp, and thud in the sand next to our queen, as a small object bounced against her damaged shell. Fighting against the stinging blood that dripped into her eye, our queen opened her eyelid. Before her, sprawled in the sand, was a small human child.

"Holy smokes, Almighty," whispers Anna, as she stares eye-to-eye in awe at this elegant queen of the sea. Despite being dwarfed ten to one in size and weight and never before seeing such an imposing creature, Anna is not afraid. Rising to her knees, Anna examines every inch of this once in a lifetime discovery. "Where did you come from?" Anna waits for the answer until her fingers discover the ugly wound in the queen's shell. "Oh no." Our queen, so very weak, summons strength from places in her soul not before known. Pushing with massive flippers, she gains several more inches toward her goal, the buoyancy of the water...escape.

Seeming to read the queen's mind, and feeling her pain, Anna, coaxes and encourages, "It's only 12 feet. It's not that far." Anna places her own weight behind our queen, pushing with all her might, "Come on. Try again." Anna pleads and pushes as sweat drips from her forehead, glistening in the moonlight, but she might as well be trying to move a house. Anna collapses in the sand, and then crawls around to face our struggling queen. Urgency is in the pleading eyes of both.

Urgency by our queen to remove herself from the shore where her children are hidden, as she is a mountain of evidence to their existence.

Urgency by Anna, knowing she must find help, "Keep trying. Please. I'll come back as soon as I can." Jumping to her feet, Anna runs with the speed of a marsh swallow—the cold night air searing her lungs with each breath, but giving her blessed pure oxygen to fly, her feet barely touching the ground.

Over fallen limbs, Anna leaps. They are obstacles on a familiar path where she can run blindfolded. It is a lickety-split, one-girl race down a winding, curving path along the bay's edge, in and through the swamp, and back along the shore, making a three-mile, crow's flight, into five by land. Tonight, only the wind could have traveled faster, or with more purpose than Anna.

The afternoon and evening had been a long and tortuous one for Clay Herschell Buchanan. The racking coughs, spasms of eternity taking his breath away seemed never to end, but his physical pain was not the source of Clay's agony. He had yelled at his daughter. She deserved it though, "I told her. I showed her. Carve away. Always carve away from yourself," Clay shook his head. *Too many hours have passed since I sent Anna to town,* Clay guiltily worries, as he sits in the Great Room. The fire's dry warmth has freed breathing room in his congested lungs. He watches the flames leap, prance, and dance, but what he sees is the glow of his wife's face. It has been three years since her burial in Angel Hill cemetery, where a small wooden marker, carved by Clay's own hands, reads: Beloved. Vigorously rubbing his forehead, Clay does not understand why it seems as if Jennifer has been dead forever, as he cannot remember the feeling of her arms around him, or the sweet song she sang with each word, but then why is the pain of her passing so fresh? He aches to the point of vomiting. Unscrewing the cap on the laudanum bottle, Clay runs his finger around the lip to coax out any remaining syrup. He is not coughing, but would like to numb his grief.

"Why, Jennifer? Why did you have to leave me...and with a daughter?" casting his eyes toward the ceiling and heaven, where he knows Jennifer is, he asks for the thousandth time, "Why does she have to look so much like you?"

Crackle. Pop. Water pockets within the wood grain explode, startling Clay, and returning him to the here and now.

"Father," Anna's distressed cry is heard just above the crackling flames, momentarily making Clay wonder if he had heard her at all, but concern for Anna's safety mixes with Clay's anger over her long absence and the need for his medicine. Clay stands, and then steps to open the door. As his hand reaches for the latch, Anna bursts through, colliding with him, and together they fall against the table, knocking over a chair.

"Father...father," in a panic and out of breath, panting heavily, Anna attempts to untangle herself from her father's arms. Her face is flushed. Her clothing and hair disheveled as if she has been wrestling the devil. Clay peers out the door expecting a madman to be in pursuit of his child.

"Anna, what is it? Anna, calm down," Clay shakes her. Her wild eyes stare at him. Clay stares back waiting. Anna opens her mouth to speak, but cannot think of words appropriate to describe her needs.

"Are you hurt?" Clay asks.

Anna shakes her head, no.

"Is anyone chasing you?"

Again, Anna shakes her head, no.

Still confused, but relieved that Anna is not hurt, Clay asks the next logical question that is of importance to him, "Do you have my medicine?"

The question is a slap in the face to Anna. Blinking her eyes, as if coming out of a trance, she reaches into her pocket. The bottle is not there.

"The turtle!" shouts Anna in defense to the unanswered question. "Father, you have to help. It's hurt. Hurry." Anna pulls free, turns and then runs out the door. Clay remains standing in place. Anna runs back in. Her urgency, her few words, they have befuddled Clay, who is perplexed, and only wants to know where his medicine is, and why Anna is hours late in returning?

"It's with the turtle. Father, please, she has to get back to the water," grabbing Clay's hand, Anna pulls him, stumbling, out the door.

The mystery of where the medicine is, and how a turtle fits in, piece itself together, as Anna's inconceivable description forms in Clay's head, *Anna doesn't lie, but a turtle as big as a season of shucked oyster shells?* Curiosity, more than compulsion presses Clay forward. His strides lengthen to a run, as he keeps pace with his fleet-footed daughter.

Through the swamp the two pairs of legs sprint. Coming around a bend in the path with the shore just out of sight, the barking of an excited dog is heard. Clay recognizes it as Dog's, and where Dog is, a Joiner is sure to be nearby. As Clay passes a stand of cattails to emerge onto the sand, he stops running. There is no urgency now.

"No!" screams Anna, as she races forward, throwing herself upon the upended shell of the deposed queen. She is only three feet from the lapping waterline.

Three feet from her domain.

Three feet from her home and safety.

Anna's tears stream down her cheeks. They are wet trails in the moonlight. Her accusing eyes search the face of the assassin for answers, "Why? Why did you have to kill her?"

August Joiner, the accused, stands convicted, but without remorse, over the corpse. In his hand is a large cutting knife. Next to him are Chet and Lloyd, now in their teens. Chet is holding a bloody axe, and Lloyd is clutching the severed head of the queen.

"Why did you have to kill her?" Anna demands more than she questions. Clay steps forward to pull Anna away from the carcass.

"Clay, this meat will feed a dozen families for two weeks." Not excusing his deed, nor needing to justify his act, August simply states, "Dog found the leatherback...and it is within my swamp. I got the right."

"No one's accusing you of anything, August. Anna spied the creature on her way home from town tonight. She was bringing my medicine, and well, you know how little girls can be," Clay explains.

"Can't say as I do, having only boys," August looks over at Lloyd as he parades around with the queen's head like a hard won trophy. "Must be confounding at times, and oh, this must be yours," August tugs the medicine bottle from his back pocket. He hands it to Clay, "Found it in the sand. And Clay, I don't think it would have survived. Its shell was badly crushed. Probably came ashore to die anyway."

Clay nods in understanding. He turns to spy Anna. She stands several yards up the bank, talking to Delbert, and shuffling her feet in the sand. *Poor girl,* Clay thinks to himself.

"You must have eaten turtle eggs before, Anna?" Delbert questions.

"That's beside the point. You tell anyone they rest here, and I'll...I'll," Anna threatens.

"You'll do what? You're just a girl," Delbert teases Anna, goading her to anger, and curious as to what kind of retaliation she could threaten him with.

"I'll tell what you do in the pond when you think no one's watching," Anna pokes Delbert's chest with her finger. Her eyes focused, unblinking. This is no bluff. It is a drastic threat, but this situation calls for extreme measures if she is to prevail and save the turtle eggs from the frying pan. Delbert's knees wobble. The moonlight reveals wide eyes filled with shock at the realization that his private playtime has been discovered, and fear at the possibility of being exposed, ridiculed and humiliated.

Anna has won.

"You better not," stammers Delbert, pleading.

Anna spits into the palm of her right hand, and then holds it out to Delbert, as Dog sniffs around their feet at the buried treasure.

"Secret?" Anna asks with a tone that is unmistakable for its seriousness, while wiping tears from her eyes with the back of her left hand.

"Secret," defeated, Delbert reluctantly spits into his own hand with the saliva he wishes he was using to savor spiced turtle eggs. With a wet and squishy grip he shakes Anna's hand. The deal is done, sealed by the most solemn pact known to six-year-olds. Delbert grabs Dog by the scruff of her neck. Dog yelps, as she is pulled away from the nest.

Anna turns back toward the trail and the long walk home. She does not want to witness the Joiners' joy in carving turtle steaks out of the queen. She was a grand dame whose life of travel and adventure will be measured by the sizzle of her juice over hot grills. Tears again trickle down Anna's cheeks, but she refuses to cry aloud.

"Concentrate on the babies," Anna sternly repeats to herself.

Delbert, wanting his pond time games kept private, keeps his promise not to reveal the location of the leatherback turtle eggs. Only once did Anna catch him scratching in the sand to check on their progress. He only saw a clutch of several dozen white spherical eggs at rest. Neither Anna nor Delbert know how long the incubation period will last.

"Why can't we ask someone?" Delbert whines.

"Because people would want to know why we are asking, and if we're asking, they'd know we had a stash some place," is Anna's stern reply.

"Why can't we take a few of the eggs to eat and leave the rest to hatch? I mean, look at all of them."

"It wouldn't be right. Would you like it if you awoke one morning to find that someone had taken one of your brothers?" Anna waits for Delbert's answer. "Well?" Delbert takes in a long, slow, and satisfying breath, contemplating this possibility, and its implications.

"Well?" Anna asks again, amazed by Delbert's hesitation.

"Maybe if I awoke to find one of the puppies missing."

"Puppies? When did you get puppies?" squeals Anna.

"Dog had a litter two weeks ago. Pop has been selling them, but says they have to be a little older before separating them from Dog."

"Hmm..." Anna casts her eyes out across the bay. A half-mile from shore a dozen skipjacks with sails filled by an easy breeze glide across the surface, while below, metal tongs grab at oysters nestled in their crowded beds.

"Anna," Clay calls from somewhere along the trail.

"I'm here," Anna calls back. To Delbert, "I got to go to town with my father, but I'll see you later...and cover up those eggs."

Reluctantly, but knowing he does not have a choice; Delbert pushes sand back into the hole and pats it smooth. Seeing a long stalk of grass within arm's reach, Delbert pulls it easily out of the sandy soil, and then places it between his teeth for a chew. Laying back against a mound he built for himself, Delbert contents himself with a morning of skipjack watching.

Back and forth, the skipjacks' oversized sails pull the V-bottom bateaus.

Back and forth swing the long booms in a tack or jibe.

Back and forth across the beds of tasty morsels.

Hypnotized into a state of complete relaxation, Delbert's chin falls to his chest in slumber. The stalk of grass falls from between his lips to be blown away on the gentle breeze. Boyish snores vibrate downward through the sand, but do not interfere with the growing, strengthening leatherbacks sleeping below.

Nathaniel Joiner sits cock of the walk, center stage, on a stool in Tavern Bouvard.

"He's just back from the Klondike," whispers a wide-eyed 20-something patron to Clay as he and Anna enter the tavern. "Look when he smiles. He's got a mouthful of gold."

Clay looks over the shoulders of the men standing around Nathaniel. Sure enough, there is something yellow shining from that mouth of rotting and missing teeth.

"It was like a communicable disease," Nathaniel speaks in a warning tone.

"What was?" asks Umbrella George who is sitting off to the side.

"The fever—Klondike fever," Nathaniel's words carry an ominous warning. "I was in San Francisco. That's in California for those of you who never step foot outside the county. I met a man named Jack London.[4] He said he was a writer. To me, well, he looked more like a wet-behind-the-ears schoolboy even though he was in his thirties. Doubt if he could even spell, let alone write anything worth reading."

"What about the fever?" a waterman holding a foaming mug of beer interrupts.

"I'll get to it but my mouth's a bit dry," Nathaniel eyes the mug, as his gray tongue licks cracked lips that are forever thirsty.

"Here you go," the waterman hands Nathaniel his brew, fascinated by the adventurer standing before him.

Tossing back the mug to swallow the chilled libation, Nathaniel continues with a robust belch, "Well, this Jack London fellow says they're scooping up fist-size nuggets in the Klondike snow."

"They said that about the gold rush to California in '49," says Jim Currier, a local guide and hunter with heavy disgust for pie-in-the-sky dream chasers. "My uncle was lured to those killing fields with such fanciful tales of easy pickings. He barely made it back, broker than when he left." Many in the room nod and grunt with agreement, having heard similar stories from

---

4 London, Jack (1876-1916). Novelist and journalist. Notable works: *White Fang, Call of the Wild,* and *The Sea-Wolf.*

old friends and relatives, all who spit at the mention of gold, as they feel they were suckers, and do not want to be reminded of their folly.

"Jim, I didn't say it," annoyed by Jim's negativity, Nathaniel attempts to regain center stage. "I said, 'London claimed it,' and men, and even women were packing a year's supply of food, over a ton of goods onto ships to make the voyage north. I acquired a ticket, and the necessary provisions through a chance meeting with a young gent sporting a new coonskin cap, and apparently having consumed a few too many whiskies." Nathaniel flashes his rotten, gold-filled teeth with a conspiratorial smirk. Raucous laughter erupts. Many men admire an opportunity seized in the quest for adventure and advancement. Nathaniel reveled in the camaraderie, but his joy was tainted as he saw the disagreeable faces of Clay Buchanan, Umbrella George, Jim Currier, and Robert Mitchell. *What the hell do they know anyway?* Nathaniel thinks to himself.

Another hunter standing near Nathaniel slides him a fresh brew, "So what of the nuggets of gold?"

"The rush all started pretty much the year of 1898. I got off the steamer in Skagway in '99. The entire voyage, London kept pestering me with his ideas and questions he wanted answered—stuff about wolves and newspapers like I was some encyclopedic person."

"Sounds like a real nuisance," spoke a man from the back.

"Sure 'nuff he was. Thank the Almighty the steamer finally rounded a bend in the river to the sight of town or I'd have had to toss the man overboard." Laughter again, as another round of drafts are served by Olivia, whose eyes sparkle with hopeful anticipation, though what she wants, what is she expecting, has nothing to do with Nathaniel or his story.

"Soon as the gang plank hit the pier I ditched him. I didn't even unload my gear. I figured I'd come back later in the day."

"So what became of London?" Jim asks.

"Not much, probably," Nathaniel shrugs his shoulders, "Likely died in a snow bank. As I said, he didn't look like he would amount to much." Several heads around the room nod, agreeing with Nathaniel's sound judgment.

The heavy oak door to Tavern Bouvard is thrown open, banging against the inner wall. A swath of sun blasts in, silhouetting a man standing on the threshold.

"Houdini's[5] in our jail," shouts Henry O'Neill. Following O'Neill through the doorway is Madison, the young son of Robert Mitchell.

---

5 Houdini, Harry (1874-1926). Born Eric Weis in Hungary. He was the son of a rabbi. He took his stage name from the French magician Jean-Eugene Robert-Houdin. Harry Houdini died of peritonitis that stemmed from a stomach injury on Halloween.

"And he's buck naked!" squeals Madison.

"What?" Clay turns to question Henry.

Beside him, Anna is bugged with excitement. "Houdini's here? What did he do?" yelps Anna, fit-to-be-tied at the thought of a real celebrity, a famous person setting foot in Havre de Grace.

"Oh, he hasn't been arrested. He had the constable lock him up to prove that no cell can hold him," explains Henry. "It's a publicity stunt as he travels through towns on his way to New York."

Nathaniel's face scrunches, creating deep wrinkles of consternation. He is losing his audience, an audience that has been liberally plying him with refreshments.

"Why's he naked?" asks Umbrella George.

"To prove he has no keys hidden up his sleeve, I suppose."

"Can I go, father?" Anna asks desperately, while tugging on Clay's arm. "It's Houdini!" A half-dozen men hustle out of the tavern, all led by Henry. Anna watches them leave, feeling anxious that she will miss the big event, "Please, father. Pl-eee-ase." Anna wiggles, dancing in circles, as if needing to pee. Her eagerness is overwhelming her, as she wants to scream. *Finally, something exciting. If I miss it, I'll just die.*

"I'd be happy to take her along, Clay," offers Robert. "She can tag along with Madison. I'm sure this Houdini chap will be an interesting diversion for this quiet town of ours. I've heard he's been quite a success touring Europe."

Anna sees this as the perfect solution. Madison, a year or so younger than Anna, looks with fawning eyes up into her face, and hesitantly takes hold of her hand. They are now a unified force against any and all evil.

"That'll be fine, Robert. Thank you. How long do you expect this spectacle to take?" Clay asks while quickly glancing toward Olivia who is wiping down the counter. Catching her hopeful expression, the spark of fire grows within her eyes. Olivia, to Clay's surprise, blushes. Her cheeks, dotted with freckles, turns redder than her hair, and is visible even in the dimly it and smoke-filled room, causing her to turn away.

An understanding passes between Clay and Robert. It is an understanding that all men acknowledge. It is a confidence among males, to be kept as a secret with only a wink and a nod.

Robert scratches his stubbly chin, pondering the question, and the desires behind it, "Tell you this, we're dining with the O'Neills tonight. Why don't you collect Anna there when you're ready? I'm sure they wouldn't mind. Besides, my wife's cousin, Sam Barnes, will be there, probably bragging about all the success the sports are having gunning over the rigs he's carved."

"Don't get me started on those rich hunters," Clay spits venom. "They may pay well for their day's fun, but they then return to their fine city homes to pester legislators to pass laws against men like us who are trying to feed our families."

"My point exactly, we need to hear both sides of the argument, and isn't some of his rig your work?" asks Robert, but without waiting for an answer, he changes the subject as he tips his hat to Olivia. "Clay, enjoy your day." Robert turns toward the door, "Let's go children."

Anna and Madison sprint out the tavern door, hooting and hollering, raising a small dust cloud in their wake. On his way out the door, and watching his charges quickly disappear in the stampede of good citizens on their way to jail, Robert shrugs his shoulders, laughing heartily, "I've lost them already."

Half the patrons in Tavern Bouvard have departed to witness the magic; some say the black magic, of The Great Houdini. He is a man who has escaped death in its many forms, many times, with many saying, "He can't be killed."

Clay takes a seat at the bar next to Umbrella George. Nathaniel, no longer the king, but reduced in rank to a mere duke, tries to regain the floor.

"As I was saying," Nathaniel pauses in thought, allowing those remaining to move closer.

"You were saying how you ditched Mr. London," Olivia pipes in, as she rinses a mug in a copper basin behind the counter.

"Yes, thank you, Missy," Nathaniel continues, irritated by Olivia's restatement of the facts. "After I left Mr. London to his own devices, I reconnoitered Skagway. She was one giant mud hole. Seems every one of the 30 odd thousand folk was covered in it, livestock and buildings, too. Some folk might have said, 'What a dismal, pitiful sight,' but not me. I saw opportunity. That's when I met a Mr. Soapy Smith. He said he was from Georgia. I should have known right then and there he was no good, being a Johnny Reb and all, but he keeps on about an honest card game at his establishment." Nathaniel rubs his chin, a chin that is peppered with gray hair, as he ponders the story, the memory as he remembers it. "What a place that Carlson's Saloon! Fancy as the days are long up north it was. Stepping through those swinging mud-brown doors was like stepping into any one of the fine Frisco establishments I'd had time to peruse. Anyway, there I was, sitting with all manner of folk. There were diggers, merchants, sailors, and even a..." Nathaniel glances at Olivia, and then leans forward while lowering his voice a little, but purposely not enough to prevent Olivia from hearing, "a lady of fleshly pleasures." Nathaniel's black eyes glint of flint as the word pleasure drips off his tongue.

Astonished, Umbrella George blusters, "I'm not going to judge her manner of employment, sinful as it may be, but to allow her a seat at a table with men, a sure distraction from their cards, well, that's outrageous."

"Maybe so, but she did have collateral that was highly valued," laughing, Nathaniel slaps Umbrella George on his back. "Even you'd put down that tired old Sampler to say a prayer or two at her divine temple."

"Sir! You've gone too far," Umbrella George leaps from his stool with surprising agility for a man of his advanced years. Raising his neatly tied umbrella, "If I weren't commanded to turn the other cheek...I'd...I'd..."

Nathaniel holds up his hands in mock defense, shaking his body, as if trembling in fear. Umbrella George realizes his protests are fruitless and turns his back on Nathaniel, "Stay behind me, Satan." Umbrella George composes himself to walk calmly out of the tavern, leaving an amused Nathaniel and several debased supporters, all remaining silent and salivating by where the story may lead.

"It's too bad he left so soon," Nathaniel halfheartedly chuckles. "He would have enjoyed the next part of the story."

"Tell it anyway," urges the 20-something patron.

"Right," continues Nathaniel. "The game appeared to be on the up and up as far as I could tell, but this one fellow named Trump[6] was taking every pot. Besides the fact that he was cleaning house, he was very personable. Told each of us that if we were ever in Whitehorse, to stop by the Arctic Restaurant & Hotel. He said it was the beginning of an empire. I asked him why he hadn't named it Trump's? I mean if you're going to build an empire, people should know whose it is. Mr. Trump thought about what I'd said, nodded agreement, and simply replied, 'You make sense.'"

"So what part would Umbrella George have liked?" asks Clay.

"Maybe I didn't make myself clear," Nathaniel's tone lowers in defeat. "When I said, 'Mr. Trump won every pot,' I meant every pot, every pan, every sack of flour, salt, side of pork, every blanket and shovel. He left me and most others without a pot to piss in."

"But what about the gold? Without a grub stake, how'd you manage?" asks the waterman, disappointed.

Nathaniel downs the last of the offered beer, straightens his worn suit jacket, a garment incongruous over a torn cotton shirt and mismatched wool pants. Then turning to look into each and every set of eyes waiting

---

6 Trump, Fred. (The father of The Donald, the American entrepreneur, real estate developer, and billionaire). Together, with his partner Ernest Levin, they owned the Arctic restaurant. Originally operated out of a tent in Bennet before they built a two-story. Shortly after completion, the partners relocated to the new boomtown of Whitehorse to open a grandeur establishment.

for the happy ending, "Well, boys, remember I said the fever was like a communicable disease?"

Heads nod, anticipating a fantastic turn of events and fortune.

"Well, like a disease, this fever makes you crazy. And in a crazed way, madness overcomes you, and you do what must be done." Standing as straight and tall as a man of diminutive stature can, Nathaniel strides out of Tavern Bouvard, leaving his audience to marvel or bewilderment, depending on each man's knowledge of Nathaniel Joiner's nature, his character, and stubborn determination.

Luck reveled, tasting the bitterness it had heaped upon Nathaniel, especially at the Golden Stairs. It should be remembered that Luck has no personal vendetta against Nathaniel. He is simply a hobby, a pastime to toy with, the flip side of heads on a tossed coin, and the bruised shoulder from repeated shotgun recoils on a perfect day of hunting.

Clay walks and Anna skips, each in their own world, as they head toward home, taking a shortcut through the Joiner's swamp. Neither one notices the orange and lavender sky off their right shoulders, as the sun falls out of the western sky. Clay, quiet and introspective, puffing gently on his hand-rolled, replays the afternoon adventure with its tantalizing sensations. For an instant, a pang of guilt by feelings of betrayal stab at his chest. An image of Jennifer appears before him on the trail. Her face is a mixture of softness and contentment. She is smiling. There is not a hint of anger or hurt. The pain in Clay's chest eases, as he realizes his hand is over his heart. The beat is calm, rhythmic, and without distress. Clay's fears are allayed. He has not betrayed Jennifer's love. His love of her and her love for him will continue, never dimming, regardless of life's twists and turns, the unexpected, and the unplanned surprises.

"You should have been there, father," Anna is bugged with excitement, bouncing forward and back along the trail. "Houdini was really locked tight in that cell. It was a basement cell, all dark, damp and gloomy. I know 'cause I saw him and I got to shake the lock. It was heavy and strong. No way could he break it. I'd hate to ever be a criminal and get thrown into that dungeon," Anna skips around Clay, not noticing her father's far away gaze. "Everyone was there to watch. At first I couldn't see, but then Madison and I squeezed through the crowd and down the jail's steps to watch." Giggling, Anna shares a secret, "Father, I think Madison likes me, because after we got to the front, he didn't let go of my hand." Anna looks to her father for any reaction. Clay's slate gray eyes are calm. His expression is neutral. Anna takes this as a positive sign, one meaning that it is okay to be liked by a boy, and to have one's hand held. Mulling the event over in her mind, *Madison's hand was warm and kind of sweaty*. Anna looks at the palm of her right hand that was squeezed tighter when Houdini emerged from the locked cell. *Did I like it or not?* She asks herself, and then switches gears back to the original subject of her excitement. "There must have been a million-billion people waiting for Houdini to come out. No one said a thing. It was absolutely quiet," Anna continues her bunny bounce-hop back and forth. "Then with only a towel wrapped around his middle," Anna bangs her small fist into her other palm for emphasis, "out steps Houdini, his arm raised. Ta-dah! You should have been there, father."

The pleading of a child reaches Clay's and Anna's ears from up the trail.

"Pa, please don't do it," the trembling voice wails. Even from a distance the cry is unmistakable. It is Delbert.

Clay and Anna are alarmed by the panic in his voice. They hurry forward to emerge upon the creek that marks the Joiner's boundary to Clay's property.

"I'll take care of her. I promise," begging with tears streaming from his eyes, Delbert clings to his father's pant leg. August stands next to the lazy creek holding a burlap sack.

"I've told you, 'We can't keep her,' It's not about who'll care for her. Now stop your whimpering, and get home if you can't stomach what needs to be done," August looks up from his son as he hears Clay's and Anna's footsteps on the path as they approach. "Evening, Clay. Miss Anna," August tips his sweat stained, droopy brimmed, felt cap. Something within the burlap sack wiggles. Clay knows immediately what is about to transpire. Anna only knows that Delbert is crying and trying to grab the sack from his father.

"Evening, August," Clay nods to August. "We're just passing through on our way home, back from town."

"I saw Houdini," Anna says with dwindling enthusiasm. Her concern for Delbert's distress suppresses her earlier excitement.

"Come on, Anna," Clay scoops Anna up to forge the meandering creek. "No need for you to be chilled on this cool evening." It is Clay's way to keep Anna moving toward home, and to hopefully avoid an unpleasant explanation of a harsh reality.

From within the sack a weak yap, not quite a bark is heard.

"It's a puppy!" squeals Anna. "Can I see it?" Anna struggles in her father's arms, causing him to stumble on the slippery rocks, as he crosses the thigh deep water of the creek to the far side.

"No, Anna. We need to be getting home," Clay is firmer in his tone than expected, as he takes hold of Anna's hand to pull her away from the unpleasant scene.

Looking back over her shoulder, Anna is becoming upset, disturbed by August, as he ignores Delbert's tearful pleas.

"Why is the puppy in the sack?" Anna's confusion is nearing fear for reasons she is unable to put words to.

"It's none of our business, Anna," Clay's strides lengthen. Today was perfect. Tonight, he prefers not to discuss the fatal consequences that animals face if they do not measure up.

"Clay," August shouts from across the creek. Clay stops walking, turns, and watches, as August says something to Delbert, who wipes his eyes, and then they both nod in agreement. August crosses the creek carrying the wriggling sack.

"Don't want to put you on the spot," August begins, while placing the bag on the ground. "Dog had a litter, and I've sold all the pups, but one."

Anna kneels beside the sack, untying it. A tiny black face with big onyx eyes appears. "Oh, look," Anna hugs the shivering Labrador puppy.

"You can see it's a runt. Wouldn't be much of a replacement for Rebel."

"Can we keep her, father?" Anna's forgotten all about this afternoon's hand holding and Houdini's magical escape.

"I'll give her to you without charge," August motions back across the creek toward his son whose apprehension and tear-streaked cheeks are visible in the fading light. "Peace at home would be more than enough payment."

Clay appreciates August's dilemma, but it is a runt, not worth the waste of a good sack for drowning. It is not likely going to grow strong enough, or muscle up sufficiently to stave off the chill of a Chesapeake winter. It has to be fed, and even if it were the pick of the litter, it could not replace Rebel. No dog ever would, and that is why Clay has turned down all previous offers, suffering the exhaustive work of retrieving his own kills and losing many cripples. There is no good reason to accept a burden that will amount to nothing.

"Oh, father," Anna laughs, as the puppy licks her face excitedly. Its pink and black toe-size tongue coaxes every ounce of affection that is possible from a small girl's heart.

A pardon, a reprieve, salvation is imminent. A familiar glow, a purity of love; Jennifer's gifts to Clay carries many forms. Tonight, it is the joy reflected in his daughter's eyes, as Anna carries home Beauty.

Beauty's rambunctious yapping does not disturb Clay's deep and dreamless sleep. Compared to Clay's resounding snores that shake fall leaves off the eaves overhanging the porch, Beauty's lonesome barks are only a little louder than the occasional desperate field mouse that burglarizes the Buchanan larder to chew on a morsel of bread crust missed during Anna's fastidious cleaning.

Being Beauty's first night away from the comfort of Dog, Anna speaks softly, cradling Beauty gently within the warmth of her quilt bed on the floor by the stove.

"Shush, Beauty. We don't want to wake father," are her words of tender pleadings. Beauty nuzzles her soft furry face into the warm curve under Anna's chin. Her cold, button nose sends a shiver along Anna's spine. It is a pleasant shiver. Beauty drifts off to sleep, relief flowing through her veins and relaxing her muscles, as instinct tells her that the events of today were monumental, but her life experiences are too few to understand exactly why. She does know that this new place and these new arms surrounding her are ones of safety and love.

The creaking of a swaying tree limb in the modest wind outside is unfamiliar. Ticks of twigs scratching against the shack are unfamiliar. A low-pitched whistle of wind through a crack in the wall's pine tar sealing is unfamiliar, but all these sounds are part of the natural. What Beauty is now hearing, what woke her and startles her, does not come from nature, or from within her new dwelling. These unfamiliar sounds are alien, and come from out there in the dark...and they are coming closer.

Standing stout, legs tense, barking at the inside of the door, shouting a warning to the sleeping household, Beauty holds her ground. If it comes through the door, whatever it is, it will have to come through her, too.

There, right there. Something outside passes by the window. *Get up! Get up!* Beauty's paltry barks ring out the alarm.

From behind and above Beauty, Anna reaches for the door latch. Her vision is unfocused, as her awareness struggles to awaken. She swings open the door. Beauty is prepared for battle, but before she can attack, Anna scoops her up into her arms. Standing at the door is Madison Mitchell. The cat-who-ate-the-canary grin on his face begs a question, but before Anna can speak the words, Madison gestures with his thumb toward the two dark figures standing behind him. Anna rubs her eyes to focus past her hand-holding friend to recognize Madison's father, Robert, and...

"Houdini," Anna shouts, so surprised, that she drops Beauty, who plops on the floor. Anna runs shouting into her father's room, leaving the unexpected guests to the perils of Beauty, who has not been given the order to stand down.

I'll take them on one at a time or all at once, barks Beauty. Her puny body shakes with each ferocious yap.

Clay climbs up out of his deep slumber to a house in chaos with amused guests waiting patiently at the door.

"Father. Father, come quick, Houdini's here," Anna cries as she pulls her father from the warmth of his bed.

A bit unsure of the madness that has overtaken his home, Clay pulls on his pants and shirt, and then follows his manic daughter to the Great Room. Anna is bounding like a springer spaniel anticipating the throw of a ball.

"That's some guard dog you got there, Anna," jokes Madison. His eyes resemble Beauty's, big puppy dog's, full of affection and awe, but to cover his crush on her, he continues with the jest, "You think you could chain her up so we can safely enter?"

"Anna, hush your dog," Clay pleads more than orders. Anna quickly picks up Beauty to reassure her, but never once does she take her gaze of wonderment off The Great Houdini.

Anna had strongly protested her exclusion from the morning hunt with Houdini, but not too strongly. Her father gave her more latitude than she had witnessed other fathers when their children spoke their minds. She was not sure if it was due to her being a girl or because there was no wife and mother in the home, or because Olivia repeatedly told Clay, "Silence the child—kill the spirit." Whatever the reason, Anna felt privileged, but when Clay gave her a certain look, that unmistakable look, one rarely seen except when he was overly tired or among adults, that look where the eyebrows furrow, his jaw tightens, and the shimmer of light deadens within his eyes, well, Anna knows the conversation is over...at least for now.

"But it was Houdini," exasperated, Anna explains to Delbert, as they walk, and to Beauty, as she gallops along the shore to check on the buried treasure of turtle eggs. Two months have passed with Anna and Delbert diligently checking daily on their eggs, hoping to catch sight of the tiny dinosaurs.

A false dawn lightens the horizon. The black night hesitantly retreats with the passing minutes, allowing the lazy morning to turn the foliage, first gray, and then the remaining hints of summer color are spotted under the overcast sky. The greens of grasses and leaves and among them are the reds, yellows, and pinks of the last of the summer flowers. Beyond the vision of the early risers, a storm front is pushing in from the north. Riding high, like foam on a breaking wave, the migrating birds are charging south. They are an annual army, massed in the millions, incalculable legions, driven to conquer the hundreds and thousands of miles, to converge on the Chesapeake region in a perfect pincer move. Many arrive from the Arctic, many more from Canada's tundra, and the rest from mid-northern states of America. All are seeking a more hospitable place to winter and feed; some to mate and raise the next generation; Canada geese, black duck, blue-winged teal, canvasback, green-winged teal, mallard, oldsquaw, pintail, scaup, scoter, widgeon, wood, and ruddy. Many will find refuge. Many will not.

Bang! Bang! Bang!

Anna cocks her head, listening. *Is that my father's shotgun?* Anna does not know where her father is taking Houdini to hunt, so she can only guess. *The shots did sound like her father's Remington.* They came from a blind not far off.

"Let's go have a look," Anna suggests, hoping to show off Houdini to the doubting Delbert. The turtles are forgotten for the moment, as Anna leads Delbert; with Beauty bounding alongside, up along a trail toward a productive duck blind fronting the Flats.

"It's a coffin," Houdini blurts with gaiety, as Clay rows them out to a two-man sinkbox off Swan Creek Point. This prized location is below Clay's property, and on the north side of a cove. Robert Madison had asked Clay to act as guide for Houdini.

"I'd be honored to take him myself, especially since it's a favor to McQuay," Robert explains, "But I have a previous engagement in Baltimore tomorrow."

Clay's nose wrinkles in disgust at the mention of Frank McQuay. "You can have use of O'Neill's double sinkbox if you'd like," continues Robert. Clay extends his calloused hand to shake Houdini's firm, but smooth one. For a moment, Clay believes he is seeing a Doppelgänger. Houdini is a dead ringer for Nathaniel Joiner. At five-foot six-inches, Houdini is only two-inches taller than the swamp rogue. Houdini's clothes are considerably newer, but they are sloppy, as if removed from the hamper. The spell is broken when Houdini smiles. His mouth contains a full set of white teeth. Otherwise, Clay needs to blink twice to confirm that a middle of the night joke is not being played upon him.

"It'd be my pleasure," Clay states cordially, but without the enthusiasm that shooting usually brings, as he thinks, *Here's just another sport.*

"I appreciate you stepping in for me, Clay," Robert is relieved by Clay's willingness, and then nudges Clay aside to whisper in confidence. "O'Neill's rig is hidden in the bushes under a green tarp, 20 paces from the row boat."

Clay smiles, and then winks at his old friend, "Mums the word." Though there is not a hunter on the Susquehanna Flats who does not know the secret hiding place of Henry O'Neill's famous James T. Holly cast iron and mast wood canvasback decoys.

Houdini settles into his section of the sinkbox. Clay passes two 10-gauge shotguns and a canvas sack of shotgun shells to Houdini, whose ever-present ear-to-ear grin is unnerving.

"It's called a sinkbox," Clay explains. "It's built on the principle of John Ericsson's[7] Monitor.[8]" Handing several iron decoys weighing roughly 25 pounds each to Houdini, Clay instructs the magician, "Place these on the surrounding framework to sink her to the waterline. You then lie back in the box. When the birds toll in for a visit and a snack, you pop up and shoot."

"It's ingenious," Houdini marvels at the sinkbox's construction while Clay rows out to set the rig of 201 decoys in a proper pattern for an effective lure.

Houdini bounces gently at first and then with more force. Waves radiate outward, and then back, but the canvas-covered framework attached to the edges of the coffin's platform dampens the wash of the waves, allowing only a minimum of chilly water to enter the box. Houdini lies prone, folding his hands across his chest as if prepared for burial. The sky above is featureless, gray, and unwelcome. The cold of the shotguns' barrels seep through his heavy jacket as they rest on the crook of his arms. He closes his eyes and then slowly releases the air from his lungs through his mouth. He imagines the escaping warmth to be his last breath. Houdini savors his mock death. Not a breeze dips in to disturb Houdini's fantasy, yet something is wrong. It is something familiar, but forgotten, not forgotten...suppressed.

A memory?

An experience?

A fear?

A fascination?

Houdini hears it now. His eyes shoot open to see it. Near the head of the coffin, two boards unevenly fitted together allow droplets of water to form

---

7 Ericsson, John (1802-1889). A Swedish engineer and inventor credited with designing and building the *Monitor*.

8 *Monitor*. An armored warship with a very low freeboard. Steam propelled, it was used for coastal defense during the U.S. Civil War. One such vessel battled the Confederate ironclad warship *Merrimack* at Hampton Roads, Virginia (1862).

and fall. Drop by drop, one after another, slowly, but surely to fill his coffin, to drown little Eric Weis. Eric struggles. His lungs fill with choking river water. Eric's body convulses, as his lungs struggle, trying to pull oxygen from liquid.

Panic!

A brother's hand pulls Eric up by his hair.

Houdini is sitting up. His breath is brought under control...slow and steady...regular. His vision focuses on his own hands. He wipes his sweaty brow with his monogrammed silk handkerchief, "I am The Great Harry Houdini. I'm no longer little Eric Weis. I am the King of Escapology. Not even death can hold me." Houdini's ear-to-ear grin is broader than ever. Belief is a powerful thing.

Twenty yards distant, Clay ties a floating object to the stern of the rowboat. He rows toward Houdini, who sits sublime in the sinkbox. As Clay nears, and then rounds the shooting apparatus, Houdini sees that it is an arm attached to a body that Clay has tied to the rowboat.

"My apologies, Mr. Houdini, but I have to take this poor soul in and report to the constable." Houdini examines the bloated, disfigured body of a boy in his late teens whose milky eyes stare vacantly. They are eyes of fish too old, spoiled and rotten with death. What flesh is visible is graying purple. The limbs are ridged and distended. His clothes are rags belonging to a poor city boy, possibly from Baltimore, or maybe New York.

"Mr. Buchanan," Houdini begins in a tone not disrespectful, just insensitive. "I doubt the lad would wish to deny us our day's hunt. Please secure him to the corner of this sinkbox and I'll see he doesn't escape."

"I think the lad's need for proper..."

"The lad is dead," Houdini states, his cleft chin jutting forward. "He has no needs or cares. You can do as you wish later, but now I wish to hunt. Please see to *my* needs."

Clay Buchanan is not a man to be given orders to. If it were not for his friendship with Robert Mitchell, Clay would have left the Great Houdini sitting alone with stinging ears from a verbal rebuke, as no other has ever endured. As Clay climbs into his coffin, and lays back next to, in his eyes, the not-so-great Houdini, he is repulsed by the uncaring remarks concerning the deceased.

"Simply drowned, you think?" inquires Houdini with a touch of disappointment by the seemingly common death.

"I would guess he was given the boom, either accidentally, or on purpose, by the condition of his face and chest," responds Clay, a touch of sadness in his voice over the loss of life, thinking: *Such a waste of potential.* "Given the boom?" Houdini adjusts his position so he can reach out to turn over the corpse for a closer examination. Deep fascination creases his otherwise smooth forehead. *Intrigue?* He wonders, while licking his full lips.

"The boom of an oyster skipjack. A dishonest captain hires on a crew, some from the city, to work the oyster beds. Instead of paying wages at the end of the week, he'll jibe the boat without warning," Clay remains lying on his back as he explains. "The inexperienced deckhand is caught off guard as the deck tilts with the sudden heeling over by the erratic turn. The lad struggles to keep his balance. He turns, frightened, to see what's happening, but seeing only the massive sail boom as it swings over the deck to smash into his chest and chin, swatting him overboard. From the bruising on his face and caved-in chest, I'd say he died for his wages."

Houdini gingerly touches the boy's battered face, "There's a peace about him. Did you notice?" Houdini pauses to remind himself of his motto: *Do others, or they'll do you,* and then continues. "While on tour in America's heartland, I heard of children that had burned to death in a school fire, so I traveled a day and a half out of my way to see them. When I arrived, their charred little bodies where just being removed from the still smoking building. I tried to picture each corpse as a laughing, happy child, but they no longer seemed human. I was drawn to them though. I looked into what used to be faces, and though only blackened skulls remained. I clearly saw terror." Again, Houdini strokes the fish-nibbled face of the body tied to the sinkbox, wishing a camera was near to record this event. He could add the photograph to his collection of grotesque tortures...*given the boom. How inventive.*

Flying in a knot, fast and low, two-dozen redheads aim for a landing in the opening left by Clay when he set out the decoy rig. Clay remains motionless, no longer listening to the morbid prattling of a man who seemingly is obsessed with death.

"C'mon, beauties. A little closer," Clay whispers. "Don't break." The redheads, seeing other ducks resting and content on the water are lured by the inviting scene. The leader checks his air speed as he wings past the outward most decoys.

Clay is both tense and calm. An instant more will determine meat or soup for dinner, life or death.

The leader, tired, hungry, and overly confident, tolls. His wings flare with feet down to skid across the surface. His webbed toes never touch the placid water. Catching a shot blast in the breast, the leader is blown backward into others of his clan as three redheads fall to the flying lead pellets. The remaining 18 birds, disorganized and frantic, bolt off in all directions, some to safety, and some into the barrel sights of other hunters secreted in their own sinkboxes and blinds.

The Great Houdini never took a shot.

Frank McQuay could have been an ad for L.L. Bean. Spiffed to the nines in the latest, most expensive gentleman's sports gear, he would ingratiate himself with the upper crust, the old moneyed men, willing himself to believe he is their equal, with the hope of being invited to join one of the many exclusive hunting lodges along the Chesapeake. On the occasion where his presence at a haughty function was that of a guest, he would mingle freely, feeling that this is where he rightfully belonged, among astute businessmen, and the movers and shakers of this nation, his peers; senators, governors, a President or two, magnets of industry and agriculture, but farmers, not a one. Pompously, smoking a three-dollar cigar, he once told President-to-be Woodrow Wilson, "Sir, the difference between myself and a farmer who scratches in the dirt is simple but quite significant. He has less than one thousand acres, dirt under his fingernails, and knows nothing of wise investing." Frank McQuay wiggles his manicured fingers in the air while chuckling, "By the way, have you met my wife, Dorothy?"

This is the first in many days that Frank McQuay has taken the morning off from overseeing his holdings. He woke early without prodding to kill fowl. This isn't a sport to him. There is no art to it. He does not care, nor does he appreciate the efforts Roman takes to dig, and then build the blind, or arrange the decoy rig, or oil the guns so they will function properly. It does not matter to Frank McQuay that Roman is black, his servant, and in his fifties with painfully swollen and disfigured joints. Frank McQuay is an equal opportunity discriminator and wannabe elitist. He treats those with less as being less. It does not matter if the person is black or white; only wealth and power matters to Frank McQuay.

"Damn it. You're still shooting behind the birds," Frank McQuay snarls at his son. "Lead it. Anticipate."

Roman reloads the oversized Remington scattergun for William, and then lies back down on the damp ground, out of sight of roaming birds. There is no lantern or blanket for warmth for Roman in the early dawn. His body aches, as the chill seeps though his clothes, and deep into his bones. Roman shivers. *Be grateful,* he says to himself. *I ain't digging in the fields. I got a bed. No beatings and I have my freedom.* Roman's litany, repeated for years beyond count, is a pitiful contradiction. Outward, Roman is a tall-walking, sure spoken manager of an elegant country mansion with a salary, paltry though it may be. "What Negro has it better?" he challenges others of his color, especially those who rarely felt the cut of a whip. "I'm Roman, named for an empire. Such as it was, so it shall be." This is his introduction. Inwardly, Roman quivers at the sight of any white man. He has seen their worst, and believes their best to be only a cunning mask to befriend, and then betray an ignorant "niggah" who has forgotten his mama's gospel, "Never trust whitey."

William sits on the wooden bench watching the featureless zinc sky, as the butt of the heavy gun weighs painfully on his foot. "Never let it touch dirt," Frank McQuay would growl. "Don't you know what that shotgun cost?"

"Why do I have to go?" whined William when Roman gently woke him in what seemed to be the middle of the night, and the worst part, it interrupted dreams of cricket with his school chums at Sandhurst. William is not the best at knocking over the wicket with the ball, but he can swing a bat, and that assured him to be picked for a team in the second or third round.

"I don't have a gun," mumbled William, as Roman helped him gather the appropriate clothing that would be suitable for sitting in a freshly dug hole next to the Flats.

"Did you forget that pretty over-and-under your father bought you during your last visit home?"

"But I was going to go sailing with 'Chief' today," griped William, as he washed the sleep out of his azure eyes, and then wetted back his wavy auburn hair with warm water from the porcelain basin that Nana Maude had carried in while Roman was rousing him from dreamland.

"You can sail any day with Millard. Besides, your father passed on hunting with an important man to spend the day with you. You should feel special."

Roman had not grown up around duck hunters, but he learned their craft, as if born to it. His arrangement of 71 decoys of several species: mallards, scaups, and brants, is an attractive respite to those long on the wing.

"Seventy-one, not 70, or 72," Roman chants, "Got to be odd, never even. Ducks, they'll find a human pattern in an even number. You always make it odd."

"Ssst," Roman alerts father and son to incoming birds. Roman may be the oldest of the three, but his eyesight is legendary. Both McQuays, father and son, strain to acquire the cluster of specks rising over the horizon.

Frank McQuay shrinks into his coat collar. William holds his breath, but does not know why. Roman, concealed in bushes, pulls and tugs on several groups of strings buried in the mud. These strings, twine that has been waxed for strength, lead out under the water to decoys anchored to weights of various constructions with metal eyelets. Pulling and tugging, then releasing the strings causes the decoy riding on the surface to dip its head, or disappear completely, as if dining on succulent underwater eelgrass. It is quite a show Roman puts on.

A master puppeteer.

Deadly convincing.

There must be 30, no, 40, possibly even 50, wildfowl. Their numbers swell as the flock of fat mallards nears the McQuays' hiding place. Roman smiles, his body aches are forgotten with the pleasure of impending success. The birds fly straight in to join their wooden companions whose smiles are permanently carved and repainted each season. The old squaw, the eldest and wisest fugleman of the group is confident.

"All clear," the old squaw signals, as he coasts in on tired wings. His belly is empty. He is ready to rest and replenish.

"Wait...wait..." Frank McQuay whispers orders to William.

"Break left!" the old squaw calls, snapping his wings, rocketing away from danger, as he leads his flock to safety.

"Son-of-a-bitch. I told you to wait," Frank McQuay bellows at his son.

"But I didn't move."

Frank McQuay slaps William with the back of his gloved hand; knocking him against the dirt wall, "Don't talk back."

Forty-feet from the blind, Anna and Delbert watch in stunned silence. It was they whom the old squaw saw, as they emerged from the cattails along the marsh path.

"That bastard," Delbert mumbles under his breath.

William's eyes moisten. He holds his hand to his reddening cheek, as nutrient rich soil from the edge of the blind sprinkles down on him like black rain. Frank McQuay grabs the lapels of William's coat, yanking him off his feet.

"What are you?" he growls as he again slaps his cowering son. "A girl? Damn it. I didn't send you to the finest military school in England for you to come back a dandy." Frank McQuay shoves William backward. He falls hard against the shotgun. The barrels dig deeply into his spine. "C'mon, Roman, the hunt's ruined." Frank McQuay climbs out of the blind. As he stomps away, he tosses one last barb in an attempt to instill character in his son, "I expect those guns to sparkle. Can a dandy do that?"

Seething with rage, grimacing with physical pain, and crushed by his father's harsh words, William grabs his shotgun, shouldering it, and through bleary, tear-filled eyes, levels the sight squarely on his father's back, whimpering, "I'll show you what I can do."

Pressure is applied to the trigger. The striking pin trembles. Its job is to ignite the powder to propel a deadly volley of pellets. The trigger, the pin, the powder, and the volley—it is teamwork, and once set in motion, there is nothing that can stop it. It is life or death. Forever. A decision determined by an infinitesimal change in pressure of a son's finger.

The weapon is snatched from the boy's hands. Through salty tears, William looks into Roman's face. There is no accusation. No pity. No malice, just a blue-black face, wrinkled by a great passing of time, now set in neutral.

"Quit your dallying, Roman," Frank McQuay calls back over his shoulder, unaware of the decisions concerning his future that are being made behind him. Roman hands the instrument that affords no second chances, back to a child, "This too will pass." A spark of understanding, compassion, flits across Roman's charcoal irises. He turns, and then trots to catch up to his master.

William sits on the plank that was driven into the blind wall. Moments pass, as he stares at his father's back, and then at the faux ducks bobbing in mock imitation of the real thing. Except for the diminishing sound of Roman's and his father's footsteps as they walk away, the world is quiet... holding its breath.

All is waiting...waiting...waiting for his decision.

Life or death.

Decide.

Jumping to his feet, the shotgun held at waist level, William cries out, while jerking the weapon's double trigger. Shots resound to shatter the silence and to end the waiting—teamwork.

The smoking barrels are evidence of humiliation.

The decapitated decoys testify to a rage released, at least for the moment.

The nine-year-old, sobbing, crumpled in the bottom of a pit dug for killing is a harsh sentence by a father who has only one idea of what a man should be and how to create him.

"I give them hope," Houdini explains to Clay. "Each time I escape the impossible, whether I'm using handcuffs, a jail cell, a steel safe, a strait jacket or ropes, to the masses it represents the drudgery of their everyday lives. Their chains are poverty, ignorance, prejudice, and religious intolerance to name just a few."

Clay listens to this strange man who is revered by millions, but Clay wonders how many have spent a morning hunting, shoulder to shoulder, in a coffin built for two, with a bloated corpse tied alongside.

"Those decoys are a simple trick, like my act. Designed to bring in the uneducated. It's presentation that counts, showmanship," Houdini rambles on. "If they knew the secret they'd be disappointed in how easy they are taken in."

Clay remains silent while searching the horizon. Now only half listening, he wonders if Houdini is talking about his audience or the ducks. In either case, it is going to be a very long morning.

Anna, Delbert, and Beauty pause at the "T" in the path. One leads deeper into the birch swamp to Delbert's home, the other leads back to the Buchanan shack with its waiting chores.

"William wouldn't have wanted us to comfort him," Delbert tells Anna. The word comfort seems girlish, but that was the word Anna had used, "Anyway, boys don't cry."

"But he was crying," Anna knows what she saw and has heard. "And you were crying when I got Beauty."

"Listen, Anna, boys don't cry and even if they did, they sure-as don't want no one seeing them," Delbert huffs. He turns in a show of exasperation, whacking a drying cattail bloom with the palm of his hand. An explosion, bright yellow, of furry pollen fills the widening gap on the trail between the two friends.

"That's stupid," Anna says defiantly, her hands on her hips.

"You're stupid," Delbert calls over his shoulder, a tit-for-tat reply.

Anna watches Delbert stomp away down the narrow dirt path. She wonders where boys learn such things "See you later, Del?"

"Okay. Yeah, see you later, Anna."

Turning for home, Anna's mind is secure in her friendship with Delbert, though she admits to herself that comfort was not the true reason for wanting to approach the blind. It was to take a better, closer look at him.

"William McQuay," Anna speaks his name aloud. Even with her dislike for his surname, his first name, "William, Bill, Billy," tastes sweet, as she plays with the variations. Anna giggles, invoking yaps of curiosity from Beauty who is at her side. *Could this be what a crush is?* Anna wonders. *Is this what Madison feels for her?* She has heard other children at school using the term, but usually referring to a boy toward his teacher.

A trickle of sweat squiggles down Anna's back as the humidity rises with the dawn. It tickles her with a hot chill.

"Houdini," Anna sets aside her fascination with William to race Beauty home. Father will soon return, and she wants to be waiting with refreshments, and wearing a clean outfit, her only other one, a handmade dress.

"Do you think maybe tonight?" asks Delbert of Anna, as the two walk one behind the other, south along the shore—left feet splashing clear water and right feet stomping speckled sand. Both youngsters are bronzed of skin from the brilliant July sun. Their matching coveralls, long sticky with sweat, are slowly releasing their wet grip from the day's play, as a cooling breeze skips across the expansive Flats. The refreshing wind chases the fading mauve light over the western horizon. Anna groans and Delbert sighs as they hold their bellies that are overstuffed with copious jumbo scoops of multi-flavored ice cream that was offered free by the blue-hair church ladies during the day long Havre de Grace celebration of the nation's 131st birthday.

"Could be tonight. I don't know," Anna replies, annoyed by the repetition of Delbert's singular question. Sixty-three days later, her answer remains the same.

Rounding a finger point jutting rudely into the bay, the two friends are distracted by the frenzied squawking and wing snaps of squabbling ring-billed gulls who are engaged in aerial battles with the great black-backed gulls, whose five and one-half foot wing span, dwarf their smaller, though equally aggressive cousin. The battle is over protein-rich hors d'oeuvres with tiny flippers.

"The turtles!" the companions shout in unison, erupting into an unfair race. Anna kicks up sand as her ten toes dig deep for traction; Delbert lopes on an uneven frame, his arms pumping, and jaw clenched with straining effort.

At the nest site, carnage reigns. Two fat and furry brown bandits, identities well known, despite wearing masks, alternate between dexterous filching of the newly hatched, as the turtles emerge from their sandy womb, and fending off sharp-billed competitors. Miraculously, as mouthfuls of sleek black hatchlings are devoured, there are a number of two-inch tracks in the sand, 10, 15, maybe even 20, leading from the nest and into the water. Once there, safety exists, at least from land and air predation.

"Get away. Get away from them," cries Anna, as she reaches the crime scene.

The thieving raccoons, reluctant to give up this rich cache, hesitate long enough to grab one last unlucky hatchling each, before skulking off to disappear among the ripening stalks of wild rice. Having vanquished the bandits, Anna and Delbert, panting, and he just arriving, split their rescue mission. Waving his arms, shouting, and weaving in crazy circles to little effect, Delbert tries to scare away the angry gulls that are taking small notice of this bizarre two-legged creature. Anna crouches over the violated nest to shield the innocent newborns, as each defenseless turtle pokes its sand speckled head up into a violent world. Two moist heads appear, followed by bodies, fresh from their shells. Gently lifting them with loving hands, Anna carries them the dozen steps to the water's edge. She tosses the tiny creatures away from the shore with the hope that they will have a jump start in their paddle to the open sea. Destroying this hope, two ring-bills, propelled by powerful wings, snatch the turtles in mid-air, to fly off with their prizes. Other gulls, hungry and envious, molest the first two, even after they have gulped whole the tasty morsels down their gullets.

"No," pleading more than a command, Anna turns back to the nest. A half dozen great black-backs have commandeered the nest, their bills digging deep for any remaining turtles, born or still shell-bound. The birds' wings are slapping and flapping sharply, cracking the air at one another, with feathers flying at each new discovery of a tasty treat, or the frustration of having one stolen from them. Delbert continues to harass the newly arriving gulls, delaying their landing for only a bemused moment or two.

Tears roll down Anna's cheeks, as despair at the indiscriminate killing and feasting, overwhelm her. She is about to sink to her knees for a shoulder-heaving sob, when, silhouetted in the dying orange ball that is the sun, sitting on an ancient mound of oyster shells some 30-feet back from the nest is—

Anna wipes away the tears blurring her vision and shades her eyes from the glare, "Umbrella George." Anna scrambles up the short, sandy shore, climbs over the brown grass-covered bank, and up the bleached mound of crumbling shells. She is greeted by a face that is sagging, skin wrinkled to leather from the elements, but with eyes wide in the wonderment of God's glory surrounding him. Umbrella George's lips and finely trimmed beard glisten with the drippings of fresh-shucked and swallowed-whole oysters. On his left sits a bucketful patiently waiting their turn; on his right, the Sampler, and his ever-present umbrella.

"Umbrella George," Anna falls to her knees before him, "please help."

"Call your friend, Anna. His strenuous antics are wearing me plumb out."

Anna, exasperated, but respectful, reluctantly obeys, "Del. Del, come up here."

Flailing and dripping sweat, Delbert turns toward Anna, and seeing Umbrella George, gives up his futile task.

"Have a seat children," offers Umbrella George with a sweep of his arm, an arm forever covered by a faded black suit jacket, pin striped, and aged like he is, but not worn out or ready for retirement.

"Won't you help?" asks Anna, still trying to urge him to action.

"Help who, Anna? Help you? Help the turtles? Help the raccoons or help the gulls?" Umbrella George asks tenderly.

"The turtles of course," replies Anna, confused.

"Would you two care for some oysters?"

"Yes, sir," Delbert quickly pipes in, never one to pass up victuals, no matter how full he may be.

Umbrella George lifts a fine fat oyster out of the tin bucket, placing a small blunt knife at the oyster's lip, and then pauses, "Hmm? Should I help these oysters and toss them back into the bay? Anna, what should I do?"

Anna's lips part, as to reply, but no sound escapes. Umbrella George looks into Anna's root beer eyes, so familiar, so like her mother's. Anna returns his compassionate gaze with indecision. Delbert fidgets. He licks his lips with sweet anticipation of the meaty-wet morsel dripping in Umbrella George's hands.

"C'mon, Anna. What's your answer? Little Cigar here looks hungry."

Coming slowly with her answer, Anna sighs, "If Del's hungry, he should eat," and with a small rebuke, "though I can't see how after all that ice cream we ate you can still be hungry?"

Delbert shrugs with only slight embarrassment, but happily accepts the shucked oyster.

"That's right, dear. If one is hungry, one should eat. It's nature's way. God provides this bounty to all creatures." Umbrella George stretches out his arms to encompass the world surrounding them, "Look at it. There is abundance for all."

From a throne of discarded oyster shells, Delbert slurps down his second helping. Anna follows Umbrella George's lines of sight. On the bay, several skipjacks are returning to the wharfs of Havre de Grace to unload their catches after licking the rocks. Their triangular sails filled with a comfortable home bound breeze. Their decks are awash with baskets of oysters. Close by, the last ravenous gulls take to the air, to harry and beg the oystermen for scraps. Closer still, white-tailed dragonflies flit here and there, protecting their territory, and their claimed banquet of insects. Behind and invisible, hidden among the reeds, rice, grasses, creeks and streams that make up the marsh and tidal estuaries, a multiplicity of species: mammal, reptile, and fowl, that are terrestrial, aquatic, and airborne, are all in search of flora or fauna in which to feed upon to sustain them for another day.

Disheartened, but accepting, Anna softly asks, "Did any of them make it?"

Smiling, Umbrella George's wrinkled face glows with warmth, as he places his arm around Anna's shoulder, reassuringly, "Yes, I watched many throughout the night scurry into the water."

"Last night? How long have you been waiting?" Anna asks, surprised that anyone other than Delbert and herself knew of the turtle eggs.

"Just like you and Cigar, I've been anticipating this very rare event. After hearing of your discovery of the giant leatherback, and being blessed with a delicious steak, courtesy of your father," glancing at Delbert, "I got to pondering. Why was it here? Injured I'd heard, but if it were a female, then there could be eggs, so I poked around and found the nest. Then, while I was in Baltimore, picking up the orders of Bibles I'd sold, I inquired as to the incubation period for the eggs. Best estimate was between 55 and 74 days. So I began my nightly vigil eight days ago."

"Eight days ago," exclaims Delbert, his eyes wide with indignation, as he uses the back of his hand to wipe the juice that is dripping down his chin. "We've been checking on them almost everyday for more than two months," Glaring at Anna, and vexed with her stubbornness, he snipes, "See, Anna, we should have asked someone."

"Eat your oysters, Del," Anna replies, a smile growing warm within her.

– 1907 –

Tavern Bouvard.

Olivia holds an empty shot glass up, turning it slowly in front of a lantern flame burning brightly behind the bar, examining the glass for streaks or cracks. Saliva wells up in her mouth. She swallows it with a smile and remembrance. Her father, God rest his soul, would spit into each glass before wiping, and then shelving it. "Keeps the dust away," he would chortle. Long time patrons, used to this procedure, would remark to the uninitiated, "Turns the hardest whiskey smooth as a beaver's pelt." Her father was a lanky, scarecrow of a man: Chester 'the jester' Bouvard. The jester is a backhanded title of respect for a man who held court every night. He presided with a perpetual grin, his teeth stained brown from the plug of chewing tobacco crammed into his freckled cheek. Sometimes it was pondered if the man had a facial defect, or brain seizure, because his lips never turned down, but one fact was not in dispute. No man who entered Tavern Bouvard could remain blue. A drink was to celebrate, not drown in. Olivia did her best to uphold the tradition...except the spitting part.

Olivia placed the glass on its proper shelf with a clink to its neighbor. The clean up from the night's revelry was never left for morning. "Always wake up to a sparkling establishment," was her father's instruction. "It starts the day off proper." All was in order except for one table still cluttered with detritus in the form of Nathaniel Joiner. Walking up to the snoring pint of a man, Olivia sniffed the familiar odor of iodine. Men who work the marsh carry this unique fragrance. A smirk crosses Olivia's lips at the thought that Nathaniel worked at anything. He cruised through life, one lucky man, so it seemed. Most likely the odor was coming from the clothes he wore, borrowed from a line or hook at an unattended shed or shack. She reaches out to wake him, but pauses, as her eyes catch upon the title of a small news article. It's not the headline, but still on the front page of the Havre de Grace *Republican*, left of center under the date. The paper is stained and wrinkled, but legible, even with the smeared ink. Olivia slowly tugs the paper out from under Nathaniel's resting arm.

A DAY FOR MOTHER?!

May 8, 1907: Spear-headed by Ann Jarvis of Philadelphia, saying, "The good children of America should recognize the second Sunday in May as Mother's Day to honor all that mothers do. Bringing home the bacon is only half the job. Someone has to cook it up." Congress has proposed a proclamation to this effect and awaits President Roosevelt's position on the issue.

"Damn straight," Olivia nods her approval while adding, "and some of us without children bring home the bacon as well." She stares mischievously at Nathaniel. His bear snores voice a complete disregard for Olivia. Rolling up the paper, she swats him on the head, startling him out of his dreams of silver and gold.

"What? What's going on?" Nathaniel sputters.

Olivia stands in front of the confused little man, one hand on her hip, the other holding out the newspaper under Nathaniel's nose as if he could actually read when sober, let alone drunk. "Recognize."

Nathaniel looks up into a face filled with satisfaction, but sees only hair, glowing red, and blazing from a devilish halo cast from the lantern illuminating Olivia from behind.

"What'd I do?" Nathaniel replies with an unusual timidity.

Stately oaks with muscular arms reach with politeness to shake the hands of their kin residing across the inland stream. Their lasting friendship creates a shaded cathedral wherein many come to pray. Cool water lazily meanders around the spindly legs of the lordly great blue heron. It is a magnificent bird at 50 inches with elegant blue-gray plumage. He gently nudges aside spatterduck lilies and patches of green duckweed blanketing the waterway as he moves forward with grace. His holy quest is for hidden fish, frogs, or eels to spear with a deadly accurate six-inch bill.

Disturbing the reverence like a rock thrown through a stained glass window, Beauty charges into the nave, barking irreverently at every creature in her path. They scatter as leaves thrown to an autumn storm. Startled, bronze-copper butterflies by the dozens take flight from supping curly milkweed pods; spiders race to the edges of silk webs; damselflies lose their delicate balance on aquatic grasses to flee off to seek a quieter pew, and our lord, dignified despite his croaking squawk, spreads majestic six-foot wings to depart from this sacrilege.

Following Beauty is a burdened child. Anna is returning from town with Clay's prescription of brown liquid, his medicine. Her duty is to check on the rat-wire traps for eels. These will be used for baiting crab lines; any extra will be cooked for dinner.

Wading barefoot into the stream is refreshing, and the cool breeze created by the mostly shadowed path, eases Anna's task. Clay had set five traps along the stream for the capture of eels that possess a natural intuition that seems contradictory. These creatures can somehow find their way from streams and creeks all across the Chesapeake Bay, out into the vast Atlantic Ocean to the Sargasso Sea, southeast of Bermuda for the purpose of spawning, but they are unable to find their way back out of a rat-wire trap to save their lives. Mostly nocturnal, with yellowish-brown bodies and dirty white bellies, those who view them consider these snake-like creatures to be ugly, slimy things, though they are quite useful, and tasty if properly prepared.

With a cannonball leap into the stream, Beauty joyously barks her discovery of the last trap squirming with eel. She looks back, grinning with delight, and announcing loudly, "Here it is. I've found it for you." Anna sloshes in between Beauty and the trap. Her toes wiggling, squishing in the soft stream bed of sand and mud made up of decaying leaves and other drowned vegetation carried on the current from far upstream.

Anna tilts up the wire trap to reach into the small opening to grab the eels about their midsections. Their two to three-foot cylindrical bodies, containing enlarged eyes, squirm within her firm grip. Each one, seven in total, are removed one at a time to the triumphant bark of Beauty, to be dropped with a squishy plop into a wicker basket that has been lined with oiled leather for water tightness.

"Father will be pleased with these fat ones," Anna says to Beauty, as she flings the eel slime from her fingers.

"Stay still," Clay rebukes Beauty. He has a momentary pang of guilt, as he watches her lie down in the bow of the sneak skiff with an unsettling attitudinal resemblance to Rebel. This black Labrador retriever of Anna's, a little more than 13 months old, and once destined for a watery grave, has developed into a birdie—a very eager, and adept hunting companion. "You too, Anna," Clay unnecessarily reminds his daughter. The small sneak skiff, not being designed for three passengers must be handled carefully and with caution, as Clay shoves off into the bay. Anna holds the scratchy wicker basket on her lap, a leaky seam seeping eel guts onto her coverall.

Upon arriving home, Anna flopped the eels, twisting and wiggling, onto the three-duck stone counter, and then chopped them into four-inch sections, while Clay placed his in-progress mallard decoys and tools; saw, hatchet, drawknife, and spokeshave, into the work shed. He then dragged the sneak skiff containing full-length oars, a small net on a pole, and an empty basket for the crabs, to the water's edge, while Beauty looked quizzically at Clay, as if asking, *Where's the Davenport?* In his patched coverall pocket, the cough-relieving liquid of modern science. Clay had said it before, and would repeat it many times after a soothing gulp, "Ah, that Bayer company is a life saver, though I still don't know what exactly an opiate is, I'm hooked on it."

The sparse wisps of cirrus, drifting high overhead, quickly dissipate. The feathery clouds are no match for the rising temperatures that will only tolerate a sky of pure opal. The teasing breeze, pleased to be called such, cannot raise a ripple on the bay, nor ruffle the feathers of the quick and graceful barn swallows on a rare break. These bullet-shaped, steel-blue backed, chestnut faced and buff-tan breasted birds are usually glimpsed rocketing after mosquitoes and horseflies to regain strength after their continent-crossing journey from Mexico, Argentina, and Chile.

Clay rows with powerful and exacting strokes from years of practice. Toxic smoke from his cigarette trails behind, a gray streamer waving good-bye, as the sneak skiff skims northward over the placid waters. The trio's destination is the mouth of the unnamed stream where the eel traps had been set and harvested. Offshore, 30 to 40 yards, where the bottom layer contains the correct percentage of salinity in its current, Clay had laid several hundred yards of trot line with eel tied every few feet. Now it is time to reap the bounty and replace the lure.

Clay eases the sneak skiff next to a wooden float indicating the southernmost point of the line. Anna pulls up the line, allowing it to slide through her fingers, as Clay slowly oars forward. Up they come, one after another. Blue crabs happily dining on the eel scraps. No hook is required. The crabs' claws are clamped firmly to the free meal. Their blind greed is their ruin. Anna shakes the line to dislodge the mouth-watering crustaceans. With the small net, Clay catches the falling crabs before they escape back into the depths. He deposits each one into the basket that is filling rapidly with the delicacy.

"King Arthur's table was never so splendid as ours piled high with crab," Clay says with satisfaction, while chewing on the butt of his hand-rolled, and winking at his daughter.

"Only thing tastier is a celery-fed canvasback," responds Anna, giggling. Clay nods approvingly. *She knows.*

As each crab along the line is removed, Anna checks the eel bait, and if needed, she ties a fresh one on before moving down the line. The crabbing team has developed an efficient system with no wasted movements to slow them down or to cause extra exertion in the soaring heat. An oar pull forward by father, a shake of the trot line by daughter, a leg stretch by Beauty, a net catch and flip of the crab into the basket by father, a tying of bait by daughter, a contented sigh by a summer warmed Beauty. Together they make a well-oiled machine so long as the product cooperates.

Halfway along the trotline, as it slides through Anna's fingers, a wary crab, somehow aware of a thing too good, and the likelihood of an untimely demise, releases its grip on the eel when its body breaks the surface. Anna plunges her hand into the water, over-reaching in her grasp for the fleeing crab, unbalancing the canoe-like craft, tipping it precariously.

"Anna. No!" Clay blurts.

The six-inch freeboard dips below the waterline. Cool, bay water rushes in over the rail, further upsetting the narrow craft. Beauty jumps to her feet, barking her caution. Anna tries to compensate by jerking sideways, away from the in-flowing water. Clay drops the oars to clutch the side railing. "Stop!" Clay's cigarette falls from his mouth to land on his lap, burning a hole in the many times patched fabric.

The flat-bottom vessel, not intended for rough waters, or unruly passengers, tips back, following Anna's movement, throwing her off balance. Her hands slap and splash the water in a wasted attempt to find purchase. Water again pours over the other side railing to slosh around Clay's boots and Anna's bare feet, and floating both baskets containing eel and crab. Beauty leaps onto the prow, the only remaining dry spot, while continuing her urgent instructions to Clay for salvage of this increasingly imperiled crew.

Clay recognizes his duty and the consequences of his decision. No doubt there will be a loss, but it is a choice that will save this expedition, and the majority of its crew. Using his greater weight, Clay forcefully throws himself against the high side of the craft. His violent move quickly rights the sneak skiff, but in so doing, flips Anna headfirst overboard with a swallowing splash. Her flop out of the skiff pushes it away from her entry point, and out of reach of Clay. Under water and disoriented, Anna inhales choking water, as the many tiny air bubbles popping around her, carry Beauty's garbled and panicked barking.

Anna's lungs reject the liquid oxygen. Wrenching spasms constrict her chest. Her arms struggle to breach the surface against the anchor that her water logged coverall has become.

"Anna," shouts Clay.

Anna's head breaks the surface for an instant, her mouth gasping for air, but filling only with churning water.

"Anna, listen to me," Clay is kneeling, retrieving the oars. Bucketfuls of water swirl within the sneak skiff, lowering the freeboard to only a few inches.

Callused hands of a girl who knows the work of daily chores splash the water's surface to a foaming froth. Overhead, circling gulls squawk while peering down with hungry curiosity. Anna's head rises once more in search of breathable air; her frightened eyes lock onto her father's face, his hand-rolled is safely back between his lips in the corner of his mouth.

"Anna, stand up," is Clay's command.

In her unexpected and undignified dunking into the bay, Anna forgot the cardinal rule: After falling overboard on the Susquehanna Flats, to prevent drowning, stand up. This amazing bay, in some places in excess of 20 miles wide, is in most places only a few feet deep, most notably so on the Flats.

Anna stands up. Her long black hair falls wet and dripping about her face to float upon the shoulder deep water. Embarrassed, Anna's cheeks flush red, as she coughs up the remaining bay water she has swallowed. Beauty continues to lecture Anna on proper crabbing etiquette. Clay draws deeply on his cigarette, saying nothing. It is too hot of a day to exert himself, but for the fun of it, and sporting a wry grin, Clay decides to chastise his daughter, "Anna, you've been warned about the new ordinance concerning swimming. If Constable Jenkins catches you not properly attired, he'll throw you in jail."

Moving slowly toward the skiff, and a bit miffed by her condition, Anna, retorts, "I don't think that fat ol' man can even swim."

"Jenkins doesn't have to. He'll just wait you out," Clay reaches out to take hold of Anna's hand to pull her aboard. "And mind your tongue," is all Clay says in rebuke for Anna's disrespectful remark about an elder.

"Yes, sir. I'm sorry," Anna sincerely replies, as she takes her seat. Clay takes up the oars to reposition the sneak skiff to begin again dipping crab. He thinks, *if she were a boy, I'd have tanned his hide for such a comment. What the hell do I know about raising a girl?*

The well-oiled machine, one part wet from a different type of dipping, resumes its work under a stunning Chesapeake sun.

Inquiring sheepishly, Anna asks, "Did you know that today may be called Mother's Day?"

The cacophonous mob of crickets interrupts their leg scratching to watch Clay's spasmodic swatting at invisible mosquitoes buzzing about his face. Clay stands over the garbage pit that has been dug a hundred paces behind the shack, and near the outhouse. He has added the leavings of tonight's meal; crab shells, boiled to an orange-red on the potbelly stove, to have its delicate meat meticulously picked clean with painstaking effort. "Catching them is always the easiest part," Clay comments aloud, as he breathes in deeply a mixture of marsh and bay air. Tonight, standing at this spot, it is the iodine from vegetative decay, salt carried on an impish breeze, and a hint of stink rising from the refuse and drifting up from the depths of their commode. He turns to retrace his steps along the well-worn path. Passing the outhouse with its customized door, Clay cannot help but smile by the memory. It was an unexpected, and certainly hilarious scene from his point of view. Returning one afternoon from a hunt, and in need of the facilities, Clay jogged toward the outhouse. As he neared it, he heard Jennifer singing happily, nary a care in the world. Thinking he may have to find an alternative pot, Clay was about to call out for his wife to share some paper, when he saw what caused him to skid to a halting stop, and fall to his knees in side-splitting laughter. Sitting unabashed on the throne, Jennifer had taken the handsaw, and cut the outhouse door in half, horizontally, creating a Dutch door. The bottom half was closed for modesty, but the upper portion was swung wide open to allow viewing out, and in. When Clay finally collected himself, wiping the tears from his eyes, and dusting off his knees with an expression of bafflement, he approached, what in his opinion was a cockamamie door. Jennifer smiled the smile of a thousand sunny days, and said, "Clay, our marsh is so beautiful today. I didn't want to miss a minute of it." Nothing more needed to be said.

The three-quarter moon, hanging heavy in the cloudless sky, casts night shadows with its milky luminescence. Clay's day is done, though around him, unseen, are creatures stalking the darkness, foraging, mating, fighting, living and dying. Clay stops next to the door to his shed to listen, his ears delighting in the melody of wheeper, ponker, hooter, and yowler. Birds of the night announcing, "Here I am. Come find me for love."

For a plogger like Clay, a man capable, respected among his peers, a man hardened by time, inclement weather, and constant worry over providing for himself and his daughter, sentimentality is considered a weakness. Day dreaming either under the sun or moon wastes precious time in which knuckling down to a task would be far more productive, leading to profit. Due to this credo, Clay is surprised by the enjoyment he feels by the memory of Jennifer's spontaneity, and her infectious joy by living in the Eden, as she preferred to call Buzzards Glory. The inappropriate name for their area next to the Chesapeake Bay, suggesting a place of death, when in reality, it is alive with more creatures than Clay believes could be packed into Noah's Ark.

Buzzing into Clay's ear, a voracious mosquito stabs through flesh for a blood meal. Clay slaps his head harder than intended, squashing the minuscule vampire, and replacing its buzz with a ringing in his head.

"If this is Eden, God, you must have created the mosquito to remind us that nothing's perfect except you," mumbles Clay, as he wipes the bug smear from his ear.

"Did young Mitchell make his delivery this morning, Anna?" Clay calls from the porch where he has placed the rocking chair to sit comfortably. Except for the moon's glow, the only light upon Clay comes through the open door. Insufficient for the novice, but in Clay's experienced hands, carving further refinement into the bills of the last dozen mallard heads is performed with a familiar feel by practiced fingers.

"Yes. Madison came before school, and then let Beauty and me ride back with him in the buggy," replies Anna from inside.

"You be careful. Mitchell's awfully young to be driving those ponies."

Laughing at the absurdity, Anna responds, "Madison wishes he would be allowed to drive them. He's younger than me. Anyway, one of the men from the dairy was at the reins.

"All right. Would you pour me some coffee if it's ready?"

Anna finishes cleaning the cooking pot, letting it drip-dry on the counter. "Yes, sir," she quickly answers. Pouring bubbling black coffee into a dented metal cup, Clay's favorite, from a polished copper kettle that is on the stove, Anna remembers her mother's words: "Your father's a hard working, rough and tough man through and through, but there are one or two hidden places that are kind, soft, and tender. Never speak of this aloud, but when he asks for coffee, pour in milk, and add sugar if we have any. Then when you give it to him, you look into his eyes. At that moment, just for an instant, you'll see in them why I chose him to be your father."

Clay accepts the steaming, sweet and creamy brown liquid from his grinning daughter. He looks at the miniature version of Jennifer, and is unsteadied by her searching and knowing gaze.

"Shouldn't you be studying?" Clay asks, breaking the spell.

"I did it all at school. Can I carve with you?" asking hopefully.

"Didn't you say today is Mother's Day?"

"Yes. Well, maybe it will be. It depends on President Roosevelt."

"Then wouldn't it please your mother if you studied the scriptures?"

Not too enthused, Anna replies, "Yeah, probably, but there are too many thou's, thee's, not to mention all those begets. It's confusing."

"Still, for Mother's Day?" Clay persists. He sets the imitation duck head on the porch planks facing the bay. Even without their button, tack, or painted eyes, these inanimate pieces of wood gaze confidently out upon the area where they will be called upon to *bring 'em in*. Clay picks up another, running his fingers over the contours. The sweep of its neck is not quite right.

"Okay," with a resigned sigh, Anna returns inside and enters the bedroom. On the cherubic engraved dresser rests the family Bible, ordered by Jennifer from examples within Umbrella George's Sampler.

"It's God's manual on relationships," Jennifer explained to Anna, as they cuddled under the soft quilt when Anna was very small. "In here you'll discover the instructions on the proper relationship between man and God, man and man, and man and the world that God created for us."

Plopping down in the chair next to the table in the Great Room, Anna casually opens The Book to scan chapter and verse. Her eyes stop on a particularly interesting sequence of words.

GENESIS 1: 26-28

And God said, "Let us make man in our image, in our likeness: and let them have dominion over the fish of the sea, and over the fowl of the air, and over the cattle, and over all the earth, and over every creeping thing that creepeth upon the earth. So God created man in his own image, in the image of God created he him; male and female created he them. And God blessed them, and God said unto them, Be fruitful, and multiply, and replenish the earth, and subdue it: and have dominion over the fish of the sea, and over the fowl of the air, and over every living thing that moveth upon the earth."[9]

---

9 Scripture taken from the *Holy Bible*, King James Version, 1987 printing. Public domain.

Curious and confused as any seven-year-old would be, Anna asks, "When God said, 'Let us make man in our image,' who was he talking to? Was it Jesus?"

Appropriately timed, an owl floats past the porch on silent wings with an unfortunate rodent clutched in its talons. Landing on a limb of a distant birch, its haunting call repeats Anna's question, "Who? Who?"

Clay pauses in his carving to better form his answer, "I believe God was talking with His angels."

"But why then does it say, 'God created man in his own image'?"

"Maybe there was an argument. Maybe the angels didn't like the notion of man running loose and creating chaos throughout a world that was seen as good, perfect, and complete, but God had apparently made up His mind, and so He created us by Himself in His image."

Anna considers her father's answer for a minute, and then with a self-important tone, "So that means I'm special? Handmade by God. There's no better designer."

"Yep," is all Clay can think to say.

For a few solitary minutes, Anna stares with inquisitive eyes at the words written long ago, but as pertinent today, as they were then. Clay considers whether he should set pole hooks for turkling. He had seen some good-sized snapping turtles while rigging the rat-wire traps for the eels. Beauty twitches in her sleep as she is stretched out next to the stove. There are always downed birds to retrieve in her dreams.

"When it says, 'subdue the earth and rule over the fish, the birds, and every living creature,' does that mean we're the boss?" Anna likes this concept.

Clay sighs, wishing he had allowed Anna to carve, "I think it means that we are commanded to use the blessings that God created for our needs, but I also think that we're supposed to use God as our example of how to be a good boss, and that is one who does not abuse what is entrusted to him."

"Oh," Anna's self-importance deflates. "Will it ever end?"

"What? The world?"

"All the blessings we need. The ducks, fish, crabs, and oysters, could they someday disappear if we are not good bosses?"

Clay stands to stretch. His vertebra pops as he twists, his knees cracking, as sinew pulls lean muscles taut over joints that are complaining. Clay feels old, but he is content. Carrying his empty cup into the shack to rinse under the water he pumps from the squeaky sink handle, Clay asks, "Do you remember when you were very little and I told you how the Chesapeake was created?"

" 'By ice,' you said."

"Right. Well, many years after the ice and melting water formed the bay, though no one knows exactly how many years, a great Indian tribe called the Susquehannocks settled in this area, and south of here lived a tribe called the Algonquins. Both tribes called the bay *Chesepioc*[10] but each had its own meaning. For the Susquehannocks, as it is for us today, Chesapeake means, the great river in which fish with hard shell coverings abound."[11]

"Oysters. They meant oysters."

"That's right, but I've always thought the name, what ever it is in the Indian language should mean, the great river surrounded by land, both abounding with all you need, just for the taking."

"But do you think we could use it all up?"

"Anna, all men everywhere could hunt, trap, fish, and gather from sun up to sun set, and never make a dent in God's blessings, so long as His creatures have a place to raise the next generation in peace."

"You mean rest days?" Anna begins to understand, having listened to the ongoing complaints by her father and other hunters regarding the gaming laws that prohibit shooting on certain days of the week.

"Exactly."

With the bluntness of youth, Anna states, "But you hunt on rest days."

Without a hint of remorse for violating the law, or an accusatory inflection in his voice that Anna is somehow a burden, Clay says, "I'll quit hunting when you quit eating."

---

10 *Chesepioc* (Anglicized: Chesapeake). Algonquin word believed to mean "Great Shellfish Bay." Recent linguistic studies suggest it could mean "Great Water."

11 Michener, James A.: *Chesapeake*, Random House, Inc. Paperback edition 2003, p 8.

- 1909 -

The wily old snapping turtle has reached an amicable agreement with Anna. He will not bite her toes, as she wiggles them, sending ripples across the pond to tempt him, and she will keep him apprised on the breaking news of the world. In reality, it was Anna who came up with the arraignment; the snapper merely abides by it.

"Guess what? You'll never guess so I'll just tell you. Two explorers named Peary and Henson,[12] reached the North Pole. That's the direction the geese and ducks come from. Pretty neat, I think, though they had to travel through a lot of snow, and that wouldn't be any fun. I wonder if Santa Claus was surprised to see them, or did the flying reindeer spot them coming, and warn Santa so he could hide."

The snapper eases closer for a better listen. He has luxuriated in this back-bay pond coming on 14 years, and his hearing is waning. His 30 pounds is an indication of the abundance of fish, frogs, and snakes to munch upon, and though his age and weight have slowed him down, his long neck and sharp beak still make for a quick ambush strike.

---

12 Peary, Robert E. (1856-1920): Henson, Matthew A. (1866-1955) African American. Together with four Eskimos they were the first to reach the North Pole in 1909. The Congressional Medal was awarded to each member of the party. Henson also received the Gold Medal of the Geographic Society of Chicago. Subsequent examination of Peary's diary casts doubt as to whether the party actually reached the pole. Through navigational errors, they may have been short of the pole by as much as sixty miles.

"My teacher, Miss Prescott, says this book needs to be rewritten daily because history happens every day," Anna laughs as she thumbs the pages. "Can you imagine how much stuff the kids a hundred years from now will have to learn? The book will be so heavy that no one will be able to carry it home. Maybe that'll mean no homework. Wouldn't that be great?"

Acting as vocal sentinels, red-winged blackbirds chatter a warning from overhead, as they take flight, calling, oak-a-lee! oak-a-lee! They dash, circling, spiraling upward, calling nosily until all in the vicinity have been alerted before racing off to safely perch on tall stalks of cordgrass swaying lazily under meandering pillows of cotton clouds. The snapper eases backward to suspend his body just below the surface, leaving only nostrils and all-seeing eyes above the water. Anna tries to pierce the dense foliage with her eyes to identify the approaching creature that is stomping through the brush and crunching summer dried leaves. With his recognizable side-to-side gait, Delbert pushes through a tangle of big-leaved tuckahoe plants. Plants, when in season, produce spicy berries that are craved by wood ducks. Standing across the placid pond, caked with mud, and one shoulder fastener of his coverall unhooked, Delbert holds aloft by its hairless tail his hard-won prize.

"It's a 'possum," declares Delbert.

"It looks kind of mangy, doesn't it?"

Delbert views his catch, as if for the first time, puzzled, and then with an obvious reply, "It ain't the looking but the tasting what's important." Delbert splashes his way around the edge of the pond to plop down in the dirt next to Anna, raising gritty dust in the process.

"So what 'cha doing at my swimming hole?" asks Delbert.

"Nothing, just talking to the snapper," pointing to the telltale features eyeing her and Delbert next to a clump of pond grass.

As if talking to animals is as natural as breathing, Delbert does not give Anna's confession a second thought, then changes the subject to his favorite topic, food, "My pa's been trying to catch that fellow for years. At least once a week he replaces that bait with fresh fish heads or gizzards." Delbert motions toward a stake stuck in the ground a dozen paces from where they sit. Attached to the stake is a strong line and sharp hook with a fish head. Egg-laying blue flies are in attendance, skittering over the fish head in an uncoordinated sideways dance. "My pa doesn't know how the snapper does it, but the bait keeps disappearing, leaving only tracks leading back into the pond." Sweat runs down Delbert's forehead and into his right eye, leaving a clean streak along its path. Squinting with irritation, he wipes his eye with his dirty palm, leaving the impression of a black eye.

"Del, you need a bath," Anna states the obvious.

"I came for a swim," Delbert stands. He unhooks the remaining fastener, and begins to step out of his coverall. "C'mon. Aren't you hot?"

Knowing there is not much of a chance that Constable Jenkins will suddenly appear and arrest them, Anna leaps to her feet to pull her dress up and over her head, "Okay." Standing in only her baggy cotton panties, Anna folds her dress neatly, and then places it on some leaves to prevent it from getting dirty. She turns toward Delbert, who is stepping into the emerald tinted water, "Del, where's your underpants?" Anna is shocked, a bit curious, but not uncomfortable by his nakedness. The sight standing before Anna is much too funny for her to feel uneasy. Delbert's head is covered with unruly brown hair, pointing in every direction of the compass. His tanned face, neck, hands, forearms, foot and stump are all covered with mud that is in varying stages of drying, from moist black to caked brown. These contrast with his lily white, plump, and hairless torso.

"Underpants?" Delbert speaks the word as if it is from a foreign language.

"Never mind," Anna runs past Delbert to dive headfirst, remaining underwater for several refreshing moments to allow the cool water to draw off the heat from her body. Surfacing, shaking her hair and water from her eyes, Anna turns to watch Delbert moving more cautiously, deeper into the water.

"Hey, Del. You better be careful," Anna giggles as only young girls can.

"Why?"

"Because the snapper might bite off that dangling lure thing thinking it's bait," her laugh is unrestrained. "It must be awful annoying to have that hanging there all the time." Anna swims closer to Delbert to splash him. The dried mud loosens its hold to run off, coloring the water surrounding him a light brown. He stands tall, proud, and unashamed.

"It's nothing of the sort. In fact it's very useful."

"Such as?" Anna asks, wondering what possible good that appendage could be used for.

"Such as writing your name in the snow or dust, and for stopping the sting of yellow jackets or the stinging nettle."

Imagining Delbert crawling around naked in the dust or snow, trying to write his name, is perplexing to Anna, requiring her to call his bluff, "That's a lie, Del. How would you see what you're writing with your face against the ground?"

"You're not as smart as you think. I'll show you," with a smug strut befitting a righteous gander, Delbert strolls up the path a dozen paces. Anna follows him dutifully. Her curiosity peaked. At a widening in the trail,

Delbert wipes away crumbling leaves, leaving a clear patch of dirt, "Watch, Miss Smarty Pants."

Anna's jaw drops as she watches Delbert pee. A mediocre stream of yellow urine is directed into the dust, creating a crude D-E-L as Delbert moves his hips. The grin of self-satisfaction worn by Delbert is better than a hundred *I-told-you-so*'s.

Hating to have her bluff called, Anna huffs, "If you can do it, so can I." She pulls her panties down to her ankles as Delbert watches with patient amusement. Gritting her teeth, Anna concentrates, trying to produce her own stream, but instead, a warm misdirected spray splashes down the inside of her thighs.

Delbert points at the pooling puddle around Anna's feet, laughing with superiority, "You just aren't properly equipped."

Humiliated, Anna quickly pulls up her panties, moisture welling in the corners of her eyes, "It's not funny, Del." Anna runs back to grab up her dress, and then sprints past Delbert. His triumphant grin turns down, as his achievement seems less important now, than it did a moment ago. "Anna," Delbert calls after her, as she turns the corner in the path, disappearing from sight. "Anna! You don't want one of these anyway. It would get in the way of birthing babies," is all he can think to say in commiseration.

Delbert sighs. He did not mean to hurt Anna's feelings. She doubted his word and he proved her wrong. It's not his fault she's a girl, but still. Delbert sighs again, and then plods back to the pond to resume his swim.

Fifty running strides past the turn in the path, Anna slows to a shuffling walk. "Del shouldn't have laughed at me," she states to no one, while wiping her sniffling, runny nose with her dress, and then stops to pull it on. As she settles it squarely on her damp shoulders, she realizes she has left her history book beside the pond. She does not want to face Delbert again today, but she cannot leave the book. Creeping quietly, as she believes the Indians, those proud Susquehannocks of legend and lore would do it, she sneaks back along the path. Upon reaching the corner, Anna moves into the brush, walking steadily from one birch trunk to the next, moving quietly through the tangles of brambles and under the tuckahoe leaves, stealthily on tip-toes, hiding, but moving ever closer to where her book lies. She is confident that she can snatch her book, and then retreat without Delbert seeing her, denying him the opportunity to cast more insults her way.

Moving to within five feet of her book, two trees away, Anna peaks around the trunk to observe Delbert. He is standing thigh deep in the pond with his back to her. "Perfect," Anna whispers. Stepping forward, careful of her foot placement, not wanting to step on a brittle leaf, Anna's eyes dart between Delbert, her book, and the ground.

Oak-a-lee! Oak-a-lee! The flock of red-winged blackbirds call out, as they swoop, swirl, and spiral around the edges of the pond, wanting to return to their former roost, but finding it still occupied, they dart off, over and through the branches, as buckshot after bushy-tailed squirrels.

Delbert turns to follow the flight path of the noisy red-wings, and finds himself facing Anna, who stands over her book, and not attempting to hide herself. Their eyes meet, his with guilt and embarrassment, hers with the gleam of knowledge and power. She is the one grinning now.

"What 'cha got in your hand, Del?" Anna asks coy. Delbert is frozen like a duck caught in the glare of a gunning light. He is unable to move, but when he realizes what he is doing, he releases his grip on his lure that is no longer dangling.

"It's nothing. Go away, Anna," Delbert turns away from Anna to shuffle into deeper water.

"You got that right," pleased with having the last, best word, Anna picks up her history book to walk down the path, though as she nears the bend, she is feeling that they are even and she wants Delbert to understand that, so she shouts back with sincerity, "Hey, Del. See you tomorrow?" A minute passes. Only the hum of insects being chased through the air by buzzing dragonflies is heard.

"Okay, I'll see you tomorrow," Delbert's voice resounds with all is well. His secret is safe with her. Anna turns the bend. Her skin prickles from the warmth of the sun drying her skin, and with the rays' soothing fingers massaging her face. Crossing the trail in front of Anna is a family of muskrats busily foraging for a late afternoon snack of beetles.

My-oh-my, boys are so strange. Mulling this over in her mind, Anna comes to the obvious realization that they are curiously different, perplexing... very perplexing. She shakes her head, and then asks the muskrats, "If it's so enjoyable, why does he hide it?"

The giant rodents pause in mid-chew to ponder a question beyond their intellect, but before a consensus, before a guess can be offered, the shadow of a high-soaring eagle crosses the path, causing the muskrats to scurry, and then disappear into the dense foliage that is the marsh.

It's a place of safety.

It's a place of hiding.

It's a place of secrets.

"You two deserve a treat for helping me pack the bullfrogs," Clay speaks to Anna and Delbert. Though Anna's participation was mandatory, a required chore, Clay reminds himself that an occasional reward will not spoil the child, and little Cigar, well, there is that thing called friendship. "Now don't go making yourselves sick on candy." Clay looks down at the two grinning children. His daughter, spic-and-span, scrubbed clean, before and after his return from netting and packing the squirming and leaping bullfrogs, slippery escape clearly their number one priority. Anna wears a clean but mended yellow dress. Clay hopes Jennifer, looking down from above, would be pleased by Anna's presentable appearance. Then there is Cigar, covered black with marsh mud. He said he had taken a bath a couple of days ago, though Anna corrected him, while giggling, that it was only a swim. Remembering the pregnant pause, Clay thought he had caught a private look passing between the two, but they are children, and children have secrets best not probed by adults.

"Ice cream!" the two nine-year-old rapscallions correct Clay in his assumption, as they accept the coins. Together, hand in hand, they run with long bounding and playful leaps down the Pennsylvania Railroad station stairs and out into the street located next to the Susquehanna River. Clay has sold seven cases of live bullfrogs to a New York restaurateur for $5 per case. Clay counts his bills twice, being distracted by the ear-splitting whistle of another train as it rumbles in on elevated tracks after crossing the B&O Bridge that spans the river. He chews the butt of his hand-rolled with satisfaction and bewilderment. He knows city folk pay a pretty penny for sautéed frogs' legs, especially when they are accompanied by an unpronounceable French name, *but why? They are just frogs.*

"A good night's work," Clay says, as he stuffs the bills in the pocket of his coverall.

"What?" asks the obese restaurateur with a tick in his left eye, as he rechecks the frogs, making sure they all are still alive.

"Oh, nothing. I said it's enough to replenish powder and lead."

Wiping his sweaty brow and adjusting the suspenders under his tent-sized jacket for the third time, the restaurateur presses Clay for a commitment, "I'm counting on you to fill my orders for duck and geese. Fat ones. My customers will consume all I can obtain, at any price."

"I've told you before, 'I sell to Baltimore.'"

"I'll give you a nickel more per matched pair of mallard and a dime more for the geese," a hint of desperation in the restaurateur's offer.

"I'm not promising anything, but when they arrive, if they fly and raft well, I'll consider it."

"I suppose I have to admire a man who honors his prior commitments, even if it loses both of us money. I'll accept your consideration, if that's the best I can get, at least for now, my good man," patting Clay on his shoulder. "Now is there a place where two parched businessmen can obtain a strong, refreshing drink?"

"I know just the place. You buying?" Clay asks, one businessman to another.

Martha Webster steps out of J.R. Stewart's Country Store on Washington Street, and into the heat of another clear, still, summer day. The members of her extended family go about their daily business, the men tipping their hats, the ladies stopping briefly to exchange pleasantries. Martha's arms are full of purchases for her doctor husband, preventing her from dabbing the moisture beading on her forehead.

"For a bit of breeze, dear Lord," Martha looks skyward. "Not a cloud or bird is moving about."

"Hello, Mrs. Webster," Anna and Delbert shout, as they dart between horse-drawn carriages and supply wagons; their feet, and the many ironclad wheels and hooves crunching the oyster shell paving.

Some creative Havre de Grace city official, annoyed by the ever-rising mounds of discarded oyster shells along the wharf's edge that spoil his view of the bay, suggested the shells be broken up, and then used as paving. For the most part, this was a brilliant idea, lauded by folk far and wide, as the mounds have been kept from over-running the village; the shells keep the streets from becoming a muddy bog during the pre-winter rains, and as the shells turn white with age, the streets appear to be whitewashed with speckles of mother-of-pearl. However, the beauty is only skin deep, because on gorgeous shopping days such as today, the sun's light, its heat, reflects off the shells mercilessly, turning a comfortable stroll through this quaint postcard town into a blinding, sweat-raising, shelter-seeking portage.

"Hello, Anna. Cigar. Watch yourselves," cautions Martha, as an elegant buggy occupied by Dorothy McQuay, and driven by Roman, is reined up short, just missing the two youngsters, as they plunge past, and into the country store in search of their favorite addiction. A little brass bell that is nailed above the red painted door jingles cheerfully at their entrance, and with the promise of a sale.

"Roman! Careful," Mrs. McQuay, startled and trembling, clutches her lace handkerchief, but not in fear for the children that her conveyance nearly crushed. It is held in front of her mouth and nose in an attempt to ward off the smell that is mainly in her head. Mrs. McQuay, the mistress and lady of the house, had instructed Nanna Maude, quite sternly, to sprinkle the handkerchief liberally with perfume prior to her departure for town.

"My apologies, ma'am," Roman replies earnestly. He secures the reins, and then sets the handbrake before climbing down. Roman scurries around the buggy to offer his hand to his charge to assist her down. "No. No, Roman. I can do it. Just go about your business," Mrs. McQuay reels back from Roman's offered hand, thinking, *that's where it starts. An innocent clasp of a hand...oh how he would brag that he held me...pure white within that blackness...where would it end?*

"Yes, ma'am," Roman humbly pulls back his hand, turns, and then enters the store. The little bell jingles his admittance.

"You're early, Mrs. McQuay. I didn't expect you for another hour," Martha adjusts her purchases to offer her hand. Fastidiously, Mrs. McQuay accepts Martha's assistance to disembark her carriage.

"Mr. McQuay insisted that Roman could deliver me because he was going to town on an errand to purchase something or another for running the house," Mrs. McQuay dabs her flushed cheeks, flapping the handkerchief with annoyance. "I cannot begin to explain how flustered I am at this moment, Martha, with him sitting next to me all the way."

"Now, now, Mrs. McQuay," Martha tries to soothe her distressed friend. "You've arrived safely, haven't you?"

"Yes, maybe, but I was forced to smell him the entire trip, and the rutted road caused me to bump up against him more than once. It's not civilized, certainly not proper."

The bell jingles a third time. Anna and Delbert, each holding their favorite ice cream, a thick swirl of strawberry in a sweet sugar cone, exit the store. Absorbed in his tongue-licking delight, and the revelry of being carefree and young, Delbert fails to bid Mrs. Webster a courteous good-bye. Anna chooses not to interrupt the doctor's wife, especially since she is in conversation with a McQuay. Neither lady misses their noisy exit from the store, and departure down the street. Martha sighs with love and harmless envy at the vision of exuberant youth. Anna looks back at the two ladies, and then leans close to Delbert's ear, whispering a ribald joke she just remembered. Mrs. McQuay shivers. The sight of this fresh, young, white child, an innocent girl wearing a yellow dress, in the company of a hobbling, scruffy, dark-skinned, obviously devious and sinful boy, causes Mrs. McQuay's eyes to roll back into her head, as her heart flutters in the grip of the vapors. Staggering, she collapses, falling limp against the carriage wheel.

"Dorothy! Oh my Lord," Martha's purchases clatter to the ground, as she attempts to steady her unnerved friend.

– 1874 –

Dorothy Parker ran to the barn. She was out of breath, panting with excitement. The harvest was in and drying, hanging inside. "Just barely in," her father, Captain Parker had complained. Dorothy had listened the night before, her ears straining as she stood outside the door of her father's den, while he spoke to their foreman, "Now if we can get a promise of a fair price from the tobacco agent tomorrow, we may break even this year." Mr. Jake listened attentively, but his lackadaisical demeanor outside Captain Parker's view was a clear indication that the foreman's priority was not the tobacco, but the clear liquid that produced his plum nose with broken capillaries. Captain Parker kept his eye out for a more responsible employee, but 12 years after that damnable war, men were scare, good white men scarcer still.

Dorothy's game of tag with the son of one of the Negro families, who were employed by her father, had led her to the unlatched side door of the barn. Peering between the uneven boards, she glimpsed her prey, or at least she believed she had. Shafts of light cutting between the sidings crisscrossed the dark interior of the barn. The humid air, pungent with fresh cut leaves, moved only when Dorothy slid quickly through the doorway, the door having been left ajar. Heavy dust danced a slow waltz in and out of the streaks of light in response to the swish of her dress. Its yellow pleats, so carefully ironed, were fast losing their creases in the oppressive heat. Dorothy's heart beat a steady cadence as it pounded against the inside of her ribs. She would find him and make him chase her for a while. That was the thrill of the game; to chase and be chased; to be caught was an inexplicable joy. She lost, but won at the same time.

Dorothy's eyes slowly dilated, adjusting to the growing darkness, as she moved deeper into the silent barn. She ducked under the low hanging tobacco bundles, going to her knees to crawl cautiously forward to where she believed he was hiding. The dirt and debris littering the earthen floor clung to the front of her dress. She inched closer to her target, the object of her desire, an exposed bare foot, a callused pink sole outlined in black, dripping sweat, and inviting her touch. His body hidden under a pile of drying tobacco leaves propped against the corner.

"Tag. You're it," Dorothy yelped.

"You've fared better than most," commented the tobacco agent to Captain Parker. "Many grand plantations slipped quickly into bankruptcy after losing their help." The agent, a fine gentleman out of Memphis, was neither sympathetic to the horrendous ordeal of the slaves, pre-war, nor to the financial crisis gripping the ex-masters, post war. Business was business to him. In his mid fifties, and wearing a pince-nez clipped to the bridge of his nose to improve his nearsightedness, he never forgets the poignant words of his invalid father: "One man's misfortune is another's opportunity. So long as you're not the cause, your conscious is clear."

"It's true, accommodations had to be made regarding labor, but we've adjusted well," Captain Parker remarked offhandedly, as he and the agent walked toward the barn. The two men had supped on a sumptuous lunch that was served on the expansive porch of the mansion. The lunch, the finest Captain Parker could pull together, was intended to intimidate and mislead the agent into believing that this was a gentleman's plantation, producing a crop merely for the recreation of its owner. The price per bale being of little consequence, incidental, thereby giving the grower the leisure to walk away from an agent's low bid, consequently keeping the agent honest in his price.

Laughing jovial, courteous to a fault throughout the reasonably setout luncheon, the agent's smiling, weasel eyes, though diminished in age, missed nothing, especially when it came to financial matters. The flatware was plated silver, the wine a second, possibly even a third rate vintage. The Negro server was a woman probably out of the fields that morning; her hands callused with chipped fingernails. *At least she had the foresight to wash them clean of dirt,* the agent thought as he was served.

On his ride in, he observed too few laborers. This explained the weeds growing between the crop rows, and the house itself was five years in need of paint. With each noted discrepancy, the agent sat straighter in the saddle, while he relished how little he would have to pay for this desperate man's work.

The two men walked with the appearance of shared camaraderie, discussing topics from the unseasonably warm weather to the state of Washington politics, and agreed that both were miserable. This appearance belied the true nature of their adversarial roles. Despite their polite, never to be spoken of financial antagonism that filled the air with electricity, the men strolled through a bucolic setting that was pleasant on the eyes, their ears being serenaded by late-summer songbirds until the afternoon was pierced by a child's scream. The men, startled, reacted quite differently. The agent stopped mid-step, a businessman, his eyes darted in all directions to search out the danger. Captain Parker, a father, sprinted forward, racing to rescue his imperiled child.

Dorothy's screams were shrill and prolonged as she burst from the barn. The yellow dress, her hands, and knees, were smudged green and brown, filthy from crawling among the hanging tobacco, and the detritus scattered on the floor. As she fled out the door, the protruding latch snagged her sleeve, tearing the material. Emerging from the dark of the barn and into the bright day, the glare momentarily blinded Dorothy. She failed to see her father as he ran to her salvation. Her disheveled appearance was more disturbing than her screams, and confirmed Captain Parker's worst fears. Blinded, and not seeing him, Dorothy ran away from her approaching father, the hem of her skirt flying wildly, as she ran to put distance between herself and her pursuer.

"You can't get away from me," was shouted from inside the barn.

Captain Parker collided with Dorothy's pursuer as he sprinted out of the door after her. To Captain Parker, the Negro boy's wide and frightened coal eyes were all the proof of guilt he needed. This sweaty black thing had molested his precious child, his innocent daughter.

The beating was endless. It was not a small boy who Captain Parker struck again and again with fists that had killed grown men in battle, but it was the unknown man who was responsible for the condition that he found his wife; naked, lying face down on their marriage bed, broken and ruined. Captain Parker was finally able to mete out justice long delayed.

The boy screamed longer than one would expect under the terrible assault. His blood-curdling shrieks brought a gathering of field hands, and the boy's relations to watch the horrifying scene from a distance. Still cowed from generations of forced submission, their timidity was predictable. Not a single witness intervened

The tobacco agent's reaction was predictable as well. Upon observing the gathering Negroes, outnumbering ten to one the gentile white men, he retrieved his mount to quickly put miles between himself and the unpleasant, yet understandable incident. He would consider returning in a week or so.

From her hiding place among the brambles near the stream some distance from the barn, Dorothy cast about, looking for her pursuer. He was awfully slow today. It was no fun not to be found.

An orange ladybug with tiny black spots flitted down to rest on the back of Dorothy's hand. It crawled in little circles, tickling Dorothy's tiny hairs and distracting her. Gently nudging its protective wing covering with her finger, she softly chanted, "Ladybug, ladybug, fly away home. Your house is on fire and your children are alone." With a magic that man and child witness with awe, the ladybug took to the air to continue her journey to places secret and marvelous.

Catching her breath, Dorothy decided she would wait a few more minutes, and then if there were still no sign of him, she would slip back to the barn from another direction to expose herself so that the chase would begin anew.

Inching along the wall of the barn, Dorothy peered around the corner. Before her was a nightmare. Lying quiet and still upon the ground was her friend, her playful pursuer. Kneeling about him was his weeping mother, his stoic father, his trembling brother, and many silent acquaintances from the field. Though sweaty during their game, his gorgeous glistening black skin ran with another darker liquid, its fluidity congealing with exposure to the air.

His father gingerly lifted the boy off the ground. He held his limp body, as if the boy were a delicate newborn infant, cradling the child's head against a chest broad with muscle, and containing a broken heart.

"Dorothy, where are you?" Captain Parker called, as he searched for her in the direction she had originally escaped to.

"I'm here," Dorothy responded, her voice choked and frightened.

Not an utterance was made, but every eye among the family, and the acquaintances of the boy, accused her. She was not the owner of the hands that pummeled the life out of the boy, but she was the instrument that set the trip hammer into action.

Admitting her culpability to her father, as he tucked her under the covers that night, he allayed her worries by saying, "Dorothy, you are a southern lady. Those beasts will always try to earn your trust with smiles and platitudes, but you must always be on guard for their devious ways. Now repeat after me.

They are no better than animals." And Dorothy did, but the accusing eyes were everywhere she went. They all knew of her sin.

One week later, the tobacco agent trotted his mare up the road to the Parker mansion. Breathing deeply, his lungs filled with the pungent odor of burnt and dying embers. Only the charred skeleton of the mansion remained. Not a soul was present to greet him. Upon inspection of the intact barn, he found Captain Parker hanging among his drying crop. The agent would cut him down before sending in his laborers to collect and bale the tobacco. Since no price had been agreed upon prior to the incident, no price would be paid. One man's misfortune is another's opportunity.

Unknown to the agent, nor would he have cared, during the most valiant efforts by Captain Parker to defend his home and repel the animals, Mr. Jake lowered Dorothy out her second story bedroom window. He followed her down the rope ladder where he then secreted her out of harm's way. She was spared any ill intentions, including having to witness Captain Henry Parker's demise. And though often inebriated, Mr. Jake completed his duty to deliver Dorothy to the home of her cousin, Miss Juliette Gordon, Daisy to her friends, in Savannah, Georgia.

– 1909 –

"Dorothy, are you not well?" Martha fans Mrs. McQuay's pale and perspiring face. Mrs. McQuay steadies herself, blinking and attempting to focus, as if coming out of a horrible dream that for her never ends.

Anna and Delbert have rounded a corner onto Pennington Avenue, and are out of sight, off on adventures that only two children on sugar highs can find.

"I'm just unnerved," she replies, again dabbing with her handkerchief.

"Let me call Roman to drive us to my home so the doctor can look you over."

"No. No, that won't be necessary," Mrs. McQuay stammers, and then bends to help Martha retrieve her scattered packages. "Let's walk. It's a beautiful day, made especially for ladies like ourselves."

Seasoned and split wood crackles politely within the glowing stove in an attempt to keep Anna company. She lies on her cot staring at the lattice frame supporting the ceiling. The foldaway, an unexpected present from her father, him saying, "You're getting too big to sleep on the floor." She was initially ecstatic about the new bed until she realized it was too narrow for both her and Beauty. Both girls had drawn warmth and comfort from the other over the years, but they had accepted the gift for what it signified. Anna is a big girl of ten. Snug under her wool blankets, Anna listens as the winter wind and its icy tentacles search out any flaw, crack, or missed seam in the pitch that is sealing the shack with sinister intent to slip through. Nothing...only the popping, crackling, and sizzles of a log being consumed is heard. Clay had told her the night before that snow seemed imminent so she could stay home from school. He would have many ducks for her to help clean in the morning, or at least he hoped he would.

Reluctantly, Anna crawls out of bed, slipping her coverall over her woolen long underwear. She folds the blankets and bed, and then stows them in her parents' bedroom. It is during these silent times, when Beauty is working beside her father out on the Flats and Anna is alone, that she feels her mother's absence the most. Anna straightens the corner of the quilt covering, imagining, with a half smile, her mother instructing her on the proper way to tuck-a-corner. Then she would be gathered up into her mother's arms, smothered with kisses, and made deaf from a hundred, "I love you's."

If time permits, Anna will climb under the quilt to bury her face in it, to breath deeply in search of her mother's fragrant scent. She has been frightened recently when the only smell was that of her father, a heavy earthen smell with the suggestion of burnt sulfur. At that moment, a panic set in with the belief that she has been completely abandoned. Anna squeezed her eyelids tightly in concentration and soon found the aroma she craved, whether real or imaginary, it was her mother's, with her love and hugs. Her presence, her memory, her comfort is still with her. All is well, but it is still difficult without her, and Anna misses her mother so very much, the sparkle in her eyes when she smiled, the lilting notes when she spoke, the softness of her skin, and how even in her illness, she could fill the home with immeasurable joy.

Beauty's delighted barking announces, "We're home," reminding Anna of her responsibilities. There are ducks, many, many ducks to be dressed for shipment.

Clay enters the shack with Beauty on his heels. Anna exits the bedroom donning her Mackinaw, her all-weather coat, an expense that Clay deems worthy of splurging on, as it is the finest available, durable, and the only garment that adequately protects its wearer. "Must have been designed by a hunter," Clay said, while in J.R. Stewart's County Store, as Anna snuggled into her first store-bought coat, her eyes beaming at its refinements.

Looking to her father, and expecting to take several trips to and from the sneak skiff to retrieve the birds, his expression forestalls her. "Don't bother," Clay states. "I couldn't get near them." Clay's face is drawn, downcast, with dark circles and signs of worry reflecting in his eyes, as he rubs and warms his rough hands over the stove, "All night I paddled. Perfect weather. Low clouds. Moderate wind and only a few patches of ice."

"What was wrong?" asks Anna, Clay's worry quickly infecting both Anna and Beauty who sits quietly, looking up at her master and mistress.

"The fowl are not here in the numbers this year. The Davenport was itching to tear a hole in 'em, but each time I'd near a dozen or so, the divers would disappear under the water. They are skittish as always in small numbers, and their plunge alerts the few mallards, reds, and buffleheads to take flight before I can position the skiff for a shot."

"You can try again tonight," Anna's tone has less confidence in it than she intended to convey.

"I could, but I'm afraid it would be the same. The weather fronts have not brought the birds down from the north. I don't have much of a choice, but I'm going to take Captain Smith up on his offer to work the rocks until the birds come."

"But you hate that work. The birds will come," Anna scrapes the last of the coffee grounds out of their tin, and then pumps water into the kettle for her father.

Clay messes his daughter's hair, as she sets the kettle on the stove. "A man doesn't have to like what he does, but he can still take pride in the way he does it."

"Sounds good," Anna replies, not believing a word.

Clay places the knuckle of his forefinger under Anna's chin to lift her face up toward his. "It's the way it is," looking into her concerned eyes, and then trying to lighten the mood. "And of course I'll jump ship like a rat in a storm the minute the birds arrive in proper numbers."

Sitting at the table, father and daughter listen to the crackling fire and pesky wind, as they wait for the kettle to boil with their dinner.

Clay ponders the journey he will begin tomorrow.

Anna wonders how long her father will be gone.

There is no milk or sugar to sweeten the coffee.

An independent and private man like Clay, who never took to teasing or foolishness, would have been warmly welcomed on any skipjack, pungy, or bugeye working out of Havre de Grace, and stationed close to home. He chose instead to crew on the *Loralie*, a 40-foot Chesapeake deadrise, captained by Percy Smith, some 70 miles south of Buzzards Glory. Clay made his decision based on two factors. The first being, he trusted Anna's resourcefulness to get along by herself, even if that means Olivia would appear unannounced, uninvited, but warmly welcomed by Anna, and in the unofficial capacity of a surrogate mother with hot dinners, kindly advice, and affection, and secondly, because Captain Smith had been a childhood friend of Jennifer's. At the conclusion of a hard day's work, and several shared glasses of spirits from his homemade still, the big-boned man with an easy disposition would regal Clay with youthful shenanigans perpetrated on the good citizens of Shady Side by him and Jennifer when she and her family were down from Baltimore. Whether these elaborate and fantastical stories were true or not, they were woven with a vividness that for the duration of the telling reincarnated the amazing girl who first captured Clay's attention. An added bonus was Captain Smith's mystical abilities. He would wake from a fitful sleep with knowledge uncanny, and at times scary, but never challenged. He always knew where the best oysters lay, and the *Loralie* was named before Captain Smith had met and married his wife of the same name...spooky.

There is an unexpected surprise waiting for Clay when he is hailed aboard. Coiling a rope line near the bow is Nathaniel Joiner. Having difficulty himself in bringing in birds in sufficient numbers, even with the use of illegal duck traps, Nathaniel turned to the watermen for work, but for some unexplained reason, none of the captains in the upper bay were hiring. With dogged determination, Nathaniel traveled south along the western shore until he out-distanced his reputation, finally securing employment from a young captain who Nathaniel had observed selling his catch, a rather substantial one, to brokers on the wharf. Nathaniel believed this captain to be skilled, or lucky, maybe both, but he reasoned that together their luck would be double-fold.

Standing on the salted, but still icy-slick boards of the dock, Captain Smith listened patiently while Nathaniel laboriously outlined his qualifications, and the reasons he should be taken on. Scratching his grumbling belly, Captain Smith reluctantly acquiesced. He did wonder how this old man of Napoleonic stature would be able to handle the oyster tongers, the scissor-like poles whose length can measure 30 feet, but seeing the fire in his gray-green eyes, Captain Smith had no doubt this man would work. The only question to be answered is that of character.

Captain Smith's assessment of Nathaniel proved accurate. As a crewman he worked with speed, skill, and the endurance of several men. Nathaniel was the first to arrive dockside in the morning, and the last to leave in the evening, double and triple checking mooring lines, equipment readiness, and securing hatchways, a work ethic that would confound those who believed him to be indolent. His strength and agility when handling the weighty tongers when he leaned, quite unbalanced, over the railing in search of oysters growing sumptuous on the bottom of the bay was indeed a marvel to witness, prompting Captain Smith to comment, "Nat, you're a born waterman."

Nathaniel responded with the belief of a martyr, "I'm simply lucky to be good at whatever I put my hands to."

Luck wasn't smiling. No, Luck was laughing with sinister joy that was filled with the bite of winter.

From the moment Captain Smith shook the diminutive hand of Nathaniel Joiner, the *Loralie* and its crew was plagued. From behind the two men came a shout of warning. Doby Pierce, a young lad right out of high school, was carrying an ungainly bushel of oysters down the ramp from the *Loralie* to the dock. Doby was an athletic and eager lad, hired as a dogsbody[13] to earn extra money for his family because his father was incapacitated, suffering in the last throes of consumption.

Captain Smith and Nathaniel turned in the direction of the shouts, as did the dozen or so wharf workers, to witness the unplanned and excruciating pratfall. Doby's right foot slipped on the gangplank, twisting sideways to be abruptly stopped in its forward slide by the cross board. A pop of a champagne cork under pressure echoed, making each man wince, as Doby's knee, carrying a bushel weight, and in an unnatural position, tore ligament and sinew. Doby's piercing wail was a sharp icicle jabbed into the ears of the men rushing forward a moment too late. The bushel of oysters flew forward to clatter over the dock, tripping men, as marbles would on a parquet floor. Not a single desperate hand reached poor Doby before he plunged into the frosted bay.

After a few frantic minutes, Doby was safely fished out, cold, soggy, and holding back tears, because men do not cry, not even if one is only a lad who is injured, and has failed to provide for his family. Captain Smith assisted in carrying Doby home to convalesce, and paid him through the week, while checking on him periodically. No one in Shady Side suffered alone. Theirs was a community that looked after one another.

The following morning, January frigid, with a workable eight-knot wind, perfect for sailing and pulling the natural resources from the bottom, and an hour out from the wharf, the *Loralie's* year-old and rust-free anchor chain snapped. If it were not for the quick reflexes of Nathaniel pulling the crewman working next to him in the bow away, the rapidly unwinding chain would have entangled the crewman's leg, dragging him overboard, and to a certain death. The grateful crewman profusely thanked Nathaniel, saying over and over, "Oh Lord, what luck it was to have Nat aboard."

---

13 Dogsbody. Slang. An unskilled day laborer hired to perform menial tasks.

The crew spent half the workday locating, and then retrieving the anchor, valuable time that could have been spent bringing up profit.

On the second day, the cock did not crow at Captain Smith's two-story house, an event that never before occurred on the four acres that faced the West River. By the time he arrived on dock, angry with himself for being late, he found the other oyster boats long departed, and not a breath of air to fill the *Loralie's* sails. The crew had dutifully made ready the boat, but now was sitting around Nathaniel, as he mesmerized them with tales of his wild adventures. Aristotle never had a more attentive audience.

Captain Smith introduces Clay to the crew. When Nathaniel steps forward, he grasps Clay's hand, pumping it as if they are long lost brothers who were separated at birth by happenstance, but now joyfully reunited.

"Clay Buchanan, my lordly. It's great to have a fellow Havre de Gracian on board," Nathaniel exclaims, pumping away, as if the bilge is drowning in water.

"Oh, the two of you are acquainted?" Captain Smith asks, surprised by the coincidence.

Clay answers with polite reservation, "Yes. Mr. Joiner and I are acquaintances."

The third day with Nathaniel as crewman, the first for Clay, is surprisingly uneventful. During the previous night, Captain Smith tossed and turned as a dingy on an angry sea. His sleep so distressed that his normally tolerant wife finally left their marriage bed to slip under the warm covers with their daughter who was sleeping in the next room. In the morning, there may have been dark circles under Captain Smith's eyes, but as he stepped on deck, his confidence was high with an infectious spirit that cries success. "There are rocks, fat and juicy to be picked off the bottom. Am I right?"

"You're right, captain," acknowledges the crew.

"And who will receive a premium price from the Leatherbury Brothers Packing House?" Captain Smith demanded as he leaps aboard.

"We will," the men shout, imagining the weight of the coins that will fill their pockets.

"Then hoist sail. Let's get underway."

A practiced and precise dance by skilled and hardy men begins with enthusiasm, but if the men had been listening carefully, they would have heard snickering within the bitter wind. Hour after hour the *Loralie* tacked and came about over where the oysters where supposed to be. Hour after back-breaking hour, the crew worked up a frothy sweat, tugging in and letting out the lines, and grabbing in vain at a bottom with the giant salad tongs. The sharp, wet wind constantly searches out and finds each seam in the men's clothing, chilling the sweat, and shivering the muscle to a numbing ache.

The weak winter sun is embarrassed to show itself through the charcoal blanket that some would call a sky. As night takes hold, requiring Captain Smith to light the storm lanterns to survey their meager catch of less than a half-bushel, he makes his fortuitous decision.

"We stay out tonight so that tomorrow we'll be on site at first light. Our luck is surely to change."

All men nod in agreement, despondent by the failure of the captain's mystical powers to provide.

The *Loralie* rests at anchor while the cook dishes the men steaming plates of he-stew, a favorite Chesapeake concoction of crisp bacon, large chopped onions, and stalks of celery sauté, today's fresh oysters browned, and then their own juice is poured over them until their gills wrinkled. Tapioca powder is added to simmering milk until gelled. Combine all together, and then top with saffron, and a half-pound of melted butter. The captain and crew salivate, as the steaming bowls tempt their nostrils in anticipation of the richest, tastiest, man-filling meal ever created by and for a Chesapeake oysterman. For several minutes, the only sounds heard on deck are the gentle breeze heavily chilled, the lapping of ripples that are tipped with ice crystals against the *Loralie's* hull, Clay's mild cough that is suppressed by medication, and the greedy scraping of spoons on metal bowls, as these exhausted men fill their bellies to satisfaction. When the last empty bowl is set down, and the shortest prayer known to mankind is spoken with blessed gratitude, "Ah..." Nathaniel's character is revealed.

"Nat, you started telling how you won that shooting contest," a member of the crew prods.

"Win? No, lad. I was cheated something terrible by that Kimble fellow," Nathaniel spits over the *Loralie's* railing. "It was 1885, I believe, though the year is not important. I was traveling through Illinois on my way to Jackson, Michigan, to conclude an important transaction," Nathaniel exposes the two gold rings secured to a string tied around his neck, jingling them.

– 1885 –

"Come one. Come all. The Logan County Fair will delight and thrill young and old alike," shouted the barker. His red, white, and blue cone-shaped amplifier pressed firmly to his chapped lips, "Free! Free! Free! No entrance fee. Come see the weird, the wacky, the wonders of the known world."

It was the 'Free!' that caught Nathaniel's interest, along with the poster of men shooting at flying plates displayed between posters of a bearded woman holding a bearded infant, and a medicine man promoting a cure-all. Unable to read, Nathaniel stood in front of the advertisement for a shooting contest for some time, puzzling out its meaning, until a passing farmer carrying a dilapidated single-barreled muzzle-loader stepped up next to him.

"Peoria Blackbird. What will they think of next?" the farmer stated.

"Is that what they're called? Seems like a waste of lead, being you can't eat them after they're shot," Nathaniel responded, and then he noticed the farmer's crippled left hand. "Accident?"

"The war," stated simply without malice by the 43-year-old, who like Nathaniel had experienced and witnessed too much pain, suffering, and death to complain of his own miseries.

"Are you going to enter the contest?" queried Nathaniel.

"That $50 prize money is tempting, but the two-dollar entering fee is well..." the farmer let the obvious speak for itself. Two dollars was a lot of money, especially for a farmer with a useless hand.

Nathaniel's mind, always quick to leap on an opportunity, and weighing the risk, which none appeared, offered, while digging into his pocket to present a solution, "I've got two dollars and you've got the gun. Loan it to me and we'll split the winnings."

The scratch-in-the-dirt farmer considered Nathaniel's offer. His worn-through civil war army boots, the only pair of footwear he owned, raised red dust under the comfortable sun, as he shuffled them. He saw no downside to this arrangement, and half of $50 would be a grand bonanza compared to nothing.

"Can you shoot?" he asked, no insult intended.

"I've shot mouse to men. The first from annoyance, the second by order of a President, and when the birds fly, not a one gets by," boasted Nathaniel.

The farmer hoped there was more truth than bravado in Nathaniel's claim, "All right. You've got a deal." The farmer handed over his gun, though if he had spoken his mind he would have asked, *how can such a small man accurately shoulder and shoot his gigantic four-bore, weighing 16 pounds with its four-foot-long barrel?*

Two hours into the competition, the glowing sun was setting off to the right of Fred Kimble[14] and Nathaniel Joiner, the last two from an impressive field of 38 competitors. The spectators, who observed the tense, yet raucous competition, more than 200 men of varying occupations and dispositions, attired in tailored black suits to working man's coveralls, men disparate in all aspects of life, except their appreciation for the honed skill of a marksman. The excited crowd shouted, whooped, and cheered with each nick, fracture, and splatter of each imitation bird.

Nathaniel's remaining opponent, Fred Kimble, age 39, with a slight paunch, a native of Illinois, was the picture of a consummate duck shooter, comfortable sitting for long hours in a wet blind, watching with unreserved joy as decoys worked their magic. "Am in clover," he would repeat moments before raising his shotgun to aim at his incoming dinner. His placid blue eyes hid his intensity for his vocation and love of invention. Black hair prematurely speckled silver, Kimble would claim while buying a new friend a drink, "Just God's way of reminding me that I've enjoyed more pleasure in my short life than most old men." Hailed as a local hero who has yet to lose in competition, Kimble was impressed with Nathaniel's handling of the four-bore, and silently amused by his greater than thou attitude.

"He's better than most," commented an official to Kimble. "Best be careful of this shooter."

---

14 Kimble, Fred (1846-1941) Knoxville, Illinois. Member of the Union Pacific Gun Club. In 1868 he invented the choke bore. In 1884 he invented the first competition target named the Peoria Blackbird. Enshrined on August 19, 1969 to the National Trapshooting Hall of Fame.

"Win or lose, this is just for fun," Kimble sincerely joked. "At the end of the day it's all the same, no duck—no dinner."

The men were now hitting the saucer-shaped targets at a distance of 35 yards, flung from a series of hidden mechanical flyers that were positioned either on the left or right side of the field. With each successful round, the mechanisms would be moved farther afield.

The farmer sat in a chair behind Nathaniel, his stomach queasy with nerves. Each competitor was allowed one assistant. His duty varied by need. A jaundiced, spiffed-to-the-nines sport with a choleric demeanor had his assistant hold his chubby cigar, and refill his glass with a liquid that he snobbishly called sparkling water. The sport, his cigar, and water were eliminated in the third round as he shouted protests. He argued that a baby's cry interfered with his concentration. The protest was denied. The sport, with his assistant in tow, stormed from the shooting line followed by "Boos" and "Poor sport."

"If a baby's cry will make a man lose his concentration, he wouldn't have lived long," spoken by the bat-black mountain of a man who cast a long shadow over Nathaniel. For a moment, Nathaniel thought he had strained a neck muscle, as he turned skyward to take in the kindly, fat-jowled face of the Negro standing in the adjacent shooting box. The man proudly wore a blue cap with a golden bugle affixed to the front, similar to the one stolen from Nathaniel upon his imprisonment in Andersonville.

Nathaniel recognized a quiet pride in this gentle giant. He also suspected him to be the only true competition for the $50. The farmer had instructed Nathaniel on the quirks of his gun; it threw its shot slightly to the left so lead more or less depending on the direction the fabricated bird flew. The farmer would also be responsible for loading this beast of a gun. "Because it can be fickle," he said which was fine with Nathaniel who watched the big man, quick as a snake bite, blast each shiny black target, squarely, shattering the baked coal tar and pitch to dust.

Luckily for Nathaniel, the Negro sharpshooter was eliminated with an unfortunate smoky fizzle. His muzzle-loader misfired, the wadding not rammed home quite hard enough, allowing the blackbird to fly and land safely, unmolested.

The farmer unconsciously rubbed his crippled hand, a hand moist with nervous sweat, waiting for the next blackbird to fly. The obstacle to his $25, Fred Kimble, had squarely killed his bird from the left, at 35 yards. The farmer watched Nathaniel, a man confident, a man who believed he was superior in every way, unbeatable, and a man who knew he was already the winner. The farmer waited for Nathaniel's call of "Pull!" that would initiate the launch of the imitation bird to certain destruction. What Nathaniel did not know, because the farmer had not told him, was that 35 yards was the absolute maximum distance that his four-bore would throw lead with any effect. If Nathaniel hit or missed might not be because of lack of skill, but due to the gun's limitations. The farmer prayed for two things, the prize money being third on the list. The first being that Kimble's gun, a breechloader, had reached its effective limit as well, and that Nathaniel would not blame him for his shotgun's shortcomings.

"Pull!" called Nathaniel.

The target sprung up from the left. Nathaniel led it sufficiently, and then squeezed the trigger, calmly, naturally, as if he had owned this weapon his entire life.

Bang!

Not a dead center hit, but it was enough to qualify as a kill. Nathaniel smiled and handed the heavy gun to the farmer to be reloaded. Nathaniel noticed the farmer's good hand was shaking. "Nothing to worry about," Nathaniel looked the farmer square in the eye. "The prize is in our bag. Just like a Christmas goose flying in to visit a stoolie."

Nathaniel turned to watch the officials move the throwers out to 45 yards. He looked over to where Fred Kimble stood, holding his paltry nine-bore, a far less powerful gun than he was shooting. "This will be the last round," he said confidently to the farmer who was ramming home shot and wad, a trickle of sweat ran down the farmer's sun-browned forehead.

"Pull!" Kimble shouted.

Bang! Black dust is all that remained of the blackbird. The spectators cheered and clapped. Today's contest was exceeding all expectations for those in attendance. They were witnessing artistry in a competition rooted in a man's livelihood.

"Well, I'll be a pickled egg," Nathaniel mumbled, as he picked up the four-bore, surprised by Kimble's apparently lucky shot. The spectators hushed in anticipation. Only the distant shout of the barker was heard.

"Pull!" Nathaniel called with confidence.

The bird leaped up from the right. Nathaniel shouldered the gun and aimed dead on to compensate for the gun's throw. He squeezed the trigger.

Bang!

The Peoria Blackbird flew on, sailing serene, spinning off over the horizon with Nathaniel's and the farmer's hope for prize money. Nathaniel continued to look down the barrel sight in disbelief. The farmer, fearing Nathaniel's wrath from the shotgun's failure to reach its target, flinched in expectation of the blow that surprisingly did not come. A roar of congratulatory cheer erupted from the spectators, as those closest to Kimble thumped him on his back with hometown pride. Fred Kimble held his shotgun aloft in victory.

- 1909 -

"I don't see how you were cheated?" Clay asks while sipping throat-scalding black coffee, and missing the special treatment that Anna provided him when the condiments were available.

Nathaniel jumps to his feet, still angry by Fred Kimble's deceit, "You don't see? Well let me clarify it for you. The man was shooting a nine-bore. There is no way he could have hit anything at a distance of 45 yards."

"But he did," interjects Captain Smith, as he adjusts the storm lantern to cast more light upon Nathaniel's reddening face.

"He sure enough did because he cheated," Nathaniel states as fact.

"How?" a crewman asks perplexed.

"Don't you men know nothing of your history?" Nathaniel pauses for affect. The men aboard the *Loralie* look to one another, searching blank faces for an answer.

"Fred Kimble invented choke boring of the barrel. By constricting the muzzle, you get a smaller pattern when the lead leaves the barrel, which will kill at a farther distance, and he also invented those dang Peoria Blackbirds we were shooting at," Nathaniel sat down, satisfied that he has made his point.

"How'd you find out?" the crewman asks.

"When the bum was accepting my prize money, he had the nerve to announce in a voice so humble it dripped honey, 'I was just tinkering with the barrel and muzzle, and would have abandoned my experiments if I'd been a better scholar, because as early as the 1780s, British gun makers were experimenting with the same idea, but they had given it up as a bad idea.'"

"So what did you do?" Clay asks, knowing this unpredictable man would not stand still for a perceived slight.

"What'd I do? I'll tell you what I did," grinning like a skunk who had bested a badger. "When Kimble wasn't looking, I took his shotgun."

Nathaniel, unquestionably right in all matters, is surprised by the mixed reaction from Captain Smith, Clay, and the other crewmen. Two of the crew believes his actions were justified. Captain Smith, Clay, and the remaining crewman agreed that if Nathaniel's telling of the story is accurate, and that is always in question, then Kimble did possess an unfair advantage, especially because the choke is so successful it is now commonplace on all shotguns, and no disclosure beforehand of its use by Kimble was forthcoming. What these three men of the field, Flats, and water could not get past was Nathaniel's taking of Kimble's shotgun, the instrument of a man's livelihood.

"You might as well have cut off the man's hands," a crewman, shouting in disgust, stands up, and then walks away, he spitting over the railing with contempt.

With grumbling all around, the men wander off to their sleeping quarters, the captain, Clay, and one crewman aft, Nathaniel and two crewmen forward. The placid evening is spoiled by friction, as bitter as the coffee, enhanced by empty pockets.

Clay lies awake in his bunk. He desires sleep, but it eludes him, even with the easy rocking of the deadside coaxing him to slumber. He stares into the blackness that is the cabin and the emotional conflict that Nathaniel has placed within him. Clay knows he is not the only man uneasy by the story because the cabin is peaceful. There is only the steady breathing of the captain and crewman. Not a single snore between them to shake the cups or vibrate the utensils. All the men in the aft bunks are mulling over Nathaniel's admission of theft in the name of fairness.

"I say give the thieving bastard the boom, Cap'n," grumbles the crewman, his verdict shattering the darkness with its harshness.

"The man's too short," Clay states with unintended levity. "The boom would simply swing over his head to no effect."

"Get some sleep, men. I'll deal with Mr. Joiner in the morning," Captain Smith's word is law on the *Loralie*. In the dark, Clay hears the sounds of a man fitfully tossing and turning from indecision, or possibly mystic dreams, interrupted only by a few intermittent snores.

The eastern sun rises to a crisp and cloudless winter day, sporting a five to seven knot wind. On deck, acidic coffee, thick warm bread slathered with melting butter, and piping hot scrambled eggs are served, and heartily consumed by the captain and crew, as they slowly awake to the bright day. Aching arms, legs, and backs are stretched to loosen sore muscles. Puzzled smiles, curious, but accepting, are the prominent expressions on the men's unshaven faces, as they look upon the vacant stool, extra plate, and unused cup.

Nathaniel Joiner is not among them.

As the empty plates are cleared by the cook, Captain Smith looks at each man, who is waiting for the command, "Ready the deck, boys. It's time we dredged ourselves some oysters."

Crushed ice mixes with bow spray flying over the men as the *Loralie*, pushed by the wind, plows through the dark water. Their numb fingers and frozen faces are ignored, as the men pull with all their strength to lift the long metal tongs, dripping with bone chilling water, and heavy with oysters onto the deck for sorting. The only interruption in this many times repeated procedure is the sporadic honking from high overhead as Canada geese arrive to seek refuge. Clay gazes up at one passing family with a wizened gander in the lead. Clay wonders what Anna is doing at this moment.

"Coming about," Captain Smith calls. The crew crouches down as the captain spins the wheel. The boom swings safely over the men. The *Loralie*, a vision of sleek sensuality, with the sun illuminating her triangular sail, and raising sparkles on the many bushels of rocks licked from the generous bay.

Captain Smith wonders if the *Loralie's* rowboat will be tied to the dock when they arrive at the wharf tonight.

Anna hugs herself with the comforting feeling of *deja vu* as she walks the frozen marsh path toward the birch tree protected pond. With each footstep her rubbers crunch the newly fallen snow. Last night's storm left a blanket of frosting to cover and quiet the world surrounding her. Beauty trots contented alongside her mistress, looking back and forth between Anna's far away gaze, and the many unseen critters heard skittering beneath the four inches of fresh packed flakes.

After a late night gabfest, Anna and Olivia had retired. Anna to her too narrow foldaway, Olivia to the unoccupied marriage bed, and Beauty to curl at the base of the glowing potbelly stove. Anna's mental alarm clock that rarely fails to wake her before dawn is overridden this morning by her mother's arm holding her within a cocoon of love and tenderness.

There is that place between the dreams of sleep and the reality of wakefulness where the mind mixes the two states to create a reality out of dreams, wishes, and desires. This was the moment that Anna continues to hug, never wanting to lose the joy that it brought her. Sometime during the night, Anna left her cot to crawl into bed with Olivia, followed by Beauty who did not want to be left out. As she climbed out of sleep, it was her mother's arm, her smell, her softness, and love that held her tight in a sorely missed embrace. This embrace of unconditional love, of protection, of safety, is known by children, and longed for by adults. It is the embrace that says, "All is right with the world." It is perfection. It is as close to heaven as any mortal can find while still alive. It is the embrace that brings the deepest sigh of contentment from which Anna did not want to end, but a joy this great, this wonderful, is always fleeting. That is what Anna told herself as she unwillingly acknowledged the arm holding her was not quite as soft; the fragrance was more like autumn than spring, and the love, though motherly was not her mother's. The arm belonged to Olivia, not her mother's, but Anna's smile remains, as the memory makes her steps along the quiet path light and pleasurable.

Olivia had asked Anna to check the fish traps along the streams and in the pond to see what might be caught within them. The fresh fish would be buttered, floured, spiced, and then fried along with the cackleberries[15] that Olivia had brought with her the night before. Anna prefers her eggs to be scrambled, like her father, but she will not complain.

Beauty stops, cocking her head, her ears perking up, as she tries to locate, and then identify a strange sound. Anna pauses to listen and to watch Beauty. The sound, or call, could be that of a mallard, or wood duck, but its staccato rhythm is unnatural, other worldly, but possibly that of a bird that has been injured, though usually wounded birds hide and remain silent so not to bring attention to themselves, which would alert predators eager for an easy meal.

Excited by the prospect of duck meat, Anna locks eyes with Beauty who is obediently sitting on Anna's left side, facing the direction of the unseen bird. Anna places her left hand near Beauty's head, as her father taught her, and then slowly moves her arm to point in the direction of the injured fowl.

"Back," Anna gives Beauty the command to retrieve.

Kicking up snow, digging deep for traction, Beauty sprints toward that which nature over tens of thousands of years has imprinted into her genes. It is an all consuming target. An object that must be acquired, and that training by Clay, the alpha male, has made into a disciplined exercise. Anna chases after Beauty in a fashion comical even to herself, giggling, as her floppy knee-high rubbers with their minimal traction, slip and slide on the snow pack. Her winter coverall, the same as her summer one, is purposely

---

15 Cackleberries. Slang. Eggs of any fowl though usually chicken.

loose fitting to allow room for a pair of warm long underwear to be worn underneath. The extra material flaps between her running thighs and against her sides with each swing of her arms. Anna flippity-flops around the bend in the path, following Beauty's tracks in the virgin snow. As she nears the pond, Anna sees Beauty standing at the edge, barking with worried urgency.

"Sit," Anna calls. Beauty obeys, but continues to bark, waiting for Anna to reach her side.

"A-a-anna, pl-ple-ease quiet your d-dog," Delbert pleads, shivering uncontrollably.

"Oh my God, Del. What are you doing?" Anna asks, stupefied by the scene before her.

The shattered windowpane ice covering the pond bumps against Delbert's bare calves. He stands in the icy pond, naked except for a cloth tied loosely around his loin. He is holding a toy bow and arrow.

"C-can't you s-see? I'm hunt-ting f-fowl," Delbert's lips and fingers are past blue with cold. They are white. The rest of his exposed skin not smeared with pond mud in a war paint fashion is tinged purple. Hanging precariously from his nose is a snot-cicle. "T-the In-jins did it th-is way. S-so-so can I," he determinedly stammers.

"Del, you'll freeze to death, besides, my father says the birds are late this year, and even if they were flying, you don't have any decoys to lure them in." Anna sloshes into the water toward Delbert. He turns his toy arrow, ready to shoot, toward her. The tip of the toy arrow grows large in front of Anna's eyes, as she realizes it has been sharpened to a frighteningly deadly point.

"St-stop! I-I've got my tumps[16] o-over th-there," Delbert motions to the handmade lumps, poor man's stool,[17] with feathers stuck into them along the pond's edge. "O-only men n-n-need fancy p-painted decoys. B-birds t-t-toll to anything that re-s-sembles."

"Tumps?" Anna tries to reason with Delbert. "So then you're an Indian brave?" Delbert blows awkwardly into the wooden duck call while searching the gray sky. Beauty's ears flatten, painfully listening to the sickly duck call.

Delbert lowers the duck call from his numb lips, allowing it to hang from a string around his neck. His eyes laugh at Anna, "Not-t-t just any b-brave. Not an Algonquin fr-om the l-lower shore. Not a Ch-Choptank from the-the Eastern shore." He raises his arms toward the sky, the arrow in one

---

16 Tumps. Handmade decoys made of mud and feathers. Crafted by American Indians and used by early settlers.

17 Stool. A group of decoys.

hand and the little bow in the other. "THIS IS THE SUSQUEHANNA! I am a-a Susquehannock[18] brave."

"Please, Del. Come out of the water and put your clothes on. You'll freeze to death."

"N-No! My pa freezes every d-day and night out th-there on the Flats tr-trying to provide. I c-can freeze too. Now g-go away."

Tears roll down from Anna's eyes as she watches her best friend shiver in an endeavor that will not be fruitful and could bring about his death.

"Beauty, stay." Anna orders Beauty to remain where she is sitting on the bank a few feet from Delbert, hoping, just maybe he will come to his senses and leave the pond. If he does, he can hold Beauty close for warmth. Anna runs in the direction of the Joiner's house that is deep in the frozen marsh.

Inside their cozy lodge, secure from sharp-clawed eagles, marsh hawks, felonious raccoons, and crafty foxes, and sheltered from the harsh bite of winter storms, a pair of beavers nibble starchy rootstocks they have dug from the surrounding peat. Interrupting their peaceful breakfast is a thumping, a whomping, distant and soft at first, but approaching and growing louder, vibrating their two-chamber home. It is keenly felt through the webbed back feet of these aquatic mammals. Curious, the two broad-tailed rodents scramble one after the other, through the underwater egress. Cautiously, the furry pair pop only their heads through an ice hole that was left by a rambunctious juvenile otter, to spy a creature familiar, yet odd. The creature passes quickly on the nearby trail. It stands upright, but ungainly, wobbling off-balance in its strides. Its outer fur is loose and cumbersome. Its long, black, flowing mane flies wild in a wind created by its forward propulsion through the still air. The creature is snorting steam, and its eyes drip liquid that fall to the pathway, freezing quickly to tiny clear marbles. It possesses a call most shrill and alarming. The beavers conclude that if this creature is filled with fear, their best course of action, being smaller, even if only by 25 pounds, is to retreat to their stick, grass, and mud fortress until the danger passes.

---

18 Susquehannock (or Susquesahannocks). Captain John Smith who explored the Chesapeake Bay and lower Susquehanna River in 1608 called the local Indians by this Delaware Indian term meaning "muddy river."

"Chet, don't waste the kindling. You're not cooking the corn," August Joiner shouts at his eldest from his birch chair, as he bangs his walking stick on a log he uses for a footstool.

"Right, Pa," Chet answers, rearranging the wood for a perfect smudge under the steel tub that Lloyd has filled with melting snow and corn kernels, "I'm just knocking the smoke out of it." Though to his younger brother he whispers with a smile, "I ain't sticking my hands in ice water. I chopped the damn wood and I'll burn it as I see fit." Quick to follow his older brother into mischief, or adventure, even at age 20, Lloyd winks back, emphasizing the expletive, "Damn straight," though not loud enough for August to overhear.

"You boys listen to your father," Claire calls from the doorway. Her hair, wrapped in a bun has gone white. Her motherly smile is missing several teeth, and her gray-green eyes must squint to focus, but her ears are as sharp as ever when it comes to detecting dissension among her brood.

"Yes, ma'am," Chet and Lloyd answer as one. Claire places her small hand on the square shoulders of her man, squeezing it reassuringly. "They're good boys."

August rubs his right hip that spasms with debilitating sciatica. The walking stick helps with mobility, but the knifing pain makes sitting in blinds, or laying in sinkboxes, a suffering experience, knocking the pleasure out of the hunt. "Thank you, Claire, for giving me sons—even these rebellious rascals."

"They're good boys," Claire repeats, ending the subject, and returning inside.

From his hand-cut, homemade throne stationed in front of his castle, August surveys the expanding camp. The dilapidated 20x20 foot earthen floor house originally built by Nathaniel stands no more. After the fire that turned their home to cinders, and disfigured Delbert, August rebuilt for Claire a proper home. Chet and Lloyd, whose youthful enthusiasm exceeded their actual contribution, assisted their father with construction where possible. Clay and several market hunters would spontaneously appear to raise the heaviest beams, trusses, and framed walls. Payment was an appreciative nod, a callused handshake, or satisfied grunt, and the confirming knowledge that a neighbor, no matter the distance, ever leaves another alone, or in need.

The new home would never be compared with the fancy Victorian houses built with lattice and dormers within Havre de Grace proper, but it is Claire's pride and joy. The rough sawn floors are swept daily. The unpainted interior walls were sanded smooth to the touch. And the two, three-foot square windows, one with a view to the front, the other over the cast iron kitchen sink provides a picturesque view of densely forested birch trees in spring and summer, giving way to stark, white skeletons standing at parade rest in winter. These two panes were unimaginable luxuries for Claire. Great care is taken in the supervision while they are wiped, streak free, twice a week by young men who are more or less willing. There is no indoor running water, but that is what strong boys are for, pumping and toting from the outside well, and for bodily functions, a new outhouse was constructed over a freshly dug hole. This outhouse has a severely slanted roof that was liberally smeared with loblolly pine pitch. A user of this facility can sit comfortably during the worst nor'easter and not get wet.

From the narrow plank porch of the four-room marsh extravagance, August oversees his boys while they separate the corn from the chaff. Off to his left is the smoke shed used for fowl, beaver, fish, and turtle meat. Built next to the smoke shed is another shed for the storage of tools, chopped and seasoning wood, and decoys that have been finished, or are in various stages of completion. Behind the two sheds is the Joiners' new venture. It is a large pen enclosed by chicken wire containing two geese, one male, and one female. It is August's plan that the offspring of these two can be trained as Judas birds, live tollers, to call in their kin to the gun.

Farther beyond the pen, and visible through the leafless winter birch trunks, is a construction project in progress. Chet and Lloyd, wishing to break free of their parents' direct supervision, and with eyes casting about for female companionship, temporary or permanent, made a pact. They would build two houses; one at a time, and the first brother to bring home a permanent mate could claim the first built house. To date, more hours have been expended seeking a willing partner than on completing the house.

When the two lads first presented August with their agreement and proposal, he was pleased that they wished to remain within the marsh and close to home, but he often wonders if his way of life, that has been satisfying for him, could keep his boys down on the farm, as the colloquialism goes. His way of life is changing. Every year there are new restrictions on how a man can hunt, the type of gun he can use, the number of birds he can bag, and those pesky, persistent, and intrusive game wardens levying fines and confiscating weapons in their attempt to force the government's laws on the hard working man, "Hmmpf, government laws, my ass; just some rich sports blaming the every day man."

"What's that, Pa?" asks Chet, his sleeves rolled up, arms deep in the warm water.

"Nothing. Keep stirring," August resumes his mental musings while stroking the head of his new best dog, Snap, a one-year-old descendant of his beloved Dog.

Dog met her untimely end last year while retrieving a colorful pinchbreast pintail that Lloyd had crippled, and that was hiding among the cattails. To

Lloyd's credit, the pintail had been his fifth shot in a row from a new repeater shotgun. The first four shots knocked the leaders of the small flock out of the sky, all dead before they splashed into the easy flowing creek that let out into the bay.

From the blind, August signaled with his arm the direction of the cripple for Dog to follow. Leaping into the cattails she disappeared from sight. Only the rustlings of stalks were heard, as Dog sought out her master's desire, and then came that heart-piercing yelp.

Silence.

In a retelling of the incident at Tavern Bouvard, Chet swore that the look on his pa's face, it was a mixture of fear and concern, never before witnessed by his boys, stopped the wind...

Two-dozen yards upstream, a poisonous copperhead snake lazily slipped into the creek from between the stalks. Its shiny penny color was unmistakable. Its rope body, covered with hourglass markings, undulated across the water's surface to vanish among the reeds.

Silence.

...and Lloyd added, while crossing his heart as a showing of truthfulness, that the sun dimmed in the sky.

August, Chet, and Lloyd stood in the blind watching the cattails. Their ears strained for any sound. Their eyes were useless in seeing through the impenetrable wall of brown. Then a black nub appeared. A moist nose over a mouth cradling a feathered body colored purple, green, white, black, and cream. Dog pulled herself from the tight constraints of the stout stalks, dragging her left hind leg limply behind her.

Lloyd leapt from the blind, only to be pulled back in by August.

"She wants to bring the bird in," August said. "We'll let her finish."

Dog's black eyes, watering and intense, never left August's, as she slowly, painfully, limped to the edge of the blind. She placed the pintail into August's open palm. August handed the fowl to Lloyd.

"Boys, tell your ma, I'll be along shortly."

Without a word spoken, Chet and Lloyd gathered their guns, shell buckets, and birds, leaving their father with Dog who was lying next to the blind, her breathing labored. August sat on the edge of the pit. He lifted Dog onto his lap.

"You're a good dog," August said quietly, just above a whisper, while stroking the soft fur of Dog's head until it only mattered to him.

The wind raised small swells on the bay. The 31 decoys, mallards, pintails, and widgeons, set out before the blind, rode well. Their painted eyes searched blindly for company crossing the expansive sky. "Rest here. Rest here," was the message this rig communicated.

Snap, true to his name, snaps his head around, his ears perked skyward, rotating toward the noise not yet heard by his human companions. Snap barks to sound the alert. All heads turn right, peering down the snow-shrouded path, waiting for something unseen to appear.

"Mr. Joiner!" a familiar, though winded voice is heard crying out.

Claire appears in the doorway, wiping dry a plate from the morning's meal, a mother's intuition working overtime.

"Mr. Joiner," Anna materializes in the path, arms flapping wildly, her feet whomping-thumping in flippity-floppity rubbers, crunching, and then slipping on the snow. With her tear-streaked face showing panic, Anna races straight to August, falling at his feet. Chet and Lloyd gather around Anna, peering back down the path, half expecting some sort of marsh monster, maybe an east coast relative of Sasquatch,[19] to next appear.

"It's Del," Anna pants, looking up into the curious and alarmed eyes of the various Joiners.

"What about him?" August asks, not too concerned.

"He's in the pond," Anna says, as if that is explanation enough.

"Did he fall through the ice?" Claire asks, wringing the small towel in her hands.

"No. No. He's standing naked like an Indian hunting fowl," Anna blurts out between gulps of oxygen, not understanding why no one is doing anything.

Chet and Lloyd laugh at the thought, "That's our Cigar for you."

"He'll freeze to death," exasperated, Anna looks to Claire for support.

"Boys, fetch your brother," Claire orders.

Chet and Lloyd dawdle a moment too long for Claire's liking, "Right now." She snaps the dish towel at them to hustle them on their way.

"Yes, ma'am," the boys reply as one, acting as if they are eight instead of 20 and 22 years of age, Chet and Lloyd trot down the path making Indian war whoops and woo-woos.

"Did Del say why he was acting like an Indian?" Claire asks Anna.

"He said he had to suffer like his pa does every day to provide," Anna turns toward August who feels Claire's disapproving stare.

"I merely told the boy that more often than not, men must suffer, and learn harsh lessons for our meals," August refuses to be stared down, especially

---

19 Sasquatch. Sometimes referred to as Bigfoot. It is a large, hairy, humanlike creature that lives in the timberlands of the Pacific Northwest. It's true. Really it is if you believe in the wonders of nature.

while sitting on his throne. "I said it's cold and miserable at times, but a man never gives up."

Snap barks. Beauty returns his welcome with several lively barks of her own. Beauty's tail flips left and right with excitement, as she charges up the path to where Anna is kneeling.

August, Claire, and Anna turn to witness the joyful arrival.

"Ha! Here they come now," August relaxes, relieved to be out from under Claire's displeased scrutiny.

Carried in triumph on the shoulders of his astounded brothers, Delbert holds aloft the black and speckled-white bodies of two adult loons. One still with the deadly toy arrow through its breast, and the other limp, its mortal wound not apparent. Chet and Lloyd continue their mimicry of Indian whoops and woo woos, but this time with respect for their brother's dogged determination. His scheme appeared to be folly, but he followed through to success despite the obvious obstacles and inherent dangers.

Delbert had yet to clothe himself, and being close to hypothermia, has stopped shivering, but he feels no discomfort. He is high on adrenaline, adventure, and glory.

"Here, Pa. I got two loons for dinner," Delbert drops the two birds at August's feet. An offering. It is proof that he too would suffer to provide for the family.

"I never had any doubts in your abilities, son," August picks up the birds. He pulls the arrow out of the male, and then examines the female. He asks curiously, "How'd you kill the hen?"

"Well..." Delbert smiles proudly.

"First things first," Claire instructs. "Put him in the tub to warm him up and wash away that mud."

Normal procedure by Chet and Lloyd would be an ungainly toss in, and splash down by a struggling Delbert, but today, with the honor due a conquering hero, they gently lower him into the tub. Delbert scoots down, submerging to his shoulders. In place of soap bubbles, corn chaff covers the surface, making Delbert's head bodiless.

"So, Del, how did you catch them?" Anna asks.

For the first time in Delbert's life, he has reversed the line of ascension to the throne. It is Delbert who is holding court to a rapt audience, not his older, stronger, more physically perfect brothers. He pauses to savor this moment as all eyes are focused on him. All ears wait for him to speak. If he had been asked to choose between the warm soothing water massaging his tingling limbs and torso back to life, or the approval spread across his father's face, it would not take a second to reply: "Throw me back in the pond." Graciously, thankfully, mercifully, in return for his courage and daring, Delbert is blessed with not having to choose.

Speaking with a teasing annoyance, and the air of one who had no doubt as to the outcome of his venture, Delbert begins, "Well, I had scattered the corn for bait as you taught, Pa," acknowledging his teacher. "Making sure there were no tell-tale signs of chaff left floating, or along the edges of the pond for LeCompte to find. Then I made tumps so the fowl would feel safe, but then Anna and Beauty burst in, and started stepping on the corn."

"But I didn't know," Anna replies.

"Just like a girl," teases Chet.

"We'll have none of that," August corrects his eldest, knowing even a comment said in jest can take root in the ear of those listening. August glances at Claire, knowing that over the years he has taken stern measures to correct what he believed to be disobedience on her part, but he has come to realize her true value as a partner in life, and that she is a woman whose dedication to the family is unerring.

"Anna ran off before I finished explaining," Delbert smiles at Anna. "Beauty then laid down quiet as a church house mouse to watch. I then heard the cry of the loon. I stood like a cigar store Indian. The drake walked out from between the tree trunks, eating, and following the corn stringer I'd laid out for any bird to follow around the pond. He kept eating and coming closer. It was only a minute or two before he was close enough to shoot. I was afraid Beauty would bark, or move, but all she did was stare. She's a good dog."

Beauty sits proudly, knowing she acted properly, as Anna strokes her head with compliments.

"I couldn't feel my fingers, so I carefully drew back the string, making sure the arrow wouldn't slip, and then I let fly. The loon died on the spot without a sound. I stepped out of the pond to pick up the bird, and was about to let out a war whoop when I heard the call. It gave me the willies. I thought it was the loon's ghost come back to haunt me."

This revelation brought snickers from Chet and Lloyd, but they were not laughing at their brother. They were covering their own remembrance of spine tingling chills on the first occasion of hearing the spectral call from one mate to the other.

"The hen followed the drake's footsteps, looking for corn, or for him, I don't know which, but she kept coming. I didn't have another arrow so for a moment I just stood there. When the hen reached the place where the drake lay, she looked at him, and then for some reason, maybe I shivered, but she looked up at me. I remembered that loons are now in molt so she couldn't fly away. I reached down, grabbed her by her ringed neck, and then twisted. She died instantly."

"No muss, no fuss. I like that," August says, nodding his approval.

Delbert sits in the tub, full of the glory that today's suffering achieved. Chet and Lloyd shake their heads in amazement, never again to dismiss their younger brother as a gimpy hanger-on. Anna playfully splashes Delbert, "Don't do anything stupid like that again, even if it did pay out."

"Make sure you wash behind your ears," Claire reminds her boy. She turns to return to her indoor chores. A weight carried since Delbert's disfigurement has been lifted from her heart. Her precious Delbert, different from, and occasionally ostracized by Chet and Lloyd, is finally accepted as a full member of the family, with any doubts to his ability to contribute and succeed dispelled forever. Claire pauses on the threshold to glance back at the Buchanan girl. Anna is a growing beauty, who Claire reluctantly suckled in infancy. She watches Anna and Delbert interact. Both were born of and nurtured by the marsh and bay, but they are not two peas of the same pod. Put a dress on Anna and she will be a lucky catch for any man. Delbert, though kind of heart, will be lucky to ever catch the eye of a woman with his unique ways. Claire knows these two will only be friends, but Anna is sincere in her affection for Delbert. As a mother, Claire can be grateful that her precious milk did not go to waste.

– 1910 –

The sky over Maryland, the Chesapeake Bay, the Susquehanna Flats, and Buzzards Glory, finally darken with the passing of the New Year. This darkness is not from winter storms but from the millions of fowl blocking the sun with wings spread wide. Each seek shelter and refuge from harsher winters that have finally overtaken Canada and the Arctic tundra. Day and night the wind thunders with wing beats reverberating over the Flats, announcing the arrival of duck, swan, and geese. The spines of men tingle. Their mouths salivate, as their hands make ready the implements of their chosen vocation. Their guns: shotguns, punt guns, and batteries are cleaned, oiled, loaded, checked and rechecked. Their platforms: sneak skiffs, sinkboxes, and blinds are painted, sealed, and camouflaged. The lures: decoys, purchased new by the better off, carved by the hunter himself or seasoned decoys that have years of experience are repaired and repainted to save a few coins. An armada of men and means preparing to take a piece of the delightful pie that nature provides. The birds are fat and succulent. The men are eager. The families who barely get by are hungry. The diners in New York's and Baltimore's finest restaurants demand something other than filet mignon. The market hunters will provide for all, taking only a small slice of the pie that flies from horizon to horizon.

"Anna, will you please get me more nails from the shed?" Clay asks.

Anna leaps to her feet from the rocker to scamper to the shed to fulfill Clay's request. He returned in the middle of the night to Beauty's excited barking, signaling, "Welcome home." Anna, awakened from her deep, dream-filled sleep, jumped into the arms of her father, hugging him tightly.

Clay, a man of his time, always reserved and slightly uncomfortable with exuberant displays of affection, responded with a tentative squeeze with one arm after dropping a kerosene lantern he had been carrying. With the other arm, he carefully sets the two, 18-inch square panes of glass on the table that he purchased with a portion of his oyster dredging earnings. "Whoa. I'm happy to see you, too. Careful of the glass, Anna, I don't want you to cut yourself."

Clay had never seen the need to use a gunning light to hide behind when he took the Davenport out in the sneak skiff. His skill and stealth was sufficient to bring home all that he and Anna needed to fill their stomachs when the birds were abundant, with multitudes left over to sell to the duck brokers. There was also an unspoken agreement among the market hunters on the Flats not to use this old Indian trick of fire-lighting, because it was feared that its use would frighten away the fowl that were trying to find respite at night.

Clay reasoned he would break this trust for two important reasons, both dealing with his family's financial security. The first being he did not have a sinkbox to use on a permanent basis, and second, half the winter season was over, and he had yet to down a duck. Oystering will do in a pinch, but it was not his way of life. It is ducks and geese that paid the bills and it will always be the ignition, the explosion and flash of powder, and the flying lead that excites Clay, causing his blood to surge through his veins.

As a child, Clay would listen to the old men weave their stories of the hunt. History was in the telling, and the telling was always peppered with one-upsmanship. If one man was soaked to the bone, the next would be frozen with frostbite. If one man's gun misfired, the next exploded. If one man brought home a record number of kills, the next would have far surpassed the record if only his barrel had not melted. Surprisingly, to a man, hard men with faces of leather, fists ready to brawl in defense of their kinsmen, drinking men spinning the yarn high and wide where a common retort is spoken with a lifetime of friendship to back it up: "Only a fisherman lies more than you," credit is always given to the man or folk when it's due, even if the folks' skin is red or black. Tall tales are tall tales, but honor is honor, and the two can coincide peacefully with these men who provide for their families and walk tall within their small community, all others being hypocrites who call these hunters criminals, but greedily purchase the products of the hunter's hard labor through back doors.

It is then expected, when the subject of the gunning light, or its traditional name of fire-lighting, is discussed, the Indian and his ingenuity are marveled upon. It was not only waterfowl the Indian successfully hunted with this technique, but big game as well. For fowl, the Indian would burn bark on a small stone slab set on the bow of their canoes. Another larger stone was polished smooth to reflect the firelight and to hide the hunter with his bow and arrow as his companion eased the canoe within range.

After giving the ungodly Indians their due, further credit and accolades were heaped upon the early settlers for refining this skill. Early Europeans used pine tar torches, though gradually this old fashioned method transformed itself with the use of boxes for aid in reflection. Candles made of beeswax, tallow, or spermaceti[20] replaced the torch as a source of light, the last was preferred because it burned longer and cleaner, though all candles were replaced when kerosene became widely available.

Clay is building his box to accommodate their new, though used kerosene lamp that can burn all night, and the light's intensity can be properly adjusted to suit the environment. A bonus to using the light is the heat it gives off, warming the hands of the hunter during the long forays into the winter nights. Clay places the two panes of glass in a "V" shape in corresponding grooves he has carved into the flat base of the box. The back of the box that makes up the open end of the "V" is flat. Clay nails shiny tin cans to the flat surface to act as a reflector for the lamp's light. The top of the box will be hinged at the back and contains a smoke bell with several holes for ventilation.

"Here, Anna, use the flat end of the hand axe to nail the hinges secure," Clay instructs.

"How will this box set on the bow of the skiff if the Davenport's barrel rests there?" asks Anna.

Clay is pleased by Anna's intuitive question, "I'm going to build a base that raises the box. Then I'll cut a hole for the barrel to slide through, though I am a bit worried that the barrel will cast a shadow that could frighten the rafting fowl, so I may have to use a shotgun."

Gritting her teeth for added strength to swing the axe, Anna pounds in the nails, only slightly bending one, which she gives an extra powerful whack to, while playfully mocking her father. "A shotgun? Isn't that for sports and their pay by the day guides?"

Laughing, and realizing that like her mother, Anna never lets him forget anything he has said, whether it is in jest, or with conviction, "Yes, I said that, but I admit the new repeaters, especially if a shell extension tube is added, can knock the hell out of the birds."

"But never as many as the Davenport," Anna states defensively, and with family pride.

---

20 Spermaceti. A waxy substance found in sperm whales and dolphins, used in candles, cosmetics, and ointments.

"No, never as many as the Davenport, and like the Davenport, this gunning light is just between us, family. There is no need to speak of it with others, even Cigar, because the game wardens have ears everywhere, and LeCompte would enjoy nothing better than to add this to his list of items to confiscate from us."

A conspiracy with her father against those who would harm the family excites Anna. She recognizes the many blessings of friendship with Delbert, the Joiners in general, Olivia, and the extended Havre de Grace family, but at the core it is just her father, Beauty, and her. They stand together as a unit, watching out for each other's needs, secrets and all.

"My lips are sealed," Anna raises her hand to her lips, turning her wrist at the corner with an invisible key. Beauty barks agreement.

In the weeks following the arrival of the wildfowl and Clay's return from Shady Side, the cold nights on the Flats are stalked by a man with the gunning light, and his two faithful companions, Beauty and the Davenport. For Anna, the days and nights consist of picking and cleaning the fowl caught by the Davenport's lead, and on the rare break, watching the various species of fowl fly about in search of food. The white blanket of winter is wearing thin as melt water trickles off the shack's roof. Snow is no longer a frosting on the tops of the birch trees surrounding the Joiners' encampment. The ice sheet covering the snapping turtle's pond is breaking apart of its own accord, and during the day, the blustery bay is more white-capped swells than ice floes.

Clay is determined to make up for lost time and lost income, and graciously, the tired birds cooperate by rafting close together in the tens of thousands for easy shots by an accomplished predator. Most years, Clay would take one foray out onto the Flats each night to *blow a hole in 'em,* but after Beauty retrieved all the dead and injured, Clay noticed the ducks, geese, and swan quickly regrouping, inciting his cupidity.

Anna has all but forgotten what sleep is. In the middle of the night, whether her attempt to catch a few winks is interrupted by Beauty's barking, or Clay's shout for assistance, both meant, "Get up." Exhausting trips, too numerous to count, from their shack to the sneak skiff, carrying back arm loads of bloodied fowl are required. Her beloved Beauty carries a share to ease Anna's burden, but Anna does not count on her father for help, because he spends the brief moments ashore carefully cleaning, and then reloading the Davenport.

"Going out again," is all Clay says, which is more than needed as he exits the shed holding the charger, a measuring cup with shot and powder; a ratio of about five-to-one. Sitting on the porch planks, the corners swept clear of lingering ice, Clay removes the Davenport's hammer from its tube so that as he rams the two different waddings down over the powder he has poured in, all the air will escape from the magazine.

Anna watches this practiced procedure while stoking the outside fire sparking to life under a rusted, 50-gallon, steel drum she has laboriously filled with water.

The waddings are oakum, old rope that she has teased apart, to be inserted over cork. Paper can be used, but Clay insists that it be cork since it can be found for free, and paper is an additional expense. Next, Clay pours shot down the Davenport's throat.

At this point in the loading, Anna always detects the slightest upturn in the corners of her father's mouth. Something deep within his being is rising to the surface. All the suffering from the numbing cold and aching muscles, the uncertainty of whether the birds will be found, the patience of endless hours of stalking, and the danger from exploding guns, or capsizing, coalesces to carve the character of a man who is willing to pay nature's high toll of discomfort and risk to life and limb to reap the benefits. This is who Clay Buchanan is. It is what he does best. It is in moments like this, when the world consists solely of Clay, Beauty, the Davenport, and Anna that her pride swells. She stands surrounded by dozens of birds that are waiting to be dunked in the boiling water to ease in the plucking. Anna pauses, watching silently as her family works with quiet precision—teamwork.

With blood stained fingers, Anna tucks an errant strand of hair behind her ear. Clay loosely packs the final wadding over the shot as the short hairs on the back of his neck stand up with the tickle of a ghost. He looks up. There is no ghost, only Anna smiling at him as her eyes sparkle, lit by the growing flames. Clay knows she has caught him revealing a truth, and that future telling by him of the hardships he must endure to provide for his family will be listened to with respect, but with the knowledge that there is no line between suffering and joy when it comes to duck hunting.

"Those birds won't clean themselves," Clay blurts while pushing very fine black powder into the tube leading into the Davenport's chamber. Holding a small piece of rubber over the tube, Clay replaces the hammer. The monster fowling piece is ready. Clay looks up again. Anna is now leaning over the bubbling drum dunking a mallard. Clay salivates. Beauty barks unneeded encouragement, her tail anxiously swinging left and right as she sits in the middle of a patch of mud left by melting snow.

"Let's go," Clay hefts the weighty punt gun. Beauty runs on ahead, the energy of youth never waning. "I'll be back before dawn. Remember, pair 'em up, drake to hen." The last instruction given night after night, year after year, is not spoken with harsh recrimination due to any failure by Anna, but said, and received with acknowledgement and appreciation, as she has correctly tied and strung birds for more than half her young life. Anna knows this is how her father says, "Thank you," and "I love you." What Anna does not know while listening to her father's boot steps in mud, snow, and slush fade, is that Clay always glances back to watch her dutifully and without complaint attend to the task at hand. Clay shakes his head with wonderment at this girl, so much like her mother, and full of mysteries unfathomable. He would never let the words be said aloud, for it is not his way, but even more than a reliable gun, a well-trained retriever, or a sound skiff, he needs Anna. It is true that Clay wanted a son to mold into a man, and he still has no clue as to how to raise a girl even with Olivia's constant advice, but Anna has become that integral footing in the foundation of Clay's life. If he were to glance back to find her missing, all that would remain is a dark and empty shack where his love died.

Clay slides the Davenport into place on the sneak skiff, securing it in the chock. He adjusts the patent buoy that is attached under the barrel ahead of the trigger, then double checks the burlap bag that is wedged between the Davenport's butt end and the skiffs transom that he has filled with fresh pine needles to soften the recoil, "In you go, Beauty." For a moment, Clay rubs his chilled hands over the kerosene lantern burning bright within the open box to warm them. Watching Beauty curl under the Davenport's barrel, her black rump against the buoy; Clay chuckles at the recent thwarting of the game laws to Warden LeCompte's frustration.

The sun had set, the Davenport removed from its hiding place, and Clay and Beauty had made their way out onto the Flats toward a rafting flock. Clay had spent four hours patiently inching closer to the nervous, but unaware birds, when suddenly they panicked and took flight. Something had spooked them, and without hesitation, or self-examination, Clay heaved the Davenport overboard; its splash lost within the wings slapping the water and air and their calls to escape. Grabbing the ever-present fishing pole, sans bait, Clay tossed the line overboard as a light enveloped him. Warden LeCompte accused and threatened fines and imprisonment for hunting at night with an illegal punt gun, but without the Davenport, or a single dead duck as evidence, he had to row away, knowing he had been defeated, foiled, but never discouraged, because the law is a patient watchman that always wins out in the end.

Clay returned to the site of the confrontation the next morning to retrieve the Davenport. There it was; the bobbing buoy, telltale on the surface. A timer made of rock salt is used as a stopper, holding a coiled rope. After the gun is pitched overboard, the salt slowly dissolves, releasing the rope, and allowing the buoy to pop to the surface, long after the threat of the law has passed.

Clay adjusts the lantern's wick to the proper illumination then closes the box. He takes a deep, lung-filling breath of salt-spiced Chesapeake Bay air, knowing that his eluding of LeCompte that night was more luck than planning. A second's delay in discarding the gun would have caught him red-handed. If LeCompte had been stealthier, he would not have startled the birds, allowing Clay time to take his shot, and adding more evidence in the form of fowl killed at night. However, the proof that Luck is on the side of the hunter is that Clay was not using the gunning light. He had run out of kerosene. His lack of planning had first irritated him, but later, Clay thanked God for the miscalculation that saved him from going to jail.

The soft croaking, mewing, and sneezing of divers and dabblers, wafts across the water to reach Clay's discerning ears. He points the skiff toward the invisible quarry, and shoves off the icy sand bank, out onto the windless Flats. The only ripples are slight, and quickly dissipate, produced by a talented man using small hand paddles who is hiding behind a diffused light and moving purposefully forward with inexhaustible patience and stealth. The surface of the bay is alive with the chatter of fowl rafting contentedly. All that float upon the Susquehanna Flats is in harmony until the man from Buzzards Glory releases the Davenport's fury.

An unexpected fog, a vapor so dense that one would think Clay paddled into the midst of a thousand campfires smoking with green wood as it rises as salty upside-down rain from the still waters of the bay. Fat fingers gloved in white quickly creep up the banks to smother Buzzards Glory. The marsh and shack disappear with a wave of God's mysterious hands. Caught in the middle of the nothingness in a void without limits, Clay's shoulders strain with each powerful pull on the one full size oar. The sneak skiff skims across the bay with its cargo of fowl, Beauty, the Davenport, and the cooling gunning light, its wick extinguished. Clay had focused squinting eyes on the distant fire burning bright under the dunking drum until it, too, was swallowed.

It was Clay's personal lighthouse.

It was Clay's beacon of salvation.

It was Clay's way out of a death trap, but it has either gone out, or the impenetrable fog is obscuring it, and he fears that he is paddling in circles. And somewhere within the blanketing whiteness a warning whistle wails repeatedly. A shiver runs up Clay's spine as the whistle can only be from the side-wheeler *Emma Giles* on her night run from Havre de Grace to Baltimore. This 549 ton vessel, a three deck monstrosity with its massive churning steel and wood plank wheels will grind Clay and his vulnerable craft into something less than tooth picks, leaving only detritus to slowly sink to the bottom if he falters in concentration or fails in strength.

I will not be a feast for the crabs, Clay tells himself as he doubles his efforts, ignoring the burn of salt stinging his eyes. It is either from his sweat or from the salt suspended in the fog. Regardless of its source, there is no time to wipe his eyes, as one paddle stroke can be the difference between life and death when a goliath is bearing down.

Blind to the distant world, and not knowing the direction the *Emma Giles* is coming from, Clay can only watch Beauty. He has no choice but to trust the instincts of this retriever to lead them to safety, to determine the direction of their small craft. Emerging as a monstrous phantom from the fog, the side-wheeler roars belching malevolent smoke from its stack and shrieking its whistle. Its spinning wheels are claws bearing down and reaching out to crush the tiny craft and its occupants. Clay's profane screams are unknown to the captain who is sitting comfortably in the round wheelhouse. The fur on Beauty's neck bristle, but her forward gaze does not waiver, even as the spray from the side-wheeler's prow douses her. She trusts in her master, though Beauty does not know that Clay failed his former partner. Pulling with his last ounce of strength, and then finding more as Anna's image flashes in front of him, Clay feels the stern of the sneak skiff rise with the passing wake of the enormous vessel. The skiff is pushed just beyond the reach of the merciless wheels, rocking unsteadily, and causing two ducks that where neatly stacked to be lost overboard. Their value is nothing compared to Clay and Beauty's lives. Beauty's body rocks side to side to remain balanced— her head steady, eyes on a course invisible to Clay. One danger has passed, but Clay is still lost on a wide bay that cares nothing for the hunter. Beauty continues to be his fixed compass. She is honing in on the place she calls home, guided either by sounds too slight for Clay's ears, or by vision capable of penetrating the wall of fog, a talent that Clay lacks, but that he is betting his life on. A man is no match for nature, but a man who lives within it and utilizes its blessings with great humility, will be amply rewarded. Tonight the reward is life.

Hours pass with only the sound of the paddle dipping into the water; the swirling of eddies, as the paddle is pulled backward. Clay feels as if he has held his breath forever, not wanting to make any noise that might distract Beauty. Without notice, without a hint or warning, the scraping of sand and ice is felt through the weathered boards of the flat-bottomed hull, allowing Clay to finally breathe a sigh of relief. Hearing this exclamation, Beauty turns her head to look with contempt at this doubting Thomas. She knows how to get home, so why worry. As if this were only a pop quiz by the Almighty on the subject of survival, as suddenly as the fog materialized, it begins to dissipate.

Beauty picks up a widgeon, and then leaps out of the skiff, running the short distance to the shack that is still hidden in the fog. Clay follows with the gunning light and the Davenport. His weary body seeks the warmth of a bubbling cup of coffee and several hours of comfort under the soft quilt of his marriage bed to restore his energy and to recover from frazzled nerves—*too close...that was much too close.* Sitting in front of the porch steps wagging her tail with the widgeon held softly in her mouth, Beauty looks upon a fallen warrior with compassion.

Suppressing a cough, Clay swigs his brown medicine while taking in the scene before him. He realizes this brave young warrior vanquished all comers before collapsing. The fire beneath the drum is now embers winking red and gray. Feathers blanket the ground, sticking where they fell into mud, or slush, giving the shack an elegant, multi-colored approach fit for royalty. The birds, too numerous to count, have been picked clean, tied hen to drake, and hung from hemp cords strung between the porch posts. Sitting and leaning against a post, fast asleep, and snoring prettily, is Anna. Next to her knees is Clay's favorite tin cup with coffee now cold, waiting patiently for his return that was long delayed, and that almost did not happen.

Beauty eyes Clay, asking, *Well, you decide.*

With Clay's return, there are many more birds to clean, evidence of the Davenport's triumph. The duck brokers will be arriving soon to purchase the night's harvest. Clay makes his decision. He reaches down and picks up the cup, its strong brew mellowed slightly by milk and sugar is still a sharp slap in the face as the chilled liquid is swallowed. Clay returns the Davenport and the gunning light to their hiding places. Clay notices the fog clearing overhead. He watches as the stars blink out with the coming day, "There may still be time." Clay trots into the shed for another long oar, and then around front to where Anna has slouched down, curled up. Beauty stands sentinel.

"Anna. Anna, wake up," Clay gently shakes Anna. "C'mon, girl. You don't want to miss the show."

Leaving Beauty to guard their plunder, Clay and Anna paddle south along the crooked shore. He does not answer any of Anna's questions, but says, "Just paddle and be quiet."

Steering the sneak skiff farther away from the shore until the shoreline finally disappears in the remaining fog, Clay stops paddling, and then touches Anna's shoulder. He points toward where the edges of the bay and marsh would meet, if they could see it, and then places his finger to his lips as a reminder for silence.

As a knife cutting through an up-ended loaf of fresh baked bread, slice by slice, the mist is stripped away from the top down. Anna glances up. The black sky changes first to gray as the distant dying moon falls into the west, pulling the moisture out of the air. The moon acts as a lever to lift the weak winter sun above the eastern horizon. The gray imperceptibly changes to mauve, and then deep purple. Orange, red, and hints of yellow streak overhead, and then dance among the water droplets hanging uncertain in the air.

The curtain of fog dissolves to an unsure mist, slowly rising to reveal the show for an exclusive audience of two, father and daughter.

The fore stage is the bay, its water as a mirror reflecting those who float upon it and enhancing God's illumination from above. The background is a patchwork of rich black earth and milky snow making up the marsh edge. On stage is a chorus of raucous ducks. Their brown, black, and blue-feathered heads plunge underwater to nibble on the grasses below the surface with bills of yellow, brown, and blue. Their tail feathers point skyward, wiggling in a comically obscene gesture fit for the burlesque of any French cabaret.

Anna forgets her exhaustion. Gazing at the follies unfolding before her, she puts both hands over her mouth to stifle giggles.

From within the marsh, a skein of whistling swans take to the stage. They are the headliners, whiter than snow, graceful, commanding, elegant, and proud. There is a cast of hundreds advancing. The ducks, bit players, move aside to allow the main performance to commence. With the precision of a dance troupe, the swans dip their long slender necks in unison, nodding politely to one another before their heads disappear beneath the water. Plunge rings radiate outward, bouncing against its neighbors, interweaving the spirals on the placid surface.

Floating, gliding in circles, pairs of swans spin around each other to music only they can hear. Music created through millenniums of seasons for those who can appreciate its subtleties and who are patient enough to learn the intricate harmonies.

Anna looks to her father. Her eyes are wide with amazement. Her mouth is wide with wonder. Clay knows this look all too well. It is the same one Jennifer expressed when he first shared this event with her, though to Clay, the swans are simply feeding. To Jennifer, they were dancing a ballet of romance and undying love.

"Your mother knew their beauty. I know their flavor and price per feather weight," Clay explains. "I believe she would want you to know both."

Anna turns back to watch the performance until the remaining mist evaporates to nothing. The sky changes colors once more to a pale blue. The sun breaks free of the horizon's sticky grip to brightly spotlight the dancers who take their last bow, spreading grand wings to depart this performance.

Expecting Anna to applaud and cheer at the conclusion of the Swan's Spectacular, Clay is rattled when she turns back to face him with tears streaming from her eyes.

"Am I responsible?" Anna asks.

"Responsible for what?"

"Did I kill my mother?" Anna's shoulders sag with guilt. Her sobs flow freely in fear of her father's answer.

"No," Clay says without hesitation. He sits quietly in the skiff with his daughter, remembering his paralyzing grief when Jennifer closed her eyes for the final time. Clay momentarily looks away from Anna to collect himself and his thoughts. Before his eyes is the world where he works. The marsh and bay are utilitarian environments. If you understand them, your meals will be provided. Jennifer would say, "The more I understand about the marsh and bay, the more beautiful it becomes." Clay did not understand the way she saw the world, but he loved her for the way she marveled at all of God's creations.

"Your mother said it's God's will," Clay begins slowly. "That I disagree with. It was an accident, nothing more, nothing less. No God I'd ever acknowledge would take a wife from her husband or a mother from her child."

The yellow sun, reaching higher, shines on Anna's soft cheeks. Her black hair shimmers. She wipes her eyes with the back of her sleeve while absorbing each word as their meanings hold condemnation or absolution.

"It ain't right though I would never have told your mother that," Clay involuntarily takes a drink of his medicine—it's just habit—then returns the bottle to the pocket of his Mackinaw. "I suppose God could have allowed your mother's passing for some reason I can't fathom, but if you can find in the Bible any scripture where God, Jesus, or the prophets said, 'I take this life,' well, I'll do your chores for a month of Sundays, but it ain't in there." Clay picks up his oar and begins to row, "Promise me this, Anna. When you bury me, don't let the preacher say, 'God giveth and God taketh away.'" Clay is surprised by his anger. His grief has so long concealed a desire to lash out, to confront those who are responsible for his loss, and to beat justice out of them. But it was only an accident, a simple fall, gravity. Clay cannot even blame nature. It is just the way it is.

A large chunk of wood thuds against the sneak skiff momentarily distracting father and daughter. Anna reaches out to push it away, but notices it has an eye hook screwed into it with a trailing cord and there is a definite shape to the wood. Clay reaches out to lift into the skiff what he quickly recognizes as an old and rare swan decoy. It has broken away from its mooring, escaped so to speak from its rig, and was floating up-side-down as its lead ballast is missing. The cork body is peppered with errant shot. Its paint is badly worn and chipped, and its long slender neck is cracked. It is an old warrior, lost and forgotten, but with many stories to tell.

"Look at this," Clay points to a Roman numeral incised on both the shelf of the body and the bottom of the curved neck. "This is an old Sam Barnes' decoy. I wonder how many years it has cast about."

"You're not going to die, are you?" asks the vulnerable 12-year-old child in Anna.

"Not now," Clay calmly reassures his daughter, his grief and anger coming back under control. "Not for a long time, but it is the way of things. Everything and everyone has its time."

Clay sets the ancient wooden mariner into the skiff. He rolls and lights a cigarette. The skiff glides lazily forward as Clay draws the pungent smoke deeply into his lungs.

The moment has passed. The show has ended. Jennifer is gone. There are birds waiting and the brokers' arrival is imminent.

"Thank you."

Clay is unsure if Anna's softly spoken words of gratitude were referring to the Swan's Spectacular or his reply to her question. Either way, a new moment is created, lasting the entire way home. It is a moment for father and daughter to share with quiet contentment. It is a moment to be cherished for the rare intimacy that it brings to them, and will be remembered without the need for embellishment when times are difficult.

Anna's hair, unrestrained by tie or bow, and reaching to the middle of her back is matted and stringy. The tip of her nose drips with the remnants of a passing rain. The Mackinaw bulges with pouches of black power that she has slung around her neck as the coat keeps her body warm against the chill of the night and dry from the large drops that land with a splattering plop-plop. Under one arm, Anna carries a two-gallon can of kerosene, and under the other, she carries a ten-pound box of round shot. Anna had volunteered to stroll to town and back to purchase these items for her father as she felt the need to be out and about, especially since the previous two days had been warm. The sun had been bright with cotton ball clouds dotting brilliant blue skies. The breeze has been a tickling feather upon her cheeks. The marsh mammals have come out of hiding, and the first signs of cold-blooded creatures who had laid dormant, buried deep in the insulating mud through the freezing winter are poking about, seeking a place to sun themselves.

Anna had argued with her father that she knew best, that she did not need to carry the coat on such a beautiful picnic-weather day. Clay had argued with himself whether to forgo the debate and to let her learn the lesson the way most pre-teens do, the hard, cold, wet way, but considering Anna would be carrying black powder that he is loath to stir dry over a hot stove if it got wet, he laid down the law. This home, even in peaceful, contented times, is still a dictatorship, and even though he allows his subject wide latitude, Clay is the ruler of his kingdom, and his word is law. Clay knew spring to be fickle, and the clouds on the distant northern horizon foretold a change by late afternoon. Anna may be a learned student of her environment, but she does not know everything.

Being warm and relatively dry, Anna is grateful for the Mackinaw's protection. She is embarrassed by the tantrum she threw, stomping out of the house, clutching the coat in one hand, and the fistful of dollars in the other. *Boy, was I a brat,* she thinks while splashing through a puddle that formed in a rut in the road.

Leaving the unpaved road that separates the fields drained and cleared by the McQuays and land left in its natural state by the Joiners and her father, Anna follows a path alongside the creek leading to the snapper's pond. From above, she is suddenly accosted by an avian of recent arrival. It is a distance traveler from across the Gulf of Mexico. Its small, five-inch, bright yellow-orange body with blue-gray wings, flutters among the budding branches in the maples, warbling chastisement at Anna for being a child, who in the face of facts to the contrary, occasionally disputes her father's wisdom and good intentions. Satisfied with a rebuke well delivered, the warbler turns its attention to a resting flock of greater yellowlegs that are pausing on their journey from Patagonia, at the southern tip of South America, to spread themselves out across Canada's tundra. Larger by three times, with brown backs, white rumps and tails, and bright yellow legs, this small flock of 12 respond with clear whistling calls of three to five notes each. Anna stops on the trail to watch with embarrassment. Their chatter, their banter, their arguing is a replay of the scene between her father and herself. From Anna's perspective, neither the birds nor she and her father seemed to understand each other—a very frustrating experience. But as Anna thinks about it, it was she who was unwilling to listen, or take the time to understand.

Leaving the warbler and greater yellowlegs to their lively discourse and vowing not to act like a child again as she is almost a grown up, Anna continues along the path. Night is quickly taking hold, and she wants to be home, sitting next to the glowing potbelly stove where she can dry her soaking hair. There will be no recriminations from her father, only a hopeful look that Anna will get it through her head that father knows best.

Approaching along the trail, bent over, and backside first, is Delbert. He is struggling with something hidden from Anna's view. "Del, what 'cha doing?" Anna calls. Startled, Delbert whips around. His wet hair and coverall fling water in every direction. Disheveled and appearing wild, deranged, and drenched, a mongrel of the mud, his surprise changes to a toothy grin. With the fingers of one hand, he combs back his unruly hair as if he really cared about his appearance, and then proudly points to that which he is fighting to keep hold of with his other hand.

"Caught it on one of our hooks," Delbert proclaims.

Walking closer, Anna clearly sees in the twilight that Delbert is holding onto the tail of a large snapping turtle, though thankfully it is not Anna's granddaddy, but still a sizeable one by any measurement.

"They're coming out after the long winter and are they ever hungry. This is the second one today," Delbert grips the stubby tail with both hands to prevent the turtle from regaining purchase and pulling away from him. "You should check the pond. I know your pa baited there, too."

Anna hopes that her snapper, who has survived these many years, is wise to this trick, but if he does take the bait that he will not get caught on the hook, "Okay. I'll check."

"Got to go. Ma's waiting," Delbert resumes his tug-of-war with his doomed opponent, pulling it along the path, it leaving long, squiggly, turtle claw marks in the muck.

Anna looks into the pleading eyes of the turtle as Delbert drags it away. She is pained by its predicament and fate. She wonders why Delbert does not hit it with a rock to put it out of its misery, but she knows he has his ways, and constantly amazes her by his no-nonsense approach to life in the marsh. For the first time she recognizes the similarities between Delbert and her father. Maybe it is a male thing to use what is available for profit and provision, missing the wonderment of its simple existence. Maybe because she has always been provided for that Anna has the luxury to look around and consider the difficulties the migrating birds contend with in avoiding, not always successfully, predation from one end of their journey to the other. Foxes, rats, snakes, raccoons, and otters feast on the eggs, while man, eagle, and hawk attack them in flight. If the birds survive the flight, they often find their nesting sites drained and plowed for crops. The birds that remain throughout the year must forever forage for sustenance while avoiding other larger and hungrier creatures as well as man's guns, snares, and nets. It is a miracle, a wonder, and a marvel that any wildfowl survive the gantlet, but somehow the intricate web that has been designed and kept in balance since creation remains. For this reason, Anna hurries toward the snapper's pond, hoping her friend, who has lived longer than she, will continue its domination in the deadly game of life over the men who desire snapper soup.

Beauty lies contented on the porch taking her cue from Clay who is leaning back in the rocking chair. His feet are propped against a post. His face is obscured by cigarette smoke that is occasionally blown away by a wind uncertain in its direction. The distant bay is a black sheet with thin slices of white traveling across to splash harmlessly upon the shore in the dimming light. Their lullaby rhythm is a timeless clock set by the moon and wound by the wind. The sun nods its good night, leaving Buzzards Glory to creatures and folk who stir only in its absence. This is the time, the transition from light to dark when all the chores are complete, when his world is quiet, that Clay affords himself a satisfied sigh. The latest strings of plucked birds wait for the duck smugglers, black marketers, or brokers, which Jack Grosso prefers to call the enterprise that he and his son have involved themselves in.

Clay chuckles thinking of these two characters; Jack and Jack Jr. They are former punt gun and battery operators on Spesutie Narrows, south of Plum Point below Buzzards Glory. Caught red-handed by Game Warden LeCompte, the imposed fine was painful enough, but to watch their guns being confiscated, and then broken apart, "It tore my morals up," Jack related in his heavy Italian accent. Clay always wonders about that. The Grosso family, hard working, church-going Catholics, arrived in the New World a generation or two before the Buchanans walked out of the Highlands of Scotland. Father and son retain not only their accents, but also their mother tongue, especially when arguing with arms flailing, fingers gesturing, lips spitting curses, and finally the re-waxing of bushy mustaches that a child can do a pull-up on. Clay believes their violent disputes are all part of a negotiating tactic used on uninitiated sellers and buyers. He quickly spotted the affection sparking between their eyes during a recent encounter with them, and so remained firm on his request for a price increase, or he would sell to the New York restaurateur.

Exasperated, but with a few winks between one another, Jack and Jack Jr. threw up their arms, feigning impending bankruptcy, and then agreed to the new price. The only irritant with this arrangement is their inconsistent arrival. Clay never knows when the pair and their wagon will arrive.

"Depends on LeCompte," Jack would cry in frustration.

"A man gets no rest from his harassment," Jack Jr. would wail piteously.

The agreement, in the event that Clay or Anna are not at home is for the Jacks to leave the bills and coins on the kitchen table under the lantern. In the three years of *doing business*, there has never been a concern over, or a shortage in, the calculated price. A man who has no lock on his door is the trusting sort. A man who is allowed to enter must do so with honor.

Beauty's ears twitch. Clay picks up the faint flutter of primary feathers of wings and tails catching air, spreading wide to slow large bodied birds as a dozen drop into the water in front of the shack. They are the size of Canada geese, but their lack of honking indicates some other species. A moment before the dark gray twilight turns officially to night, Clay sees that these sleek birds are double-crested cormorants with bodies entirely black, with long square tails, and necks that are crooked in the middle, seemingly broken. Hungry, and in search of fish, they quickly dive beneath the surface without leaving a ripple, to remain underwater, swimming and searching for prey. Clay tries to focus, blinking, but sees and hears nothing, wondering, *were they really there to begin with?*

Beauty jumps to her feet, barking excitedly.

A newfangled contraption bumps, bangs, shakes, and rattles on the rutted road toward the shack.

Clay stretches his arms, assuming it is the duck brokers.

Skidding to a sliding halt in front of the shack, two mustache-wiggling men grin from the cramped cab. The younger lays on the horn.

A-ooo-gah!

Jack and Jack Jr. have arrived. "Sorry we're late," Jack Jr. states while climbing down from behind the wheel of the new Ford, stake bed truck. "Had to outrun LeCompte."

Clay shakes his head, thinking, *You're kidding. How can you be late when you never say when you'll be arriving?*

Jack stands proudly on the truck's running board, "She's fast all right," then reprimands Jack Jr., "But you almost crashed into something a couple miles back."

"Well, if you'd let me turn on the head lamps I might be able to see," Jack Jr. throws his arms up into the air.

"And so would LeCompte," Jack replies, transitioning into rapid and emotionally charged Italian.

Beauty stretches back out, contented.

Clay sighs deeply.

The lazy moon has failed to rise to help Anna in her search around the pond's edge for pole hooks. The few twinkling stars peeking between drifting clouds and the incomplete canopy are a poor substitute for a lantern that Anna wishes she possessed. Crawling on her hands and knees, she has to rely on her senses of hearing and smell, the latter being more effective. Anna does not hear anything struggling to free itself from a jagged hook, but the stink of rotting fish is her guide to each pole's location. The three that Anna finds are empty.

If it had been day, Anna would have been immediately relieved to see the winking eyes and nostrils poking above the water as her confidant floats just below the surface. For several days he has watched from a safe distance as men erected their devices, all the while desiring his demise. A snapper's grotesque mouth is incapable of a smug smile, but his cold-blooded heart is afire with cocky joy. This old man of the pond possesses a piece of wisdom that will never change: Nothing is free. There is always a catch. It is what he lives by.

Screams for help streak down the path to Anna. Her first thought is of Delbert, but the pitch is too high. The snapper submerges with a soft pop of water filling the space his nostrils left vacant.

Anna scrambles around, feeling with her hands to locate the kerosene and shot she had set down. Finding them, she snatches them up and runs back along the muddy path.

"Don't scrimp on the ice," Jack shouts from the shack's porch.

"I think I know how to pack ducks," Jack Jr. shouts back while stuffing the ducks in, a hundred to a barrel. The barrels are specifically designed with ventilation, the staves making up the sides of the barrels having been left with spaces between them. Jack Jr. scoops ice from one barrel to cover the ducks before hammering down the lids. The flatbed holds ten barrels, two less than their old wagon, but still a pride to the Jacks.

"Some of these roads may be hell on wheels," Jack says, "but I hear the State Road Commission has geared up to make more improvements."

"That's what the government is supposed to do," Clay says. "Make a man's life easier, not make it more difficult."

"Well, this baby's doing that for us," Jack Jr. replaces the wooden stakes on the sides of the flatbed. "She'll outrun LeCompte. At least until the government retires his sway back horse and issues him an automobile."

"Someone should do something about that man," Jack spits off the porch.

"All we can do is outsmart him," Clay replies.

"It will come to a head one day. You can't avoid him forever. Look at us, Jack snarls, and then asks, "How many in total?"

"One hundred and twenty-seven pairs," Clay answers.

"Any mismatches?" Jack asks Jack Jr. for no other reason than to see if he can raise Clay's ire.

No response. Clay does not take the bait.

"No mismatches," Jack Jr. shouts from the cab.

"How much of this do you want?" asks Jack.

"Twenty will do," Clay holds out his palm for Jack to count out the singles.

"The rest as before? Baltimore?" asks Jack.

"Yep."

"Clay, we really should be thanking the law. All they've done by passing laws against our trade is raise the price of a duck, making it more profitable," Jack nods toward his new truck.

A-ooo-gah! Jack Jr. playfully taps the horn.

"And made it more fun," Jack concludes, stepping off the porch.

"What they've done," Clay says, his voice raising an octave, "is change a respected profession to one of public disdain and skulking around at night."

"Po-TAY-to, po-TAH-to, Clay. The money spends the same," Jack chuckles, punching Clay in the arm. "But if you ever get tired of paddling around the bay you could try breeding live tollers. I hear the Joiners are raising them. Properly trained, they'll bring in their kind, and if they don't learn quick enough, you can always drop 'em in the pot." Jack places his thumb and fingers to his mouth then smacks his lips.

A-ooo-gah! Jack Jr. taps the horn again. "Yep. Drop 'em in the pot."

"I'm afraid Anna would just make pets of them," Clay laughs, his irritation at the mention of LeCompte, subsiding.

A-ooo-gah!

"All right already," Jack shouts. "Boys and their new toys." Jack climbs back into the cab next to Jack Jr. as Jack Jr. turns the truck around. As it shakes, bangs, and rattles away from the shack, Jack leans out the cab holding dollar bills in his raised hand, "Whether you're buying or selling, it's all the same. No duck—no dinner."

A-ooo-gah!

Thoughts of the last seven days visiting with her dear cousin Dorothy Parker McQuay at her baronial home cast Mrs. Juliette Gordon Low's mind to distraction when she should have been concentrating on the operation of the Rauch & Lang as it bounced silently along at the breakneck speed of 25 miles per hour. It had been years since the two had chatted like magpies over tea and cucumber sandwiches. Each playfully blamed the other for abandoning their sisterhood to marriage and travel. Dorothy, a child refugee from tragedy arrived bedraggled, but physically intact at the handsome Savannah, Georgia, Regency house owned by Juliette's parents, William Washington Gordon and Eleanor Kinzie Gordon. Juliette may have had five other siblings whom she adored, but as the road grime was sponged from Dorothy's trembling body and she was fed spirit-raising spoonfuls of spicy gumbo, an immediate intimacy of gab developed between the two. They were inseparable, attending the finest private schools in Virginia together, and traveling farther afield for French school in the bustling city of New York. Headmistresses at these edifices of higher learning applied the wooden ruler more than once to the girls' ruffle-padded backsides for gross violations of quiet study time.

It was while in New York that Dorothy met her beau, the handsome and financially driven Frank McQuay, who spirited her off to Maryland and a life as the idle mistress of an ever-expanding plantation. It is a life well suited to a lady of proper pedigree, privilege, and leisure. "Birth has its rights," Dorothy would comment to Juliette while rebuking a servant for some minor infraction, or for failing to remember his place in the hierarchy of man, not to mention good society.

Sisterly tears were shed upon their greeting embrace on the expansive and meticulously clipped deep green lawn fronting the pillared home. There was delight in their reunion, and sympathy for the loss of Juliette's late husband, William Mackay Low, the wealthy Englishman Juliette married at the matronly age of 26. His death in 1905 left Juliette to drift without purpose about Europe and the British Isles until she met Sir Robert Baden-Powell. He enthralled Juliette with his views of the new youth movement and enlisted her, heart and soul, re-energizing her at age 52.

With unabashed enthusiasm, Juliette explained her new zeal to Dorothy as they took lunch on the second story balcony that overlooked fertile fields recently turned in preparation for planting. Nanna Maude stood quietly in the opening of the French doors. She held a silver tureen of vichyssoise waiting for permission to serve. This epicurean delight was hovered over by Mrs. McQuay to ensure Nanna Maude had properly prepared and chilled it to European specifications.

"It's only cold potato and leek soup," Nanna Maude complained to Roman as he toted ice in from the delivery wagon. "Any ninny can make it."

Dorothy, wearing the latest fashion design, fanned herself on an afternoon that provided its own cooling breeze, did not see Juliette's point. "Why would any lady choose a profession outside the home?" Dorothy asked, patting her lips with an embroidered cloth napkin.

"Women these days need to develop self-reliance and resourcefulness," Juliette responded, her tone polite, and her heart filled with conviction.

"Women maybe, but not for ladies," Dorothy shakes her head dismissively, then shoo's away a pesky fly with her gloved hand, "And to willingly spend time out-of-doors in nature, no, dear cousin. This is as far out-of-doors as I wish to ever be. If I want to experience nature I'll go to a zoo where it's in cages where nature should be."

A late afternoon rain and Dorothy's negativity toward Juliette's new purpose in life dampened the departure. Dorothy even commented that for Juliette to operate an automobile was undignified and embarrassing. But regardless of their differences of opinion, while standing under the protective portico, Juliette hugged her cousin passionately, kissing her cheeks good-bye. As she steered with the tiller of the maroon and black electric car, Juliette watched her cousin, her closest sister, in the rear view mirror. Dorothy waved her handkerchief, then dabbed sincere tears from the corners of her eyes. To Juliette, Dorothy grew smaller, less important, a product of a fading history, becoming inconsequential, soon to be irrelevant. "Change is sweeping the world, and women must be a part of it, or we will always be subjugated, and made an afterthought," Juliette proclaimed aloud while pulling the throttle control lever to full speed. Large drops of rain splattered the windshield as this phone booth of an auto slides on dainty whitewall tires from the long majestic drive of the McQuay's to the worrisome dirt road that gleamed slippery with the accumulated moisture. Juliette flipped on the head lamps of her horseless carriage.

Anna emerges from the path, panting for air, and weighed down by her load. She turns her head left then right, trying to peer up and down the wet, brown ribbon of road, searching for the source of the cries for help. Drizzle keeps her blinking water out of her eyes while wiping her face with a useless wet sleeve. Her hair, black as the night, creates rivulets of chilled water that runs down her neck to invade the Mackinaw, bringing on shivers.

Dark clouds, still pregnant and hanging low, bump apart to provide Anna with a moment of starlight. Up the road 50 paces, in the direction of Havre de Grace, is a large object glimmering askew of the road, leaning awkwardly, half in the drainage ditch dug by field hands employed by Frank McQuay.

"Help me!" screams a woman. "Please...someone."

Arriving out of breath, Anna drops the kerosene and box of shot with a squishy plop in the mud. The sight before her is shocking to the point of hilarity. An old woman, dimly illuminated by flickering beams cast by head lamps, her citified clothes covered in mud. She is flopping around in the ditch that runs with half a foot of dark water, runoff from the field. The owl-wide eyes of this pathetic woman show a panic that no words can describe. The flailing woman looks to Anna as if a dark apparition has come out of the terrifying night to add tortures to her already unbearable plight.

Anna moves into the fading light of the lamps, hoping to calm this hysterical woman, "It's going to be okay. Are you hurt?"

Recognizing this dripping creature as only a young girl, Juliette redirects her fear to the original terror, pointing with trembling fingers toward the half buried front wheel, "Snake!"

Swimming inquisitively between the metal spokes of the sunken front wheel is a three and a half foot long snake. Its dark brown bands are barely discernible in the glow of the head lamps.

"Where?" Anna asks, searching.

"There," Juliette continues to point with one hand while futilely pulling at the muddy bank, attempting to drag herself away from the menacing spawn of Satan.

Anna jumps into the ditch with a splash. She leans closer to the wheel to see what the fuss is all about, and then grabs hold of the snake by its tail. "Got it." Held within the beam of light, its yellow-white belly shimmers, "Just a water snake. It's harmless." Anna presents the snake to Juliette as a present.

"No. No, please. I believe you," Juliette cowers. "Please, just throw it away."

Surprised by such a silly suggestion, Anna swings the snake, whacking its head against the auto's fender, killing it instantly, "That would be a waste. It can be simmered in a stew or cooked on a stick over a fire." Looking closely to confirm the snake is dead; Anna then stuffs it into her pocket.

Cold, wet, sitting in and covered with mud, her new automobile stuck in a ditch, and stranded on a dark and deserted road, Juliette smiles as she asks, "What's your name, dear?"

"Anastasia Nicole Buchanan, but everyone calls me Anna for short. What's yours?"

"I'm Mrs. Juliette Gordon Low, but my friends call me Daisy," she replies, reaching her hands out to Anna for assistance. "Anna, please help an old woman up. I've sprained my ankle."

Anna bends down to allow Juliette to put her arms around her neck, to help her out of the ditch, and to sit on the running board of the Rauch & Lang.

"What happened?" asks Anna.

"It was frightfully awful," Juliette wipes her face with a soiled handkerchief, accomplishing nothing except to redistribute the mud. "I was tooling peaceably along; when out of the darkness a truck loaded with huge barrels came straight for me. Its head lamps were out. Can you imagine such a thing? I swerved to avoid a collision, but lost control on this dreadfully slippery road. Before I could stop, I slid into this ditch. When I got out to check for damage, I twisted my ankle, tumbling quite undignified to lie where you found me. Then that snake appeared." Juliette shudders, wiping her face again. Anna imagines it is quite flushed under all that mud.

"Anna, dear, you are my savior," Juliette hugs Anna affectionately, "but what shall we do now?"

The large imposing drops of rain, gradually turning to drizzle, finally peter out to leave behind a night with a cool breeze that pushes the clouds slowly south into Baltimore County. The clearing sky is crowded with bright stars, better late than never, to provide a ghostly light to replace the one's now dead in the automobile's head lamps. A thousand unseen animals scurry and flutter about the marsh, shaking off water that is coating their insulating fur and feathers. Nature always provides the perfect protective wear for those expected to weather its storms.

Anna gathers sticks and branches, piling them in the shape of a teepee by the side of the road.

"A fire is a nice thought, Anna, but I only have two matches in my bag, and that wood is too wet to ignite." Anna does not reply. She casually opens one of the pouches of black powder, sprinkling the wood liberally. Next, Anna unscrews the cap to the kerosene can to pour a half-cup onto the pile.

"Matches please," asks Anna, holding out her hand.

Juliette hands the matches to Anna who smiles, mischief dancing in her eyes, "By the power vested in me, I command fire to come forth." Anna strikes the match, throwing it flaming onto the damp wood.

Whoosh.

Whumph.

Crackle.

A fireball erupts with the ignition of the powder, followed by the slower burning kerosene that quickly burns away the surface moisture of the wood, leaving a fine cracking fire. Blazing unselfishly, the fire casts warmth in all directions while illuminating the narrow road, the Rauch & Lang, a mud-covered Juliette, and a pleased with herself 12-year-old girl.

"That's superlative work, my dear," Juliette claps her hands with elation, scooting along the running board to edge closer to the flames to better enjoy the heat.

Anna curtsies, "It's nothing really. I learned it from my father." Anna sits down next to Juliette.

"You're very resourceful. Where do you attend school?"

"Mostly right here," Anna indicates the marsh that lies in darkness beyond the firelight. "My father teaches me. I think of him like the principal of an outdoor school, but my mother's friend, Olivia, when she can get hold of me, sends me to the fundamental school in Havre de Grace, but they don't teach anything of real value," and, laughing at herself, "there's nothing *fun* about it."

Juliette marvels at Anna. Here is a young girl, miles from anywhere, traipsing alone, confident, resourceful, self-reliant, maybe a little too homespun in her fashion sense, but practical, and possessing a positive self-image. Anna has all the character traits that embody the spirit and soul of what Sir Robert explained to Juliette that a Girl Guide should be.

"Anna, would you like to be the first member of an American organization called the Girl Guides?"

"What do they do?"

"Basically they do what you do, but they earn proficiency badges for accomplishing tasks such as building fires, treating snake bites, learning how to stop a runaway horse, homemaking skills, and participating in community service projects," Juliette explains with enthusiasm.

"I already know how to do those things."

"That's what is so perfect. You would be an instant role model of what a modern woman can be. I can picture you now, standing in your pressed uniform during meetings, teaching others what you know, and with the membership dues, you'll be able to take trips with the other girls to museums and other places of culture."

Anna's excitement is quashed by the mention of a uniform and membership dues. These are financial extravagancies that she knows are out of reach for her little family, even as she is tempted by the coins she is clutching in her hand within her pocket from today's purchases, and to travel, no. Her father and Beauty need her here in the marsh at the edge of the bay. Here is her place among the critters and fowl.

"I don't think..." Anna begins sheepishly, not embarrassed by her lack of funds, but does not want to disappoint this lady who only wants to help, but may not be aware of the limitations of others.

"It will be wonderful," Juliette continues, "I have a pen and paper somewhere in here." She turns to rummage in her carryall bag. "Yes, here we are. Now, Anna, help me with this. I've been composing what I call the Girl Guide Law. It's what the members will live by, a code of behavior."

Reluctantly, not wanting to be rude, Anna sits beside Juliette making suggestions for a law that other girls, fortunate girls; girls of means and privilege will aspire to live by, a pledge of sorts that Anna finds almost silly. If one is a human being with morals, and any sense of character, these laws are automatic, but maybe, just possibly there are girls who are not lucky enough to have a father like hers to be guided and taught by.

Wiping the caked dirt from the crystal of her diamond watch, Juliette realizes she and Anna have been working on drafts of the law for over an hour, "I believe we've got it. Let me read it to you in its entirety:

THE GIRL GUIDE LAW

> I will do my best:
> to be honest,
> to be fair,
> to help where needed,
> to be cheerful,
> to be friendly and considerate,
> to be a sister to every Girl Guide,
> to respect authority,
> to use resources wisely,
> to protect and improve the world around me,
> to show respect for myself and others
> through my words and action.[21]

I think it's perfect." Juliette hugs Anna again, delighted with their accomplishment. "Now, if you're ready. Raise your right hand to recite the pledge."

"What's going on here?" demands a gruff and slightly accented voice coming from beyond the firelight's reach.

Juliette stares into the darkness. She is a doe caught in the gun sight of a hungry woodsman. There is nowhere to run—nowhere to hide. Juliette

---

21 Girl Scouts of the U.S.A.: *Highlights in Girl Scouting 1912-1991*. The Girl Scout Law.

freezes, pupils dilating. Anna's smooth forehead furrows with wrinkled annoyance. Familiar with this harassing voice, she leans in close to Juliette, and whispers, "It's the duck police."

The long brown head of a tired-eyed gelding, its mouth frothy from exertion, enters the glow of the fire, followed by its middle-aged rider. Juliette relaxes, seeing a uniform of a governmental agency, pinned with a gleaming badge that is worn by the diminutive rider. Juliette's pleased that reinforcements have arrived. Standing off balance on her injured ankle, Juliette smooths her wrinkled and soiled dress to properly address the man.

"I'm Mrs. Juliette Gordon Low. As you can plainly see, I've had a mishap while returning from a visit with my cousin Mrs. Dorothy Parker McQuay. Are you acquainted with the McQuays?"

Anna is surprised, and a bit confused. *Juliette is related to Mrs. McQuay?* They are so different, however, Juliette is frightened by everything, and the plush interior of the automobile she is operating resembles a miniature red velvet sitting room for ladies, which screams, look at me. I've got money. *Hmm, Juliette seems so kind, caring, and charming, even covered in mud.* Anna decides to give Juliette the benefit of the doubt, admitting to herself that the entire bloodline of the McQuay's may not necessarily be bad.

Smartly dismounting, standing eye-to-eye with Juliette, and careful to extend every courtesy to this mud-caked woman who is apparently related to a man of distinction and influence, he offers his hand, after removing his calf skin riding gloves, "It is a pleasure, Mrs. Low. I'm Game Warden Felipe LeCompte at your service."

Anna crosses her arms and gives LeCompte the best stink-eye she is capable of, wondering how this pudgy lickspittle[22] keeps his uniform and boots dry and spotless through a rainstorm. If she did not already have enough reasons to hate him, his immaculate grooming and attire in comparison to her manginess would be reason enough to start.

"As you can see," Juliette begins, "my auto is stuck, and unfortunately even if we could right it, the batteries have lost their charge, so it will not move of its own accord."

"Hmm...This is quite a predicament," LeCompte acknowledges.

"Yes, but blessedly I have had the company of this dear child. Anna, this is..." LeCompte turns his attention to the dark haired girl in the Mackinaw coat, recognizing her immediately, "Ah, yes, Miss Buchanan," rudely interrupting Juliette, feeling the need to inform her of who exactly she is associating with. "She, Mrs. Low, is the daughter of a local criminal."

---

22 Lickspittle. Slang. A contemptible fawning person. A kiss-ass toward authority figures.

"My father's not a criminal," Anna cries, rising quickly to her feet, fists clenched in defiance and rage.

"And what are those?" LeCompte points to the pouches and rain-soaked box.

"Powder and shot. Nothing illegal about 'em," Anna stands firm.

"No, they're not in their present form, but in the way your father puts them to use, they are."

"They're put to use to feed people."

"So you admit your father is an outlaw hunter, shooting for the market?" LeCompte presses Anna, itching for a confession he can use later in court.

"Mr. LeCompte, I don't think this is the time, or place, for an interrogation," Juliette attempts to come to Anna's defense, uncomfortable with her distress.

"I beg your pardon, Mrs. Low. Seeing how you are unaware of whom you've associated yourself with, I can understand your good intentions to protect this child, but it's better if I deal with her."

Anna, knowing she has let her tongue get the best of her, and possibly endangering her father, she seizes the opportunity to skedaddle while LeCompte and Juliette converse. Picking up the pouches, shot box, and kerosene can, Anna dashes past LeCompte to vanish into the darkness of the marsh.

Seeing Anna flee, Juliette calls out to her, "Anna, wait."

"Let her go, Mrs. Low," LeCompte attempts to calm Juliette. "It's better for all. You don't want to entangle yourself with people of her ilk. Now, let's see what's to be done to right your vehicle, and a fine one at that, if I may say so."

Warden LeCompte walks around to the submerged wheel, studying the dilemma. Juliette, despondent over losing her first recruit for the Girl Guides, limps to the far side of the road to squint into an eerie world possessed of animal sounds: hoots, croaks, soft whistles, rustling in the underbrush, flutters among the tree limbs, and cloaking a darling of a girl.

"If I had a rope I could tie my horse to your automobile and drag it free," LeCompte calls from across the road.

From the recesses of the path leading into the marsh, Juliette detects Anna's soft voice, "Tell him to use a branch and a rock."

"You mean a lever and fulcrum? Brilliant," Juliette whispers back, pleased that her first impression of Anna was correct.

"Yes. And Daisy, call them Girl Scouts. It sounds more adventurous."

The mud drying at the corners of Juliette's mouth cracks with her widening grin as she admits to herself, *what a terrific suggestion,* and then asks the game warden, "Mr. LeCompte, is her father truly a criminal?"

"I don't say he is. It's the law that makes him one," LeCompte removes his cap to scratch the short, oiled-back hairs on his head, unable to figure a solution to Juliette's problem. "And where would we be without the law?"

Juliette remains standing on the road, her weight on her good ankle. On one side, the order of plowed fields and her modern conveyance mired in muck. It has produced a rigid enforcer of laws. On the other side is the chaos of nature that contains a bewildering, and to her a frightening environment. It has produced a gifted and fascinating child.

Warden LeCompte walks up next to Juliette as she continues to gaze into the darkness. He pulls on his gloves, "I suppose he is feeding his family."

Juliette is relieved that a man of Game Warden LeCompte's unwavering view of the infallibility of the law may allow, though hidden within himself, a private sympathy for a father providing for his family. She turns to this scrupulous man, and sweet as cherry pie, asks, "Do you suppose your horse can carry two?"

- 1912 -

Clay sits at a scarred and oiled oak table late in the evening in Tavern Bouvard. He is surrounded by Olivia, Doctor Webster, Pastor Isaac Davies, the lighthouse keeper Henry O'Neill, several other townsfolk, and market hunters. The group edge close to Clay in stunned silence as he reads solemnly from an EXTRA!!! edition handed to him by the typesetter of the Havre de Grace *Republican*, a frantic man whose fingers were stained black with printer's ink.

TRAGEDY AT SEA!

April 16, 1912: The unsinkable sank. White Star's luxury steamer the *Titanic* struck an iceberg during the night while on its maiden voyage from London to New York. Calm seas belied the danger of a record-setting speed run across the Atlantic. Survivors plucked from the icy waters report from the rescue ship *Carpathia*, panic among *Titanic's* passengers when it was discovered there weren't enough lifeboats. One man, who kept his wits, John Harper, a Baptist minister, was seen running up and down the decks urging people to allow women, children, and the unsaved into the lifeboats. Once in the frigid water, dying himself, he still tried to bring others to salvation before they perished.

The death toll is expected to exceed 1,500 unfortunate souls. Some of the notables lost to Davy Jones' locker include Colonel Astor, Mr. & Mrs. Straus, and Washington Roebling II. An official inquiry has begun into this maritime disaster, but it will have to go forward without Captain Edward J. Smith's insight. Keeping with navel tradition, the good captain, with a previously unblemished seafaring record, stood faithful at the wheel to go down with his ship.

A sad irony is the captain's pre-sailing statement that this would be his final voyage.

A somber mood has draped itself over those who had come in for a few laughs and a momentary escape from life's difficulties.

"A toast. On the house for the living and the dead," Olivia announces, trying to break the morbid spell.

"A toast," Pastor Davies agrees, adding. "There's a lesson here. All the money and notoriety in the world couldn't save them folks. Only Jesus provides eternal life."

Olivia pours shots of rattle-belly pop all around.

"Hold the lemonade, dear," O'Neill asks, "but you may double the whiskey if you'd like." He winks with a mischievous eye.

"A man," Pastor Davies looks around the room while holding up his glass, then acknowledges Olivia, "and a woman must be sure they are right with God, and their fellow man, because when the sickle man comes a-calling, he rarely comes to bargain."

"That's the truth of it," Doctor Webster slurs, being piffled.[23]

Snickers and guffaws escape many mouths of the men who are witness to the uncommon condition that Doctor Webster has allowed himself. Each man believes he knows the tongue lashing Doctor Webster subjects himself to from Mrs. Webster who probably claims she is only looking out for everyone's best interests. "Think of the town," she's likely to argue. "What if someone needs medical attention? You're in no condition to help."

Unknown to the men is Doctor Webster's sure-fire, never fail, tried-and-true response. He gathers his adoring wife into his thick arms and speaks the words: "Martha, you are not only a fine and caring woman," planting a lip-to-lip lengthy kiss, "but the finest skirt north or south of the Mason-Dixon line."

"You're not that well traveled, and just because we live south of the Mason-Dixon doesn't mean the south will rise tonight," is Martha's playful response, feigning annoyance with a tease of schoolgirl innocence. Her pulse races, seeing the wanton desire in her husband's amorous eyes as her flesh flushes pink with the needy grope of his unusually clumsy hands.

"Oops...too late."

Husband and wife retire to their marriage bed, laughing with an excitement that will be sated before the first morning birds begin their sweet sunrise song.

---

23 Piffled. Slang. Half-drunk.

"To the living and in remembrance of the dead," Clay toasts.

"To the living and in remembrance of the dead," all gathered within Tavern Bouvard toast, and then swallow down the harsh liquid.

Life, with its difficulties goes on.

The disturbance that began in Constable Jenkins' office has moved to the sedate chambers of Judge Jeremiah P. Hathaway.

Judge Hathaway had been steeping tea and admiring through his second story window, a morning whose sky was painted by a God who cared about the details. A descendant of Quakers from the Eastern shore, the judge is an unassuming man who keeps God foremost in his daily activities, especially when contemplating punishments for violations of the civil peace. The case before him is a drunk who has thrown a rock through a store window during the night. The accused defense was that a bug-eyed monster was staring at him, attempting to steal his soul. The representative for the People, and a personal friend of the victimized spectacle-store owner, passionately demanded a harsh sentence and full compensation. He emphasized each word by pounding his fist into the palm of his other hand, always the crusader for justice. This same prosecutor, two minutes ago was standing in the judge's chambers begging for leniency for the faded boogie. His Honor listened without remark to the Janus[24] prosecutor, not appreciating the use of the deprecating slang for a Negro informant.

"He serves a useful purpose," was the prosecutor's bottom line.

Judge Hathaway cared little for men who bartered information to bend the law to their favor, or for the officials who assisted them, justifying the means for the ends. Equity is what the courts stand for. If they do not, they will fall, along with the society it supposes to judge. Restitution would be the obvious answer, but for the defendant being penniless. Jail time in lieu of financial compensation solves nothing. The store owner is left with a broken window, although privately the judge agreed that the window painting of the giant eyes wearing glasses was a least monstrous, at worst, soul sucking, and the public coffers would have to sustain the man while incarcerated.

The American form of *juris prudence* is based on England's Common Law and it is based on common sense, though everyone agrees that good sense is not common.

---

24 Janus. The Roman god of gates that is represented with two faces looking in opposite directions. Two-faced, double-dealing.

His Honor scans the shelves of leather bound law books looking for precedent. None call to him. He turns back to the window where at the notice of the congregation of agitated men approaching along Pennington Avenue toward the courthouse, a familiar and ever-correct voice of his deceased wife speaks her gentle words of guidance: "What would Jesus do?"

"Now there was a man of good and common sense," the judge speaks aloud as he blows to cool his steaming cup of tea. The answer is simple, equitable, and logical. The defendant will work for the store owner at a fair wage, half of which will be deducted until the cost of replacing the window is paid. The store owner is made whole. The defendant, his wife, and children are not left destitute, and the coffers of the community are not taxed.

The offended men shattering Judge Hathaway's refuge are arguing among themselves, demanding action from the perpetually sweating constable, who is presently out of breath from lugging his obese body up the flight of stairs. Each man vies to be heard by the judge who is the calm eye of the storm. Wishing for his gavel that rests on the courtroom bench to bring chaos to order, his Honor is reduced to raising his voice. This is an act rarely observed, and to the judge, a vile recourse, a symptom of failed communication.

"One at a time," Judge Hathaway looks to the trembling man not shouting, but obviously in the most distress. "Mr. Weiss, would you please be kind enough to explain the reason for this riot?"

Unaccustomed to and preferring to travel through life in anonymity, the owner of Havre de Grace's State Theater timidly steps forward. He has learned from an unkind history that to stick one's neck out, to be front and center, usually results in being the first to be singled out and made an example of by one despot or another. Fortunately, he has heard only kind remarks regarding this judge. Respectfully removing his cotton cap, squeezing and nervously fingering the brim, his bald pate covered only by a white yarmulke and gray side locks, Mr. Weiss speaks with difficulty as his mouth is dry as cotton, "I've been...I mean to say, we've been swindled."

Again, the undisciplined chorus erupts with each man wanting to give his account of the fraud.

"Gentleman!" cries the judge. "We are not making progress in this fashion. What is it you wish of me?"

"A warrant sworn out for the arrest of Charles A. Pryor," says Constable Jenkins.

"I'm not familiar with that name. What is his alleged offense?"

Constable Jenkins flips through his pocket pad searching for the correct notes that he had jotted down while first being assaulted by these men who pay his salary, "It appears that Mr. Pryor, who is a journalist and filmmaker of some repute, had recently returned from interviewing and filming survivors of the *Titanic* disaster. He approached Mr. Weiss to offer him a firsthand exclusive newsreel that included someone dubbed the Unsinkable Molly Brown."[25]

"For $500," Mr. Weiss interjects, "but I didn't have that much money on hand."

"Who does?" his Honor sympathizes, always living frugal within his civil servant salary.

"It seems," the constable continues, "that Mr. Weiss approached these other gentlemen, offering a percentage of the ticket receipts if they'd be willing to syndicate the $500 advance fee."

"Which they did, and Mr. Pryor accepted, signing this agreement," Mr. Weiss simpers, "but on the scheduled date for showing, no newsreel was delivered."

"And Mr. Pryor seems to be in the wind, your Honor," Constable Jenkins concludes.

Judge Hathaway removes a document from his desk, writing in the pertinent information, "What is the date of the agreement?"

"May 15th, your Honor," answers Mr. Weiss, slowly moving backward, wishing to blend into the background.

Gratefully accepting the signed warrant for arrest in the name of Charles A. Pryor on one count of larceny by deception, Constable Jenkins, thinking this man is obviously not a credit to his journalistic profession, ushers out the wronged, but mollified men, and apologizes for disturbing the judge's peace.

Adjusting his 60-year-old body in his deeply padded leather chair, Judge Jeremiah P. Hathaway sips a tea that has gone cold. He ponders the question that has eluded an answer for all of time: *Why don't men consider the suffering of their victims when they commit criminal acts?* There are always consequences.

---

25 Brown, Margaret Tobin. "The Unsinkable Molly Brown" was anything but the boisterous rough-around-the-edges tomboy of the Broadway musical. Called "Maggy" never "Molly" by her friends, she was a dedicated suffragette, a staff writer for the Denver Times, helped to establish a separate juvenile justice system in Colorado, and received the French Legion of Honor for her relief work after WWI. She died October 26, 1932 in New York of a cerebral hemorrhage.

Grinning like a skunk eating stink beetles, Delbert is in his element as he splashes knee deep in sucking muck within a forest of towering cattails. The legs of his coverall are rolled up in a meager and futile attempt to keep them clean. Delbert's only view is straight up to an afternoon sky that reminds him of a placid pond with clouds in the shape of spatterdock lilies. Hearing the lapping water on the unseen sandy shore, he calculates he is within a stone's throw of the bay. Through trial and error, Delbert knows he is in the area with the proper ratios of fresh to salt water that will produce the tastiest stalk hearts. Those that he does not eat now he will carry home in the burlap sack slung over his shoulder for ma's salad.

Creating their own wind as they swirl above Delbert's head, and leaping from brown stalk to brown stalk are wave upon wave of chattering red-winged blackbirds crying, oak-a-lee! A few are annoyed by the young teen's invasion into their domain, but most ignore his passing. The majority of the males are busy showing off their bright red shoulder patches and buff gold chevrons in the attempt to impress females. It is a waste of strutting and posturing because the ladies are preoccupied with gossiping, specifically passing on the locations which contain the fattest grubs, caterpillars, worms, and insects, all delicacies to strengthen feathered bodies prior to selecting a preening mate, and the production of eggs.

Delbert grasps a chosen stalk at the base of its 12-foot structure. He pulls gently, but firmly, his feet sinking deeper until the telltale sucking, almost a slurping, that signals the cattail's release from its tentative grip within the mud. As the stalk is agitated by its uprooting, the swollen spike at the top bursts. Bright yellow pollen floats down to cover Delbert in rich gold. *You're such a dim-whittle at times,* Delbert chuckles, musing at his failure to bring along a tight weave bag to collect the pollen to add to flour for golden pancakes, his ma's specialty. Gazing up to examine the wealth contained at the top of each stalk, Delbert smiles. Being forever the pragmatic marsh man, and not wasting time, energy, or worrisome thoughts on what he does not have, he returns to the tasty task at hand.

Being unable to sit due to the tightly packed stalks surround him, Delbert leans back, creating a comfortable lounge chair to support his weight and to relax as he peels back the leaves to expose the tender white heart. Lacking flowing water that is clear of suspended soil particles to rinse the few specks of mud clinging to the heart, Delbert brushes it as clean as muddy fingers are capable before biting down. A crunchy and mild, somewhat cucumber taste fills his mouth. *There is nothing I can imagine that would be more enjoyable at this moment,* he thinks while wiggling his backside against the stalks supporting him to create an even more comfortable living chair, *except maybe to share this snack with Anna.* Taking another bite and closing his cyes, "And maybe a pinch of salt." Pieces of cattail heart spit from his mouth as he laughingly speaks aloud his small desire for company and a bit of spice. All the while, the late May sun, a relaxing sun, a gleaming yellow sun that can coax idleness from the most industrious lad works its tranquilizing magic. Its shimmering rays massage Delbert into resting for only a moment, to take a catnap, to count to 50 winks, but only once or twice, maybe three times.

Oak-a-lee...oak-a-lee, does not disturb Delbert who sleeps snug within the cattails' embrace. His legs sunk deep in five-toe squishy mud that is warmed by the passing of a long afternoon. The red-winged blackbirds' calls are not a continuation of their intra-species chatter, but a warning from many alert eyes to one who possesses only two...if he were using them.

The blackbirds tried.

The danger is moving among the stalks.

The blackbirds warned.

Delbert's snores attract the danger.

The blackbirds flee saddened by having to leave one unaware.

Sweat trickles down Delbert's forehead from the heat and humidity.

The blackbirds fly; self-preservation.

If Delbert's eyes had opened, the sweat would be from fear.

The danger slowly wraps around his leg.

Clay exits the Bank of Baltimore. His yearly meeting with the mortgage holder of his property went well. Payments have been on time and any surplus has dutifully, per Clay's instruction, been used to purchase interest-bearing bonds that are guaranteed by the government. "The future is uncertain," the banker warns. "It's always wise to hedge your bets." Clay's friendly response each year is the same, "I don't gamble with money." And the banker's playful retort was expected, "Clay, life is a roll of heavenly dice. We all gamble whether we like it or not." The men shake hands, wishing each other a good day. High overhead an engine sputters, and then roars back to life, regaining power. Clay shades his eyes from the glare of the afternoon sun to view a fragile monoplane performing daring loops and breath-taking dives. *Now that's gambling*, he thinks as he strides to a nearby field packed with gawkers.

Somewhere within the hundreds of awe-struck, neck-craning spectators is Anna. Hearing from a passerby on the street in front of the bank that the pilot of the wood, wire, and cloth-covered aircraft is a woman, caused

Anna's interest to instantly turn from the practicalities of finance to a fancy unimaginable.

"The pilot's a woman?!" cried Anna to her father. "Can I go watch? Please, father."

Using Anna's enthusiasm as an excuse to give in to his curiosity of the flying machines, Clay acquiesced, "All right, but don't get into any trouble. I'll meet you there after my business is concluded."

Anna was off and running, lickety-split, before Clay finished his sentence.

Squeezing through the crowd of men, women, and children, Clay alternates looking for Anna and watching the tiny airplane twist and turn overhead.

"Whoa!" cries an elderly man; his wobbly grip on his cane handle is as if he is the passenger, dizzy with each spin and tumble.

"Oh my!" gasps a lady holding a folded parasol, her knuckles white within her gloves with a mixture of fear and excitement.

"Wow!" escapes from the mouths of many awed spectators who have heard of these flying machines, but thought them to be fanciful dreams, the story of the Wright brothers and their Flyer I being a hoax.

Clay overhears an envious comment from a young Negress who is standing in front of him, her gaze skyward as she unintentionally blocks his way. "That lucky girl," she says, apparently to a Negro man who could be her older brother. This comment, for some unexplained reason prickles Clay's skin. His full attention is focused on the rickety plane as it streaks low over the crowd. Its wooden propeller grabbing at the air as the engine roars while puffs of oily smoke trail from behind. The wings flex, the wire struts strain as the pilot rolls the plane over onto its back, upside-down. To Clay's horror, streaming from the seat behind the goggled pilot is the long black hair...of...his...DAUGHTER!

Rushing roughly past and knocking the Negro woman to the ground, Clay races forward. The Negro man who has never become accustomed to the rude behavior of whites, bristles, wanting to lash out, but restrains himself by reaching down to help his sibling back to her feet. "You okay, Bessie?"

Unfazed, wearing a thousand-foot stare, imagining herself, not as a passenger of the spirited plane, but the pilot. This is who this part African, part Indian from a poor family from a small Texas town was referring to when she said, "That lucky girl."

"I'm fine," Bessie says, dusting off her knees as she resumes flying, even if for the moment it is only vicariously. Then, softer, not realizing she spoke aloud, she whispers her dream, "That's going to be me."

Bessie's brother, who has been kept in his place longer than his sister, suffering the disappointments of denials and rejections, all based on the color of his skin, even after moving north, scoffs, "Yeah, you will. Right after they make you queen, Bessie."

Bessie Coleman,[26] at the age of 20, does not hear her brother. Her ears are deaf to what she cannot do. She has picked cotton and washed clothes for pennies, she has walked more than four miles each way to school every day in her hunger for knowledge, and now her head is in the clouds. She vows, if she has to cross oceans and travel the world, she will hold the aviator's stick in her hand...a hand that already vibrates with the pumping pistons and spinning propeller.

A soul-piercing scream from above stops Clay's heart.

Delbert cradles his swelling hand. Tears roll down his cheeks. He knows the only creature that heard his scream is a great blue heron that was disturbed while spearing fish for its afternoon snack along the edge of the bay. Its response is to take to the air to find a more tranquil spot. Delbert watches the elegant though indifferent bird with knobby knees fly overhead, taking with it the knowledge that he is in peril.

It was only a feeling, a small intrusion into Delbert's slumber. Real or dreamed, it was not worth waking for, but the thing around his thigh bothered Delbert's subconscious. Oak-a-lees were tuned out as were the occasional buzzing of wondering bees and the dragonflies that hungrily pursued them.

Brush the thing away, was the instruction Delbert's mind gave to his hand, a hand that rested comfortably on his plump stomach with a half-eaten heart held gently in his fingers.

The fangs that punctured the skin of his palm were painful, but watching his bleeding hand swell, invaded by deadly poison is excruciating. The angry copperhead slithers away between the cattail stalks, not once glancing back to concern itself with the aftermath of its reaction to a boy's touch. Delbert's mind tumbles over the imminent and life threatening problems and the too few solutions.

The poison—a problem.

A racing heart—a problem.

Far from home—a problem.

---

26 Coleman, Bessie (1892-1926). First woman to earn an International Aviation License and the world's first black aviator.

Caged within cattail bars—a problem.

No help—a serious problem.

Get to the bay—the only solution.

Life begins and ends with the Great Chesapeake Bay. Above and below the water, its animals, its fowl, its fishes, thousands of species thrive and live. This is what the loud and desperate voice in Delbert's head repeats—*LIVE*.

For over 200 miles the bay's edges fold, wrinkle, crease, and crinkle with coves, sloughs, and oxbows. If symmetry was wanted, if nature preferred rigidity, God could snap the Chesapeake into straight lines, though its shore would measure in excess of 8,000 miles. Delbert pleads, begging aloud to whatever power there may be for only a few feet of precious shoreline. Maybe a passing boat can be signaled.

Maybe...

Delbert lifts with strong thighs to extricate his pudgy legs from the muck. Not a sucking sound is heard. Only the sloshing of black water as his muscles contract and relax. Warm salty water coats his legs and acts as a thin membrane between skin and mud. Skin that is renewed every few months from its original formation 13 years ago within the womb of a marsh woman versus mud deposited grain by grain for thousands of years. Young skin designed to slough and scrape away versus ancient mud designed to hold and absorb that which passes its way.

The snakebite brought fear.

Caught, trapped, and betrayed by the element Delbert so loves, brings on hysteria.

Dizzy with a thrill that is beyond the moon and stars, all Anna can do is shake her head and scream with delight as the ground and crowd streak past below her, a blur of colors, clothes, faces, and cheering voices. Her eyes stream tears from wind created by propeller wash and an air speed Anna believes no mortal can possibly survive for too long. This physical excitement is only half her joy because *Harriet Quimby*[27] *is a woman!* Laughing between screams, Anna realizes that this woman whom she was told is the first licensed pilot in the United States is a perfect example of what her mother meant when she said: "Shoot for the stars, and if you only reach the moon, you're still out of this world."

A woman can do anything, Anna now knows this to be fact.

---

27 Quimby, Harriet (1875-1912) America's first licensed pilot and the first woman to solo across the English Channel.

Halfway across the open field used as a takeoff and landing strip, Anna sees a man in a coverall break from the crowd. He is charging the ground-skimming plane like the madman of ancient times who battled windmills. Waving his arms, he is shouting something unintelligible at the plane, or is it directed at her, maybe at the pilot?

Harriet Quimby, a veteran of numerous air shows, is use to mobs crowding around after she has landed, but seeing the man run out in front of her plane as it races full throttle is surely the act of a lunatic. Pulling sharply back on the control stick as her feet manipulate the rudder pedals, the nimble plane leaps up, over, and around the idiot who is still shouting, a cigarette somehow stuck in the corner of his mouth.

The shouted words are indiscernible, scrambled by the turbulent air. Anna's ears fail her, but her eyes send the distressing signals to her brain with clear understanding, as she recognizes her father to be the crazy man who is waving and shouting.

"It's my father," Anna shouts with a catching breath above the engine's whine

"It's obvious that he'd like a word or two with us. I'd better set her down."

"Can't we keep flying?"

Harriet laughs a deep hearty laugh, understanding a girl's apprehension at the thought of an angry father, "It's always better to face the turbulence head on."

Fighting the mud only intensifies its steel grip on his entombed legs.

Calm. Be calm, Delbert begs of himself, his thoughts running wild. *Struggling raises the heart rate...the poison will circulate faster.* Twisting the burlap sack around his wrist in an attempt to form a remedial tourniquet, Delbert leans back against the stalks to force himself to relax and think clearly. He smacks his lips, but feels nothing as they are numb, and his mouth is dry as he wishes for a cool drink, though he does not believe there is enough water in the world to quench his thirst—*the poison is moving swiftly.*

With his uninjured hand, Delbert scoops a handful of mud away from his trapped legs. Black water quickly fills the void. The water contains sediment but not sludge. *This might work,* encouraging himself as the race will be to the most determined.

Quickly circulating poison versus a slow hand...*be calm, deliberate, one scoop at a time.*

Refusing to acknowledge the fear that grips his body, Clay releases the energy in the form of anger. He runs alongside the flimsy airplane as it comes to a bouncing stop on the grass.

"What the hell do you think you're doing?" Clay shouts.

Spectators cheer and crowd around the airplane to touch the magic that is the fabric-coated wings giving lift and to feel the glass-smooth propeller that pulls the craft skyward. Tiny puffs of blue smoke drift from the ticking engine as drops of oil leak from a cylinder to vaporize on the glowing hot manifold.

Anna unbuckles her seatbelt and timidly, stalling as long as she can, begins to climb out of the passenger seat as Harriet double checks the shutdown procedure—safety first.

"I'm sorry, father," Anna begins.

Clay snatches Anna off the airplane, setting her forcefully down on the ground. Envious and awe-inspired spectators clap Anna on her back, clasp her hand for a quick shake, and congratulate her for her daring bravery.

"I can't expect a child to always act sensibly," Clay responds, the smoke around his head is not from the hand-rolled, but his burning incense, and not the sweet-smelling spice stick, at Anna's reckless behavior. For an instant Clay considers the corrective value of a switch liberally applied to his daughter's backside.

Anna is crushed by her father's use of *child* in referring to her. She would have preferred a sharp slap across the face, or a whoopin' as Delbert calls it, but she knows her father would never hit her. This knowledge is more of a puzzle than a relief, because harsh words from a beloved parent can do damage that will sting the soul and remain long after a purple bruise heals.

Harriet extricates herself from the confined space she believes is inappropriately named, *the cockpit,* though she will admit her joy after each flight makes her want to crow. Jumping down into the waiting arms of the cheering crowd, Harriet removes her leather helmet and bug-smeared goggles, and then steps toward the enraged man clearly abusing his cowed daughter.

"Excuse me, sir," Harriet interjects.

Clay rounds on the pilot with a building fury, but before a caustic syllable can leave his mouth, it is swallowed whole to reform itself to fit his chauvinism, "You're really a woman."

"I'm pleased that your powers of observation are keen. As this fact is out in the open we can summarily dispense with it," Harriet states without a hint of sarcasm. "Now to your concern. If your daughter being on board during the demonstration has alarmed you, I'm very sorry, and I do apologize," Harriet grins at Anna who melts in admiration. Clay stares down at this diminutive woman with her chipmunk cheeks and chestnut doe eyes that drip with sincerity. His over-the-top anger dissolves to allow Clay to reveal the core cause of his distress, "Isn't flying extremely dangerous?"

With her disarming smile filled with pearl white teeth, Harriet steps close to Clay, invading his personal space to evoke a feeling of intimacy despite the throng surrounding them, "Mr. Buchanan. Clay, is it?" Clay nods in affirmation. "Clay, I'm a licensed pilot who has passed many rigorous tests. I'm bound by oath and profession to uphold the highest standards of safety, but adding to that I'm also a human being, and a woman who cherishes life. I would never place a precious young woman in jeopardy," Harriet emphasizes the words young woman for Anna's benefit and a gentle reminder to Clay. "A flight in my aircraft is as safe as playing in one's own backyard."

Clay considers Harriet's remarks, obviously sincere and from her heart, "Miss Quimby...Harriet?" Clay leans in close to Harriet's cheek as if to kiss her, then whispers, "That's what I was afraid of."

Standing back from the crowd, alone with their thoughts, Bessie and her brother contemplate their futures. Bessie licks her full lips, anticipating the sweet desserts, the white cotton candy that flying among the clouds will bring. Her brother's heart breaks, knowing it is inevitable that like his own dreams, Bessie's will crash and burn. The only question is whether she will survive the fall. He spits, the bitter taste never quite leaving his mouth.

The lumpy pile of mud next to Delbert's hip grows with each labored handful. His thighs and knees drown in a pool of black water, but they are free of the mud. Delbert can wiggle each leg back and forth with the hope of some future release, but his attempts to lift them are met with a vacuum that holds him firmly in place.

Beyond the wall of cattail stalks are resident ducks feeding along the water's edge. They may be unseen, but Delbert clearly hears their greedy gulping of corn kernels left by a hunter illegally baiting, and their splashing as they dip their heads beneath the surface to nibble on tender grass shoots. Why some fowl fly hundreds or thousands of miles in migration and others stay the year-round, is at this moment a strange curiosity to Delbert when his survival is on the line, but in his delirium, thoughts come and go, priorities are skewed. It makes sense to stick around to enjoy the bountiful food sources that bloom with the spring, summer, and fall seasons, forgoing the long, arduous, and dangerous journey. Delbert believes that if he were a fowl he would stay happily in the Flats year-round. Choking on his words, "If I were a duck I could fly home." Tears flow afresh as he tries to breathe deeply, but a sharp pain, a constriction grips his chest.

Contemptuous of man's failings, fowl of all species will dine contentedly in the company of the dying, so long as the afflicted pass into the hereafter quietly.

Decorum must be maintained at the dinner table.

The bay's dark water churns white with spray flying off the *Emma Giles'* powerful side-wheels. A wake of fine mist is left by the ship's passage. Tiny rainbows dance within each drop, catching, and magnifying the last light from the sun whose day's work is done. On its northbound passage from Baltimore to Havre de Grace, the *Emma Giles* carries a plethora of cargo; staples for milling, pig iron for smelting, textile fiber suitable for spinning into yarn, and crates of chickens stacked head high, their incessant clucking destined for the pot. Its human cargo varies in appearance, occupation, and financial status as is evident by the level of comfort and accommodation supplied by the captain for their passage.

A shoeless family of five whose dinner consists of yesterday's bread sits together on the starboard side of the open upper deck. The three little ones fidget in the arms of a mother whose leathered skin and gaunt features of a woman of 45 belie her true age of 22. Time is not measured by a clock for this family, but by empty bellies, hard labor, and deprivation. The father stands over his family, silent, and looking forward into an uncertain future, he still has hope that it will be kinder. He only needs one good break to turn around what has been an unending series of misfortunes and disappointments.

Directly below, in one of four posh suites capable of sleeping six, another man of the street, Wall Street, swirls his glass of port, relaxing after a seven-course meal. To prevent indigestion of the mind or stomach, families like the one above are kept from his sight, though they are invisible to him anyway.

After a brief sermon on safe conduct by Clay, he and Anna boarded the homebound vessel. Though content, Clay suffered a brief shiver as he stepped aboard the vessel that nearly ate him as a midnight snack. Father and daughter's stalwart relationship remained intact. Anna beams, her lips chapped, and her cheeks burn a rosy red from the wind that her mind still feels buffeting them. Clay's fears are allayed with his daughter's feet solidly on the ground, and admittedly he is slightly amused as it is clear her experience with Harriet Quimby will keep her mind in the clouds for some time to come.

Chamber music, being played by a traveling quartet that has positioned themselves on the fantail of the middle deck, draws Anna's attention. She and Clay are leaning on the port railing of the upper deck, marveling at the colors, too numerous to count, that make up the sunset as the day transitions to night. Walking toward the stairs as she is following the sound of music, Anna notices the squirming children; their sunken eyes and bony frames resemble skeletons. Anna stares, not meaning to be rude, as her heartstrings are tugged to generosity. Her fingers jostle the handful of lemon balls that her father purchased for her from a vendor on the dock. It was a kind gesture, an overt act, a physical something, not a hug, or sentimental words, which is in line with his character when reestablishing harmony.

Without a second thought, Anna walks toward the ragged family, removing a handful of lemon balls to share with the children. The mother's tired eyes widen with worry. The hungry children gaze up expectantly. The father's expression hardens. Instinctively, Clay grasps Anna's arm to forestall her, and prevent an unpleasant scene.

"Anna, let's go downstairs."

"But I want to give this candy to them."

Clay lowers his voice, "Sometimes pride mistakes kindness for pity." He glances between Anna and the destitute family. "Wait here," he tells Anna as he casually hooks his thumbs into the loops of his coverall, then strolls over to the man who stands protective in front of his family. The men converse and shake hands. Clay motions Anna over and introductions are made. The father instructs his children to take only one lemon ball each. The mother reminds them to say thank you. Garbled words of appreciation are heard as the lemon balls are stuffed into each mouth.

Descending the stairs to the middle deck fantail, Anna is mystified, "I don't get it. What did you say to the man so he'd let me give his children the candy?"

"In his eyes you were a stranger pitying his family."

"I only wanted to share. I thought they'd like some."

"Why?"

"Because they didn't have any."

"Exactly. They didn't have any. It's offensive to a man to have a stranger provide for his family that which he cannot do himself."

"But what did you say to him?"

"I introduced myself. We spoke of the drudgery of travel, the pleasant music, and I asked him if he was of the mind to help out a friend of mine. I know that Madison's father is in need of hands at his dairy. I told him to ask for Robert Mitchell."

"Anna's cross-eyed expression upon reaching the main deck speaks to her continued confusion, "So you to told him where he can find a job?"

"No. I asked him if he would help out a friend. There is a difference. The man's pride remains intact. He sees an income forthcoming that will allow him to provide that which you are now only sharing."

Slowly nodding her head as the subtleties take hold, Anna replies, "Pride is a silly thing."

"Pride is many things but rarely is it silly."

On this gentle night at the end of a wondrous day, Anna's only irritant is the pungent smoke from her father's cigarette. Her only concern is his stifled cough. Both are soothed away by the dancing notes from the strings of Mozart's concerto. Anna leans back against the railing, her head lolling back with eyes closed. The fresh smell of the bay, the soft thrum of the engines underfoot, the music lifting her soul, and the warmth of her father as she leans against him—nothing could be better. Then opening her eyes, Anna watches as the God of Heaven flicks on the lights to distant planets. They sparkle brightly as if just for her.

Shafts of starlight stabbing between the tall stalks carve Delbert into segments. Night sounds, so familiar, usually comforting, are ignored as are the voracious mosquitoes drawing their own doom in Delbert's blood. He lies on his side, propped against the cattail stalk chair that finally collapsed under his weight. His muscles quiver from the poison's destructive effect. He is unsure if the contradictory smile within his mind is correctly formed on his face.

It's the music.

...so beautiful.

...so serene.

...so calming.

Delbert's joy is based upon one of two assumptions reached in his delirium. If he has died, then the music is from the Host, and despite his sinful activities at the pond he has made it to heaven, or within earshot are people playing instruments which mean he is still alive, and if alive, there is still hope. Delbert moves his right leg with the deformed foot. Not really a foot anymore, long since burned off, but a gnarled stub, scarred and blackened hard. *It's free of the mud!*

The music fades, leaving Delbert more alone than he could ever imagine, desperate in his struggles. He cries out to the night sky, "I never complained about my cigar foot. I never ask for anything." He pauses to lick his chapped lips. He thinks he licked them but he cannot feel them. "Okay, maybe everything has already been provided," turning his face, Delbert sips at the thin layer of water as it rises with the incoming tide, but immediately spits it out—salty! A boy whom everyone believes can take care of himself whimpers, "I don't want to die here to be buried by cattails and absorbed by the marsh."

Anna squints, shielding her eyes from the glare skipping off the bay from the morning sun that is leaping into the sky above the Eastern shore. She and Clay walk on the temporary path created between the marsh bank and the receding tide. Anna rubs the kink in her neck. She had fallen asleep at a table in Tavern Bouvard, the excitement and exhaustion of the day in Baltimore taking their toll. She woke early in the morning, stiff of neck and chalk mouthed. Her father and Olivia were exiting the storeroom. One of Clay's shoulder straps on his coverall was unhooked—strange—because her father is never lazy or sloppy when it comes to his apparel, even if his entire ensemble consists of several flannel shirts, a coverall, sox, and boots. Noticing that Anna was awake, Olivia nervously glanced at the wall clock. Its brass hands were nearing seven. Wringing her hands, Olivia asked, "So how long have you been awake, dear?" "Just woke up," was Anna's honest response as she wiped sleep from her eyes.

Clay's stride is purposeful. Chores, endless and varied, wait for father and daughter at home, including Beauty, who will be excited to the point of annoyance by their return. Anna smacks stalk after stalk with her open palm like a stick on a picket fence. Cattails are far more enjoyable because the golden bloom at the top explodes, leaving in Anna's wake a trail that Midas[28] would envy.

"I want to be a pilot," Anna begins, almost challenging.

"That would be fine," Clay casually answers. In his state of contentment, his relaxed physical being and mental bliss, Clay would likely allow his daughter to be a circus clown if she wished. "Just make sure your chores are finished first."

Anna stares at her father, a quizzical expression on her face by his acquiescence. Having provoked no objection to her new vocational goal, she happily smacks another stalk to be showered in gold.

One eye blinded by the poison, the other severely blurred, Delbert fumbles around with his uninjured hand to locate and grasp another cattail stalk. Half a dozen lie as fallen soldiers in the mud. They are victims of Delbert's previous attempts to pull his leg and perfect foot free. He never thought his normal foot would ever be a hindrance, but with its right angle acting as a one-sided anchor, Delbert cannot budge it free. His cigar foot digs a sloppy trench as he uses it as leverage. Pulling and pushing with the last of his strength, his ears detect a sound more heart-warming than the laughter of a baby.

It is a sucking, a slurping, a sloshing, a slight loosening of the mud gripping his left calf and foot, and then the terrible SNAP! The cattail breaks in two as the marsh regains its grasp. Delbert holds onto a worthless stalk, its agitated bloom sprinkles gold onto his muddy face and into his eyes. He has no more tears to wash away the pollen that would so enhance a breakfast, but is gritty sand against his pupils with each painful blink.

"Anna, do you see this?" Clay points to golden nuggets scattered in the sand and mud along their temporary path, "It's corn. Someone is over-baiting." Clay shakes his head in disgust, "And look over there. A duck trap." The thin trail of corn leads to the narrow opening of a chicken wire

---

28 Midas. Myth. A Phrygian king who could turn whatever he touched into gold...and no, he never installed mufflers.

cage supported by wooden stakes. "LeCompte will find the corn and cage and automatically assume it's mine or the Joiners'."

"But you do bait, sometimes," Anna says.

"Yes, but I don't draw attention to myself. And when I'm done with the cage, I break it down so it won't be discovered. Whoever placed these here didn't know what he was doing, or worse, he didn't care if we are blamed."

Curled into the fetal position with mud for a womb, Delbert debates, seeking an uncontested victory. His teammates are periwinkles, salt-marsh snails that are climbing higher on the stalks for a better vantage. His opponents are fiddler crabs scuttling about, brandishing their oversized claws in an attempt to intimidate.

Those are the voices of Joseph and Mary, Delbert asserts.

Joseph and Mary would not concern themselves with duck cages, counter the crabs.

Reaching for another stalk, Delbert tries again, but his muscles are not following his brain's instructions. His fingers will not clasp the stalk.

Delbert's mind orders: *PULL!* His arm lies still.

Delbert's mind orders: *PUSH!* His leg lies still.

The voices are lost with a breeze that rustles the stalks and makes the periwinkles dizzy. Delbert is drifting farther from himself. There is no sensation of wet or cold or pain. There are no odors of salt or iodine or decay. Delbert is drifting in a nothingness that has no hold except for a hint of a memory from another time. The memory is from another life, from an adventure experienced a millennium ago, from a successful folly that brings a chill, anchoring Delbert to the present. He cries out, "This is the Great Susquehanna!"

Rolling the chicken wire around the stakes, Clay dismantles the empty duck cage. Anna uses the heel of her scuffed leather, city-going shoe to push the remaining corn deep into the mud, "Did you hear something?"

"Hear what?" Clay pushes the stakes and wire under an overhang in the mud bank to conceal it.

"I'm not sure, but I thought I heard something."

"What you're hearing, young lady, are your chores calling you home."

"No," Anna laughs, "that wasn't it."

Father and daughter resume their journey home, his stride purposeful, and her smack on the cattails golden.

Paddling in after awakening from their overnight slumber while rafting on the Flats, a dozen resident ducks swim to where yesterday's corn was found. Anna glances over her shoulder at the birds waddling ashore, then without warning, or probable cause, they take flight.

"Did you see that?" exclaims Anna. Clay turns as Anna points to the flock hastily departing. "And there. Did you hear it that time?" The small patch of skin between Clay's eyebrows furrow as he sees the fleeing fowl, but he still does not hear anything but the ducks' quacks and frantic wing flapping. Anna runs back to where the ducks had come ashore. Clay watches perplexed as his daughter cocks her head as if discerning stories told by the wind to the ordained. Anna climbs the short muddy bank to disappear into the forest of cattails.

"What in heaven's sake?" Clay retraces his steps.

"Father!" Anna cries, her wail a panic.

Clay's adrenaline surges with a father's fear as he follows the trail of bent and broken stalks that Anna left as she forced her way through the cattails. Stepping into a small clearing made by a desperate hand, Clay's eyes refocus to force his brain to accept the terrible signals they are sending it.

Anna is kneeling in the mud, cradling Delbert's head. His brown eyes stare sightless into the brilliant sun.

"I'm a Susquehannock brave," Delbert repeats, his lips are cracked and mud caked, but continue to move, stating as fact what is only whispered to a dying breeze.

Anna's cheeks run with tears as she looks to her father with the eyes of a child, pleading for him to make everything all right.

Sipping steaming coffee of varying strengths at the table in the Great Room of the Buchanan home, Clay and Anna listen as Doctor Webster updates Delbert's progress.

"It's really a miracle he's alive," the doctor states for the third time. "The snake's venom did a lot of damage. He's lost vision in his left eye and there's some paralysis in his right hand that may or may not improve with time, but knowing Cigar as I do, I predict he'll be bounding through the marsh in a couple of weeks. He's an amazing boy."

"He's a brave," Anna states proudly of her friend.

"Yes, he was very brave," Doctor Webster says, not understanding Anna.

"No. He is a brave."

Finishing their drinks, Anna clears the table as Doctor Webster pulls on a light jacket against the evening's chill. Clay opens the front door to see the doctor out. A blackened copper-cooking pot with a heavy lid sits in the middle of the porch.

"What do we have here?" Clay steps out to investigate. He lifts the lid. The mouth-watering aroma of snapper soup drifts pleasurable to tantalize the three.

Beauty had barked at something earlier, but it was assumed that her commotion was directed toward Doctor Webster's new Model "T" automobile. "It's a tin *Lizzie*[29]" the doctor called it as the contraption sputtered and backfired to a stop.

Claire Joiner watches from the cover of several maple tree trunks set back from the Buchanan home next to the trail leading into the marsh. Clay, Anna, and the doctor inhale the rich culinary concoction, re-igniting a Pavlovian[30] response requiring the wiping of their moist lips even before a tasting. Preparation of this delicious victual is not only time consuming, but also a task taken on with great care. The turtle's head having been cut off, it is stood upside-down to drain. After it has bled well, Claire scrubbed it with a stiff brush and then placed it into boiling water until the skin and upper shell peeled away. Fresh water with vegetables of celery, carrots, and onions were added with herbs, garlic, salt and pepper. She simmered it for two hours then strained, saving the broth. Claire cut the meat into bite size pieces, and then browned all in butter as she blended in flour, then poured back the broth, and added her prized and precious sherry, all the while rapping the knuckles of Chet and Lloyd with her wooden stir spoon as they tried to filch pieces. To top it off, a few hard-boiled goose eggs where sliced and added as accents.

Claire fretted and cursed herself, being ashamed for thoughts long past regarding Anna, that being whether or not she as a newborn should be allowed to live when her mother could not feed her. Not only was her shame for these thoughts overwhelming, and an apology wholly inadequate, Claire could not ask forgiveness of Anna's mother. If Claire's prerogative had won the day 12 years ago, her precious Delbert would be lost to her now. Claire pounded her head against the maple's bark, raising a lump sure to be a black and blue bruise, in her attempt to knock away the sickening grief at the mere thought of Delbert dying. Claire thought to hug Anna to show her gratitude, but her shame prevented such intimacy, and words from her heart were

---

29 Tin *Lizzie*. Slang. During WWI British seamen referred to H.M.S. Queen Elizabeth as a tin *Lizzie*. In America the term refers to Henry Ford's Model "T" automobile, or any cheap vehicle. Partridge, Edic. *A Dictionary of Slang and Unconventional English*. Eighth edition by Paul Beale. Macmillan. 1984.

30 Pavlov, Ivan Petrovich (1849-1936). Nobel Prize winner. Most remembered for his classic experiment where he trained a dog to salivate at the sound of a bell, which was previously associated with the sight of food.

simply inexpressible. Having never spent an hour in schooling, Claire was stunted in vocabulary. She expressed her feelings by acts in the bedroom for August and the labored preparation of meals for Lloyd, Chet, and Delbert, along with an absolute defense of her family. Claire decided that her only course of action would be to provide with a willing heart that which she once desired to deprive—sustenance.

Clay, Anna, and Doctor Webster re-enter the shack erected on the best fast and wetlands next to the Chesapeake Bay to share a supper that Jennifer Darling Buchanan would be proud to serve her loved ones. As the door closes, Claire is satisfied that her first offering, in lieu of an apology, in place of an inadequate thank you, has been accepted.

- 1914 -

In the bull pen consisting of three scratched and chipped desks of the Havre de Grace *Republican* sits a lone reporter. His thin lips move as he silently reads the continuous stream of news stories coming over the wire. The sun has long set and his eyes are dry, blood shot, and burn from over use.

"Anything yet?" the editor shouts from his office. The deadline for putting the paper to press looms with the need for one more story. The incessant ticking from the large-face clock nailed to his wall over the calendar grates on his last nerve. The 29th of June 1914 is circled in red ink. Today is his 15th wedding anniversary and he promised his wife he would be home early. *Another broken promise,* the editor worries. *Why she stays with me I'll never know.* His wife, as if knowing her destiny, wears a patient smile in the wedding photograph staring at him within the silver frame sitting at the corner of his cluttered desk

"There was an assassination yesterday," the reporter calls out, perking up with the hope that this story will be acceptable.

"Who? Where?" suspicion tints the editor's voice.

Reading as the ticker spits out the brief story, the reporter says, "Archduke Franz Ferdinand.[31] Oh, wait. He was killed in some place called Sarajevo. You ever hear of him?"

---

31 Archduke Franz Ferdinand of Austria-Hungary and his wife Sophia were assassinated on June 28, 1914 in Sarajevo. The killer was associated with a student terrorist group, Young Bosnia. Austria-Hungary believed that Serbia's government was behind the assassination and declared war. Ferdinand predicted his murder

"No, and it's too far away and of no consequence to us," the editor wishes he could throw his paperweight at the irritating mechanism to shut it up, but the clock was a gift from his wife. Her intent was that he would no longer have the excuse of not knowing the correct time. Its effect was to create guilt and frustration. The paperweight, carved by his own hands, is a one-third scale of a mallard drake, perfectly proportioned, and painted by his five-year-old son. It is an artistic mess, but its value is immeasurable. It is also the editor's daily reminder of why he works like a dog...to hunt...to enjoy the out of doors...to savor tasty duck meat, "Keep looking."

"Anna? Anna Buchanan?" a post-pubescent though still tentative male voice asks.

Anna turns from studying her arithmetic book to look into the sky blue eyes of every young girl's dream boy. Throughout the evening, sitting at her table in the corner of Tavern Bouvard, she had heard the heavy door squeak open and slam shut many times. The slamming door was not from disgruntled patrons, but from the door being caught by the rising wind of fall. It announces a storm front on the northern horizon that brings a sudden chill requiring mittens. For those men whose bellies ache for wildfowl, the grumbling will be quelled by a productive hunt, for tomorrow the birds will be aloft.

Anna cannot be blamed for being caught unaware of his approach, or for the frothy mustache that lines her upper lip. Over time she had learned to ignore the door, the clink of glass mugs, the pungent air heavy with tobacco smoke, the raucous laughter, and the rough jostling of inebriated men as she focused on her studies while peacefully sipping root beer.

"Yes," Anna stutters, taken aback by the handsome face. His is a face that edges close to femininity with a soft full mouth and elegant long eye lashes. She does not recognize the 16-year-old standing before her as the little boy who she once sympathized with, and had playfully tasted variations of his name on her tongue. Now from the perspective of her 14 years, he is the vision of a man; straight of stature and clothed in pressed garments purchased from a New York tailor.

"I apologize for interrupting your studies as you looked so involved, but seeing you sitting here, I asked who you were, hoping for some conversation other than that of my insipid father."

---

shortly before the event, sullenly saying, "The bullet that will kill me is already on its way." His killing sparked World War I.

"Uh-huh," Anna says, nodding as if her neck is on a loose spring and having no idea what insipid means.

"As we haven't been formally introduced, I'm William McQuay, recently returned from studies in merry olde England." William extends his hand in a gallant expressive greeting. A twinkle of mischief in his eyes as he bats his lashes flirtatiously.

"I'm Anna," extending her hand by rote, and feeling foolish for stating her name as he already knows it, but excited as the light of recognition glows hot with the memory of that brief observation of him many years ago.

"Here, let me get that," William holds Anna's calloused hand in his soft one and uses the fingers of his free hand to gently wipe away the foam above Anna's lips. She is torn between two emotions; the thrill of the lingering hold on her hand and mortification by the root beer mustache she was wearing. With unabashed flair, William tastes the foam.

"Ah, root beer," winking at Anna to put her at ease. "It's my favorite, second only to sarsaparilla."

William had accompanied his father to town with the hope of diversion from his boredom from wandering aimlessly around the mausoleum his parents call their home. He was looking to find his friend, Millard, known affectionately by the nickname of Chief. Chief acted as surrogate older brother to many Havre de Grace youth who looked to him for adventure, unwavering friendship, and sound advice. Chief may be seven years senior to William, but if available, Chief always found time for him. Millard Evelyn Tydings[32] was that way, reliable, a friend to all, and that is why he is Chief.

To William's disappointment, he learned that Chief, who is now a practicing attorney in Havre de Grace, was temporarily absent on a legal matter. This is how William found himself still by his father's side as Frank McQuay entered Tavern Bouvard in search of a guide for an associate from New York, specifically the investment firm, House of Morgan.

Embarrassed as she hears herself giggle like a little girl, Anna attempts to compose herself. "It's a pleasure to meet you, William."

Still holding her hand and giving it an affectionate squeeze, William responds, "Some may say so but only time will tell. Won't it?"

Hating her stupid heart for betraying itself by sending too much blood to flush her cheeks, Anna reluctantly withdraws her burning hand. William, sensing that Anna is tongue-tied, and trying to put her at ease, explains his presence. "I came with my father," pointing toward the bar where Frank McQuay is engaged in discussions with several market hunters and part-time

---

32 Tydings, Millard E. (1890-1961). Nicknamed "Chief." Born and raised in Havre de Grace, Maryland. He was a lawyer, war hero, congressman and state senator.

guides. It is clear, even from across the crowded tavern, and by the shake of the market hunters' heads that they are either unable or unwilling to guide for the elder McQuay. "A V.I.P. is arriving late tonight on the train and he wants to go hunting tomorrow. My father claims to be a hunter at his core," William looks around, and then leans in close to impart a secret, "but his bravado never seems to match the number of birds in his bag." The truth is spoken with a surprising amount of poisoned delight, but Anna misses his venom toward his father as she sits spellbound by the attention of this gorgeous boy.

"William," Frank McQuay calls from across the room.

Looking again toward the bar, Anna and William see his father motioning William toward the door. Standing next to Frank McQuay is Clay, making an unlikely pair.

"Looks like your father is to guide," William says.

"Really?" Anna is surprised, knowing the animosity between the two men.

"Will you be coming along?" asks William.

"Will you?" Anna's unsure of what answer she wants, or what the consequences will be of his answer.

"Maybe we'll see each other again." William says, a wry grin curls his lips as he tips an invisible hat to Anna, turns, and is swallowed by the crowd of men. A squeak and slam of the door is Anna's only clue that William has left the tavern.

"Another root beer, Anna?" Olivia asks.

"Huh? Oh, can I have a sarsaparilla?"

Olivia immediately recognizes the faraway gaze in Anna's eyes. It foretells of complications, and likely trouble that no amount of reasoning can prevent. Olivia knows this because it is the same gaze she saw in her mirror when she thought of Clay while Jennifer was alive. The face that now looks back at her is guilt ridden, but she cannot help herself.

Crisp leaves of orange and red that swirl with the wind are briefly illuminated in the bright headlight beams. The Buick touring car, with Frank McQuay white-knuckling the wooden steering wheel, races down the gravel road. He drives as if the devil himself is chasing him. Sitting in the passenger seat, William believes that it is his father's conscience that he is running from.

William rubs his bruising thigh that was injured when his father shoved him against the curved fender of his new status symbol.

"Don't ever let me catch you talking to that dirty tramp," growls Frank McQuay.

The trail through the Joiners' swamp is a checkerboard of light and dark as clouds pass across the face of the moon. Unseen, but distinctly heard overhead are the honking of geese returning from the Arctic tundra accompanied by ducks arriving from across Canada and the midwest. Anna burps from deep in her belly from one too many carbonated drinks. It is a loud, robust, and throaty reverberation that brings laughter to father and daughter as they walk with brisk strides against the rising wind.

"Don't ever let me catch you doing that with others around," Clay chuckles. "It's not very lady like."

William: "Anna isn't dirty and I doubt she has ever kissed a boy."

Frank: "Don't be smart with me. You're not too big to be smacked."

Anna: "It just slipped out."

Clay: "You're lucky you're too big for a switch. There are a lot of good birch trees along here."

Frank: "You shouldn't even know the girl's name let alone be conversing with her. Her kind wants only one thing."

William: "And what is that one thing? To be treated decently?"

Clay: "I saw you talking with Mr. McQuay's son."

Anna: "His name is William and he was quite the gentleman."

Frank: "You know damn well what it is. It's money. Our money and for me to have the rotten luck to have to ask Clay Buchanan to guide for me galls me to no end. He thinks he's as good as the next man."

William: "I've heard he's one of the best."

Clay: "I don't know the character of William, but I'm familiar with his father's. I trust you to be a good judge of character, but sometimes it's wise to err on the side of caution."

Anna: "You think there could be flaws hidden behind his friendly smile?"

Frank: "What you heard is relative. If Clay Buchanan is the best at anything it would be living in a shack on valuable land not utilized for profit and his daughter will turn out no better."

William: "Shouldn't I be the judge of that?"

Clay: "I think it would be difficult for William to grow up under Frank McQuay's influence and not have acquired some of his father's traits."

Anna: "I'll keep a close watch but he has been living in England."

Both fists are used to beat William. His insolence demanded that his father take immediate corrective action. Using both feet, laced up warm to the calves in moccasin leather boots, he stomped the brake pedal to the floorboard, causing the elegant vehicle to slue violently. William was thrown from the convertible and before he finished rolling across the rough road, his father was upon him.

Clay reaches out to briefly hug Anna as a cloud crosses the moon. When its light reappears the two are again walking along the friendly path with hands in their pockets.

Splashing cold water from the sink onto her face to wash away the deposits left by the sandman in the corners of her eyes, Anna chastises herself for oversleeping, "Why today? You idiot!" Now she can only guess where her father took Frank McQuay, the V.I.P., and maybe William.

Pulling on her Mackinaw, Anna rushes out the door, nearly knocking Delbert over as she collides with him on the dark, pre-dawn porch.

"Hey, where you going in such a hurry?" Delbert asks as he picks up the otter with the snare around its neck.

"Oh, Del! Did you see my father this morning?" her heart beats with hope. "He's guiding for Frank McQuay and I have to find him."

"Nope. Didn't see 'em," Delbert licks the index finger on his gimp hand and holds it up to gauge the wind. "But today with the wind as it is I'd say he'll probably be using the hogsheads at Swan Creek Point."

"Thanks," Anna hugs Delbert and then runs off into the darkness. "Why do you need to find him?" Delbert calls after Anna. "Need something," is her disembodied reply.

Strange, Delbert thinks as he latches the door closed.

Lawrence Fitzgerald Remy stares down at the blind; three old barrels planted level with the rough surface and camouflaged with living vegetation.

"My goodness. If you hadn't pointed them out, Clay, I would have stumbled right in," jokes the House of Morgan partner.

"If only the birds had the poor eyesight that we humans do, bagg'n 'em would be a lot easier," Clay replies.

"True, but where would the sport be in that?" Mr. Remy concludes.

Frank McQuay sniffs the air as an out-of-place aroma...no; it would be classified as a smell, wafts past his wrinkling nose.

"Mr. Remy," Clay instructs. "Please take the center one. I'll take the one on the right to better direct Beauty, and Mr. McQuay, you can shoot from the one on the left."

The center hogshead is the largest and most comfortable, though Clay has brought along extra blankets for each of the men to sit on and for warmth. Frank McQuay gags as he slips into his allotted barrel, recognizing that his was originally used to pickle cucumbers. It was not with malice aforethought that Clay sentenced Frank McQuay to sit in the malodorous pickle barrel while he and Mr. Remy inhaled aged oak permeated with fragrant olive oil, but a perverse smile did briefly cross Clay's lips in the minutes preceding dawn upon his realization of this happenstance.

"What's say we let Clay call the first shots," offers Mr. Remy.

"Fine," Frank McQuay responds, his stomach doing flip-flops with nausea from the powerful odor.

Gliding in on tired wings from another long night's flight south, the old gander, the patriarch of his family, peers through the darkness for any signs of danger. Following in his air stream is his mate. She is his one true love. She is his lady for life. He will protect her even if it means sacrificing his own life, for without love, life is not worth living. Behind her are their three offspring on their first migration to the Chesapeake Bay that is their winter refuge and feeding grounds. The gander and his family broke off from the main "V" formation to reclaim their prized piece of marsh just inside the bend of Swan Creek Point. Down the family glides with the gander constantly honking, his varied tones are words of guidance, constant teaching, and most importantly, reminding each member to keep vigilant for anything suspicious.

Like a beam of light, a sliver of day breaches the eastern horizon, spotlighting the incoming geese. These Canada geese are dark gray of body with black heads and necks with startling white chins traps, heavy with tender meat, and coming straight in to the gun sights. Still within the shadow of darkness, Frank McQuay and Lawrence Fitzgerald Remy tense with anticipation. Clay remains relaxed, unconcerned, almost uninterested in the dinner on wings that are approaching.

"They'll break just out of range," whispers Clay.

Black tipped wings test the wind as they adjust slightly their flare to break their air speed. The gander surveys again the peaceful marsh and the gathered ducks with a smattering of geese bobbing near the shore.

That's it! Honking the warning call, the gander, with his family close on his tail feathers, snap wings to veer left, catching a gust of wind that rockets them safely away.

Bang!

Frank McQuay leaps to his feet to shoot. It is a wasted shot that echoes embarrassed across the marsh and Flats. Lawrence Fitzgerald Remy shakes his head in disgust at McQuay's impatience, "Clay, how'd you know they'd break?"

"None of the decoys in this rig are feeding," Clay states the obvious. "They'll fool ducks but never geese."

Beauty would never betray her mistress, but between retrieving the dead, or in the case of Frank McQuay's poor shooting, crippled birds, she keeps a curious eye on Anna who is hiding a safe distance from the hogshead blind.

For Beauty, the morning hunt has been exceptional. Mallard, widgeon, and black ducks, tired and hungry, flew in to find eternal rest among their wooden relations. On command, Beauty would leap and bound across the shallows with her tongue flapping out the side of her mouth to carry as a lone pallbearer the fallen traveler back to her master. Why she so enjoyed these wet, windy, and cold mornings is a mystery even to her. However, this is the first winter that her joints ached, not from the cold, but from life's equalizer—age. She is still quick, and her energy level remains high, but when the hunt is finished there is now a pleasure equal to retrieving, and that is a nap in front of the glowing potbelly stove.

"Now, Mr. Remy," calls Clay.

Leaping up, Mr. Remy shoots, and quickly and accurately downs two fat canvasbacks. The remaining flock of eight darts left. Frank McQuay leads the group and fires three times, killing one and nicking the tail feathers of a second. Clay, patient and generous, waited for the two gentlemen to take their shots, and then fires once, killing instantly the duck that thought it had a reprieve.

"Magnificent shot, Clay," says Mr. Remy. "I would have believed that one was outside our range."

"Back!" Clay sends Beauty plunging in after he marks the spots where the ducks fell, and then addresses Mr. Remy. "I can't take all the credit as this Remington holds a tight pattern that will reach out and knock 'em down."

From her crouched position among the tall grass, Anna watches Beauty watch her. For a moment she feared Beauty would run to her, but as each spied the other, unspoken words of acknowledgement and understanding passed between them. Then as the faint glow in the east increased to shorten the morning shadows, Anna is disappointed when only three stand to shoot; her father, Frank McQuay, and a third man who Anna assumes is the V.I.P. that William spoke of, but no William.

This is a fool's errand. Wishful thinking, Anna chastises herself. *If William were not invited, why would she believe he would be here? For her?* Anna sits back on the grass. Her ego is bruised and the seat of her coverall is soaking through from the dew that clings to the grass and permeates the black earth. Sighing with a surprised amount of sadness that the main attraction is a no show, Anna decides to watch the men bring down the birds.

The flocks of wildfowl: geese, swan, and duck, that at one time in the not too distant past were massive to the point of blotting out the sun and moon, fly overhead sporadically and at varying altitudes, but still in sufficient numbers to cause a man's trigger finger to flinch. The many different species, mingling their variety of calls, all coalesce to form one continuous discordant sound. *Oh to be able to decipher their language.* Anna considers the stories these wildfowl could tell, the places they have been, the things they have seen...

Bang! Bang! Bang!

...and the losses they have suffered.

It is a complicated puzzle that never adequately explains why some birds are lured to the gun while others pass over without a sideways glance. The young man who believes he is superior to all creatures will boast that his success lies with the spread of his perfectly carved decoys, the placement of his blind, and the accuracy of his shot. This lad quickly finds himself humbled when at the end of the day his bag is empty and his ears ring from the ribald laughter of old men who know better. These veterans of the hunt who have seen their vocation change through the flintlock, muzzle loader, punt, armada, breechloader, side-by-side, over-and-over, and slide action will confirm that a man's success is wholly dependent on the individual fowl. A man can set out mud decoys and stand as if a tree, and then injure his back carrying home a bag of birds so plentiful that if it were not for neighbors the meat would spoil. Another man with the finest, elaborately carved and painted decoys, hidden in a perfectly dug and camouflaged blind, is at a loss to explain the expenditure of not a single shell, but the very next day the fortunes of these men are reversed.

The best a man can do is study each species and its preferences, provide for its needs, but in the end pray for the blessings of a merciful God, a kind glance from Luck, and a stupid duck.

Segments of words and partial phrases of the men's conversation are caught by the wind and delivered to Anna's ears during the times that Beauty is collecting.

V.I.P.: "Amazing numbers..."

Clay: "Decline...past years..."

Frank: "Market hunters...excessive hunting..."

The angle of the sun in the morning sky indicates the time to be somewhere in the neighborhood of 9:30. Anna's grumbling stomach indicates it is long past time for breakfast. Crawling a good distance away from the blind to ensure she is not detected, Anna begins her trek home.

William sits on a vacant muskrat den by the side of a mud hole. The den's previous owners were careless and became hearty meals for a pair of nesting eagles. The mud hole, having been a shallow winter's pond, was choked to muddy muck by thirsty marsh grasses. William decided that he should sit for a moment to consider his situation. He is not lost. He knows the sun rises in the east and there it is, though it is higher now than when he began his foray into the maze that he has found the marsh to be. If the east is indicated by the position of the sun then the bay is in that direction. The opposite direction would be the gravel road that runs north to Havre de Grace, south to Baltimore, and somewhere in between is his family's holdings.

"It is simple enough," William says aloud, trying to impart confidence in himself.

But it's not simple at all. After leaving the road in search of Swan Creek Point, the path mcandered, circled, arced, and seemed to cross itself, making direct headway difficult and confusing, especially when he passed through tall grasses, towering cattails, and trees of species he could not name that obscured his line of sight in all directions except up. Everything looked the same but different to him. William was no longer sure if he had passed this tree, or that stand of cattails on his left or right side, and when finally a rabbit trail of a path let out onto the bay, he could not be sure if the distance he had traveled placed him north or south of the point and so he did not know which way to turn.

Delbert found his morning adventure to be amusing. Curious as to Anna's need, he followed her to the hogshead blind, but was surprised and puzzled when she stopped at a distance and appeared to hide. *Very strange,* Delbert thought. He watched for a time, but was quickly bored, and so he headed home with his otter slung over his shoulder. A mile or so from the blind, Delbert noticed imprints in the soft soil made by new boots. The ridges on the soles were crisp and well defined. Catching up to the wearer of these boots was easy as the owner kept getting caught on the switchbacks and was delivered directly to where Delbert first noticed his presence. For fun, which Delbert always pursued when an opportunity presented itself, he decided to step into the tall grass to observe the wanderer undetected.

It was a game of cat and mouse, though the mouse had no clue that he was being stalked. The mouse was a great source of amusement for Delbert each time he retraced his steps when a trail appeared to dead end, or he circled back around in ignorance and frustration, looking around exasperated. The boy touched a familiar chord with Delbert, but he could not put a name to the face, though his fine clothes and inability to navigate the marsh bespoke of one not from around here. Delbert was about to put the boy out of his considerable misery by revealing himself and leading him to wherever it was he had come from when...

"William!" Anna cries.

William is pleasantly startled by the human voice; a familiar and friendly voice attached to a smile that could challenge a summer sun for its radiance. Fearing he would expose his true situation and the relief he felt by Anna's presence, William took on the posture of one completely at ease with his surroundings. He affects boredom by yawning then conspicuously checks his pocket watch as if to verify that it is Anna who is late.

"Well, Anna, it's certainly a pleasure to finally see you this morning," William says as he stands to brush an annoying twig from his pressed trousers.

"What are you doing here?" Anna says. "I expected to see you at the blind."

"I thought that as this is the path you'd follow I'd wait a reasonable time to see if you'd pass. No sense in being under parental scrutiny all the time."

Delbert claps a hand over his mouth to prevent either a burst of laughter or the charge of damn liar from escaping his mouth as he listens to the hogwash spewing from William. Then without warning, Delbert's stomach twists with an emotional pang as he realizes Anna has lied to him. She did not need anything from her father. She wanted to meet William who Delbert connects with the surname of McQuay. Delbert peers between the bending, wind blown, grasses to observe his best friend and an interloper walk away down the path in amicable conversation. There could not be two more incongruous persons on earth. William is an alien lost in a world where the state of being requires a casual acceptance that nature will impose itself on all who dare to enter. Only the fowl preen themselves here. And Anna, apparently smitten with this strutting buffoon, still herself in all basic ways, unconcerned with the rump- size water spot on the rear of her coverall, leads him to safety. Would she be so gaga if she were aware of Delbert's assessment that William's only attribute is a silver tongue?

Anna's hunger is forgotten.

William's geographical uncertainty is assuaged.

Delbert follows the two at a respectable distance. Feelings of hurt, jealousy, and curiosity swirl between his heart and mind, confusing him with their complexity, and surprising him by their existence.

"Someone once said the Good Lord doesn't subtract from our allotted time on earth the hours spent in duck hunting," Mr. Remy loads fresh shells after downing three ducks. "Do you believe that, Clay?"

"I believe in: no duck—no dinner."

"Ah, a practical man."

"Lawrence," Frank McQuay interjects, "Mr. Buchanan can be practical. He has the luxury of hunting every day. It was likely a businessman who was relying on God's grace to provide gentlemen such as us with extra time, rare time, to hunt this bounty, though Clay was correct earlier when he said there is a noticeable decline in the number of fowl returning each year."

"Clay, do you have any thoughts as to why this is happening?" asks Mr. Remy.

Clay is not intimidated by any man, and when asked a direct question will answer it, but he also knows that it is not what you say, but how it is said that is important. Looking past Mr. Remy, staring at Frank McQuay to reiterate beliefs that Frank knows all too well, "It seems to me that the loss of nesting sites..."

"It's caused by market hunters," Frank McQuay rudely interrupts. "They use outlawed guns and questionable tactics while ignoring rest days."

"Where's the law enforcement?" questions Mr. Remy.

"The duck police?" Frank McQuay scoffs. "Oh, we have very dedicated game wardens, but as with the majority of government enterprises there are too few of them and they're under funded." Frank McQuay fumes, annoyed with the House of Morgan partner's encouragement of conversation with the hired help, and wishing his words were knives in Clay's chest. *How dare a cultured man like Lawrence Fitzgerald Remy think to ask an uneducated, impoverished man as Clay Buchanan is, a question that would require extrapolation of cause and effect when only a portion of the whole, the migration-reproductive system is visible, and when in all likelihood his answer will be biased?*

Anna believes she is giving William her full attention as he relates comical stories of his chums back at Sandhurst, but a corner of her mind is mulling over two thoughts. The first is William's apparent lack of concern for her less than fashionable apparel which relieves her feelings of self-consciousness. Anna may be a product of the marsh where frilly things are unheard of, but feminine instincts, a desire to be viewed as attractive by the male brought about a sudden concern for her appearance. The second thought is of the distinctive prints in the path—Delbert's. Anna wonders, *were they made before or after the collision on the front porch early this morning? If they're from after, is he following her and William?* Anna knows that if Delbert is stalking them Indian style she will never catch sight of him, though at each bend in the path she sneaks a peak, but sees nothing. Delbert's that good.

What William would have called Sandhurst gruel as he sat in the immense stone chow hall of the esteemed English military facility has by some miracle been transformed by Anna into a steaming bowl of sweet and creamy porridge topped with dried wild strawberries. He never imagined oatmeal could taste so delicious that he would ask for a second helping.

As the two approached a structure that William assumed was a hunter's cabin, Anna unabashedly welcomed him to her home, asking if he would care for breakfast as she herself had yet to eat this morning. Watching her prepare this simple dish, William observed the orderliness of the small home, and Anna's quiet efficiency. After he had shut up from babbling about anything he could think of, Anna picked up the conversation without a moments pause. William was deathly afraid of those uncomfortable silences that normally occur with developing relationships. He may be pressed and dapper, all put together on the outside, but he was still a nervous, less than confident 16-year-old on an unchaperoned date. His friends would admire his cleverness in arranging, so to speak, this clandestine rendezvous though it is likely they being English gentry would at the very least tease him for fraternizing with a country peasant, and at their crudest would chastise him for associating with a caste they would deem untouchable.

"Drying the strawberries is easy. The difficult part is keeping the black birds from stealing them," Anna lifts another spoonful to her mouth and then swallows. "Would you like more milk?"

William nods, not wanting to speak with a full mouth. "Manners make the lady and gentleman," his mother would say.

As Anna gets up from the table, William notices that the rear of her coverall has dried; leaving the baggy material the same faded blue as the rest of her garment. There is no reason for William to be staring so intently at her developing frame, but he cannot help himself. *Why am I drawn to her? She's nothing like the fancy girls of London or the prissy town girls that mother parades before me.*

Anna turns from the sink with a pitcher of milk in her hand. William continues staring as she walks the two paces to the table. Her face beams, unblemished, fresh, and natural.

THAT'S IT! William knows why she captivates him. It is not because Anna is a raving beauty because in comparison with other girls she is not as pretty, but actually rather plain. It is not because of some intoxicating perfume because William can detect no aroma other than the freshness of the out-of-doors. Anna is neither demure, nor timid, but once started on a topic of preference she reveals a confident, robust, and animated spirit. And it is certainly not her dress. Compared to ruffled gowns, whimsical dresses, colorful bonnets adorned with flowers or feathers, and elbow length gloves that he is accustomed to seeing on young and not so young girls, Anna's clothing is drab, but practical.

Natural.

Practical.

Real.

Anna's exterior provides William with a rare truth. There is no pretense with Anna. She conceals no agenda other than the obvious interest in the young man who sits before her, accompanied by hospitality afforded any guest entering the Buchanan home, and then there is her smile.

God, why does he keep staring at me? He probably thinks my teeth are too big. I've got to stop smiling. I must look like a retard. Anna's hand shakes as she pours milk onto William's oatmeal.

Anna knows she is just winging it. She has no reference to rely on, no experience to compare with, or instructions to follow when it comes to boys, except Delbert, but that is completely different. Olivia had described the ridiculous mechanics of sex and its implications when her monthly cycles began, and her mother, if Anna remembers correctly, had said something about the joy of pleasing the one you love within the marriage bed. Anna also knows she is not going to be having sex and is definitely not in love.

Anna is dizzy. She is sure her face is flushed. Her cheeks hurt from grinning too much and for the life of her she does not remember preparing the oatmeal. *I don't know what this is,* Anna's brain hurts as she tries to place her body's irrational reactions into an emotional category that makes sense, but as she is failing miserably, she pushes this quandary aside to focus on keeping the conversation flowing, "I was surprised to see the bittern so late in the season."

William tries to remember which bird Anna is referring to. She had pointed out so many creatures that he would have walked right past, and even with her directing his eyes, he still did not see several because their camouflage was perfect, "Ah-huh."

"It's funny the way it stands when startled, so straight, stick-like, with its head and long beak pointing skyward to blend in with the plants around it."

Now William remembers the skinny brown bird standing frozen, "Why didn't it fly away?"

"Their kind never flee when frightened," Anna wishes she was as brave as this small marsh bird. She is afraid to chew her meal, fearing she will bite her tongue under the scrutiny that is William's penetrating gaze. "Are you late?" Anna notices William glancing at his pocket watch.

"No. Sorry. I didn't tell my mother where I was going and if my father returns while I'm away..." William's voice quavers as he leaves the sentence unfinished.

It is fortunate that Beauty is with Mr. Buchanan because Delbert is keenly aware that she would have found him out as he sneaks from hiding place to hiding place around the shack where Anna is entertaining William. Then again, if Mr. Buchanan and Beauty were home it would be Delbert who would be inside, warm by the stove, entertaining and being entertained.

Clay loads the heavy bags stuffed full of birds into the backseat of Frank McQuay's Buick that is parked a mile from the blind on a dirt cutout. Frank McQuay climbs behind the wheel, anxious to leave the morning hunt and Clay Buchanan behind.

"Excellent hunt, Clay," Mr. Remy extends his hand to shake Clay's. "I've hunted at some of the finest private lodges up and down the bay with guides of some note, but I can confidently say that you and Beauty are the best. You never call the shots too soon as I've seen many an anxious person jump the mark," looking briefly at Frank McQuay who has started the engine, "and then watch as the birds swing off, never to return."

"It's always a pleasure to sit a blind with a man who is a good listener," Clay replies sincerely.

"I recognize it's a sport to some and a livelihood for others. Let's hope a balance can be found." Lawrence Fitzgerald Remy climbs into the passenger seat as Frank McQuay pops the clutch, jerking the vehicle forward, wheels spinning.

Clay and Beauty are left in a spray of dark earth. Clay shoves the $50 bill that was passed during the handshake into his pocket without looking at it. The tip burned his hand.

"That son of a bitch!" Clay slams the door after entering, shaking the shack to its foundation, and almost catching Beauty's nose as she follows, but does not make it inside.

"Who?" Anna turns from her preparation of a duck stew for lunch. She is frightened because she has never heard her father utter such curses. She also fears that her father had seen William walking along their rutted road after leaving her on the porch.

It was a bumbling affair, a clumsy, comical farewell. Anna and William stood on the porch, he thanking her again for the meal, delaying the departure for a reason known only to him, but making her anxious and hopeful. They could not look directly into each other's eyes for more than a moment before turning away to gaze off into the distance as if in anticipation of something important was going to occur, and then it happened.

"I hope to see you soon," William held out his hand to shake.

Anna placed her hand in his, and while he squeezed hers, without thought, preamble, or realization of what instinct was driving her to do, she lifted up off her heels, onto her toes, and kissed William softly on his lips.

"Frank McQuay," Clay stares at Anna. "Who else would be a son of a bitch?"

Anna shrugs her shoulders afraid to say anything that might give away her guilty pleasure.

"He spent the morning blaming market hunters for the decline in wildfowl and lobbying for tougher laws and more game wardens," Clay paces between the bedroom and the Great Room, casting off jacket and over shirt. He slugs back a mouthful of brown liquid to quell a rising cough, "I don't know if he's just a hypocrite or a fool as well." Beauty whines and scratches outside the door. Clay yanks it open, "Get in here if you want to." Beauty runs to Anna's side for mutual protection from the thing that has possessed her master. Clay strides the six paces to tower over his daughter and hunting dog, pointing a shaking finger at them. "No man will ever stand between me and providing for my family. Is that clear?"

Uncertain as to why her father's tirade is directed at her, other than she is the only one available, all Anna can think to do is nod silently. Clay grabs his favorite cup off the shelf to pour a cup of bubbling brew from the kettle on the stove, and then begins to break down his Remington for a thorough cleaning, "Where the hell does McQuay think those ducks and geese come from for all his fancy dinner parties?"

William finds himself sprawled beside the gravel road. A moment before he was walking blissfully, whistling with tingling lips. As he rubs the rising lump on the back of his head he wonders where the dead otter lying next to him came from.

As a southern lady of fine breeding, Dorothy Parker McQuay could not bring herself to vocalize her annoyance that caused her eyes to tear. Between dainty bites, and in a meager defense, she placed a perfumed linen napkin under her nose, attempting to endure through an elegant supper that should have been a delight. Courses included salad of romaine lettuce sprinkled with slivered almond, grated cheese and a light dressing, fresh vegetable soup, caramelized duck with stuffing, baked ham covered in brown sugar, candied yams and wild rice, and for dessert, fresh baked pumpkin pie, vanilla flan, and peaches shipped in by train to add to ice cream turned only 15 minutes prior to serving. Dorothy's delicate ears may have burned from the words uttered in the kitchen, but she would whole-heartedly agree with Nanna Maude and Roman: "That Mr. McQuay stank like hell with the sulfur turned up high." "Dang pickles gone bad, I'm thinking."

As the last dish was removed from the expansive burl dining table, Dorothy was able to excuse herself, using the customary reasons that she wished to allow the gentlemen their pleasures of cigar and brandy, and the freedom to discuss topics for which a lady need not be concerned.

Reclining in a high-back brocaded chair in front of the den's hearth that crackled with seasoned oak, Frank McQuay is predisposed to anger as he is already irritated by his odor that an hour's scrubbing did not wash away, muttering, "Damn smell's gotten into my pores," but he is also forced to entertain an unwelcome guest. It is not the distinguished gentleman sitting across from him, but the news he is delivering.

"Frank, normally I would never recommend moving money out of our firm, but with Wall Street flat, and as your friend, I believe your interests would be better served if your investments were in tangible assets, not stocks," Lawrence Fitzgerald Remy advises while inhaling the rich aroma of the brandy.

"What, into more land? Crop prices are down, labor wages are up, and I've barely recovered from the losses I incurred in 1910 when you recommended I put money into oil speculation in California, the Lakeview and Union Oil Company. Where was it located, Taft?"

"They did strike oil."

"They sure did. Their Number One[33] rig gushed uncontrolled for 18 months, losing 90,000 barrels of crude a day. I heard they built dykes to create a 60-acre lake and rowed around on the oil in boats. Fun for them, but the price of crude fell by nine-tenths."

"Frank, the advice was sound. I certainly cannot be held responsible for the incompetence of the wildcatters."

"And of course you're not responsible for my losses, are you?" Frank McQuay snaps back.

The tension that follows Frank's ill-mannered quip is broken by Roman who taps on the open door, enters, refills the men's brandy snifters, but before he can offer fresh cigars he is dismissed with a wave of the master's hand.

"There will always be ups and downs. That's a fact, so let's get past it," Mr. Remy resumes. "The tax laws favor land holders who are involved in its exploitation. Whether you develop for commercial, mining, or agricultural purposes, there are handsome write-offs including your labor costs. I would suggest changing to a subsidized crop and expand. Bold men of vision take risks and profit follows fearlessness."

"Ruin follows folly," Frank retorts. "Besides, I've purchased all the available holdings adjacent to my land and all but 160 acres have been cleared and are in production."

"What about the land east of the frontage road extending to the bay?"

"Part of it is owned by Mr. Buchanan and north of him it's owned by a mongrel family by the name of Joiner."

"Is the land owned outright or is there a mortgage?" Mr. Remy swirls the relaxing liquid within its pear-shaped glass. "Look to all possibilities, Frank, because I needn't tell you that on your present course of diminishing returns

---

33 Lakeview Gusher Number One. Located about a half mile east of the Taft-Maricopa Highway in the Midway-Sunset oil field in Kern County, California. Identified as State Historic landmark 3485, it is the largest U.S. oil well gusher. The gusher spouted on March 14, 1910 as the drill bit hit a depth of 2,440 feet. After producing 9 million barrels in 18 months, the gusher was brought under control, but to no profitable ends as the oil was spent and the new rig produced less than 30 barrels a day.

the end result is bankruptcy. It's not imminent but within the foreseeable future the bank could come knocking."

Frank McQuay sits in his stink listening to what he already knows and to advice that is improbable under the current situation. Frank McQuay has found himself in that unenviable position of being land rich and cash poor. If he could sell he would retire wealthy to New York and travel, but a person of means, capable of buying him out, which to Frank McQuay equates to a man of fiscal intelligence and business savvy, would never purchase a plantation that is sliding into the red. He could sell at fire sale prices, but that would defeat the purpose, leaving him far short of the means required to sustain his family's lifestyle.

Lawrence Fitzgerald Remy, a man whose personal fortune is increased with each stock trade regardless of whether profit or loss follows, extinguishes the three-dollar cigar in a golden ashtray, and then leans toward the humidor, "May I?"

"You're my guest. Indulge," Frank McQuay says aloud, but to himself, *it's time to cut costs.*

Roman pokes the glowing coals with an iron rod. It is the last act of the night after the McQuays have retired. The servants have completed their assigned tasks and are crawling under quilts in their individual quarters attached to the main house off the kitchen. It has always been assumed that Roman and Nanna Maude are married since they arrived together decades ago to serve at the behest of the family McQuay. Due to this assumption, their room is a few feet wider with a double-size bed and small brazier for heat. On their first night, when the two were presented with this sleeping arrangement, Roman eyed the youthful Nanna Maude with assumed expectation, but found himself groaning on the floor with bruised testicles. A year later, after careful scrutiny of his character, Nanna Maude allowed Roman to join her with the promise that hers would be the only bed he would ever enter.

Out-of-date newspapers cleared from the den are read by Nanna Maude to Roman and then used along with kindling to ignite the coal. Due to the extra labor involved in the special meal for the McQuays' guest tonight, she is too tired to read, and allows Roman to feed the paper, crinkled and twisted to the flame. If she had read it, front to back, as is her custom, a particular article would have brought Roman fond memories and sadness.

EXTINCTION

September 1, 1914: The last American Passenger Pigeon is dead. This species that once made up one-third of the entire bird population has gone extinct to the chagrin of its keepers at the Cincinnati Zoological Garden and the anguish of all bird lovers. Individual birds were 17 inches in length and hunted for their meat. The squabs (babies) were killed for their fat and were used as butter or oil. Is this a case of Darwin's[34] natural selection where a species is no longer relevant to the world and simply perished, or did man have a hand in its demise? We may never know, but this writer will forever miss those Sunday dinners of baked pigeon pie.

---

34 Darwin, Charles (1809-1882). English naturalist. He is renowned for his controversial study of evolution and for a theory on survival of the fittest known as Darwinism. In 1859, he published his abstract entitled *On the Origin of Species*.

– 1875 –

May and June in New York's Catskills was a time of festive fattening. Roman had celebrated his 20th birthday a week ago, receiving his yearly set of rough homespun pants and shirt and the largest slice of sweet potato pie. As he reclined on a gentle hill, cushioned by new grass and fragrant with seasonal flowers, Roman pictured in his mind the fluttering and flashing of grayish blue and reddish-fawn feathers of the thousands of pigeons to be caught within the baited nets strung from trees.

Roman kept one eye and an ear on the sky for the arrival of the flock that would cover from horizon to horizon, thick and deep, with incalculable wings creating their own wind, and that require several days to complete its pass overhead. His other eye and ear was on the dusty road for the migrant netter. Utilizing the modern telegraph to keep abreast of the birds' whereabouts, the netter would whip his weary draft horse to pull his wagon a little faster as he chases the flock across the continent.

Roman remembers the pride he felt when last year he was told that with his help, and the combined efforts of other pigeoners throughout the region, for weeks on end, more than 100 barrels a day of adult pigeons were shipped to New York, and not less than 15 tons of ice was used to pack squabs. The jingle of coins in Roman's pocket at the end of the season was thrilling, but when he scattered them before his ailing mother, the delight that was evident in her eyes and the extra hugs brought him a joy that could never be surpassed.

Roman chuckles with the memory of how as a child his mother needed to comfort him when throughout the night at this time of year he heard boughs breaking under the immense weight of the roosting birds. His fear was rooted in the children's rhyme: When the bough breaks, down comes baby, cradle and all.[35] Roman believed children were falling out of trees and being hurt, though the reality was far more cruel. With more than a hundred nests to a tree, the ground would be strewn with broken limbs, eggs, and dead squabs that were feasted upon by hogs and wild dogs.

"We used to use guns to shoot them out of the trees until the barrels melted," reminisced the netter the previous year, "but powder and shot add up, reducing a man's profit. Now a net with clubs, stones, and poles are sufficient to kill the birds. The only limiting factor is a tired arm."

Roman did not know the exact date, but he began to become uneasy with the passage of balmy days with neither the great flocks passing overhead, nor the arrival of the netter. He was not alone in his worry. Men and boys throughout the country scanned the sky for the pigeons, called by various names in different regions: passenger, wild, wood, red-breasted, and blue-headed. Conscientious men denied the pang of guilt growing inside them at the possibility that their exploitation of the birds, including the harvesting of young could be affecting the overall numbers within flocks where the total bird count could exceed two billion. The Indians of Canada and the United States begged, pleaded, and even threatened the white man to not disturb the breeding places until the young were able to fly, but to little effect. "What does a savage know?" was the response by God-fearing white men.

The small numbers that did reach Roman flew on, scattering farther north as the forests they traditionally nested in or feed upon; primeval beech woods, pine, and hemlock were largely cut away, or ruined for many seasons by fires. The sloping pasture that Roman rested on was as of last year a mighty stand of hemlock abundant with seed.

With one last look to the empty horizon, one last look down the lonely dirt road, Roman hiked up his pants to wander home, steeling himself for the look of disappointment in his mother's eyes.

The pigeons did not disappear overnight but with constant molestation by man, season after season, they finally lost their ability to succeed in communal ways. Scattered far and wide, adults were killed, leaving orphans to starve, or the squabs were taken, denying a future generation. Nature, being a heartless mother, killed the remnants through unseasonable storms.

---

35 Grimm, Jacob Ludwig Carl (1785-1863) and Wilhelm Carl (1786-1859). *Rock-A-Bye Baby*. German brothers who collected folk songs and folktales. The most notable are known as *Grimm's Fairy Tales*.

– 1914 –

Flustered, Mayor Carroll[36] surrenders the podium and broken gavel to the perspiring Constable Jenkins in the hope that he can return this conglomeration of angry men to an assembly where Robert's *Rules of Order*[37] has some meaning. Tossing away the useless gavel, Constable Jenkins raises his breechloader, charged with only powder and wad, and then fires. The explosion, confined within the walls of the city council room, is magnified many fold, bringing the mixed bag of men under control, at least momentarily.

"The next one will be a live load," Constable Jenkins informs all in attendance while inserting a shell containing shot into the breech.

Under normal circumstances the variety of men who gathered on this blustery night would not be found together at any organized social event, except at Tavern Bouvard where an accidental elbow bump would garner a grunt while accepting their jigger or mug and a welcoming smile from Olivia.

The expansive council room within Havre de Grace's city hall is located on North Union Street. It was built in 1870 as a combination school, opera house, and town hall. Its overhanging gable roof shelters three stories of

---

36 Carroll, Tomas M. Mayor of Havre de Grace 1913-1915.

37 *Robert's Rules of Order* (1876). A set of rules for use in non-legislative assemblies devised by Major Henry M. Robert, a military engineer, after researching rules of Congress including an 1845 book known as *Cushing's Manual*.

activities: education, entertainment, and the machinations of governmental employees who are charged with acting in the interest of the everyday man.

Sitting as a knight on the dais, Frank McQuay has assumed the position of representing the moneyed elite with his son beside him as squire, believing it is his duty to remind the rabble that through good government all will benefit. Another in an elevated chair is Judge Hathaway, representing the judiciary, though he would prefer to be home with the Good Book and a cup of sweet tea. Down the line sits Doctor Webster, just in case volatile words turn to action and his skills are required; Mayor Carroll who knew this meeting would have no outcome to further his political ends, but who is still required to officiate, and several local game wardens. Felipe LeCompte, sitting with arms crossed, wants the criminal behavior to cease, the consequences be damned, "The law is the law," is his mantra. Whispering among themselves are Robert Mitchell, his cousin Samuel (Sam) T. Barnes, and Captain William E. Moore. These three men are pragmatists when performing their part-time positions of policing their fellow citizens. Each hunts, owns businesses, and believes that offering education and viable alternatives to the men whose sole source of income is market hunting better serves the needs of the community than are fines, confiscation of guns, or jail time. Why take food from the mouths of families and breed animosity when the possibility exists to improve the lot of a neighbor?

Clay Buchanan, with Anna in tow, stood as two among a hundred irate men. Chairs had been supplied in neat rows with the erroneous belief that this meeting would resemble the cordiality of the Daughters of the American Revolution.[38] The chairs were quickly overturned or used as raised platforms to stand upon to better hurl curses, accusations, and demands to know— Who's responsible? Clay had told Anna that he was skeptical that the views of the hunter would be heard. He restated this opinion to those men around him, pointing out that absent from the stage were the very men from Harford County and Maryland elected to Congress who had voted to restrict their trade.

"You watch and listen," Clay offered. "We'll be rebuked like unruly children."

Clay's motive for attending is to gauge the solidarity of the men standing shoulder to shoulder with him and to learn if there will be an increase in monies or men allied against him. Tonight's meeting is also a good excuse to arrive in town the night before Havre de Grace celebrates the re-dedication of the Concord Point lighthouse. Its associated festivities are a magnet to

---

38 Daughters of the American Revolution (D.A.R.) organized in 1890. A patriotic society of women whose forebears were Americans of the Revolutionary period. A social organization.

Anna and provide Clay with a viable cover story for a nocturnal visit with the proprietress of his favorite watering hole.

Absent from the homespun-clothed men is August Joiner. When Clay informed him of the purpose of the meeting, August shrugged, and with indifference replied, "They're gonna do what they're gonna do and I'm gonna do what I've always done." He then returned to tossing grain to his growing flock of live tollers. Clay could not argue with August's philosophy in light of his agreement with it.

Anna's shoulders are squared with pride to be included, even if only as a witness, to another aspect of adult life, and to events which directly affect her family. Listening to the truths expounded by the men standing on the floor and the impositions taken by the vocal few sitting on stage, Anna becomes keenly aware of the disparity of influence. The only saving grace to the evening is the wavy-haired lad sitting next to his father. Anna has to stand on the tips of her toes and still can only snatch glimpses of William between the men who stand in front of her. She convinces herself that he has seen her because about 20 minutes into the meeting his sour demeanor perked up and he keeps leaning right and left as if to keep sight of her among the jostling men. William's movements are quickly staunched by a remark from his father. William's defiant response is to sit as tall as his frame allows, stretching his neck as an ungainly goose to keep his eyes on the object of his concern; rules, regulations and laws be damned. Inexplicably, the foul odor of close-quartered men and the smoke from their stinkweed cigarettes change within the mind of William to a fresh, out-of-doors fragrance.

"Gentlemen," Constable Jenkins announces. "To continue where the mayor left off, please give your attention to Judge Hathaway."

The judge steps forward to the podium. Constable Jenkins walks to the side of the stage, his breechloader cradled in his arms.

"I was asked to explain the Weeks-McClean Act that was signed by President Taft last year," Judge Hathaway begins without the need for notes, as he has had to study the pertinent laws in the course of sentencing its violators. "I know you are all men of intelligence so I will summarize the points. Migratory birds, that being ducks, geese, swan, crane, or any of the many species that fly from one point geographically to another for the purpose of nesting or avoiding inclement weather have been placed under federal custody. The Act prohibits shooting of duck and geese except November 1st through January 31st." Frank McQuay nods his head in agreement, selectively forgetting that last week, the beginning of September, he paid Clay Buchanan to guide for him and Lawrence Fitzgerald Remy. The men hunted out of season and bagged enough ducks to feed the entire McQuay household, including the servants, for two weeks so long as the ice can be replenished to prevent spoilage.

"...There is a closed season on swan, curlew, willet, gray back, calico back..."

"You're gonna starve us!" cries a voice from the back of the hall. The cry is mingled with a grumble that grows with the naming of each species.

"...dowitchers, knot, plover and other beach birds." The judge pauses for a moment, looking out upon the sea of surly faces, glad that the only man armed tonight is Constable Jenkins, "And last, the Act forbids hunting from sunset to sunrise." The judge looks up in time to step back from the podium as a chair thrown from the crowd crashes into it. Applause erupts from the hunters. Remaining calm, ever the dignified jurist, and holding up his hand to prevent Constable Jenkins from overreacting, the judge straightens his plain gray suit, and then steps to the edge of the stage.

"My sympathies are with you," Judge Hathaway speaks softly, making the assembly quiet down, "but that is all the law will allow me. If any of you are brought before me by these game wardens I will follow the law and impose the penalty mandated by statute." The judge turns as if to retake his seat then turns back to again address the men, "Change is never easy. We as human beings believe we want things to stay as they are; status quo, but think for a minute, do you really want your lives to remain as they are? Change can be for the better. I know you men to be resourceful and creative. I'm confident you will find a legal path that will bring prosperity and self-respect."

Clay hopes the meeting will be adjourned on the judge's somewhat positive words, though words are easily spoken, and rarely do they fill the mouths of families who have always relied on a gun for sustenance.

"Quiet! Quiet down," Game Warden Felipe LeCompte's accented words pierce the room as he steps forward. The hunters, many of whom are also property owners in some small fashion or another, glare with contempt. Their hatred of this man begins with the occupation he has chosen and ends with his ability to trespass onto a man's land without warrant to protect a bird that was destined for the dinner table. *What happened to the sovereignty of the king, his castle, and his land?* This question has been pondered by many fathers confronted on their own porches as meals and means to procure them are confiscated in front of his children, their rumbling stomachs are a protest that is ignored by the government man.

"As the judge failed to remind you, I will. This state enacted in 1872, rest days that prohibit hunting of any fowl, and in 1900, the Lacy Act made it a federal offense to transport illegally taken birds across state lines."

Boos and hisses resound throughout the hall, but LeCompte continues his harangue, "Why do you persist in violating these laws?" LeCompte points to several men standing near the front, "You men. Joseph Dye, Norris Jackson, John Thompson, I know each of you are in possession of illegal punt or armada guns." Then addressing the general audience, "I continue to find illegal duck cages and there are reports of the use of a gunning light. These are crimes and they will not be tolerated. This is your final warning. If you men persist in breaking the law the full weight of the state and federal government will fall upon you. You can surrender your illegal weapons or we," with the sweep of his arm, LeCompte indicates Robert Mitchell, Sam Barnes, and Captain Moore, who are caught chatting, and who wish to be anywhere but sitting in the spotlight, and in association with a fanatic, "will pursue you, catch you, and have you hauled off to jail."

This last statement of *hauling off to jail* does not sit well with Judge Hathaway, as it is not statutorily correct, at least for the first offense, but to publicly correct this firebrand of a game warden at this moment would serve no purpose.

Clay fears an old fashioned lynching may be the closing act, and then watches as Frank McQuay takes over the podium. He unfolds several pieces of paper, clears his throat, and with an unseemly glee, he leaps into the fray.

"Market hunters of the Susquehanna Flats, I address you tonight to help each of you gain a broader understanding of why these restrictions are being enacted. There have been some of you who have shouted, 'Who's responsible?' Well, I'll tell you," Frank McQuay pauses as the men's attention is piqued. "It is you."

Curses and shouts fill the room. Constable Jenkins' profuse sweating rises to a new level of soppiness. Rivulets of water run off the breechloader from where he grips the barrel. William is mortified and seeks an escape route from the lion's den that his father has not only led him into, but he is now jabbing the antagonized beast.

"I have copies of several of the many news articles that are framed and nailed to the walls of Tavern Bouvard," Frank McQuay waves the papers accusingly. "Starting as far back as the 1880s, on one November day, more than 10,000 ducks were shot on the Flats for the New York market."

An old man, crooked, and lean of hair except those stringing from his ears and nose, nods, grinning toothless. His memory still intact, visualizes that incredible day.

"Yes," Frank McQuay catches the gleam in the old man's eyes, "you should remember that day, Mr. Dobson. You shot 540 ducks before your gun burst. Then there was the day in 1893 when 5,000 birds were shot. The article reports that many thousand more would have been killed except for the calm weather that stopped the flying." Frank McQuay scans the crowd, seeking one particular man. This middle-age man of rotund features is unsure if he should stare unflinching at his accuser or look away as his memory re-visits the past with delight. "Raise your hand, Jesse Poplar. You alone knocked down 235 from your sinkbox."

Jesse's grin is a confusion of pride and guilt, as several men standing nearby shake his hand and slap his back in recognition of superb shooting.

Frank McQuay's point, whatever it is, is lost on these men, "There are more examples of excessive gunning, but you know the score better than I do. What we don't know is the count taken, the tens of thousands killed by the night gunner who skulks in the dark. There are no news articles written about him and his sneak skiff. He steals from all of us, not only the ducks, but the pleasure of the hunt itself." Frank McQuay misjudges his audience, believing that the night gunner is a small fraction of the whole that makes up the water fowling community. Little sympathy is gained by this tactic because most of the men gathered tonight have at one time or another hunted after sundown. Frustrated, Frank McQuay cuts short his last two points, "I continue to hear cries of poverty and starvation because of the new restrictions, but it seems that with blackheads selling for a buck and a half a pair, redheads for two-fifty, and mallards for three dollars, one day's shoot would bring a man a standard of living far above the 22 cents per hour laborer's wage."

"No man's bag is filled every day," shouts a grizzled hunter who spits chewing tobacco on the polished floor.

Frank McQuay continues undaunted, "Listen to reason. If the ducks and geese continue to decline, who is going to pay to be guided? Not me. Many of you make a tidy sum guiding for those who you disrespectfully call sports."

"We don't have to listen to this," cries a voice from the back. The double oak doors are thrown open. The hunters stream out into the night, some to regroup at Tavern Bouvard to begin tomorrow's celebration early. Others disappear into the night to prepare for the morning's hunt. No man would acknowledge his concern, but those who attempted to sleep did not rest easy. Two thoughts disturbed the men: the many great flocks that within memory, joining as one to cover the entire sky are now distinguishable as individual entities with time and space separating each group, and those forces beyond their control are tightening their grip on their livelihoods.

Frank McQuay shouts his own parting shot at the thinning crowd, "Wealthy men like myself who are busy during the week have a right to hunt, too. We'll not pay the cost for a guide, or exorbitant fees to outfit sporting yachts if the birds are scarce." His voice trails off. The last hunter standing in the middle of the large hall has his hands in his pockets, a chewed cigarette dangling from the corner of his mouth, and a teenage girl by his side. Clay Buchanan shakes his head slowly, whispering to Anna, "With all his education he still knows nothing." Anna only half listens to her father's words. She is taking in the destruction surrounding them. The chairs, overturned, strewn about and broken symbolize the dead waterfowl and the desperate men who depend upon them.

Filled with rage by the discourteous nature of the walk out, Frank McQuay folds his papers, creasing them between his fingers, and then turns to the men sitting on the dais in expectation of their sympathy. What he finds are frowns. The mayor is worrying about the next election. The judge is disappointed in the breakdown of communication. The game warden is perturbed by the snubbing of the law. The three part-time duck police are annoyed with themselves for their poor judgment in showing up tonight.

Conspicuously absent from his chair is William. He made his escape while his father was engaged in riling the masses. William believed he could survive his father's wrath for abandoning him, but if a riot broke out, he would not be perceived as any different than his father—like father, like son—and one fat constable could not protect him.

His dirty hands paw her yellow dress and grab at her bare legs as he tries to pull Anna down. Shrieking, kicking, and dripping sweat from frantic exertion, Anna triumphs as she is first to reach the hatchway into the lantern room at the top of the Concord Point lighthouse.

"Anna Buchanan, you cheated," out of breath, Delbert climbs through the hatch to grudgingly accept second place.

"Did not!" Anna replies. All thoughts of maturity disappeared at Delbert's challenge to race to the top. It is rare for anyone to enter the sanctity of the lighthouse keeper's domain, let alone to have the opportunity to gallivant, but today's special occasion allows all comers that freedom.

"I said, 'We race on Go.' You started when I said, 'Three,'" Delbert points out Anna's failure to follow instructions which led to an unfair advantage and her ultimate victory.

"You said, 'After one, two, three, then go.' So I went after three," Anna takes on the haughty manner of an uncompromising wordsmith in defense of her devotion, play-acting annoyance with Delbert's picayune grievance. "If you meant we go after you say Go, then you should have made that clear, which you didn't. Regardless, I win. You lose."

Dispensing with the controversy, the two escape through a glass-topped hinged panel to plop down on the exterior walkway. Their legs hang over the edge. Their arms rest on the lowest of three iron railings circling the walk. A brisk breeze lifts Anna's skirt and crackles the 48-star flag flapping on its newly whitewashed pole next to the lighthouse. From their vantage, the whole of Havre de Grace is literally at their feet, and the view of the vast Susquehanna Flats spread out for miles with its working sail boats and active sinkboxes. Despite the previous night's lecture on hunting restrictions, blasts from distance shotguns can be heard when the wind's erratic direction shifts momentarily onshore. Anna and Delbert squint against the mid-morning sun to watch stupid ducks decoy in, then plummet out of the sky to splash into the bay, now dead ducks.

The lighthouse was built at the point where the muddy Susquehanna River meets the tidal flow of the Chesapeake Bay. The area was originally known as Point Conquest as it was a true triumph for sailors to navigate the dangerous area. Constructed of Port Deposit granite by John Donohue, a local contractor, the lighthouse walls are more than three feet thick at its base, narrowing to 18 inches at the parapet. Its total height may only be 36 feet, but its nine whale-oil lamps reflecting through Fresnel lens can be seen for miles to guide mariners to a safe berth.

Along with other sightseers standing or sitting on the walkway, Anna and Delbert listen to the town's brass band that has been assembled next to a temporary rostrum. The enthusiastic band strikes up patriotic tunes between the speechifying. The rededication of the lighthouse runs with a popular theme of reminding Havre de Gracians of the pride they share in the bravery of one of their own. The original lighthouse keeper, John O'Neill, who is the ancestor of the current keeper, single-handedly fired cannons at the attacking British navy during the war of 1812.

Later, when John O'Neill was asked why he stood his post when others ran away, he modestly replied, "I'm a simple Irishman trying to protect the town in which I live and my new country that I love."

– 1812 –

Unrelenting pounding on the door of the small cottage that sits across the street from the lighthouse woke its inhabitants. Stumbling and groggy, the 44-year-old John O'Neill yanked open the cottage door to determine the cause of the pre-dawn commotion.

"The British fleet, sir," cried a terrified lad, the lone sentry for the entire town. "They're sailing in!"

"Muster the militia at the cannons," John's sleep was swept away with a wave of adrenaline. "King George shall not burn this town."

It was King George's plan to use his fleet of war ships to blockade the Chesapeake Bay, burn towns, and destroy factories along the shore, specifically targeted were the cannon foundries near Havre de Grace. The goal was to cripple and punish the upstart nation for its audacity to attempt to dictate trade and declare war against a king over a paltry matter of seizing American ships and imprisoning its sailors.

John pulled on a heavy shirt and pants against the cool May morning as his wife and daughter, roused from their slumber by the clamor rising in the street, looked to him with worried expressions.

"My darlings," John comforted his family with a warm embrace, "you needn't worry about me. There's yet to be born an Englishman who can best an Irishman in a fair fight."

With tears in her young eyes, 15-year-old Matilda squeezed her father tightly, "When have the English ever fought fairly?" From the Irishman's point of view, no truer words had ever been spoken, but as a father he dared not acknowledge it, "Get dressed the two of you and take refuge in the woods. I'll be along to fetch you after I've dissuaded these limeys.[39]"

Racing to the three cannons situated adjacent to the town at Potato Battery, John's spirits were crushed when he found only a handful of men milling around waiting for instruction. John O'Neill had been commissioned a lieutenant over the local 50-man militia. They may have been mostly undisciplined, non- uniformed, older and disabled men, but John expected all 50 to answer the summons.

Reviewing the scant assets before him, John ordered the men to make ready the cannons for firing. Offshore, debarking into barges from several ships of the king's admiralty, came British landing forces, 400 strong, a number equal to the entire population of Havre de Grace, including women and children.

"Fire!" shouted John.

The three cannons spewed ineffective iron balls that missed their many targets. Disciplined to a fault, the musketed Marines riding in the barges did not blink or flinch as water thrown up from the cannon balls impacting the water drenched their red coats.

Aboard the *Maidstone*, commanded by Rear Admiral George Cockburn, the officers and crew were surprised and delighted by the showing of a defense, meager though it was. With a wry grin, Admiral Cockburn, who was standing next to the helm, handed his porcelain teacup to the ship's best boy. Clearing his throat so all on deck would hear, the Admiral bellowed, "Finally, a town with starch in its britches." His desire was to infect his crew with the thought that their skill would finally be tested. "Captain! Show them the guns of a ship of war."

Onshore, John and his ragtag men were reloading when an explosion of cannon and the roar of rockets from the *Maidstone* shook the ground beneath them. With no time to run and no place to take shelter, the exposed men crouched down, praying for salvation from the fire and brimstone that rained down upon them in no less quantity than that which destroyed Sodom and Gomorrah.[40]

---

39 Limey. Derogatory slang for a British person originally used to describe sailors because limes were first used aboard British ships to ward off scurvy during long voyages.

40 Sodom and Gomorrah. Biblical cities that God destroyed because the sins of the inhabitants were unpardonably grievous. Genesis 19:24-26. *Holy Bible.* King James Version, 1987 printing. Public domain.

Between British barrages, John shook off the concussions to find that he was still alive, but alone beside the cannons. His men had not been killed but were fleeing into the woods. Their spines were broken by fear.

"Cowards!" John called after them, but the loud ringing in his ears made it impossible to know if he had actually uttered a sound. Wasting not a moment, John fired the three loaded cannons, one after the other. The third and largest recoiled awkwardly, its wheel caught his pant leg to roll over his thigh as John was pulled to the ground. Injured and unable to lift the heavy balls to reload, John retreated to town to join another man who had taken refuge in the nail factory. Taking up an extra musket, John fired repeatedly at the Marines in the oncoming barges until the ammunition was exhausted.

The gun crews aboard the *Maidstone* adjusted their aim toward the town to cover the landing Marines. Cannon balls smashed through house and store as rockets set ablaze this quaint hamlet whose name is credited to the Marquis de Lafayette. This young Frenchman had come to America during the Revolutionary War to aid the colonists during their struggle against a mutual enemy, Great Britain. As Lafayette crossed the Susquehanna, he was so taken by the idyllic village nestled at the junction of two pristine bodies of water, he burst forth with, "C'est La Havre de Grace," as the village's resemblance to La Havre de Grace in France was undeniable in its natural beauty. After a time, the Maryland General Assembly incorporated the community as Havre de Grace.[41]

"We must flee," cried the man as the last musket ball left John's gun.

"I'm afraid I'll only slow you down. Go on ahead. Find that cowardly militia and implore them to defend their homes, if not for country, but for the sake of honor."

Alone again, John limped to the village common in search of a single brave man with munitions. He found only his town on fire and the advancing Marines led by an English officer on a prancing stallion. Outnumbered 400 to one, without powder, wad, or ball, and by order of the mounted officer, John O'Neill reluctantly laid down his musket to be taken prisoner.

Clapped in irons, deep within the damp hold of the *Maidstone*, John learned that he would be hanged for the crime of firing on soldiers of His Majesty's service. John's despair was not from remorse over his acts against a cruel king that has brought him to this dire end, but from breaking his word to his wife and daughter. John was willing to die for them if a good would come from his sacrifice, but to die in vain with his town destroyed and his family left without its provider, seemed sinful.

---

41 Havre de Grace. French for "harbor of mercy."

Two decks above John, in the Admiral's cabin, standing courageous with knees knocking beneath her fire-charred dress, Matilda again pleaded her father's case with the Admiral with the goal of a reprieved sentence. Two days ago, upon learning of her father's capture and fate, Matilda broke away from her mother who had crumbled with grief. She set out alone in the first undamaged skiff she could find to row out to where the *Maidstone* was anchored. An amused sailor standing by the rail and observing the solitary rower, called out to his superior, "Officer of the Watch, should we prepare to repel the boarder?" Having witnessed the young girl approach his mighty war ship, determination in every stroke of the oars, the always serious, commissioned officer replied, "Only if you are a cad."

Upon climbing the rope ladder to the deck, Matilda swallowed, then licked her lips so that her voice would ring clear without a hint of the fear that filled her, and demanded to speak with whoever was in charge.

Admiral Cockburn admired spunk, so long as it was presented respectfully. The Admiral then opened a leather bound book and read the law to Matilda: "Any civilian firing on soldiers must pay with his life." Matilda pointed out that her father was not a civilian, but a commissioned officer in the militia. Admiral Cockburn was not convinced, as her father wore no uniform or insignia. Matilda begged for time to prove his commission. Admiral Cockburn allowed her three days.

Wearing the same dress from two days ago, now fouled with soot from rummaging through her partially burned home, Matilda presented the Admiral with official Maryland State papers that left no doubt that John O'Neill was a lieutenant commissioned to command the state's militia.

"The law is the law," boomed the Admiral. "Release the officer and escort him to the deck."

Standing on deck with a glorious afternoon sun shining down, the Admiral addressed Lieutenant O'Neill, "Lef-ten-ant, your attire needs attention, but there's little doubt that your bravery can stand up to the strictest inspection." And to Matilda, "Keep this in remembrance of Admiral George Cockburn, who admires loyalty and bravery in his enemies as he rewards the same virtues in his men." Into Matilda's hand the Admiral placed a token of respect, his personal gold-mounted tortoiseshell snuffbox.

This token represented the courage of two acts: John O'Neill's defense of town and country, and Matilda's defense of family, both in the face of overwhelming odds. The snuffbox and what it symbolizes; courage, bravery, loyalty, and willingness to sacrifice was handed down through the generations of O'Neill's as a reminder of what it took to create a great nation, and what is required to maintain it.

– 1914 –

With grandiloquent intonations and arm gestures, the mayor continues, "...
the snuffbox is now in the possession of one of our favorites. Will the son of
Millard Fillmore Tydings and Mary Bond O'Neill step up here? Come on,
Chief, let's take a gander."

The band's two snare drummers, one a raucous teenager, the other an
ancient veteran, rat-tat-tat in competition with each other, attempting to
mimic the blinding beats of a passing humming bird's wings. The rattling
snare coaxes Chief to the front and excites the crowd for the grand reveal.
The citizens of Havre de Grace part as if commanded by the hands of Moses
to allow Chief to walk forward with only claps on his back and brisk hand
shakes to impede his progress. All are done in admiration of the keeper of
the town's holy relic. Millard E. Tydings holds the polished snuffbox aloft
in his tapered fingers that are usually reserved for slashing the air to skewer
opponents on one legal point or another. At 24, Chief radiates confidence
and ambition with a charming and whimsical demeanor toward his friends,
qualities attributed to the genial O'Neills. His adversaries find him humorless
and hot tempered, traits imposed by the Tydings' side of the family tree.
These contradictory characteristics are carried within a frame that is tall,
muscular, and athletic, topped by an aristocratic profile, granite chin, Roman
nose, and penetrating blue eyes.

Chief steps up onto the rostrum. The frenetic drumming is drowned out
by applause and cheers. The polished gold and tortoiseshell glints in the sun
as Chief slowly turns the treasured relic. From the point of view of every

citizen, the snuffbox is emitting its own light, bathing men, women, and children with inspiration and instilling the belief that each are endowed with the same courage that ran through John O'Neill's veins, regardless of their personal lineage.

"Do you believe some Admiral gave a girl his snuffbox?" Delbert asks, his legs swinging in time with Anna's.

"Don't you believe a girl can be courageous?" Anna replies.

Delbert changes the subject, wise enough not to get into that sort of a debate with Anna, "My pa told me that O'Neill was also awarded a sword by the folks of Philadelphia, but I've never seen it."

Led by the mayor, the band plays a rousing rendition of *In Defense of Fort Henry*. Proudly adopting the song as their own anthem, the adults recite words they know by heart while the children mouth Francis Scott Key's inspiring poem commemorating the dawn of September 14, 1814, when after a night of British navel bombardment, the American flag still flew over the fort:

> "Oh, say, can you see, by the dawn's early light.
> What so proudly we hail'd at the twilight's last gleaming?
> Whose broad stripes and bright stars, thro' the perilous fight."

The beats of his heart are strong. His skin prickles under the blue suit. Deep in his marrow, Chief vows to God that he will uphold the honor and memory of the brave men and women who have gone before him into battle if he is ever called upon to defend this nation.

> "O'er the ramparts we watch'd, were so gallantly streaming?
> And the rockets' red glare, the bombs bursting in air,
> Gave proof thro' the night that our flag was still there.
> O' say, does that star-spangled banner yet wave.
> O'er the land of the free and home of the brave?"

All eyes are on the American flag waving red, white, and blue. Flying overhead from the bay, in simulation of that fateful day one hundred years ago, black ducks acting the part of cannon balls mix with streaking red-wing blackbirds playing rockets. The reciting words catch in the throats of many, who for a brief moment feel the fear of their forebears, but are spared the dire consequences.

> "On the shore dimly seen thro' the mists of the deep,
> Where the foe's haughty host in dread silence reposes,
> What is that which the breeze, o'er the towering steep,
> As it fitfully blows, half conceals, half discloses?"

The mayor scans the crowd, each face aglow with pride to be a citizen of Havre de Grace. Every eye is on the flag that he personally raised, and every mouth uttering the words that he leads them in. Today's celebration is what the populace will be reminded of when it is time for them to vote, not last night's city hall debacle. Turning his gaze toward Chief, the mayor is unsettled by the tears running down the younger man's cheeks.

"Now it catches the gleam of the morning's first beam,
In full glory reflected, now shines on the stream:
'T is the star-spangled banner: 0, long may it wave
O'er the land of the free and home of the brave!"[42]

The crowd erupts again with cheers and applause. The mayor wraps a comforting arm around Chief, "Steady man."

With steely eyes and a forward jutting chin, Chief whispers a desire that may as well have been a prophesy, "If God answers prayers, may I be the instrument to make that our nation's anthem."

On such special gatherings as a rededication ceremony, patriotism surges, but it has to compete with a far more primal instinct brought about by the smorgasbord of olfactory delights permeating the air. The ladies of Havre de Grace are known for several fine qualities; fear of God, love of family, and the ability to set a table. This last quality, in any other geographical region might only be considered fair, but elevating their recipes out of mediocrity is the town's location that provides the ladies access to a vast variety of fresh fish, fowl, crustacean, venison, and other small mammals of the marsh and bay. Milk from Mitchell's dairy is delivered daily and vegetables are picked from one's own garden or purchased from the market only hours after leaving the field.

Treasured as a special blessing is the McCormick Spice Co. The founders built their warehouses on the waterfront of Baltimore's sheltered harbor. Condiments from around the world are gathered here for processing, packing, and re-shipment. It is a mandatory pleasure for any citizen visiting Baltimore to stop in to fill orders for the kitchens of neighbors, or for a few extra pennies, to ask the Grossos to pick up a package when they make their nightly run with barrels of black-market ducks.

Following their noses to the lunch banquet provided for all, Anna and Delbert spiral down the lighthouse stairs, squeezing by other lookee-loos.

---

42 *Star Spangled Banner*. Composed by Francis Scott Key as a poem in September 1814, entitled: *In Defense of Fort Henry*. In 1931, Congress proclaimed it the United States National Anthem on legislation sponsored by Senator Millard E. Tydings (Chief).

Racing out of the lighthouse door, the two teens collide with Chief, nearly knocking him over.

"Whoa. Slow down you two," says Chief as he regains his balance.

"Sorry, Chief," Anna replies as she bounces off him to continue on her quest with Delbert. Their goal is to gorge on the tasty dishes that cover the tables extending from Concord Street and around the corner onto Lafayette.

"Wait!" Chief calls out. "I have a message for you, Anna."

Anna and Delbert skid to a halt.

"There's a young man who wishes to have a word with you."

"Really?" Anna is delighted by this news. It is not completely unexpected, but she had been unsure as to when another meeting would be arranged. Delbert's face scrunches with consternation.

"Anna," Chief continues solemnly, "I'm a member of the Maryland Bar Association, an officer of the court. As an attorney, I would never lie." Chief pauses to let his words sink in until all three are laughing at the joke, "But seriously, he's down past the cannery by the mounds if you're interested."

"Of course, thanks," Anna sprints off. Her hunger for food is forgotten. A different hunger has taken its place though Anna cannot describe what it is she craves or what will satisfy her.

"Anna!" Delbert calls after her. He is standing where Anna left him near the base of the lighthouse.

"What?" Anna stops 20 feet away.

"What are you doing?" Delbert remains where he is, raising his voice while adults and children walk and play around him.

Anna hesitates in answering, not sure of the truth, or what will suffice as an answer.

"He's just a friend, Del."

"No. I'm your friend," Delbert decides to throw caution to the wind. "He's a McQuay."

With this surname spoken aloud, her presumed secret rings out for all to hear. Anna is taken off guard and surprised that Delbert somehow knew who she was going to see, and then remembers his footprints on the path. Anna scans the crowd with a fear that all gathered will stop in their celebrations to accuse her, but of what?

Deceitfulness?

Maybe.

Betraying her father?

Possibly.

The moment of apprehension passes with only Delbert continuing to confront her.

"Del, his name's William, and as you are my friend," Anna half pleads and half hopes to guilt Delbert into accepting her decision, "I ask that you trust me." Anna breaks away from his stare to run off to her meeting. She hates it that she is the one who feels guilty.

William's frustration is not from his inability to skip bleached and broken oyster shells across rough, wind-blown water, but by the apparent failure of his perfect plan. His father had absented himself early from the rededication ceremony to spend the morning betting his money at the racetrack in the company of wealthy men who were up from Baltimore. The Graw was completed in 1912 on the outskirts of town and had quickly acquired two reputations. The first, highly promoted, was that of championship races at one of the best racing strips of the American turf where owners who had hopes of winning the Kentucky Derby trained their thoroughbreds. The second, down played by the track owners, and not surprisingly its embarrassed victims, is that betting depleted the purses of men from all economic levels.

When his father informed him of where he would be and for how long, William calculated the possibilities. He could not directly approach Anna, but he could send word through a trusted friend. Checking his silver-plated pocket watch, its minute and hour hands nearing 12, the time his father mandated they meet to return home, William's frustration over his failed plan mixed with disappointment over not seeing Anna. Admitting defeat, he began walking along the shore, his boots crunching forcefully on the scattered shells. From this distance, a quarter of a mile, and secluded behind the mounds twice the height of a tall man, William was surprised that he could hear the flag next to the lighthouse flutter. Cocking his head, perplexed, the corner of his eye catches a glimpse, revealing the true source of the flapping material. Turning his head, William sees Anna looking down from the top of the mound. Her dress lifts and falls, a careless victim to the brisk breeze. Anna's face beams, delighted, and excited to find William.

Modesty seems to be an affliction brought about by the passing of many years and the curt instruction by those who envy. Anna cannot be blamed for her slow reaction in smoothing down her dress when crisp gusts of wind whip it up as a spinnaker sailing before the wind. Her youth and free spirit have yet to be contaminated by thoughts of vulgarity. Two years her senior and curious as a raccoon in a pantry, the brief exposure of Anna's legs and undergarment sends William's heart rate racing and his thoughts to the exploits of braggarts.

Anna and William are frozen to their spots. His immobility is attributed to his delight in Anna's appearance upon the high mound; black hair blowing devil-may-care in rhythm with her bright yellow dress and with legs still tan from the frivolities of summer swimming in violation of the swimsuit ordinance. To William, Anna is Joan of Arc[43] cresting the hillocks in wild defense of her people and in the name of God. Muscles still tense with frustration dampen his joy in her presence. With an unfamiliar anger that is rising, he knows their encounter will be too brief. *Dang it! Why is she so late?*

Anna's hesitation is rooted in indecision. She wants to throw herself into this young man's arms, kissing him from ear to ear until her lips hurt, but a shyness not known before causes doubt. *I'm such a silly girl.*

An instant later, as if startled by the gun at The Graw, filly and colt bolt toward each other. William scrambles up the steep mound, slipping on shells that slide as if made of shale. Gravity assists Anna's unbalanced descent. Her shod feet fly out from under her. Her backside ungracefully smacks the incline, sending her tumbling into William's arms, exactly where she wants to be.

"I've been waiting," pants William, his words tinged with a note of annoyance.

"Chief just told me," pleads Anna, hoping William's displeasure is with the lateness of the message giver and not with her.

"I can't stay. My father will be waiting," William's expression is agonized, but instead of complaining more, he kisses her, exactly what she wants.

Her hunger has returned, and it is William she wants to devour.

His anger evaporates in Anna's embrace, and then it is replaced by a growing fear of what his father is going to do to him for being late, so William makes his offense worth the punishment—Anna gasps.

---

43 Joan of Arc (French: Jeanne d'Arc) (1412-1431). At age 17, and under the belief of divine inspiration, she led French forces to victory over the English at Orleans. It was the turning point in the Hundred Year's War. The English saw Joan as an agent of the devil. Captured in 1430, she was convicted of witchcraft and heresy and burned at the stake on May 30, 1431. In 1456, Pope Callistus II granted a hearing where Joan was pronounced innocent. Known as the Maid of Orleans, Joan was canonized on May 16, 1920.

Silly, lighthearted, giddy and gay are not adjectives used to describe Clay, except this evening as father and daughter walk the gravel road home. Anna is witnessing a side of her father that is quirky and amusing at the very least and strange to the extreme of worrisome.

Clay is drunk.

Holding a tenured position in Tavern Bouvard, Anna has a lifetime of experience in judging a man's demeanor after the spirits take a hold of him. There is the sad drunk of the merchant who wallows to the extent of tears in every grief that life has thrown his way. There is the buddy drunk of the hunter who loves his dog, his current best friend who sits a blind with him, and every patron who will allow his embrace. There is the happy drunk of the skipjack captain who jokes and cajoles all within hearing to merriment, and then there is the angry drunk whose chosen occupation is a perpetual state of mind of the dispossessed. He finds ridicule, despisement, and disrespect in every eye and discordant tone of voice. Flying fists and kicking feet are his justifiable response. Anna has always admired Olivia's instinctive response to each:

Sad drunk — compassion, with a tear-drying handkerchief.

Buddy drunk — hug, with a subtle defense of her pinch-worthy derriere.

Happy drunk — ribald joke, with a playful tease.

Angry drunk — cudgel[44] with a cot to sleep it off.

Anna judges her father to be a mix of buddy and happy as he recalls, to exaggeration, the day's festivities at the lighthouse and the post celebratory party at Tavern Bouvard. Clay's walk, inspired by the dancing limbs of playful loblollies responding to the blustery wind, turns to a two-step jig to the left, and then three sliding boot steps to the right.

"C'mon, now. Don't be a stick in the mud," Clay grabs Anna's hands to spin her in wobbling circles.

Anna's unsure of the tune playing in her father's head, but revels as they jig, twirl, and high step under the fading light of an orange sky. Dragonflies accompany the madcap gyrations down the lonely road. Zooming about and around Clay and Anna to vigilantly defend their aerial domain, the dragonflies snack on the few insects stirring this late in the season. Anna loses herself in the wonderment of the moment. Clay's gray eyes twinkle above a face in need of a shave, and his grin, though stained from tobacco, is smiling at her. Anna allows herself to believe that she sees in her father a love for her equal to the joy he has for hunting, even if it is a by-product of excessive drink.

---

44 Cudgel. A short, thick, heavy stick used as a weapon. A club or small bat.

In the midst of a twirl, Clay stops. His nose wrinkles, sensitive to the smallest changes in his environment. The smile falls from his face, pulling the twinkle out of his eyes. Clay turns to stare down the road ahead of them. Anna follows her father's sober gaze. Adrenaline strips his veins of intoxication. Rolling toward them, rising silent and menacing, a wall of smoke covers the road and turns the remaining orange light to brown then black.

Fire.

Man is the only creature who will run toward a fire. Whether in a heroic act to save others, in defense of one's property, or merely in fascination of an all-consuming entity, the individual's motive depends on his character. All other creatures that have the means, wiggle, crawl, scamper, leap, run, flit, or fly in fear of the destruction that a conflagration brings to their home and habitat. Even the ferocious dragonflies abandon their posts.

Anna's flight instinct is strong, but her desire to remain beside her father sets her feet moving forward at a run as Clay's long strides plod steadily ahead. The erratic wind, a blessing to the hunter as it encourages the birds to fly, opens and closes pockets of air within the enshrouding smoke. Heavy embers swirling gray within their cloud, dream enviously of being admired as their dainty cousins, the snowflakes, but they must accept reality and choke the lungs of the living while hoping to extend their lives by spreading the hot seeds of their creation.

Clay passes his handkerchief to Anna to cover her mouth and nose as he pulls up his undershirt to cover his own. His eyes water and burn from the acrid smoke as he peers ahead looking for its source. He can clearly hear the crackling and popping of bursting water within the trunks of oaks, pines, and maples, and the roar of fire consuming brambles and crowning to devour the majestic trees, some of which have stood for decades, others for centuries over a landscape rich in the diversity of life.

Clay feels Anna's hand clutching the back of his coverall as he struggles forward. Her eyes are closed. She follows by touch then stumbles into Clay as he stops at an object materializing out of the smoke and night. "Oh," Anna's startled by her collision with her father, and then peeks with watery eyes at her surroundings that reveal little but confusion and disorientation. Choking, she asks, "What is it?"

"It's Frank McQuay's Buick," Clay uses his hands to guide him around the stationary vehicle and to feel the seats, searching for unconscious occupants who may have succumbed to the smoke. His concern for human life supersedes his dislike for the Buick's owner. A lump catches in Anna's throat, fearing for the safety of the boy she adores.

"Do you see anyone?" cries Anna, her eyes squeezed tight against the smoke, hoping that the hysteria welling up within her is not heard in the tone of her voice to betray emotions beyond that of neighborly concern.

Mixed within the roaring flames and whipping wind, jumbled shouts tell of men in the distance. Clay is unable to determine if they are shouts of panic, instructions toward combating the fire, or warning calls, but he is confident they are coming from the western side of the road.

"There's no one here," Clay shouts above the din while leading Anna down the short embankment, "This way." Together they move over blackened ground that was once resplendent in tickseed sunflowers that would radiate gold in the sunlight. Old timers call them butterweed. Their seeds are high in protein and vital to waterfowl. Clay and Anna hurry between the skeletons of oaks and maples, their massive trunks still sputtering with flames that crave raw material to consume, the pines are ashes that scatter within the wind-driven smoke. The shouting becomes discernible words of one man, not panicked, but abusive in his instructions: "Move it!" "Put your backs into it." "We'll work all night if need be." "You two! Get axes on that one." Anna believes the men are fighting the fire to stop the destruction of more wooded fast lands. Clay and Anna cross the fire line to clear the curtain of smoke, its flames dancing in fits.

A dozen yards distant, Frank McQuay stands upon scorched earth. The ground smolders under this boots. He is the general commanding troops involved in a fire fight, except they are the aggressors of the one-sided battle. Half a dozen men employed as field hands by Frank McQuay run along the advancing fire storm throwing lighted brands to encourage the holocaust. Another dozen soot-covered men wield axes to fell the damaged and destroyed trees.

Rising in desperate flight, fleeing their nests containing young ones yet to be fledged are pairs of wood ducks, drake and hen, father and mother.

One pair.

Two pair.

Fourteen pair.

Thirty pair.

The birds taking flight at the last possible second look back, despairing as they leave their nests. They are a fluttering wave of singed primary and tail feathers. Known to the locals as summer ducks they are colorful fowl that nest along creeks and the forested lands above the marsh. Their calls are cries of anguish at the loss of their brood, a generation of birds that will never take flight, that will never view this vast and wondrous continent from on high, and will never have the opportunity to perpetuate a species both beautiful in their markings, and for the fortunate hunter, a feast.

For many creatures, fire is destructive. For others it is an unexpected bonanza. Bobolinks, small playful birds so named for their call, challenge red-winged blackbirds for dominance in collecting fried and fleeing insects. Diving between and before the flames to gobble fat beetles, crunchy grasshoppers, and succulent snails; these excitable birds that normally dine on rice seed gorge themselves with the high-energy morsels.

Frank McQuay's sour disposition this evening is rooted in his failure to restrain his betting exuberance this morning that resulted in grand losses despite his pledge to economize. The excitement at the Graw is always infectious. Moneyed men, gentlemen from Baltimore and New York threw sums in excess of prudence into the betting windows after their favorite steeds. Frank McQuay's pride in being one-of-the-boys goaded him into the same wasteful behavior. Upon arriving home, instead of enjoying the remainder of the weekend in relaxation, Frank McQuay took his financial frustration out on his workers and ordered all hands, including his tardy son, to the northern edge of his fields.

"I cannot waste another day," spat husband to his annoyed wife when she complained about having to dine alone in the company of the Negro servants. "That acreage must be cleared to prepare for planting," was Frank's departing remark. He is a man irritated by having to explain his actions or motives.

The two ash-covered specters emerging from the smoke are first taken by Frank McQuay as loafers from his work crew. A rebuke that includes: pissing away my time and money, never leaves the general's mouth as he begins to recognize the two for who they are as they charge toward his position, the Buchanans, father and daughter. Frank McQuay spits into the burnt black earth, as these are the last two people he wants to encounter tonight.

"Get off my land!" orders the general. "You're trespassing."

The field hands, including William, are distracted from their assigned tasks. They watch, knowing a confrontation between two similar men from opposite sides of the road will erupt into sparks that create their own fire. Frank McQuay is a man driven to bend his surroundings to his will even if it requires breaking it to then rebuild in the image of his creation. For God said: "Rule over the fish of the sea and the birds of the air and over every living creature that moves on the ground." Frank McQuay takes this edict to heart and certainly no man shall dare stand in his way for dominance over the land and everything upon it.

Clay Buchanan may be backslidden in his church going, but if pressed, he can cite McQuay's scripture as portions of Genesis 1:28. Portions, Clay would establish, benefit the narrow-minded seeking selfish goals, and damned be the man to point out the spiritual implications and responsibilities as a ruler, that being: As God's representative in the creaturely realm, he (man) is steward of God's creatures. He is not to exploit, waste or despoil them, but use them in the service of God and man.

Clay is no saint. He is a man who will kill to provide for his family. There is no creature that can be smoked, simmered, sautéed, fried, boiled, or skewered over a spit that will be granted a free pass across his gun sights, his traps or hooks. The difference between these two ornery men is that Frank McQuay will destroy much in his singular pursuit for wealth while Clay Buchanan focuses his sights narrowly, one meal at a time, except in the case of the Davenport.

Both men have blood on their hands.

"McQuay," Clay accosts the general, "your fire's spreading across the road."

"What of it? It should all be in cultivation."

"You don't own that land and have no right to cause its destruction."

"I may not own it yet," Frank McQuay leaves the threat hanging as he crosses his arms in smugness.

Clay moves nose-to-nose with McQuay, "I'd never sell and the Joiners would die before they'd be moved from their land." Spittle flies onto Frank McQuay's face with every defiant word.

Frank McQuay shoves Clay. He stumbles on the broken ground to land undignified in the ashes. Anna rushes to her father to help him up. Frank McQuay shouts orders to his field hands, "Get these two off my land!" Five men, muscled from long hard years working at tasks fit for mules, encircle Clay and Anna, each reaching for an arm or a leg of the toppled man.

"Leave him alone!" screams Anna, fighting with ineffectual fists against the men dragging her father along the ground. From behind her, circling her waist, and pulling her from her defense of her father are arms familiar, yet acting in a fashion now horrible. Anna turns to confront the black-faced boy with eyes white and frightened.

"Anna, stop it," William's words are filled with pleading, but looking past him, Anna's view is of a cruel man ordering others to dirty their hands at a task he himself would not succeed in. Anna slumps in William's arms. In defeat, she sobs, breaking his young heart.

– 1916 –

Two years pass without the McQuay name being spoken aloud in the Buchanan home, though a tension remained as it was constantly on the minds of father and daughter, but for two very different reasons.

Two years with drifting smoke irritating the eyes, lungs, and spirits of those who dwell east of the dividing road as Frank McQuay and his fire gobble up land to the west.

Two years with the too-frequent spark trespassing the legal boundaries drawn on a map and registered at city hall.

Two years of impotence before Judge Hathaway in obtaining a cease and desist order against Frank McQuay's all-consuming appetite for land, his practice of slash and burn, and for compensation for damages to adjacent lands by errant flames.

Again and again, the judge, with clipped legal precision, and a noticeable tone of annoyance by Clay's and other land owners' persistence, would cite the law, "Statute does not provide for redress when the claimant cannot prove a loss. A few burnt trees, shrubs, and grasses that grow wild and are not a part of the landowner's production for timber or scheme for agricultural harvest have no value. Wildlife, by its very name is not attributable to the landowner as it is not part of his livestock and it is free to transit boundaries established by survey and deed." Judge Hathaway, a patient man by practice, tried to explain these intricacies of law in terms that a hunter would understand, "Mr. Buchanan, if from your property you shot a mallard, but in its dying it landed on your neighbor's property and expired there, should your neighbor be allowed a claim against you for the dead duck? Of course not, so until the law establishes a value for nature, which is unlikely as it would be fraught with speculation and subjectivity, these claims against Mr. McQuay for destruction of nature will continue to be ruled as frivolous. You own the land and the improvements to it such as your home. If Mr. McQuay illegally takes your land, or through his burning causes your home to be destroyed, then you would have a cause of action for which this court would address. Case dismissed, again."

Clay's fight is against external forces whose technical use of the law, financial superiority, and the prevailing attitudes toward the intrinsic value of nature are destined to defeat him. Anna's battle is an internal one between an emotional heart and a supposedly rational mind. Arriving at a final resolution regarding her attraction for William, weighed against his actions that to Anna were reprehensible, allowing men to humiliate her father as he was tossed onto the road, is frustrated by her inability to discuss her dilemma with a neutral party. Her father would explode in astonished disbelief at the hint of an interfamily relationship. Delbert would listen attentively, but would be inclined to side with her father. Olivia would react with understanding, but Anna could not risk Olivia spilling the beans to her father. Martha Webster, bless her heart, would hug Anna, and delight in the follies of youth, but the news would somehow reach both fathers before sunset. Anna considered talking with Umbrella George. His wisdom and love of God spoke of compassion. His advice would come from a lifetime of contemplation and worldly observation, but Anna has been unable to approach him when curious ears were not in attendance.

These are the confusing and frustrating times when Anna dearly misses her mother's love, support and guidance.

While tending to her daily chores, washing clothes, cooking the meat of the day, cleaning the shack, and assisting her father in hunting, Anna hoped that busy hands would mean happy hands, but this has not been the case. Her thoughts continually wander back to her first kiss on the porch; William's clumsy fondling of her coverall-protected breasts as they kissed and touched tongues on that day of celebration, and the tragic ending in the burning field. Anna smiles inwardly at the pleasure of the kisses. She softly laughs at the thought that William was groping for bosoms that at age 14 had yet to sprout, but now at 16 would be a prize for any young man to hold. She is still surprised by the tongue thing...very strange...yet somehow inciting her to want more of the same and more of...what? Him? Anna hated him for being part of the McQuay family, for not defending her father. If William cared for her at all he would side with her...but against his own father?

Am I being unfair? Anna asks herself this question repeatedly, but receives no answer. Worse still have been her fruitless walks within the marsh and fast lands on her side of the road. Occasionally, she stands on the road that, since that painful day, has been paved, and looks across vast lands in transition from wooded forests teaming with life to burning, burnt, then mono-culture fields tended by scores of men, not one being William. The solidity of the asphalt is a sad metaphor for the permanence that separates her from him. Anna had hoped that William would find her as he so skillfully did the first time, or at least send a message, but by whom?

Two years without resolution.

Two years without a confrontation to end her physical and emotional misery.

Two years. He probably doesn't remember my name, Anna thinks as she stands over the empty sink. The last supper dish has been washed and placed on the counter to dry. She does not remember washing any of them.

"Finished already?" asks Clay, as he carves a canvasback decoy body while sitting in Jennifer's rocking chair. "Why don't you get another knife and help me with these? There are three dozen left to detail and fall is upon us."

"It's still early. I'd like to go for a walk," Anna steps toward the door half expecting Beauty to accompany her. The two girls look to each other, one with graying fur, stiff joints, and a wish for understanding, the other with love and compassion. Beauty lays her head on her paws to remain in front of the low burning stove.

No words need to be spoken.

Indian summer is a brief interlude between the oppressive heat of summer and the chill that announces the hammer of winter. For the sluggard, these lazy days are a perfect excuse to keep handy a fishing pole and to put off until tomorrow what the wife needs to be completed today. For the hunter, it is a time of the itch that cannot be scratched, the undefined irritation, and anxiousness unresolved. It is a time to re-oil the guns, re-check the boat's caulking, repair and repaint the decoys, double-checking their anchor weights, and then do it all again.

Anna kicked off her boots on the porch to walk the warm soil as she treads a meandering path northward. Wearing a sleeveless overall and an undershirt left her arms bare to enjoy the late afternoon sun and faint breeze that today carries no smoke. The only benefit that had come from the smoke drifting across Buzzards Glory was the suppression of mosquitoes. They are a marsh pestilence that swarm in clouds of their own making and together can suck a body dry of blood leaving the appearance of a bad case of the chicken pox. This benefit has gone largely unnoticed by man, beast, and fowl, because it was replaced with an annoyance of equal proportions; red, watering eyes, scratchy raw throats, and the inability to take deep hearty breaths. With the air clear today, these ravenous insects rise from their hiding places among the high grasses and cattails in search of a blood feast.

Without conscious thought as to her destination, Anna found herself at the snapper's pond. Wiggling her toes in the tepid water, she signals to her ancient friend her presence, and her desire to talk, though today a pouring out of her confusion and frustration better describes her anguished and desperate pleadings for closure. A minute passes and then the familiar nostrils and eyes appear above the water. His presence is a comfort by itself. Each may face his or her own tribulations, but Anna has always sensed a camaraderie that transcends species and language. The snapper is her wise friend whom she would acknowledge as a neutral listener. Because of his advanced age, he has many of the attributes of Umbrella George. Her secrets and desires have always been safe with him and he is safe with her.

Anna is distracted in her melancholy tale by the leisurely passage of a viceroy flitting above the pond. She watches as this local butterfly floats boldly past the all-seeing eyes of the many predatory marsh birds anxious for a meal. Wearing the royal colors of deep orange outlined in brilliant black of the monarch, this usurper of the sovereign's right of passage offers Anna insight into her confusion over William's true character.

Is William deceiving me by his showy exterior?

If there were such a concept as admiration between species there would be none more deserving than the monarch butterfly for their yearly feat of migration. This regal insect with four broad wings weighs less than a goose's flight feather. By any measure it is miraculous that the monarch's migratory route forces it to cross a continent. A heavy rain, a sudden chill, an evil wind blowing in the wrong direction, or an ill-timed drought that dries up the life-sustaining nectar of the poisonous milkweed plant can doom the delicate creature.

Beyond the miracle of migration by all species that traverse unimaginable distances and dangers in their lifetime is the mystery of how several successive generations of the monarch follow the same route to complete one migratory cycle. A young goose, duck, swan, or egret need only follow their elders to learn the route. If they survive predation, one day they will teach it to their newborns. For the monarch butterfly, the distances are great, and their flight slow. They fly only a portion of the route then die off, leaving their offspring to transition through larva, pupa, then to adult, who tackles the next segment of the incredible journey on their own. The monarch repeats this process several times. No generation of the monarch will ever see the entire eastern states' route from Canada to Florida's panhandle and back, but the success of the species depends on each to complete its allotted portion.

Lacking admiration from the marsh birds, the monarch relies on respect. In its larva stage it eats milkweeds and as an adult it feeds on the plant's nectar. The poison of the milkweed accumulates harmlessly in the monarch, but if a bird tries to eat it, the taste is so horrible that the bird will vomit it up. The bird remembers the bright orange and black colors and allows the monarch to transit through its territory unmolested.

The viceroy is a crafty insect, mimicking the colors and pattern of the monarch to openly sneak its fat and tasty body past the birds that erroneously believe it to be distasteful.

Tears well up in the corners of Anna's eyes. Sobbing loudly, she admits to herself that William's handsome appearance and smooth demeanor duped her.

"Hey, little Miss," a crusty voice calls to Anna. "What's with the waterworks?" Emerging from a thicket of brambles is a stump of a man, bent shorter with advanced age. His hair points in all directions of the compass. His clothes are mere tatters. The glint in his eyes shows concern, but his sudden appearance with a shotgun and intrusion into her sanctuary frightens Anna.

The snapper dips below the water.

"Whoa. Didn't mean to startle ya," the dwarfish man shoulders his pump shotgun. "Don't s'pose we know each other. I'm Nat Joiner. You may know my kin?"

Anna wipes her eyes, relaxing, "Del's my best friend."

"Little Cigar? Well, there ya go," Nathaniel slaps a mosquito sucking at his neck. "I'm his gran'pap." Nathaniel plops down next to Anna. His odor is pungent, gritty to her eyes. His smell is of a man who not only lives off the land, but also carries it with him, unless by accident he falls into some creek. "So why is a pretty young thing such as yourself in a state of distress?"

Anna sniffs her runny nose, not wanting to appear too unladylike by wiping it with the back of her hand.

"You can trust me. I've seen and done it all. Probably more'n once. Be your problem that of treasure, adventure, family or foe, I've succeeded in all of it. Some say I'm lucky. I'll agree with 'em but it's also wisdom from experience," not a note of gloating or ego is in Nathaniel's voice. It is his humble truth. A fact as he sees it every day.

"It's romance," Anna blurts out. She is surprised by the ease at which these two words flow from her to the ears of this stranger. These words and their meaning which Anna had held as a secret of greater importance than the whereabouts of the Davenport. Not caring if he will understand, be empathetic, laugh at her juvenile crush, or spread her long-kept secret across Harford County, she is desperate to speak with someone about her torn heart, even if her old friend feels slighted. She promises to make it up to the snapper later by telling him all about the Hanging Gardens of Babylon,[45] supposedly one of the Seven Wonders of the Ancient World. Anna doubts it was as wonderful as her teacher described because if it were that great, built by some king named Nebuchadnezzar II[46] for his wife, Amytis of Media, because she missed the mountains and greenery of her home, people would have maintained it. And it is obvious whoever chooses these Wonders never strolled through this natural garden that is the Chesapeake.

"Ah, troubles of the heart," Nathaniel yanks a length of grass from its root, chewing the stem to release the bitter juice, poor man's tobacco. He sits straighter, his eyes gazing skyward as he remembers his many conquests over the fairer sex, "Now that's a subject in which I excel. Spare me no details. Ol' Nat will direct you onto the correct path."

Anna takes a deep breath to prepare to empty her body of a long held burden. In the telling, it is not explained from beginning to end, but from curiosity to excitement, from shyness to revelation, filling in details of familial relations, grudges, feuds, and jealousies as an afterthought. Through Anna's purging that takes her from giggles to swooning and into tears, Nathaniel sits patiently. He is attentive to every word with only the involuntary scratch of his whiskered chin, a slap at a pesky mosquito, or the intentional twitch of his eyes toward the center of the pond as distractions.

Anna's shoulders slump with exhaustion and relief at the conclusion of her tale. She turns toward Nathaniel hoping for words of wisdom and his proclamation for her direction in life. Licking his chapped lips, the pearls spill forth, "All fathers are bastards." Unintentionally shocking Anna, he continues, "It's like this, young Miss. Fathers do what they think is best, but always it's what's best from their point of view. It ain't our fault." Nathaniel naturally includes himself within the exculpatory acts, "We can't see life from another's point of view and shouldn't be held responsible when our best intentions conflict with the natural course of things."

Anna nods her head, beginning to understand the two fathers, but she is still conflicted over William.

---

45 Hanging Gardens of Babylon. An ornamental garden planted on the ziggurats (a temple shaped in the form of a pyramid with a series of terraces) of ancient Babylon (now southern Iraq).

46 King Nebuchadnezzar II (604-561 B.C.). A king of Babylonia who conquered Jerusalem. 2 Kings 24-25. *Holy Bible*. King James Version, 1987 Printing. Public Domain.

As if reading her thoughts, Nathaniel elaborates on his theory, "You want to please your pa? Of course you do, and your beau wants to do the same, so there is conflict, but fathers aren't going to be around forever, so if you've found love, you grab it and hold on. Damnation to the consequences." Nathaniel sees a spark of hope growing in Anna's eyes, but realizes that one last point needs to be clarified, "Folks say apples don't fall far from the tree, but in my opinion, it's the fall that gives hope for the next generation."

Anna is once again perplexed.

"I'm saying that children aren't doomed to be just like their parents even if they act like 'em at times."

Ignoring Nathaniel's odor, Anna embraces him, giving a bone crushing hug and a thankful peck on the cheek. Anna wants William, and Nathaniel has provided her with the excuses she has needed to overlook his act and take the risks to seek him out, "Thank you." Anna leaps up to run off, to where, she is again unsure, but her decision being made she must move or she will burst from the excitement within her.

Nathaniel is pleased with himself, as always, then raises the cracked butt of the shotgun to his shoulder, pointing the barrel toward the middle of the pond, "You have to breathe sometime."

Dust bombs explode beneath Anna's feet as she skips along a path lined with maples and loblollies that have been spared the fire's insatiable appetite. The hues of bark brown and tan, leaf green, grass yellow, and deepening sky blue are again vibrant in her world with the freeing of her heart and the shedding of her burden of uncertainty. Adding an exclamation of awe to her joy, Anna encounters those whose rightful place is upon the thrones of empires. Within a grove of pines where the branches intertwine in a circling embrace, monarch butterflies by the millions dance about in a playful diversion from their journey south. Their great number turns the very air orange as they float in mass from crowded limb to crowded limb. Their fanning wings animate the stoic trees in a vibrating waltz. Anna moves carefully into their midst, extending her arms as hundreds of the beautiful creatures settle on her hair, arms, and cling with minuscule feet to her clothes. She giggles and shivers as the butterflies scurry about, tickling her while greeting each other with pomp and circumstance.

A lazy moon rising above the Eastern shore shows only half its face. Its pale light bequeaths the stalks of cattails with a yellow tint, and the black soil gathers the night's moisture with sparkles of diamonds in the rough. Anna allows her feet to carry her home through the semi-darkness after the monarchs retired for the evening. A light wind blows flight dust from Anna's body; powder left by the monarchs' wings to bestow upon her a lightness of spirit.

Without warning, the hairs on the back of Anna's neck stiffen, not from fear, but by the disturbance to her enchanted evening. Hidden within the jumble of marsh vegetation, a beast crashes about, grunting and moaning. Anna's fairly confident that it isn't a predator that would harm her because of its lack of stealth. Whatever it is, it is not comfortable, nor is it designed for this habitat, because Anna clearly hears its stumbling and fumbling about.

"Come out of there," calls Anna, assuming the creature understands English or will heed the tone of her command.

Silence...except for the drone of mosquitoes zeroing in on exposed flesh.

The creature is disoriented and crazed by the relentless insects that are thrilled by the meal delivered into their domain. Hearing Anna's words it pauses, twisting its head left and right, seeking direction, and desperate in its hope for rescue from the prison the cattails have become.

"I said, 'Come out of there,'" Anna stands with her hands on her hips, impatient, knowing that if Beauty were with her, the dog would flush out the creature, even if it required a convincing nip or two.

Charging toward Anna through the cattails that are knocked askew by its stumbling run, the creature cries out pitifully. Anna braces herself for it to materialize on the path in front of her. What appears, Anna could never have been prepared for. It is wild of eye and swaying on all fours. It is covered in dirt with a smattering of seeds cast adrift by smartweeds, wild rice, and millet that seek a place to germinate. Numerous tickseed bristles cling to its matted hair for the sheer pleasure of irritating their host. What trembles before Anna is a young man far diminished from his former larger than life self.

Looking up at Anna as if she is an angel that requires an explanation before she will assist, he whimpers, "I'm lost," as he slaps mosquitoes from his tear-streaked face.

"Not anymore," Anna kneels beside William, wiping dirt and the smears of blood from his face—blood that had been siphoned by insatiable insects drawing off another's life but lost their own by the defending hand of a crazed teenager.

"Please forgive me," he repeats in his delirium.

"There's nothing to forgive. I understand," Anna covers his mouth with her own.

The two teenagers ignore the distant echo of an off-pitch shotgun blast as their needs are filled; Anna's desire for William and his desperation for anyone.

"They won't bite us in here," Anna whispers between pillow soft kisses. "The itching has stopped, too," a relaxed sigh disguises William's nervousness. The stories of bravado told by dorm room braggarts never mentioned anything as intimate as this. The tales were always filled with rough verbs: bang, poke, hump, and screw. Never was there mention of the closeness where through the thin material of a wet undershirt he can feel her heart beat. William thought Anna was joking when she suggested they take a swim in the pond to escape the mosquitoes. His thoughts turned to astonishment when without hesitation she shed her coverall to tiptoe into the warm water wearing only her white undergarments. Sheer articles of clothing that left nothing to the imagination even in the dimmest light and that were pressing against his lean body.

William stared without apology as Anna slowly immersed herself in the dark water, moving slowly away from the edge. Her Cheshire cat[47] smile had coaxed William out of his shyness and away from the torment of the insects that attacked his bleach-white skin.

Clinging together as Jimmy and Sook, soft-shell crabs before coupling, his arms encircling her body, hers around his neck, and lost to each other's kisses, William is grateful for his nervousness. His case of the jitters are preventing the rise of what to him would be an embarrassment in timing at the very least, and at worst, it might frighten off Anna.

All thoughts of the many arguments with his parents that left him trembling and bruised over his many unexplained absences these past two years melt away as Anna pulls him tighter against her contradictory body. Her body is soft and supple in some places and hard in others. This moment of simple pleasure makes up for the numerous wasted nights he made his way down the dirt road toward Anna's home, only to be frightened away by a barking dog. He had considered venturing into the marsh and woods to search Anna out, but he was afraid as the trails confounded him. Tonight as he approached the simple shack, he caught a hopeful glimpse of her, but dared not call out. He tried to follow on a parallel trail, but it led him to the disaster in which Anna had rescued him from. William is grateful that her eyes hold no pity or ridicule toward him for an inadequacy that he should not be held responsible for. He was not raised in the marsh.

Anna sighs into his mouth, content.

William worries; will she walk me back to the road?

---

47 Cheshire cat. A creature in Lewis Carroll's *Alice's Adventures in Wonderland & Through the Looking Glass* that would disappear, leaving only its broad toothy grin to mark its spot.

Uninvited, certainly unexpected by the Joiners who are sitting down for a late supper, Nathaniel kicks open the door to their home. He unceremoniously and without concern for the meticulously maintained pine floor, drops his useless shotgun. It clatters, metal against wood. Nathaniel's eyebrows are singed, his face is charred, and blood drips from several pellet holes.

"Dang breech burst but never you mind about me. I brings satisfaction," Nathaniel smirks as he tosses the old snapper to land with a thud next to the implement of its demise.

Chet leans close to Lloyd, "Luckiest old man I've ever known." Luck, if it had lips, would be pouting at this moment by its failure to put an end to Nathaniel Joiner, but it is a patient adversary. Time is always on Luck's side.

The jet stream is a narrow current of strong westerly winds undulating in the upper troposphere.[48] It is the invisible breath of God unknown to the majority of man, but through its control of the weather it determines the destiny of all life on the planet. High pressure and low pressure systems are guided across oceans and continents to bring comfortable variations in temperature if kept on the move, but the stream can bend itself to block that which barometers measure, causing drought, deluge, or winters that in the clocks of men last but a moment or never seem to end.

Anna shivered under her quilt until she moved her cot closer to the glowing stove. Turning herself as a duck on a spit, front side, backside, she tries to find a happy medium. Whichever side faces the stove burns while the side away from the heat quickly chills. She tried to divert thoughts of discomfort by concentrating on the creaking limbs of the maple outside the shack, but with the dying wind the only sound is the breaking of burdened limbs as a blanket of heavy Arctic ice settles upon them. Anna cannot remember a winter that arrived with such savageness. She began to feel sorry for herself then remembers that her father and Beauty are hunting outside in this madness.

---

48 Troposphere. The inner layer of Earth's atmosphere that varies in height between six and twelve miles where nearly all cloud formations occur.

Exhausted from turning backside to front side, and fading into and out of a restless and worried sleep, Anna's weary mind does not fully register the advancing crunch of ice under boots or Beauty's subdued barking. To her they are fragments of hopeful dreams expressing the desire to have her family at home and safe, never mind ducks or dinner. Only after the wave of biting cold air washes in from the open door, does Anna realize her father's voice contains substance.

"Get up, Anna. We've got work to do." With reluctance, Anna looks up from her cot. Dark circles hang in bags under her eyes. Expecting to clean ducks she is confused by the two axes held by her father.

The trek along the shore is an antithetical affair. Clay's heavy foot falls dig into the ice to propel him forward with purpose. The only impediment is the ice crystals suspended in the air that sting his eyes. Clay's double-headed axe is balanced on his shoulder. His bare hand, with thick fingers that are rock solid with calluses, holds the ball of the oak handle. He repeatedly clears his irritated throat with growls of a cornered black bear.

Weighing half that of her father, Anna's rubber soled boots slide as if on rails of steel. Her focus on foot placement is distracted by the wonderment of ice cementing the bay and decorating the bent and twisted vegetation locked in winter's slumber beneath. A summer fawn on its spindly legs has less difficulty walking than Anna as she again picks herself up off the frozen ground. Gloved in stiff leather, her hands reach for the razor-edged axe that buried itself into the ice bank upon her fall. Her breath, an emission of vapor is the only stirring of air.

Clay does not look back but continues on as Anna gathers herself together, his thoughts his own, his purpose undisclosed. Anna neither expects her father to delay on account of her, nor is she upset by the appearance of indifference. It is her belief that his inattention is a measure of expectancy and respect. Clay expects that she will rise to the tasks placed before her and respects her shortcomings as part of the learning process.

Beauty is torn between her master and mistress. She trots forward on padded paws with Clay while keeping a watchful eye on Anna. Beauty's muscles may be cold and her joints stiff, but she is ready to leap to Anna's assistance if required. Beauty may work for Clay as a dedicated employee, but she loves Anna, never forgetting who fought to extract her from the blackness that was the burlap sack.

Two miles into the trio's northerly push, shadows of men and boys come singularly, in pairs, in threes and fours, emerging on trails known only to those who live their lives within the marshes and woods. These are hard men with muscles lean, nary a pound of leisurely fat. They are whiskered if not bearded with maturity. Their skin, leather tough, is wrinkled from sun and wind, and scarred from accidents, mishaps, and the occasional knife fight. Their eyes are ageless, deep windows to wisdom hard-gained. All are hunched against the bitter cold in jackets and coats, Mackinaws and Sears' catalog, homespun and hand-me-downs. Each carries an axe of varied description, several are lugging picks. Not a gun is found among them. Not a word is spoken in wasted energy. The only disturbances in the pre-dawn silence are the stomping of feet in frozen boots and heavy breaths of fog on numb hands in the futile attempt to warm them.

If folk from town, or a sport had dared climb out of their comfortable nests to witness this rare gathering, they would be frightened by this mob of more than 60, when as a unit, all but 10 turn east, and proceed out over the frozen Flats, the mobs' faithful Labradors and Chesapeakes having been ordered to remain behind.

Twenty minutes pass before they are heard, the croaking and meowing of canvasbacks and mallards and the flapping of frantic wings against ice. The mob fans out in an encircling maneuver, their pace remaining steady and deliberate as the battle is about to be engaged. Tightly packed together and covering an area in excess of half a mile are thousands of waterfowl, their legs locked into the ice. The last open water of the upper bay froze solid during the night as the birds rafted together for warmth.

Anna licks her numb lips, the moisture quickly freezing, as she approaches a fat canvasback that is struggling to free itself from the ice.

Clay clears his throat as he adjusts his grip on his axe for a powerful swing.

From somewhere along the line of men, attack instructions are shouted, "Swing true boys. Watch the legs."

And it begins. Swing after powerful swing, the heavy axes and stout, pointed picks ring out as metal impacts the ice. Ice shards and shavings fly about as they are chipped from the sheet that covers the bay. Muscles burn with fatigue and sweat forms on brows and drip into beards to form icicles. Hour after hour, and into the gray dawn that denies the existence of a sun, the men's labors continue. It is a thankless job, but strangely satisfying as each bird is freed, its wings cracking the air with flight.

Anna leans on her axe, exhausted. She looks about, bewildered by this confounding act by these men whose lives are dedicated to killing as many fowl as there are shotgun shells in their hunting buckets.

Between swings, Clay grunts as if reading his daughter's mind, "If we kill them all, what will we eat next year? Get back to work." And she does, seeing that the trapped birds stretch out beyond her count.

The first mallard drake freed by Anna had enthralled her. She has seen thousands dead, diminished in their vibrant coloring by the absence of life, but the spirit, the fight to survive imbued in this struggling fowl was emblazed in the teal-black of its head and neck, the tan-tipped burnt umber of its chest, the royal blue of its speculum[49] and the snow white of its tail feathers. By the 35th fowl, it became a blur in the color palette, and when Anna gave up on her count somewhere past one hundred, the bird was an indistinguishable clump of feathers flopping about, and hampering her swing. Working by the ceaseless rhythm of axes and picks around her, she moves forward one bird at a time. Her mind is as numb as her face, contrary to her overheated body that moves by rote.

The battle against the elements ends with a grunt, a sigh, and the last mallard seeking friendlier environs. Left in the mobs' wake is desolation and nothing to prove their accomplishment. The men carry the axes and picks in their arms or slung over their shoulders. There is no hint of tiredness. A showing of weakness is against these men's nature. Young boys drag their tools as if anchors pulling them under for the third time. Anna leans on the handle of her axe waiting for a lost ounce of strength to be found to enable her to pick it up. "Tools are life," Clay would say. Anna only had to be told once to treat them with respect.

Slugging across the ice next to Clay is a man with a cheek full of wild tobacco. His name has long been forgotten as his face is rarely seen, and his age can only be estimated by the number of retrievers that have worked by his side. Unknown, but respected, unseen but constantly about, his life is wild, but always he is at peace. He glances back as Anna hefts the axe over her shoulder to begin the journey off the Flats.

"That girl of yours got real grit," he spits brown juice that splatters on the broken ice. "Yep, real grit she's got."

Clay's walk off the frozen upper Chesapeake Bay is perceptibly taller.

Snaps, nips, growls, and fur-tearing brawls are inevitable to determine social hierarchy among the two dozen canines who each believe they are top dog. Left alone without their alpha masters, these retrievers revert to the behavior of their wolf ancestors with slightly different genetic strategies.

The Chesapeake retrievers, born and bred along the majestic and challenging shores, quickly exhibit their vile tempers. They accept no attempt by others to subordinate them. No man or beast other than its master

---

49 Speculum. The secondary feathers of a bird's wing, usually lustrous in color.

can order it about, and even then, a slight hesitancy can be observed, as they are reluctant to be completely tamed. These red beasts are the first to size up competitors and engage in violence.

The Labrador retriever, a late-comer to the area, gentle, easy going, loyal and lovable, was looked upon with great doubt when first introduced to the market hunters. This breed lacks the double matting of fur and the protection of extra oil to lubricate and protect it from the frigid climate as does the Chesapeake retriever. The Labrador also seemed hesitant to leap into ice-clogged waters to retrieve the downed birds. These apparent character and genetic defects are compensated for by the animal's intelligence, desire to please, and refusal to quit an assigned task, despite the inclement weather. The Labradors' game plan is to lie down and patiently wait their masters' return while being entertained by their belligerent cousins' fisticuffs. However, if challenged, their metal would not be in doubt.

The 10 men left behind keep an eye on the fights, stepping in with a whack from the flat side of an axe only if one dog is being overwhelmed by several. A good fair fight is an enjoyable diversion from their task. After the fowl are freed they will need access to water and food. These men labor to break up sections of ice near shore to expose a gentle current and protein rich roots of eelgrass that is so cherished by wintering fowl. One hundred yards long, 10 feet wide, the open water trench follows the sensual lines of the marsh shore. The flowing water gurgles softly at the edges of the broken ice, cooing as a mother to her child.

The impacts of axes on ice and the grunts of men prevent all but the keenest ear from hearing the flutter of feathers gliding toward the trench. The man endowed with this gift looks up in time to call a warning to his companions who dive prone to avoid being struck by the excited and hungry ducks converging on their mother's call.

Scrambling away from the trench, the men look to each other, asking with wide eyes, *have you ever seen this before?* The unanimous answer is: never.

Great flocks, many not associated from the freeing labors of the mob on the iced-over bay, splash, bathe, and feed in the opening; mallards, canvasbacks, redheads, teal, and even a dozen long-necked swans glide in for a repast. Not a bird among them seems concerned by the nearness of the dogs and men staring in longing and disbelief, as if knowing a truce has been ordered. Instinct overcomes petty rivalries, as the retrievers become a cohesive pack eyeing their prey. By communication not heard, or understood by man, the dogs circle the trench, each looking for the plumpest fowl that would most please their master.

"Beauty," Anna calls out. "Come."

"Jake," a man summons his dog. "Here boy."

"Rufus," a boy shouts. "Heel."

The members of the mob whose dogs are preparing to destroy the long morning's work, order them to their sides. The entire group moves a distance from the trench to watch a spectacle that will be storied for years without the need for embellishment in Tavern Bouvard.

The war in Europe had been progressing for two years. The United States has chosen to remain out of the conflict raging across the Atlantic that had its roots in the assassination of an archduke. The war was only of interest to residents of Havre de Grace if they happened to have relatives in one of the combat zones. For this reason, the editor of the *Republican* rarely wasted copy on this distant struggle. Last evening, before the paper went to press, the editor made a decision to run a story that was war related, and had originated in *The Lancet Report*, a medical publication. The story was unusually graphic rather than dry as are the majority of health related reviews. The editor also saw a sad irony, making it worthy of print. Besides, with the cold snap gripping the region, coddling mothers are keeping the paper delivery boys at home, so it will be unlikely that this edition will be read at all.

DEATH STALKS THE SOLDIERS

December 14, 1916: A medical publication, *The Lancet Report*, discloses that six times as many men are dying of illness than from war wounds. Purulent bronchitis (Influenza) is sweeping through the British depot in Etoples, France. This depot is a stopover for soldiers from England, Scotland, Ireland, Australia, and India on their way to the front lines. On any given day more than 100,000 troops are in and about the camp. Medical personnel are stymied in their efforts to ease the suffering, or in stopping the spread of the disease. The victims sway as if drunk; fall to the ground coughing up blood, where they die of high fever and lungs choked with fluids; their faces a bluish tone from a lack of oxygen. War is the greatest destroyer of life ever devised by man, but it is apparent that nature takes a backseat to no one in its ability to end lives. Residents of Havre de Grace can rest easy with the knowledge that like the war, this tragic affliction is over there.

The newspapers remain bundled and stacked on the back dock of the *Republican* when the editor arrives at the office at eight in the morning. He has to decide whether to enlist his adult reporters to help him deliver the papers or toss them into the dumpster. Either way there is a waste of resources.

Decisions. Decisions.

Growing louder in competition with the melee of ducks and swan clogging the open trench is the honking, high-pitched and irregular, not of some hidden mechanical goose, but of an automobile rapidly approaching over the ice. Its driver is either a lunatic or inexperienced as the vehicle and its trailer careen left and right, sliding catawampus, with the trailer attempting to pass the vehicle on either side.

Shouts, whoops, hollers, and hat waving come from the occupants crammed in the speeding convertible. As it nears the mob, faces become recognizable. The driver of the Buick is William McQuay. He is gripping the steering wheel like a drowning man to a round life preserver, though it is not fear he is expressing, but a devilish joy in mischief making. Beside him, bounces Chief and August, both unconcerned with William's perilous driving skills. Riding in the backseat are Lloyd and Chet, excited as two minks playing with a mouse, and Delbert who is rather subdued as if this wild ride is an everyday occurrence.

The mob parts and dogs scatter so not to become victims of vehicular manslaughter. The Buick's slender wheels are locked in a sideways slide that would make the rider of any down-hill snow saucer envious. Coming to a twisted stop, the Buick facing west, the trailer south, the mob gather to hear the declaration.

"We've brought corn for the fowl," August states.

"And corn whiskey for the men," Chief adds.

The mob groans at the indication of handling hundred-pound sacks of corn and then cheer at the reward being unloaded by the Joiner boys.

Shouting above the re-energized men slugging back hearty, throat-burning gulps, Chief jokingly announces, "And I will defend any man arrested this day for baiting." Then with condolence he pats William on the shoulder, "But I cannot be involved with and will deny any knowledge in this lad's auto theft."

Laughter and rowdyism abound as the men cut open the burlap sacks of corn to spread across the ice for the birds to feast upon and toast one another for a job well done. During the revelry, while the men and boys are occupied with the corn, their whiskey, and stories of adventure and one-upsmanship brought on by the well-applied liquor, Anna, hoping her father is not aware, sidles up to William who is standing next to Chief.

"Ah, Anna," Chief says. "We three conspirators meet again. Don't think I've forgotten my part in your clandestine meeting. I pray all is well?"

"All is well," Anna winks at William whose blush is apparent under his red-chilled cheeks.

"I can't imagine your discussions would focus around the topic of me," Chief says, "but has William told you that he owes his very life to me?" Anna shakes her head, encouraging Chief to continue. "It was on a day very similar to today except the ice had not frozen solid; a fact that young William learned the hard way. When I came upon him floundering like a Labrador pup newly introduced to our icy bay, he was going under for the third time."

"I couldn't find my footing is all," William attempts to defend his manhood though at the time of the incident he was only eight.

"Yes, I could have given you the benefit of the doubt, but after pulling you out, my what a sight. Shivering, soggy and bedraggled with frightened eyes of gratitude and awe for his valiant savior," Chief elbows Anna in playful jest, "Well, I knew right then I'd be looking after his sorry backside forever."

"I've seen his soggy backside and I will attest that it's not sorry," Anna sticks up for her man, evoking laughter from Chief, and more blushing from William.

Delbert catches pieces of the conversation as he hefts a sack of corn out of the trailer. His scowl is not from the weight of the bag.

From a distance, and through the mingling men, Clay keeps a suspicious watch on Anna while listening to Jim Currier, a local market hunter and carver, "Did you hear, LeCompte arrested the Grossos? He also confiscated their truck as evidence for trial."

"Heard the rumor but haven't confirmed it yet," Clay sips from his medicine bottle now mixed with spirits for an extra kick.

"I'm thinking if I can get men like yourself to guarantee your birds to me I'd take over the run to Baltimore."

"Smuggling is a risky business, Jim, but if the Grossos are done for, and your prices are equitable, I'll throw in with you," Clay's pleasant expression masks the disquiet gnawing at his gut.

A practiced eye would have difficulty pointing out the exact location of Clay's duck trap. Placed snug within the wind-protected bend of two stubby fingers of sleeping land extending into the bay, the trap's position, and the limited scattering of corn is a Siren's[50] song to weary ducks seeking shelter and food.

The hunters remaining by the trench to ensure it was kept free of ice were able to abandon their post after a week of restraining their instincts. It was noon as the five men sat huddled around a timid fire, drinking he-man coffee, that as one they knew they could leave. The flames bending to the south stood at attention and saluted out of respect. Then with subdued crackling, the flames leaned to the north as a temperate breeze that had traveled from the Caribbean arrived to beat back its Arctic cousin. Its mild purpose was to break up the strangling ice with the aid of an emboldened sun. With a nod, a handshake, and mumbled grunts, each man went their way, disappearing through the snowy marsh into diminishing woods. Quietly satisfied, their grumbling stomachs foretold the kind of reception they would receive upon reaching their homes.

After walking a circuitous route from his home to the duck trap, always respecting the tenacity and tracking skill of Game Warden LeCompte, Clay reaches into the trap, grabbing and twisting the necks of three canvasbacks, five redheads, and two blacks. Clay admits to himself that this device cannot compete with the Davenport in the number of fowl it puts into his bag, but the trade-off is the ease of how the birds are obtained.

Why is one's reward in direct proportion to the risk?

A properly set trap can be left overnight, or if camouflaged, can draw in fowl through the day while the hunter sleeps, or attends to other business. A dozen or two birds can be his reward for a minimum of effort. A trap will feed a hunter's family, and a friend, but it will not put any coins in his pocket. The risk is the discovery by a game warden, but the only loss will be the trap, unless the hunter is caught onsite with a bird in hand. Then it is a fine and possible jail time.

Sitting a blind in-season with a valid license poses little risk and moderate reward if the birds are flying over the hunter's position. If a hunter is guiding a sport where compensation for a day's work is guaranteed, the upside can be fowl on the dinner table and a few dollars in his pocket to replenish expended shells. The downside is choosing a blind not frequented that day by the birds. If the birds are abundant and the sport or guide over-exuberant in shooting, and the game warden happens upon the stationary men with too many in their bag, a fine and confiscation of their efforts ensues.

Clay pauses, checking the wind for unnatural sounds that indicate the presence of an intruder with prying eyes. He becomes more cautious with

---

50 Siren. Myth. A sea nymph that was part woman and part bird, beautiful and charming. Sirens would lure mariners to steer their vessels onto rocks and to their deaths by seductive singing.

thoughts of his big gun. The Davenport, a gun becoming rare as LeCompte succeeds in confiscating other punt guns, is the centerpiece of Clay's livelihood. Solidly forged and milled with care, this cannon is a reliable killer of waterfowl if properly handled from loading to the pulling of its formidable trigger. The reward for its use is compelling. A single night, one shot, can bring over one hundred birds to be dispersed among family and friends with a barrelful left over for sale to hungry markets. These duck dollars, if prudently spent can ease a hunter's life with the purchase of newer, warmer clothes, seeds for a spring garden, and a long put-off visit with the dentist to pull an ailing tooth. If saved, the funds will provide during times of seasonal scarcity and a modest nest egg during retirement that only comes with incapacitation.

The risks when using the punt gun are manifold. Unlike a legal shotgun that can be displayed on a wall or kept in a gun case, the Davenport requires a resting place that is secret and safe from inquisitive eyes and the law, a location close by and ingeniously concealed where it would not be discovered by a game warden desiring its capture as a fugitive from another era. Its loss to Clay would be incalculable, the fine and jail time a second consideration. Working in the depths of night in a craft prone to capsizing on the broad Flats is a dangerous affair. Sudden storms with rising waves, blinding snow, or disorienting fog can end the life of the big gun hunter. Increasing the hazard is the gun itself. A misfire, fizzle, or hang will end the hunt without a single bird in the boat. A miscalculation in powder or packing can cause the gun to leap out of the chock and recoil through the cushioning sack of pine needles to break out of the transom, exposing the hunter to hypothermia and drowning. If a punt gunner were forced to choose the method of his death he would say a breech explosion. Shards of metal ripping away skin, bone, and brain would be painless for the hunter. Recognition of his passing would be the distant echo of exploding black powder carried across the water for none but the ducks and a tenacious game warden to hear.

Sitting on his haunches against the bank, its coating of snow thinning, its brown grasses poking through, Clay scans the choppy water as he stuffs the ducks into a canvas bag. With sails full, two skipjacks work the distant oyster beds. Clay shivers with the memory of his days working the tongs. He does not envy the unseen men fighting against the weight of the immense oyster grabbers, the chill in the wind, the bite of ice in the water, the cuts to their hands from razor-edged shells, and the constant ache of fatigued muscles. Clay is grateful for past opportunities, and the open offer of a berth aboard Captain Smith's deadrise, but prays that he will never again need to accept.

Clay's thoughts of Captain Smith wander easy to his beloved Jennifer, to Olivia, and his daughter. Clay is at peace with Jennifer's passing; the years grinding down the sharp pain of her absence with his slow realization that her love will remain with him throughout his life. On the other hand, there is no peace with Olivia as she is a constant enigma to Clay. She was a rock throughout Jennifer's illness, showing no emotion toward Clay other than a stalwart friend.

The skipjacks tack together, partners in a laborious dance.

After Jennifer's death and the passage of a respectable time, without pretext to Olivia's intentions, and before Clay had consumed a single draft of beer in her tavern that night, Olivia placed her hand upon his, stating, "You'll be staying after closing." Clay's history with women is singular where courting, coaxing, and comforting were the precursor to commitment, marriage, and then consummation. Clay and Jennifer's intimacy was developed, nurtured, and brought to passionate fulfillment over a period of years. Olivia's statement, bordering on a command was not unwelcome, nor brash in its delivery, but placed Clay in a position far out of sequence from familiarity. Clay entered Tavern Bouvard late that evening expecting companionship among friends. He left before the rooster's crow, physically exhausted from a sexual encounter, and emotionally conflicted as to Olivia's new place in his life. Returning the next evening expecting to find Olivia gushing with affection, Clay was quickly rebuffed by platonic platitudes with only a sideways glance from her to indicate any change in their relationship.

Through the ensuing decade, Clay has made sincere overtures to legitimize their private affair, hinting at marriage, only to be dismissed by a laugh or sigh. Olivia never directly said, "No," but her attitude of contentment at the status of the relationship was apparent. Olivia would be his lover but not his wife. Her relationship with Anna was nurturing, and in all respects they acted the mother and daughter role, but Olivia would not accept the title.

The light coming from behind Clay, skipping across the muddy water, reflected brightly on the sails wet with spray. One boat stayed its course toward Havre de Grace, the other turning southeast, possibly to a mooring on the Eastern shore.

Scratching his short-cropped hair, Clay makes an accounting of Olivia's refusals. From his casual questioning as they lolled together after a sweaty encounter, Clay is confident of their compatibility in all areas save two: location and vocation. Olivia lives in Havre de Grace, a proper town, and owns a successful business. He lives in Buzzards Glory, in a marsh, and is an outlaw gunner. *Do I expect Olivia to give up a respectable life and a secure livelihood to join with a man whose income, if not his freedom is precarious?*

Clay's chauvinism collides with his common sense. *A girl is suppose to leave her parents and family home to cleave to her man, but Olivia is not a girl, and no sensible person would walk away from a comfortable lifestyle, not even for the sake of love.* Clay chuckles at his inflated ego. The topic of love had never been discussed between the two of them. He simply assumed their intimacies were physical manifestations of feelings too powerful to be expressed in words. He now considers, for the first time, and with distaste, that their affair may be nothing more than the rutting of two lonely people. This possibility would answer the questions of: *why hasn't Olivia asked me to move to town and join in a partnership in the tavern?* Clay double knots the canvas bag, tearing its worn fibers, *if she did ask would I give up my way of life?* Clay reluctantly admits that to do so would better provide for Anna's needs; a proper home, social interaction with those of her age group, better supervision, and the instruction from a lady in the ways of a maturing woman. However, this life, life in the marsh and on the bay is all he and Anna know. Some say you cannot teach an old hunting dog new tricks. That is true, especially when he does not want to learn. Then is it stubbornness, selfishness, or fear that prevents Clay from giving up what he knows and admittedly provides him with a sense of self worth? Clay does not have to answer this question because Olivia has not asked hers.

"Hey, Mr. Buchanan."

Clay spins on the balls of his rubber boots, "Cigar." Clay is startled and quietly chastises himself for losing focus that allowed someone, even one as silent in his movements as Delbert is, to sneak up on him.

"Did ya trap enough ducks for her birthday dinner?"

Clay adjusts the grass and brushes snow over the top of the trap to better conceal it. From within his pocket he methodically dribbles golden kernels of corn to create an inviting trail to the trap's narrow opening, tossing the remainder inside to lure more ducks, "I believe we have enough. What do you got there?"

Delbert proudly holds out a pigeon-size bundle that is wrapped in pink and yellow cloth with a white ribbon securing the ends, "They're hunting mittens. The kind with a slit for the trigger finger."

"Now why would Anna need a pair of hunting mittens?"

"The day the birds were chopped free from the ice I overheard you speaking with my pa."

"Oh really. You overheard?" Clay scrutinizes Delbert, causing him to squirm with his admittance of eavesdropping on adults' conversation.

"Ah, yes, sir. Just in passing, you said you were going to buy Anna a shotgun so I asked my ma to make the mittens," even at 17, and master of his swamp and surrounding marsh and fast lands, Delbert's maturity, his self-assurance crumbles under Clay's accusatory stare, "I mean, doesn't every hunter, even if Anna is a girl, need proper attire when bringing in the birds?"

Feeling like a bully, Clay lets Delbert off the hook, a hook that Clay, by his own failure in discipline, was caught, "That was very thoughtful of you and kind of your mother. I'll make sure Anna properly thanks her."

"It's pronounced, woos'tĕr shēr'," Olivia shakes the slender bottle. The black marinating sauce sizzles as it splashes into the heated iron skillet. "Now stir in the butter and current jelly."

"What's this called?" Anna asks as the Great Room fills with a strong yet delightful aroma.

"Shotgun sauce," Olivia laughs at her joke that Clay would appreciate but only puzzles Anna. "It's a new recipe, but I'm sure you'll like it poured over fried duck, which I know is your favorite," Olivia checks her watch. "Now where's your father with those birds?"

Lying by the door, Beauty's sensitive ears twitch at hearing unfamiliar footfalls outside in the slush. She begins to growl as she rises to her feet to defend her family from a possible threat.

"Easy, girl." Anna worries that William may be sneaking around being anxious, and too early for their post birthday party get-together. The creaking of rusty hinges penetrate the thin wall as the shed door is opened. Beauty barks, warning of violence.

"Someone's in the tool shed," Olivia backs away from the shared wall. The shotgun sauce boils unattended. "Anna, let Beauty out." Olivia glances toward Clay's Remington shotgun hanging on the wall over the table; a shiver of uncertainty runs up her spine. Cut wood, stored in the shed for the stove, or for use in carving decoys is being thrown about by the intruder, clunking against each other and thudding as they impact the dirt floor.

Anna opens the door.

Beauty attacks.

– 1884 –

Dogs have always been the bane of Felipe LeCompte's life. As a boy of seven, living in the Pyrenees Mountains of France, a stray dog attacked him. Felipe cannot recall the breed of the animal, only the horror of being thrown around by his wrist that was crushed in the jaws of a monster that Felipe had only wanted to pet. The damage to his wrist was substantial, ripped skin, torn muscles, and broken bones. These injuries would heal in time with only a minimum of paralysis and scarring. What has not healed is the guilt that the subsequent series of events were his fault. If he had not been bitten, his father would not have used their meager savings for his medical care. This money had been earmarked for the purchase of a badly needed billy goat for their farm to replace the old one that died during the harsh winter. Without the goat to sire kids for sale at market, his father was forced to seek work away from home. On his return trip, he was stabbed during a robbery, and he died alone by the side of the road.

Without an income, the family, comprising his mother, teenage sister, and himself, lost the hillside farm to foreclosure. Felipe's mother believed that Marseille, a coastal town of some importance could offer them hope, possibly as servants for the well-to-do. Upon entering the town on the back of a turnip wagon pulled by an ox, the family was engaged by a man, dashing in appearance, with black cape, feathered felt hat, pressed trousers and polished boots. He offered employment with the offhanded remark, "For the price of a bath and decent dresses, I'm convinced I'd be looking at two comely ladies." The man turned out to be a wanted corsair[51] with a price on his head.

Felipe's mother and sister would return from work early each morning to their drafty, one-room, second-story apartment. Their only heat rose through the rough flooring from the ovens of the bakery below. Their tired faces were heavily caked in makeup to cover bruises, their eyes distant and empty. A few coins strewn onto the wobbly table by his mother was their paltry compensation for the ancient vocation that always takes more from one's soul than it gives to the purse. This scant tinkle against wood was Felipe's cue to wake up and begin his day delivering bread.

Three weeks later there were no coins to wake him, only the evil barking of the landlord's dog that was restrained by a fraying leash. The landlord's angry words that were predominately curses, accused the absent corsair of cheating him out of rent as he dragged Felipe by his hair into the filthy, garbage-laden street where Felipe was summarily deposited. His mother and sister never returned and the corsair lost his head to the guillotine for crimes too heinous to be fully explained to a child.

The baker offered a modicum of pity by allowing Felipe to retain his position, but charged him full price for the bread he would eat. Felipe slept on the back stoop where he was harassed nightly by alley dogs that regularly nipped at him to determine if he were alive or dead.

All the mongrels wanted was a free meal.

Reduced in weight, and wearing clothes that stunk and hung as rags on his bony frame, Felipe was rescued by a letter from America that had taken seven months to reach him. The letter was from relatives unknown to Felipe and contained three prepaid tickets on a schooner to Baltimore, Maryland. The letter was addressed to Felipe's mother and delivered to the frightful landlord as his was the last known address. As his fee for reading the letter to the illiterate Felipe, and delivering him to the ship, the landlord cashed in the two tickets meant for mother and sister. With a kindness unbecoming a businessman of his stature, the landlord reluctantly gave Felipe several sou that if used with extreme frugality, would purchase food for nine of the 66 days' passage.

By the turning faces of The Fates,[52] and a gentle hand of Luck, Felipe found favor in the American ship captain whose best boy had not returned

---

51 Corsair. Pirate.

52 The Fates. Myth. The three goddesses of destiny: Clotho, the spinner who spun the thread of life; Lachesis, the disposer of lots who assigned each man his destiny; and Atropos, she who could not be turned who carried "the abhorred shears" and cut the thread at death.

to the ship prior to sailing. The voyage across the vast Atlantic and up the splendid Chesapeake Bay was one of adventure and enjoyment. Even while being at the captain's beck and call, Felipe had time to learn the ship's workings and observe the birds and marine animals that rode the currents of air and water. Two of the many were the soaring albatross and the mighty blue whale. Felipe's stomach was full for the first time in over a year. His clothes, though used, as they were taken from the best boy's abandoned trunk, fit well and were warm. He was learning a new language, and the profound aphorism that America was the land of promises kept if a man worked hard. Felipe was confident that the United States must be a good place; why else would France have supported it financially and militarily for more than one hundred years?

Felipe LeCompte's American relatives were prosperous business folk who could afford to educate their children. When he arrived alone on the quay, Felipe was quickly assimilated into the fold without a hiccup. Along with formal, in-classroom education, Felipe was given heavy doses of the merit of the *Rule of Law*. There was a strong belief by the adults in the family that a government, properly administered, laid down laws that were intended for the good of the people, and these laws should be upheld. Therefore, when as an adult, the opportunity presented itself to Felipe to work as an agent for the government of the country that did so much for his relatives that came before him, and in turn, would save his life, Felipe LeCompte proudly raised his right hand to take the oath of a federal game warden.

What he did not realize by accepting this post is that he would have to face, almost on a daily basis, the territorial and aggressive animals that had so terrorized him as a child—dogs.

– 1916 –

Four hundred square miles, which included Havre de Grace as the northern boundary and south to the Gunpowder River halfway to Baltimore, was the area originally entrusted to Game Warden Felipe LeCompte. His duties were to educate the inhabitants to the laws regulating hunting and to apprehend violators. It was a Herculean[53] task made impossible by the terrain that included thick forests of hardwoods with a floor a tangle of fiddlehead ferns; flooded swamps with sucking muck to swallow a man if he somehow squeezed through the stands of cypress that barred his way; marshes made impenetrable by big-leaved tuckahoe plants, cattails, and shoulder-high grasses; and an undulating shoreline, that if walked would measure 800 miles. Therefore, it was not surprising that most of the hunters regularly violated the restrictive laws with impunity. This did not mean that LeCompte was failing to make an impact. He focused his efforts on the greatest offenders, the market hunters. By tracking their movements he quickly confiscated the big guns of the careless. He fined those who he caught with too many birds, or hunting out of season or without licenses, and arrested those who he caught with their hands in a duck trap or hunting at night. With successful lobbying over the last several years, Congress increased budgets to the agencies tasked to oversee the welfare of the country's land and wildlife, nearly doubling the number of game wardens. This reduced the area LeCompte patrols to 200 square miles, a reasonable area to his dutiful mind.

---

53 Hercules. Myth. The son of Zeus and Alemena. A hero of Greece who possessed exceptional strength, bravery, intellect, and compassion.

During his southward sweep along the shore, LeCompte regularly dismantles duck traps by the dozen, recording in his log the exact location for future reference. Today he found one in plain sight, no apparent attempt to hide it, obviously a finger in the eye of the law. Normally he would release the captive fowl and dismantle the trap, but because it was adjacent to land owned by a market hunter, LeCompte decided to invoke his powers of warrantless search, and toss the residence. He always hopes to catch a break and discover implements of illegal activities, but if his actions merely serve as a strong reminder that the law is being enforced, he believes he is fulfilling his oath.

Felipe LeCompte heard the warning growls and challenging barks of the Buchanans' Labrador retriever. He knew this breed to be of temperate disposition, but no matter how he tried, he still flinched at the primeval sounds that took him back to childhood with its accompanying nightmares. He also incorrectly assumed the occupants of the shack would investigate who was trespassing before unleashing the dog. Kneeling to rummage under the workbench, LeCompte is vulnerable as Beauty charges around the corner to sink her canine teeth deep into the meat of his right thigh. Somewhere, someone is screaming, but the white pain blinding LeCompte and short-circuiting his senses, prevents him from realizing that the screams are his. He vaguely feels Beauty's growls vibrating through damaged muscles as he is roughly dragged out of the shed.

"Beauty, heel," Anna calls as she peers cautiously around the corner of the shed. Olivia aims the Remington at the man rolling in the slush, clasping his wound, and moaning. Beauty backs off a few feet, keeping a wary eye on the man for any indication of false movements that will require another bite.

"Felipe?" Olivia lowers the shotgun. "What are you doing here?"

"What the hell?" Clay shouts as he and Delbert approach at a run.

"What the hell is right," LeCompte cries, his accent heavier than usual. "I could have that dog destroyed for attacking and you jailed for siccing him on a federal officer acting in the commission of his official duties."

Anna moves to Beauty's side to pull her away, "It's not her fault." Her tone beseeching, fearful of the loss of her companion,

"Damn right," Clay affirms. "LeCompte, you have no business here. Now drag your sorry self off my property." Clay takes his Remington from Olivia.

"My right comes from the power of the government to enforce its laws and that evidence," LeCompte points to a roll of chicken wire and four poorly sharpened pine stakes.

"Evidence of what?" Clay asks.

"That was a duck trap I pulled from south of here. It was on your property," LeCompte limps toward Clay pointing an accusatory finger.

Clay stands his ground, "You may have a right to trespass onto a man's land, but you have no right to frighten Olivia or my daughter. I can't imagine any judge denying them their attempt to protect themselves."

"Buchanan, let's not play games. I know how you make your living. I will find your big gun, and then I'll lock you up for good."

Clay loses his temper, shoving LeCompte with his Remington, "Get the hell out of here while you still can."

LeCompte stumbles backward as Beauty strains against Anna's hold, growling, teeth bared, and wanting to get back into the fight. LeCompte recognizes that he is outnumbered and outgunned, making retreat the better part of valor at this time. He hobbles in the direction of the shore where he has hidden his boat, "This isn't over, Buchanan. Not by a long shot."

Satisfied that LeCompte has quit the immediate area, Clay safeties the Remington and shucks the pump to eject the chambered shell. It is empty.

Olivia shrugs her shoulders, admitting with a sheepish grin her ineptitude.

On two prior occasions, William asked Anna to lead him to the designated spot a few paces off a secluded trail that was fading from lack of use. He did so under the guise that he wanted to make sure she knew precisely where they were going to meet for their special birthday celebration. William's mistake was that each request had been during the day, and now it being night, the trail took on a new appearance. With its deep shadows from cattails scissoring against each other in the wind, and the temporary indentations in the waving needlebrush grasses made by wondering raccoons, foraging muskrats, or burrowing rabbits, they added unexpected side trails not accounted for in William's mental map. His all too familiar fear bubbled up from his stomach, the fear of losing his way. William's arms were tired from lugging the heavy horsehide blanket into the marsh, a distance of two miles from his family stables. He accepted the fact that Anna was unlikely to be willing to lie down in the melting snow, and he did not know of any other position to accomplish the act, so dreamed of, and after they are finished the blanket can be abandoned.

Turning to Anna's call, William loses all thoughts of his burden as she runs toward him. Her black hair shimmering in the moonlight flies out behind her from under her knit cap as she falls against him, their mouths soft and wet, hungry for each other. His excitement grows with her embrace. He is still nervous, but has mentally prepared to go forward. Anna is not pulling away from what she must be able to feel. William concludes this to be a good sign.

Preparing a cozy nest for his lady with the blanket, William is distracted by Anna's dancing. She says something about a new dress, but with the flocks of noisy geese flying overhead, dimming the moon, the dress' color and style are indiscernible to him. William assumes Anna's twirling is a delay due to shyness, a hesitancy to disrobe, though she showed no reluctance when they went swimming, although this is different; this is the proverbial leap into the deep end. William decides to be gallant and help her before she slips in the slush and ruins the mood. Taking hold of her waist, he inhales to begin a night that will be remembered for the rest of their lives.

Beginning with caresses to her thighs, William offers a compliment as he feels her warm bare skin, "So soft," then he flashes on what he has been told is the truth, confirmed by discussions with, and listening to older boys, and a few talkative men, that when it comes to sex, ladies are to be treated like whores, and vise-versa. A lady is to be dominated, taken, so that she never has to admit she enjoyed it. One old runt of a man at Tavern Bouvard, who was telling adventure stories for cool mugs of beer, offered proof in the way nature does it, "And don't you think God set forth examples for us to follow?" He looks around the room for signs of dissent. Finding none, he elaborates, "Have you ever seen the bald eagle? He flies higher than a man can see. A most noble and awe-inspiring creature, if there was every one. Now, while he's high above the clouds, he spots his mate, then dives with talons ready to strike. The female feigns objection, turning in mid-flight, her talons toward his, but does she fight against the inevitable? No sir. She clasps his, hanging on, and together they plummet in ecstasy, spiraling down as the ground races up to kill them, but an instant before certain death they release to soar as only eagles can." The runt with a healing pink scar on his face gulps half his beer, "Dangerous? I'd say so. Violent? Possibly, but she allows him to do it again and again, and ain't that the point?" He pauses, as men of questionable character grunt with approval. Unseen, and unacknowledged, except when serving, Olivia shakes her head, disgusted by these ignorant men, but she will tolerate them until their pockets are empty. The runt concludes with, "If you dominate the lady, she'll always be your happy little whore."

To William, Anna is a lady in the making, so he will be her eagle.

Even in this poor light, as William presses down on her, positioning himself, he sees in Anna's eyes that she is holding back, exactly as his tutors said a lady would. William accepts the restriction of his trousers rolled down around his ankles, the inconvenience of Anna keeping her boots on, and her dress scrunched up, because she has to be taken in a hurry. He is comforted by her arms tightly wrapped around him and her quivering legs, both unmistakable indications that their need for each other, their coming together, their years of forced separation and waiting will be equally satisfied in the next minute.

Anna imagines what a sight that the geese passing across the midnight moon must have of the tangle of arms and legs exposed in fumbling, and then quickly withdrawn under her Mackinaw as a turtle into its shell. The honking, a chastising substitute for giggles and tears that Anna holds back at her and William's graceless escapade. The pilfered blanket, scratchy to Anna's skin was used to tramp down and cover the tall grasses to fashion a rough hollow. Plopped down within the encircling needlebrush that act as a natural curtain, muffling the nearby waves and wagging with the rising wind, Anna is chilled by slush leaking through moth-eaten holes in the blanket, wetting her neck, lower back, and in spots, her lavender dress; a gift from Olivia, now twisted and bunched around her abdomen, hopelessly wrinkled.

Anna located William south of her home. He was only slightly off course on the carefully marked trail. Clay had not questioned her as she departed after dinner, neither did her uncoordinated outfit of cap, nor her birthday dress, rubber boots, and Mackinaw that was buttoned to her collar concern him. He assumed she was so pleased with the store-bought dress, that after modeling it at the insistence of Olivia, Anna just did not want to remove it.

Anna opened the Mackinaw to pirouette in front of William, her dress twirling as an ecstatic dervish[54] for his inspection, and to show him that she knows how to get all dolled up for his pleasure despite the floppy rubber boots. She hoped for a compliment, but received what she first believed was William's concern for her modesty as his hands smoothed down her dress, murmuring, "So soft." Then quickly, with an aggression that surprised her, his hands were running up the insides of her thighs to roughly tug at her undergarment. Anna had given her implicit consent. Though the nervous look in William's eyes showed disbelief that she was going to go through with their intimacy and an expectancy that she would renege at any moment.

---

54 Dervish. A member of any of the Muslim ascetic orders, sometimes referred to as "whirling dervish" because they perform ecstatic observances such as dancing, whirling, and chanting.

Anna tries to concentrate with all her senses. She wants her mind to catalog everything William is doing to her, to retain each sensation of this first wonderful experience, her grand step into womanhood. But she is not getting cooperation. Uncomfortable and comical distractions interfere. The Mackinaw may be the finest coat ever designed to keep a hunter warm and protected from inclement weather; wind, fog, rain, and snow, but it is to be worn by one person. It was not conceived to cover two bodies fidgeting with inexperience. Anna is unable to control her shaking legs, pushed apart. Out from under the coat's protection, they shiver, not from pleasing caresses, but from the sting of winter's frosty night. Her white undergarment swings as a flag of surrender from her rubber boot. Her knees rudely reflect the moon's glow as unsteady beacons. To Anna they are pale and knobby, ugly as those of great blue heron chicks.

Anna has watched these ancient birds for hours during their nesting time on the bay. They are mysterious creatures, changed little from prehistoric times. As adults engaged in courtship they are elegant and sensual. With admiration and respect toward their intended, the birds bow humbly, moving slowly closer to playfully rub thighs. Nodding approval to one another, their great beaks and feathered breasts touch with care. Their long slender necks bending in gratitude, each forming half of a perfect heart, signifying acceptance of the other as two equal parts that make up a whole.

Anna stifles her laughter. Tears of disappointment moisten her eyes as disgust pokes holes in her passion, though hopefully it is hidden from William because she does not want to dampen his pleasure. She relates their lovemaking less to the beautiful great blue heron and more to the desperate chicks. These young, grasp rudely, ravenous for food, triggering regurgitation from their provider. Anna clutches tight to William, wanting his affection, a closeness, his heart to be felt beating with hers, but his searching hands, roaming over her body are triggering a response in him that makes her want to vomit. This is not the tenderness that Anna had believed foreplay to be.

His kisses turn to bites.

His fondlings are grabs at sensitive skin.

Anna believes she is ready to prove her love, to transition from a girl to a woman, but William's attempts to join with her are worse than a clumsy assault. It is absent the emotional connection that Anna desires and is met by a body that William has made tense. Anna's mouth was readily willing to return words of comfort and encouragement, but it takes all her willpower not to laugh out loud at William's ridiculous and crude antics.

Game Warden Felipe LeCompte sits huddled in the bottom of his rowboat with only the fire of a zealot to warm him against the spray of an incoming tide. Rowing south along a shore tall in needlebrush he found a cut in the land that at low tide would be confused for a dying creek frosted at the edges in slush. With the last light of day dimming in the west, he squeezed his small craft between the two banks flush with leaning grasses. LeCompte was confident that even with tonight's full moon, a casual passerby on land or water would not see him or his boat. His leg throbbed with an ache that ran up his spine to pound at the back of his eyes. The bleeding from the bite had congealed within the torn fabric of his hemp pants to create the beginnings of a scab woven with cloth. The painful removal of his pants, tearing off the scab, is inevitable, but LeCompte ignores his present physical discomfort, and the nagging thoughts of a future filled with days of convalescing to focus on a rare opportunity—to bag Clay Buchanan in the act of poaching.

In advance of any game warden making his rounds is a communication system connected by what could only be a hunter's telepathy, because no telephone or telegraph wires have ever been found. Poaching significantly declines in advance of the game warden's arrival, and the constructor of a duck trap is far from the scene. Conversely, after the game warden has passed through, all forms of hunting resume with an increased vengeance, apparently to make up for lost time, or to spite the law. The poacher believes he has a free hand because the game warden is now harassing some other God-fearing, family provider, down the line. LeCompte is relying on these facts, and what would be a natural assumption that he fled home to lick his wounds, to lull Clay into exposing himself by using either the fabled Davenport or building more traps.

The odds are still against LeCompte but he accepts them. Clay, if constructing duck traps, may work north from his shack. The odds are 50-50 that Clay will pass LeCompte's way. If Clay employs the Davenport, he may paddle his sneak skiff north, straight out from his shack, or south in search of rafting fowl. The odds are three-to-one, but regardless of where Clay fires off his punt gun, the blast echo will reverberate across the Flats to LeCompte's ears. He can then race to the Buchanan home to intercept Clay holding the gun and birds.

Several factors are working to decrease the likelihood that Clay will be venturing out with his cannon: the clear sky and full moon make it difficult to sneak up on the fowl, but it is the increasing wind raising the waves that are, in the end, the determining factor. A sneak skiff, even in the hands of an expert paddler, would quickly be awash in water flowing over the low rails. A market hunter's life is filled with calculated risks. Hunting without a license risks receiving a fine, which is a hardship because most hunters only earn a meager income. Using outlawed duck traps or guns risks jail time. That takes him away from his family and their needs, but does not damage his character as honest citizens do not consider outlaw hunters to possess any, though these same upstanding citizens buy his birds on the black market. The greatest risk, which is devastating, is the confiscation of the hunter's traps, guns, gunning light, and sneak skiff. A dedicated market hunter will use his innate ingenuity to persevere in a trade that has sustained his family for generations, but the loss of his life, well, that ends it there.

Felipe LeCompte, admitting that Clay Buchanan is an expert in his nefarious field, who has so far outwitted the law-and-order man at every turn, would weigh all risks carefully, especially as a widower with a daughter to provide for. Therefore, Clay will likely leave the Davenport in its resting place tonight, a secret place that no bribe or threat has ferreted out. An unknown factor that the game warden is not certain how to equate is the discovery of Olivia at the Buchanan home. LeCompte is surprised that Olivia would be found in the company of a man like Clay, but as a tavern owner, she would be prone to corruptibility even being from a respectable family.

At the time of LeCompte's hasty departure from the uneven confrontation at the Buchanan residence, his instinct was to row south, though he could not have said why. Now shivering in darkness with needlebrush slapping his face, and tempted to light his rarely used lantern for warmth, he realizes, to his good fortune, why he turned south instead of north. Absent from his boat are the pine stakes and chicken wire that he used as proof of Clay's criminal activity. He clearly told Clay where he had discovered the trap, "South." The odds were now in LeCompte's favor, better than 50-50, that Clay would return the trap to its original spot, as the placement of traps is a carefully thought-out affair.

Clay will have to pass along the shore in front of LeCompte or behind him on a nearby path. The incoming tide making shoreline foot passage difficult, suggests the path is where LeCompte should turn his attention.

It is difficult for a person, regardless of their discipline to remain focused on any one task while in the marshes next to the Chesapeake Bay. Men, women, and children, who have succumbed to this phenomenon, will swear that a supernatural force exists within this bewildering and magnificent region. The grandeur takes hold of the mind to mesmerize, and to cause one's jaw to slowly become slack in wonderment at the glory that lies before him. During daylight, the senses are overloaded, inducing a stupor as the observer tries to process by sight, sound, touch, smell, and feel, the thousands of exuberant plants challenging the color spectrum, and the myriad of animals great and small that make up the Chesapeake stage and are on parade. The massive trunks of great oaks, pines reaching for heaven, and fragrant ash and birch trees unite to stabilize a fluid environment, holding the background in frame. Snakelike streams that are in no hurry to arrive at any destination meander to charm those who gaze into their sparkling waters. Cattails, needlebrush, and spartina grass run to the bay's edges to cover pungent soil as a quilt on the softest bed. Sprinkled liberally as spice to a Sunday stew are shy deer peeking around blueberry bushes; grasshoppers springing from stem to leaf; soaring eagles surveying their territory; ladybugs searching for a new home; noisy geese just in from the tundra; barn swallows rocketing after insects; turtles climbing onto rocks to sunbath; and fiddler crabs combing the mud. The creatures that inhabit and transit the region may change with the seasons, but the miracle of their diversity never diminishes.

At night another world dominates. Shadows trick the eyes with the moon's light playing slight-of-hand to allow vagueness to rule. Creatures of all sizes, skitter, hop, slither, crawl, leap, paddle and fly, abounding in a realm of wistful invisibility. The faithful trees that held the daytime scene together, sponge away all light. Cloaking themselves in the darkest black, they force the viewer's eyes onto repetitive waves that began on the bay and continue to whisk across an ocean of grasses, leading a person to hypnosis.

Game Warden LeCompte's head twitches. The muscles in his jaw tighten. He blinks as his pupils refocus as he awakens from a mystical trance. Only the moon at its zenith, LeCompte's stiff joints, and his buttocks so numb that they have lost all feeling offer hints at the hours that have passed. He is reasonably certain that his eyes never closed in sleep, but his mind only perceived what the spirits of the marsh allowed. LeCompte has an itch that he has missed something, *Did creatures, two legged or four, move quietly along the trail without being challenged?* His eyes, less than trustworthy, argue with his confused mind. *Something passed! When? When did it pass?* Uncertain, LeCompte wonders if his odds-making rolled snake eyes. He begins to rise, his joints creak and pop, but he is stopped in mid-stretch as his lawman's instinct calls a warning.

Sounds —out of place in the natural chorus of the night.

Squeaks —not from arguing marsh mice, but from metal against metal, growing louder, approaching from the north along the trail.

Fearing he will prematurely spring his trap, LeCompte lies as if he was an opossum, dead quiet, in the bottom of his row boat. He holds his breath and prays that Clay will pass him without notice.

A light, attached to the squeaks, creates a warm ball, engulfing the man carrying the swinging lantern. His labored breathing betrays the burden he is toting; a duck trap? LeCompte dares not lift his head above the taunting needlebrush to eyeball his prey, allowing him to pass.

Waiting...

Waiting...

Game Warden Felipe LeCompte licks his lips as he savors the victory to come, then crawls after his quarry.

Luck will see the end of a hunter tonight.

Anna's skin sizzles slippery with friction and sweat. She grits her teeth preparing to make her transition.

LeCompte tingles. His blood surges, pumped full of excitement as he nears the man splashing in the shallows...the criminal's capture is imminent.

William's muscles tighten, frantic to accomplish his task. He is the eagle with talons clamped on his mate. The ground races up at him with unexpected speed to put an end to what has just begun.

The man's back is to LeCompte. The lantern placed upon the bank casts a shadow, large, eerie, and freakish, but clearly shows that he is scattering corn about a newly installed duck trap.

Sweat falls into Anna's eyes causing her to blink away the salty sting. Trying to focus, she catches a glimpse of a lonesome heron passing across the watchful moon.

LeCompte uses a tried-and-true technique to disarm the criminal, "You're surrounded. Stand where you are. You're under arrest." The man turns. The light cast from the lantern illuminates his startled face, "LeCompte?" Game Warden LeCompte hesitates; shocked, "It's you?" then remembers his oath. "Drop the shotgun. You're under arrest."

An explosion and cry of physical pleasure by one of the teens masks the nearby mechanical blast and scream of pain.

The heron's guttural call protests these disturbances to the peaceful night.

William glances back; bravado turns his walk into a strut. He is all that a man should be. He took his lady and she admitted no pleasure. Anna stands in the middle of their disheveled nest with her Mackinaw buttoned tightly around her, the coat's protection warming her where William left her cold and wet. Anna loves this boy, but at this moment she pities him, as he is unaware that he left her still a girl, his mission unachieved, she unfulfilled. Pushing the pity aside, Anna has a contradiction welling up from deep within her. The honest grin spreading across her face as she fingers the gold bracelet that William gave her, whispering in her ear, "It's a family heirloom," is a true reflection of her happiness. Tonight was neither the uniting of two souls as Anna had hoped for, nor did their bodies fuse together in passion as she expected, but their attempted act was a new beginning in their relationship. It is a tightening of their bond. It is something she will categorize as special and together they can build on it. Their lovemaking can only get better...she hopes.

Nurturing this consolation, Anna runs along the shoreline. Her boots splash playfully in the water of a receding tide as her dervish twirling carries her forward with carefree abandon. She hums a childhood tune while dizzily watching geese glide in overhead. The feathers on their outstretched wings whistle a sigh to mark the end of a long and dangerous journey; rest is at hand.

Spitting out brackish water that is draining chilly from a cut in the land, Anna finds that she is face down in the muck, giggling at her clumsiness. The skirt of her dress that is exposed below the Mackinaw, acts like a sponge to soak in the water blown back by the persistent wind. Anna turns around to discover what tripped her. Her eyes grow wide with horror as her scream is silenced by vomit. Tears blur her vision as she scrambles away from the body of Game Warden Felipe LeCompte. Anna is not crying for LeCompte, as he was the instrument of a government that made her father's life so difficult, but for what his death will mean to her family.

Unless...

Any daughter who enjoys the out of doors, or simply loves her father and the company of an affectionate dog, would be delighted to be spending the afternoon in mutual pursuit of a duck or goose dinner, but Anna is miserable. Her muscles are fatigued beyond memory, making the simple act of carrying her new shotgun, a Model 97 Winchester pump with a carved and lacquered stock depicting a huntress and her retriever, a strenuous burden. But this weakened state did not prevent her from flinching in response to the sharp cut inflicted by the tongue-pincher.[55] The artificial duck call she is attempting sounds more like that of a cat whose tail has been stepped on as Anna tastes the copper tang of blood; a substance she scrubbed from her hands and clothing in the early hours of the morning.

Anna feels deep in her marrow her father's mumbles of chastisement more than she hears them as Clay stands in the damp, earthen duck blind. Clay had chosen a blind near the northern end of their property to shoot from. Anna does not know if this location was chosen because her father believes the birds are more likely to pass over, or does he want to be as far from the scene of the crime as possible? Smoke from his hand-rolled cigarette wafts past his weathered face. For the first time, Anna notices the deep lines permanently creasing the corners of her father's eyes. Are they from years of squinting in the bright sun, or from worry? Clay sighs as he watches their last hope for fresh meat today veer off into the darkening sky and out of shotgun range. Anna wants to shout her annoyance at having to use this antiquated duck caller because her father will not spend the 55 cents to purchase the latest model that she saw advertised in the Sears fall catalog, but her frustration is lost within the swirling fear that by speaking any word she will betray herself, and the previous night's activities.

---

55 Tongue-pincher. Slang. Wooden duck call.

It seems hypocritical to pray to Jesus at this moment, but Anna is willing to accept help from anyone who will convince her father that it is only the evening chill flowing off the bay that is causing her arms and legs to shake within her warm long underwear, coverall and Mackinaw coat. She squeezes shut her eyelids to concentrate in the hope of regaining control over her nervous limbs, but as she re-opens them, her father's accusing glare causes her frame to rattle. Her shoulders, now doubly weighted with guilt, slouch as she sits upon the rough, wooden slat that is intended to be a hunter's bench.

Staring at her father, Anna desperately craves the answers to questions she is too afraid to ask: does her father know who she had been with last night? Could her father ever understand that the fresh bruises on her back and inner thighs are not borne of punishment? And should she confide in him that she knows he has broken the Sixth Commandment[56] of God, or tell him that she has helped him get away with it?

"The cold froze him stiff," Constable Jenkins says as he peers down from the Havre de Grace wharf into a row boat tethered to the stern of a skipjack just in from the beds.

"He don't smell much either," says an old oysterman who is stuffing a handful of tobacco into his cheek to suck on.

"Where'd you find him?" asks the constable of the skipjack captain.

"We'd just made a westerly tack off the northern tip of Spesutie Island. I've always been lucky there. I came about and saw what I thought was a dingy adrift so I told my boys to put a hook into her as we passed. Finders-keepers sort of thing, but when she was drawn close we saw him lying just as you see him."

"When was this?"

"I'd say close to seven this morning."

"Seven? Why didn't you bring him in then?"

"Wouldn't have helped anyone and I've got mouths to feed."

"Well then, did you notice which way the tide was running when you found the boat?"

"Did I notice? My life is ruled by the tide. It was receding," the captain hands Constable Jenkins a small notebook and leather wallet. "Now, if your next question is; where do I think he drifted from? I'd say somewhere along Buzzards Glory."

---

56 Sixth Commandment. Deuteronomy 5:17. "Thou shalt not kill." Scripture taken from the *Holy Bible*, King James Version, 1987 printing. Public domain.

"What are these?" Constable Jenkins examines the objects.

"That's what ol' Benny found on him. That's how we knew he was a game warden; the badge and all."

"No money in his pockets?" Constable Jenkins addresses this question to ol' Benny who stops his winding of a deck rope to pause in thought, as if he is pondering the mysteries of the universe. Brown tobacco juice dribbles down his chin to splatter on the deck, "Nope. Can't say there was any." Ol' Benny's toothless grin says otherwise, but the constable realizes it is not important, and lets the issue drop.

Judge Hathaway walks up next to the constable, "I hear we've got a body?"

"It's Felipe LeCompte. He's been shot."

"What a pity. He was a good man and a credit to his profession," the judge rubs his gloved hands together for warmth. "Do you have any thoughts?"

Constable Jenkins flips through the pages of the notebook, stopping at the last entry, "Normally I'd say we'd have a countryside full of suspects, but unfortunately, though it's not surprising, I believe I know the culprit."

The judge pats the constable on his shoulder, "Let's get this cleared up quickly. We can't have folks thinking they can get away with murder."

Clay keeps watch for a stray duck or goose flying low enough to take a shot at as he, Anna, and Beauty trudge home from their failed hunt. The towering cattails they are navigating act as a natural blind, obscuring them from all but the keenest avian eyes. Throughout the day, Clay was aware of Anna's quiet, almost nervous demeanor, changing what should have been a relaxed, post-birthday hunt, into one where the air was electric with what Clay would define as fearful tension. He is never comfortable raising issues of emotion, and will push all eccentricities by Anna into the category of women's issues, thus relieving him of responsibility. This too shall pass, is Clay's absolution, but her mood swings are more frequent and dramatic of late, inducing Clay to conversation when he prefers the crunch of slush under foot, the whisper of wind through the cattails, the soft slurpy splash of icy waves against an ever-changing shore, and the teasing calls and brassy chatter of ducks and geese high above in the clouds.

"Madison Mitchell stopped by the other day," Clay begins with a neutral topic.

"Hasn't he been working with his uncle in Baltimore?" asks Anna.

"He's learning the undertaker business."

The abrupt discussion of the business of death causes Anna to stumble and her stomach to lurch at the too-fresh, face-to-face with the dead game warden. Anna wonders if her father, in a roundabout way, is attempting to confide in her that he killed LeCompte, "Sounds ghoulish."

Pushing aside a tangle of fallen and decaying stalks, Clay chuckles, "I suppose it is rather ghoulish, but I imagine it's a steady business since we all gotta die."

Tears burst from Anna's eyes. Her lips tremble with the burden of the secret she carries, but she is unable to fashion the words to release them. Clay is unnerved and confuses her tears for sadness at his mortality.

"Hey, what's this?" Clay wipes Anna's cheeks with his rough fingers. Looking into his daughter's eyes he perceives a profound anguish that reminds him of the moments before Jennifer died. His beloved wife was not fearful of dying as her faith, the cornerstone of the household, brought her a peace in knowing that she would soon be with her Savior. Her grief was over all the moments she would miss with her family. Hers was the anguish of loss. Upon review, Clay would attribute his act of tenderness to the memory of his wife. Standing in two inches of marsh muck mixed with black slush, surrounded by dead cattails, and his shotgun balanced on his shoulder, Clay pulls Anna into an embrace that she clings to, burying her face in his coat to sob out her fear that their days together may be numbered.

"I told you before," Clay turns his head to cough. "I'll be around for a long time. My point in bringing up Madison is that he asked to use the hogshead blind. He is in town for a few days before heading off to Michigan. Apparently he has secured a job at General Motors building automobiles. I thought you'd like to say, 'Hello,' before he leaves."

Anna clings tighter to her father.

Madison Mitchell was not overly disappointed when his mother's cousin Sam T. Barnes, Madison's mentor when his father was occupied, begged off joining him hunting this afternoon as he had too many decoy orders to fill. Madison, thought of as likeable, but a little odd, enjoys the company of others, but is content to keep his own counsel. This is probably why he took to undertaking with such enthusiasm. His work environment was one of quiet solitude where he could think in peace. For the last several days, Madison had been thinking about the drastic change about to take place in his life. A change of his own choosing that will enable him to rapidly obtain his goal of becoming a licensed mortician with his own funeral parlor in

Havre de Grace. Madison had decided to temporarily give up the solemn apprenticeship of preparing the deceased for burial to work a chaotic Detroit assembly line. His compensation will be the incredible wage of six dollars a day. With his salary niggardly saved, he will have ample funds to complete his education, and return to his preferred vocation.

Madison sits comfortably in the fragrant barrel after adding foliage to better camouflage the edges of the blind. He inhales the scent of aged oak with a hint of olive oil as he looks out across Swan Creek Point; acreage that seems to slumber in winter's silent affection. The only disturbances are the sweet and varied calls of fowl feeding out on the Flats, hidden in the grasses of the marsh, and flying high overhead. There are no decoys bobbing in the shadows, though Madison could have his choice of the finest that Sam carves, neither did he borrow his father's Chesapeake retriever to chase after downed birds. Madison prefers to sit quietly, warm and snug, clothed within his goose-down coverall, gaze at the serenity around him and ponder.

If a duck, or if Luck allows a goose to fly close in, he will take a shot. If not, to Madison, it is just as well. For this young man, watching the birds come in, wings flaring, webbed feet skidding across the water, to toll in front of the blind, now that is the glory of the hunt, not the killing. For some, the killing is a necessity, but Madison can take it or leave it. His dinner is secure.

With overlarge ears, oddly, yet adorably shaped like his personality, Madison hears the subtle sounds of nature as a chorus. He closes his droopy eyes to find the strum of chords, then with concentration the individual notes, singular and pure, that the wild outdoors plays free of charge for the person who is willing to appreciate what makes up the symphony of life.

Madison snuggles, comfy and cozy, deep within the wooden cask, his shotgun sagging in his arms; *what a grand world a hunter lives in.*

Black storms with frightful lightning that electrify the sky, send men running to shutter their homes in fear, are but amusing entertainment, a happening far below for the wise old gander as he leads his family at the edge of heaven where the angels sing the mighty birds' passage.

For 80 million years, birds in their many distinctive forms have ruled the skies, masters of the air, subject only to the call of an unknown voice that drives select groups to migrate hundreds and thousands of miles each year. For the Canada goose, husband and father, this call came near the end of the short Arctic summer with the depletion of the protein-rich insects. The flight feathers that molted six weeks ago, leaving him and his beloved grounded and vulnerable to predation had grown back. His fledglings were fat and anxious for adventure, and a son and daughter from last year's mating had hung around seeking familial comfort and companionship for the long journey down the Atlantic flyway to the marshes of the Chesapeake Bay.

Rising to 28,000 feet to level off in the thin air of the stratosphere,[57] this family joins other geese to create a perfect "V" formation. This configuration, dramatic and poetic, made up of varying numbers from 20 to 20,000 during the southward push, acts as would a sharp bow of a sloop cutting through an ocean of air. Only the lead bird exerts effort while all who follow ride the invisible aerodynamics, each drafting its predecessor to glide on wings broad and powerful. Their bodies, feathered black at the wing and white of belly, are sleek at 15 pounds with necks long and straight to point the way.

Men, scurrying about, confined to earthy business, peer skyward with envy at hearing the constant chatter, honking from far above. These same men long for the freedom of birds they cannot see, traveling to places they can only dream of. This constant chatter from husband to wife, parent to child, is guidance, reassurance, and reminder to trust in the sun, stars, and the earth's magnetic field to lead them safely to where thousands of generations before have found food and rest.

This wise gander, ever cautious, discerning, contemplative, yet daring, and some would say foolhardy in his fierce and unwavering protection of his mate and their children, is of a rare lineage of male geese who die of old age in their sleep. He strives, by every decision, every act, to continue to outsmart foxes, eagles, and the men who hide in holes in the ground with deadly weapons, all desiring to have him and his family for dinner.

His mating did not occur until the second journey to the secret courtship grounds. Being unusually large and powerful at less than a year was due to a combination of having the genes of a champion, and being well fed on tundra insects by attentive parents. His physical stature would easily have attracted the attention of any female, but due to his parents' insistence on patience and that quantity of prospective mates does not equate to quality, he fought his natural urges. When the time for pairing off ended, he flew back north, still a bachelor. His parents both warned that it behooves the young to find a mate who reflects an expectation of deserving the best, with enduring qualities fit for a lifetime. This is important because the pairing of geese is until death do they part. Few species in the world are truly monogamous,

---

57 Stratosphere. A layer of air above the troposphere. It extends to approximately 30 miles above the Earth's surface.

and many of those who claim this distinction rarely succeed. Geese are the exception. Caring and nurturing each other in all they do, they are God's model for fidelity.

One year later, when finally he was set free to parade himself on the battlefield of love, hidden deep in the marsh, he challenged all contenders with hisses and snaps, extending to their fullest his seven-foot wings to attack, pummel, and crush would-be suitors for the prize. His parents had surveyed the field to find who they were looking for and would accept as suitable for their son. Though physically indistinguishable from the other hundred or so ladies-in-waiting, her bearing was one of careful instruction, showing promise. Modest, and feigning disinterest in those fighting for her attention, she merely preened herself, or focused on the ground at her feet as if a fat bug taunted her, but she weighed carefully each potential mate, because her choice now, and his decisions later would determine her life expectancy.

Soon it became evident to her that one male in particular would be this year's catch. He was larger, obviously older, likely circumspect in thought and wary of rash decisions. He was by far more powerful and skilled in combat, for when the fighting became serious, he would quickly grab the opponent's head in his beak to shake some sense into him. The males who stepped forward, bowed out quickly, or were tossed from the field. Other challengers backed prudently away, allowing the victor to reign, and the opportunity to woo without interference.

With hesitancy and modesty not from shyness, but with respect and courtesy, he approached the preening female in a refined manner, his grand body swaying gallantly, unlike the crude waddle of a lustful duck. Nearing her, he stretched his neck to further raise himself above all others to make it impossible for her to ignore him. The critical part came as he leaned his neck back and forth, from side to side, waiting for her acceptance or rejection. Finally, after what seemed an interminable amount of time, she mimicked his movements. Their intimate dance with elongated necks twisted around the other's, never quite touching, was a loving foreplay with the promise of eternal devotion.

This year's fledglings are a success for husband and wife. As parents they outsmarted or fought off hungry tundra foxes that were eager to make a meal out of eggs or the helpless young birds. All are alive, healthy, and nearing the end of their journey. Together, they have flown over states with sleepy farms, bustling cities, and large tracts of wilderness; Maine, Rhode Island, Massachusetts, Connecticut, New York, New Jersey, and part of Delaware before entering Maryland. Here, they swing west from the Eastern Shore to glide across the Susquehanna Flats. As a small peninsula appears far below, its features familiar and inviting, the father gives the appropriate call. The close-knit family dips their wings to begin to swirl down in long graceful arcs as every eye checks carefully for danger in any form, chattering all the way.

Men and their machinations would be humorous to the gander if not for the deadly consequences attached to their successes. The gander's vantage point is his greatest advantage. From on high he is able to detect the traps that are designed to kill him and his family. They are safest aloft in and above the clouds, and though imbued with supreme endurance, they cannot stay airborne forever. Once on the ground, they are relatively safe. Hiding within dense grasses, they are difficult to find, or out on open waters, predators are rarely able to sneak up without being detected. The danger, the dread, the tension, and if the gander were honest with himself, or forthcoming with his family, his fear, which is almost paralyzing, comes with the last one hundred feet. It is within this zone that death comes instantaneously from a blast never heard, or slowly, painfully, with ears ringing and eyes weeping, in the jaws of a beast who has given up his birthright of freedom for the guarantee of a meal and the comfort of a warm fire.

The paradox of wisdom gained by the old gander is experience that comes with facing that which will kill him. His parents' tutelage was only the foundations to build upon. Every year, the return to Swan Creek Point is a matching of wits, a challenge to his wisdom, and a new experience brought about by the changing tactics of men.

This evening as the weak sun dropped out of sight to change the winter sky from opal to aquamarine and casting long, low shadows, father and family search out the telltale signs of ambush. Chattering agreement, the last word falling to father to confirm their findings; he being ultimately responsible, he notes with some comfort the absence of imitation birds pretending to assemble peaceably near shore; there is no canine attempting to hide within the sleeping grass, and nothing but empty blackness is visible from three poorly concealed holes next to the bay. He can never be absolutely certain that passage through the hundred-foot killing zone will be safe, but this landing appears to be void of man, and that is a cause for celebration. The tone of chatter becomes jubilant as tired wings flare and legs lower in preparation of a landing just past the hogshead blind.

Madison awakens to what he believes are his own snores disrupting the harmony of life that sung him to sleep. His eyes cast about to re-orient himself. Madison quickly realizes that Luck is offering him a rare opportunity. A small flock of fat geese are tolling, appearing to land on top of him. Their exuberant honking echoes within his barrel. Grabbing his shotgun, Madison leaps to his feet, materializing out of the shadow, to fire off a hastily aimed shot as the flock passes close overhead.

As a father's concern for his family's safety never rests, it is the gander who first detects a change in contrast within the shadow of the blind, then the alarming glint of blue steel in the fading light as the hidden menace rises to threaten his family. Father's warning call ignites reaction, split-second and obedient. Wings snap against crisp air to change direction and to pull with straining muscles out of gun range. His beloved, focused on instructing her young in their tasks after landing, is a heartbeat late in reacting.

Bang!

Madison's aim is not true, and only wings the second goose. She spins mid-air to tumble crazily, landing with a shallow splash on the sandy spit extending a dozen yards out from the blind. The gander flinches at the gun's terrible blast. He turns, horrified, to watch his mate, his beloved, his life, crash to earth.

The saying, "Leave no one behind," has become an anthem to American military forces, but it was spawned from observations of waterfowl. When transiting distances, if one bird becomes sick or injured and must drop out of formation to rest or heal, one or more fowl will follow to keep the fallen company and protected if need be. The birds will travel on only when the fallen has died or is again fit to travel. Then, as a group, they are able to fly faster together than would a singular, lone bird fending for itself against the elements.

Instinct and abiding affection drives the family of geese to turn back toward the gun to rescue the one that has fallen. Harsh words from father order the eldest son to fly on, to guide the fledglings to the safety of the alternate landing area. His eldest daughter disobeys, recklessly refusing to abandon her mother and lands beside her. The injured matron struggles to gain her footing; her broken wing splayed in the water, her breathing labored from a punctured lung shot through with pellets. The gander, distraught over failing to protect his mate, and charged with fury, lands between the blind and his beloved to confront the man who is tearing his world apart.

Pleased with his quick, nearly from the hip shot, Madison climbs out of the hogshead to retrieve the crippled goose, but finds his way blocked by the largest, angriest gander he has ever seen, alive or dead. His automatic shotgun, with an 11-shot extension carries enough fire power to kill this hissing goose many times over, but instead of sending this fowl to the hereafter, Madison stands transfixed with sloppy slush washing against his mink-oiled leather boots. His gaze is locked beyond the challenging gander to witness a sight that shakes his soul. A smaller goose standing next to the cripple; nudging, seeming to encourage what must be her mother, tries to help her to her feet with the hope of fleeing to safety. The mother, flopping in the throes of suffocation, lays her head against her daughter's feathered neck, trying to console her as a mother would do, and then her head falls with a final splash into the water at her daughter's feet. The small goose spreads a protective wing over her dead mother, her head bowed in silent anguish.

Madison has heard stories of how a fowl will be shot out of a flock, and other birds, with what are thought of as suicidal intentions, turn back to face the gunner, who with a light squeeze of the trigger dispatches them to his bag. Madison reflects on the grief he has witnessed from family members of the deceased who come to his uncle's funeral parlor; wailing over sudden loss, inconsolable weeping, and lashing out in anger at a God who did not answer their prayers. A cold sweat breaks out on Madison's brow at the similar reactions exhibited by the gander and offspring to the loss of the goose, a father and daughter to his killing of their mother.

With the kick of a mule, the gander crashes into Madison's chest, knocking him flat on his back. The shotgun, the instrument of death, sails out of his hands to splash down, where it is quickly covered by several inches of bay slush. The gander's powerful wings slam repeatedly against Madison's forearms as Madison covers his face to protect it from the savage attack. Retreat being his only option, Madison rolls away, hoping to escape from the wild bird's furry. He scrambles to his feet to run, stumbling down the shore with the gander snapping at his heels.

"Never again...never again," cries Madison, his brief, but repeated elegy.

The eldest son, a prodigy in the making flies on. Grief-stricken but always obedient, he leads the nervous fledglings to the alternate landing area. It is a lightly wooded patch surrounded by protective marsh lands several miles west of Swan Creek Point that his father had shown him on his first migration. As he makes a cautious pass from a safe height, the young gander is momentarily confused. The landscape has vastly changed. The comforting pines and birches are gone as are the deep grasses with thick fleshy roots and the many wandering streams. Checking his bearing and distance from the peninsula, where terrible and painful events are taking place, he is still confident that this is the precise area, but below, spread out for a great distance are fields plowed bare, the raw black earth turned and exposed with patches of snow.

Wanting to prove his worth, to make his father proud in this time of crisis, he circles again, his brothers and sisters in tow, to analyze the situation, and then he spies what brings relief. Near the corner of the wide field, standing together, apparently feeding on some tidbits, are 20 or so snow geese, cousins of sort. He almost missed them as they are in dark shadows near a hedgerow of prickly shrubs. Honking encouragement and comfort to his siblings, the young gander leads them down.

The hilarity of a man being attacked, disarmed, and run off by a goose had Nathaniel rolling on his back, slapping his knees, and squirting tears as he laughed himself hoarse. Nathaniel had been walking the shoreline trail looking for duck traps. He reasoned that since trapping is illegal, if he found one, and ducks were already inside, he would be within his rights, and somewhere within the gray area of the law to release the ducks from the trap, keeping a few as an informal service fee for his good deed.

Nathaniel had watched with drooling lips as the flock of geese prepared to land near the vacant hogshead blind. He was too far away to take a shot, even if he had had a shotgun. His last one, found leaning against a dilapidated oyster-shucking shed having exploded. Oh how he wished he had not bet his chokebore shotgun on a sure-thing hand of cards.

"I know he cheated," Nathaniel had complained. "I'm the luckiest man alive. Only a cheater could have beaten my cards." These last words were shouted as he was thrown from the back room gaming establishment for impugning the character of its owner, a man who rarely lost a hand when he dealt the cards.

Nathaniel had been as surprised as the geese when Madison sprang from deep within the hogshead to make his badly aimed shot. Even with the birds' quick reaction, they were less than 30 feet from the blind, sitting ducks to coin a phrase, but the lad only managed to cripple one. Nathaniel knew that if he had been at the trigger, right now he would be figuring out how to carry home the seven birds, likely weighing close to 90 pounds.

What now holds Nathaniel's attention is a spot 10 feet from the wave-washed bank where Madison's shotgun rests beneath the slush. It is clear to Nathaniel that Madison threw away his gun, and to emphasize the act, Madison's parting words of, "Never again," was a statement proclaiming his quitting the field permanently. Remembering a term a shipwreck hunter once used, "salvage rights," Nathaniel believes this situation would apply:

property lost or abandoned beneath the water may be salvaged and the finder has the right to keep it.

Being confident that Madison is not returning, Nathaniel creeps as quietly through the brittle brown grass as is possible, watching the giant gander and small goose stand sentinel over the dead one, a very strange sight indeed. Also, a very foolish and dangerous act by birds who Nathaniel respects as being one of the wisest, canniest creatures he has ever matched wits against, and that he is unashamed to admit that he has lost to on most occasions. Scratching his chin, Nathaniel calculates the chances of a successful dash to the gun, draining it of water and whatever debris; mud, pieces of eelgrass, and sand that may have oozed into the barrel, and firing off several shots at the two live geese—not good, unless he wants to risk another exploding barrel.

It was the smallest of twigs, actually the lower three inches of a clump of needlebrush broken off by the weight of the last snowfall that alerted the two mourning geese to the softest of snap under Nathaniel's mud-caked boot, but in that moment, the wind had held its breath as if pausing in silent respect for the dead goose. Father and daughter twist their heads to stare at the new threat. Nathaniel knows his chances just went from not good to no chance in hell. With honks sounding choked with grief, the two geese look once more with sorrow at the goose that was an adoring wife and loving mother, then sprint, with their broad wings rapidly flapping, tips slapping the water's surface to soar into the air. Nathaniel keeps a curious eye on the two geese as they circle several times above, just out of gun range, as he casually retrieves the shotgun and dead goose.

A very lucky day indeed, Nathaniel smiles at the soundness of the shotgun and the weight of the goose, and then considers how best to take advantage of another unexpected opportunity that recently presented itself.

Father gander flies toward the alternate landing area with his daughter gliding off his wing tip. His honking is more formality than anything else. His thoughts are of a lonely future without a mate who is irreplaceable. As he scans the changed terrain for his other children he concludes that his eldest son has led his siblings to the third landing site because even with only the dimmest of light remaining, being quickly replaced by twinkling stars, father's practiced eyes can discern the oversized wooden cut-outs of snow geese staked into the overturned soil.

Together, father and daughter fly on.

By the radiant glow of the multi-stick candelabra held high by Roman, Nanna Maude carries a large, silver-serving platter into the formal dining room where the McQuays are seated, resplendent in their finest Christmas apparel.

"Smells delicious," Dorothy remarks.

"Tastes even better when you've shot them yourself," Frank boasts.

"I've heard geese are the hardest of the fowl to coax in," William adds, tucking in his linen napkin.

"It's all about experience, son," Frank's chest is puffed up. "Savor each bite."

- 1917 -

Anna sits red-eyed and sobbing on the wooden porch surrounded by the Davenport's latest kill of 54 mallards, 16 black, 9 goldeneye, and 3 teal.

"A decent night's work," Clay had said, as he stretched the kinks out of his back in the rays of the brilliant January dawn.

The drum of boiling water was overturned in the scuffle, the fire beneath now sputtering to sustain its life. Anna's broken fingernails attest to the desperation she fought with when Constable Jenkins and his two deputies came for her father.

Clay initially believed LeCompte had filed charges against him for Beauty's bite, or this visit was a surprise inspection to determine compliance with bag limits, but when his excessive kill was ignored, and the constable stated that he had an arrest warrant for the murder of Game Warden LeCompte, Clay stood stunned, silent, appearing to the officers of the law to be guilty by his failure to deny the charge. Adding to Clay's lack of denial when he turned to look at Anna, she burst into tears with grief that she had failed to protect her father. Constable Jenkins mistook Anna's outburst to be an admittance of knowledge. He made a mental note to interrogate her at a later, more appropriate time.

Though he believed he was facing a murderer, one who would be desperate, the pleading look in Constable Jenkins' eyes was an indication of hope that Clay would accompany him peaceably back to the jail, but knowing in his gut that this was unlikely, he brought along two of his stoutest underlings. This precaution turned out to be barely enough to wrestle Clay, grunting and throwing effective, gut-busting punches, to the mud. The constable, in his calculations of necessary force, failed to consider Anna and Beauty's response. Anna leapt onto the backs of the two deputies pinioning her father, scratching and clawing at their eyes and faces, screaming profanities she herself was unaware she knew. Regardless of her father's sins, no man would take him from her without a fight. Beauty went for the Achilles[58] tendon of the closest deputy, but before she could inflict real damage and turn the tide of the battle, Constable Jenkins swung his billy club,[59] connecting with a crack against Beauty's skull, knocking her unconscious with a withering yelp.

With an embarrassed frustration by the debacle that has unfolded from a simple arrest, Constable Jenkins took hold of the collar of Anna's coverall to yank her from his struggling deputies. She landed on her backside to find the constable's muddy boot pressed firmly to her chest, and no matter the effort, with which she kicked, squirmed, or beat at his leg, Anna could not free herself to help her father. She was forced to lie in the mud while the deputies hog-tied Clay to roughly deposit him in the backseat of a borrowed automobile, a vehicle familiar to Anna—the McQuay's.

Unseen, but heard, slightly muffled and straining under the weight of the two deputies sitting on him, Clay called out to Anna as the Buick bumped on the ruts, slid in the snow, and rattled away.

His parting words were not, "I love you."

And they were not, "Don't worry."

Neither were they, "It will be all right."

Instead, they were, "Take care of the birds!"

Beauty, having recovered from the clubbing, comfortingly nuzzles Anna, but also indicating by her nudges that there is work to be done before the duck broker arrives, in spite of the circumstances that paralyze her mistress. Wiping her eyes, Anna rights the drum, and stokes the fire. She will make her father proud in this time of crisis.

Under the jail, in a basement cell that is cold, damp, and with one barred window placed high in the wall to let in light, is where Clay has been placed

---

58 Achilles (tendon). Myth. He was the greatest Greek warrior of the Trojan War, also the hero of Homer's Iliad. He was killed when Paris, a Trojan prince, wounded him in the heel—Achilles' one vulnerable spot. (Tendon connects the heel to the calf muscles.)

59 Billy club. Slang. A police officer's baton.

as punishment for the bruises he inflicted upon the deputies. These same men-of-the-law promised to provide Clay with a blanket for his cot, and clean, dry clothes to replace his muddy ones, but with the afternoon shadows walking mutely across his cell, these items have yet to materialize.

Sitting comfortably at their street-level desks and nursing their modest injuries with ice packs, the two deputies hear, but ignore Clay's coughing and calls for medication, for Doctor Webster to prescribe what was left on the dining table in the Great Room. With Constable Jenkins processing the stack of paperwork at the courthouse, then off on other business, the deputies feel free to administer their own form of justice through deprivation.

Anna is let into the narrow corridor that contains Clay's lonely cell. Her arms are heavy with a wooden stool stolen from upstairs, dry clothes from home, and a quilt and basket of hearty food to hopefully lift Clay's spirits. The latter two provided by Olivia who had earlier been denied access for not being related to the accused. A flickering storm lantern wired to the corridor wall casts a feeble light. Cut by the bars, the slices of light create grotesque shadows dancing rudely in the cell where Clay lies shivering from the cold and the beginning stages of drug withdrawal.

The brown, syrupy liquid; the thick, viscous solution derived from the decorative, red poppy bulb prior to its blossoming; exotic, potent, designed by the very best scientists where just a sip or spoonful whisks your problems away. It is marketed by Bayer as a wonder drug, a cure-all for whatever ails you until you stop, or are denied your doses. Then, as a vengeful lover wrongfully scorned, the angry face behind the caring mask is revealed with all its horror.

Twelve hours by the tick of an unseen clock had passed, a mere half revolution of the world, but the strain, the stress, the physical exertion of the dawn fight, and worry over whether Anna processed the fowl had quickened the drug's passage through and out of Clay's system. His brain, losing its altered chemical balance began asking the body for more of *the cure*, first as a nervous suggestion, but being ignored, requested more firmly with itches, shakes, and sweats. Clay's focus, his concentration on pushing down, holding back his inner turmoil and choking on phlegm filled coughs, is broken by Anna's familiar cadence. Whether on dirt, wood, stone, brick, or concrete, father knows his daughter's footfalls.

Looking into the cell, Anna holds her breath, fearing what will be revealed when her father turns over to face her. From the semi-darkness, Clay's faltering voice echoes off the stones, "Did Jim Currier stop by?"

Anna's fingers wrap around the clammy cell bars to steady herself, "Yes, but he only gave me $20 for all the birds."

"That's our arrangement," coughs rack Clay's body, his back heaves, his muscles contort his torso.

"I've brought clothes and Olivia gave me food and a quilt for you," Anna wants to cry, to release fresh tears. She has no idea of how to help her father now that LeCompte's body has been found and her father's been arrested for his murder. Her ears still ring with Olivia's strenuous proclamation that her father is innocent, but the words fell flat on Anna as only hopeful desires. Anna's mind, her concerns, confusion and worry travels so far afield that she becomes startled when Clay places his cold hands over hers, his drawn face presses between the bars.

"Anna," Clay's piercing eyes demand her full attention. "Take the money to Doctor Webster and have him bring my medicine." Shivers run up his spine as Clay braces himself for his daughter's reaction to the next demand, "Then stay home."

"What? No!"

"Anna, the household must be taken care of."

"You need help. Besides, it's only a shack by the bay without you," Anna reaches through the bars to cling to her father, the cold metal of the bars digging into her shoulders, the significance of the separation stabbing her heart. "What's going to happen to you?"

"Anna, I can't explain, and I don't have to. I'm your father. You'll do as I say. I've taught you what you need to know to survive. You'll make it through this no matter the outcome."

Anna wants to hear her father proclaim his innocence, but knows he would not lie to her. She believes he is avoiding the ugly truth by diverting the conversation, hoping, possibly, to save her from additional anxiety and shame.

"Anna, you must promise me you won't come back here," the words catching in Clay's throat as he fights down a coughing fit.

Even as her father speaks these harsh words, she feels his grip on her tighten.

Sitting naked on the edge of her cot, Anna stares at her toes as William's off-key whistling fades with distance. Wondering why the length of each toe seems odd tonight, she remembers as if from a dream her curt instructions and stern reprimands to William, but his performance under the covers did improve, and his ego did not suffer too much. He accomplished this time what he believed he had done the night of her birthday. She is now a woman, sore and messy, but at least there will be no bruising as Anna kept his vigor in check. His only complaints were having to use a too narrow cot, and their inability to use a larger, more comfortable bed in the other room. The corner of Anna's mouth rises in a half smile, causing the always-watchful Beauty to cock her head with curiosity. Anna visualizes the hurt look of a chastised boy in William's face, and the depletion of his spirit that she was holding in her hand when she sternly told him, "No. That's a marriage bed," but then how quickly the compromise of the floor revived both his mood and spirit.

Anna had been so happy to see William waiting for her, actually pacing the porch with worry, when she arrived home after dark. She was immensely relieved to learn that he had no knowledge that his family automobile had been used to take her father away. Holding her in his arms, William exhibited a moment of indignant consternation, coupled with a string of profanity, at his father's complicity. His outburst endeared him further to Anna in her need for any ally that his sudden transition from comforter to molester went unnoticed. William's physical attention was a welcome distraction, though it was impossible for Anna's thoughts not to be filled with images of her suffering father and feelings of self-doubt in her ability to manage on her own. Anna's secure world, appearing to be crumbling around her denied her what should have been the second attempt at the joining of two hearts and bodies. Their first attempt ended with neither being accomplished; their second ending with the success of only the latter.

"Do I look like a woman?" Anna asks Beauty. Beauty responds with a neutral bark, and then drops to the floor from her cushioned seat on Jennifer's rocking chair to stand by the door. "I know. We have work to do," Anna reaches for her coverall and boots. "Do you trust me?" Beauty cocks her head again; a non-committal but faithful expression crosses her face.

Balanced precariously over the gap between the shed and maple tree, one foot standing on the wood shingled roof, her other wedged in the elbow of a branch, Anna reaches once more into the dark hollow of the tree in an attempt to lift out the Davenport. Anna has watched her father remove and replace the punt gun innumerable times from its hiding place without so much as a grunt. She now appreciates the brute strength that is required to dead lift an object weighing in excess of one hundred pounds wrapped in slippery oil rags. Anna begins to despair as her numb fingers again slip from the gun's oak stock. She recognizes the leagues separating her physical ability and that of her father with this simple task. Wiping her sweaty brow,

Anna is not yet willing to admit defeat, or acknowledge the mocking of the mackerel sky. Tonight's spotted moon diffused through thin white clouds is a hunter's dream. This type of sky helps to highlight the birds from a distance and gifts the operator of a sneak skiff with safe paddling across calm waters. Only a night with a canopy of low-hanging clouds, pregnant with snow, is more productive for the night stalker paddling as a wraith across the Flats. However, with added rewards come increased risks of being caught out in a sudden disorienting snowfall and becoming the ghost he is only imitating.

From below, Beauty barks encouragement, and needlessly reminds Anna of the passage of time. Anna leans back on a bare branch, "I'm trying. If you have any suggestions I'm willing to listen." Beauty looks up at her mistress in silent contemplation, her moist tongue hanging from a mouth breathing steam. Accepting the challenge, she sprints off as if hearing a thieving raccoon, to disappear around the corner to rummage inside the shed.

From Anna's elevated position, she looks through the skeleton that winter has made of the maple's branches to scan the vast blackness, the inky waters of the Susquehanna Flats at night. An involuntary gasp of fear grips at her throat by the loneliness spread out before her. At the same time a soft breeze kisses her cheek. It is either a reminder that her mother is watching over her, or it is a deceptive lure with whispers of ducks rafting just out of sight to entice Anna to venture into a realm where only the most experienced dare to hazard; all others being fools.

Anna's current frustration could easily have been avoided except for that promise made so long ago: The Davenport's hiding place and its use must never be revealed. It is a family secret.

William would have helped her to prepare for the hunt, but upon seeing the massive punt gun, illegal gunning light, and unstable sneak skiff, he would balk at the foreign nature of the objects and their wicked purpose. Anna, believing that William possessed disposable funds, proof being his expensive clothes, his English education, and of course the elegant plantation home he lives in, along with his generosity in giving her the gold bracelet with the strange symbols, he would offer, and if she hesitated, cajole Anna into taking money to get by on. This would not please and assuredly anger her father for obvious reasons. Delbert would be delighted to help, and, if he finds out that she did not ask for his assistance, he would be hurt by the slight, but he, more than anyone would understand promises and secrets.

A garbled bark calls attention to Beauty sitting at the base of the sturdy maple, her tail wagging a mile a minute. A coil of rope trails from her mouth. A heart-warming grin curls Anna's lips with intuitive understanding of what Beauty is proposing.

"So you think I weigh that much?" Anna asks as she nimbly climbs out of the tree, slides down the shed's roof to the overturned dunking barrel to retrieve the rope.

Beauty barks excitedly, running in small circles, expressing her belief that, *now we're making progress.* Beauty has always been proud of her mistress's innate abilities to size up a problem and solve it with little wasted energy, and Anna's attentiveness when being taught has made her invaluable to the processing of fowl and running the household, but as Anna has not been hands on when it comes to the Davenport, Beauty needs to be vigilant for missteps that could prove deadly. The first step is to get the dang gun out of the tree.

Climbing high into the maple, Anna throws the loose end of the rope over an upper branch. She has tied the other end around the butt of the gun, double-knotting it to prevent slippage. Twisting the dangling end around her wrist for a better grip while saying a silent prayer, and then shouting, "Here goes nothing," Anna leaps from the tree. Beauty jumps at the trunk with hopeful anticipation, but Anna merely hangs in mid-air, 25 feet above the ground. Swaying like a pendulum between the outstretched branches, and twisting with kicking feet, Anna cannot help but to laugh out loud at her predicament: *Whose idea was this anyway?* To add taunting ridicule to her misstep, a saucy flock of ruddy ducks zips in overhead to splash down just offshore. The gang of birds roughhouses in the shallows like rowdy teenagers without parental supervision. Then in a blink of their all-seeing eyes, they sense a change in their security. As one, the 30 ruddies sprint with frantic wings across the surface of the water. They skim to a distant stop within the safety of a mixed raft of fowl that are floating with the tide.

Imperceptible at first, then with minute jerks, the stretched rope moves, scraping off bark as it slides over the limb, dropping Anna an inch, then another. "Beauty, it's working." Anna kicks her feet harder and bounces with Beauty tugging on the rope from below. The oak and metal killing machine slowly rises as Dracula[60] from his wooden coffin.

Anna is thankful for her father's practice of reloading the Davenport prior to putting it to bed. She is confident that after watching him clean and load the gun, she could do it, but tonight as she is running late with

---

60 Stoker, Bram (1847-1912). Author of the horror tale *Dracula*. Using supernatural powers, the Transylvanian vampire makes his way to England where he drinks the blood of innocent people to sustain his immortality. Likely based on Vlad IV, the Impaler (Vlad Tepes), a prince from Walachia, a region south of Transylvania in the 1400s who murdered hundreds of his own people and placed their heads on pikes to put fear into the invading Moors. It worked. They retreated without engaging Vlad Tepes forces.

the moon racing across the sky, anything to save time is appreciated. After dragging the punt gun from the base of the tree to the shore, its stock carving a telltale trench in the muck, Anna strains, but is able to carefully set the barrel into the notch in the bow and then the stock on the chock in the center of the sneak skiff. She double-checks the small piece of rubber Clay placed between the hammer and the powder tube leading into the breech. It is a safety precaution to prevent an accidental spark igniting the fine powder, causing an unintended and dangerous discharge. Anna decides to wait to remove the rubber until just before cocking the hammer—safety first.

There has never been a need to hide the sneak skiff, as its possession is legal, but the form of its construction makes it apparent to any knowledgeable person that it is used in an illegal fashion. The chock's design and placement in the skiff can only be used for one object, a punt gun. The innocuous wooden wedges screwed into the top of the bow hold the box for a gunning light. The copper sheathing attached to the sides and bottom of the skiff prevent ice damage when paddling between or sliding over ice floes. And to eliminate shadows at the waterline from the overhang of the sides that would create a defining line to alert the resting fowl of an approaching menace, Clay has tacked whitewashed canvas to the railings that hang as a skirt to the waterline. Except for the occasional use for soft shell crabbing, the sneak skiff's use by Clay is strictly nocturnal, and thus a casual passerby during daylight will find it resting just above the high tide line, a strange looking vessel seemingly abandoned among the grasses.

Unlike the sneak skiff, which among seasoned market hunters is a proud possession, the gunning light carries a stain upon its user's character and, rightfully so, a measure of guilt for cheating one's neighbors. It is not the confused birds that Clay worries about, but that ultimately, his use of the light will cause the fowl to quit the area to seek a respite from a puzzling moon that keeps moving and brings death. If this occurs, many families hunting within the code of honor will go hungry.

Anna is aware of her father's hesitancy to use the gunning light as she removes the brush camouflaging the burlap sacks covering the light, but she will use every device to increase the odds in her favor. Set only a dozen paces from the garbage pit and outhouse, the gunning light's concealment is so absolute that one unaware of its precise location would be likely to stand on it thinking it a rotted stump or a long-abandoned muskrat den. Anna hefts the box back to the skiff with Beauty trotting by her side. In her mouth she carries the two burlap sacks as is her habit for Clay; an important and necessary task. At the skiff, with its bow floating in the water prepared to launch, Anna orders Beauty in as all appears in order; the Davenport is loaded and anxious in its chock, the gunning light is lit and balanced on the bow with kerosene filling the lantern's well; the hand paddles are securely tied with strings to nails protruding from the sides of the skiff, and an extra, long oar lays in the bottom for propulsion before and after the stalking.

"C'mon Beauty. Get in," Anna motions with her hand for Beauty to take her place in the bow under the Davenport's barrel, but Beauty remains sitting, wagging her tail with the two sacks in her mouth. "Let's go, girl. Time's a-wasting." Feeling the hunter's pull to *get-on-with-it*, Anna is not pleased with Beauty's stalling. Anna grabs the sacks from Beauty; tosses them to the ground, and lifts Beauty into the bow. Beauty leaps back out to take up the sacks in her mouth, further frustrating Anna, "Beauty, I promise to cover the light with the sacks when we return. We don't need them now."

Beauty does not possess the words, or the pantomime to explain the burlap sacks' purpose: filled with pine needles or sea oats, they are needed to cushion the recoil of the Davenport. Without them—catastrophe.

"Fine. I'll go without you," Anna shoves at the skiff to launch it. As it slides free of the shore, Anna climbs in, kneeling to take up the long oar. She looks back, perplexed by Beauty's actions, "Well? Last chance."

Beauty's duty, her love, and dedication to Anna, makes her decision an easy, but fearful one. She will accompany Anna out onto the Flats, and somehow try to protect, and if need be, save Anna when the unchecked recoil from the cannon's blast causes the gun to jump out of the chock, its weight overturning the unstable craft, or propelling the gun backward, breaking through the transom and sinking the skiff.

Beauty leaps into the bow but continues to stare at the receding shore until the sacks disappear in the darkness.

"Relax, Beauty. Tonight will be an adventure," Anna says, her confident words betrayed by the truth of her nervous tone.

Beauty lays her head under the cold silent barrel, it waiting to make a kill...that is what it is designed for...that is its nature. No one can blame the Davenport, only its user.

Tender swells rolling softly north to south down the Flats gently rock the sneak skiff as Anna paddles serenely, enjoying the quiet of the night. Worries for her father are suppressed to focus on the task at hand. Beginner's luck and the outgoing tide make progress easy as she paddles southeast toward Spesutie Island. Following her ears, Anna directs the diffused beam of light toward what she hopes are the coughs, sneezes, purrs and croaks of a sizeable raft of fowl congregating in the distant channel. With each stroke of her oar, Anna comes closer to facing a fact that she has yet to admit to herself. Except for the fundamentals listened to over dinner, or at Tavern Bouvard, Anna has neither witnessed nor has she ever been schooled in the intricacies of stalking with a sneak skiff, or shooting a punt gun. It seems straightforward: find the birds; drift or use hand paddles to get close; keep the light pointed toward the birds, and then pull the trigger. Beauty retrieves the dead and rounds up the cripples—straightforward.

"It can't be that difficult," Anna whispers to Beauty, selectively forgetting the many mornings her father returned, cold, wet, and full of aches without a single bird to show for a long, lonely night's efforts. Beauty remains silent, her jaw muscles grind her teeth, not from irritation at Anna's greenhorn act of talking while on the hunt, but from worry at what will happen if Anna somehow manages to get close enough to pull the trigger.

Prayers are a foreign concept to Beauty, though she does dream of an afterlife of warm summers with birds without number, and in contrast to her character of success at any cost, Beauty hopes for failure tonight which may be their best chance for survival.

Anna discovers the rafting fowl she has been hearing for the past hour. Vaguely visible and slightly opaque at half a mile, bobbing en masse, their varied colors are muted by the night's black paintbrush. Rafting together, floating as a single organism as they roll as corks in the swells, their grouping provides a measure of comfort for these social creatures chatting each other up. A few birds, weary, weak, sick or injured, feeling the security of numbers, tuck their bills under waterproof wings for a recuperative rest from foraging and avoiding the hunter in his blind or sinkbox. Divers, the more industrious among the talkative or sleeping birds, splash with their wings with each submersion in search of the tender roots of eelgrass waving gently below the surface. Snipping off the less tasty green portion upon surfacing, the divers give a little sneeze to clear water from their bills before swallowing, then interjecting their two cents into the ongoing conversations. Not equipped with heavier feathers and the extra protective oil of the divers, widgeon, brant, and other opportunistic ducks position themselves to the lee of the divers to nibble on the drifting castoffs.

A low-pitched purr rumbles across the Flats, carried with the breeze, and running with the swells. This cat-like sound produced by contented geese indicate their presence to Anna. Its sudden absence would have signaled a warning to the practiced hunter that the approach is too swift and the birds are nervous, even at this great distance...but Anna, being excited by finding the birds and the prospect of a great kill that will gladden her father, paddles faster to close the gap.

Sighing with relief, Beauty knows that to the birds' sensitive hearing, the water falling drip-drop from the long oar each time Anna lifts it clear to take another stroke in their direction is like the crashing, churning paddle wheels of the *Emma Giles*. It is the sound of man, and to a fat duck or goose, any sound made by man signals danger. Beauty's ease comes with the fact that fowl will never allow the menace of man, a disturber of their peace, and threat to their lives to approach.

Silence now carries the night, perking Beauty's ears...waiting for the explosion of fowl. Geese stare into the glow of the false moon as they consider their options. Swan and brant swim about feeding, unaware and without a care, relying on others to keep watch. Older ducks, suspicious of a two-moon night, lead their flocks to the edges of the area the light is encompassing to peer around its beam for a cautious look-see, and despite Anna finally shipping the oar, it is the baldpates who are too uppity to join in the gossip, sitting in singles far out on the perimeters of the raft who give the warning to bolt.

Boiling and frothing white fire, the surface beneath the thousand birds erupts in a cauldron, as wings beat the water to blast skyward. With a gulp of air, the divers splash into the black depths to vanish forever. Above, raising a thunder in a stormless night, the decibel level of wings snapping and cracking the crisp air, battle for supremacy over the airborne birds' harsh calls to escape. Fleeing in a coordinated chaos, the swirling mass, an organism that for a time bobbed as one, fills the sky to split dozens of times in a frenzy of mitotic reactions spurred on by a confused and frightened nucleus.

At a hundred yards, Anna presses her palms against her ears to protect them from the booming wing beats and jarring calls. "No...no...no!" Anna cries, but the wild chorus swallows her words. Beauty hears a vague reference to: "...they're leaving," then stretches, content to take a nap. The cupboard will be bare, the paddle home will be long and against the tide, but they will arrive safe.

Anna's hands fall to her lap. Her shoulders slump as she watches the birds grow smaller, becoming dots against the mackerel sky to disappear with only distant echoes of their warning calls, now ridicule in her ears for her failure. She was not even prepared to shoot the few lost ducks that in the madness to escape flew directly over the skiff, as she had forgotten her Winchester. A mistake a practiced hunter would not have made...and one that would disappoint her father. The empty surface of the Flats spreading out before the small craft containing two passengers, a gun, and a puny light, emphasize to Anna, with a stab to her heart, the emptiness that she will return to when she enters the shack by the bay. And regardless of how many logs she stuffs into the potbelly stove, no matter the thickness of the quilts she covers herself with, or even if her body heat is raised by Beauty snuggling close or William's passionate embrace, Anna is all too aware that her core, deep in her heart where her soul resides, will always be cold until her father returns to make the shack a home—if he returns.

In her debilitating state of depression, Anna allows the sneak skiff to be pushed and pulled along with the tide. The gunning light sways as a drunken watchman with the gently rolling swells that tempt Anna to lie down in the bottom of the skiff for a forgetful sleep, but there is no place to curl up. The Davenport's placement, center stage in the craft speaks to its importance, the nature of the mission. Anna places her gloved hand on the steel barrel. Its cold, unfeeling demeanor seeps through the glove to infect Anna with its stern rebuke: Are you a little girl; one who wears petticoats and nibbles tea cakes, or are you a huntress?

The voice ringing in Anna's head is taunting, familiar, and oddly accented, challenging her to knuckle-down, grin-and-bear-it, and rise-to-the-occasion: you are Anastasia Nicole Buchanan, daughter of Clay Herschel Buchanan and Jennifer Darling Buchanan. Clay made no excuses and raised a huntress. Jennifer bore the pain of your birth to instill endurance, and to smile while suffering sorrow.

It is Delbert's taunts, "You want to be a Susquehannock brave? Well, you can't be, because you don't have one of these...a dangly thing."

It is her father's instruction, "You don't punish a dog for what you haven't taught it. Patience, practice, and then the reward."

And though Anna does not know him, it is the voice of the father of the sport whose first-born was a double-barreled punt gun. His name was Colonel Peter Hawker[61] whose oddly accented voice resonates as the English ghost in every punt gun; distinguished and haughty, "I am the Davenport, crafted for kings, an instrument to do the bidding of royalty. Anastasia, claim your right, and I will do as you command."

Trying to stoke the fire in her own belly, and gritting her teeth to impose determination, Anna sits straighter in the skiff, "We're not beaten yet."

A shiver runs up Beauty's spine as an English ghost dances on her grave that has yet to be dug. One eye opens to view the imposing barrel of the

---

61 Colonel Peter Hawker (1802-1853). Authored *The (Shooting) Diary of Colonel Peter Hawker and Instructions to Young Sportsmen*. His famous double-barreled punt (boat) gun, one-side percussion, the other side flintlock, had a barrel length of 8'3½", a muzzle diameter of 1½", a weight of 193 pounds, and was designed to throw one pound of shot per barrel. This revered gun rests in state at The Wildfowlers' Association of Great Britain and Ireland.

Davenport suspended over her, full of powder and shot, and nothing to restrain it.

Running with the tide, the sneak skiff arcs around the peninsula of Swan Creek Point. The gunning light casts a dull sheet into the darkness of the cove. Colors other than black flash in a prism of feathers. A classroom of swan surrounded by a playground of brant glows dimly in the wavering light.

Anna holds her breath as she lies, belly-down, in the skiff. Using the short, hand paddles, Anna cuts across the tide, struggling to keep the light steady and move slowly, silently toward the birds feeding close to shore. Finding it impossible to look around the box containing the lantern, Anna peers down the barrel to discover her father's ingenuity. Next to the notch, cut out to hold the Davenport's barrel, is another small notch framed by the bottom of the box and the bow of the skiff. It is the perfect peephole to orient the skiff and aim the gun. With cold fingers numb within wet gloves, their ache contrasting with forearm muscles burning with fatigue, a tear drops from the corner of Anna's eye to freeze on the breech. Her frustration, desperation, and fear that she is not making headway, runs through a spinning wheel of emotions to land on despair.

Beauty's alarm drains her mouth of moisture, aware that through accident of tide, direction of approach, lack of strength in Anna, the light distorting distance and size, and the two species of fowl with their particular foibles, the stalk is perfect. Beauty fights her nature, her training, and her instinct to acquire the birds. To save Anna's life, and possibly her own, Beauty must alert the birds with a warning bark to give them a chance to escape, but time has run out.

The paddles tethered by strings float beside the skiff as it glides within range.

The swans stare at the growing light, transfixed, dazed, and confused.

The brant splash in the shallows content in their assumption that the sun has chosen to rise early today.

The Davenport vibrates with anticipation.

Anna cocks the spring-loaded hammer that is half the size of her hand. It is a curved piece of metal in the shape of an *S* for slaughter.

The small piece of rubber used for safety sake falls away.

Taking one last calculated look through the cutout at the ignorant swans and ducks, Anna closes her eyes, and instinctively turns her face away from the breech. With three fingers wrapped around the trigger, she squeezes, flinching at the...click.

Beauty's head snaps around, her vision focusing on the hammer.

Anna quickly cocks the hammer again and pulls the trigger... click... nothing.

No spark.

No fizzle.

No anything.

No percussion cap.

Clay's practice of using the piece of rubber is to prevent accidental sparks from igniting the load, but it is also to keep moisture from seeping down the tube causing a misfire from damp powder. He keeps the percussion caps that fit over the tube, and that are struck by the hammer to fire the cannon, in his coat pocket until the last minute, another safety precaution. Clay's coat containing the small packet of percussion caps hangs on a bent nail outside his basement jail cell.

A groan, deep, heavy, and spirit breaking emerges from Anna's throat, long and painfully slow.

Preventing shadows at the waterline, and doing double-duty concealing ripples, the whitewashed canvas skirts turn the unchristened sneak skiff into the Flying Dutchman,[62] the infamous ship of the cursed. Floating silently across the waters, it brings death to any that cross its ghostly apparition...the Davenport be damned.

With a soft hand, the breeze pushes from behind and encourages the changing tide to move toward shore. The ship with Anna as captain and Beauty as first mate continues to glide forward with the gunning light staring down the small flock of perplexed birds. As if a ghost herself, fading in and out of solid form, pushing through a dream where she is only a witness, Anna is amazed, and a spark of possibility grows within her, as the skiff eases in between the mesmerized swan and feeding brant. As the sharp prow nudges between the birds, their feathers scraping the canvas, they hypnotically swim past the light's illuminated edge. Their eyes blink, attempting to focus on the master commanding the silent vessel they are still unsure exists. Anna's hand slowly reaches out, guided by hope and from the ethereal world of hunters past. Grabbing the closest swan by its feathered neck, she squeezes, feeling warmth and a pulse through her glove. Anna twists the long elegant neck with the strength of purpose.

The swan floats dead.

Anna reaches for a brant.

---

62 Flying Dutchman. Legend. A Dutch ship whose captain is supposed to have been condemned to sail the seas until the Day of Judgment, always beating against the wind.

Sweet pungent aroma from his smoldering cigar and the thought of Clay Buchanan charged with murder are the only two pleasures lifting Frank McQuay out of the pit of economic despair his account books are pulling him into. The advice to expand his holdings has kept the creditors from knocking on the door, but they still stand on his doorstep calling his name. Each new acquisition of land brings profit and loss, increasing risks with modest rewards depending on labor availability and the flux in crop prices. What are not listed in the ledgers are his poor choices of horses to bet on which further diminish his purse. The only certainties that come from Frank's vast agricultural holdings are heavy bags with dark circles under his bloodshot eyes and long, exhausting hours. The hours of daylight are spent supervising in the fields. Come night, the dragging hours are monitored by an antique grandfather clock. Its incessant ticking is Frank McQuay's only company while he is stationed at his desk, scribbling in his books. These pages of columns, line after line of numbers, have become master, he their servant. What little sleep he steals is filled with disaster. Dreams of bills crushing him under their weight and the law dragging him off to debtor's prison causes fitful nights. Worse still is the nightmare of another type of prison with the horror of losing his reputation and community respect. This possibility sits him upright, sweating and suffocating next to his snoring wife.

The quiet of the masculine mahogany room, its reddish-brown hues set off by the yellow-orange flames flickering timidly in the stone fireplace, is fractured by the softest of sounds...silk slippers padding down the hardwood hallway to stand accusing in their ignorance.

"Frank, are you coming to bed?" Dorothy asks, her hands on her full hips.

"When the work is done, dear," Frank replies with the bite of a snake.

Dorothy walks into the room to warm herself by the fire, her heavy robe fringed with lace drawn tightly about her, "Well, since we're both up, I'd like to revisit a concern that affects the entire household."

Frank, all too aware of his wife's concerns, has no patience for petty annoyances.

"He must know I hear his prideful mumblings," Dorothy pleads, expecting sympathy. "Roman says he's named after an empire. Can you imagine such a thing?" Dorothy looks at her husband for a reaction that does not materialize. Frank slouches in his pleated chair, drawing deeply on his cigar, hoping the smoke surrounding his head will cause his wife to disappear.

"That will be the day the sun's brilliance is extinguished," Dorothy rattles on, "and the moon's cheese stinks to high heaven; Negroes running the world. They can't run their own lives. That's why they're always under the whip." Her hands wave away the cigar's drifting smoke as her nose twitches with irritation.

Frank takes in a chest full of air through his mouth, hoping in the pause that he will find patience, "We don't whip 'em any more."

Dorothy advances on her husband, stomping her feet to make her point, "That's the problem. At best their mendacity when communicating is the least of their daily offenses against us. Those of us with fine genealogical lines must not tolerate their subtle defiance. If we do, they'll forget their places."

Ignoring his wife when she blathers on about a topic without relevance has been Frank's usual defense, nodding occasionally to give the impression that he is participating, but cornered in what used to be his sanctuary, he is forced to respond, "What is it that you'd like me to do?"

"I want white servants," states Dorothy as if choosing the color of a scarf or the flavor of ice cream; it is that simple.

Picking up his gold-banded pen to return to his despair, Frank dismisses his wife, "They're too expensive. They'll demand larger quarters, and will quit at the first distasteful task."

Refusing to bow from the field, Dorothy relies on the tried-and-true feminine response to a husband's insensitivity, "You don't understand my needs." Then punctuates with a perfect excuse for firing the staff, "Besides, I believe they're stealing. I can't find the gold bracelet that you gave me when we were courting."

Disregarding his wife's ludicrous accusation of thievery by staff who have proven their loyalty, Frank throws his pen down while shoving back his chair to stand to confront his once-promising, but empty-headed wife, "You don't understand anything. Now leave me be!"

Frank's words, delivered with the punch of a bare-knuckle fighter, stun Dorothy. Too shocked to respond and too frightened to cry, she runs from the room clutching her throat as if her husband were strangling the life, the safety, the serenity out of her that she believes she is entitled to—good breeding and all.

Roman fills the vacuum left by the lady of the manor, carrying in a tray, with the elegance, a stature and presence that few majordomos[63] could match. His attire is impeccably pressed and starched, not a speck of lint on

---

63 Majordomo. A man in charge of a great household as that of a king or head of state.

the black wool jacket and pants, or a scuff on his polished shoes. His back straight despite his advanced age, pride and self respect his ramrod. On the ornate tray, two brandy snifters are filled halfway with the rich intoxicating liqueur.

Still in a huff, Frank snatches one of the pear-shaped glasses, spilling a few drops on the way to his lips, "Mrs. McQuay does not drink brandy, Roman."

"I'm aware of that, sir," Roman sets the tray on a side table, lifts the second snifter and swirls the liquid in a practiced fashion as if born into the life of privilege. He inhales the woody fragrance and sits down in a nearby chair, its soft leather wrapping his frame in cozy comfort. Ignoring Frank's sour visage, Roman sips the sweet cordial and relaxes, enjoying true security.

In her younger years, Beauty would be beside herself, splashing overjoyed and exuberant, to bound in circles to encourage Anna as she plods home, towing the sneak skiff along in the ankle-deep water and through the sparse grasses that attempt to delineate the line between marsh and bay. As a senior citizen, Beauty prefers to remain in the skiff, snuggled among the fowl, using them as a feathered blanket against the rising wind and falling mercury. Nearing dawn, the clearing sky with its preamble of light, teases the shivering that with the sun's bright face, its yellow rays offer false hope that skin will prickle with warmth, but tittering at their weakness, winter's hand rises to slap the outdoorsman's cheek until it is red.

With the morning light reflecting off the Davenport, the gunning light standing tall, and the nine swan and seven brant lying dead in the sneak skiff, Anna is exposed to the eyes of a daytime world coming to life. Though there is not a human in sight, she is vulnerable to every fear and anxiety. Suspicious snaps of twigs or an unexpected splash from within a cutout poke at Anna's paranoia. She conjures game wardens with handcuffs, ready to spring from around each turn, and out from behind every mound. Their sole purpose is to toss her into a cell next to her father, completing the destruction of the Buchanan family.

Why can't they leave us alone?

The short tow rope digs into Anna's shoulder as the first hour turns into two. The pain is worse than any strap from the uncomfortable brassieres that Olivia makes her wear when attending church. Olivia's argument is, "God prefers modesty." Anna cannot argue with that, but believes that bras are a contradiction, since they lift, separate, and force the bosoms of women to stick out prominently, calling as much attention to themselves, and their owners, as possible. Besides, at her age, Anna does not need an artificial contraption to proudly display her bouncy breasts, or to attract attention, especially as the only response she is interested in comes abundantly in the yearning gaze of William when his mischievous eyes drink in her voluptuous form, clothed or not.

To push away the pain, Anna counts her footsteps; starting over each time she reaches one thousand. The uneven shoreline has been memorized since childhood. No conscious thought is required, allowing her to slip into a trance as step after step into mud and sand, and splash after slushy splash around her boots, a sucking and swirling, act as a metronome or the swinging gold watch of a hypnotist. Anna's extremities are numb with cold, her shoulder numb with pain, and her mind made numb to *get-it-done* and make it home.

Focus on the steps, the splashes.

Pulling the skiff around the last long arcing bend, 40 yards from the shack, Anna squints against the harsh but futile sun cresting the Eastern Shore to her distant right. The glare skipping off the growing white-capped swells that blow spray into Anna's face, jars her roughly out of her meditative state. She glances up and toward the clearing fronting her home, where her worst fears are realized. Anna chokes on her heart as it lurches into her throat. Standing tall, staring straight at Anna is a man whose composure commands authority, even at this distance.

Running, to where she does not know, would only delay Anna's arrest, and any chance to escape would require abandoning the skiff and all on board. She being exhausted, and he longer of stride, he would quickly overtake her unless Anna orders Beauty to attack him, but that risks injury to her beloved dog.

Bowing her head in shame, Anna trudges forward, dragging her boatload of guilty evidence behind her. Anna grimly pictures her father's crestfallen face when gloating authorities tell him that she has failed him in every respect; a lifetime of tutoring wasted on a girl who cannot successfully hunt alone for one night.

The weight of Anna's failure crushes her instinct to flinch as he leaps from the raised bank. Beauty barks at the assault Anna does not see coming, but she looks up one last time at the clearing to glimpse the man's blowing hair above a wry smile within a bushy beard peppered gray. The gears of Anna's befuddled mind click forward to register that game wardens do not have beards and always wear a creased fedora or a starched cap. Within a twinkle of Anna's root beer eyes that are speckled yellow, she sees the man tug on two thin cords as the honks of live tollers, geese on leashes, reach her ears on the confused wind.

"Hey, you!" Delbert exclaims as he splashes down in front of Anna, her hand rising to ward off a blow that was not coming.

August and Delbert welcomed the returning warrior home with applause and bearing gifts. There were no recriminations from August by Anna's failure to fire the Davenport, only amazement at her steadfastness to muscle through a task that has defeated many full-grown men.

"She sure suffered for her meal, didn't she, Pa?" Delbert stated as fact more than a question as he placed the pot of possum stew on the potbelly stove. Claire had sent it with her men, keeping her word to provide victuals. "I believe she's worthy of brave status, even without..." Delbert winked at Anna, leaving the private joke unfinished.

After tying the Judas birds, one male and one female, to the porch post, August hefted the Davenport back into its tomb while Delbert muttered, "Wow," repeatedly. His heady amazement was not only from being privileged to see and handle the legendary punt gun, a weapon that in its lifetime that has exceeded four generations and has brought home or sent to market in excess of 1,200,000 birds, but that Anna connived a rudimentary system to remove its weighty mass from the hollow. "All this time, hiding at hands reach—brilliant," was Delbert's second mantra.

Stacking the swan and brant to overflowing on the three-duck counter, Delbert challenges Anna's telling of strangling the 16 birds while floating within their midst. August comes to her defense with one heartwarming statement, "It's not only possible, but commonplace, but it requires the stealth and skill of an old squaw. Clay would have taught Anna to be nothing less." Anna accepts the compliment for her father, but knows she failed, and only dumb luck and strange circumstances found her in the position to bring home fresh meat to eat.

Before stepping off the porch to leave, August turns back to Anna, feeling the emptiness at Clay's absence. He is about to speak words of reassurance that Clay will return, but August knows Anna will see through to his uncertainty. Instead, August says, "These tollers are well trained to bring 'em in and I'm confident you can breed 'em and sell the offspring."

"What do I owe you?" Anna asks, not expecting charity, but anxious, her palms sweating as she has nothing to pay for them with. August runs his thick fingers through his beard, calculating the noisy birds' value, and then glances at his son whose mussing Beauty's fur, "I've never thanked you for saving my boy's life," and with that, August steps off the porch, his sciatica forgotten for the moment.

The atmosphere of celebration quickly leaks out under the closed door with the departure of Delbert and his pa. The playfulness of kinship diminishes. It is scattered by the blustery wind. Anna checks and re-checks the door. With each rattle she hopes for an unexpected visitor who will help occupy her mind with mundane conversations about the weather, the price of shot and powder, suggestions for a spring vegetable garden, or even the musings about the war in Europe. Will President Wilson keep our boys out of it, leaving those on the other side of the Atlantic to settle their own disputes? But like a carnival balloon, so filled with cheer when purchased, its invisible contents, like Anna's hope, vanish, leaving both limp and miserable.

Anna stands peering out the window, holding a half-plucked swan by its neck and ignoring the five-gallon ducking pot that is boiling over. Its water sizzles as it runs down the side of the stove, turning to a hissing steam. A distracting conflict erupts between the animals within the confines of the small dwelling; a residence that is not at peace and seems to be shrinking. Anna turns away from a picturesque view of the world. At a glance, it is bright with a noonday sun floating in an ocean of blue where the dome enclosing the earth is without boundary. A glorious day for the illusionist tricking the mind with sleight of hand. Tiny cracks in the shack's sealing whistle an unhappy tune. Its discordant melody is the reality played by the gusting wind that lays flat the smoke escaping the stovepipe. Icy spray flies from the tops of breaking swells that have become wild waves crushing the brown grasses that stretch bayward, wanting to expand the territory of the marsh. Above, the birds, from mallard to sprigtail, eagle to owl, shiver as the sharp blow slices between carefully preened feathers to chill the best insulated as they wing from bay to marsh, woods to roost, in search of foodstuff and refuge.

The argument for dominance within the Great Room between Beauty, who believes her territory is being invaded, and the gander, a proud and ornery Canada goose, is interrupted to neither's satisfaction by Anna's stern, but ineffectual warning to Beauty to let the birds be, and by tying the geese to the rocking chair to limit their mobility. Anna had brought the honking, continuously gabbing birds inside to protect them. Wild and free, the large and powerful geese can easily defend themselves against foxes, raccoons, snakes and eagles, but tame and on a tether, they are susceptible to predation. Until Anna can construct a pen of sorts, she will have to put up with their cockiness, their apparent understanding of their value as a meat winner, and their incessant prattling.

Returning to the sink and her plucking, with Beauty at her feet, Anna tries to tune out Beauty's throaty growls lobbed across the room at the geese whose hisses are none too subtle. Down feathers ripped from the swan's flesh float about the room in a snow without moisture. The unlucky land in the bubbling dunking pot to drown, or to settle on the glowing stove to wither, curl, and then fall away as burnt cinder to the worn-smooth plank floor. The lucky will live on as stuffing in a pillow, or in some future quilt, soft and warm.

Lifting a brant by its webbed feet to immerse in the pot, Anna catches Beauty's knitted brow and sideways look of contempt.

"Why are you looking at me like that? You think I failed?" Anna blows an errant strand of loose hair from her face. "I got the birds, didn't I? Or is it the Judas birds that are annoying you? I would think you'd appreciate all the help I could get, but no, you have to throw a fit."

The geese tempt fate by raising the stakes, honking and flapping their expansive wings to pull the rocking chair around the small room, banging into the table and jarring the stove.

"Stop it and shut up!" screams Anna, throwing the dead brant into the rioting birds. Beauty's shocked expression is misinterpreted by Anna as silent condemnation of her means and her ends, because a paltry 16 birds may feed her and Beauty, but they will not support a household now increased by two belligerent geese that have to be cared for, "Fine, I admit using the Davenport didn't work out as planned." Anna remembers August and Delbert's praises, but they now ring hollow looking at the puny stack of naked and gutted birds lying on her counter. They are not worth the fuel the duck broker will burn driving down the rutted drive to her home. "I'm doing the best I can."

Anna places her hand against the sink to steady herself as her mind reels. She sees the Great Room for the crooked, slanting, eight steps across hovel that it is; filled with chaos and burdens overwhelming to a 17-year-old girl who is unable to control her dog, the squabbling geese, not even a boiling pot of water, but thought that an act of love-making was all she needed to make her a woman. Anna wonders what happened to that young child who so impressed Daisy on a dark and rain-driven night for her to express such amazement at her self-sufficiency. *Who am I kidding? I can't handle this,* Anna thinks as her frustration rises beyond her limits. Swinging her arm, she knocks the pot off the stove. Hot water sprays the room, splashing across the floor to startle the geese and evoking a yap from Beauty who hides under the table. Anna grabs her Mackinaw off the hook by the table to storm out the door, leaving it swinging as a broken jaw on its hinges, and abandoning the inhabitants to their own devices, "Kill each other for all I care."

Her beloved pond provides no solace as Anna sits rocking with knees pulled up against her chest. Without her old friend and confidant it is simply a lonely body of water with ice crusting the edges. A stone's throw to the dark middle, above the quiet depths, feeble ripples run back and forth in irritation. They wish to be set free to grow to maturity as those pounding the distant shore along the bay, but they are denied the full force of the wind by a balustrade of close-knit birch trunks skirted with ever-growing prickly brambles.

On other occasions, found by accident with a lover, friend, or family member, this same setting, idyllic, peaceful, a refuge from all storms, would be a joy to discover; a fond memory to be recalled in one's later years; a place where the world's troubles could be made right if God would allow every man's heart to be filled with this tranquility.

Anna's anger, a surrogate for fear and failure, blinds her eyes and steels her heart to all but the cold and isolation. However, a Benedict Arnold[64] is in her midst. His presence betrays pity and challenges Anna to stop sucking on the sour teat she is nursing from. Her ears, cold without the wool cap detects a sweet warble, a lively melody whistled as a single swinging note that encourages winter chickadees to flit from their nest to add their musical voices to the happy song. Wishing this intruder with his cheery disposition will pass on by, leaving her to wallow, Anna closes her eyes to will herself invisible. *Why shouldn't I be a part of the cold earth, the rough bark, and the twisting brush?* Anna's gloom starkly contrasts with the soil rich in nutrients feeding dignified trees in winter slumber, and empowering brambles to produce red berries by the bushelful for wandering fowl, that she stands out as a lump of coal on a snow bank. To Anna's relief, the angelic melody ceases, but disappointing, the steady footsteps crunching ice underfoot approach without invitation until they stop directly in front of her. Anna

---

64 Arnold, Benedict (1741-1801). As a brigadier general during the American Revolutionary War, his successes against the British aroused the enmity of other high-ranking military men, and he was passed over for promotions. Crippled by battle wounds and, after marrying Margaret Shippen, a Loyalist, he made secret overtures to the British and informed them of a proposed American invasion of Canada. At the end of 1781, Arnold escaped to England where he lived out his life ostracized and ailing.

opens her eyes. She slowly raises her head to take in the threadbare, blackish suit worn by a man, whose grin keeps him warm and that could persuade a bear to give up its honey. His bearded face is topped by a bowler hat. All are framed by the brilliant blue sky. In his hand is the Sampler, and under his arm, tied securely closed against a sudden gust of wind is his umbrella.

Looking down at Anna, forever a child to him, a sparrow broken in spirit, Umbrella George's heart swells to surround this daughter of all men with an embrace of unconditional love. Ignoring the rheumatism in his hip to squat down to be on her level, to be eye-to-eye and willing to share her pains, Umbrella George takes Anna's cold hands in his wrinkled ones and remains silent until she is ready.

The two remain in a world without words. Anna's pupils dilate as she seeks a toehold within the bottomless green eyes of Umbrella George's that swirl with endless eddies of warmth. As if Anna and Umbrella George are the center of the universe, where all surrounding elements humble themselves to the needs of these two, the ripples accept their modest place and retire, leaving the pond relaxed and at peace, The tops of the trees that battle the truculent winds broker a temporary truce so they may turn their energy toward healing the broken one at their base.

Anna tries to look away, to smother the words rising with the pain, but Umbrella George's tender gaze holds her focused on admitting the truth.

"It's so hard."

"Darling girl, life is supposed to be," responds Umbrella George as he squeezes her hands. "How else would we learn anything?"

Anna blinks back tears, still fighting the sobs that want to flow, "What if it's more than I can handle alone?"

Softly, Umbrella George's words are whispered as a sage careful when imparting secrets, "The Good Lord never gives us too much. It may seem like it at times, but that's only because we don't yet realize our potential." Umbrella George's back straightens to pull away, to lessen the blow, "Child, how dare you say, 'You're alone.' You have a whole community to rely on. They rallied around you and your mother. Bless her beautiful soul, when you were born. Do you think they'll give up on you now?"

Anna's tears fall freely, wetting their clasped hands, "But what my father did..."

"Allegedly did. He's a respected man in these parts and thank God that Lady Justice is blind. We must trust in both."

A deep sigh escapes Anna's lungs. She believes what Umbrella George is telling her, that there are many in Havre de Grace whom she can rely upon as she has always relied on her father. She could always rise to any task because he believed in her, and though he is a stern father who rarely praised her, it was in his assigning her the tasks of carving, cleaning of fowl, and hunting, that was praise itself.

What Anna must also accept is that justice may be meted out to her father because Umbrella George's belief in her father's alleged acts cannot stand scrutiny, "Why do you always carry that?"

"The Sampler?" Umbrella George's hope soars. "Well, you never know when some folk will be touched by His Spirit and wish to order the Good Book."

"No," Anna corrects his misunderstanding, "I mean the umbrella."

Umbrella George chuckles, as the answer is the same, "Any fool will carry one when it's raining." He leans forward to kiss Anna on her forehead, knowing she will have difficult times, but she will never give up. Using his umbrella as a cane he stands, and then turns on a worn heel to stroll off while whistling a tune that Anna now recognizes as *Amazing Grace*.

Approaching the shack with a bounce in her step, buoyant from the encounter with Umbrella George, and humming the spiritual that is warming her heart against the cold gusts of wind, Anna finds a strange scene awaiting her. In the shadow of the late afternoon sun, sitting outside on the porch, to the left and right of the open door are sentries, alert and watchful. To the right, the geese have dragged the overturned rocking chair through the door and are alternating between preening and twisting their long necks, always wary and on the lookout. Fronting the left door post is Beauty, her tail wagging an indication of her pleasure at Anna's return. A disquieting calm reigns between the two species. Displeased by being in each other's company, but accepting the reality, a détente has been worked out through means other than political.

Stepping onto the porch, Anna is torn between laughing at or consoling these battle-worn creatures. Tuffs of fur are missing from Beauty's graying head and shoulders. Giving as good as she got, patches of black and gray feathers are absent from the necks and wings of the geese who work to put their mauled coats to right. These tear-offs swirl in and out of the doorway as dead soldiers aimlessly seeking a final resting place.

"I see you've come to an understanding," Anna says, deciding that laughter is due. She rights the rocking chair, plumps the cushions and sits down between her faithful dog and the birds, laughing herself hoarse at their disheveled appearance and wounded pride until tears salty and sweet cover her cheeks.

Despite the carnage inside, the shack is at peace, a place for its inhabitants to dwell.

The purity of the drug did not make up for the lack of quantity. Standing wobbly on weak legs on his side of the bars, Clay emptied the small brown bottle that Doctor Webster had provided, and impatiently waits for him to return with another. Their argument concerning the proper dosage to suppress the effects of his ailment continues to reverberate within Clay's cell.

"There's enough there for two weeks," the good doctor stated through bars whose solidity spoke of permanence. Doctor Webster was gravely concerned by Clay's reduced state; his shaking hands, the heavy drops of perspiration clinging to this forehead, but most alarming was when racking coughs shook his thinning frame they produced bloody purges, particles of lung from late stage tuberculosis.

Doctor Webster is as perplexed by this wasting disease, the consumption, as is the medical community as a whole. It is so misunderstood that the fashionable of Europe believe it is a genetic trait passed down through the elite, and to die before the age of 30, spitting up blood was a mark of distinction—a romantic and spiritual passing. The wealthy, sequestered in sanitariums, failed to acknowledge the cries, the watery, throaty gurgles of those unwashed and ragged wretches in crowded slums or alone in isolated country towns suffering the painful drowning death.

Hanging on with one hand to his side of the bars, Clay upturned the bottle. He did not hear the doctor's declaration as to the lifespan of the bottle's contents, only his own swallows as the dizzying opiate flowed down his throat to momentarily appease his cravings, comfort his raging nerves, and conceal the extent of his affliction.

"Clay, your disease is farther along than I thought. You can't hide it any longer. You'll need to tell Anna."

Wiping his mouth with his blood-speckled sleeve, Clay argued, "I've told her not to come back here. Besides, I've beat this thing all these years, and I'm not ready to give in yet." Exhausted from suffering withdrawal and the fatigue that accompanies the inability to breath as the tubercle bacillus in the affected lungs explode to attack the host body, Clay hung his head—its weight heavier than the burdens he shoulders.

"I'd never challenge your will," Doctor Webster stated as he watched Clay's vise grip on the bar squeeze the color from his fingers, "but your decision to keep Anna away, is, in my opinion, unfair to both of you."

"I don't need your familial advice, doc. I need you to bring another bottle."

"I'm not sure it will help anymore."

"Well it can't hurt," Clay slammed his hand against the bars, rattling them, and scraping his palm on the rough, rusted surface. Clay's outburst was a transparent masking of pain and pleading, clearly evident in his tired eyes that spoke volumes to Doctor Webster. His Hippocratic Oath[65] tugged at his heart to provide comfort to a tormented patient, who is also a dear friend, but tugging also at his conscience was "to do no harm." Doctor Webster feared he had already done the harm by allowing Clay unsupervised and unfettered access to laudanum with the mistaken belief that this hunter, a master of all that he endeavors, would be the ruler over the drug. Though sadly, stealthily, a *coup d'etat* had occurred, and the doctor, with only the best intentions, missed it.

"I'll consider your request," Doctor Webster turned to leave, but with the speed of a striking snake, Clay reached out to grab hold of the doctor's wool coat, pulling him forcefully back to the bars, his fat belly pinched between the metal separating the two men.

"You've been paid. Now bring me another bottle."

Shocked by Clay's violence, Doctor Webster stood as if stupid, caught by a gunner's light, and smelling the harsh odor and hot breath of a man who had not bathed, and who feared another night without his fix.

Feeling dirty, as a drug pusher, the doctor stammered, "I...I'll b...bring another, Clay. I promise."

Clay released his friend, a confidant and conspirator to keep secrets, who only stumbled twice on the stairs as he fled as fast as his rotund physique would allow.

---

65 Hippocratic Oath. Ethical code attributed to Hippocrates. There are two parts: the first part sets out the obligation of physician to student and vise-verse. The second part is a pledge that the physician prescribes only beneficial treatment; refrain from causing harm, and to live an exemplary life. Hippocrates (460-377 B.C.) a Greek physician of antiquity who is regarded as the father of medicine. His name is associated with the Hippocratic Oath although he did not author it.

Tink...tink...tink.

The used bourbon bottle filled with warm horse blood slides down the rough cell wall. Tied with twine at the neck and lowered through the high window from street level, it is a present from Olivia to Clay, the cure *du jour* for the consumption.

The owner of the tannery is a crotchety old man suffering from a lifetime of scleroderma. The painful disease causes his skin to become increasingly hard, tight, and shiny, easily torn or ripped. His pores forever ooze the retching stench of dead animals that are being processed into items for future usage. He grinned yellow teeth as he accepted the coins for the bucket full of film-encrusted blood recently drained from a filly who lost one too many races. Personally, he did not believe heated blood contained curative powers, but he was not a man to dim the hopes of the desperate, especially when it fed his pockets.

Olivia suspected that Clay's cough was more than a persistent scratchy throat, and though she was a woman who freely spoke her mind, never afraid to ask questions, a most unbecoming attribute for a *lady*, she was also respectful of one's right to privacy. Olivia would be patient until Clay decides to share the true cause of his night sweats and chest pain, as she no longer believed it was from colds or over exertion.

Waiting on Clay's admission did not mean sitting idle. Olivia acted on her beliefs until proven wrong, which happened rarely. This was the reason for her night trip to the tannery across the Susquehanna River for the foul bucket of wishes and prayers.

Still restricted from visiting, Olivia resorts to evading the jail guards' forays for fresh air, which thankfully on this icy night are few. Shots of post New Year's schnapps thrown back in front of the office stove produced contented snores even from these vigilant deputies.

"Clay?" Olivia whispers as she kneels in the snow outside the street-level window. "Are you there?" She jiggles the twine to clink the bottle against the floor to get Clay's attention in a room filled to overflowing with nothing but a man's thoughts. Clay smiles for the first time in two days, thinking: *where would I be?* But an anchor of sadness drags down the upturned corners of his grin. Shaking his head and wringing his hands a he watches the bottle dance like a marionette, he proclaims to the yet to be seated jury, "No. LeCompte did not deserve to die. He was only doing his job, but why did he have to come to my property that day?"

Wrapping Olivia's quilt tighter around himself, Clay steps to the wall and picks up the bottle. Its contents warm his hands through the glass; his mind grateful at the thought of spending the night with a bottle of joy-juice, but as he pulls the cork his nose wrinkles. "I'm here," he gags, turning away from the sickly-sweet smell. Clay holds the foul bottle at arm's length, an abomination to his senses, "My God, what is this?"

"It's hot horse's blood. Drink it. It'll help you," Olivia's voice rings with jubilance as if her belief in the thick animal claret was inspired by whispers from heaven instead of overheard from a blind-drunk patron at Tavern Bouvard.

"Doctor Webster promised he'd return with my medicine. I don't need or would I ever take a swig of that," Clay states with finality, crushing Olivia's joy as an unseen beetle on a darkened path.

Silence...the twine falls through the window to curl at Clay's feet.

Spoken as a coo to a child, but felt as a swinging boom from a tacking skipjack, "He's not coming, Clay."

The cell, built solid of stone, mortar, and metal, immovable, fell in on Clay, knocking the wind from his chest and sending his thoughts to panic.

"Clay? Clay, for God's sake, tell them and forget about what happens to me. Think of Anna. Clay?" Olivia's tears make no sound as they fall into the snow. With no response forthcoming from the black hole that is a window, Olivia reluctantly rises to walk off into darkness made bleaker by Clay's stubbornness.

A faint light bleeds through the cell window with the frosted dawn. A hungover guard peers into the cell where Clay is curled under the quilt, his boots protruding from the covers at the foot of the bed. Unseen by the guard is Clay's shirt. It is drenched with ripe sweat as his body secretes the poison through his pores; a poison that Clay calls medicine. The guard scratches his pounding head, puzzled by the sight of the bourbon bottle lying empty on its side.

The heady musk of a protective father intertwines with spring blossoms that are the faint scent of a mother, who together wrap Anna in a safe harbor of slumber. Warmth from the thick, goose-down quilt, its aged patchwork soft against her bare skin, is a loving embrace of textile tenderness; memories of her parents found deep within their marriage bed. Succor from conscious troubles; golden moments for the impoverished spirit. A dance of the heart and mind where they yearn for more, and the sandman, leader of the dream band, complies with melodies filled with laughter, tickles, hugs, and kisses.

Woven as drum beats to the delightful song is a pounding, a hammering, distant, yet near, close by, but outside.

Mingling as a fragrant additive, an aroma, a scent distinctive and pleasing, wood-smoked bacon sizzles in a frying pan, infusing the rooms with mouth-watering delight to coax Anna out of the land of Nod.[66]

Anna stretches under the covers, refreshed from a long needed sleep. Her joints popping as a contented, "Ah," escapes her lips. Then as if a bucket of ice water were thrown in her face, her brain springs awake. Anna lifts the covers. Except for cotton panties she is naked and does not know how she got that way, or for that matter, how or when she left the rocking chair to climb into her parents' bed. The answer to her questions pops his head through the doorway.

"Sleep well, princess?" Delbert's snickering drips with sarcasm.

"Did you undress me?" huffs Anna. However, her voice lacks conviction as she pulls the covers modestly up around her chin.

"Yes," feigning annoyance, "I thought I was disrobing a corpse as you were dead to the world." Delbert holds up a short-handled axe that has a blade on one end and a flat for hammering on the other, "I came to help you build a pen for the geese, but like a girl, I found you sound asleep in the rocking chair, snoring like a bear."

"Snoring?!" Anna sits up abruptly to defend her femininity, the quilt forgotten, it falls away to expose breasts whose nipples stand in defiance at the coarse accusation, "I don't snore. You take that back!"

Delbert's teenage hormones race at seeing Anna's excited bosoms, but they are overridden by the perverse satisfaction that he can still get his friend's goat. *She's too easy*, he thinks, and then playfully responds, "If only those had been that big when we skinny-dipped, I might have been interested, but now...eh."

"Get out!" cries Anna as she covers herself, frustrated.

"Children," Olivia calls out, emphasizing *child* to make a point at their juvenile antics, "breakfast is ready."

Anna pulls on an undershirt and coverall before entering the Great Room that has been restored to order. The rocking chair is back in its rightful place; the geese are honking happily and secure in their new outside pen; Beauty lolls by the crackling stove, again, queen of her castle; the dead soldiers and their spirits have been swept out into the wind; mounds of bacon, crisp and dripping with juicy fat crowd a platter of spiced and scrambled goose eggs that sits center stage on the table, book-ended by a basket of browned and buttered biscuits and a pitcher of frothy milk fresh from early milking.

---

66 Land of Nod. The mythical land of sleep. A pun on land of Nod (Genesis 4:16. "And Cain went out from the presence of the Lord, and dwelt in the land of Nod, on the east of Eden"). *Holy Bible*, King James Version, 1987 printing. Public domain. Note: Nod means wandering.

"This is just what I need," Anna hugs Olivia, who squeezes back, wishing Anna's statement was true.

Olivia knows that even with all Anna's skills and determination, she faces an uncertain future. To succeed in a marsh along the Chesapeake Bay, Anna will have to find within her that skill, her special gift, that will consistently provide food to feed herself, Beauty, and the geese, including an income sufficient to make the payments on the land this shack sits on. Anna will have to do this without her father. Olivia fears that Clay's desire to protect Anna from life's harsher realities has placed her in a position she is unprepared for, because if Clay remains silent, the law will convict him for the murder of LeCompte. If he speaks the truth, that is still a condemnable act, and when he is freed, the disease will take its toll. Although Anna's friends will assist her whenever she calls upon them, ultimately she will succeed or fail on her own.

Olivia holds Anna tight as Delbert begins to serve.

Now in his mid 60s, Judge Hathaway has served the community of Harford County for 35 years. He has done so with distinction, dispensing justice with an even hand, and when the circumstances became obvious would joke on the record that, "If it quacks, it's a duck," to the joy and amusement of his coverall and wader-booted constituency. His re-election every four years was as expected as the migration of fowl to the local waters, but with the birds' decline and the strict enforcement of game laws that upset his stalwart supporters, the judge's tenure is now as precarious as a hunter in a leaking sinkbox.

The judge decided a few years back that the life of a widower in retirement, sipping tea, and reading the Bible would quickly become a lonely affair, even in the company of the Holy Spirit. He reluctantly admitted to himself that the law was his earthly mistress, and vain though it may be, it provided him with his identity and standing in the community, and he does not want to lose either. This was the reason he sat uncomfortable, queasy even, as the guest of honor in President Grover Cleveland's[67] gold placarded

---

67 Cleveland, Stephen Grover (1837-1908). A lifelong Democrat who, as the 22nd and 24th President of the United States, followed policies of reform and independence, transferring thousands of jobs from patronage to civil service. In foreign policy, he was an isolationist and opposed territorial expansion. He retired to Princeton, NJ where he was trustee (1901-08) of the University and lectured

chair. Judge Hathaway has found himself surrounded by the moneyed men of the Wellwood Club who are eager to support his re-election. The judge's queasiness, his rolling stomach is not from the orange sauce poured liberally over the roasted duck, or from the heavy cigar smoke hanging foul in the air of this famous duck club, but the expectation of *quid pro quo*[68] with every hearty handshake, wink, and the touch of soft fingers to the brim of their top hats.

This tipping of Lady Justice's scales is not spoken aloud as it would be far too crass for gentlemen such as these of noble breeding, especially when rulings in their favor would be for the good of all, at least in their opinion, so no harm done. For the time being, the Honorable Jeremiah P. Hathaway, proud of his half Quaker heritage, ignores the voice in his head, the sweet voice of his dear wife calling a warning. He suppresses his conscience as its strings are tugged upon, to listen to stories told by the old heads sitting court, commanders of all they see in a club of kings so exclusive that it has no address. Men of power, prestige, and influence know its location on the western shore of the Northeast River. Many citizens living in Charlestown, Maryland, north of the Susquehanna Flats who will never see the inside of the hallowed halls just south of town, a club that regularly hosts Presidents, refer to it as the Well-heeled Club—but only with reverence and a hint of envy.

"I hunted with the man himself," one old head continues. "We simply called him Grover. One of the boys he was." The white haired gentleman pauses while the Negro attendant in pressed livery and white gloves re-lights his Havana. "From 1885 to 1896, no it was '97, we'd go after the ruddy, ignoring all others. Sitting a blind or sinkbox, Grover would say, 'That duck is the finest for the table. A gentleman, dapper in his appearance, and look at him fly. My God, in a strong wind he'll fly backward to avoid the shot.'"

Sitting off to one side, at a lesser table, Frank McQuay listens, rapt with interest, dreaming of becoming a full member of this club instead of a probationary. As it was Frank who suggested to the members they support the judge in his time of need, they could add another tentacle to their far-flung influence, and his own position would be elevated within the Wellwood as well as securing his interests in other areas.

"If you glance over there," the old head jabs his smoldering cigar toward a gilded cabinet fronted with glass, "you'll see what we call our Cleveland Canvasbacks, a couple of drakes he shot over. You'll notice their design is

---

in public affairs. Cleveland enjoyed public admiration as a staunch exemplar of integrity in government.

68 *Quid pro quo*. Latin. One thing in return for another.

flatter and wider, not like today's rounder, higher profile decoys. Grover preferred the flatter ones, not that he was adverse to change, but he had a theory. Even though they are weighted, I believe those have iron keels made from old horseshoes; they couldn't right themselves in rougher waters. Grover's theory was if the decoys are reluctant to assist further in the hunt, it was a sign to him to get off the water and return to the club for a spirited game of gin rummy, a fat Cuban," the old head manipulates his cigar between his fingers, "and a bottle of the club's finest."

The history of the each member and V.I.P. guest was expounded upon late into the night to ensure each member in good standing was reassured of their importance, praised for their business astuteness and command of the hunt, but also to instill in the judge that these are men who are winners, and the judge should hitch his judicial future to them. Judge Hathaway's smile was a pasted strain, amazed by the boastful nature of men who should exhibit quiet contentment from the obvious success and blessings in life. The judge could sum up the evening by saying, "I dined in an opulent room filled with the trappings of wealth, sitting among men, barons of industry, who, if you believed their stories, never missed when shooting at a passing duck or goose."

Throughout the entire evening, including the drive back to Havre de Grace over the Susquehanna River with Frank McQuay, not one mention or acknowledgment of the carvers of the decoys these men shot over, or of the experienced guides who placed the rigs just so to entice the birds down. Listening to the well-heeled members of the Wellwood Club, you would believe they did it all themselves.

Judge Hathaway finds himself deeply disturbed by the remarks, the platitudes lathered on him by members of the Wellwood Club as he departed. Their words were spoken with a confidence that surpassed a guarantee for his re-election, with whispers of machinations in place for such an event; the plot for winning already conceived; the intrigue to sway the populace to an idea, a way of thinking not their own—but for the good of all, so no harm done.

If you had to say, "...no harm done," then there probably was, is the sentiment that keeps swirling in the judge's mind, occupying his thoughts, and screwing his face to appear as one suffering from blocked flatulence. His concerns deny him the pleasure of an early morning that is backlit by a cresting sun turning the night's frost that covers resting fields to a sparkling display. Farther than the eyes can see, a magical carpet spreads out, glistening on black earth, dazzling on naked trees. A wonderland held in twinkling crystals; perfect, peaceful, where the only disturbance is the occasional oily backfire from the Buick whose engine, like its driver, is not in tune.

"It's an interesting case you have before you," Frank McQuay begins, wanting to ease into a conversation where a specific outcome is desired, while at the same time concentrating on avoiding potholes that might jostle the judge, having noticed his Honor's ill mien.

It is not only unethical, against the cannons of an officer of the court, but also statutorily illegal for a judge to discuss a case before him. Within the halls of the judiciary, this is common knowledge, and Judge Hathaway is never queried by those who regularly surround him regarding a case on which he is sitting in judgment. Therefore, Frank McQuay's statement is startling, and off-putting. Though giving the benefit of the doubt that he is unaware of this prohibition, and likely passing the miles with small talk, his Honor does not want to be rude or unresponsive, especially to the man who has for all intended purposes secured, by means this half Quaker lacks the courage to ask, his judgeship for as long as he wishes. Therefore, the judge hopes a neutral response will suffice, "The jury always has difficult decisions to make in a case concerning capital murder."

"Constable Jenkins seems to think that Buchanan fella is the guilty party," Frank McQuay presses, probing for the judge's leanings.

"What the constable believes is irrelevant," his Honor states, squirming in the padded seat, and then turning toward Frank McQuay as a recollection tickles his brain. "Didn't you and the defendant have several suits against each other some time ago?"

Quickly correcting the judge, he hopes to distance himself from Clay so that his questioning of the judge will seem innocuous, "No. Mr. Buchanan and several other poachers filed nuisance suits against me which your Honor dismissed as frivolous."

Crossing above the vibrant Susquehanna River, its banks slick with slush, the Buick vibrates as its slender Firestone tires hum while running over the bridge's metal decking.

"Hmm..." the judge gazes out through the windshield that is fogging at the edges from their warm breath. A flock in excess of 60 ruddy ducks, flying fast and low, crossing under the bridge, skim the shoreline toward the Flats. The judge reflects on a winter's day such as this about a decade ago, though maybe it was overcast, if memory serves, where he stood a blind north of Havre de Grace on this magnificent river. His concentration that day on the distant horizon with the hopes for a fat mallard to drop into his bag left him vulnerable to the diabolical and reckless flight patterns of these boobies. He was struck in the back of his head, knocking him forward into the screen of vegetation he had erected to hide himself. Recovering quickly as he spit out wilted leaves, he emptied the entire magazine, all nine shots at the fleeing fowl. The judge achieved nothing but raising a bruise on his shoulder and filling the blind with expended shells and acrid burnt powder. Later in the day as he ambled home, keeping his shame, his failure to himself, he overheard three men telling how they fired 22 shots and downed only one.

Who's the booby now? snickered the judge.

"It doesn't surprise me that a law-breaker, a man who indiscriminately kills fowl to the detriment of all honest citizens who patiently wait for the season, would take the next step and murder such a good and valiant defender of the law as Felipe LeCompte," Frank McQuay hopes to stir the emotional stew.

Judge Hathaway feels his equilibrium slipping; his judicial balance being upended simply by listening to theory or speculation that would not be allowed inside a court room, at least not his. Words spoken will color thoughts that influence actions. To slander a man; to jump to conclusions even if circumstantial evidence points in a particular direction is tortable in the very least, sinful when standing before *The Judge*, doubly so when that man is not present to defend himself and his name, good or otherwise.

Steering the Buick down Judge Hathaway's lane, the gingerbread homes all neat and respectable, Frank McQuay concludes with his point, puncturing the judge's innocence once and for all, "Your Honor, men placed in positions such as yours have a duty to ensure that the defendant does not go free. Regardless of the difficult decisions the jury has to make, you control the court." Stopping in front of the judge's empty home, and ratcheting the emergency brake in place, Frank McQuay turns to stare into the swimming eyes of the astonished judge who is fumbling with the door handle, attempting to escape. Frank McQuay softens his tone, but his expression, steely, is anything but gentle, "Clay Buchanan is a menace to society. He's lived outside the law. His kind needs to be corralled, regardless of the means, so upstanding contributing folk can walk these streets in safety. Justice must be done for Felipe LeCompte, and, it's for the good of all."

Judge Hathaway sits bundled in a knitted afghan in front of the roaring fire in his parlor, still decorated, as it was when his wife was alive. His old hands shake. The tips of his fingers, stained from decades of following the law inked within innumerable volumes, now clasp tightly to the cup of steaming tea as he raises its weak brew to his lips. Judge Hathaway wonders if he will ever be warm again. His center, his soul is infected with a cold blackness. It is the pooling of the sacred ink draining from the pages by his want of a thing, a possession, a position that might not rightfully be his, and the parting words of Frank McQuay, planter, businessman, gambler, Wellwood Club probationary, and now owner of the judge's moral compass, "No harm done."

The bags under Judge Hathaway's sleep deprived eyes are black as his judicial robe. Peaceful slumber is the true measure of a man's conscience. The judge's nights have been filled with turmoil. His sleep, what little there was, has been denied him respite from the battle raging between the stated, "...good for all," by men whose agenda is self-serving, and the Word, written for guidance and societal harmony in Leviticus 19:15,[69] "Do not pervert justice; do not show partiality to the poor or favoritism to the great, but judge your neighbor fairly." Sitting in his raised chair, his throne, exalted when presiding over matters civil or criminal, his Honor's concentration drifts between droning questions of the special prosecutor brought up from Washington D.C.—and the labored answers of the skipjack captain recalling the discovery of the body—its location, the date, time, tides and wind direction—and the defendant at the defense table sitting accused.

The judge avoided characterizing the physical features of defendants brought before the bar on matters of criminality as they are afforded the mantle of innocent until proven guilty, but he has found that an inordinate number of convicted persons have stereotypic features and mannerisms of lower animals; there is the pinched face of the ferret whose pointed nose sniffs out trouble; the beady eyes and nervous twitches of the weasel who is always on the lookout for the correcting arm of the law; the fidgety hands of the raccoon who is into banditry; the heavy brow of the ill-tempered, brawling badger, and the warped curiosity of the mischievous otter. All these traits start a man on his path of criminal behavior; some remain in the realm of the petty while a select few, the more industrious and adventure-driven, advance to grander, more nefarious acts; murder being the culmination of a career, long and sordid.

Examining Clay, Judge Hathaway sees a man in great distress, suffering from a disease that has diminished him in spirit and physicality. Though he could be mistaken, the irritating and interrupting coughing fits of the defendant are from a throat tickle that will not be quelled. The clothes the defendant wears are a faded blue coverall still damp from an early morning hand washing, a patched gray flannel shirt, and scuffed workman's boots in need of a presentable polish. The coverall and shirt are another's, two sizes too big, or has the man been so diminished by his incarceration? Clay's head, shorn to the scalp with small razor nicks, red and raw, is bowed in embarrassment, shame, or guilt. The evidence will soon tell. His shoulders

---

69 *Holy Bible*, King James Version, 1987 printing. Public domain.

are slumped in despair or defeat. Only his lips, held firmly together by his clenched jaw indicate any measure of defiance by a man not in control; not the master of his environment; wholly out of place in this bastion of jurisprudence with lacquered oak tables, polished pine chairs, and suited men speaking highfalutin language that argues for or against his guilt.

The defendant no longer resembles his peers; huntsmen, marsh men, oystermen, the salt-of-the-earth, calloused-handed men who make up the jury. These men are well fed, refreshed after a night's sleep in beds designed for slumber and recuperation in the homes, arms, and hearts of love ones. They have not been isolated, deprived of hot meals and consortium. Nor does the accused seem of the same species as the spectators crowding the public benches. The wooden, hip-wader-high wall separating the detained and the free-to-roam is thin and low, flimsy in its construction, with a simple swinging door that a child can push open. But the full strength of the law, backed by the society that created it; the town, the state, and the country, makes the wall ridged and impossible to scale. Clay is the creature to be gawked at, in need of being kept for judgment. The spectators who make up society are the gentle folk, the keepers, empowered by their own sense of morality to judge.

These good citizens are divided. Half are the curious who rarely witness the drama of murder with all its sordid details and sensationalism attached to motive. It is the why of the matter that pokes at the human psyche and must be sated or the audience will leave without satisfaction. The other half is made up of staunch defenders of the defendant's character and his innocence. They are believers in the man through love or association, but rarely can they account for his whereabouts at the time of the crime.

Judge Hathaway chews on his lower lip as he ponders excuses, none legitimate, to recuse himself from this case because a tiny piece of his ethics indoctrination holds tight to the axiom of innocent until proven guilty despite Frank McQuay's coloring words to the contrary and his desired outcome. And even if the accused appears to be a shell of a man, he shows no physical features of any animal. And though his coughing fits are disruptive to the judicial proceedings, his eyes and mannerisms are apologetic; a higher order civilized response.

"The prosecution calls Doctor Hiram Webster," Dieter Nelson, the rising star among Washington's elite, announces as a command to Lazarus[70] as if he were the Healer and commanding the doctor to rise from the dead.

---

70 Lazarus. John 11:1-44. The Biblical story of Lazarus' death and Jesus raising him from the dead saying "Said I not unto thee, that, if thou wouldest believe, thou shouldest see the glory of God?" *Holy Bible*, King James Version, 1987 printing. Public domain.

Pushing his girth through the small swinging door that separates the spectators and official actors, the good doctor keeps his eyes squarely on the witness stand; not that he is afraid of the uncomfortable chair where a man is examined to the depths of his being, but he is unable to face Clay for abandoning him during his greatest time of medical need. For Clay's part, he looks up at the call of the practitioner's name, hoping that if only for the briefest of moments his friend would catch his eyes that express deep shame over his actions during their last encounter. The voice screaming in Clay's head demands that he shout his apology, to heal their emotional wound, to mend the tear in their friendship, to span that chasm created in a rash moment of panic, and to make amends before the abyss of pride takes hold to separate them forever.

It is not Clay's jaw that keeps him muzzled but decorum, propriety, the observance of conventions, and the rules of court. Besides, Clay has been appointed an attorney. Clay had originally asked for Millard Tydings, believing the young aristocrat of Havre de Grace would guide him through the judicial process, that to the ignorant can quickly become a miasma.

The pie-faced man now patting Clay's hands in reassurance, Clem Mathers, Esquire, had informed Clay at their first meeting that Chief was unavailable. Asked to explain, "Call me Clem," related, "Chief joined the militia," a faraway gaze in his eyes, dreamlike as if he was transforming his soft gut, a protuberance to minimize his stork nose, into a muscled, fighting man of 20, instead of the alcoholic barrister racing toward 60.

"Like his forebears, Chief is leading Maryland's finest, Company D, under General Pershing.[71] They're chasing that riffraff Pancho Villa[72] back into Mexico." Seeing Clay's disappointment, Clem combs the remaining half dozen red hairs on his otherwise bald and freckled head; wisps of hair that are confused as to which direction to lie. "Don't worry. I've never lost a murder case. I've never tried one either, but how hard can it be?" Clay felt the last reserve of hope wash away, yet as Clem wiped his bifocal glasses

---

71 Pershing, John Joseph (1860-1948). A general who commanded forces in pursuit of Pancho Villa and the American Expeditionary Forces in Europe during WWI (1914-1918), and Chief of Staff of the U.S. Army (1921-1924). Known as "Black Jack" Pershing because he had once commanded an all-black troop.

72 Villa, Pancho (1878-1923). He was a Mexican rebel general during the Mexican Revolution (1910-1920). The United States supported Villa, and then President Woodrow Wilson turned his support to President Carranza. Villa retaliated against Americans in Mexico by stopping trains and shooting people. In 1916, his troops raided Columbus, New Mexico. President Wilson sent thousands of troops under General Pershing after Villa but failed to capture him.

with the lapel of his blue-black coat; he smiled, exuding a calm confidence in his abilities that his folksy appearance masks.

Special Prosecutor Nelson, having elicited from Doctor Webster the cause of death, "Exsanguination due to massive trauma, the result of a shotgun blast to the upper torso," follows up with a question that appears to be off the cuff, but in fact is calculated. "Doctor Webster, have you met with the defendant since his arrest?"

Quicker than a Carroll's Island dog after a cripple, Clem leaps to his feet, jarring the table and upsetting his glass of odorless clear liquid, "Objection! Relevance?"

Prosecutor Nelson turns toward the judge, "Your Honor, my question goes to the defendant's state of mind," annoyed by the interruption from this country lawyer.

"Objection overruled. You may answer the question, Doctor," Judge Hathaway rules, readily acceding to minor victories for the prosecution, arguing to himself that the leanings of a battle here and there does not guarantee a decisive war, nor should it make him a traitor to impartiality.

"I was summoned to his jail cell on an unrelated medical issue," the doctor's words are chosen carefully, still not looking at Clay, but rather for any face in the room offering sympathy for his unease; his chosen role as the quiet healer shattered by the shot causing an unnatural death.

"Doctor, the court will decide if your visit is unrelated to the killing of Game Warden LeCompte," the prosecutor stresses the word killing.

Among the curiosity seekers in search of gossip, or bored citizenry on break from their everyday work wanting warmth, shelter, and camaraderie from winter's barren streets, are the expected faces, their expressions are placards to thoughts both obvious based on their relationship to Clay and palpable in their intensity.

"Mr. Buchanan suffers from an ailment and needed his prescription refilled."

Martha Webster sits in the second row, absently crocheting either a sock or sweater, one never knows until it is completed. Her fawn eyes, brown and large, are a mix of worry for Clay and confusion over her husband's refusal to treat him.

"Did you refill that prescription?"

Anna is slumped in the rear of the courtroom next to Cigar, the representative of the Joiner clan. Both teenagers had entered as if criminals themselves, purposely sitting behind those whose height and girth would obscure them from Clay's roaming eyes, if he had had them. Doctor Webster caught glimpses of her pained expression between wide shoulders.

"No."

Umbrella George wears his only suit, pressed with creases that could cut flesh. To the uninitiated, he appears to be asleep, except for his beard that vibrates with lips moving in constant prayer for His Spirit to comfort, to reveal the truth, and to guide the lost.

"No? You're a doctor. Your patient is suffering and you refuse medical attention. Why?"

Jack Grosso and his son, Jack Jr., out of jail on bonds are obnoxious in their support of Clay, not crying his innocence, but in his justification. Father and son's trial has been thrown into chaos because with the death of LeCompte, the warrantless search of their truck and the uncovering of the black market birds under ice and oysters cannot be justified without explanation.

"He was becoming addicted to the medication."

After overseeing the milking of the dairy cows, Robert Mitchell and his brother-in-law, Sam Barnes, slipped in to check on Anna's emotional state after a two-way telegraph conversation with Madison, whose hands still work the automotive assembly line, but his heart, mind, and soul remain firmly in Havre de Grace with his childhood crush.

"In other words, the defendant was out of control."

Two individuals sitting on opposite sides of the courtroom, and seemingly the wrong sides, are Frank McQuay and Olivia Bouvard. Frank, sitting behind the prosecutor, focuses not on the testimony of the witnesses, but with folded arms and a sharp glare, stares at the judge with impatience, his brow knitted tightly. Doctor Webster is aware of the animosity between the patriarchs of the McQuays and Buchanans, based on their perceived culpability in the decline of wildfowl, but their disagreement did not seem to prevent Clay from guiding for the McQuays' guests, or from preventing the McQuays from purchasing Clay's catch, in season or out, but appearances are often deceiving.

"I didn't say that."

"Then, Doctor, tell us, in your words, what did the defendant do to warrant your denying him care?"

The real puzzle, the enigma that befuddles the doctor is seeing Olivia seated directly behind Clay. With each word spoken against him, this daughter of a respectable business family sheds a tear. Gentlemen of discretion, if forced to acknowledge presumptions would reluctantly nod in agreement that lingered glances containing sparks that could be affection have passed between Clay and Olivia, but these infatuous moments are inconsequential considering Olivia and Felipe's relationship.

Doctor Webster knows the prosecutor has trapped him. Dieter Nelson, whose tailored, pin-striped suit hangs on his rail thin body as he leans against the jury's box, directing Doctor Webster to look into their hungry eyes as he answers.

"Clay attacked me."

Prosecutor Nelson's eyes, too close together, and seeming never to blink, twinkle, "No further questions."

"Your witness?" the judge offers the defense.

"One question," Clem begins, walking close to Doctor Webster, an open and friendly expression on his soft, comforting face. In his hand is a small paper sack. Clem withdraws a bottle of Clay's medicine. "This bottle, which is half full, was recovered from Mr. Buchanan's residence after he was arrested. We therefore can assume he had sufficient medication before, during, and after the time of Game Warden LeCompte's demise. The active ingredient in laudanum is opium. Now, Doctor, what is the effect on a person who takes opium?"

"They become calm, very relaxed," Doctor Webster breathes a sigh of relief believing he is being pulled from the lion's jaws.

"Thank you," Clem returns to his seat.

"Re-direct?" asks the judge.

"Yes," the prosecutor remains seated. "In your medical opinion, doctor, if an addict is threatened, or perceives his ability to obtain his drugs, his fix, could be cut off, what is the addict's response?"

Doctor Webster feels the teeth of this beast bite down, refusing to let him go. He now looks to Clay for forgiveness, but Clay's head is hung, anticipating the noose, "Adrenaline stimulates the body and the addict lashes out."

"No further questions," the prosecutor picks at a pimple on his chin as he recalls an appropriate colloquialism: *like shooting ducks in a barrel.*

Lunch was an assorted affair, obtained from various eateries near the courthouse, including coat pockets and knapsacks that contained meat sandwiches of sliced duck, boiled possum, grilled chicken, or baked rabbit, wrapped neatly in wax paper. Conversations were lively or subdued depending on which side of the scales Lady Justice held that they wished to weigh heavily upon and whether the eatery sold liquor or soda pop.

Upon the gavel's bang for order, the defendant's table contained, in addition to Clem's glass of clear liquid, there was placed for Clay's benefit, a brown ceramic mug filled with a mixture of Martha Webster's berating of her husband and Olivia's belief. Sweet, thick, reddish-brown, and pungent, a liquid that is lip staining and cough suppressing; equal parts laudanum and steaming horse's blood; another mare now glue.

Clay sits straighter in his chair, revived to a small degree, wondering why the prosecutor is staring at him with a wicked grin stretched across his acne-pitted face.

"The prosecution calls Anastasia Nicole Buchanan," Dieter announces while closely observing Clay's facial contortions to see how close to the mark his subpoena struck; how on target his aim is at uncovering the truth. A defendant's reaction is a clear measure of the damage a particular witness will be if he, Dieter Nelson, first in his class from Harvard Law School, editor of its prestigious *Law Review*, two years running, can tease, pull, trick, or connive out of the unprepared witness. This is especially so when the witness is a young female whose emotions can be exploited to betray the truth.

The unprepared part is especially important. The surprise attack being imperative. So much so that when the special prosecutor arrived at Constable Jenkins' office to pick his brain, he forbade the constable from interrogating the daughter. "Not a single question," Dieter stated three different ways so there would be no misunderstanding, and explaining in the simplest words: "If the daughter knows the questions before I ask them she will have had time to concoct a story. I want her off guard. It's the best way to the truth and a conviction." Constable Jenkins was in some respect relieved. It was not that he had any qualms about putting the figurative thumbscrews[73] to a material witness in a murder case, especially when he believed he had the culprit locked up, but still, how much punishment should be inflicted upon the daughter for the sins of the father? Constable Jenkins decided that he had done his part in arresting the man. Now he will let the "Suit," a man too good to accept the offered chair, even if it did wobble, prosecute the case.

Clay's mind, made numb by the opiate, took a moment to process the significance of the prosecutor's words. When they become clear, the corners of Clay's mouth begin to rise in deviltry, believing his daughter is safe from judicial abuse in the recesses of the marsh, where if a person wants to remain lost, even a trained hunting dog will have difficulty nosing out their location. Clay's mouth freezes in mid-grin when all heads turn toward the back, their heavy clothes rustling against one another.

---

73 Thumbscrew. A torture device used to slowly and excruciatingly crush the thumbs.

A grumble runs through the spectators as they agree a foul move has been made on the part of the prosecution whose apparent strategy is to win at all costs.

"Objection, your Honor," Clem shouts, rising in protest, his arms outstretched in a beseeching manner. "To have a man's kin, his daughter testify, is a moral outrage."

"It's neither immoral nor illegal, and as it is only a wife who cannot be forced to testify against her husband, distasteful as this is," the judge's words are directed toward Mr. Nelson, "there's nothing I can do about it. Objection overruled. Miss Buchanan, please take the witness stand."

Clem places his hand on Clay's shoulder. Reassurance is not his purpose, but to prevent Clay from springing out of his chair to pummel the smug prosecutor who now stalks his daughter in a familiar method of sneak skiff after an inexperienced swan.

Aware of the conservative nature of these backwoods folk, and the grumble, which came from the jury members as well, Dieter began his questioning of Anna with the gentleness of a loving uncle. This tactic was not because he cared for Anna or the feelings of the jury members, because he did not. It was to regain the support of the men on the jury who likely had daughters of their own. It was also to put Anna off her guard, whereby she would be more likely to implicate her father with a slip of a relaxed tongue. Dieter calls it: "Massaging the witness to wow the jury." However, if this tactic fails, he is the master of the twisted word and phrase to rattle the witness, to confuse the befuddled into saying, "Yes" or "No" at his will. That is where *turn of a phrase* originates; in the minds of great attorneys, which of course Dieter believes himself to be one.

Dieter casually waves LeCompte's logbook in front of Anna as if it is unimportant, but to her it is a club to beat her with, "Miss Buchanan, do you know what a duck trap is?"

"Yes," Anna shifts, uncomfortable in her chair, "but they're illegal."

"Have you ever witnessed your father build them?"

"I've seen him dismantle them."

"That wasn't my question."

"Oh," Anna looks to her father for any indication of how to answer. Clay hates himself for placing his daughter in this position to either condemn him or herself depending on her words whether they are the truth or lies. Anna tries to split the goose egg without breaking the yolk, "I've not seen my father build any traps since they've been outlawed."

Dieter glances toward the jury. He sees several men elbow and nod to each other in mutual pleasure at Anna's quick thinking. Dieter decides to ask a question that presumes the answer has already been given, a trick that has a higher than average percentage of succeeding.

"Miss Buchanan, why did your dog bite Game Warden LeCompte?"

"Because he had broken into our shed," defiant and justified as the answer bursts from her mouth, but the pleased expression on the prosecutor's face, the further narrowing of his demon eyes, makes her choke on her words.

Turning toward Clay, Dieter straightens his narrow tie that does nothing but accentuate his reed-thin frame, "Now that you've established that Game Warden LeCompte was at your home the day he was murdered..."

"Objection," Clem rolls his eyes in exasperation. "There's no evidence to indicate murder occurred. The prosecution is assuming the jury has already reached a verdict."

"Your Honor, the man didn't shoot himself."

Clem latches on to a theory, unlikely, but if finagled just right could be plausible: *This big city attorney ain't as smart as he thinks,* Clem muses, *he just stepped in wet duck droppings of his own making,* "Maybe he did shoot himself."

"That's absurd," Dieter approaches the judge's bench. "What? The man shot himself with a shotgun, dragged himself over the railing into his rowboat, paddled out into the bay to discard the shotgun, and then died?"

"You said it," Clem, pleased as a pup with his first retrieve, hooks his thumbs in the belt loops of his pants and gives a slight nod of satisfaction that could be perceived as a bow to the spectators.

Anna sat relieved at not being the focus of attention, at least for the moment, as the verbal battle commenced. For the first time in almost a month she examines her father. He has shrunk in size and presence. The man who was larger than life; whose knowledge had no limit; who to Anna commanded the sun, stars, and moon; who always provided for the family, and who depended on no one is now infirm. He is almost a child in need, reduced to relying on others for everything. Dependent for his meals, his clothes, and for the medication that helps him hold his head up with a measure of pride, even if that too has been stripped away by confinement and accusations too horrible to comprehend.

"Gentlemen," the judge weighs in, "the objection is sustained. Mr. Nelson, refrain from using the word, 'murder.' That is a determination of fact for the jury alone to determine." Judge Hathaway feels his chest being pierced by Frank McQuay's scowl even before he glances toward the spectator seats to confirm the displeasure.

"I'll rephrase," Dieter continues. "On the day Game Warden LeCompte died of a shotgun blast to the chest he was attacked by your dog at your home. You stated he had broken into your shed. What happened next?"

"He accused my father of setting a duck trap. He had brought chicken wire and several rough-cut stakes, claiming he'd found them on our property," Anna realizes she has to offer an explanation, but she will keep her answers as brief as possible, thereby hoping to deny this awful man more ammunition.

Dieter flips through the pages of LeCompte's logbook, nodding as if confirming a fact, "That's exactly what it says here in his log. Can you read, Miss Buchanan?"

"Yes, I can read."

Dieter's surprise was momentarily betrayed by the stereotype he had developed of these country bumpkins. They may know their way through the backwoods, and may be able to skin a 'possum and clean a fowl, but Dieter believed they would be hard-pressed to accurately recite their A-B-Cs. There may be more to this coverall-wearing teenage girl than one would first assume, and then again, this witness is probably the exception to Dieter's rule, "That's good. Please read this second to last entry—by my finger."

"'Found: One chicken wire duck trap secured with cut and sharpened stakes. Location: Buchanan property, approximately one-third mile south of residence.'" With each word read, Anna's voice becomes softer; hoping the words on the page will disappear with the fading sound.

"Thank you."

"But it couldn't have been my father's trap," Anna blurts. "The rough way the stakes were sharpened indicates a man who doesn't know how to handle an axe or he has no pride in his work."

Frank McQuay inhales with satisfaction as Anna's outburst indicts her father in trapping even if it was meant to throw doubt on the trap's ownership.

"Thank you for your opinion on your father's craftsmanship, but please now read the last entry," Dieter holds the log close to Anna. Anna scans the handwritten words. Their meaning is clear. The brown splotches, dried blood, staining the edges of the page are LeCompte's, but they might as well be covering her father's hand. Anna cannot speak these words. She looks to the judge, hoping he will hear her heart franticly beating in panic and come to her rescue. At his advanced age, he assuredly must be a grandfather who would want to protect all children from pain and harm and therefore he will protect her.

"Read the words, Miss Buchanan," Judge Hathaway breaks the fairy tale spell of salvation.

"'Received dog bite from Buchanan Labrador. Staking out location of discovery of duck trap to arrest poacher.'" Each word is a slice into her heart, a cutting away of her father piece by piece, lost to the scribbles of a dead game warden.

Olivia's knuckles are white. Her fingernails dig into her palms, breaking her skin and drawing blood. Her body trembles with compassion for Anna as she is forced to undergo public grilling and frustration which makes her head ache to the point of anger by Clay's silence. His gallant chivalry will be the destruction of them all. It is better to cut off a diseased limb than to allow it to inflect and kill the whole body.

"Now, Miss Buchanan, where was your father the night Game Warden LeCompte," Dieter chooses his words carefully, "received his gun shot?"

"I don't know."

"Weren't you home?"

"No. I was out."

"Out where? Out on the town?" sarcasm drips with Dieter's question.

"It was my birthday and I'd been given a new dress," Anna grins for an instant at Olivia whose drawn face expresses only agony, "and a shotgun. I went out to show it off."

"To show off the dress and shotgun? To whom?"

Blood races to Anna's head, *stupid, stupid, stupid!* Anna decides anger may be her best defense, "It's a marsh. To the raccoons; to the owls; the otters; who else would be out there except a sneaky game warden hiding in a cutout."

The courtroom becomes dead silent. From the judge to the jury, from Clem to Dieter, including the spectators, all mouths are agape at the self-implicating words shouted by Anna, as the logbook did not state LeCompte had secreted himself in a cutout. How would Anna know where he was hiding is everyone's question.

Only Frank McQuay is enjoying himself as both Buchanans may end up in prison by the time this trial is over.

Dieter is unaccustomed to being thrown such a curve. Great attorneys know the answer before the question is asked, no surprises. To regain composure, Dieter returns to the prosecution table where he absentmindedly thumbs through pages of paper while making a quick decision: *follow through on the father's conviction. Worry about the daughter later.* "Fine. You showed off your new dress to the forest creatures," Dieter purposely omits the mention of the cutout and her shotgun.

"Marsh animals," Anna corrects the prosecutor with an indignant huff; unaware of the dangerous legal position she has put herself in.

"Marsh animals. When you returned home, was your father there?"

"No."

"Do you know where he went?"

"Objection. Calls for speculation," Clem states.

"Objection sustained," Judge Hathaway mumbles.

Frank McQuay's momentary smile turns downward.

"How many shotguns do you and your father own?" asks Dieter.

"Two," Anna's relieved he did not ask, "How many guns?" because with the Davenport it would be three and she does not want that secret revealed. Neither does she want to lie, believing it is safer staying with the truth, or at least as close to it as possible.

"When you returned from being out, how many shotguns were in the home?"

Anna always assumed her father had taken his shotgun that night, knowing that LeCompte had to have been killed by a shotgun due to the size of the wound. If her father had taken the Davenport and shot LeCompte with it, the game warden would have been cut in two. But now, having been specifically asked the question, remembering only the confusion of the night; a mix of excitement and disappointment over the disaster of her sexual encounter with William and the shock of discovering LeCompte's body, Anna does not know the answer. That night she was not thinking clearly, moving on automatic, trying to dispose of the bloody body, and now, looking out across the many faces waiting on her reply, there is one face missing—where is William?

With sadness over William's absence during her time of need, Anna answers truthfully, "I don't remember."

"So could we assume your father took his with him?" Dieter hopes Anna's slumping shoulders, her defeated and downcast expression, are the marks of surrender, and that to end her misery on the witness stand, her response will be in acquiescence.

"Objection. Speculation," cries Clem.

"Withdrawn, your Honor," Dieter returns to his seat, not overly disappointed that the question was not answered. He knew any half-wit defense attorney would object, but you never know if court appointed attorneys are really paying attention. Besides, the question was for the jury to assume the answer, "No further questions."

Lying on his back, stiff as a corpse, wishing for a moment's sleep with the dead, Judge Hathaway stares at his bedroom ceiling watching swaying shadows that are cast from an old chestnut tree outside his window, its skeleton being shaken by the rising wind.

Sliding his hand under the covers to the side of the bed that has remained vacant since 1889, when his beloved Mildred shivered to death from yellow fever, the judge ponders for the first time why he has never found, or actually looked for a replacement; someone to cook, clean, to chat with, and to perform other womanly duties. As the judge runs through these activities in his head he realizes he has described a person whose occupation is a cross between a maid and a prostitute. Defining what he wants, it occurs to him that his needs, even in Mildred's absence, have been fulfilled. She loved him so completely; with unashamed abandon, not because he was exceedingly handsome; no, she never called him that. It was not because he was wealthy, and as a small-town judge, it was unlikely he would ever be; no, she did not look to him for monetary comfort. It was not because he excelled in outdoor activities, was the fastest runner, or the best shot; no, she never applauded him for those. Mildred, the petite fireball whose eye-pleasing oval face lit up every room, would coo with adoration and the love of angels, "You're a good man. That's why I love you."

For the first time in 28 years, Mildred's side of the bed is cold; sleep will not come to him wherein his dreams she is with him, to love and support him and upon waking, her living essence surrounds him as if her embrace is never-ending. The judge realizes that one only replaces that which is gone or broken. It is he that betrayed her trust, her love and faith in him, and now she has left him.

Judge Hathaway is not a man to tolerate deceptive men, and finds his breathing difficult due to his own prejudiced behavior bartered for a want. His court rulings, seemingly only slightly tilted are of a magnitude to pervert justice. They are also denying him peace of mind at the very least, and at worst, are placing his soul in jeopardy. The words of 2nd Chronicles 19:6-7 flood forth, recited by Mildred in a tone of hopeful correction, "Take heed what ye do: for ye judge not for man, but for the Lord, who *is* with you in the judgment. Wherefore now let the fear of the Lord be upon you; take heed and do *it*: for *there is* no inequity with the Lord our God, nor respect of persons, nor the taking of gifts."[74]

Considering his options, the judge decides that retirement in a home filled with his wife's love, his needs satisfied, is favorable to a judgeship where the price of his wants will always exceed his ability to pay.

Snoring rattles the window pane in its bedroom frame as sound slumber in the cocoon of Mildred's warm embrace is the Almighty's immediate

---

74 Scripture taken from the *Holy Bible*, King James Version, 1987 printing. Public domain.

blessing to the judge whose decision has brought him back to the narrow and righteous path.

Hastily summoned from his warm ale and toast breakfast by a panting bailiff, Clem rushes into Judge Hathaway's chambers, his coattail flying as papers tumble from his folio. Closing the door and gathering the scattered documents, Clem finds that he has entered a heated shouting match between two unlikely characters, presided over by a black-robed sexagenarian serenely sipping what smells like mint tea. Clem tries to catch his breath and legal bearing, at the same time calculating the words he is hearing in relevance to his case.

"No, I can't prove it," Olivia, red-faced, argues. "I wasn't a virgin and there were no witnesses."

"So I'm supposed to accept the word of the harlot of Havre de Grace that the accused was half a day's walk from the crime, in the back room of a tavern copulating?" Dieter argues to the judge, wondering what lunacy has come over this courthouse that he would even be having this discussion behind closed doors.

Smack!

For his defamatory remark, Dieter receives an angry slap across his face from Olivia with the force of a barroom brawler, knocking him backward into Clem. Olivia is incensed by the remark, but at the same time feels the sting of her self-satisfying, weak-fleshed coupling.

Zeroing in on what he surmises is the subject of this meeting, Clem licks his lips, the bitter ale ignored as his salivary gland produces sweet saliva at the inkling of an alibi for his client; a man, fast sinking in the mire of evidence more substantial than mere circumstantial.

"Clay was with you that evening?" Clem asks, hopeful, stepping toward Olivia.

"All evening, throughout Anna's birthday dinner at the Buchanan home; all during the walk north, and until he left my..." Olivia pauses, not wanting to be indecent any more than she has been in front of this judge whose bearing and moral fiber has always been an inspiration to the community, "...left my side at three in the morning."

"For the sake of this ridiculous argument, if he were with you, as you claim, he could have ridden a horse or hitched a ride home, and then killed the game warden," Dieter pro-offers.

"Not if the skipjack captain is correct about tide, current, drift and location, and he is, as his life and livelihood depends on it," Clem interjects.

"It's still just her word—a desperate attempt to save her lover." Dieter hisses. "Even if she were to take the stand, the jury would see right through to her motives."

Judge Hathaway continues to recline in his cushioned chair, eyeing these three passionate individuals in a tug of war of logic, emotion, and desire: Dieter Nelson, the out-of-towner, up from Washington, here to ensure justice is done for the deceased, an honorable and many times thankless task; Clem Mathers, an average man of modest intellect, scraping by on the leavings of court appointments, and Olivia Bouvard, who by her admission of adultery places herself in the position of public scorn, to be levied a fine against, if not jail time if she takes the witness stand and swears an oath. *Is a woman's reputation a fair trade for a lover's life?*

Having lived in Harford County his entire life, the judge is aware of a fact that the two counselors are not, making Dieter's assertion that Olivia's pronouncement is merely to protect Clay, folly. There is likely no other person than Olivia who wants the killer of Felipe LeCompte captured and punished more than she. Setting his china teacup on its saucer, he leans forward, and holds up his hand for silence.

"The prosecution speaks of motive," the judge's voice is deliberate, but without the hard edge of a jurist without compassion. "The defense grasps for a tangible alibi, and Miss Bouvard, who is right now coming to grips with her less than moral actions, though in this instance, her dalliance may have saved a man from a wrongful conviction as I believe she speaks the truth."

Dieter opens his mouth to begin a tirade based upon case law precedent, judicial partiality, and what he believes is local bias, but before a syllable leaves his throat, Judge Hathaway addresses Olivia.

"Miss Bouvard, please tell these gentlemen who Felipe LeCompte is to you."

Olivia collapses into a chair by the window, sobbing as she is overcome with grief by his loss and the overwhelming fear that Clay will be lost to her as well, "He is my first cousin, raised in my parents' home as my brother." As a woman who loves Clay with all her being, she wants to please him in every way possible, and will obey him out of respect, except when he is wrong. She made up her mind during Anna's grilling on the stand to come forward and bare the intimate truth, regardless of what happens to her standing in the community, and knowing that the law casts a harsh shadow on sex outside of marriage.

Clem, stunned by this revelation, is slow in moving to Olivia's side to comfort her. His knees are weak at the thought that he may win this case.

"It's still just her say so," Dieter refuses to give up. "If she goes on the stand and tells her story, she's admitting to a criminal offense of fornication. I'll demand she be prosecuted for it, and even with her relationship to the deceased, they may not believe her. In the end, it's what I can make the jury believe, and I'm very persuasive." Dieter finishes his rant to a vacuum, expecting Clem to pontificate on behalf of Olivia, but instead Clem chooses discretion over valor and looks to the judge for wisdom.

Folding his hands, his two index fingers forming a church steeple, the judge sets forth the course of action which will be followed, "I do not see the gain in having Miss Bouvard testify to her and the defendant's debauchery. Felipe LeCompte is dead and that's a tragedy. Clay Buchanan's reputation has been disparaged simply by the charges leveled against him. Poacher or not, that label, that charge, is for another court at another time. There is no good reason to hang upon Miss Bouvard the scarlet letter and ruin her life, too."

"But it's a crime," Dieter persists. "Doesn't this community stand by its laws?"

Judge Hathaway scans the walls of his chamber, shelf upon shelf, rising to the ceiling with leather-bound books crammed with laws, "Are you aware that relations outside of marriage used to be a whipping offense? It was a despicable punishment laid well-on to female offenders who where stripped naked to the waist. It was degrading and so offensive that an ancestor of mine, in...I believe it was 1774, and at the time a God-fearing upright innocent Quaker, a great-grandmother, bared her own wrinkled and sagging flesh to stand side-by-side with the guilty, whose bodies were young, ripe, and filled with enticements. She did this to expose the lascivious nature of this act and to end a deplorable public humiliation."

Wiping her eyes, Olivia whispers, "She sounds like a courageous woman."

"She was a strong woman of moral convictions, but that's a story for another time," Judge Hathaway stands, indicating this meeting is over. "I do not want to be a judge who requires a witness to endure public scorn or encourage titillation when there is an alternative. Miss Bouvard, you will wait here. Gentlemen, please join me in the courtroom."

Dieter Nelson, believing his conviction is slipping away throws in a cannon ball, "If you're planning on letting the father off, then I'm going after the daughter." Whether Dieter's threat struck a nerve, or was out of line, the strength of his remark stopped the judge and Clem in mid-step.

The judge adjusts his pants, or maybe it is his briefs under his robe, no one dares ask, then speaks as if with a friend over a game of pinochle, "Could a 17-year-old girl kill a man to protect her family? I believe she could. Did Miss Buchanan kill Felipe LeCompte? At this point it is speculation. But I would hope that you would find more evidence than her own words to convict her. And by the way, if you were more familiar with our shoreline, you'd know that a cutout is the only logical place to hide if you're a man with a rowboat."

A song is being composed in Clem Mathers' head to dance to with the words: case dismissed, as the repeating lyrics. Prancing along the street to a tune only he can hear, the wind blustering at his heels, Clem replays the judge's brief speech that was music to his ears. "In light of newly discovered evidence, the case before the court, in the matter of the State of Maryland versus Clay Herschell Buchanan is dismissed."

Unlocking the door to his puny office, Clem is startled to find that his morning newspaper has been placed neatly on his cluttered desk, and stacked on the floor in front of the desk is a brace of canvasbacks.

Whistling as he walks toward Tavern Bouvard for the celebration party, his cap pulled down tight against the wind, August Joiner picks away several down feathers that somehow got stuck in his beard.

Unable to read, when August placed Clem's newspaper on his desk, he did not comprehend the words written in bold face across the top and its ominous implications:

DANGER FROM BELOW!!!

The contents of a secret telegram from Berlin, the home of Germany's Kaiser, to his minister in Mexico is revealed. Dubbed *The Zimmermann Telegram*[75] after Arthur Zimmermann who drafted it, the words are crystal clear. Germany means to bring the European war to our underbelly. If Mexico, our good, though sometimes troubling neighbor to the south, sides with Germany against the United States, Germany would help Mexico recover

---

75 Zimmermann, Arthur (1864-1940). The German foreign secretary during part of World War I. He authored a secret telegram (January 16, 1917) sent through the German ambassador in Washington, D.C. to the German minister in Mexico. It offered Mexico's President Venustiano Carranza an alliance if Mexico sided with Germany. The British Admiralty Intelligence intercepted and decoded the telegram and made it available to U.S. President Woodrow Wilson who caused it to be published on March 1, 1917. Zimmerman was removed from his post.

Arizona, New Mexico, and Texas. OUTRAGEOUS! This reporter will eat a large helping of humble pie, admitting he was wrong, in that what goes on over there in distant lands does affect us here. We Americans can no longer stand idly by and accept German atrocities. There was the unprovoked sinking of the passenger ship *Lusitania*[76] by a German submarine, which cost the lives of 1,198 innocent souls. There is the ongoing German harassment and sinking of non-combatant merchant ships involved in free trade. And now a direct threat to take our land. It seems President Wilson's "Peace Without Victory" approach is naive and so are we. The Kaiser has thrown more than the first punch. How long should we keep ducking?

Timothy Ross, the apprentice to the mortgage and loan manager of a particular Baltimore bank, the lad with two first names, an energetic go-fer, is always willing to prove his worth. He readily volunteered to take the bank's tin-*Lizzie* to Havre de Grace to deliver assorted documents. Tim is a contradiction to his peers. City-raised with a comfortable two-story, red brick home to live in, he prefers to rough it, sleeping outdoors and exploring the crooked, ever-changing shorelines, and the snaking creeks. He is continuously enthralled by its creatures. With his perpetual eager expression, that of a playful puppy dog with astonishment radiating from brown eyes, and his curly salt-and-pepper hair that refuses all combing, regardless of vigor, he is likable and accepted in any company.

Tim cannot get enough free time among wild things, but has learned to appreciate the opportunities that the indoors of a sometimes stuffy bank has to offer. Thus, he began his apprenticeship two years ago under a friend of his father's, with the adage: a seed is the foundation of growing plants; money is the seed of business; business is the mechanism that gives people what they need: food, clothes, tools, houses, automobiles, amenities.

Tim cannot create a seed, only God can do that, but as a future mortgage and loan manager, he can be a part of the machine that provides the seeds of business to better lives.

There is, however, a down side, a sad side to the business of banking and loans, and that is when Tim is delegated to deliver notices of missed payments on notes due. Tim hates to be the bearer of bad news. He prefers

---

76 Lusitania. A Cunard ocean liner that was torpedoed May 6, 1916 and sunk off the coast of Ireland. The ship had sailed from New York and was heading for Liverpool, England. The Germans suspected the ship of carrying arms and munitions.

to see the excitement on a man's face when his loan has been approved and he is able to run after his dream.

Within Tim's satchel of documents is just such a notice where some family, who likely is already too aware of their financial shortfall, is officially notified to send funds they do not have. Tim is embarrassed for the family, as with the handing over of the notice, he drives away with their pride, leaving the family desperate, knowing their business, their home, their automobile, their amenities, and their dreams will soon be lost to them.

Bumping down the rutted road, an easily missed turnoff that he had to ask two people directions to find, Tim pulls up next to a shack, wondering still if he is at the right place; the *home* of Clay Buchanan? Stepping out of the Ford two-door, wind off the bay whips up under his cotton slacks, chilling him. Approaching the porch, Tim wonders if the place is abandoned until the angry, protective barks of an unseen, but obviously ferocious dog resounds from behind what Tim hopes is a secure door.

"Mr. Buchanan?" Tim shouts. "Hello? Anyone home?" The only response is from the devil dog, now scratching, attempting to get out, and from somewhere close by, are perturbed hisses and honks. Tim folds the delinquent notice and cautiously wedges it between the door and its jam. He then retreats with quickened steps, leaping among the patches of mud and snow, to slide behind the wheel of his automobile and make his escape. Tim wonders what type of man could survive in such a rough and dilapidated structure. Tim is also puzzled as to how, in the name of God, did the bank ever determine it was a reasonable risk to loan money to this man, where on the first glance, there is no viable source of income that can be derived from this property; a tract of land left in its natural state.

Two minutes later, as Tim is tooling north along the road toward Havre de Grace, admiring the neatly plowed fields west of the road, he recognizes his inner conflict: *my desire is to explore among the seeds God has planted to my right, but progress needs the seeds that business has planted to my left.*

Unknown to Tim, two life-altering events were occurring at the same time as his musing. Judge Hathaway is dismissing the charges against Clay, while a gust of wind that buffets the tin-*Lizzie,* also carries off the folded paper printed in red ink that Tim had left as an un-"Welcome Home" to the shack's occupants.

The mid-morning sun pulls mountains of clouds, sinister and brooding, over the horizon, to counterbalance the wild merriment that explodes from inside Tavern Bouvard each time a new celebrant enters through the front door. True to form, Martha Webster, after giving Clay an immodest kiss on his lips after the judge's decree, but respectfully declining Olivia's invitation to the party, set about, in her mysterious and miraculous way, to inform the populace of town and county of Clay's release, and of the drunken riot to follow at Tavern Bouvard.

A parade of men and a smattering of adventuresome women, abandon their work to beat against the wind for the promise of a drink or two, on-the-house, and to toast justice. The social taboo of intoxication before lunch is blown away with hats not firmly held to one's head. The congratulatory claps on Clay's back are punctuated with, "I knew you were innocent;" "Rooting for you the whole time;" "Prayers are answered;" and a few whispers of, "LeCompte got what was coming to him;" "Good riddance;" and, "One for the working man." As the jubilant mob squeezes through the tavern door, Jim Currier, who had been chosen as jury foreman, pulls Clay from the clinging vine that Anna has become to enlighten him of the jury's own conspiracy, "The evidence be damned, Clay. We had agreed to find you not guilty because a man's got to feed his family, and no government enforcing rich men's laws got the right to stop him. Not at least while a wildfowler has a jury of his peers."[77]

Clay began to assert the truth of his innocence and his confusion over the substance of the new evidence that all of a sudden set him free, but Jim waved him off with a more pressing matter, "Anna's done a fine job of providing for the household, but nothing for me or the market. I've got orders to fill."

The adrenaline high of freedom surging through Clay's body masks his true, weakened and infirm condition. It is his sunken eyes that are the clue that prompts Jim to ask a man of Clay's usual fortitude the delicate question, "Are you up to it?"

"How many?" Clay asks.

"Minimum of a hundred by tomorrow morning."

Clay turns his face to the wind to calculate the advance of the menacing clouds towering over the Eastern Shore, "Storm's coming."

Jim Currier remains silent, allowing Clay to make the decision himself. Jim will be home and safe, warm next to his stove with nothing to lose but a few dollars. Clay will be *out in it*, come what may, battling not just against

---

77 On July 8, 1905, a Floridian, Monroe County Deputy Guy Bradley who had been hired as a game warden was killed by Walter Smith, a Florida plume hunter on Oyster Key. A local jury, honoring the tradition that wildlife is expendable, set Smith free, ruling he had acted in self-defense. However, the facts contradict the jury's verdict as Smith had threatened to kill Bradley if the game warden attempted to arrest him or any member of his family.

the skittishness of the elusive fowl, but a potential maelstrom brewing across the bay. Jim shudders at the thought.

"Come by around ten," answers Clay, his eyes now showing a mixture of concern and determination, but no fear. His medication numbs that emotion.

Nathaniel Joiner enters Tavern Bouvard with the setting sun, happy to be in out of the weather turning nasty. His tattered long underwear, a poor comfort as the wind cuts through his thin and patched coverall. This misery is a ripe source for gripe and the braggart statement, "True men need no jacket."

Olivia looks up as the old man enters. A smile crosses her lips while continuing to mix drinks for the heavily sauced, commenting to the closest hunter with the brew-soaked beard across the counter, "That man can sense a free drink a county away." As the drinks flow, so do the stories, the reminiscences of cat-and-mouse with the lawman LeCompte. As Olivia listens to these gritty men, half without teeth from fights won and lost; hard men whose sympathies lie with themselves, their rancor for the symbol of government intrusion slowly changes to respect for a hard job done well.

"That man was wound so tight you couldn't shove a whisper up his backside," notes ol' Benny as a mixture of beer and tobacco juice dribbles from the corner of his aged and wind-cracked lips.

"The man seemed never in need of sleep. Always on me like mosquitoes in summer," a hunter states as he thinks back to a specific winter's day, heavy with sleet, where he had to lie prone in the icy mud among drooping grasses, soaked to the bone, to avoid the persistent game warden that refused to quit the area.

"He found my traps no matter where I hid them," a man of the marsh tosses in, remembering the grumbling of his son each time he was informed that more stakes need to be cut to replace the confiscated ones.

"Never a wrinkle in his clothes—not a spot of dirt," another says, as he wipes spilt foam from his wool shirt.

"Remember, Jim, when we'd hidden the extra ducks in the hollowed-out bottoms of swan decoys?" a sinkbox gunner relates. "He sniffed them out."

"Captured three big guns!" shouts a man from the back of the smoky room.

"His little mustache tickled," a giggling voice full of sweet memory recalls, her femininity slurred by the cocktails.

Laughter, ribald and honest, catches as a wildfire in the dry brush. The dark room is alight with honor for a man few really knew and less ever wanted to meet.

"A toast," Nathaniel shouts, "On me!" Nathaniel plops down a stack of bills on the counter. The unexpected slap of paper against oak silences the astonished crowd as not a person alive or dead has ever known this runt of a man to pay for a drink. His pronouncement causes Olivia to drop the whiskey bottle she had removed from a shelf behind the bar. It shatters—an exclamation of the unexpected.

"What?" Nathaniel smiles, his gums black from chewing tobacco. He looks around the room at the stunned faces, looking as if the Second Coming[78] has arrived and they being unprepared.[79] "Are you telling me you've never known of a man compensating another for a story well-told, and then that story teller sharing with his friends?"

Olivia snaps up the bills before Nathaniel changes his mind.

"To Felipe LeCompte," Nathaniel leads the crowd. "The best God damned game warden this side of the Chesapeake." Glasses filled with mixers and mugs sloshing with beer are raised high and clinked in salute. Several celebrants, old-timers more observant than others, notice tears running down Olivia's cheeks to fall as nectar into the next round of drinks. Not a one comments negatively. They are aware of her loss.

Jack Grosso and son, Jack Jr. are snockered. Sitting slumped at a corner table that is sticky with beer, peanut shells, and the crumbs of a dinner of hardened bread and mallard stew, father and son attempt to avoid the jostling crowd who have decided that Tavern Bouvard is home tonight. Jack Sr. tries to read a news article printed in the evening edition of the *Republican*. To his son he mumbles a prediction of woe.

TEMPERANCE BREWING

February 12, 1917: Gaining speed with sobering consequences, the Women's Christian Temperance Union, established by the God-fearing ladies

---

78 Second Coming. A common reference to the return of Jesus. Acts 1:11 "Which also said, Ye men of Galilee, why stand ye gazing up into heaven? this same Jesus, which is taken up from you into heaven, shall so come in like manner as ye have seen him go into heaven." *Holy Bible*, King James Version, 1987 printing. Public domain.

79 Luke 12:40 Jesus said, "Be ye therefore ready also: for the Son of man cometh at an hour when ye think not." *Holy Bible*, King James Version, 1987 printing. Public domain.

of Cleveland, Ohio, are likely to win a vote on the nationwide prohibition of alcohol. Their cry: 'Liquor is the root of all evil, the base of moral decay,' has made vast inroads in the conscience of good society across the country. If Congress passes this amendment to the Constitution, it would be the 18th. Two-thirds of all state legislatures will have to ratify the amendment before it becomes law. This writer, who admits to enjoying a libation occasionally, wonders if the absence of what some deem a vice will have any affect on men's or women's morals."

"It'll never pass," Nathaniel states from the next table, overhearing Jack Sr. Only a drunk can understand the garbled words of another one.

"Stranger things have happened," Jack Jr. says, blinking his eyes, trying to focus on Nathaniel, or at least one of them. "The people, blind ducks flying toward the gun, have passed laws against us hunters, making what we do for a living illegal. And we're the very men who put meat on their plates. No duck—no dinner. Why wouldn't they pass laws against what we do for enjoyment?"

The last thought running through Nathaniel's muddled mind when his head hits the table in unconsciousness is: *another opportunity. I'm the luckiest man alive.*

Filled with ice splinters, spray flies up and over the bow of the sneak skiff as Clay muscles through rising swells, the broad-bladed paddle digging deep while the Davenport's menacing muzzle points the way. A man of lesser skill, without a mortgage or a family to provide for would have begged off, using common sense and the dangerous surf as his excuse to stay home. Curled in the bow, Beauty is jostled, bumped, and jarred against the thin boards holding back the bay, but she is able to avoid the majority of chilled water that hits Clay square, stinging his eyes, and freezing the incongruous smile that is plastered across his suffering face. Clay holds tight to the paddle and a pleasing memory as he shifts his body weight, struggling to maintain balance, upright on his knees.

Anna had scampered with the speed and ease of a squirrel up into the maple tree with the rope to show her father how she had pulled the cannon out of the hollow—*amazing*. He had asked, not simply for the sake of nodded praise, but to save his dwindling energy reserves. The four stiff drinks and then the long walk home wore away the adrenaline that had Clay walking tall after his release. Clay now moves with deliberate efficiency, not wasting an ounce that is needed against the dark monster driving wind, wave, rain and snow in his direction; the whole of the Eastern Shore is swallowed into the waterman's nightmare called: storm.

"Find the fowl. Blow a hole in 'em. Then paddle like the devil on fire before the world crashes down," Clay repeats, surprised that he spoke these words aloud, a vein of worry creeping up his spine. *I cannot force it...use the elements to your advantage.* But a disquieting voice hisses into Clay's ears: "No time." And from the bow, bright as a candle in a dark room, Beauty's eye chastises her master: *Voices carry. Focus!* Clay feels the rebuke. He shivers, not from the cold piercing his clothes, but from the warnings of a ghost, a friend, and a companion he let down. *Rebel, have you forgiven me yet?* Clay's eyes narrow with the seriousness of his decision to challenge what God has set in motion. He pulls with long practiced strokes to make headway.

Before pushing off, Clay declined the gunning light. Its high profile would further unbalance the skiff as the precarious craft rides up, over, or crashes through swells that come in uneven sets and disorganized directions. "It would be impossible to hold the light's beam steady," agreed Anna.

Estimating three hours of paddling, that to Clay's aches is a week, he spins the skiff on the crest of a swell, angling toward Spesutie Island that lies somewhere to the south, hidden in a moonless night. There are no landmarks in the expansive bay, no beam of light from the Concord Point lighthouse, and no flickering flames beneath the boiling dunking barrel to guide an insignificant man paddling in a toothpick of a boat. It is only Clay's senses, his earned skills, his experience, his years of practice in weather more varied than the species of duck he hunts that guide this sane man into an insane position without panic.

Clay knows if there are any birds in the area they will be in the lee of the island, resting near its western shore, and hiding from the brunt of the wind. Bobbing, feeding, and sleeping, the fowl have a right to believe that no rational man would venture out tonight. And if any man were to attempt the crossing directly from Swan Creek Point, he and his craft would easily be seen cresting the swells that run around the island from the east, prompting the birds to flee.

Clay lays belly down, the skiff becoming a wayward log rolling with the swells. The hand paddles, plunged into black water, twisting left and right, are used more as rudders than propellers to keep the ominous eye of the Davenport staring blackly, waiting to blink death at a raft of ducks that may or may not be where Clay hopes he is heading.

There will be time for only one shot tonight. One chance to make his kill, to overload his boat with birds to fill the orders made from the comfort of restaurants or palatial mansions.

Clay believes if he rides the swells whose crests are quickly becoming topped with caps blown white and frothy around the northern tip of the island, he will catch the birds with their defenses aligned in the wrong direction.

The dropping barometer pulls down the angry clouds—their weight knocking the air out of Clay's diseased lungs. His faithful Mackinaw puts up a valiant fight to protect Clay from the pellets of rain that begin peppering his back and legs. Beauty scoots further up under the two boards that make up the bow decking as Clay, for the first time, questions his own judgment.

Hail beats against Jim Currier's bedroom window. It is an unrelenting snare drum that rudely wakes him from a cozy slumber. Climbing out of his toasty bed, he peers out a window that is quickly freezing. Ice crystals form geometric designs in the shape of frozen spider webs. Its spinner carries the shroud. Jim anticipates a morning where the town of Havre de Grace, the county of Harford, if not the entire Chesapeake region, will be covered in a blanket of snow. How deep is the question yet to be answered?

"Come back to bed, honey," Jim's wife murmurs from the darkness.

A shudder, but not from the cold radiating through the window, runs through Jim's body, "God be with you, Clay."

"What did you say?"

Adjusting his red-flannel night shirt, Jim crawls back into bed, and into the arms of his wife, "Nothing. I'll be sleeping in tomorrow."

Spesutie, an upside-down horseshoe of an island, two miles in length, and a crooked mile wide, is half an hour paddle in calm waters out from Swan Creek Point. It sits flat except for the swishing grasses, proud cattails, and desperate crabbing shacks, all clinging precariously to the island's shifting silt. Its foundation is made of detritus laid down and built up over many millenniums and is continuously being washed away or redistributed. With each gentle ripple or pounding wave, centimeters or feet of tenuous land slough away; silt, particles, or chunks of rich, life-teeming muck returning to the mother of rivers, the Susquehanna, transformed into the Chesapeake Bay, to continue on a meandering journey south. These particles, minute in their individuality are continent builders when united, but for the castaways of Spesutie, they will drift, toss and tumble until gathered up by eddies along the western or Eastern Shore, or will be added to one of the many other islands of the bay that are frantic for sustenance in their struggle to survive. Only Spesutie is honest about its fate. Its luck is emptying out. One day it will be completely reabsorbed and lost to memory. No longer will there be a refuge for waterfowl during storms and a hope for the hunter in need of food for his family or to fill his pockets with coin at the birds' expense.

As a house built on sand is destined to fall with its shifting foundation, an island built on pulverized rock and the bits and pieces of dead things, is temporary. It may be present for generations of man, but fleeting in the eyes of God who is never satisfied with the status quo, who abhors stagnation, and as the Alpha and Omega,[80] He alone can claim permanence, to be the same today as He was yesterday, and will be tomorrow, forever.

Wanting only the faith of a mustard seed[81] to survive, vulnerable Spesutie is taking a beating. The island is stripped of its essence by the barrage of wind and wave as a nest woven of grass is torn apart by the plow. The water-logged storm originating in the south Atlantic built its strength in warmer waters to pile-drive against the states of Florida, Georgia, and the Carolinas, and then teased Virginia as it veered back out, eastward, to refresh itself in the open ocean. Without a name, just a hideous roiling face, malefic in its intent, it joined up with a cold front racing south from the Arctic to swing back landward. Embracing the best, or worst characteristics of each other, the storm throws itself upon New Jersey, Delaware, and Maryland, slowing over land long enough to be able to count the dead before assaulting the western shore of the Chesapeake. The land's and its residents' only defense is a wide shallow bay...ducklings before an angry eagle.

---

80 Alpha and Omega. Revelation 1:8. "I am the Alpha and Omega, the beginning and the ending," saith the Lord, "which is, and which was, and which is to come, the Almighty." *Holy Bible*, King James Version, 1987 printing. Public domain. Alpha, the first letter of the Greek alphabet, the beginning. Omega, the last letter of the Greek alphabet, the end.

81 Mustard Seed. Matthew 17:20-21. He (Jesus) replied, "Because of your unbelief: for verily I say unto you, If ye have faith as a grain of mustard seed, ye shall say unto this mountain, Remove hence to yonder place; and it shall remove; and nothing shall be impossible unto you." *Holy Bible*, King James Version, 1987 printing. Public domain.

Clay did not see the pleasure in any aspect of the Chesapeake Bay. That luxury was for romantics and poets. The bay and its surrounding marsh and fast lands are seen only as challenges to his skill as a hunter. Its function as a repository of plants and animals is there to sustain him and his daughter. And contrary to lovers of nature, Clay imparts no emotion, no anthropomorphic qualities of good or evil. In Clay's words, "Critters ain't cute and storms ain't ugly. Critters want to live and storms got to blow. If I do my job right, I'll catch the first and stay out of the way of the second." Clay holds no animosity against the bird or beast that outsmarts him, or grudges against the gales that soak and chill him.

If Clay had not been straining, required to use all his strength to keep the unseaworthy sneak skiff from capsizing, and angled in a southwesterly direction, he might have enjoyed the ride. The skiff with its flat bottom, copper-plated for protection, also made the craft slippery. Using wind and wave to its best advantage, Clay propels the skiff, sliding it down the swells as an oyster over a tongue. However, joy was kept at bay as Clay busies himself, shifting his weight forward and back to keep the bow on its downward slide, and with the massive weight of the Davenport's barrel, from plunging into the trough between the swells and swamping the craft. Despite the rain that now falls as ice, chilling Clay to the point that only by visual inspection can he determine what his doughy hands are doing, his internal fire burns hot with muscles tensed, twitching and reacting to pitches and yaws that could overturn the skiff and cause him to be lost in the night

Wiping his eyes with his wet sleeve, Clay spies the breakers crashing into the headland, the northern point, the top of the arc of the horseshoe of Spesutie off his left shoulder, exactly where they should be. Hearing in the twisting wind for just an instant, then the happy sound is snatched away; his belief and hope are confirmed. Fowl, in a quantity yet to be counted, ride happily the rise and fall of swells that are splashing up to meet their plummeting brethren falling as hail. Playful ducks cough, sneeze, and meow, while geese honk in chatty conversations.

Please let them hold, Clay prays as he cocks the Davenport's hammer, deftly pocketing the piece of rubber and placing the percussion cap over the firing tube...all is ready.

Beauty shifts her position, crouching. Her muscles tense over joints painfully stiff, swollen with inflamed arthritis, *if the old man can do this, so can I.*

Rounding the point on the crest of an agitated swell, Clay chokes down a cough of bloody phlegm at his excitement by what he sees spread out in the calmer water of Spesutie Narrows. Blinking away the icy film covering his eyes to confirm this spectacle, the feathered treasure trove, the honey pot of webbed meat, Clay's counter, his estimator of numbers of individual birds snaps a spring. The ducks and geese have massed in a number remembered only as a child at his father's side—incalculable. Every species of duck: mallard, booby, canvasback, sprigtail, brant, bufflehead, to geese: Canada and snow, have all come to congregate in a tiny eye of a blunderbuss of a storm. They revel, presumably safe from the killer that is man.

Instinctively shrinking within the sneak skiff to lower its profile, Clay uses only the paddle in his left hand to steer the craft. His right arm embracing the monster, his two fingers stroking the trigger covered in ice. Clay scoots backward to lower the stern and raise the muzzle as a following swell takes up the task of propellant. The Davenport's black eye transforms to a mouth impatient to vomit flaming lead. It is always ready to inflict death on a massive scale.

Closer, Clay urges the erratic swells. At 100 yards, the birds are seen as a mirage through the downpour of hail with only their individual antics to distinguish species and sex.

Closer, at 75 yards, Clay angles the paddle, pointing toward the noisiest birds, their proud and bragging chatter indicative of fat birds heavy with meat.

Closer, at 40 yards Clay wishes he had 10 Davenports or a dozen men with batteries: pipe guns fanned out as shotguns lying side-by-side and fired as one. The number of birds Clay could kill tonight would surpass an entire season. Focus, concentrate, it is all about the aim, and it is all about the birds.

Closer, at 15 yards from the rafting birds, the swell falls away with its energy spent, leaving the sneak skiff to fuss, rocking forward, ever nearer to the unsuspecting birds.

"Perfect!" Clay cries out, surprising the birds by his unexpected presence and shout. Startled, they leap into air as icy as the water they were frolicking in, attempting to escape with ear-splitting thunder. The wash of air from their wings slaps Clay in the face. It is the birds' only rebuke to his cruel intent.

Clay jerks on the trigger.

Balloom!

Night turns to day as flames belch forth. The Davenport cannot kill all the birds as thousands upon thousands escape, but close to 200 are blown from the sky or are crippled in mid-leap.

Beauty hurtles from the skiff after the first bird.

Clay is no longer aware of the cold or the pelting hail. There is only exhilaration at his triumph, and a measure of relief from his concentration that was so fixed upon the birds that were his goal and his financial salvation. Clay's single-minded focus causes him to miss the awkward rise in the skiff's stern after the Davenport's recoil is taken up by the bags of pine needles. Clay has always been a fast learner, never making the same mistake twice, so he remains prone in the skiff to avoid the birds flying in a panic, helter-skelter. Unfortunately, in this position, he is unable to quickly adjust his weight to compensate for the extreme pitch as an unexpected wave overtakes the craft. Though, even if Clay could react faster, the size and force of the wave still would make it futile.

Swells, whether on an ocean or bay are a product of the wind. The greater the wind traveling over longer distances, the larger the swells that ultimately release their pent-up energy in the form of breaking waves. Because the storm came primarily from the east, the wind created swells originating on the Eastern Shore to race across the Flats toward the west. Within the protection of the north to south Narrows of Spesutie Island these east to west swells could not build into anything more than turbulence. This storm, however, was formed by a collision of two, with pockets of erratic winds, where swells created and pushed from the north to the south intermingled with their east to west relations, creating directional chaos and size variations.

Upon rounding the tip of Spesutie Island, and entering the Narrows, the sneak skiff found calmer waters compared to the open, unprotected bay. This was the deception, the trick, and the trap Clay fell into. Wind, from the Arctic parent asserted itself and blew a rising swell, traveling south with nothing to impede its progress, or diminish its strength. It cut across the westbound swells to steal fragments of their energy and rise up into the phenomenon called a rogue wave; an aberration in nature, a fearsome beast to sailors and watermen. As this wave was squeezed, its racing energy forced into the undersized mouth of the Narrows and collided with the headland of Spesutie Island, its power was released and the freak wave broke with cascading whitewater. Its tumbling fury, a steaming locomotive, was masked by the thunder of wings and the Davenport's blast. Other than the sudden rise in the sneak skiff's stern, Clay's only indication of the hazard charging up from behind is his lurching stomach. Too late to avoid capture by the wave, Clay can only cling to the railings as the skiff, rising to the wave's tumbling crest, twists, spins, then is tossed, flung and tumbled into the washing machine that is the marauding wave. The Davenport is thrown dangerously from its chock. Its protruding hammer catches on Clay's coat as he spills out of the sneak skiff. Clay is pulled down by the punt gun, its weight acting as an anchor to drag him to the bottom of the bay.

Pinned between the Davenport and the bottom, Clay struggles to free himself, wrestling against the massive weapon and ripping at his clinging Mackinaw. Clay's back and sides are sliced, cut by the razor-sharp oysters that tear through his all-weather clothing, and whose bed he has rudely invaded. With weakened lungs, filled more with disease than air, burning for breath, Clay's struggling scream wakes only the sleeping shellfish.

At 77, Beauty has seen 11 winters of plunging into frigid water, breaking through ice sheets, retrieving without complaint the innumerable kills and paddling after the many cripples. Quietly, she prefers to luxuriate next to the crackling stove while watching over her master and mistress as they carve and cook, as any grand dame would, but until a replacement comes along, she will obediently find her place in the bow of the sneak skiff and maintain her perfect record of retrievals: zero dead missed, every cripple hunted down and returned in a soft mouth that all black Labradors are famous for—never bruise the meat.

Therefore, it was having the mallard pulled from her mouth and its possible loss that concerned Beauty more than her own confused tumbling over and over in the churning water foaming white above and inky black below. So suddenly did the wave swallow her, to fling her about, that after it passes, Beauty flails about, struggling in the darkness in search of the surface with its life-sustaining air.

One positive that ice water imparts, a grace even, is its numbing affect. The muscles that Beauty needs in her fight to the surface are connected to aging and infirm joints that normally would protest against such frantic exertion: screaming, sending signals implying that shards of glass have been inserted—STOP IT! This numbing of Beauty's inflamed arthritis, the silver lining on a bleak night with black clouds, allows Beauty's spirit, which is still young at heart, to order her muscles to overwork the joints, to ply and pull at the suffocating water as only a starving pup after its mother's dry nipple would.

Beating to part bobbing birds, still buoyant in death, Beauty thrashes her way to the surface. She gulps in air mixed with hail and water. The water dances on the crazy surface as the hail splashes down in a barrage of miniature cannon balls. Mouthing the nearest duck, a bufflehead, Beauty resumes her duties: instinct, training, obedience. Paddling to where the sneak skiff should be she finds only water.

No master—no boat.

The anxiety gnawing at Anna's innards turns her stomach sour with worry and helplessness. "Cowering against the storm," she says to the geese huddled between the blazing stove and empty rocking chair that wobbles with the shuddering shack. "That's what we're doing." Her berating declaration is unfair as she stood fast, remaining outside stoking the fire under the dunking barrel from the time her father shoved off in the sneak skiff, which seems a lifetime ago. Anna dutifully fed the wild flames against a sideways wind that blew them flat; she crouched protectively between the slanting rain and the failing embers. It was only after the marble-size hail bruised her back and knocked one of the geese unconscious did Anna abandon her post with a guilty, over-her-shoulder glance toward the bay that has disappeared in the black night and white ice. The only evidence of the bay's existence is the encroaching slush, the build-up of ice pushed inland and covering the first step of the porch by waves beating over the shoreline. The once-in-a-lifetime storm surge belittles the high tide line like an insignificant stepsister, to run under the shack, and erode the soil surrounding foundation posts that Anna hopes are sunk deep.

Restless ghosts of the night, wayfarers who never returned home in storms past, call out to Anna in voices familiar and familial; her father's and Beauty's, both haunting and in need of help. Grabbing her dripping Mackinaw, Anna again races out the door to splash a dozen yards toward the bay she is already standing in. She again discovers nothing but the evil trickery of wind that howls for its own delight and to further distress the despairing.

"Father!" cupping her hands to her mouth, Anna shouts. Her wavering cry, a combination of alarm and desperate command to appear is shoved back down her throat by a bare-knuckle fist of wind whose heavyweight title reads: Relentless.

Morals and decorum be damned, "I should have hugged and kissed him; demanded that he marry me immediately," Olivia yells, her frustrated words echo back at her from a room of drunkards passed out where they sat. Olivia wipes the same place on the spotless bar for the fifth time as she listens to the heavy door rattle on its wide steel hinges.

"The light is life," Henry O'Neill states firmly to his wife as he pours in more whale oil. The Fresnel lenses magnify and direct the beam of hope.

"Henry, look out those windows," his anxious wife points toward the white void that is kept at bay by trembling windows which threaten to shatter. "This light doesn't reach a dozen feet in this storm. Besides, only a fool would be out there tonight." Henry embraces his wife who shivers in the heated room, "Man's very nature is foolish, and whether or not any can see the light, it is my duty to attend the flame and pray for them."

As with the game of horseshoes, there is a narrow margin between the toss that sounds a ringer and the one that leaves a man a loser. There is also the thin line between love and hate, and the unfortunate ease in which too much of a good thing, even a blessing, can quickly change into a curse.

Beauty has been paddling in circles for what seems an eternity, seeking the sneak skiff and listening for Clay's shouts among the rising and falling swells, but to no avail. There is no place to put the bufflehead that she carries and the only sound is the howling wind.

The blessing that has numbed her aching joints, allowing Beauty's muscles to fight to the surface after being run over by the rampaging wave, continue to penetrate to her core, a curse now slowing her movements and causing her to gradually sink. Struggling, pawing at a surface that has no solidity, Beauty's mouth, clogged with feathers, barely remains above the rolling water. The downpouring hail makes the separation between water and air indiscernible. Beauty's world is in turmoil. She is being attacked by a cold that creates corpses: from above by blowing wind and falling ice; from each side the frigid water, and tugging at her body, unrelenting gravity is bent on pulling her under for a final time.

Spesutie Island is close by, only a hundred yards, but tide and wind pushes Beauty farther and farther away, killing a moment's thought of swimming to its crumbling shore. Beauty's refusal to relinquish the bufflehead, her stubborn pride in a job done until completion is her undoing as her open mouth swallows choking black water.

Beauty's exhausted body, frozen numb, is unable to revolt against the invading liquid, and is overwhelmed.

Blackness envelops her as she slowly sinks.

A memory long forgotten returns. She is a pup without a name, struggling, and frightened by the unknown meaning of gurgling water until a hand reaches down to pull her out of the darkness that was a burlap sack.

The hand, soft and gentle, belonged to Anna, her mistress, who held her close, safe and secure, next to her heart.

The hand that has taken hold within this darkness is anything but soft and gentle. It is a rough, calloused hand pulling Beauty by the scruff of her neck out of the abyss as her muscles were relaxing, surrendering to a fate destined from birth. Beauty, with the bufflehead still in her mouth, is dragged up onto the hull of the overturned sneak skiff. Clinging with frozen hands to its copper bottom, Clay lays his head next to Beauty as she tries to shake her coat free of water. Clay's Mackinaw, which had served him for years without number, is gone. His only protection is his torn coverall that expose the cuts on his back to the pelting hail that turn red with Clay's blood upon impact with his raw flesh. His whole body shivers, shaking the skiff that is a slave to the erratic current. With teeth chattering, Clay looks to his partner, admittedly his friend and companion, who this time Clay did not let down, who he did not abandon.

Beauty stands on shaky legs as she presents Clay with the bufflehead. A warped smile cracks apart Clay's blue lips to stammer, "What? Only one duck?"

Even without the double matting of fur and extra oil of Beauty's ornery cousin, the Chesapeake retriever, now that she is out of the water and able to throw off the heat-sucking liquid, her core temperature revives, rising rapidly. The affects of whipping wind that is decreasing and the beating hail changing to flakes of snow that seem to dance down upon a premature grave are only irritants to Beauty.

Clay is not so fortunate.

Staying warm through the years, able to perspire renegade poisons, and suppressed by medication, Clay's illness was kept in relative check. The disease was held to only small, incremental advances, but the emotional and physical strain, the toll that came with the accusation of murder; being held in a frigid solitary cell, and before he could recoup his strength and stamina, coupled with suffering exposure to rain and ice and the turbulent dunking that has cost Clay his protective Mackinaw, soaking and chilling him to his marrow, has triggered a violent attack on his weakened defense system. Waiting in the darkness of Clay's lungs for just such a moment, the incubating, simmering, silent massing forces of bacillus, the nodules of tuberculosis that have colonized Clay's lungs, burst forth in legions with the vile design to take full control of Clay's body, its host, its keeper and unwilling provider, and to consume it. The strange irony is if that which wages war against the man wins, he is destroyed and dies, and so does it. Victory is fleeting, bitter sweet, and hollow as the coffin waiting to be filled.

Clay has made only mumbles since his remark. Whether his question was in reference to his marksmanship or Beauty's retrieval skills will have to be answered later. His breathing is shallow, gulping, as a thirsty man at a spigot. His hands are clamped to the spine of the skiff as if welded, permanent. His eyes gaze at a point fixed somewhere in infinity, but he does not see. As the minutes pass, one leg, and then the other, kicks at the water. To Clay's delirious mind he is vigorously propelling his disabled craft toward Swan Creek Point. It is a place of vague recollections, a destination for a purpose he is uncertain of. Clay feels nothing. Lungs that will not accept breath, no longer trouble him. Clay simply is being covered, flake by delicate flake, in a blanket that carries no warmth.

Beauty stares at her master who is unresponsive to her nudges, who suddenly mumbles something, "I came back for you, Reb," and whose legs have quit kicking altogether.

Beauty turns her head to peer through the falling snow. She calculates the distance she would have to swim to reach Swan Creek Point, and though the storm's angry face is turning away, allowing the turbulent waters to settle, land is still too far. It would be suicidal to attempt a crossing. The biting cold water would eat away her strength that has been returning. The grasping hands of gravity would succeed in pulling her under; to be nibbled upon by passing fish; to be feasted upon by crabs that poke their heads out of the incubating mud. If only the current were stronger; the incoming tide greater than the back flow from the surge that inundated the western marsh.

Beauty's lamenting howl is heard, but ignored by the returning waterfowl that have determined that the threat has passed. Clay hears the mournful sound, but neither recognizes it, nor does he understand the splash that follows.

Standing where the shore should begin and end, Anna braces herself against the persistent sucking, the tugging at her rubber-booted calves by the black water heavy with slush, as it returns to its normal confines of the bay. Anna's knit cap, topped with snowflakes, is pulled down tight over her ears against the cold. Her hands, sleeved in mittens, are tucked under her armpits as she hugs herself within the Mackinaw's warmth that brings no comfort on this morning that is yet to see the dawn.

Except for the air that is breathed out through her nose that turns instantly to fog, and Anna's grumbling, confused stomach that hungers for food, but which nerves would immediately reject, all appears quiet, tranquil, serene, a wonderland of lightly falling snow on a land and waterscape at peace. Affectionate flakes kiss the marsh and bay, each to add their delicate, one-of-a-kind crystalline structure to the previous, magically building mountains, or by the magician's wand, to vanish as if it never existed, except in the minds of amazed children.

The ghosts of storms past have quit taunting Anna and have moved on to other worried souls. She has stopped calling for her father and Beauty; her voice gritty and throat raw. Her desperate shouts wasted as the curtain of falling snow absorbed each cry. Anna bites her trembling lower lip to the point of drawing blood, a physical pain, and a distraction. It is her defense against tears that would admit her loss. Anna cannot allow herself to give in to the obvious. She will never be ready for that emotional upheaval, and so she refuses the inevitable devastating truth, the reality that her father and Beauty could not have, and did not survive the night's gale.

Whispering, hoping no one or anything will hear as Anna is in fear of being contradicted, "Father will not leave me and Beauty will never hurt me."

It is not an actual voice that answers, but an immediate constriction to her chest that forces her lungs to exhale an absolute, to face and acknowledge the power set against her loved ones: *What is their puny will matched against You? You are...a storm that runs over the face of the world. You create and destroy. You ask to be feared even by those who have faith.*

Anna is crushed, crouching on her haunches and weeping into her mittens because she has too much of one and not enough of the other. Her tears instantly freeze as they fall from her eyes.

From the open door of the crooked, shook askew shack, the two Canada geese, tentative and always cautious, poke their heads out...a ghost is returning.

It is distinctive, almost rhythmic. It is different enough from the draining slush, the retreating water, and the rivulets not yet frozen solid to cause Anna to catch her breath between sobs and to turn her head. Something is there, invisible in the falling snow. Something is approaching from along the shore at a quick pace, a run. It is splashing, throwing up water and ice with each rapid impact.

Anna slowly stands, guarded in her hope for any sort of a happy ending, as she believes it is beyond her grasp, but her heart reaches for it anyway. Her heartbeats rise to match the growing impacts, the nearing splashes of the something that is closing in and almost upon her. Anna stares at nothing and everything. All is a white veil. Taking a small step of faith, Anna asks, "Father... ?"

Leaping out of the whiteness and into Anna's arms is the answer to her question.

"Beauty!"

Steam rises from Beauty's coat with each snowflake that alights, melts, and then evaporates on her overheated body. Anna hugs and rubs her face in the sweet-smelling fur, repeating, "Beauty," again and again to reassure herself of the existence of the impossible which, she clings to, never wanting to let go. Beauty's tongue, long and wet, slobbers, panting, out-of-breath and exhausted. Wanting to sleep for a week, she fights the impulse, knowing that her arrival home is only half the mission. She is alive and safe, but her master is not. He is somewhere, alone, drifting with a current that ebbs and flows, as does his life. Beauty barks excitedly while struggling to free herself from Anna's embrace. Beauty's resistance to the joyful reunion, to a premature celebration, sends a jolt through Anna who now looks to the nothingness from where Beauty sprang. She asks the question that frightens every daughter who adores and cannot find their father, "Beauty, where is he?"

Between exhale and inhale, between the beats of every heart, after the exertion, there is a moment of pause, of rest. For the ill or infirm, the aged and weary, it is a moment of trepidation when one hopes for one more breath, one more beat of the heart, another moment of life. God, through His will or charity creates storms, which in their exertion destroy civilizations, but saves the butterfly. The human inhabitants of the Chesapeake region are awakening to this pause, this rest, to discover what has been damaged or destroyed. The animals of the marsh and fast lands crawl and dig their way out from under the layers of ice and snow to skitter, hop, and scurry in their scavenging. The fowl take to the air to see what morsels have been uncovered along the changed shoreline by the turbulent waves. The bald eagle spreads its wings, waiting for the first thermals to lift it on high. Its nest, woven secure in the tallest loblolly pine, held fast while the nesting pair faced down the storm with majestic defiance.

Anna's overworked lungs burn with each intake of bitter-cold air. Her leg muscles are spent, wasted, as she runs in heavy boots through the ankle-high slush along the shore, and down trails covered with foot-deep snow that explodes with each footfall as a blunderbuss loaded with the whitest of powder. Refusing to quit, to slow the maddening pace, Anna stays close on the hightailing heels of Beauty. And though there is desperate urgency in Beauty's speed, Anna nurtures the miracle of Beauty's safe return, hoping, expecting even, that around each bend or turn she will plow into her father who will be loaded down with ducks and geese, dragging the Davenport, and crudely complaining, "Do I have to do all the work?"

Arriving at the tip of Swan Creek Point, breathing heavily, and dizzy with exhaustion, Anna pauses to survey the placid cove, the bay, and the Narrows separating her from Spesutie Island in the distance. A thin layer of ice covers the surface. She can hear it crackle as it hardens. The dark clouds that threw rain, hail, and then snow all night are moving on to leave behind brightening skies. The morning light turns the fallen snow to a creamy icing topping gentle ripples that have been captured by the ice and held still, a pause in their exertion. Beauty barks encouragement to continue, but Anna does not know to where. They have reached the end of the land and her father is nowhere to be seen.

Refusing to wait, Beauty bounds forward across the shallow sand bar. Her weight breaking through the crusting ice to continue forward in belly-deep slush to what appears to be an elongated clump of raised land dusted in sparkling snow. Beauty leaps onto it and barks for Anna to catch up.

Anna watches, perplexed by Beauty's meaning, and in a panic, shouting, demanding, "Where is he?" Then, as with the passing of the last cloud on a gloomy day reveals clear skies; to allow vision to that which was hidden, clarity of understanding, horrific in its meaning, drains the flushed coloring from Anna's cheeks. Anna rockets forward, scrambling through the broken ice and screaming with the wrenching reality that the mound of snow is a winter's sarcophagus entombing her father.

Falling upon the shrouded sneak skiff, Anna grabs and tugs at the snow-covered body, trying to turn it over. The powder, white and fluffy, sloughs away to reveal her father. What is left of his tattered coverall is frozen to the skiff: Clay's hands are rigid and fixed to the bottom, his face turned away as if in shame for being found defeated by nature, a force that he is suppose to have dominion over, or at least the wisdom to stay out of its way.

Whimpering, "No...please, God, No!" Anna throws off her mittens to get a better grip. Wedging her fingers between her father's graying yellow wrists and the copper bottom, Anna cries out to the rising sun as she rips her father free. Clay's stiff, ice-hardened clothing cracking as his body tears loose of its bonds.

Cradling her father, Anna brushes away the remaining flakes from a face she does not recognize. This man appears already as a ghost, a body without a soul, a house without an inhabitant. This is not the face of the man she idolizes, adores, and loves. His eyes that were hypnotizing gray are now glazed and his skin has the waxen clarity of a tallow candle, the translucence of fish whose flesh is white and pared thin. Anna's tears falling upon his face possess more solidity. Her hands, hot with blood surging full of life, rub a face that is doughy and dead. Anna groans a deep guttural moan full of denial and despair.

Anna screams at her father who she believes has abandoned her, but at the same time refusing to accept the frozen body in her arms. She shakes Clay with a violence that causes his head to flop side-to-side as if his neck were rubber.

"Jennifer..." is muttered, heard as a delicate brush of lips against Anna's ears. "Jennifer." Clay blinks, his focus is distant, his pupils contracting and expanding, seeing what his lost mind conjures.

Hope fueled by desperation is eternal as Anna rocks her father as a sickly newborn, willing him back to health, back to her, "Father, I'm here. You'll be okay now. Please don't leave me."

Clay's shriveled hand rises to touch Anna's face. His fingers are cold, a shock even, as his calluses that were hard as stone wither against her hot skin, "My beloved, I've never stopped loving you."

"It's me, it's Anna," Anna frantically looks around for any sign of help. Father and daughter are alone on a bay slowly icing over, next to a marsh covered in sparkling snow. It is a desert without a life-saving oasis, not even a mirage of a working skipjack or passing paddle wheeler.

"I'm sorry for doubting you, my love," Clay's voice is tender, barely above a whisper. "You were right. You are always right. Our baby girl is amazing."

Anna sobs for her father as in his delusion he believes she is her mother, and for herself at his words that she has always hoped he would say, emotions he would reveal, a love expressed, but always held back with the belief that they were unnecessary and unmanly.

"I've never been disappointed. No son could make me prouder," Clay's eyes glass over and close. "No!" Anna shakes her father. "Wake up. Wake up!"

A bloody cough erupts from Clay's mouth. His eyes open and refocus on Anna as she wipes his lips.

"Anna?" gurgling for breath, Clay chokes on his words. "I lost the Davenport. You'll have to find it. Look for the buoy." Clay's chest heaves. He gasps for that which will not fill his lungs.

"I'm here. I'm here. Tell me what to do," helpless, Anna holds her father tight, hoping to warm him, and trying to give him her strength to fight for his life against a triumphing disease and malicious cold that has sunk deep to freeze his heart, conspirators in ending his life.

A peace settles on Clay, a moment of illumination, angelic, brightening the hunter's face, and frightening Anna as her father's hand falls from her cheek. Clay's lungs muster its last reserves to allow for one deep sigh to escape, the kind that lifts a great weight, or as an expression of acceptance.

The gurgling from deep within Clay's compromised lungs returns. Bubbles foaming at the corners of his mouth are filled with blood. His body no longer fights the drowning as a crooked grin crosses his stained lips, "There's nothing to be done." Clay's head lolls toward the east where across the Narrows, lit by a brilliant yellow sun, ducks and geese are visible feeding and chatting contented. "I believe it's a rest day."

Clay's final declaration, in reference to himself, or the waterfowl he menaced his entire life is confusing. Though it could be appropriate considering the changing times and restrictive laws that turned an honorable man and his worthy profession into an outlaw with the stroke of a legislator's pen. Possibly his statement is his last instruction to a daughter he cherished. Either way, his words are lost, as at that very moment the mixed flock of waterfowl takes to the sky, swirling and confused, sensing a new threat, but unable to determine where it is coming from. Their wings, strong and imbued with endurance, carry with them a father's spirit. The thundering wind rising to heaven masks the sobs of a daughter.

A male mummichog, stockiest species of the killifish, often referred to as bull minnows by bait fishermen, is having the dark vertical bars of its flank ripped away by the raptor's powerful beak. The hungry eagle had spotted, with its telescopic eyes, several of these ubiquitous fish trapped in a marsh stream that is in the process of freezing solid. These unfortunate silver-gray fish squirmed within their shrinking confines, their limited wiggle room making them easy pickings for the elegant bird that is not too proud to scavenge.

Killifish are of little direct value to man; never seen on a dinner plate, but if caught in a seine, they are a delight for the inquisitive child to play with. Their indirect value, their true worth comes from their hardy and adaptable nature that allows them to flourish throughout the Chesapeake region in all seasons. Residing in marsh ponds, streams, and the bay proper, the one to seven-inch bait fish are dined on by larger predatory fish: pickerel, bass, yellow perch, and catfish which in turn, all find their way, dipped in batter, to a sizzling frying pan—sumptuous.

The four semi-frozen mummichogs are a delightful appetizer on a cold, bright day with the sun reaching for noon. The sun's placement is perfect for the eagle to scream from the apogee in the sky on silent wings after a main course that will be shared by its mate who is tending the nest.

As the last chilly swallow slips down the eagle's throat, a racing flock of green-winged teal speed overhead in a tight formation. Twisting and turning as is their way and coincidentally matching the wandering stream as the teal follow it from the old snapper's pond on their foray from the woods to the bay. Cocking its head, eyeing the prospective hot meals, the eagle leaps into the air, flapping broad wings to gain altitude. There are no clouds to hinder visibility or to inhibit thermals for the eagle to rise on, quickly becoming a mere speck, a memory, deadly in a vast blue sky, a predator that should never be put out of one's mind, even if it is out of sight.

The waterfowl that are rafting together in open water, and which appear to be the most vulnerable to an attack by the eagle that can dive with blinding speed toward the tightest concentration to pick any duck out of the group, are nonetheless at ease as they go about their business. Oddly, ducks on the water are secure, and will even nap with the knowledge that an eagle looms overhead. It is only when ducks take flight that they must be wary.

From its lofty height among angels, this eagle's heart is out of place in the company of God's celestial attendants as it is black with only one desire, and that is to kill. Adjusting its remarkable vision, the eagle has the ability to enhance an object by 40%. Zeroing in on a group of mallards, the eagle seeks to identify, by even the tiniest indication of a weakness, an injury, or the sluggishness of old age, the one among many that will make for an easier target. Casually leaving the bay, the mallards fly up a narrow estuary leading into the Joiner's swamp—an even easier kill, and the eagle will not have to lift itself and the dead weight of the duck out of deep water after the neck breaking collision.

Arcing over with its wings angled back to decrease drag, the eagle plunges as if shot by Sagittarius,[82] a white-tipped arrow hurtling toward earth. The eagle streaks ever faster—its eyes constantly adjusting and refocusing; its tail feathers on fire with speed, bending, compensating for the changing angle of attack and the target's moving sweet spot. At a hundred feet above the flock, dead on a lagging hen, without an apparent signal or call between them, acting as one, the 20 mallards pirouette from tree top height, to fall as tumbling dancers to the icy water. They scatter as buckshot, paddling frenzied in all directions across the slushy surface.

---

82 Sagittarius. Astronomy. The archer. A zodiacal constellation. Sagittal: pertaining to or resembling an arrow or arrowhead.

Undaunted by prey that somehow sensed its approach, the eagle quickly scans the marsh and tree line for another victim before pulling out of its dive to veer back skyward.

Nibbling winter bark from a sleeping sweet gum at the transition from marsh grass that is covered in snow, except for its brown tips, to the fast lands forested in a variety of soft and hardwood trees, is a cottontail. It is taking a break from raising its young that are sequestered within a deep burrow. If the sweet gum still possessed autumn leaves; one falling from its highest branch would make more noise on its drift to the ground than the eagle as it bends its wings to change trajectory toward the new target. The beating heart of the snacking cottontail stops as the eagle's mighty talons sink deep, piercing vital organs to end the cottontail's life. So sudden is death that the cottontail did not have time to swallow.

The nesting eagles relish their hot meal as they take turns tearing chunks of meat from the ravaged carcass that steams as the innards are exposed to the frigid air. Sated, the two eagles, resting high in the loblolly under the brilliant winter's sun, survey a landscape that is stark white and cruel.

In their dark burrow, the cottontail's young wait for a parent who will never return. They have two choices: sit and starve, or venture out into a world where they are viewed as prey. Either way, their chance of survival depends on what they have learned from a parent that has been taken too soon.

Angel Hill is bathed in the rays of the afternoon sun that dance over undisturbed cotton ball snow that is radiating between hues of blue and yellow. Overlooking the tranquil Susquehanna Flats and Havre de Grace, Angel Hill is an enchanted acreage for anyone who is not wearing mourning black. The only signs of human intrusion onto this sacred ground are the deep foot prints leading up the rise to a rectangular hole, where standing solemnly around a plain pine box; the last sinkbox Clay Buchanan will ever enter, are the Joiners, sans Nathaniel, the Websters, and several dozen men, hunters all, and their significant others, some claiming they are wives. Closest to the rough casket, Olivia squeezes Anna's hand to the point of inflicting a pain that at any other time would garner a yelp, but today it is ignored as Anna is unaware of any feelings; not accepting sensations from outside her body because her insides, reflecting the tempest which brought her to this place today are consuming all sensory perceptions and distorting reality. Anna watches Pastor Davies' lips move in his soliloquy that no one is listening or responding to, as the gathered are occupied with their own thoughts. Through the whirlwind that is her mind, Anna tries to answer the question asked by all who grieve: "How can a loss so great fit into such a small hole?"

Concentrating on breathing, having to remind herself to inhale and exhale, is the extent of Anna's physical control over her body. She tried to encourage her heart to beat, but its reply was, "What for?" Then, as if flicking a switch, Pastor Davies' baritone voice touches a chord that Anna's brain believes is worthy of attention.

"Each man has two fathers, the one called God, who is in heaven, who chastises with tribulations and loves with blessings. The second called Pa, who chastises with the belt and loves through instruction..."

Useless, Anna concludes as her brow furrows as her pain is mutating into anger.

"...Each man also has two mothers; one called Ma, to suckle from in life, and the second called earth, whose arms he rests within in death..."

Poetic but pointless, Anna's gaze wanders to the sad faces surrounding her who are pondering death, possibly their own mortality, which is in stark contrast to a day that God, who apparently mocks the weeping, has made bright, too brilliant, full of the goings on of life wherever Anna looks. Skipjacks with golden sails are skimming the waters with placidity, its crews bustling. Folks are strolling sidewalks freshly swept of snow as if it were a summer day. High above the water, swirling, rising and falling, turning, grouping and separating are flocks; the myriad of waterfowl raising an excited raucous for no other reason than to announce to family and friends, "I'm still here."

"...It is this mother that Clay is laid into beside his beloved."

A stab of guilt pains Olivia's heart and conscious at the pastor's words. She clings to her belief that she loved Clay as deeply as Jennifer, but the lack of a band on her finger somehow taints this purest of emotions, especially standing before her best friend's grave. Jennifer may be dust in a rotted pine coffin, but somewhere among the decaying remains is a small gold ring that will always elevate Jennifer above Olivia, and without one herself, will saddle the child growing within her with the moniker of bastard.

"...Man is supposed to find peace in his final resting place, but I also believe that Clay, regardless of life's hardships always knew a peace that we all seek. As the inscription on the temple of Apollo reads: 'Know thyself and the universe is yours.' Clay was a hunter from head to toe and he knew the universe that is this splendid bay..."

Anna resists slapping this preacher and screaming in his pudgy face, a face so full of caring, *the splendid bay killed him!* But she knows this is not exactly true. The bay just helped wield the hammer onto nails that were already in place, a disease destroying him from inside.

"...so it's more than appropriate that Clay rest here; on this peaceful rise overlooking that which he knew and loved so much, the Susquehanna Flats..."

This stupid, stupid preacher, Anna's head aches, knowing there was nothing her father loved about the Flats. He worked the Flats for what it provided. *He loved my mother and me.* Without quite understanding why she did it, Anna swivels her eyes, casting a glance toward Olivia, whose drawn and pained expression, whose dark circles under her eyes, and disheveled hair and clothes speak of pain more than associated with the loss of a friend. There was never a doubt in Anna's mind that Olivia loved the family Buchanan, but was Olivia also in love with her father, and did her father love Olivia in return?

Anna's misery seems to be shared equally by this woman who has been Anna's surrogate mother; who never attempted to supplant her real one; only exalted her mother with her endless stories of childhood deviltry while reaffirming Jennifer's love for husband and daughter. Visualizing these moments of storytelling, with her father sitting nearby, carving and smoking his cigarettes, Anna now clearly sees the glow, an energetic radiance surrounding Olivia's face when she spoke of love for Clay. Was it her own love for her father that shone through? Slowly shaking her head, Anna is amazed by how she could have been so blind to the true nature of her father and Olivia's relationship, except to use the excuse of childhood self-centeredness and adolescent preoccupation with her own heart's desires.

Anna's affection for Olivia grows beyond measure in their shared grief. Olivia's loss is as great as her own, only in a different way. Through this shared agony, Anna finds the emotion that had been crushed by sorrow, frozen as she held her dying father in the shallows of a cold bay icing over... compassion. Within this newfound bond, Anna returns Olivia's squeeze to her hand, but with a gentleness that expresses understanding.

As Pastor Davies concludes his eulogy with Psalm 23, his voice rising to magnify the Lord's inspiration, something about, "...quiet waters, ...valleys of death..." Anna observes a true homage to her father, though probably just a strange coincidence. A group of Canada geese, led by a wise gander who knows there is no threat to his family here, flies low over Clay's casket, not honking, not a chatter among them. They glide so low, at barely 10 feet, that Anna believes she can lift her hands to stroke their soft, gray-feathered underbellies. In unison the birds dip their wings to land a dozen yards away.

These magnificent birds stand in silence, reverently, among tombstones engraved with the names of men whose lives were dedicated to killing them.

These men are gone, but others remain to harry the birds.

These geese are still here, but too many have fallen to the gun.

The remnants of this flock are not gloating or dancing on the snow-covered graves. These geese, in quiet contemplation, are seeking the same thing that all who come to Angel Hill Cemetery are in search of—a place to rest in peace.

Steam from the Ford's ribbed radiator rises into the chilly air, hissing as a snake as the four-cylinder engine idles with a rackety-boom, but it is Constable Jenkins that is prepared to strike. Waiting patiently for the mourners to conclude the lowering of the casket, he savors the idea, rolling it sweetly around on his tongue, that with Clay dead, the infamous gun can be his. To achieve its confiscation, an act that all others, even the clever and persistent LeCompte failed at would be a splendid feather in his career cap—at the very least garnering him a photograph in the local paper, maybe even a commendation for removing the beast, the marauder of the Flats. However, it is the scratching of that unreachable itch, it is finally having the mystery solved of where the punt gun has been hidden all these years, where it has lain in darkness from the prying, desiring eyes of the law that impotently could hear the gun's mighty thunderclap of death, but could never feel, never could hold its cold metal in its hands, that gives the constable his greatest relief and pleasure.

He licks his chapped lips. *Besides*, he thinks, *what use could Anna have for the gun? She may be fit and healthy, but she is still just a girl. The gun would be far too heavy for her to lift, and she could never launch or maneuver the sneak skiff with the skill necessary to stealthily approach the fowl with any success.* Constable Jenkins chuckles at the thought of Anna's fright at the gun's blast if she did get up the nerve to pull the trigger. And with Anna's disclosure and surrender of the Davenport, this act of conformity to the law will go a long way to remove the stain of outlaw hunting that is attached to the name Buchanan. Voluntary forfeiture of the cannon will be a symbolic hand washing permanently preventing the sins of the father from attaching to the daughter with all the societal stigma and legal consequences that are connected. The daughter can step out from under the cloud of her father. Today is a bright new day, but even as Constable Jenkins drinks in these warming thoughts, a shiver crawls up his spine like an unseen spider. His hands squeeze the black steering wheel with worry. *What if she sells it?* Watching Anna shuffle through the snow down the slope, Constable Jenkins realizes that she is surrounded by the who's-who of outlaw hunters. If Anna passes along the Davenport, the gun's new owner would immediately be the envy of his peers; his ability to generate income would vastly improve, and the law would continue to be snubbed, to Constable Jenkins' consternation.

From the corner of his eye, the constable watches as Sam Barnes and Jim Currier trudge up the slope to meet Anna. At this distance, the constable can hear nothing, but reads the two men's body language as if it were shouted. Sam, a prolific decoy carver and guide, who also fishes for a living, stands straight while shaking Anna's hand, apparently offering condolence. On the other hand, Jim, a fine carver in his own right, had made his living as a market hunter, but of late has not been seen attending a blind or sinkbox though he is flush with greenbacks. He appears weighed down, as if carrying a heavy burden. His broad shoulders are slumped and he is not looking Anna in the eye. Could Jim, feeling the timing inappropriate still be asking to be considered as a contender for the purchase of the Davenport? Whatever their brief discussion, it ends with Anna giving him a hug, and then she continues down the hill past the two ancient Negro men who are entrusted to open and then close the final resting grounds. Sam and Jim remain fixed to their snow-covered spots, their heads turning to greedily stare with mouth-watering desire at the resting flock of geese.

Nearing the newly purchased vehicle, an automobile that Henry Ford offers in any color so long as it is black, a vehicle bought with town funds to be shared by all officials, if they can somehow pry their constable out of the driver's seat, Anna and the mourners eye the rattling contraption suspiciously.

From inside, Constable Jenkins unlatches the passenger door and pushes it open. "Miss Buchanan, please get in."

"Constable Jenkins, so good of you to pay your respects," Olivia steps forward, "but Anna was going to come home with me."

"Yes, my respects," the constable stammers. "My condolences, but I wish to offer Anna a ride to her home," an undertone of malice coats his words, "and to discuss a matter of legal importance which does not concern you, Miss Bouvard."

"I'll be all right," Anna hugs Olivia, and surprisingly, Claire Joiner steps forward to embrace Anna while staring at the constable who now shivers at Claire's unspoken warning; a threat he knows this woman would carry out if he is not gentle with Anna, but the law must be upheld...finally.

While holding Anna tightly, Claire whispers, "Clay raised a good girl. You always remember we're neighbors. You can call on us any time."

As Anna climbs into the first automobile she has ever ridden in, she does so with trepidation, believing she knows what to expect, her answer already formed, but this will not make the coming interrogation any easier.

"I'll catch up with you later," Delbert calls out.

An oily backfire and spinning wheels in the snow are the last rude words as Constable Jenkins pops the clutch, sending the creation of the assembly line swerving down the road and past paperboys standing on every corner, yelling: "Extra! Extra! Read all about it," as they wave a special noon edition of the *Republican*.

WAR! WAR! WAR!

April 6, 1917: President Wilson asks for and receives from Congress a declaration of war against Germany, after stating, "To make the world safe for democracy." This reporter applauds, for now we can come to the aid of France who has, since the forming of our country, assisted us, and though we have struggled to free ourselves from the grip of Great Britain, we are honor-bound to assist her as she is still our mother, whose sons, our brothers perish by the tens of thousands alongside men from more than 25 countries, including an army of Bedouins commanded by Lawrence of Arabia.[83] God speed our boys to victory as the battle is engaged. There is no turning back now.

Anna's toenails are smashed against the insides of her boots as she braces her feet against the wooden floorboards in anticipation of a crash. She presses firmly on an imaginary brake pedal, an instinctual response to Constable Jenkins' reckless driving. The speedometer needle points at 35 as the sedan careens along the icy road that divides the past which is the natural, the unspoiled forested lands, from the future, the orderly rows of plowed fields. Anna's teeth clench in fear for her physical safety, but she is unflinching against the threats from the constable.

"I don't know what you're talking about," feigns Anna.

"Don't play stupid with me," growling his irritation at her repeated denials, Constable Jenkins glares at Anna while ignoring the road. "I want the Davenport and you're going to tell me where it is."

"I didn't know my father's shotgun had a name, but it now belongs to me. You have no right to it."

---

83 Lawrence, Thomas Edward (1888-1935). Byname Lawrence of Arabia, also called T.E. Shaw. He was a British archaeological scholar, a military strategist, and an author. However, he is best known for his exploits with Arab warriors during World War I against Germany. His life is the stuff of legends. Unfortunately, at age 46, his life was cut short when he was involved in a motorcycle accident and died six days later.

"I'm not talking about a shotgun and you know it. It's the punt gun that he's used; and his father before him used to slaughter waterfowl with. Now stop jerking my chain or I'll arrest you for obstructing a law man in his duties."

This threat of arrest, instead of instilling cooperative fear in Anna, which was Constable Jenkins' intent, backfires. The simmering anger that bubbled at the grave site from the ignorant pastor's words boils over at the raw memory of her father's arrest, and how, with the weight of the boot on her chest, the constable pressed her to the earth while his deputies hog-tied her father, a large nail pounded into a coffin being prepared for Clay.

As if fired from a gun that was assumed to be empty, Anna's wild and vicious attack so surprises Constable Jenkins that he cries out in alarm that startles winter finches from their cozy nests among the sleeping trees as the Ford barrels past. Trying to protect his face, he releases his grip on the steering wheel. Anna's chipped fingernails find the fat folds of the constable's face and neck to scratch and tear flesh. Her scream is one long anguished wail of grief and anger.

Without human guidance the sedan's direction chooses that of least resistance without heed to the battle going on within its cotton fabric lined interior. The crowned road, designed to shed water, but now blanketed with snow covering ice acts as a gradual slope, a slippery winter slide, easing the vehicle toward a perilous future edged with drainage ditches.

Constable Jenkins' girth puts him at a great disadvantage in the small confines of the front seat against Anna whose bantamweight allows for freedom of movement. Her clawing with change-ups of fist and elbow swings batter the constable who can only turn and cover his head.

As slowly as the sun descending from its long journey across the broad sky, the sedan's spinning wheels creep closer to the road's edge. Then like a stick thrown into a bicycle spoke to flip its rider, a rut hidden under the snow catches the narrow right front tire. The Ford, First-On-Race-Day or Found-On-Road-Dead, depending on the owner's experience, flips onto the driver's side with a metallic crunch, to plow up a mound of snow as it slides down the lonely road.

Dazed, with the wind knocked out of her, Anna finds herself crumpled on top of the moaning constable. Looking out the broken windshield, she finds the world has turned on its side. An urgent voice encourages escape. "Flee!" is repeated, ringing in Anna's ears. She crawls through the shattered glass as shards tinkle down from the bent frame, cutting her palm and scratching her scalp. Anna tumbles to the ground, a soft but cold impact. Rising to her feet, Anna staggers toward the past, the natural, and the unspoiled as a grunt slaps her from behind, "I'm coming for the Davenport."

Anna turns around to face the scene: her footprints lead away from a wreck she caused; the fat, sweaty constable is pinned in a crippled automobile he hogs. He is a lawman who harasses children too poor or immodest to wear a swimsuit, who was part and parcel responsible for her father's death in a roundabout crazy connect the dots way a daughter would do; whose face bleeds from her talons on a day when the sun's bright rays hurt the eyes, and she laid to rest her father. A smile of satisfaction curls crooked on Anna's mouth. It is both cruel and deadly serious, frightening in its formation, especially coming from a 17-year-old girl, "You just come. I'll kill you like my father killed LeCompte."

Watching Anna disappear among the elms, maples, and oaks, their branches enveloping her with protection, Constable Jenkins' male pride helps him to decide that when telling the tale it will be a wild doe that leapt out of nowhere which he tried to avoid that caused the wreck.

Not a soul would believe the truth, and if they did, he would never live it down...the big, strong, lawman bested by an unarmed girl.

Steam hisses from the Ford's cracked radiator.

Constable Jenkins waits to be rescued from the bite he knows was self-inflicted.

Snow, turned purple by the setting sun whose diminishing rays faintly illuminate a sky of reds and blues, flies up in wide plumes with each angry step; footfalls, better described as frustrated kicks as Anna strides along the wooded path toward home. Her blood-stained hands are crammed deep in her pockets. Her head is down, eyes focusing on nothing. Her thoughts tumultuous as she is unable to finish a train of thought, all ending with a wreck. Gut-wrenching sadness thrown overboard by anger at adults who did not understand her father, or who are trying to take advantage of his death. Sadness and anger, two powerful emotions struggling for supremacy while a third demands recognition: fear, which is harassed by a nagging brother—worry. These last two emotions, fear and worry, Anna cannot blame on others, as they are a result of her attack on Constable Jenkins, though she believes she was justified as he provoked her. A strange feeling, slightly rebellious, squares her shoulders, and with a hint of pride in defense of her family, Anna declares for any and all who are listening, animal, fowl, or human, "Buchanans will not be fucked with!"

Embarrassed by her choice of the off-color word, Anna covers her mouth with her hands. She does so with the hope that she can retroactively silence her gutter mouth to preempt it from being slapped for profanity and then summarily washed out with soap when she arrives home.

With her mouth still covered, Anna's eyes swivel about. There is no sign of another human. Her ears, pink from the cold without her cap that she lost during the brawl, hear only the snapping of an ancient limb brought down by the weight of snow.

No rebuke is heard.

No slap to the face is forthcoming.

There is no one home to apply the soap.

Anna's crippling sadness from the death of her father places her thoughts beyond the everyday, the mundane, the routine, and the ritualized activities of day-to-day living. The magnitude of loss is a blinding squall which tormenting gives way to reveal that which made up the storm, the individual drops and puffs of wind that create stabs of pain. Each act, the nuance of the deeds that by themselves were simple, almost insignificant acts of kindness, considerate courtesies, and thoughtful reminders, but when combined over a lifetime are love: a precious entity, a privileged offering, an indefinable necessity.

"How am I supposed to live without my father?" Anna cries out as twilight deepens around her.

There will be no more she-man coffees prepared for that most intimate of looks between father and daughter, the mischievous smile. There will be no more instruction in carving decoys with suggestions on how to improve the shape of the bill or the angle of the neck for swimming or sleeping mallards. There will be no more reminders to take the Mackinaw for protection against an approaching storm.

Anna's rational brain reminds her that she is not alone. There are friends and neighbors to call on. This comforting thought is snatched away at the realization that her profane declaration was mere bravado beginning with a lie. Anna admits, with words barely a whisper, "There are no longer Buchanans. There is only me."

Anna's hands are back in her pockets. She decides not to wipe her nose that the cold air has made run. Shuffling her boots through the snow, it is sadness that has won the moment, but her head is up and her eyes are focused on an uncertain future.

Something that could be mistaken for a palm-sized snowball on furry feet crosses behind Anna on the dark path. It is a young cottontail. It may be frightened by every sound and movement, but it still chose to come out of its hole.

Objects which during the day reflect prisms of light, that take on colors, whose hues relate a character, a quality and purpose that is either pleasant, obscene, memorable, or forgotten in a passing moment, at night become the enigmatic black hole with only a vague outline for the viewer to grasp at in identifying its true form and function: this is the Buchanan shack by the bay.

It is behind such objects, forms, and structures that those who cannot show their faces during the day wish to be shadows, hiding themselves, and lie in wait to pounce on the innocent, the unaware, the unwitting, and upon the unescorted woman. That is the desire of the man who has learned that Clay Buchanan no longer stalks the marsh or reigns king of his crumbling castle.

There is no father.

No man of the house.

No protector of the maiden.

There is nothing to fear; yet he is thwarted by an aggressive dog and two challenging geese with each attempted approach. They are black shadows on a dark porch, a strange and unnatural alliance of two species marching post to post in protection of a home where the majority of its original inhabitants are dead, and the lone survivor absent.

He retreats, stumbling blind over the snow-laden marsh grass to hunch down next to the garbage pit and behind the outhouse. The pit's contents; discarded leavings, rotting, returning to dirt; its odor is deadened by winter's covering. Uncomfortable and exposed, he considers taking refuge inside the outhouse where at least he would have a place to sit, and the element of surprise, but light breezes sneaking in and out of cracks and knot holes of the privy tell of a gagging stench behind the cross-slatted door.

Animals, he thinks, though snickering at himself, as he is the one prowling the night with a carnal hunger that fails to ever be satisfied. Not even the dance hall ladies in the city, who demanded payment up front for services yet rendered, and a tip for salacious extras, could quell his cravings. In fact, what they showed him, what they did to him on a stained and bug-infested mattress in a squalid basement room only intensified his base urge.

It was fortuitous that upon his arrival in Havre de Grace that he learned of the death of Clay Buchanan. It is a miracle that he found his way in the darkness to this isolated place along Buzzards Glory. It is by Luck, God, or the devil, that he hears the unmistakable crunch of snow under a single pair of boots.

His eyes strain. She is there, approaching through the darkness. He wishes for the vision of a barn owl so that he may better see her, the object of his appetite. As with an owl whose ears evolved to be one higher on the head than the other to detect the exact location of its desire, he cocks his to help determine closing distance and speed.

From the starless night, on an inky trail with nothing but specters created by his anticipating mind, he watches as she materializes in the form of a Mackinaw-clad creature. Her walk is of misery, but her bearing is upright, not defeated, no sign of surrender, and obviously feminine. The stout boots, the baggy coverall and coat cannot conceal the youthfulness, vitality, and sensuality of a woman in her prime—so desirable.

Shifting his position behind the outhouse so she will pass him unaware, allowing for an ambush from her rear, he unwittingly steps on untrammeled snow. Its crunch is a trumpet sounding, a jarring announcement of his presence.

Anna stops.

She listens.

He holds his breath.

The night is silent but for the waves lapping at the shore a stone's throw away. Their motion, pushing ice together, and pulling it apart are a rhythmic crunch, a slushy mixing. A dozen steps away the familiar outhouse sits awry from the gale. Her home, a hundred more, waits for her return.

Strange, but Anna knows the marsh, and when it is in cahoots with the night, it can produce images that are seen out of the corner of one's eye, but are gone at the turn of the head, and sounds, when investigated have come from nothing...or from a clumsy, masked bandit foraging in the pit—a raccoon. Continuing on, Anna is surprised by pleasant feelings coming over her by passing the outhouse; a closet with a faithful seat. It is an enclosure wherein an accumulation of uncountable hours of thoughts of the serious, mundane, important, and ridiculous have been worked through. And nearing with her every step is a home wherein a cot calls, luring her into a slumber that may or may not bring refreshment. At least she has Beauty to snuggle with.

Anna opens her mouth to call her faithful companion, "Beau-,"

Slammed to the ground by a hurtling weight, Anna's face is mashed into the frigid snow. Her scream is cut off as her mouth is plugged with the cold compacted crystals. Then roughly, she is rolled over to feel a hot... tongue wiggling in her mouth. Its heat turns the snow to a choking liquid. Her gag reflex is held in check, as is her initial fright and instinct to fight off her attacker, to use the power of the adrenaline racing through her veins and unleash her fury, still only a hair trigger from a violent explosion.

With their mouths welded together, he brushes the snow from her eyes. Anna's heart already knows his weight and the twirl of his tongue, but her eyes are relieved to confirm the identity of her assailant who fumbles to gain access under her clothes. She exhales through her nose with pleasure as Beauty's barking and the geese's honks raise a commotion. They race to her aid after hearing her call cut short. Their rage at the intruder, at William, is a vivid reminder of her own anger, raising the lid on Anna's stew that has been boiling since his unexplained absence.

Anna bites down on William's tongue as she knees his groin. His squeal and pained grunt are sweet satisfaction for Anna. These two sensitive and vulnerable protuberances; one probing, the other swollen; the first assuming its invasion of her will bring about the welcoming of the second. Both are in need of lessons in manners.

Anna shoves William off of her as Beauty and the geese attack, biting without worry to bruising the meat, nipping and snapping through pants and sleeve with painful results as William covers his head. He rolls in the snow as if on fire, kicking and pleading, with cries, wails, and howling from a torn and bleeding mouth. Shock and surprise color his every sound.

"Where have you been?" Anna shouts as she weighs in with a kick or two to William's exposed mid-section. "I needed you during the trial and you weren't there."

"Call 'em off!"

"You weren't here when my father died," her cries punctuated with another swift kick to the ribs.

"Please, Anna," William screams, trying to roll away, but Anna, Beauty, and the geese stay on top of him, delivering physical pain equal to her hurt and disappointment. "Let me explain...please. I was there for you."

Anna grabs Beauty and holds her arm between the tormenting geese and William, "What do you mean, you were there for me?"

Scrambling to his feet, but remaining bent over in pain with his hands cupping his injured crotch, William stutters, "I was there to comfort you almost every night while your father was in jail."

Anna fumes at William's definition of the word, "Comfort? You were here, but after I fed you, all you wanted to do was work up a sweat under the covers."

"I thought that was pleasurable for you, too," baffled, William's words are slurred as his tongue swells, the other protuberance now deflated and cowering.

"Yes, that's pleasurable, but only for a moment. Comfort is what lasts. It's being with me. You don't have to say or do anything. Just be by my side. That's comforting. That's what I needed."

"Oh," chastised, William retreats to a defendable position, a seemingly rational response that is ill timed in an emotional moment. Silence would have served him better. "Well, you could have told me then."

"I'm telling you now, but what about the trial and the funeral? What's your excuse there?"

"I went to the courthouse, but my father was there, and I couldn't risk him seeing me. I'd have no explanation," William's eyes light up in the darkness. His growing excitement causes him to spit blood as his words tumble out faster, becoming more difficult to understand. "Then, you're not going to believe this, but several chums from England, whose fathers had sent them to 'the colonies' as they still call us, for an extended vacation, and to get them out of harm's way of the war, surprised me with a visit and invited me to go with them to New York. The city is an incredible place— amazing and wildly diverse in the entertainment that's available."

"You're right. I don't believe it," Anna believes William absolutely. What she cannot believe is that William finds his absence justifiable.

"It's the truth," William continues. "And the best part is they want me to sneak off with them to join Lafayette Escadrille.[84] It's the French Air Corps. They take all comers and train them to fly." Then as if it is a motto he has repeated a hundred times, probably accompanied by drunken, adventure-seeking lads still wet behind the ears, with dance hall ladies gripping their manhood to pump up their egos with one hand while emptying their pockets with another, William raises his arms, fists high in the air to shout, "For the glory of England and America, we'll show those Jerries!" Sensing his point, his excitement, his excuse is not fully being embraced, he adds, "Besides, nothing I could do would have made any difference. Your father's death is a tragedy, but we must move forward."

Dumbfounded, Anna's jaw is slack at hearing William's reasoning, his obtuseness, and the perfect example of his lack of concern for her. Closing her mouth and releasing Beauty and the geese; these small acts, to grind her teeth, seething, and loosing implements of her rage, her vengeance, is gratification beginning with two soft-spoken words, "Sic him."

---

84 Lafayette Escadrille. This all-volunteer air corps was created in April of 1916 as the Escadrille Americaine but the name was changed due to German diplomatic complaints. Later, in February of 1918, the 38 American pilots were absorbed into the U.S. forces as the 103rd Pursuit Squadron. Their fame exceeded their actual accomplishment, though they did down 57 German planes in 20 months. Raoul Lufbery who was killed in action was the squadron's leading ace with 16 shoot downs. Ten other pilots also reached the status of ace.

Walking toward the empty shack that she calls home, Anna is comforted by the screams of a boy who is blindly running, being chased by relentless warriors through a landscape covered in snow and cloaked in darkness.

William will learn to prioritize—a lesson with severe consequences when the test is failed.

Riotous children of all ages celebrate victories in the same wild fashion, especially when they are long overdue: with joyous laughter, with ecstatic leaps and bounds, and triumphal pilings-on, which are referred to as dog piles, but in this case, geese outnumber the dog two-to-one.

Beauty and the geese tumble through the open doorway in this state of exhilaration, to present themselves before the mistress of the house, their general through ascension. Anna does not appear to share their revelry at their total victory, even though she set the charge in motion. Sitting slumped in her chair at the wooden table, Anna stares in through the curved glass of the lantern at the wick flickering with a weak flame. She turns to gaze upon Beauty, whose tongue hangs, panting, with a mile-wide grin, her tail wagging side-to-side, thumpidy-thump. The two geese are flapping and folding their wings. Their feathers askew even in the one-sided battle, as it is not unexpected that the vanquished would get in a few lucky defensive blows. What a sight is her little army...her family. "I did the right thing, didn't I?" Anna searches their faces for signs of confirmation, because there are always doubts, second thoughts, and those mental naggings that other options should have been explored before what may have been a rash decision prompted by hurt feelings; a reckless act of retaliation, and a too hasty destruction of an all-consuming relationship, which even now she craves. Sure, William was not here when Anna needed him, but did she take the time to consider, to listen, really listen and try to understand his side and the difficulties and pressures he is under as he resides in a museum-piece of a mansion run by a tyrant?

Beauty's harsh barks, high-pitched exclamations are easily interpreted, "Didn't like the smell of him: too much starch in his store-bought clothes; too much musk oil in his annoyingly chic hair; too much polish; and too much shine without substance. Simply put—good riddance!"

The geese twist their heads in that herky-jerky fashion to look to one another to form a consensus. The female, not deferring to the male, but allows him to be her spokesman on this issue of agreement. He stretches his neck to its full length while shaking his head as if trying to extricate an annoying bug from his ear, and then fills the Great Room with a decisive honk. It is meant to be the final punctuation, the period, the conclusion to a subject not worthy of further discussion, "Victory is ours! General Buchanan deserves a medal."

Accepting their counsel, Anna nods, appreciative, "Then I guess we need a fire and some food." She closes the door on a painful night, allowing the geese to remain indoors; a respite from the chill. They settle in the corner next to Jennifer's rocking chair. Anna begins to crumple and stuff the stove with old discarded newspapers before adding the kindling and cut logs. "Not too tight," Clay would always remind her. "Allow the flames to breath. A little space is a good thing." Her father's words ring with warmth and relevance.

Will there ever come a time when I won't miss his gruff instructions? Anna wonders, as a headline in the *Republican* catches her eye.

ENDURANCE LIVES!!

December 18, 1916: Sir Ernest Shackleton's[85] ill-fated 1914 quest to traverse the Antarctic on foot ends in success; not for crossing the loneliest continent at the bottom of the world, but for surviving 19 months stranded, with all lives saved.

A day's sail from the white continent, Shackleton's ship, *Endurance*, was trapped in sea ice. Frozen in place for 10 months, the ship was destroyed by the slowly closing fist of pack ice that had encased the Weddell Sea.[86] The intrepid explorer and his men were forced to endure the unimaginable and camp on the exposed ice for five months, hoping and praying for a rescue that was not coming.

Shackleton realized that if his band of men were to survive, bold and decisive action would be required. He undertook to launch his own rescue by making two daring and treacherous 800-mile open boat journeys to South Georgia Island. There, Shackleton and two other determined men crossed the wind-swept and snow-covered mountains of South Georgia to reach the island's remote whaling station of Stromness.

---

85 Shackleton, Sir Ernest Henry (1974-1922). An Irishman educated at Dulwich, England. He led several British explorations to the Antarctic. For his contributions, Shackleton was knighted and made a companion of the Royal Victorian Order.

86 Weddell, James (1787-1834). An English explorer navigator, and seal hunter, he commanded Antarctic voyages. The Weddell Sea is named after him. His book, *A Voyage Towards the South Pole* (1825) is a record of his exploration.

The station manager, Mr. Sørlle, shocked at seeing men dressed in rags and covered in black from blubber smoke, faltered in his question, "Who the hell are you?" Adjusting his tattered clothing to better present himself, a knight of the English realm, the leader replied, "My name is Sir Ernest Shackleton. I have come to requisition a ship to rescue my lads still on Elephant Island."

After four months, and on the fourth attempt, the previous rescues prevented by ice and foul weather, the *Yelcho*, a tug loaned by the Chilean government succeeded in reaching the island. As the shipwrecked men ran about in jubilation at their salvation, Shackleton, from the deck of the *Yelcho* was witnessed weeping as he exclaimed, "They're all there!"

These adventurers, led by a never-say-die man, whose spirits were instilled with endurance, lived to tell a tale that is unrivaled in the annals of expedition history.

This writer, who sits in a comfortable office, never ceases to be amazed by the human spirit that can overcome incalculable odds.

Finding inspiration in their triumph against adversity, Anna realizes she is nodding in agreement with the newspaper reporter...amazing.

Knocking, tentative, but a definite rapping, sounds outside the door.

"You want more of the same?" shouts Anna, her confidence building.

Beauty growls.

The geese focus on the door handle as it wiggles.

The door swings open with a creak of rusty hinges.

Delbert stands on the threshold, and with a measure of caution, answers, "I'm not William."

His statement, delivered gently is still a belly blow to Anna. From her squatting position next to the stove, she plops down onto her behind. Looking to Delbert with exasperation, embarrassment, and hoping for understanding, Anna admits her closely guarded secret, "He's an idiot, but I love him. *I'm an idiot.*"

With a perverse smirk that only a friend is allowed to wear at the expense of another, Delbert states matter-of-fact, "I've come to help you retrieve the Davenport, and yes, you are an idiot." Delbert steps forward and extends his open hand, knowing Anna, the proud daughter of Clay Buchanan, will accept a hand up, but never a hand out.

The hunter feeding his family or gunning for the market works to overcome the wise and wary waterfowl. The weight of his bag is the measure of his success. He works to overcome the weather: gusting wind, soaking rain, chilling ice and snow. A roaring fire and a cup of steaming he-man coffee at the end of the hunt is his reward. He works to overcome the calendar; a futile endeavor where there is not the faintest chance of success or hint of reward for undertaking the challenge.

With the advancing days, there is only the slumping of shoulders and a collective sigh of resignation in every home, gunning club, mercantile, sinkbox, and blind, signaling the moment, the instant each hunter dreads, when, based on the tilting earth, the lengthening day, and the rising temperature, the ducks and geese depart. Heeding their instincts; the call to take flight; the birds abandon the Chesapeake Bay region. This moment is the closest men come to shedding tears.

The waterfowls' departure from the bay is a rending of a vitality that has no comparison. As individuals who are part of families join groups of birds to rise into the sky, they call out to one another to organize, to form immense flocks pointing north. They will not land again in the bay or surrounding marsh for another nine months. The ruckus raised in their departure creates a deafening silence by their absence. To the people of the Chesapeake, the birds are the breath of life. Without them, it is crib death.

The birds are going...gone.

The punt guns are hidden away for summer.

Only the stories remain to sustain the men in Tavern Bouvard.

Racing up the Atlantic flyway from Brazil, crossing the Caribbean east of any landmark, with a bead on the Chesapeake, with the intent to refuel before dashing off to Cambridge Bay in the Arctic, are red knots. These dove-size shorebirds are on a tight schedule that must be adhered to if they are to reach the Arctic to breed, and raise the next generation during the short northernmost summer. Any ill-timed spring storm along the way will delay these dainty birds whose window for fattening opens only a crack for the briefest of periods.

The red knots, speckled brown and white to blend in with the sand, have to arrive in the Chesapeake during the first week of May. This is to coincide with the spawning of a creature of primeval origins. Its eggs are the red knots' protein for survival; the source of life for a migratory species that flies the world, bottom to top, and back again, with only one stop—the shores of the great Chesapeake Bay.

"Ugly and useless. Not a bite of meat in its entire body," proclaims man.

"Beautiful and perfect. No need to change a thing," declares God.

The speakers' points of view differ, but the object under scrutiny is the inoffensive horseshoe crab.

This animal, the size and roughly the shape of a large, upside-down dinner plate, was 150 million years old when it witnessed the supercontinent Pangaea[87] split apart to create the Atlantic Ocean some 250 million years ago. For the majority of its life, this dark brown creature with a menacing looking tail: straight, narrow and spiked, that doubles its overall length, remains in deeper channels and rivers. It crawls on slender legs, feeling its way along to pick up and munch on bottom-dwellers such as small mollusks and worms.

Then in May, and with the full or new moon pulling with its invisible hands to create extra-high tides, these horseshoe crabs, who are more closely related to the grotesque and repulsive spider than the beloved and tasty blue crabs of the bay, crawl up to the water's edge in the tens of thousands. Each female drags around at least one male who is mounted to her back. He has attached himself by way of a specialized hook with the aim to be the one to fertilize and pass on his perfect genes.

With their mates in tow, the females dig shallow nests to deposit their pearly green eggs. Of the more than 75,000 laid per female, it is fortunate if 10 survive incubation and the nine years to maturity, to breed, and repeat the cycle. Feasters on the horseshoes' eggs, who did not exist to devil the hard-shell crustacean until the last few ticks of the world's timeless clock; eels, killifish, and other small fishes, gulls and other shorebirds probe the sand to disturb and uncover the caches by the millions.

It is before the crabs' hatchlings escape from their birdshot-sized eggs that the red knots must arrive. With only two weeks to gorge before the next high tide, when the remnant of miniscule crabs, after molting five times in the egg, will break out to swim for the depths, the red knots zip in, out of the east on waves of wind. Exhausted and emaciated from their non-stop oceanic flight, the birds, using their long, narrow bills, frantically poke here and there into the sand. There is no time to rest and no time to waste. They need to double their weight or they will perish before reaching the nesting grounds still far to the north.

---

87 Pangaea. Believed to have been formed approximately 500 million years ago, Pangaea was a supercontinent containing nearly all of earth's land. It was comprised of connected landmasses, the southern region Gondwanaland, and the northern called Laurasia. About 250 million years ago, Panagea began to break apart under the theory of continental drift.

The red knots' stop-over in the Chesapeake is so brief that their arrival and departure often go unnoticed. However, for the lucky and observant who are enjoying a lazy spring afternoon, this darling little shorebird, flitting about, running to and fro on scrawny legs, in and out of the foam-edged waves, is a delight to watch. That is until it is understood how desperate its situation is; how the clock, the calendar, and the weather align to imperil its future.

God set the heavens and earth in motion, and that imperfect creature, a work in progress called man, named it Time. And Time, as man and beast know, waits on neither.

All that can be done is to root for the little bird.

The shrill and cheer-filled voices of girls who are on a serious mission, call out from the middle of the gathering crowd in front of city hall.

"Support our boys!"

"Support the war effort!"

"Buy war bonds!"

Anna squeezes through the crowd of working men on break and ladies of leisure, to edge her way to the front to investigate the commotion.

Several tables decorated in red, white, and blue bunting are set up at the base of the steps. Behind these, placed on the rising steps are a dozen striped flags with 48 stars each. Standing ramrod straight or sitting at the tables are primary and secondary school-age girls, all smartly uniformed in khaki, the older ones with sewed-on merit badges, and the younger without. They chat up fellow Havre de Gracians, encouraging them to contribute to a worthy cause, "President Wilson says we're saving the world. It's the patriotic thing to do."

Standing off to the sides are proud mothers. Their little dimpled darlings with bright smiles, curled hair bouncing with each flip of their heads; the vision of the American girl; future good wives in training. Men go off to fight and die—heroes all. The women remain pressed and preened, stalwart, regardless of the outcome. They will weep in private, clutching their returning husbands or sons with joy, or the telegram in sorrow.

Approving of the scene, but wanting more for these young women; a future where they are self-sufficient, capable, seen as equals to men, is the orchestrator, organizer, and tireless supporter of these Girl Scouts—Mrs. Low, Daisy to her friends. In spite of her advancing years, Mrs. Low flits from one girl to the next, encouraging, assisting, and seeming to whisper a question in each of their ears. Each girl, as if trained from birth, when asked a question she does not know the answer to, will furrow smooth brow, bite her lower lip, then coquettishly bat long eye lashes while hesitantly shaking her head, no—an answer that is never supposed to be uttered by a good woman; a wife to her husband. Mrs. Low knows there is a lot of work to do before these capable girls are confident in their abilities, whether innate or learned.

One girl, a year or two younger than Anna, who Anna recognizes as one of Chief's two younger sisters, though she cannot remember her name, nods at Mrs. Low's question. Pausing for a moment in her sales pitch to the town barber, she squints, focusing on each face in the crowd, and then coming to a stop to stare straight at Anna. Grinning with accomplishment, she raises her arm to point a manicured finger. Mrs. Low's eyes follow the accusing digit.

Every wrinkle on Mrs. Low's grandmotherly face lifts in a smile that is topped with eyes sparkling of diamonds. Together, they wrap Anna in the warmth of a thousand hugs; so very precious, but given freely to a long lost friend. Mrs. Low reaches out, hoping to embrace with her arms the object of her affection, and then motions Anna to come to her. Surprised at seeing Mrs. Low after all these years, and pleased that she is remembered, Anna hurries around the tables that are bustling with patriotism to receive her hug. Mrs. Low's khaki colored coat, a match to all the little daisies budding in the midday sun around her, is so soft, of a fabric light and caressing that Anna melts into it as Mrs. Low throws her arms around Anna with abandoned restraint.

There is no substitute, no comparison, nothing that equals the feeling of security and safety, of acceptance, of affection when enfolded into the loving arms of a grandmother, anybody's grandmother, even if the aged woman has no offspring. The energy imparted; the tingles received; the love that oozes from one to enter and fill every fiber, marrow, and cell of another cannot be described by words, but expressed only as all granddaughters do, as Anna does, collapsing into, with a long, full body, lung-depleting sigh.

In Mrs. Low's arms, the world that of late has been cruel and unfeeling toward Anna dissolves, disappearing with all its problems. There is only the love of her mother and father wrapped into and given freely by this old lady, who in all likelihood could not dream of surviving the challenges that Anna has faced, but can still give without restraint what is sorely missed— love without strings; tenderness, sympathy, interest and complete attention without uttering a syllable.

Anna is comforted, and to her own astonishment, she begins weeping. She squeezes Mrs. Low as she did her dying father; then, hoping he would not leave, and now, hoping that this moment of bliss will never end. Within the security of Mrs. Low's embrace, Anna prays that she will never have to return to the world with problems and responsibilities, or if she does, that there is a mother and father to worry for her about where the next meal, or the money for shotgun shells will come from. Mrs. Low caresses Anna's hair and coos words without meaning into her ear. These sounds are sweet and accepting, not needing to know the reason for Anna's tears. Mrs. Low stands unabashed with a hundred pairs of questioning eyes seeking the answer for gossip's sake, but they will leave with their interests still piqued, but unsatisfied. Then as quick as a spring rain that drenches the picnickers, the deluge stops to reveal the bright sun. Anna's sobs turn to embarrassed laughter as she eases out of the embrace to wipe her eyes. Her face lights up, a fresh, rosy complexion in competition with the clear sky.

"I'm sorry. I feel so foolish," Anna begins. "I didn't mean to blubber all over your pretty coat."

Dismissing Anna's concern for her clothing, and seeing that she is regaining her composure, Mrs. Low digs around in her pockets, searching for a misplaced object, "Anna, a woman need never apologize for tears. It is our right," and without knowing it, Mrs. Low touches the soft-tender place in Anna's heart, reassuring her. "We are strong creatures, but our strength comes from our ability to express our feelings...to cry for ourselves, for our family, and for humanity as a whole." Then with a quick glance around at the throng of eager ears, Mrs. Low leans in close to whisper in Anna's ear. "Remember, dear, we as women are responsible for the joy in this world. It's a heavy burden and our tears lessen the load."

Anna nods in understanding, though she is not quite sure if Mrs. Low means it is the woman's responsibility to bring joy to the world, or that because of women there is joy in the world. With a wink from Mrs. Low, Anna settles on the latter.

Clapping her hands sharply, any eyes not already on Mrs. Low and Anna turn toward them, "Good people of Havre de Grace. Thank you for coming out today and offering your support for our valiant men fighting to preserve freedom in the world. My name is Mrs. Gordon-Low. I am the founder of what is now called the Girl Scouts. Many of you fine families have daughters involved in local troops. I thank each of you for allowing them to broaden their experiences beyond cooking, cleaning, and sewing. They will not only be better women for it, but better citizens."

The crowd claps and cheers as the Girl Scouts who are sitting, stand with the others to take a bow. Their blushing mothers accepting praise from those standing nearest them.

"Now," Mrs. Low continues with glowing pride. "I have a special announcement. As you men know, in a horse race, like those at the Graw, there is the unofficial and official winner. Sometimes they are the same, sometimes not. Well, in the Girl Scouts, the first officially registered is my niece, and though I love her dearly, truth be told, the first true Girl Scout, unofficial as she may be, is one of your own from right here in Harford County."

A clamor rushes through the men and women with surprise, excitement, and hope, as parents who desire that it be their daughter throw about prospective names. Anna edges away, allowing the uniformed girls to move closer to Mrs. Low so that one of them may more easily receive the accolades and acclaim for being the first.

Mrs. Low holds up her hands for quiet. Held in one of them is a small object, a pin of sorts, "Quiet please! I met this brave and clever scout, as a novelist might say, 'On a dark and stormy night.'"

This puzzles and disappoints the parents, as they would never allow their daughter out on such a night as Mrs. Low describes, thereby eliminating their precious, well-scrubbed offspring from contention in this race.

"Together, she and I created the Girl Scout Law recited by every girl in every troop."

Anna, listening to Mrs. Low's words, remembers back five years to the rain-soaked night she discovered Mrs. Low and her automobile, both stuck in the mud. *Could Daisy be speaking about me?* This thought is beyond Anna's wildest imagination, but here Mrs. Low is, reaching back to clasp her arm and pull her forward.

"And modest as expected, I present you good folks with the young woman whom I think of every day, inspiring, and ahead of her time in resourcefulness: Anastasia Nicole Buchanan."

Gasps are heard at this unexpected name, accompanied by a smattering of rolling eyes from those in attendance. The clapping is hesitant, with the loudest coming from the youngest Girl Scouts who have yet to be tainted by their mothers, who in horror look upon the incongruous setting. Crisp, new uniforms of coiffed girls from respectable families applauding the daughter of a suspected murderer and known outlaw hunter, who is wearing a patched and faded coverall over a white undershirt; her only saving grace is her long, silky, black hair that others would die for.

"Anna, in recognition of your contribution and inspiration, I am privileged to present you with the Golden Eaglet."[88]

---

88 Golden Eaglet. From 1918-1938, it was the highest award in Girl Scouting. The design of the Golden Eaglet featured an outlined figure of an eagle with the letters *G* and *S* placed on either side of the eagle's head. The award's name and design has changed several times in the ensuing years and from 1980 to the present, the highest award is the Gold Award.

Missing a beat in their clapping, the Girl Scouts recognize, some with the sour taste of envy, that the Golden Eaglet is the highest award possible. A goal that each girl strives for, but is rarely obtained. The few, more insightful girls learn a powerful lesson and rush to embrace Anna as an honorary Girl Scout, a sister in the struggle for true womanhood. The others swallow the salt lick of hate.

Anna's tears, running down her cheeks, are glistening under a loving sun. They are sparkling arrows pointing toward vibrant eyes overflowing with joy.

Frank McQuay slips quickly past the rear of the crowd to find a side entrance to city hall. His goal is to avoid being corralled and coerced, cajoled or embarrassed into spending money on buying a bond. Frank McQuay refuses to contribute to or get involved with other people's problems. He has enough of his own and would not think for a moment of asking others for help. Though at all times considering his lofty position in the community, Frank McQuay does not want to appear unpatriotic, so avoiding confrontation is the best move. William, intercepted before his escape to France, and denied the glories he believed awaited him in the wild blue yonder, is forced to tag along on this trip to town to observe his father *doing business*. William, despite his last encounter with Anna where he was run off, he is ecstatic by his glimpse of her. She is still his breath of fresh air. He wants only to stand by her side to support her, to lend his applause in recognition for whatever the reason she is the center of attention, but for pride and its many faces, William denies himself this pleasure.

Mrs. Low's pride bubbles over for Anna.

Anna hopes the Golden Eaglet's dazzling reflection reaches to heaven so that her parents can see it and burst their celestial buttons with pride.

William wants to be with Anna but his pride keeps him from apologizing.

Frank McQuay's pride in maintaining the appearance of wealth forces him to be selfish, dodging his communal responsibility to set a sacrificing example.

The day was a disaster for Timothy Ross, apprentice to the new mortgage and loan manager, and candidate for the draft. Timothy's sour disposition, a panic really, began with the sun shining brightly through his bedroom window to wake him. If today had been Saturday or Sunday, his days off, all would have been well, a relaxing sleep-in, but today is Friday, a workday. Even though the bank does not open to the public until nine, he is required to begin work before the sun's light touches the western shore.

In his haste to dress, slick back his unruly hair, and shave, his razor missed a patch of stubble under his chin. This violation; an unsightliness, a vulgarity, a glaring flaw in a setting of polished propriety, a bank, was harshly pointed out by his supervisor who tossed Timothy a straight razor with the curt instruction, "Clean it up." Timothy cut the stubble as well as his throat, and then spent the next 20 minutes trying to staunch the bleeding while other employees banged on the lavatory door in need of its facilities.

Upon reentering the manager's office, a bastion of decorum, with tissue stuck to his wound, the manager's displeasure was evident by the shake of his head and the longer than needed stare at his Patek Philippe[89] pocket watch; his chubby thumb rubbing the engraved hunting scene on the cover, as the watch's minute chimer punctuated Timothy's morning of mounting blunders. Snapping closed the cover and depositing it into his vest fob, the manager grabbed a bulging satchel containing documents in need of delivery. Tossing it to Timothy, he dismissed him with a rhetorical question. "You're not going to make a habit of this, are you Ross?" Wisely, Timothy kept his mouth shut. Exiting across the lobby's polished marble floor, he walked swiftly, but with proper restraint, even though he wanted to run away under the disapproving glare, the sharp raptor eyes of the other departmental heads that were quick to spy out the blood spots on his less than perfectly starched collar. Underlings kept their noses to their paperwork, quietly empathizing with Timothy, but relieved they were not the focus of negative scrutiny.

A bank, a prestigious one, with connections in Washington D.C., specifically the War Department, could keep a man who is deemed valuable, from having his number called up. It is the New World's version of a hallowed hall. In Europe, a cathedral is where a man can find refuge. In the United States, sanctuary still comes with the words, "In God We Trust," but it is printed on the almighty dollar. If a man is seeking special treatment, he better have a lot of them, or endear himself to those old men who control their flow.

---

89 Patek Phillippe. Antoine Norbet de Patek began selling high quality watch movements with decorative cases in the 1830s. In 1845, Adrien Philippe joined with Patek and "Patek Phillipe" was formed in 1851. Phillippe created the stem-wind mechanism that is used today. Some famous owners of Patek Phillipe pocket watches were Queen Victoria, Prince Albert, Marie Curie, Clark Gable, Albert Einstein, and Tchaikovsky. A rare Perpetual Moonphase Patek Philippe pocket watch repeater is valued at $80,000.

A day filled with a bright, skin-warming sun and aquamarine sky, dotted white with drifting clouds, was made gray by each dismal reception of Timothy upon each hand-to-hand delivery of the bank's precious documents. Those who expected the paperwork at a specific time were annoyed by his tardiness. These businessmen and landholders barked their irritation and questioned Timothy on his competence. Those recipients in dread of his arrival despaired at his appearance. In tears, they challenged his Christian charity: "Are you heartless? Where will my children sleep if I have no home?"

Not wanting to add rudeness to these character assassinations, Timothy stood politely, but clutching the satchel as a shield against the accuser, only departing after the caster of disparagement finished venting. With his spirit bruised and mood battered, Timothy dutifully raced off to be late for his next delivery.

In Timothy's attempt to make up time, a ridiculous endeavor as it is impossible to regain that which has been lost to the rotating earth, he drove the bank's tin-*Lizzie*, a polished product of Detroit, without care for life or limb; pedal to the metal, and damn them pot holes. The paved roads were ribbons of heaven and of little danger so long as horse-drawn carriages and wagons, which are still the majority of conveyances, did not suddenly appear from a side road. Looking both ways before crossing or turning onto a highway has yet to be ingrained in the minds of the populace.

It is the unpaved roads, the country lanes, and rutted drives that test Timothy's driving skill to keep the vehicle moving forward in a straight line, and the engineers' structural tolerances, or more specifically, their envisioning of the extremes that the operator of their automobile will subject it to.

Spokes, even turned from oak, are still made of wood. Their splintering, the snap of broken bones, sounding of distant gun shots is ignored by Timothy as he swings the vehicle wildly, careening, as it flies off the pavement, and bounces down the dirt drive. The crack of fracturing spokes is masked by the crunch of the suspension springs bottoming out against the axle. It is not until the left front wheel, its rim collapsing, tipping the front end downward to dig into the soil and bringing the vehicle to an abrupt and dirt spraying stop, does Timothy attempt to brace himself against the crash.

Shaking the blinding stars from his eyes and rubbing his chest after the painful impact with the steering wheel, Timothy climbs out of the hobbled vehicle. With a foul expletive or two, he surveys the damage: a twisted bumper, a bent fender, and the destroyed wheel. He is lucky to have escaped serious injury. Looking down the extended drive that in its disuse is disappearing under spring growth, he now remembers this property, the shack by the bay, wherein the lack of proper husbandry has required his second visit with a Last Notice before the bank takes back the property. Timothy always thought that to be a queer turn of a phrase: take back the property. It should be, in all honesty: kick the inhabitants out and sell to the highest bidder.

Remembering also, the mad dog behind the not-so-sturdy door, Timothy decides to replace the wheel with the spare before attempting to deliver the strongly phrased document, just in case a quick get-away is required. Besides, the day is waning, taking its precious light with it. Timothy's only consolation as he removes the jack and lug wrench from behind the seat is his knowledge that the president of the bank does not trust these mechanical contraptions, stating for all to hear, "I'll take a horse any day, but that thing... no, sir. It may be the future, but I predict it will be the death of us all." An accident will only reinforce his beliefs and possibly garner sympathy from this powerful and influential man.

Anna's walk, her stroll, her glide home through the fast lands and marsh is a heady amble three feet above the ground. Black-eyed Susan, daisies with cheerful faces smiling up at Anna, mingle with shoots of recent growth along the trails; yellow coneflowers and greening grasses stretch upward to catch the last rays of the day. Above in the elms and birches, the deep emerald leaf buds have unfolded to form wide varieties of geometric shapes. Dangling as puppets on strings, they dance to music whispered on the balmy breeze.

Highlighting Anna's euphoric passage are splashes, streaks, and flashes of feathers; bright yellow-orange bodies zipping through branches on blue-gray wings. The prothonotaries, a Central and South American warbler are here to nest and to encourage others to sing songs in celebration of life—new life forming in eggs of creamy white with deep red, lavender, and purple spots—or simply because they are giftedwarblers. It would be a sin to deny a passerby of their vocal virtuosity.

Stepping down from her elation to tread the rough boards of her porch, and to open the shack's door, Anna hears a metallic clank and a clunk. Beauty scrambles out the door in the direction the out-of-place mechanical noises are coming from. Her barking rouses the penned geese that are preparing a nest for their eggs. Curious, Anna looks around the corner of the shack. Her heart leaps into her mouth as she sees the outline of a vehicle: *Constable Jenkins has come!*

Anna's threat to kill the constable flashes in her mind, but she knows her words were only bluster, spewed in a fit of rage. Glancing back at the Davenport's hiding place, she trusts the maple to keep its secret. But if the constable is here for her, to arrest her for the assault on him, well, she will not run away. Somehow she will endure. Anna places her hand over the Golden Eaglet for courage.

Peering up the drive again, a wave of relief washes over Anna as the silhouette of a slender man is seen running around the vehicle with Beauty biting at his heels. Whoever he is, he is certainly not the fat constable.

In Timothy's hasty retreat, Beauty quickly assesses that this man is no threat, so the chase becomes more of a game for her, her barks playful, her bites more for fun than effect. Hearing the man's fear-filled shouts, Anna takes pity on him and runs to his rescue, chuckling at the comical scene.

Once around the automobile he runs with Beauty at his heels.

Up onto the tin-*Lizzie's* running board to climb onto the hood for safety.

Slipping off, to be chased around once again.

Slapstick.

Vaudeville, with the night providing blackface for all.

"Beauty, heel," Anna arrives with a sympathetic smile, an expression laced with light-hearted pity, that in other situations would anger a man, but Timothy is more concerned with Beauty's bared teeth than Anna's snickers. Beauty returns to Anna's side as Timothy cautiously appears from behind the automobile.

"Are you lost?" Anna asks.

"No. I'm delivering bank notices," Timothy is hesitant to simply blurt out his purpose as he does not exactly know who this girl is. "But as you can see, the wheel broke, and I've been fixing it."

Anna takes a closer look at the splinters of hardwood hurled about at the sight of the accident...dozens of feet from the pavement. It dawns on Anna that the vehicle had turned off the road before the wreck, not because of it. Uneasy, Anna asks, "We're you coming to see me?"

This question, obvious but unexpected catches Timothy off-guard.

"Umm..." cornered, but stalling for time, Timothy reaches into the front seat to pull the notice out of the satchel that is destined for this property owner. Squinting in the darkness at the name, he believes he has dodged a bullet. Timothy is glad not to be ruining the evening of this country girl, who, even in the darkness, he can plainly see is a comely lass, even if she is in need of a new outfit. "Ah, no. This is for a Clay Herschell Buchanan."

Timothy is experienced, and has begun to build up a thick skin against the sight of hearts breaking. He was not, however, prepared for the facial and physical collapse of the girl in front of him, even acknowledging that the night's shadows likely amplified the sag of her face, the darkening of rings under the eyes, and the shrinking of her frame within her clean, but well-worn coverall.

"He was my father," whispers Anna.

"Was?" Timothy's voice cracks.

"He's dead."

"How about your mother?"

"Dead."

Timothy has to say it. It is his job. He is not responsible for the situation, but the words are like glue, sticking to his tongue, and faltering as they cross his lips, "I'm sorry. Then I guess this is for you." Timothy holds the paper out for Anna to take. The paper glows with malice as the full moon rises over the Eastern Shore.

"What's it say?"

Timothy clears his throat.

Beauty growls.

The red lettering, printed in capitals, sucks what little light that glows from the two lanterns out of the room to absorb, intensify, and then radiate it back. The words LAST NOTICE burns Olivia's and Anna's retinas as it lies flat on the round pine table between the two women. The stark white and crisp paper, embossed with the bank's seal is too serious for a room built for frivolity; completely out of place; created in the consecrated halls of a financial institution, the notice from on high is in sharp contrast with the sinful patina of the tavern's table. The greening pine surface, with worn corners and carved initials, began its discoloring with an alcoholic orgy a generation ago; the first spilt whiskey saluting a cask's broken maidenhead. Three old hunters who witnessed this establishment's opening, and who keep up the tradition of drinking each other under the table, are ignored as they resemble a pile of sleeping puppies, limp and tangled, snoring peaceably in the corner, adorable except for the smell of vomit.

Olivia's blue flannel nightgown, oversized and billowy, hides her expanding middle. Her sleeping cap is pushed back, exposing fire-red bangs curling to the left and right. Dark circles under her eyes speak to sleep interrupted, while the tables still cluttered with cups, bowls, mugs, plates and pitchers of flat beer; accoutrements of the previous evening's celebrations are evidence of Olivia's general fatigue.

Anna leans forward, expectant. The sweat generated by her run through the night is drying, leaving strands of hair stuck pell-mell to her forehead and cheeks. She is anxious for Olivia's answer; for her to speak the words of salvation; her rescue. Anna looks to Olivia as she is the acknowledged adult and will provide the answer. Olivia can resolve and make disappear the threatening paper that declares the bank's intent to snatch out from under Anna the only home she has known; to remove her from the setting that molded her and created memories. Whether these remembrances are joyful or filled with pain, they are the sum total of Anna's being. The shack, the marsh, and the bay, are what make up the quilt that is her life. They are the patchwork of experiences sewn with a stitch in the tickle bed where her mother died:

a stitch beside the snapper's pond;

a stitch wading through the eel-laden stream;

a stitch strolling under the grand old oaks;

a stitch playing children's games among the cattails;

a stitch hiding, playing adult games among the grasses;

a stitch under the shack's protective maple tree;

and a stitch in front of the potbelly stove where she watched her father carve decoys, listening and learning the ways of a hunter.

These are Anna's treasures to be protected and saved at all costs. Anna is confident that Olivia understands this, too.

"Your father's Last Will and Testament names me guardian over you, Anna," Olivia takes Anna's hands in hers, and looking sympathetically into her expectant eyes, inhales deeply. "This means I'm responsible for you; for your well-being. I'm honored that he trusted me, and I'm willing to do anything, to sacrifice whatever is necessary to ensure you are taken care of, but I can't afford the monthly expenditures of this tavern and the mortgage on your home, too."

Anna pulls away. This is not the answer she expects. How can Olivia not have the money she needs? "But the tavern is always full of customers."

"Yes it is, and most nights I work until three or four in the morning, to collapse on the cot in the back when I'm too tired to walk home, but only after the last one leaves or passes out. The point is, most of the men run tabs that are paid sporadically. Some months I'm barely able to pay the distributor for the alcohol I sell. Anna, when it comes to business, appearances are often deceiving." Olivia unconsciously rubs her swelling belly.

"Mr. Ross said that if I make one payment, or even if a good-faith partial payment is made within 30 days, the bank will hold off on foreclosing."

"I'm sorry, Anna. It's just not possible."

"I wouldn't have asked," Anna stands, becoming desperate, "but the large flocks are gone until next winter. Only the summer ducks are left. The Davenport is useless against them as they don't raft in large numbers."

"The punt gun is too dangerous for you, and, if you haven't got wind of it yet, Constable Jenkins has placed spies along the shore to listen and watch for the gun's blast. Let it rest with your father."

"So I'm supposed to give up; quit without a fight?"

"I don't know what else to suggest."

"I don't either, but I know my father wouldn't give up, so I won't either. No matter the risk, Constable Jenkins and his spies be damned."

"Anna, now you listen to me. That gun, the Davenport killed your father."

"No! The law killed him, but at least he killed LeCompte first," Anna regrets her outburst the moment she spoke it, remembering Olivia's complicated relationship to both men.

"Anna, your father didn't kill Felipe. He was with me," Olivia is hesitant in her explanation even though she has been wanting to tell Anna ever since the funeral, but she is unsure how Anna will react.

"You were there for my dinner party, but he went hunting after I left."

Olivia reaches out to Anna, who sits again, but stubbornly will not take Olivia's hand, "No, your father came here with me." Olivia reaches across the table to gently touch Anna's chin, turning her so they are facing each other. "I loved your father, and though he never said the words, I believe he loved me in return. Do you understand what I'm saying?"

Anna's selfish anger at Olivia's inability to help her financially is tempered by that special connection again, and a measure of satisfaction at having guessed correctly at the grave site, that more than friendship had developed between Olivia and her father. With boldness that comes from anger, softened by her mother's explanation of what will be done for love's sake, respect for her father, and affection for Olivia, Anna asks, "Were you... pleasing my father?"

Olivia's eyes take on a faraway gaze, though they remain locked on Anna's, as she responds instantly, "Yes. And in return, he pleased me a lot."

Anna sits quietly for a moment, the Last Notice pushed aside by this unexpected, wonderful, but puzzling information, "But if he was here with you, who killed your cousin?"

Olivia's shoulders slump within her nightwear as the weight of justice denied crushes down, "I don't know, and since the majority of folk believe it was your father, I don't think anyone is looking."

Morning's light creeps in from under the tavern's heavy door as the two women consider the revelations of this early morning. The ticking of the wall clock and the snores resonating, vibrating the glassware, are anchors to the present. Anna digests the truth of what has passed. She is relieved that her father was not responsible for the game warden's murder, even if the good folk of Harford County believe otherwise. Olivia is nervous about the future and the need to reveal to Anna her other secret that grows larger with each passing day.

"Anna, you could move to town and live with me...and the baby."

"The baby? What baby?" Anna's startled expression frightens Olivia, but Anna's face quickly transforms to one of hope.

"It's your father's."

"Another Buchanan?!" squeals Anna, disturbing the three hunters in their dozing. Anna leaps across the table to wrap her arms around Olivia's neck, squeezing with delight.

"Will you stay with me?" Olivia asks tentative.

Sitting back down, Anna's eyes move between the bank's document that is threatening an abrupt closing on her past, to Olivia, who carries in her womb the future; a brother or sister. Her decision should be easy. Let go of what was to embrace what will be, but Anna cannot do it, not yet anyway, "No. I have to try to save my home first. Can you understand that?"

Olivia finds that she is smiling despite Anna's rejection. She is relieved that Anna is excited and accepting about the baby, and though she would prefer Anna to stay in town and begin a new life with her, Olivia recognizes the toughness, or maybe it is courage in Anna that was Clay's hallmark. Whether Anna succeeds or fails, what is important is the struggle in the attempt that will define her character. Clay possessed this trait and Olivia loved him for it. Anna is developing this quality and Olivia would not dare dampen it, "I understand."

The two women, both carrying responsibilities and shouldering burdens, walk to the tavern's entrance where they embrace, finding strength in the other. As Anna opens the door and the bright new day spills down upon them, a previously unnoticed adornment to Anna's coverall catches Olivia's eye, "That's unusual. What is it?"

Placing her hand upon the Golden Eaglet, which is pinned over her heart, Anna says, "It's a symbol of all that my mother and father raised me to be."

Plopping down on an upturned log, a seasoned oak abused as a chopping block and appreciated as a stool, Anna sits in the open doorway of the shed. After admitting that no rescue, other than one of her own making is coming and that the eggs incubating under her geese have no value yet, Anna puzzles out some other scheme, a way to earn money beyond subsistence living. She surveys the artifacts and tools of her father's vocation that are now hers.

Raised off the dirt on planks of pine, beneath the workbench, are tightly sealed two-gallon cans of black powder, birdshot, and oakum for the Davenport. Next to these containers is a wooden apple crate, empty at the moment, but used to store boxes of shotgun shells. Anna makes a mental note that eight shells remain in the magazine of her Winchester, four in her father's Remington.

On, above, or next to the workbench, each instrument, carefully maintained and oiled, rests in a niche or hangs from a nail. There are the two long-handle axes that have been the cause of blisters to hands, the downing of trees, and the freeing of trapped waterfowl. There is the handsaw for sizing boards, its teeth the envy of beavers everywhere. There is the short-handle hatchet, its cutting edge used for stripping off small limbs and shoots from potential logs, and its flat end for pounding nails. There is the two-handled drawknife with its straight blade for removing bark from tree trunks, and for reducing the bulk of a block of wood intended for a decoy body. And, certainly not last among the variety of tools that have become Anna's, is the spokeshave for rounding and creating contours.

Anna reaches down to rub Beauty's head and scratch behind her constant companion's ears, asking, "Do you remember how mother laughed and father grumbled when I brought the spokeshave inside to shred cheese?" Beauty casts her eyes up at Anna, acknowledging the nostalgia. Anna frowns, worrying as she more closely examines Beauty's left eye that is increasingly becoming opaque from disease. Beauty is accepting that with age comes affliction, and so she shakes off Anna's concern to settle down for an afternoon nap.

Resting on the workbench where Clay last placed them are wooden dowels, headless pegs for attaching finished decoy heads to their bodies, and a hand-crank drill for making the holes. Focusing her eyes on the twisting bit, a memory, believed forgotten, surfaces. She was eight, almost nine, and wanted to help her exhausted father. She was all too aware that her father's hunting forays had not been productive lately, and he had to spend more hours in search of their meals.

No duck—no dinner.

An order for decoys, a godsend, had been placed with her father, which he had nearly completed. The heads needed to be mounted and then the decoys painted. With little prior instruction, she took it upon herself to drill the holes. The first two bodies she drilled, though proving difficult were a success, the third was a disaster. As she placed all her weight against the top of the drill, the decoy body held between her bare feet, she began to crank the handle. The shavings spun out of the deepening hole as intended, then the bit caught, causing her to lose her balance. There was an awful metallic snap as her weight shifted. She had broken her father's only drill bit.

Hours later, when her father entered the shack, his face was full of joy as his bag contained two gadwalls, fat ones. His eyes then fell upon the decoy she had placed in the center of the table. There was no sense in trying to hide it, though for a moment she had thought about throwing it down the outhouse hole. Light from the lantern glinted off the broken end of the drill bit as it stuck out of the wood, hopelessly wedged and askew.

His whole body sagged. The joy, the light in his eyes faded to a dull gray, loosing their luster.

Sitting in the chair next to her handiwork, she buried her face in her hands and sobbed.

There was no punishment, no shouting, only the long walk together to town to trade the gadwalls for a new drill bit that was entrusted to her to carry home. Its swirling contours left their impression in her hand as she had held it so tightly.

That evening, their supper consisted of two strong cups of he-man coffee, as together they finished drilling the holes, her father holding the bodies, she drilling them.

On one of two shelves over the workbench are three horn-handled jackknifes for carving. The blades, slightly curved, resembling a waning moon, are two to three inches in length. The shorter and narrower, worn with age and use, the longer and wider, more recently purchased. Each has a comfortable grip; oil and grime from Clay's and Anna's hands stain the handles. Surrounding the knives is an assortment of duck and geese heads, canvasbacks and Canadas, completed except for bill details. The bodies are still only rectangular blocks of pine and cedar stacked to Anna's right. These decoys-to-be are only one processed step from their natural round state. The logs to Anna's left are destined for the stove or as fuel under the dunking barrel. The blocks' saving grace is the absence of cracks or from not being cut from heartwood that will cause the finished product, the decoy, to quickly split after its immersion in water.

The second shelf holds tin cans of varying sizes. Many labeled by paint spillage alone. These rainbow colors, each signifying for the practiced hand where and how much paint to apply to transform a carved piece of wood into a living lure. In trade for its exclusion from the fire for finding another use, the wood has become a trickster bringing death to others. It is a beautiful piece of craftsmanship.

Reaching for the knife that is older, more experienced in its purpose, Anna's hand pauses in mid-air. Seeing in a new light what has always been there, a rough, badly shaped head with a bill that is too flat and with eyes too high and out of alignment. It is Anna's first attempt at a goose head. Picking up this stitch in her life quilt, Anna remembers the pain when the blade, that was only doing its job, sliced into her hand, and her trembling from her father's shouted anger by her failure to follow his instructions. There is no longer pain from that cut, and the harsh voice that frightened the child is silenced. What remains is a useless piece of wood that her father kept.

Anna smiles.

The poor example of a goose head that has been preserved and kept safe is a physical thing, a tangible representation of that emotion her father could not put into words—love.

Beauty's head rises. Her ears perk up.

Growing louder, advancing along the drive, rattling and backfiring due to a lack of maintenance, is some contraption that sputters to a stop in front of the shack. Anna sets the goose head back on the shelf, its place of honor, while thinking, *Automobiles have never brought good news.*

Anna picks up a carving knife.

In lock step with each other, Anna and Beauty turn the corner of the shed. They walk out into the afternoon sun from the shelter of the maple tree's full canopy. The breeze rustling the leaves above them do so with ambivalence, waiting on the tone of the parties, their intent, and purpose. The brightness of the day could not emphasize more the shock Anna receives by seeing William standing beside his father's Buick. Dressed in a tailored, pin-stripped suit over a white dress shirt, topped by a brushed bowler hat, he cuts a vision ever so spiffy that Anna's heart skips a beat as she catches her breath at the sight of this handsome young man. However, something is off. William's stance is not of a confident, sure-of-himself lad who so many times possessed her mind and body. He is uneasy, uncomfortable, shuffling in polished shoes. William tugs at his collar that is apparently too tight or too stiff with starch; a redness, a rash is rising on his neck.

Relaxing her grip on the knife, Anna is pleased that William has found the courage to return. Her impulse is to rush into his arms and cover him with kisses, but reminding herself of the reasons for his banishment, she holds back and holds onto the knife, though feeling foolish doing so.

"William, what are you doing here?" Anna tries to keep her voice neutral, but her excitement at seeing him, and her caution over why he is here, cause the words to flutter.

William's eyes widen, showing apprehension that is out of proportion to this meeting, even if it is with an estranged lover with a carving knife and an attack-prone dog. Anna tries to read, to cipher out the reason for his fear.

"Ah, Miss Buchanan," stepping out from under the porch's overhang and its shadow, Frank McQuay extends his hand in greeting. He is all teeth and gums as the muscles in his face struggle to maintain the disingenuous grin of one who inadvertently encounters a detestable person that they do not want to offend.

Beauty growls, but remains at Anna's side...waiting, watching, tense.

Unconsciously, Anna squeezes the knife handle as if to make it and the blade a part of her. Watching Frank McQuay's meaty palm move toward her, Anna's instinct is to strike out to cut deeply, and to fillet him to the bone. Though Anna now believes she understands William's fear, but not so much his apprehension. William is afraid that his relationship with her will be exposed, and fearful of the repercussions to follow. His apprehension can only be over the substance of this visit, especially when it is beginning with sappy cordiality from a man who has never made it a secret that he, at the very least, believes that he and his family are better than hers, and at most, disgust and open warfare.

Survival depends on discretion rather than valor...paddle away.

Anna takes a cautious step backward.

Knowing beforehand that the friendly-neighbor approach probably was not going to work, though believing, too, that it is always better to try the honey before vinegar, Frank McQuay assesses Anna's level of hostility toward him: high. He quickly changes to a pre-rehearsed tactic as he drops his offered hand, "William."

Casting his eyes about to land anywhere except on Anna, William's avoidance, his shrinking before her is as a man caught by the duck police with a full bag of off-season birds—guilty. His punishment is Anna's silence. Whatever the reason, whatever concocted conspiracy the McQuays may have for their invasion into her sanctuary she will wait with the calmest of exterior. The best bird dogs show no fear when confronted by skunks and weasels. And if her silence, her waiting, causes William to suffer a little agony, some discomfort by having to speak the words he has come to say, apparently words that will hurt her, maybe he will learn another lesson—empathy, and will grow a backbone. If not, Anna will have some satisfaction watching him squirm.

"Anna, sorry. I mean, Miss Buchanan," William's hands are nervously in and out of his pockets, wiping the sweat from his palms. "We would like to...what I'm saying is...this property is not being worked, and as your father...no one is paying the mortgage.'"

"For heaven's sake, we rehearsed this," Frank McQuay's exasperation with his son's fumbling of the situation does not give rise to his own recklessness as he gives a wide birth to Beauty whose curling lip bares teeth equal to the threatening blade in Anna's hand. Frank McQuay dismisses his son by stepping in front of him, making him as irrelevant as a preacher when opening day, the first legal hunting day of the season falls on a Sunday. "Miss Buchanan, I'm here to offer you a way out of your financial difficulties."

Being defensive that, if anyone, it is Frank McQuay who knows of her troubles, Anna chooses to play ignorant, "What difficulties?"

"Well..." Frank McQuay is not prepared for Anna's lack of knowledge and understanding of her dire situation. He did not consider for a moment that she would be clueless. It could be problematic if he is the first to enlighten her, as she being female will likely become hysterical and unable to rationally consider his more than generous offer. He could always wait for the bank to foreclose and throw her off, and then purchase the property, but that is risky and more expensive, as he will have to bid against others, likely raising the price, and he could be outbid. Frank McQuay needs this land. He decides to go forward with a sympathetic approach that will be sprinkled with a few drops of vinegar where needed. "Then I will have to assume that the bank's system for notification to those who are in arrears is ineffectual."

"What?" Anna feigns ignorance. She cocks her head, glazing her eyes as if Frank McQuay's words were spoken in a foreign language.

Rephrasing and unconsciously speaking slower, Frank tries again, "The bank has not been paid what is owed on this land. In less than a month they will have the right to have Constable Jenkins remove you. Do you understand?"

Anna's eyes clear, the pupils becoming pinpoints as she hisses, "I understand, but how do you know this?"

"An astute businessman always has his ear to the financial wind," Frank McQuay says with pride as he hooks his thumbs in his vest pockets. His ego, oozing from his pores, contains such an offensive odor that Beauty's eyes water.

"Even if it's true, I don't need your help."

"It's a fiscal fact, and you do need my help if you want to remain..." Frank McQuay pauses, glancing around at the structure, the hovel that Anna lives in. "If you wish to remain in your home."

This offer, allowing her to keep her home is unexpected, as Anna assumed the McQuays wanted everything, the whole kit and caboodle, "What are you offering?"

Frank McQuay holds in the grin that wants to explode across his face at his own brilliance. His quick-on-his-feet, last second change to what he intended offering could seal the deal. "I'll purchase the mortgage, which means I'll own the land," though he knows this is not exactly true. Frank McQuay will take over making payments on the outstanding debt, thus saving a bundle, and assuming all the equity, the payments that Clay has already made. "I'll have a contract drawn up that allows you to live in your home for as long as it stands." Frank McQuay's mind is already drafting the document so in no improvements or repairs will be allowed, hastening the shack's deterioration. There will be no mention of the outhouse, only the physical footprint of the shack and a narrow path to and from the bay will be for Miss Buchanan's use. All else will come under the plow. *Under these depravities, I'll wager she'll abandon the property completely within 60 days.*

Frank McQuay closely watches Anna's face as the wheels in her head are turning, being swayed by the prospect of living in her home without the worry of mortgage payments. She can live as she always has, almost. As with all hunters wanting to bring in that wary bird, the lure must be just right, the decoy real, or at least perceived as real. The bird must trust the decoy to be honest about safe waters. Frank McQuay sweetens the deal, "And, I'm also willing to offer you a small stipend, a percentage of the profits from the crops that will grow in place of the marsh and fast lands." This is another piece of genius. Offer that which will never be. These lands, folded into his other holdings will be swamped, not with sparkling or brackish water, but with current debt, and will be used, on paper, to dump all expenses. Profit and loss is an equation to be manipulated by Frank McQuay as he sees fit.

Anna's thoughts race with excitement, *I can keep my home and be paid. It's a miracle...and too good to be true.* Anna glances past father to son. William is miserable. His hat is in his hands, the rim's fine curve is being crushed by fingers twisting it. The cause is not only his father's curt dismissal, but from worry...paddle away.

"Mr. McQuay, I'd as soon lie to you as spit in your face, but as it doesn't matter, I'll speak the truth. I don't know much of financial matters, and maybe that's my father's fault, but I do know this land. So before I decide to accept your offer, I need you to answer my questions. Are you going to cut down all the trees?"

"Yes, cut 'em and burn 'em to make way."

"And the marsh, are you going to drain it?"

"Yes, of course. My workers will dig trenches. Soggy soil never produced a salable plant."

"The streams and pond?"

"We'll divert the streams at the highway into the culverts and trenches, and then fill in the pond with dirt.

Anna is horrified by this vision of barren land. What will be left is a single crop, maybe two, if there is a rotation, in place of plants and animals too numerous and diverse to name. The comparison is life in abundance to sterility, a palette of colors scraped clean except for one. Anna wonders...

Where will the otters play?

Where will the butterflies rest between dances?

Where will the muskrats build their lodges, and from what?

"What about the ducks and geese? When they come off the bay, where will they find shelter and food if all of this is gone?" Anna asks, as above all other concerns, the answer to this last question is critical to her final decision.

"They can find some place else to go," Frank says flippantly.

William cringes, knowing at least one thing about Anna, and that is to a Buchanan the wildfowl is life. Take everything else away and a Buchanan will still survive, but without the birds' coming and going, the pulsing blood of Buzzards Glory, without the wildfowl's sociable chatter during the day and eerie calls in the night, all that remains is an empty body. There is no soul, no character, and no charm, just a void that is equal to death.

Frank McQuay does not know this. His measure of value, what is important to him is determined at the bottom of an account book. Value to Anna is her father's way of life. What is important is the way her mother saw the world around her—magical.

Choosing sides, a swirling gust of wind inserts itself into the middle of the negotiations. It carries the aroma of salt and iodine, the breath of the bay and marsh. This was Anna's first breath and her parents' last.

Squaring her shoulders Anna answers, "No. You cannot have this land." These words taste sweet as they roll across her tongue.

"Don't be stupid. You're going to lose it to me or to someone else," Frank McQuay spits out. He is tired of niceties. Business is cutthroat. If this foolish girl wants to cut her own, well, she is already holding the knife.

"Then I'll lose it, but I won't sell it or give it away. Now I think you should leave." Without conscious thought, Anna pushes up the long sleeves on her coverall. Blood rushes to William's head, causing him to nearly faint as the golden glint of the bracelet he gave Anna reflects the sun. Frank McQuay no longer sees the shine of the sharpened blade but his wife's treasured bracelet.

Believing their discussion is concluded, Anna turns on her heel with Beauty dutifully at her side.

Tasting both her own blood from biting her lip and grit from being held face down in the dirt, Anna hears Frank McQuay's growls between Beauty's aggressive barks, "How you stole it I can't imagine, but you're finished on this land." With his full weight upon her, Anna is unable to breath. Fading into unconsciousness, her last sensation is the gold bracelet being stripped from her wrist.

Terrified that his grip on Beauty's neck will slip, giving her freedom to use her gnashing teeth against him or his father, William holds onto her fur with desperation. Backing toward the Buick as his father climbs in to rev the irritable engine, his last heart-wrenching glimpse of the girl he loves is her body slowly curling into the fetal position. With his grip slipping, and using his last ounce of strength, William throws Beauty to give himself an instant to escape, a moment to leap into the Buick that his father already has rolling.

Looking to his father, who holds the bracelet in his left hand, William pants, "That didn't go as rehearsed."

Dazed and feeling his cheek swelling, William finds himself lying in the backseat of the Buick that is parked next to their home. His father stands over him, rubbing the back of his right hand, clenching and unclenching his fingers. William shivers as he looks into the evil darkness of his father's unflinching stare while listening to the sweetness of his singsong words, "Dorothy dear, I have a surprise for you."

Beauty follows Anna's footprints that lead around the corner of the shed after returning from chasing the vehicle with its two vile occupants down the drive, all the way to the paved road, keeping to its left side so that her good eye could keep its spinning wheels in focus. Coming to the open door, Beauty finds Anna with the spokeshave and a rectangular block of pine in her hands, her face smudged with dirt, and her lip bloodied.

"They're gone?" Anna asks Beauty who barks affirmative. "Then we've got a lot of work to do."

Anna pushes the shaping tool across the block, ignoring the tears that fall onto it. She knows there is a canvasback body under the excess wood, and only by revealing it does she have a chance to save her home.

Carrying her precious cargo, the drake in her left hand, the hen in her right, Anna's forearms ache as she holds the two mallards away from her body. She had departed her marsh home for town before noon, holding the two decoys in the palms of her hands so as not to smudge the fresh paint still drying. Anna had carved all night and painted all morning, stopping only twice. The first was for a trip to the outhouse with the time spent in contemplation that lasted longer than anticipated. In her exhaustion she had fallen asleep, and if not for Beauty's rousing barks, Anna would still be snoozing, sitting on the throne with her coverall scrunched around her ankles. The second break was to brew a half kettle of he-man coffee to prevent a repeat of the first, though its aftertaste was bitter without her father to share it with.

Walking down South Washington from Revolution, two of Havre de Grace's many streets whose name was inspired by patriotism, Anna enters the long shadow of Harford Memorial Hospital,[90] the former grand Victorian home of the George A. Baker family. Prior to 1912, when the Bakers strode the halls of this 21-room, multi-floored leviathan, Anna secretly wondered what it would be like to live there—all that space. She had tried to befriend one of the pretty little Baker girls, hoping to be invited to their home to play, but the welcome mat never materialized. Now as a hospital, with room after room of sick or injured, some taking advantage of the wraparound porch to convalesce in the sun or shade, Anna hopes never to enter its doors. Then for a painful moment a *what if* question lands heavy on her shoulders. *What if she somehow had gotten her father to the hospital, would he have lived?* The question is unfair as are all *what if* questions asked after the fact. Anna knows God does not give "Do overs," but as Umbrella George believes to the point of infecting others, God will grant us the strength to get past the *what if* and overcome the *what is*.

Exiting the shadow, Anna passes two ladies on a leisurely stroll. They glance at Anna and her wooden baggage, but their gaze is neither condemning nor long enough to imply that she is worth a second thought, denying Anna a satisfying pronouncement that her father was innocent of the charge of

---

90 Harford Memorial Hospital. In 1910, Mrs. Mattie Baker Thomas sold her family's 21-room Havre de Grace mansion for $10,500 to a group headed by General Murray Vandiver for the purpose of establishing the first hospital in Harford County. The hospital opened New Year's Day of 1912. By 1944, a new brick hospital was opened on the property abutting the Victorian original.

murder. Continuing along the sidewalk where ash trees line the way to her destination, beads of perspiration run down Anna's back despite the late afternoon breeze that gently rustles the fresh leaves on the thin, skyward reaching branches. Her hands are moist, slippery against the horseshoe keels Anna has hammered into the decoys' bottoms. Entering through the picket fence gate of the Barnes' residence, Anna's stomach gurgles, but it is not the rumble of hunger. It is her unsettled nerves that are twisting her innards into knots and causing her to sweat. Anna has helped her father fill numerous orders for decoys; carving a mallard head, rounding a goose body, sanding a widgeon's tail, and adding touch-up paint to a multi-colored wood duck. They were a good team, working together, usually in silence unless she got it wrong, and then her father would instruct in the refinements of bill curvature, or the mixing of paint so that the feathering of brush strokes along the speculum and tail feathers created realism. What Anna has come to offer, proof of her skills for sale, are, but for the roughed out heads, solely the product of Anna Buchanan.

The mallards are good but are they good enough?

Mrs. Barnes, a robust woman in all regards, is within a year or two of the age Anna's mother would be if she had lived. Her physical size would lead the uninformed to believe that sloth and gluttony were her vices, but to her family and neighbors, the openly spoken jest is God made her that large to contain all the love that fills and then flows from the vessel that is her body. Though, not a soul mentions, except as an accolade, that Mrs. Barnes' perfume has the familiar essence of oatmeal cookies. This is the inviting aroma Anna finds herself inhaling as she is enfolded within Mrs. Barnes' heavy arms, to be mashed against watermelon bosoms, while tears of sympathy freely fall, "Oh Anna. Dear sweet Anna. I'm so sorry I wasn't able to attend your father's funeral. I've been in Baltimore at my sister's and only returned this morning."

Anna cannot prevent the silent tears from rolling down her cheeks. The freshness of her father's death, her attack on the insensitive constable, the impending foreclosure, and the proposition by the McQuays that led to the revelation of the source of William's gift to her, he having stolen it, is all too crushing, one heaped upon the other. Mrs. Barnes pulls back. She wipes Anna's tears with the softest of fingers, as her too-big teeth, even for her immense smile that accentuates every laugh line, imparts a gentle strength and truth, "Those who knew your father know that he was a good man."

Before Anna can respond with an appreciative, "Thanks," Mrs. Barnes changes the subject, "My, what do you have with you?"

"A pair of mallards," Anna holds up the drake and hen for inspection.

"I can see that, darling. I'm not completely blind," Mrs. Barnes removes her thick spectacles from the pocket of her flowered housedress. "They are gorgeous. You certainly went the extra mile on the details."

"I'm hoping Mr. Barnes will approve of my work and place an order," Anna's voice softens, "Like he used to do with my father." Not wanting pity work, Anna refrains from sharing her desperate need to raise money to save her home.

"Well, if he doesn't he's a dang fool. Those are pretty enough to place on the mantel."

"I hope they're good enough to shoot over," Anna replies, wondering, *what use is a decoy on the mantel?*

"He's out back in the carriage house with Florence, and I believe I saw Mr. Currier stroll that way a while ago. Go on back, dear. I'll bring out some lemonade and cookies in a few minutes."

The sounds of industry and enjoyment come from the open doors of the rusty-red and brown carriage house. It is creation at its purest. Grating zzz-zzz-zzz of cedar blocks being cut to length, rhythmic sscra-sscra-sscra of shaving and scraping away of square edges, and the swoosh-bang of a hammer as it arcs through the air to pound in lead keels to craft a working decoy, mix with laughter to draw Anna into a dust-filled structure framed with the contentment of productivity. The two-seater carriage had been permanently exiled to the side yard, its void replaced years ago with worktables and row after row of shelving on three walls that hold a multitude of imitation wildfowl going through genesis. On the lowest shelf are blocks of wood in varying sizes for different species: from duck to goose to swan. On the lower to middle shelves are bodies carved to shape, but lacking heads. Sitting atop them all lay the essence of the birds to be: bodies with heads sanded smooth, all leaning to the right with weights attached so their lives on the water will be upright. All they lack is the color, that which is the spirit of their being, and of course eyes to see who they work for. These finished specimens are placed on the higher shelves, at the creator's eye level, to marvel for a brief moment before they are carted away by the huntsman who commissioned the rig.

Approaching the open double-swing-out doors, Anna is puzzled by the companionship of the two similar, yet polar men before her. Sam and Jim to her father, Mr. Barnes and Mr. Currier to her, are best of friends for as long as Anna has known them. Though to an outsider, due to their 30-year age difference, they appear to be father-son, but as Sam's hair is coal black and Jim's is Scotch-Irish red, parentage would certainly be called into question. Therefore, mentor-apprentice better fits the relationship. Both men hunt, fish, guide sports occasionally and are known for consistency in carving decoys that are sought after throughout the Susquehanna Flats region. They are identical in all respects except two—Mr. Barnes attends St. John's Episcopal Church and is a law-abiding, chip off the block of a father who took the Duck Police oath, and dreams of one day becoming Johnny Law himself; Mr. Currier attends the United Methodist Church and is a part-time duck broker who yearns for the days before market hunting became illegal. Anna assumes there are many heated arguments between these men over religion and the law, the former are the offspring of God, and the latter is the product of politics. In her lifetime, she has witnessed arguments turn into bloody brawls, all ending with cursed vows to never speak to, "That damn ignorant fool," but with the first flutter of wing feathers, these same men are sitting a blind together. This proves the old adage that a good friend, like a good hunting partner, is a rare thing, and if the two are found in one person, any difference becomes inconsequential.

Mr. Currier, leaning precariously backward on an ancient chair with one too many cracks in the weathered seat, referred to as the butt pincher, balances against the door frame. His hands, working autonomously of his brain, whittle away with a pocket knife at a piece of wood that is too small for a decoy head, but perfect as a future duck call, "That bass, a big mouth for sure, as it splashed green and yellow had to be at least a 10-pounder, if it was an ounce, to have snapped my rod."

Bent over his nicked and scarred workbench, Mr. Barnes has his back to his tale-telling friend as he twists a canvasback head onto the dowel protruding from a body that is progressing through its evolution, "Sounds like a whopper, Jim."

Taking the bait, Mr. Currier replies, "I've rarely seen a larger fish."

"No. I meant your story," Mr. Barnes guffaws, slapping his knee to raise a cloud of sweet-smelling cedar dust that had come to rest in the weave of his new Levi Strauss & Co.[91] pants.

It is Florence, taking a break from sweeping, per her mother's request to keep father's workshop tidy, who upon seeing Anna approach the carriage house, is distracted from a dream-like gaze at her left hand. Dropping her broom, Florence, usually shy and reserved as she too slowly transitions through her lanky and awkward late teen years, rushes past her father, and

---

91 Levi Strauss & Co. Formed in 1853 by Levi Strauss (1829-1902) and his two brothers, Jonas and Louis. Levi was a Bavarian immigrant who arrived in San Francisco in 1850 during the gold rush to sell textiles. Learning of the miners' need for durable pants, Levi hired a tailor to make garments out of tent canvas. Later, denim was substituted, and for strength, copper riveting was used on pocket seams. Today, the company headquartered in San Francisco is the world's largest maker of pants.

nearly topples Mr. Currier to share news that she hopes Anna has yet to hear, "Joe finally got up the nerve."

Becoming excited and bouncing on the balls of her feet, but unsure as to why, Anna asks, "The nerve to do what?"

Offering her left hand, fingers wiggling, Florence shows off the narrow gold band, "I'm to be Mrs. Joseph Davis."

Hugging Florence with sincere affection, Anna asks, "When's the special day?"

A cloud passes across Florence's face, dimming her joy and replacing the light in her eyes with the darkness of fear, "As soon as he returns. He's with the Blue and Gray,[92] training before being sent to France. I so wish he had gone to train in Aberdeen[93] then he could visit on weekends before he ships out."

"Why didn't he?"

"Said he wanted to serve as a machine gunner under Chief."

"I'm sure he'll return soon with many tales of heroism."

"Joe told me not to worry because, even in the face of court martial, he would always wear his lucky hunting socks; one red and one blue."

"Then the only ones who need to fear are the Jerries."[94]

Stepping out of the carriage house, Mr. Barnes wipes the dust from his hands and face with a gun-oil stained red handkerchief, and then stuffs it into his back pocket, "What do we owe the honor of this visit, Anna?"

Anna's giddy, girlish expression changes to a serious, though nervous business face. She has come to make a deal, a sale, to a man whose livelihood requires attention to detail—no foolishness. His product is his reputation. If the wildfowl do not toll to the decoys he offers for sale, next year there will be no orders.

"Mr. Barnes," Anna begins, trying to swallow the lump in her throat as she presents her mallards, "now that my father has passed, I'd like to offer

---

92 Blue and Gray Division. The adopted name of the 29th Division out of Camp McClellan. It is a Southern camp named for a Northern general. The adopted name of Blue and Gray was a respectful acknowledgement that garnered a special esprit de corps between the men from families who were still proud of their historical support of either the North or the South during the U.S. Civil War.

93 Aberdeen Proving Grounds (APG). During World War I by presidential order, the U.S. Army took possession of nearly 70,000 acres and more than 100 miles of waterfront along the western shore of the Chesapeake Bay for weapons testing and personnel training. APG is located south of Swan Creek Point and west of Spesutie Island.

94 Jerries. Slang. German soldiers.

my services. I carved and painted these two since last night. I'm fast, and if I may quote Mrs. Barnes, 'They're gorgeous.'"

This last statement brings a soft chuckle from Mr. Currier as he has never heard anyone refer to a decoy as gorgeous. Functional, balanced, sturdy, and rugged are usually the catchwords to compliment a decoy, but gorgeous—never. Though, as he folds the blade of his pocketknife and steps forward to examine Anna's handiwork, he admits to himself that she did put more work into the feather detail than he ever has.

Giving Anna the respect her offer deserves, but also requiring of her work the quality he expects, Mr. Barnes responds, "Barring the prospect of these winning any beauty contest, granting they do possess the likeness of mallards, how do they ride?"

Only the rustle of leaves in the branches above their heads and the clink, clink, clink of Mrs. Barnes stirring ice in the glass pitcher of fresh squeezed lemonade in the kitchen is heard. Anna's hesitation in answering is the sad admission that she does not know. The pinkish color in her cheeks drains away, leaving only ashen embarrassment. In her haste to finish the pair, the few extra minutes she allotted herself was spent scratch texturing the green head of the drake and blending the hen's breast and wing feathers, Anna forgot the dreaded rain barrel test.

"Florence, pick out any one of the finished canvasbacks," Mr. Barnes instructs his daughter, and then leading the procession, he carries Anna's mallards to the corner of the house where the roof's gutter spigot drains into an old pickle barrel. "Drop it in, Florence."

With an undignified plop, Samuel T. Barnes' canvasback splashes into the barrel, bobbing briefly, rolling right to left, and then quickly settles down, upright, buoyant, balanced, and eager for the report of a shotgun. Mr. Currier nods, expecting nothing less from a man who has honed his craft for decades. Floating before the four is the standard that Anna, by her solicitation, states she can equal. With reverence, Florence lifts the canvasback from the water.

"Let's see what you're selling, Anna," Mr. Barnes drops the hen in. "Ladies first."

The hen bobs happily, enthusiastic, quickly lifting her head out of the water, as if scanning the sky in search of friends to join her for an afternoon swim. A good start. Anna begins to sigh with relief, but her breath catches, as her decoy droops in the rear so that the tail is nearly submerged.

"Hmm... What do you think?" Mr. Barnes asks as he pushes the hen around the barrel, trying to make the wooden bird rest properly.

"Too much weight toward the rear," Anna says, attempting to keep her voice neutral, business-like, and refusing to allow tears to form in the corners of her eyes.

Lifting the hen out of the barrel, Mr. Barnes tests the handsome drake. It is a striking specimen, but because of his wooden heart, all the ladies that he would attract, their lives will be ruined. With an upside-down dunking, Mr. Barnes submerges the male, and then pulls his hand back. Believing itself a diving duck returning to the surface after feeding on the roots of eelgrass, the confused mallard pops to the surface, its perfectly placed eyes showing surprise at the appraising audience surrounding him. Florence bites her lower lip, wanting to say that she heard it sneeze to clear its accurately detailed nostrils, but levity at this moment would not be appreciated.

Mrs. Barnes watches the trials from the screened back porch. Her lungs are full of air that she is afraid to breathe out as she wills the decoy to ride high and level. Her hands hold a wooden tray, inlaid with intricately carved pieces of wood depicting geese flying past Concord Point lighthouse in winter. Topping the tray are summer's taste treats.

Relaxing on its wide belly, ignoring the settling ripples bouncing off the rusty metal rim of the barrel, the drake is a success with a promising future in the eyes of Anna, Florence, and Mrs. Barnes, the color slowly returning to Anna's cheeks. Though looking between Mr. Barnes and Mr. Currier prevents Anna from premature celebration as both men stare at the decoy, maybe expecting that it should spread its wooden wings to take flight... *what are they waiting for?*

As with a three-scoop ice cream, stacked high on a hot summer day, it does not happen all at once, but slowly, imperceptive at first to the naked eye. The sun's warming rays takes its toll on the round balls of frozen delight, and only an attentive person will observe the slippage, the first signs of structural failure, as what appeared to be perfection in its creation, leans enough to cause a toppling, followed by a child's wail.

Anna does not wait for Mr. Barnes' words of rejection. She lifts her leeward tilting drake from the barrel, saying, "I'm sorry for taking up your valuable time." Accepting the hen back, her two failures good only as fire wood, Anna strides away with Florence's plaintive words, "But they were so pretty," meant to be a plea to her father, but only sting as Anna remembers Delbert's words spoken as frozen stutters: "Only men need fancy painted decoys. Birds toll to anything that resembles."

With eyes blurry with moisture, Anna fumbles with the latch on the front gate. Its simple lift and pull mechanism conspiring to keep her imprisoned with folk who had the courtesy not to laugh at her regrettable attempt to be... *to be what? Like her father?*

"Where's that stupid Umbrella George now?" Anna mumbles as a salty drop rolls over her upper lip and into her mouth. In her humiliation, and frustration with the taunting gate, Anna does not hear her name being called until his firm hand takes hold of her shoulder, startling her, causing her to jump, and losing her grip on the drake, it dropping to the brick walk with a solid thump.

"Whoa. Easy there," Mr. Currier says, bending to pick up the decoy. "Let me look at these a minute."

"Please, Mr. Currier, don't pity me. These can't be placed with any rig. I'll have to start over."

"You are correct about that and I never pity anyone."

"Oh," Anna says, actually hoping for a little pity, but instead of soppy commiseration by Mr. Currier, his straight talk is somehow comforting, possibly because his tone reminds Anna of a younger version of her father.

"The rain barrel proved these are unbalanced and of no use for hunting over water. You could rip out the keels, putty the holes and reset them and I suppose they'd be acceptable, but I have an itch that says you'd be wasting your time, and maybe your talent."

"You've lost me," Anna wipes away her tears. Tears that seem to be without end these days.

"Refreshments are served," Mrs. Barnes calls from the back porch, her high pitch voice in competition with a squeaky, screen door hinge.

"Anna," Mr. Currier places a protective arm around her shoulders. "What I'm proposing will sound like the babblings of a man who has had one too many shots of blue pig,[95] but its something my wife has been pestering me to do for her, and if you're willing to come back and share a glass or two of Mrs. Barnes' finest, we can discuss what I believe you have a gift for."

As Anna walks back to the carriage house and into the circle of early summer merriment, the shortcomings in her decoys forgotten with the first bite of oatmeal-raisin cookie, she silently asks forgiveness of Umbrella George, wherever he may be wandering in his efforts to spread the Good Word.[96]

Constable Jenkins sits in semi-darkness on the top step of the stairs leading down to the basement cells. The cool air radiating from the thick

---

95 Blue pig. Slang. Whiskey.

96 Good Word. A colloquialism for a lay preacher who freely shares his knowledge of the Holy Bible and inspiration derived from it.

stone walls brings a measure of relief from the unrelenting heat generated at his core, made unbearable by the layers of insulating fat. As he listens to the whispering of the teenage girl in the cell, the same cell that confined her father, and the woman who believes her nocturnal visit to the street-level window is clandestine, each word uttered, either punctuated with sobs or soothing encouragement, is clearly understood by the constable's keen, some say dog-like hearing.

Frank McQuay had properly filed the complaint for theft yesterday. The constable had every legal right, duty, and obligation to search out and arrest Anastasia Nicole Buchanan, but for a reason yet to be ciphered out, he smelled a rat, and so found numerous other tasks to occupy his time that subsequently delayed the hunt. Constable Jenkins' conflict arose from the years of association with the Buchanan family. He remembered, as if it were yesterday, a bright sun-filled spring day, when the newlyweds arrived by steamer from Baltimore to occupy property Clay had previously purchased. The changing laws did redefine Clay's vocation as that of a poacher, possibly turning him into a killer, though for reasons the constable was not privy to, the charges were dismissed. Clay was not a thief in the traditional sense, and by any definition that omitted his outlaw gunning, he was an honorable man who instilled into his daughter the same values of morality and citizenry, but there is the rub, the heart of the constable's conflict.

Can a man be a law-breaker and be moral and honorable at the same time?

Does necessity trump the law?

Should the daughter be stained by the sins of the father or whitewashed by his virtue?

Using his checkered handkerchief, a perpetually damp rag, to wipe his perspiring forehead, a forehead beginning to pound with this mental wrestling, Constable Jenkins divests himself of the sudden responsibility of coming to a decision by the use of his lawman's motto: "All I do is arrest 'em. The court decides guilt or innocence." With this pronouncement comes the skipjack's boom to knock him off his solid footing.

If I abdicate judgment to the court and it released Clay, he had to be innocent.

If that stain is removed, all that remains is necessity.

If Anna stole the bracelet, was it out of necessity?

The question that causes the stench of rat to rise again is: *why did Anna keep the bracelet?*

Remaining seated on the step, the flickering flame from the lantern wired to the wall at the bottom of the stairs remains to dance on the insides of his closed eyelids, as the constable listens to Anna plead with Olivia to bring her instruments of her father's craft. There is no talk of her crime, only the looming loss of her home to the bank or to the McQuays. Anna's explanation for her need of these tools at first seem to be folly, but as the constable considers the variety of knickknacks his wife has purchased throughout their 24 years of marriage to pretty-up their home, Anna's purpose may not be crazy after all...financially risky...but not altogether crazy.

For the first time in a long career, Constable Jenkins wonders *what if* he had left for home a few minutes earlier, or finished one more report, then he would not have seen Anna and Florence on Washington Street, arm in arm, with a skip in their step, chatting as school girls do, but there she was, and he had to do his job. Anna's only words as she was wrenched from Florence's embrace and placed under arrest were to Florence.

"Please tell Olivia what has happened." Anna did not fight Constable Jenkins. She did not scream or cry as she was placed in the front seat of the town's official vehicle recently repaired. She did not appear to blame him for what he was doing. There was a fire in her eyes, but it was not kindled by hate. It was a fire of purpose fueled by hope.

Constable Jenkins rubs his tired eyes and then opens them to stare at the two decoys sitting on the floor outside the cell bars: mallards, a drake and a hen, their heads touching, a sign of intimacy, as they lean toward each other on horseshoe keels that he overheard Anna say were positioned incorrectly. Hoisting himself up with a grunt, Constable Jenkins decides to interrupt the Stewarts' dinner.

It is the clatter of metal against stone that wakes Anna from her troubled sleep. She had laid down around midnight, knowing that it would take Olivia until morning to travel to the marsh shack and back, she having reluctantly agreed, saying, "It's against my better judgment to smuggle you a knife." What Anna did not know is that Constable Jenkins had intercepted Olivia, 20 paces from the cell window, warning in no uncertain terms, "If I find a single item in Miss Buchanan's cell that I didn't personally authorize, you will be sharing the cell with her."

Sitting up with a wool blanket wrapped around her to keep off the early morning chill and wiping the crusty deposits from the corner of her eyes, Anna's mood is a mixture of worry and optimism. These contradictory emotions are the result of dreams that were jumpy and without cohesiveness, understandable in her predicament. How long a dream actually lasts, Anna doesn't know. Her legs, however, are exhausted from running down dark trails with towering cattails that swayed in a breeze she couldn't feel, sloshing through deep grasses that hid sucking muck and leaping streams that crisscrossed themselves, never making it to their destination. The course she set was familiar. There were bright eyes of critters staring at her as she passed, and a chorus of noises from crickets, toads, and screech owls, all directing her footsteps down paths that led nowhere. These paths that Anna thought she knew well, conspired to prevent her from reaching here home. When she retraced her steps in frustration, she repeatedly came upon the same party. It was a banquet, some kind of social function with ladies and gentlemen all gussied up. Chandeliers hung without support from the night sky to illuminate marble floors. The only walls that separated Anna from the parties were the darkness of the marsh that was impenetrable. Anna instinctively knew she was not welcome at any of these celebrations, but she also knew that she was a part of every toast.

A deep breath full of mouth-watering aromas entice Anna to rise, as a Sunday breakfast of fresh-baked biscuits browned flaky, covered with chunks of melting yellow butter, all surrounded in a sea of thick gravy, cover the metal tray to overflowing outside the cell. A tall glass of frothy milk sits next to the tray on the floor. They are compliments of Mrs. Jenkins.

Missing, are the mallard decoys. The drake and hen have been replaced by two dozen, three-by-three inch square blocks of pine, a new carving knife, a set of paints in a rainbow of two-ounce glass bottles, and standing, bristles upright in a tin cup are four paint brushes with heads ranging from wide to pin point. All items are stamped with the J.R. Stewart's Country Store name. They are compliments of...

Constable Jenkins exits the jail as two deputies are reporting for work.

"What 'cha got there, boss?" one deputy asks, his tone accusatory, though amused.

"Need 'em to replace two lost at anchor," responds the constable as he climbs into his official vehicle, pressing his foot against the starter button to bring the engine to life.

"Where you going?" asks the other deputy, prodding and verbally poking his supervisor, "Just in case somebody asks."

"The only somebody that I answer to is on her way to church, and I've already told her." Spinning the steering wheel to make a U-turn in the middle of Union Street, Constable Jenkins drives south, turns right on Revolution Street and then heads out of town. Passing horse-drawn wagons, carriages, and other combustion-engine vehicles that are slowly multiplying and replacing nags ready for retirement, each conveyance is filled with families wearing their Sunday best. Tipping his hat, or waving cordially, the constable is confident that he will find the Joiners within their marsh encampment and amenable to looking after the Buchanan residence while Anna is absent and it remains hers.

Judge Hathaway's courtroom is populated with individuals who are paid to be in attendance, are compelled by reason of their detainment, or are supporters or detractors of the accused. Criminals whose offenses do not rise to the level of lechery, conflagration, or homicide, do not tantalize the masses, leaving empty the majority of the spectator seats, and the courtroom to grind though the monotony of infractions, petty misdemeanors, vandalism, and at the summit of ignored offenses are theft and burglary.

At this level of criminality, the culprit is usually home grown. He is either a neighbor, an old school-days' friend, business patron, drinking pal, or hunting partner, making these procedures low key, informal to the point that each member of the judiciary feels compelled to apologize to the defendant upon imposition of sentence. And with the relocation of the Janus prosecutor to New York City, where he felt his legal acumen would be better appreciated, the court is relieved from deal making. If you are innocent, the scales of Lady Justice will indicate so. If you are guilty, the weight of the law tips to bring punishment down upon you, or so it is designed.

The replacement prosecutor, a newcomer to Havre de Grace hails from Chincoteague Island, one of Virginia's outer banks that protects the peninsula from the Atlantic's temperament. At age 35, Prosecutor John Hastings-Worth is bewilderingly hairless except for a palm-sized patch of the curliest blond mat in the center of his chest. There is not a wisp upon his head, not a hair to mark his brow, or to bat a lash with. This lack of a manly mane does not stop his wife Nancy, a choir member whose voice rings loudest with joy, from enjoying his oasis of hair. She picks at it when at play, and pulls until the roots give way when she is filled with her husband's passion. A passion that she teasingly jokes about late at night after catching her breath, "All that and we only have one son?"

John Hastings-Worth has two traits that quickly endeared him to the folk of Havre de Grace. The first is his straightforward way of communicating. If a question is asked of John, he will give an answer that leaves no room for debate, but plenty of color for conversation.

Question: "What made you leave Chincoteague Island?"
Answer: "The judge wouldn't allow my Lab, Comet, into the courtroom."

Question: "You seem so relaxed, laid back, so different than most
               lawyers in the courtroom. Why is that?"
Answer: "The law is stuffy and rigid. People don't have to be."

John's second trait is his ability to avoid, even when baited into an
argument as to who are the better decoy carvers: the men of the upper
Chesapeake Bay or those from Chincoteague Island? However, if pressed
into answering this volatile question, John's answer is given as naturally as a
bored yawn from an old retriever waiting for a sport to hit something, "The
best decoy carver is the man who purchased my last drink."

Judge Hathaway sits picking at an infected hangnail on his thumb
while listening to Constable Jenkins describe the arrest of Anastasia Nicole
Buchanan. When the bailiff called the docket, "People of Maryland versus
Buchanan," the judge was surprised, thinking that his judgment of Clay had
been incorrect as to him being an honorable man, though maybe morally off
the straight and narrow path. Then, when the daughter was led in, sadness
gripped the judge as he remembered hearing about Mr. Buchanan's untimely
death, and now, so quickly has his offspring fallen into delinquency. His
Honor has seen this before. A family living on the edge is pushed over by a
little bad luck, though the death of the breadwinner is a far cry from a little.
What the judge has not before witnessed in his courtroom is a defendant
who is ignoring proceedings that will determine where she will be residing
for the next six months: home, a jail cell, or in the case of one not 18, a
reformatory.

When Constable Jenkins escorted Miss Buchanan into the courtroom,
he whispered into the bailiff's ear, who in turn, nodded with a shrug
of indifference. Sitting at the defense table, focused on her task, Anna is
painting small objects, the glass paint jars spread in an arc in front of her.
From the judge's chair, he is uncertain as to the nature of these miniature
items. Judge Hathaway frowns at Anna's public defender, and though his
shrug is the same as the bailiff's, "Call me Clem's" is not from indifference,
but bewilderment.

Anna's serene exterior hides a fear that she is choking on. She fights the
tremors in the hand that holds the pin-point bristle-head brush, that if allowed
to go unchecked would rapidly spread throughout her body to leave her
whimpering, curled under the defendant's table in a pool of tears. Permitting
Anna to function is a phrase repeated for the 10 millionth time since her
arrest. A phrase thought lost to memory, spoken only once by Olivia when
attempting to calm herself after dropping and breaking every bottle in the
last case of whiskey in front of a tavern full of thirsty men, "*Que sera sera.*"
Later, Olivia explained that, "It was Spanish for *what will be will be,* so what
is the point of getting upset or worrying yourself sick." Deeper still, as the

foundation, are Anna's mother's words read from Scripture on what turned out to be one of her last days:

> "Therefore I say unto you, Take no thought for your life, what ye shall eat, or what ye shall drink; nor yet for your body, what ye shall put on. Is not the life more than meat, and the body than raiment? Behold the fowls of the air: for they sow not, neither do they reap, nor gather into barns; yet your heavenly Father feedeth them. Are ye not much better than they? Which of you by taking thought can add one cubit unto his stature? And why take ye thought for raiment? Consider the lilies of the field, how they grow; they toil not, neither do they spin."[97]

"If it's inevitable...concentrate on the details." Anna mumbles.

"Did you say something?" Clem asks, his voice barely a whisper as he listens to the questions asked of Constable Jenkins by the prosecutor.

"During your interrogation of the accused, did she admit to stealing the bracelet in question?"

With an embarrassed expression, redness flushes the constable's already moist cheeks, as he realizes he has not asked Anna a single question about the theft or how she came to possess the bracelet. Choosing to fudge his answer, wanting to keep his professional slip to himself, and his hard-ass reputation in tact, he replies, "The defendant did not answer a single question."

"Thank you. No further questions." John Hastings-Worth ambles back to his seat.

"Cross examination?" the judge asks of Clem.

"Yes, your Honor," Clem quickly acknowledges the question. His thoughts are clear with the gears turning smoothly without the clouding and corroding effects of alcohol. After his victory in the Buchanan murder trial, his value in the community, along with his self-esteem had risen substantially. It may be true that it was not a silvery tongue that persuaded the jury to return a not guilty verdict, but the result was the same. Clay had been freed and Clem was the attorney of record. A success of this magnitude gave Clem the courage to look in the mirror, and he did not like what he saw. Self-improvement was needed, but the steps taken were small and realistic, beginning with his excessive drinking. Excluding the celebratory blind drunkenness following the trial, Clem has not consumed a drop of any intoxicant, though each day is a monumental struggle and each night he sweats himself to sleep. Clay's death, the demise of the living, breathing symbol of Clem's success, was a blow that sent him marching toward Tavern Bouvard. If Clem had not encountered Umbrella George, who was standing

---

97 Matthew 6:25-28. Jesus' teachings. *Holy Bible*, King James Version, 1987 printing. Public domain.

quietly on the corner, as if waiting for him, Clem would have returned to his inebriation. Instead, the two men walked for hours along the Chesapeake shore, discussing the arrival of the osprey from South America, the departure of the tundra swans, and the many ways to prepare yellow perch that are just now making their spawning runs in the upper tidal ends of the bay's rivers and streams. To Clem's surprise, Umbrella George never mentioned God, or that life goes on, but to his relief, Clem saw God's handiwork and felt His presence in everything, comforting and strengthening him through the crisis.

Where is the evidence of theft or proof of possession of stolen property? Clem asks himself, and then addresses the constable, "When you apprehended Miss Buchanan, did you recover the bracelet?"

"No. It was recovered by the individual who it was stolen from, Mr. Frank McQuay."

"Constable, independent of the complaint filed by the victim, do you have any knowledge or evidence that a crime, a theft, a burglary occurred?"

Prosecutor Hastings-Worth grins inwardly, admiring the tack the defense attorney is taking, obviously hoping to make this a he said/she said case. That explains the defense attorney's request for a judge trial and the reliance on the judge to be blind to power and influence—risky. Loosening his tie, the prosecutor scratches Comet behind his ears as the Labrador lolls against his master's leg.

"No," answers the constable, "but the complaint lists both Frank and William McQuay as witnesses to the bracelet's recovery."

Clem shuffles through sheaves of paper to locate his copy of the complaint, where as he returns to stand before the constable, he flips the page to the signature lines. "Constable Jenkins, please tell the court how many signatures are at the bottom of this page."

"One. Does it matter?"

"Maybe. Maybe not. Thank you."

Choosing a home that is one block from the elementary school, eight blocks from the court, John Hastings-Worth, in his capacity as a father, has the privilege of walking his nine-year-old son, Paul, accompanied by Comet, to school before his leisurely stroll to work. Dust may collect and scuff marks may gather on his shined shoes, but these are small annoyances for the joy of spending a few extra father-son minutes together. This morning, the brightness of the sun made John appreciate that he was walking westward, but also, its warming rays tugged at the strings that always drew him to explore the countryside, savoring a new-found creek or an isolated pond for a cool dip...in violation of the swimsuit code. In his capacity as a prosecutor, John believes in judicial economy. Get to the point. Do not waste the court's time, especially when the out-of-doors is calling. John knows who his next witness needs to be.

Ignored until this moment, sitting behind the prosecutor in the spectator seats are Frank and William McQuay. Frank is as relaxed as the prosecutor, even under the intense and hate-filled stares of Olivia and Delbert. Frank McQuay's comfort comes from knowing that by lunch a guilty verdict will put an end to Anna Buchanan's tentative hold on her property. Despite Frank McQuay's failure to sway the judge to his point of view in the murder trial causing his application for full membership in the Wellwood Club to be denied, today the court will work to his favor and sweep Anna away as easy as the sledgehammers will knock down her shack. *It's strange how things work themselves out,* muses Frank.

William is miserable. Nanna Maude believed he had taken ill with vomiting and advised that he remain in bed. Frank McQuay placed the back of his hand to William's forehead, and finding no fever, jerked back the covers and ordered his son to get dressed.

"The prosecution calls William McQuay."

Anna does not look up at the calling of William's name, but she feels the stab to her heart, and the breeze as the gate swings open upon his passage from spectator to testifier, taking the solemn oath to tell the truth.

"William," the prosecutor begins, leaning on the wooden box that makes up the witness stand, chummy, as if talking to a neighbor across their adjoining fence, "did you accompany your father to the Buchanan residence as it's indicated in the complaint signed and filed by your father?"

Not looking up, twisting the buttons at the cuff of his jacket sleeve, and wishing he were anywhere but here, William answers, "Yes."

"Did you go there that day because it was suspected that Miss Buchanan had stolen your mother's bracelet?"

"No. We went there to purchase her land."

"Did Miss Buchanan agree to sell?"

"No."

"Now, William, the complaint your father filed states that, 'While at the residence of Anna Buchanan, my son and I observed a gold bracelet on her wrist. I recovered the bracelet, which was the one found to be missing from my wife's jewelry box, and then drove to town to contact the authorities.'" Seeking to corroborate Frank McQuay's statements to close the case, the prosecutor asks the only question required, "Did you observe your father recover your mother's stolen bracelet from Anna Buchanan's wrist?"

"*Que sera sera*...what will be will be," hums Anna as she puts the finishing touches on her cocktail decoys.

William raises his eyes to observe his father, sitting proud, pleased with his accomplishments, and then looks at Anna, who appears to be oblivious which causes William to again taste the bile rising in his throat. Looking back to his hands that are the cause of Anna's suffering today, he is unsure who he hates more, himself or his father. All William has wanted to do is please Anna but he fails time and again. Closing his eyes, William's fingers slowly clench to make fists in preparation for the inevitable battle, "No. I did not see Anna with the bracelet."

John Hastings-Worth shrugs his shoulders...an early lunch.

Comet stretches.

Clem is stunned—Victory!

Anna looks up from her handiwork to gaze with compassion at the frightened boy who does not want to leave the witness stand.

Holding two of Anna's miniscule decoys in the palm of her hand, the bands of the jeweled rings on her fingers slowly disappearing within the pudginess of her fattening fingers, Mrs. McQuay asks, "What kind of ducks are these, Mr. Stewart?"

Stepping down from his ladder after placing tins of canned mackerel on an upper shelf, the proprietor of the country store leans across the display counter to again admire the intricate feather patterns of these one-inch decoys, though except for the thumbtack keel, he should think of these carvings as birds due to their realistic appearance, "This one is a wood duck. You can tell by its distinctive emerald crest that extends beyond the back of the head, and of course, the drake is one of the more colorful birds with a rust bill. He has red eye rings, a green-blue head with white lines running front to back. His neck is white transitioning to a muddy brown breast finely speckled with white. His wings are varying colors of blue, white, and gray. The other bird is not a duck at all, but a swan. Its white body and long curving neck is the give-away.

Mr. Stewart was finishing his last bite of roast beef and baked potato dinner when the firm knocks to his front screen door resounded throughout his gingerbread house. Swallowing, to indicate the meal was completed so as to soften the fierce and fixed look from his wife, Mr. Stewart excused himself. Mrs. Stewart allows no interruption to their family meal. Childless and beyond the age to expect such a miracle, husband and wife live in disappointment, blaming the other for the lack of offspring. Mrs. Stewart, a sprite of a woman with the figure of a 12-year-old boy, turned her embarrassment and disgrace at being barren, regardless of the true cause, to being the perfect housekeeper. Her need to produce, to create perfection, as does God with each child's birth, manifested itself into fastidiousness and intimidation of her spineless husband who believes in turning the other cheek, and that tolerance and understanding instead of a rebuke will eventually cure his shrew of a wife.

The reason that Constable Jenkins required Mr. Stewart to accompany him to re-open the store was irrelevant. The excuse to absent himself from an immaculate house that has long since been a home was the dessert that never materializes on the dinner table. His wife's reasoning is, "Sweets are for children. Do you see any children at this table?"

Allowing the afternoon sun's warm light that shines through the storefront window to accentuate the radiance of the paint, each fine stroke glistening, Mrs. McQuay turns the carved birds in her hand, left and then right, her fingers twitching, anticipating the need to quickly close to catch the birds when they take flight, and then asks, "What would these be used for?"

Not having asked the question himself of Anna, but merely taking them on consignment for her, though always the salesman, and elevating their importance, Mr. Stewart glances around to see if any other customer is within hearing, and as if imparting a secret to not only a highly valued customer, but a person worthy of the information, he whispers, "The artist did not specify their purpose, but stated that ladies of fine households would know what they are for."

Mrs. McQuay hears only two words: artist and ladies, and quickly replies to assert her inclusion as a lady, "I was simply testing you," as she unhooks the gold latch on her crushed leather purse. She places five-dollar bills on the counter, one for each of the 24 decoys. Mr. Stewart is speechless as he carefully wraps each bird in pink tissue paper, and then places them into an empty hatbox. Each of Anna's creations sold for more than double their full size counterpart. Shaking his head, Mr. Stewart knows that when he tells of this sale, the rig carvers will never believe it. Regardless, he certainly will order more from the artist.

"I asked gently, because you know how sensitive Dorothy is, if it was in bad taste to be hosting such a lavish dinner party when so many boys are going off to an uncertain future, war being declared?" Martha confides in her doctor husband as they climb into the front seats of their automobile that is parked under the McQuay's sheltering portico. Her visit was social; his professional. "Naturally, her answer was well reasoned," Martha scoots close to her husband for warmth as with the lateness of the night a chilling dew settles on everything it comes in contact with. "She said, 'It's a family squabble among cousins.[98] The falling out among relations will likely be over before the second toast of the evening, and then we can call it a victory party.'"

"Rather naive if you ask me," Doctor Webster grunts, as he grinds the gears, not quite getting the rhythm of depressing the clutch pedal while at the same time moving the shifter. The automobile lurches forward in fits and starts down the driveway until momentum equals the second gear ratio.

"Be kind," Martha squeezes her husband's arm. "You know Dorothy doesn't concern herself with politics."

"She doesn't seem to concern herself with anything that doesn't concern herself." The four-cylinder engine whines in revolt of the doctor's miss-shift, its high pitch obliterating his words.

"What's that dear?"

"A broken arm, cracked ribs, and facial bruising..."

"Yes, poor William. That must have been a terrible fall."

"Is that what Mrs. McQuay said happened?" The doctor fumbles with the headlamp switch that instantly illuminates the smooth ribbon of road leading to Havre de Grace.

"Well, no. Dorothy was telling me about a new recipe. Apparently, Nanna Maude calls it 'fricasseed duck.' She uses a roux made of flour and bacon drippings, sautéed onions, and then adds water, a secret mushroom sauce, seasons to taste, and simmers everything in a skillet. My mouth is watering imagining its flavor. Dorothy was also excited about the party favors she calls cocktail decoys. She demonstrated how the birds float in the glasses. Dorothy kept pushing them under or flipping them upside-down, and then giggling, actually giggling when the bird popped to the surface and righted itself. She repeated, at least a dozen times, 'The artist is a genius.' I agreed with her sentiment, but as to William's injuries, I just assumed. It seemed obvious how he received them."

---

98 The original three combatants in World War I: England's King George V, Russia's Czar Nicholas II, and Germany's William II were cousins either directly, or through marriage, all descendants of England's Queen Victoria.

"Yes," Doctor Webster places his arm around his wife. "It is obvious how he received them." As a healer, he is supposed to cause no harm to his patient. In this case, the doctor feels no guilt in the perverse, and possibly justifiable pleasure he received with each wince from Frank McQuay, as he tightly applied wraps to Frank's swollen and lacerated knuckles.

Sitting on a rotting stump within a towering stand of cattails, a natural blind at the edge of the bay, Anna relaxes with her Winchester cradled in her arms, her fingertips caressing the carved stock. The September breeze, not yet brisk with winter's chill, still contains remnants of summer as it gently blows Anna's unrestrained hair—no cap needed today. Beauty naps at her feet, her gray muzzle resting on Anna's foot. The proud gander of three strapping goslings sits at the water's edge, patiently waiting for birds of a feather to call in. His mate remains back by the shack within the chicken wire pen to tend the young ones.

Anna knew this to be a fool's errand. It is too early by a month for wildfowl to be arriving from the north. Even without a paper calendar to foretell the day, the weather has yet to produce a mighty blow, and even if it did, the goslings growing fat on tundra insects are still too young to take to the wing to ride the front in. The two scrawny summer ducks that wandered in Anna's direction were not worth the gander's welcoming honk or Anna's second glance. This morning's outing is to scratch a building itch and to test her emotional stability; to put a so-called toe into the waters of winter where there will be no father to rescue her if she falls in too deep, though he is everywhere, and in everything Anna undertakes. His omnipresence is a comforting hug squeezed too tight. With each shadow that catches the corner of her eye, Anna turns, expecting him to materialize. When helping Olivia in the tavern as the third trimester has slowed her step, a gruff or gravelly voice heard from across the room that carries the right inflection will cause Anna to look up from pouring drinks to scan the crowd with hopeful anticipation. It is in these instances that all is right and good as her father is in the world with her. It is the moment when a child is given a gift wrapped with sparkling paper, ribbons, and bows. In the next instant, after the shine of fantasy has been torn away and the lid removed, a crushing despair overwhelms with the knowledge that the box is empty. These are the unintended mind tricks upon the heart of one grieving.

Spring and summer were filled with too much industry for Anna to fully process her father's passing. The necessities of self-preservation interceded, keeping Anna busier than a one-armed woodcutter attempting to use a two-handled saw. The maintenance of her home, keeping the geese, herself, and Beauty fed filled every waking hour with responsibility, the only reward being exhaustion that caused Anna to fall into a dreamless sleep each night. The whirlwind of enterprise was not all chaos, devoid of any pleasure. When Mr. Stewart handed Anna her share of the proceeds, each dollar bill more than she had ever seen or possessed, represented a growing barrier between her and the bank's intent to initiate foreclosure proceedings.

Timothy Ross, wearing the uniform of a doughboy, explained the exceptions to military service are reserved for sons of the well connected, had stopped by four times to check on Anna. He expressed joy and relief for her that surprised Anna when she turned over sufficient funds to bring the mortgage up to date, while promising more. The twinkle in his brown eyes animated his soft face as Anna slapped the stack of bills into his hand with pride in her accomplishment. Then she was ashamed because if it were not for Mr. Currier's suggestion and Constable Jenkins' kindness her situation would be far different. *No one succeeds on his own,* is the sentiment that Anna acknowledges. Then examining the pressed uniform that the bank's messenger was wearing, she wondered how this affable young man could be a soldier, but then again, Anna did not know what soldiering entailed, or what war demanded. Tim, as he had asked her to call him, while sitting on the porch step, spoke of his uncertainty of what to expect. He wished that the bank's president, who has been in England for five months, had not chosen to remain to help in the war effort. Tim believed he could garner favor from him because of the president's distrust of automobiles and the accident that Tim was in. This, Tim believed, made the two of them kindred spirits. The president's intervention might have saved him from service. Regardless, his concern was less for himself, but more for his parents; how they would handle the news if something bad were to happen to him. Anna was aware that Tim never said the word, "Killed."

Except for the cloud of war, Anna enjoyed Tim's visits between bank deliveries. He was a pleasant distraction. Tim was easy on the eyes and genuinely interested in her daily activities. His fascination with Anna rose to the level of shrugging off an occasional afternoon of responsibilities. On his last visit, bank documents remained within the satchel while Tim accompanied Anna into the cattails she now sits within to search for tasty hearts.

Anna's other distraction came in the form of Delbert. There was the purposeful capsizing of the sneak skiff by him while he and Anna were dipping soft shell crabs, his reasoning was plain, "Anna, you looked parched."

After her immediate anger, the two laughed and splashed while Beauty, who remained on shore, barked her encouragement.

Within each activity, Anna finds her father, which brings a smile and a tear, though the reminder of her father that Anna cherishes above all, a tangible product of his existence, the soon-to-be bundle of joy, kicks strongly, each time Anna places her hand against Olivia's belly. Anna and Olivia agree that the child is impatient, as are mother and sister for its arrival.

Among the bitterness of loss, there is the sweetness of renewal.

Two dragonflies, zigging here, zagging there, in and through, about and around the cattail stalks, distract Anna from pleasant daydreams, their apparent battle over territory reminding her of her own internal struggle. Her brain, which Anna wants to believe acts rationally, most of the time anyway, versus her heart that is filled with emotions: sympathy, empathy, and compassion. Her brain says her relationship with William is over, severed permanently and irrevocably by his deception that caused her arrest and left her home vulnerable to confiscation. Yes, her heart agrees, what William set in motion is unpardonable, but does the punishment fit the crime, especially, when he put things right by his statement in court. "It's strange how a lie was the only correct course," whispers Anna. "If William had said he had given the bracelet to me, too many secrets would be at risk." The truth would have done more harm than good. It is a strange paradox considering two wrongs are never suppose to make a right. Then speaking to Beauty, Anna asks, "In Leviticus,[99] didn't God say, 'Do not lie'?" Beauty lifts her head with a warning glance. "You're right, Beauty. God also said, 'Do not deceive one another.' Secrets are a form of deception. If William and I hadn't deceived our fathers, he would not have had to lie, but it is what it is. How long do I continue avoiding him?"

Beauty's ears twitch to the sounds of crunching cattail stalks being broken and trampled and the muffled call of, "Anna?" *Will she remain quiet and allow the threat to their peaceful home to pass or will she give in and announce her location?* This is Beauty's silent question.

Anna glimpsed William a total of three times throughout the summer during her many trips to town when she dropped off her itty-bitty carvings at the country store. The first time was a Saturday afternoon. The sun shone brightly, but without the intensity of a sweltering day where it is so hot that the sky itself is thirsty, allowing what seemed like the entire population of Havre de Grace to stroll leisurely through town. William did not see her as he walked with Roman, but Anna passed close enough that through the milling

---

99 Leviticus 19:11. "Ye shall not steal, neither deal falsely, neither lie one to another." *Holy Bible*, King James Version, 1987 printing. Public domain.

crowd, she clearly saw his bruised face and that his arm was held within a sling. A pang of pity ached for a second or two for his injuries, though in a strange way Anna concluded they were self-inflicted.

On the second and third sightings, their eyes briefly locked from down the block, a distance that gave Anna time to disappear around a corner and into a store to hide among the merchandise stands. Until she is ready to face him, until she has confidently set William in his proper place, a mutual and satisfactory, if not satisfying agreement between brain and heart, avoidance is the prudent course.

The entire household of Buchanan: Anna, Beauty, and geese have heard William's plaintive calls on many occasions, but he was dissuaded from approaching the shack by the loosing of Beauty or the geese who set his feet to fleeing. Evidence of apologies or overtures was found lying in his wake; a bundle of wildflowers, a box of chocolates, a summer scarf of the softest material, its colors a reflection of enchanted rainbows. These items, taken alone, were thoughtful, tasty, and tantalizing to the touch, but taken in context, they were tainted. How can she trust William or his gifts?

"Anna?" William's call is close. His course, by accident, if kept steady, will find her. Anna considers nudging Beauty and slipping between the stalks to the shoreline, gathering the gander to stealthily slip away, but one thing has weakened her resolve of avoidance. During Anna's last glimpse of William, when he ran past the window of the dress shop she was hiding in, he was wearing the identical outfit as Tim.

Beauty hears Anna's sigh of resignation that to Anna was a steeling breath of determination, the decision being made to remain on her stump. If Luck, the close relative of the Fates brings William to her exact spot, then it is time to deal with him. Gazing skyward for help or inspiration, Anna watches as patches of fluffy, cotton-white clouds, their bottoms flat, move across the blue sky as if sliding on an invisible pane. She wonders, *does the sky really go on forever, or are we all ducks under glass for the amusement or consumption of something or someone?*

With the crack of brittle stalks, William, covered in golden pollen from exploding heads, pulls apart the curtain of cattails to reveal Anna's blind, "Here you are." William studies Beauty to determine whether she will attack, but it is Anna he should be concerned with.

Leaping to her feet, Anna strikes William across his chest with the barrel of her shotgun. The swing impacts with the force of an out-of-control skipjack boom, as Anna lets loose a guttural cry, startling a tumbling flock of red-wings into a change of course. Flattened on his back, muck seeping into his army-issue and with Anna's rubber boot planted firmly on his chest,

William stares into the glowering eyes of the girl who he is used to seeing on her back.

Speaking slowly, enunciating each word, though her jaw is clenched with resolve, Anna asks, "What is it that you don't understand? I do not want to see you."

Cringing against the likelihood of another blow to his tender ribs, William stutters, "I...I just wanted to say g-good-bye."

"What?" Anna removes her foot, as she was not expecting this. She assumed he would babble apologies, beg forgiveness, and ask for another chance.

"My platoon leaves in two days. I'm technically AWOL,[100] but Joe, you know Joe Davis, we're in the same unit, he said he'd somehow cover for me."

"Why didn't he come, too? Florence misses him so much."

"Joe said, 'Someone has to do the right thing,' though I didn't know if he meant me or him, and I still don't."

Allowing William to sit up, and then helping him to his feet, Anna's determination to be ice cold melts, "You're an idiot. C'mon, let's go back."

A spark of lust flashes hot in William's eyes, but Anna quickly extinguishes it, "For a cup of coffee."

Beauty leads the group out of the canyon of cattails and through the waist high grasses to a narrow, almost invisible marsh trail. No words are spoken until Anna spies a particular plant growing in a tangle around the base of a clump of rice stalks, "Ever tried smartweeds?"

"I don't think so."

Reaching down to pull off several small leaves, Anna offers them to William, "If you eat them, they'll make you smart."

"Consensus says I could use a bit of smarts," William says without a hint of cleverness, as he tosses the leaves into his mouth, and begins to chew. His gnashing teeth release oxalic acid from the plant, which it uses as its defense against herbivores. William's eyes instantly water as he tries to spit out the foul-tasting mush his mouth has made out of the leaves, "It's hot!"

Anna laughs, watching, as William dances in blind circles. His fingers try to brush the green, gooey leaves from his inflamed mouth. With puckish[101] satisfaction, Anna says, "I didn't mean it would make your brain smart, just your tongue."

---

100 AWOL. Absent without leave. Having no official permission to absent himself from military duties but without the intention of deserting.

101 Puck. A mischievous sprite in English folklore. Also called a hobgoblin or Robin Goodfellow.

In contrast to the noble eagle that prefers not to get its feathers wet when snatching its prey from the bay and the endless tributaries that feed it, the dashing osprey relishes a full-body, feet first plunge. This long-clawed fish hawk will submerge itself completely, to reappear as if launched by springs from the aquatic buffet. Returning to a nest or its favorite branch, the osprey folds its wings as a feathered black cape, dignified, before tearing into the flesh of the unfortunate fish.

Olivia is all too aware that it would be blasphemy to announce her preference for the sharp-billed osprey over ducks and geese. Not as a main course but in admiration. It may be because the female of the species, at 24 inches, is larger than the male, and accepts no guff. It could be due to the proud way it sits a limb, but as Olivia rides an old gelding along the trail skirting the fast lands next to the marsh, and watches as parents and offspring leave their nests for the season on their journey to Brazil, Colombia, and Venezuela, she recognizes that it is envy and not admiration that draws her to this hemispheric traveler. These predators live lives of endless summers with only warm days to bask in and cool nights for comfortable slumbers.

Olivia's snippet of uncomfortable sleep was abruptly interrupted this morning by a swift kick within her womb to announce the time has come. Untwisting the covers that were wet from her water breaking, a contraction confirmed what the child already knew. Prudence would have found Olivia gingerly walking the several, short, town blocks to enter the fancy, wood-inlaid foyer of the grand old Baker mansion, and into the arms of the nurses who are now the reigning mistresses of the Harford County Hospital. Instead, Olivia pounded on the two-story double doors of the stables owned by Jim Currier's father. There were younger, faster horses to choose from that could deliver Olivia to her destination post-haste, but the tired swayback whose gentle gait would be less jarring was Olivia's pick for her journey through nostalgia.

Olivia chose to ride through a landscape filled with memories of Clay, where the desire for emotional comfort overrode the need for the safe environs of a hospital maternity ward. With each clip-clop of the shod horse hooves on the trail, the soil releases Clay's cologne for Olivia to breathe in deeply. The midday breeze, fluctuating this direction and that, south to north, and then back again with the changing season, rustles the leaves in the birches, oaks, loblollies, and massages the grasses. If Olivia wishes to converse with Clay, his words are found in the creaking limbs of ancient trees that she passes under and in the trickles of every creek and stream she passes over.

A man, who lives off the land, the water, and the creatures that dwell upon or within, can never leave them, nor can he be wrenched from them, even in death. His imprint is indelible, if not on the land itself, in his love-hate relationship and the stories of conquest and defeat. Not surprisingly, the defeats are proudly retold more often than the conquests while warming frostbitten hands in front of the blazing stove in the country store, or over a chilled mug of beer that quenches thirst in Tavern Bouvard. Being beaten, but not broken is a rite of passage to wisdom. Sweat, blood, tears, and spit is the stuff that holds the outdoorsman together, and when they are spilt, they glue the donor to that challenge for eternity.

The welcoming party of goose and goslings, all honking with raucous abandon at company newly arrived, watch as Olivia slides off her unnamed horse to curtsy awkwardly, a strong contraction bending her to one knee. A pained utterance of, "We're home," blurts from Olivia's lips.

This statement of belonging was meant to comfort the baby, but it rang hollow, echoing flat against the empty shack. The crooked structure is filled with cherished memories of laughter with Jennifer, her slow burning affection for Clay that grew to an insatiable conflagration, and her earnest love for another's daughter. However, to puncture her fantasy of belonging, another contraction hobbles Olivia's steps toward the door, where above it, still secured with obstinate tacks, and ignoring "Until death do we part," are stems, the toughest parts of all plants, with two beaten, but not broken dried flowers that at their height of beauty adorned Jennifer's hair.

Pushing open the door, its squeaking creak temporarily eliminated by Anna having dabbed the hinges with gun oil, Olivia pauses. There is no doubt that she did not think this through. Standing on the threshold, and looking at an angle through the bedroom doorway, Olivia's guilt at bedding her best friend's husband without the sanctity of joining vows, conjures an image of Jennifer suffering in labor to bring forth the blessing that was conceived in that marriage bed. And though snowfall is months away, Olivia shivers from the cold that covered the ground that night, or is it from a ghost that breathes down her neck?

The 15-minute walk from the natural cattail blind to the Buchanan home does nothing to reduce the painful fire that engulfs William's mouth from the smartweeds. However, to his benefit, the tears running down his cheeks do add a measure of realism when he speaks of his remorse for causing Anna to run afoul of the law. Anna listens carefully and believes his words are true, that he was trying to express his affection, but William fails in one important respect, in that he never says, "What I did was wrong and it will never happen again."

Forever the optimist, a character trait Anna obviously derived from her mother, because her father would say, "A skunk is a skunk. It can't change its stripe," Anna hopes that William will at any second, at the next bend in the trail, acknowledge his wrongdoings, instead, it is his problems that consume the balance of their short journey.

"My father is always flaunting his wealth and influence, yet here I am wearing a uniform, and going off to war."

"It's the patriotic thing to do."

"This has nothing to do with patriotism. My father forced me to join up, which doesn't make much sense to me because he first prevented me from joining Lafayette Escadrille. Maybe it's glory he doesn't want me to have, but he did say that a little killing will make a man out of me; somehow straighten me out."

A barn owl could roost in Anna's gaping mouth. She cannot fathom how taking another person's life could ever make a man out of anyone. More likely it would contribute to the diminishing of what a mature man should be: strong, yes, but always compassionate and caring. Only a cold-hearted man could escape the nightmares brought about by causing the death of another, and in this case, multiplied by the horrors of war that Anna cannot begin to comprehend. Her only experience with that sort of violence was her discovery of LeCompte's body. And though his dead eyes stare at her from the depths of dreamless sleep, causing shivers to run up her spine even under layers of toasty quilts, Anna is grateful that the darkness of night obscured his mutilation. She will silently agree with Mr. McQuay that William could use some straightening out. If army life is synonymous with structure and discipline, then time in service will build William's character, if he applies himself.

The goose's distant honks cause the gander to take flight to investigate the commotion, quickly followed by Beauty, whose enthusiasm exceeds her diminished ability to run down the trail. William is hesitant to follow Anna as her pace quickens. No one knows that he has snuck back to Harford County for this clandestine rendezvous. William's preference is to keep it this way lest his father be informed of his presence.

Sensing William's reluctance, Anna casts a disappointing look over her shoulder, and asks, "If you want redemption in my eyes you'll stop being afraid of others finding out about us."

William's heart seizes on Anna's use of the word *us*, and with trepidation follows, excited that she is considering a relationship of some sort with him, but silently thinks, *it's easy to be fearless when your father's dead.*

Passing the stand of maple trees that border the shack's clearing, one of which Claire Joiner banged her head against, Anna observes an unfamiliar swayback horse tethered to one of the porch's posts. It is nibbling on grass growing at the edges of the steps. Beauty and the gander are sitting quietly next to... "Olivia!" Anna runs the remaining yards to kneel beside Olivia who is sitting, leaning against the door frame. Perspiration drips from Olivia's forehead as a contraction contorts her face. The freckles that run across her nose from cheek-to-cheek flare brightly as her face is flushed.

"Why are you out here?" Anna wraps Olivia's arm around her own shoulder to help her to her feet. "You should be inside."

"You should be at the hospital," William says, standing back, and though Olivia now knows of his presence, he does not want to become entangled.

Ignoring William, Olivia, embarrassed, says, "No one was home."

"This is your home," Anna says as she strains to lift Olivia, and then looks at William, her face pinched in consternation. "If you're not going to help, take the swayback, and ride to the Joiner's to fetch Claire."

William mounts the old beast with flare, rather too dashing even in a uniform covered in pollen and mud, irking Anna, cruelly reminding her of why she fell for him. William, wanting to depart, yanks on the reins to turn the tired animal, but as he faces the seemingly impenetrable marsh, and beyond it the birch swamp, he pauses, "I don't know where she lives."

"For heaven's sake, William." Anna half carries Olivia through the doorway. "Can you find your way to town?"

William nods, not perceptive enough to catch the irritation in Anna's sarcasm.

"Then go get Doctor Webster."

"Can I write to you?"

There is no immediate response from inside the dwelling as Anna eases Olivia onto a bed where laughter and tears, beginnings and ends, life and death, stain the goose down quilt. Its many colors, some faded with time, its patches, made up of remnants both soft and coarse, are a tapestry of successes and failures within this home, but through it all, it is a comforter. Olivia searches Anna's face. Olivia wonders if Anna senses any guilt, the betrayal Olivia feels by lying in the marriage bed of another and giving birth to a bastard. Fearing the answer, Olivia instead asks between contradictions that snatch her breath away, another question that regardless of Anna's decision is life altering, "Well?"

Outside, the reluctant soldier, who if riding a stallion equal to his captivating bearing would be a shoe-in for Uncle Sam's next recruiting poster where all women would look upon him, weak-kneed and swooning, and men would follow to their deaths, he waits for Anna's reply. Any indication to the affirmative will give William an anchor, a reason to want to think of home, where there are memories to cling to and exist upon to carry him through whatever the enemy has prepared for him on the far side of the Atlantic. A negative response will...a bobolink calls to its mate from the top branches of the maple tree. It is hidden by leaves in transition from lush green to autumn's golden rust.

"Only if the doctor arrives before the baby."

William's whooping, "I promise," is ignored with the fading hoof beats as Anna props pillows behind Olivia who declares through clenched teeth, "I have to push."

Doctor Webster's tin-*Lizzie* slides to a stop in front of the Buchanan family home with a rattle and a bang. As the doctor heaves himself out from behind the wheel, he is met by a mile-wide grin that radiates from the porch. Not even the long shadow cast by the late afternoon sun can contain Anna's joy. Sitting, rocking in her mother's chair, Anna cradles a bundle in her arms. Doctor Webster steps onto the porch to gaze down at a child with a mop of red hair, freckles, and piercing gray eyes.

"May I present my brother Seth," Anna beams, unable to take her eyes off the infant.

"Olivia?" asks the doctor.

"Resting."

"Well, it seems you've everything under control," Doctor Webster says, a playful hint of hurt in his voice, and then plopping down on the edge of the porch, he surveys a landscape dying for the arrival of wildfowl. Then softly, speaking so only Anna can hear, the doctor says, "Your messenger with the half-dead horse asked me to inform you that he expects replies to his letters."

Doctor Webster may not have arrived before the baby was born, but Anna admits that William did his best, and that is all she expects of him. Though with a smirk, she replies, "He sure expects a lot."

"Hmm...a family trait I suspect," picking a long stem of grass to chew on, the doctor asks, "Ever met his mother?"

Tickling the baby's perfect chin, Anna says, "No, but I hear we have done business together...so to speak."

Chewing contentedly on the grass, a habit all boys acquire and never seem to break, Doctor Webster says, "It's a shame she will never see past the art work to admire the artist."

The bobolink calls again.

– 1918 –

The bitter January wind numbing Anna's toes and pinching her cheeks as she stalks the Flats has no hope of diminishing the flames stoked by family that warms her soul and keeps a smile on her winter-cracked lips. There is no ache from lying face down on the rough and uneven boards of the sneak skiff, as endless hours of playing on the floor with her baby brother have toughened her stomach. The dark clouds arcing from shore to shore are ignored as they hang menacing from a black sky. Tethered loosely by invisible forces that allow the clouds to say and sway, they intensify Anna and Beauty's isolation. They are alone on a great expanse of water with only the gunning light heavily diffused for guidance. It is a terrifying situation, though, for Anna, looking through the notch between the base of the light and the bow in search of her quarry that is hidden among the shifting ice floes, she stifles a giggle as she relives Seth's astonished joy and unrestrained laughter when they play—peek-a-boo!

Christmas revelry in Harford County, as around the country, and the world, had been subdued in many households due to the temporarily or permanently empty chairs around dinner tables. Mothers worried themselves sick, and fathers, whether British or not, kept a stiff upper lip. Despite the melancholy, the market for wildfowl remained a hungry and greedy one. It was only the daring outlaw gunner who could fill the larders, even if the glazed gooses and roasted ducks, regardless of the spices added, tasted flat in the absence of cherished sons.

The obligatory Christmas and New Year's parties saw the display counter at J.R. Stewart's Country Store forever empty of Anna's cocktail decoys.

This translated in the minds of customers as proof of their rarity. With each *secret* delivery by the *unknown* artisan, they were snatched up for surprise unveilings to the delight of guests who coveted each piece and sought out other lucky owners for trade or purchase, at an inflated, profit-taking price. The purchasers' stated goal is to obtain a full set for their mantels, though no one knows exactly how many different species have been or will be carved. Mr. Stewart, being tight lipped, fans the curiosity which drives up the prices. The increasing profits are generously shared.

The continuing financial windfall leading into the heart of winter's foulest weather gave rise to the suggestion by Olivia that Anna forgo hunting, "You can buy the meat you need."

Surprisingly, Beauty was the one who reacted first. Ignoring the pain in her joints, she rose from her curled position at the foot of the blazing stove to stare at Anna with her only usable eye, her left completely blinded by cataract. Beauty's intensity was a challenge, or as perceived by Anna as, "You'd dare turn your back on that which fed generations of Buchanans?"

Appeasing, Anna scratched the sagging skin under Beauty's chin, and replied without a second thought, "I'm pretty sure it's not in the Bible, but I believe it would be a sin not to practice what my father taught, what he lived and died by, simply because I have a few extra dollars in my pocket."

Satisfied, Beauty settled back down to patiently endure a session of ear pulling by Seth. This would continue until he became tired and fell asleep like a pup curled beside his mother's soft fur.

Olivia said no more other than, "If you were to use both shotguns, with their magazine extensions, you could knock down 30 birds."

Paddling slowly, careful not to lift the paddles clear of the water to prevent unnecessary water droplets, a quiet pride courses through Anna's veins. Though the shotguns lying under each arm hold only 12 shells each, totaling 24, Olivia assumes Anna not only has the skill to sneak in close enough to the rafting fowl, allowing her to open the chokes for the broadest pellet spread, but that she will knock down every bird she aims at, and that Luck would see to it that the over spray will either kill or cripple more.

The result of using the two shotguns was far fewer birds to turn over to Mr. Currier than when she uses the Davenport, her skill with the family killing machine having improved with each foray. Anna has only two annoyances when taking out the punt gun. The first is she has to spend an hour or two searching the shoreline on foot to ferret out the spies that Constable Jenkins has placed there. Anna will never be able to fully repay the constable's kindness in her time of need, and she no longer holds a grudge for his past wrongs against her family, realizing he was doing his job, as he continues to do. He will try to catch her using the Davenport and she will proceed carefully and cautiously to prevent him for succeeding.

Anna has begun referring to the Davenport as her headache gun, imitating comments made by an unashamed man from a distant marsh, who, while dribbling a quenching brew into his chest-length beard at Tavern Bouvard, described, with unconcealed boasting, the ear-splitting concussion of his punt gun, and that he required two aspirin[102] before and after pulling the trigger—another miracle from the Bayer Company.

Anna's second annoyance or difficulty with the Davenport is removing and replacing the monster from its lair. Anna has reduced this challenge with the resourceful use of a block and tackle that washed up on shore. Mood, hers and the weather's, became the determining factor as to which implements of destruction she chose to load aboard the sneak skiff. Tonight's rising wind and following swells made it safer to use the shotguns instead of the unwieldy Davenport.

Just guessing, Anna suspects that five hours have passed since she shoved off from the snow-laden shore in front of her home. The stalk, if charted, might appear meandering, possibly aimless, as she maneuvered around the drifting floes, but Anna was purposeful as she ventured first northeast, and then allowed the wind and current to push her south. Her cockamamie half circle, with occasional deliberate splashing, pushes the disturbed fowl that seek rest to the pinch point at Spesutie Narrows where the ice squeezes, limiting further the open water to congregate the birds in mass. There can be no noise from the skiff at this critical time or the birds will flee completely.

Beauty chooses to sleep until the starting gun demands her participation. On several nights this winter, when quiet reigned across the still bay, Anna has returned empty handed to the disappointment, and what appeared to be a hint of shame from Beauty. Anna accepted Beauty's mood in stride, not once saying, "You know, it was your snoring and leg spasms against the side boards that spooked the birds before I was within range." Instead, with a genuine smile and respect for the faithful old lady who now waddles like the ducks she retrieves, Anna would say, "We'll blow a hole in 'em next time."

Anna's light acts as a weak moon to light up the sparkling diamonds lying among the snowflakes that fell the day before, and are hitching rides on the flat panels of ice, their richness is a hint to the reward meowing, sneezing, and honking a hundred yards distant. Anna has skillfully worked

---

102 Aspirin (acetylsalicylic acid). Invented in 1897 by German chemist Felix Hoffmann (1868-1946). Hoffman also synthesized heroin, an achievement with unfortunate consequences. The Bayer Company obtained a U.S. patent and monopoly on manufacturing aspirin from 1900-1917. Until 1915, aspirin was only sold through doctors and pharmacists.

her way around and through the bumping, scraping, and crunching panels, always keeping the light's glow facing south and toward her target. Whether paddling forward, backward, or sideways, she did not once allow the skiff to run into the ice. It is a delicate dance of purposeful planning with intuitive guesses as to which opening will remain and which will close in to trap her, but now, an impasse.

The mystery for Anna of how individual drops of water become an ocean, one uniting seamlessly with another, is played out in solid form. Similarly, how do a billion delicate snowflakes become an impenetrable wall? And for that matter, how do a hundred panels of ice squeeze so tightly together to become one immovable, obdurate mass, solid enough to drive a vehicle across, if so desired? This is the unending plane that stretches left and right into the darkness, halting Anna's forward progression, and that separates her from the fowl.

Decisions...

Decisions...

Decisions...

Anna slowly rises to her knees, and leaning over the gray lump of rug that Beauty has become, she lifts the lid on the gunning light, and then reaches in to slowly turn down the wick until, imperceptive, the light goes out. With balanced care, Anna lifts herself out of the sneak skiff to lie on the flat white acreage of ice. Pausing, pondering how to secure the skiff to the ice, Anna sees that the wind and tide hold it firmly in place. Reaching in to retrieve her Winchester and the Remington, the latter will always be her father's, regardless of who looks down its sights or pulls the trigger, Anna tucks each under her arms to resume her stalk.

The first 50 yards are almost a walk in the park. With no moon to betray her silhouette, Anna needs only to watch her step so that she does not slip. The thin, negligible layer of snowflakes covering the floe poses no threat of a disturbing crunch to alert the birds. Between 50 and 30 yards from the splashing, feeding, chattering congregation, Anna lowers her profile by crouching, while slowing her pace. There is no rush to the contended targets. It is only Anna and the waterfowl.

"If Luck holds on, the kill will be spectacular tonight," Anna says to the wind that taps against her back and blows strands of hair into her face. She is unsure as to why she would utter such words, except for the extra shotgun shells she carries in her back pockets.

Between 30 and 15 yards, Anna crawls, or more precisely, pulls herself along the smooth surface of the ice. Her new, winter, off-white coverall with attached hood, blends in as a lump on the surface. Nearing two yards of the crumbling, sloughing, lee edge of the floe and the open, frothing water made turbulent by the several thousand ducks and geese enjoying a night of frivolity, Anna hesitates. The mallards splashing closest to Anna remind her of bath time for Seth as he excitedly kicks his feet and throws handfuls of water in every direction.

Pure joy.

Pleasure in being—alive.

Anna shakes her head to remove the pleasant image of life, and to jar her mind back to the task at hand—death. Narrowing her eyes, she focuses on the fattest drake. He will be the first to feel the pellets' deadly sting. Gripping her Winchester pump, Anna inhales a lung full of raw, crisp air to shout the birds into the air.

Balloom!!!

The explosive shock wave hits Anna square in the face, making her cringe, recoiling as if she were standing next to 10 headache guns firing as one.

The waterfowl rocket into the shattered air in confusion. Their frightened calls and frantic wing beats nearly equal the boom that set them in motion.[103]

Fracturing under the concussive shock, a spider web of fissures appear in the ice beneath Anna.

A hundred yards distant, Beauty is jolted from her slumber. Leaping out of the sneak skiff, she is startled by landing with a thud on the ice floe, when she expects a frigid splash.

Recalling stories of hunters being knocked unconscious, or worse, battered overboard by disoriented birds, Anna remains prone, but rolls onto her back. It is an awkward position to shoot from, but necessity calls for a creative response if Anna wants to remain out of the birds' flight paths. Quickly raising the barrel skyward, its curved butt firm against her shoulder, Anna sights a canvasback and a black head as they wing over her.

Squeezing the trigger, the recoil, a brutal eight-gauge punch to her shoulder is transmitted to the brittle, cracked pane of ice beneath Anna, shattering it. Anna is shoved down to be swallowed by blackness so cold that it steals her attempt to gasp. The weight of the shotgun pushes her head down. Air bubbles, as they race to the surface, rushing past shards of disintegrating ice, pop as a million firecrackers in Anna's ears. Her thick coverall makes her futile one-arm flailing like stirring a vat of congealing fat, her other arm refusing to release the anchor, the gift from her father.

---

103 On January 2, 1918, the first artillery shell is test fired at the Aberdeen Proving Grounds located south of Swan Creek Point, west of Spesutie Island. The was the first of 416,294 rounds fired in 1918, each shaking the ground, rattling the windows, and keeping the wildfowl in constant flight.

Her rational mind orders her hand to let go of the shotgun while her longing heart pleads to hold on. It is a tangible link to her father, as well as an act by him indicating worthiness, which to Anna equals love. The shotgun is priceless—irreplaceable.

Anna's lungs burn for air as she fights the instinct to gulp. Her heart races, beating to circulate oxygen-starved blood to weakening muscles. Her right leg kicks in vain, helpless; her left is snagged on something, useless. The constant current tugs at Anna's body, pulling with a winning determination to collect any detritus that falls within its grasp. Consciousness, a delicate, fleeting thing at best, ends with twinkling stars before Anna's eyes...and muffled, determined growls?

Lifting her head, her silky hair trailing behind, Anna blinks. Her vision is blurred with ice crystals forming to seal her eyelids close, but what Anna sees is something from a dream. Beauty's canines have punctured the left leg cuff of her new coverall...the snag...and she is growling as she pulls, muscling Anna backward onto solid ice.

The dark clouds above Anna have parted to reveal a heaven that sparkles brightly as if just for her, just for this moment for angels or her parents to look down to ensure that tragedy has been averted, that their child is safe, and then they are gone as the swirling clouds squeeze close again.

Beauty releases her grip and moves to stand over Anna. She wears an expression that is a cross between concern and disappointment, her message is clear: No duck—no dinner.

Again, Anna wants to exclaim, "It isn't my fault," but instead, hugs Beauty for all she is worth, while silently apologizing to Luck for her inaccurate statement. It was Beauty, not Luck that had to hold on.

After Sunday's church services throughout Harford County, ladies gossip, and men huddle around the Special Edition of the *Republican*, while boys too young to don a uniform, re-enact with arms spread wide, and lips sputtering and roaring, the historic aerial dog fight.

KILLER BESTED

April 21, 1918: The scourge of the Belgium skies, German ace Manfred von Richthofen, colorfully known as the Red Baron, and credited with shooting down 80 Allied planes, was killed by Captain Roy Brown while piloting his Sopwith Camel. The valiant Captain Brown engaged the dastardly Red Baron in an attempt to draw him away from his pursuit of a young Royal Air Force trainee, Lieutenant May. Reports indicate that after the Red Baron was shot, he was able to land his tri-wing Fokker in a field where he was quickly surrounded by Allied troops. A cheer arose among the soldiers when it was discovered that the killer of young and daring men was dead.

This reporter has learned from highly placed sources; that even though Manfred von Richthofen was feared above any man who took to the sky, and despised as a cold-hearted enemy, Allied troops intend on burying the German ace with honor. When asked about this unexpected salute, Captain Brown[104] replied, "It's all about respect."

The men clustered around the newspaper are pleased that there is one less kraut to kill their boys, and this they will happily recount to the womenfolk, but the second news article, as with all worries, will be internalized, and kept to themselves. Mothers have enough anxiety with thoughts of bullets, artillery, and poison gas taking the lives of their sons. They need not be burdened with an invisible killer.

DOZENS OF MYSTERY DEATHS SWEEP ARMY CAMP

Strapping young men, eager soldiers all, complain of fever and body aches, and two days later they are dead. Physicians at Maryland's Camp Meade [105] are baffled and overwhelmed by the number of dying. This reporter, horrified by the ghastly descriptions of those suffering, will refrain from repeating it to save the families of the unfortunate additional pain.

What is the cause? How is the illness passing from one man to another with such speed? What could take the lives of so many healthy soldiers so quickly? It is reminiscent of the tragedy, reported here, that occurred at the British Camp in Etoples, France, two years ago. If this illness is the same, how did it get from other there to here? One can only wonder if death is blowing in the wind, and if so, is anyone safe?

---

104 Captain Roy Brown (1898-1944), a Canadian assigned to the 209th Royal Air Force Squadron, firing .303 bullets, struck the Red Baron (1892-1918) once in the chest as the German's plane, a Fokker DR.I tri-wing fighter was making a low-level pass near a ridge. Controversy exists over who is actually responsible for von Richthofen's demise. An Australian machine gunner Sergeant Sedrick Popkin used identical .303 bullets as Captain Brown to shoot at the Fokker as it passed the ridge. Examination of the Red Baron's body indicated the bullet was moving in an upward trajectory when it entered his chest. As it may never be known who fired the fatal shot, is it possible that another Sopwith camel was flying that day and that Snoopy finally got his man?

105 Camp Meade. Deaths from influenza were equated to losses on the battlefield. During memorial services at the camp, when the presiding officer called the name of the soldier, the sergeant shouted, "Died on the field of honor." Forty-three thousand American servicemen died of influenza along with countless doctors and nurses who tended them.

It may be small consolation that Maryland's finest are not stationed at Camp Devens, Massachusetts, where, terrifyingly, 100 are dying each day.

The men look to their young children, who in dresses and trousers, innocently and without a worry in the world, play grown-up games, and then, as a group, the men realize their womenfolk have stopped chattering and are staring at them.

Intuitively, the older women clutch their Bibles as to life rafts against the coming storm, while daughters who are mature enough to understand, even if they cannot see the danger, weep silently in their mother's arms. The men, hunters all, either as their livelihood or for recreation, shiver at being stalked, and feel the weight of responsibility upon shoulders broad enough to carry their family's fears.

Major Tydings' muddy boots leave an annoyed trail up the opulently carpeted stairs of the centuries-old country chateau. Seeking his misplaced soldier, Chief had learned from one of his machine gunners that William mentioned he was bored. When he was not found among the men engaged in the soldiers' time-honored pastime of craps or cards, Chief knew there was only one other place where entertainment could be found—for a price.

William was not among the men sharing a bottle of *vin rouge*[106] in the heavily curtained and lavishly decorated parlor, so now it is only a matter of locating the correct door, because busting in, interrupting coitus, even with the high rank of major, is intolerable, unless there is a damn good reason.

The latest mistress of the abandoned house, the madam of this grand home, and mother to the young and not so young girls who are every soldier's diversion in times of war, informed Chief that the one he seeks is in the fourth room on the left. To his back, in broken English, she stated sternly, "No refunds or credit if not finished." Ignoring her financial policies regarding customer satisfaction, Chief squares his shoulders in front of the door, raises his boot and kicks it open, banging the brass knob against the plastered interior wall. Startled, the naked, scrawny and lethargic 20-something woman straddling William on the four-poster bed, drops the lit candle from which she was dripping melting wax onto his chest, a sadistic reminder that there cannot be pleasure without pain. The sputtering flame scorches skin and singes the few hairs growing between his erect nipples. The pain from

---

106 Vin rouge. French for "red wine."

burning flesh produces an unmanly shrieking yelp from William as he beats out the flame and leaps skyward as if struck by lightning. This unexpected bucking dislodges William's paid-by-the-hour companion. She tumbles off the quilted bed, to land, if in her current profession it is possible, undignified, with legs in the air on a rug of the thickest burgundy plush.

"What the hell, Chief?" William asks, adding a string of profanity to reassert his masculinity.

"What the hell and a brown mule[107] is right, Private," retorts Chief as he stands framed in the doorway. Major Tydings is not questioning William on his sexual inclinations as he understands men and boys have their weaknesses, but it is his timing. "Get dressed, soldier. We were supposed to be up the hill 15 minutes ago."

William stumbles past Chief, dressing as he goes. In his wake, William does not leave an apology, only an amused woman trying to make a living under wartime conditions where only God has the right to judge her. Shaking out her long black hair in a practiced way so that the remaining candles cause it to shimmer, but also to expose patches of bare scalp, she pats the edge of the bed, while licking to moisten dry lips. It is an invitation to Chief to stay awhile, and to make use of the lad's remaining minutes—waste not, want not. As any gentleman would do, Chief smiles cordially, tipping his cap respectfully, and says with the seriousness of a man on a mission, his strong square chin jutting forward, "Thank you, but no thanks. I have Germans to kill."

Stepping outside into the temperate fall night, a continuing drizzle making everything wet enough to be uncomfortable, Chief finds William lacing up his boots.

Scanning the dark Alsace countryside with its rolling forested hills leading into black mountains, Chief has a hard time imagining that this seemingly peaceful region, and its neighbor, Lorraine, dotted with pastoral lands that are green and productive, had been the first to fall to the Kaiser's cruelties. It is up in those mountains, lined with miles and miles of zigzagging German and Allied trenches that the deserving Major Tydings has been ordered to *wake up the neighborhood,* to strike a blow. Chief's goal is to inflict such carnage upon the invaders as to set them upon their heels, clearing the enemy from their trenches through a hail of bullets equal to the fire and brimstone that God laid down upon Sodom and Gomorrah. Any hostile still alive will be painfully aware that the Blue and Gray are now manning the far southeastern end of the war's Western Front. Commanding four machine gun

---

107 Keith, Caroline H. *For Hell and a Brown Mule: the Biography of Senator Millard E. Tydings.* Madison Books (1991).

companies and two regimental machine gun companies of the 57th Brigade, a combined strength of 72 heavy guns, Chief's force is a power to be reckoned with...so long as each man does his duty.

"Double-time it, William. We've got to catch up with the boys. They're impatient and can't begin the assault without my whistle," Chief starts off at a fast clip with William huffing along behind. "I thought you and the Buchanan girl were an item."

Considering his answer, and weighing the many letters of encouragement from Anna, all signed, *Affectionately Yours,* that are in his duffle bag back near the dairy farm where he and others are bivouacked, William says, "I was thinking of Anna the whole time, so it's really not cheating. Besides, she's not here to give me what I need."

Making their way up the slippery mule trail to the mathematically positioned machine gun emplacements, the precision of deadly crossfire elevated by the slide rule, Chief attempts to provide William with food for thought, though he is concerned that he may be whispering into deaf ears, "What you need is self-discipline, and what that lady at the chateau will give you, you may not be able to get rid of."

Down on his hands and knees, crawling toward his assigned gun, William says, confident, and dangerously too loud within the silence of a forest waiting for the whistle, "Don't worry about me. I may be crazy for love, but loving ladies will never make me crazy. I always choose the youngest and freshest."

While William is reassuring Chief that he has a foolproof method against madness, back in the chateau, the madam puts her daughter's mind to ease, saying, "Here, swallow this aspirin. It will help with the aches, and don't you worry. Those sores will clear up by themselves. Mine did. Now go on, there's another bored soldier waiting for you in the parlor."

Pinching her own cheeks to bring fresh color to them, the youngest orphan to join this dysfunctional family, a recent arrival from the farmlands of Belgium, thinks, *if he's so bored, he should go to Flanders.*[108] Then, reconsidering her malicious sentiment, she looks upon the eager face of the young American. He is ogling her prematurely sagging breasts through her shear, black-lace

---

108 Belgian Flanders was a flesh grinder wherein hundreds of thousands died during World War I. In 1914, the British professional army was utterly destroyed. In 1915, the Germans unleashed poison gas and the flamethrower. In 1917, in the battle of Paachendaele, Allied troops by the thousands drowned in mud and water-filled artillery craters while trying to cross "No Man's Land." In 1918, an overwhelming German attack would have broken the battered back of the Allies if not for the last minute aid of newly arrived American forces that eventually turned the tide against Germany's armies.

bodice. With a hopeful sigh, she asks, "Darling, will you be buying my dinner tonight?"

Floating with the gentle tide, Anna is an untethered decoy, but unlike the wooden lure that wants attention and company, Anna desires only solitude during her naughty pleasure. Summer baths in the cool waters of the bay have continued into fall with the unseasonably warm weather. Excluding Beauty, who stands guard on shore, and her geese, a total of five, who paddle about contented, it is only the stars that wink to each other, lust-filled witnesses to the bather turned skinny-dipper, turned spotlighted drifter.

Solitude breeds immodesty and boldness, the courage to shout to purposely disturb the silence, to throw a rock into a placid pond, to shed one's clothes along with inhibition, and to jump about against puritanical mores. Illuminating Anna's deviltry are the bay's bioluminescent creatures that outline her sensual figure with every movement of her arms, legs, and unencumbered breasts that bob as natural flotation devices. Anna could drift with the current, perfectly still, not moving a muscle, fading into the darkness, invisible and reserved, but where is the fun in that, so as she is turned with the tide, she gives a quick wiggle, a shimmy, and shake of her frame to disturb billions of the transparent planktonic animals, causing them to turn on their lights...a bizarre ability for creatures with no eyes, and the perfect indulgence for a playful girl.

Staring skyward, Anna makes a wish accompanied by a prayer. She sends it riding upon a shooting star that heads toward the east and the European continent in conflict—unimaginable strife on this tranquil night.

Numb with nauseating pain, William cannot remember if the whistle came from Chief or the star shells bursting above his machine gun that set his feet scrambling back down the mountain, tumbling alongside other soldiers fleeing German artillery.

The Blue and Gray had caught the enemy huddled under tarps trying to escape the increasing rain. Their heads and shoulders were dry, but run-off from the slopes quickly filled the trenches, soaking them to their thighs. The lines of machine gun fire, over, down, and into the German trenches were a spectacle of meticulous slaughter. Only the ear shattering repetition, the tack—tack—tack of 72 Vickers machine guns spraying molten lead at a rate in excess of 300 rounds per minute kept the American soldiers deaf to the screams of dying Germans.

William's eyes water as he is ordered to stare into the sun. He somehow understands the words though the language is foreign to him, and someone is laughing, but not at him.

Private McQuay's duties were simple, and difficult to screw up, which was the point of his assignment. While the triggerman let loose the barrage, Private McQuay would pour water across the flash hider. The hider usually consisted of a six-square-foot piece of burlap, the water keeping it from igniting and giving away their location. Private McQuay's only other task was filling the gun's built-in jackets to keep it from overheating and jamming, becoming a useless hunk of metal.

William tries not to cry-out, wanting to close his mouth to deny his captors the satisfaction of their tortures, but his jaw will not follow the command of his muscles. It seems to fall away as a barrel on a breechloader with a broken clip. The laughing man flips a page.

Major Tydings had gone over the plan several times: "Once all machine gun crews are in place, I will blow my whistle, and you'll give 'em hell. With Luck and God on our side, each of you may be able to unload two, possibly three ammo belts before their artillery finds you. Stick with it, boys, and concentrate on your fire. Let me worry about the shells. I'll be right beside you and will blow a second time with all the breath my lungs hold to signal retreat when the time comes." With Chief's unerring style, he ended his deadly serious instructions with levity, saying, "Remember, last man down the hill buys the drinks and cleans up after the mules."

William struggles against the wire bonds cutting into his writs. His own blood, a lubricant, wet and slippery, makes it possible to free himself if only he would unclench his hand. A simple act commanded by his brain, countermanded by his heart that esteems loyalty, at least William's definition of it.

"More water! More water!" screamed the triggerman at Private McQuay as the gun began to heat up, choking and coughing, clogging with expended shell casings as it neared the end of the first ammunition belt. Private

McQuay was distracted by the out-of-season Fourth of July spectacle put on by the Germans' second line in defense of its butchered first; red flares and white star shells bursting to light up the night to search out the Allies' hiding places. They were colorful preludes to deadly high explosive shells, their concussion shaking a man's bones, and could, if detonated too close, instantly stop the beating heart. Phosgene gas was a possibility but soldiers tried not to think of it. The first symptom of exposure was the immediate evacuation of the bowels. This left the embarrassed man just enough time before he died, to say good-bye to the man next to him, unless that man was already dead.

Thumped in the side with the empty ammunition belt, Private McQuay turned, and seeing steam rising from the glowing, red-hot barrel, shrugged his shoulders as he had only pre-positioned one bucket of water, it laying on its side, empty. Private McQuay looked between the outraged triggerman trying to feed the second belt from the ammunition box, which had been delivered earlier on the back of a mule, and the brilliant sky that flashed with artificial lightning. The menacing flares and star shells illuminated the downpour. Perplexed, Private McQuay shouted back, "But it's raining."

The triggerman gave Private McQuay a hand gesture that under any other circumstance would be indecent, leading immediately to a brawl.

Instead, with an undeserved pride in its presentation, Private McQuay unzipped his trousers to reveal that part of his anatomy, which is given unqualified leadership, and with a sigh of relief, urinated into the machine gun's jacket. The triggerman smiled as the gun cooled and resumed its tack—tack—tack.

William tries to open his eyes to better see what is happening to him, but one eye is swollen shut and the other is running with blood. Shaking his head and bending his neck so a quick peek will not be directly into the sun, William instantly understands the meaning of ignorance is bliss. Squatting deep in a concave crater created by an artillery shell, William soils himself as fear conquers the pain. The perceived humiliation evokes laughter from his torturer, a German officer holding a rifle affixed with a bayonet pointed at William's chest. The rifle's butt end smeared red with William's blood as gloved fists would have been too soft to beat him with. Two other soldiers, wearing head and arm bandages heavily stained, encourage the officer to run the doughboy through to quickly finish what was started. A fourth soldier, sitting on his helmet to keep his rump out of the muck, seems oblivious to William's suffering and his compatriots' amusement at William's expense. The distracted soldier with sidesplitting laughter, spitting out two accented words that ring with familiarity, "Old Bill!"[109] as he hugs a tattered magazine to his chest with muddy hands. For the briefest of moments, William believes he catches the eyes of the reader, shocking him into stunned silence by his battered condition.

Private McQuay was shaking his pride and joy for the third time when Major Tydings appeared out of the darkness, his complexion an eerie red in the floating flare overhead. "That's it, boys. Time to skedaddle." Before Private McQuay could stow his equipment and zip up, the triggerman was sprinting after Major Tydings down the mountain, slipping into and bouncing off trunks of injured and damaged trees hidden in the darkness. As promised, Major Tydings blew his shrill whistle for all to hear. As Private McQuay ran after their shadows, he recalled the terrible and frantic nights being chased through the marsh by a determined black Labrador and snapping geese....oh how he would gladly trade those nights, that fear and the possibility of a dog bite or goose nip for the deadly artillery that was chasing him.

The German officer's leer turns to an evil sneer, his grip on the rifle tensing to skewer William, but neither the officer nor his wounded encouragers are focused on their prisoner. Their stare is above William atop the crater. All are frozen in a snap shot of surprise.

Private McQuay could not be considered athletic, though he possessed the slender bearing of a distance runner, in all previous competitions, he fell short. His best showing was a fourth, beating a man suffering an asthma attack, but with exploding shells urging him along, slapping at his backside with brutal force, adrenaline put wings under his feet. Within several hyper heart beats, Private McQuay had caught his superior and was about to pass, when, after Major Tydings bounced off a sturdy fir, Private McQuay saw something fly from a pocket of his uniform, shiny and glinting.

William squeezes his eyes shut against the bayonet that is racing toward his heart. It is not darkness that he sees, but the smiling, adoring and comforting face of Anna.

Balloom!

---

109 Old Bill. A cartoon character created by Bruce Bairnsfather (1888-1959). *Old Bill* depicted life in the trenches. It was warmly embraced by soldiers and distributed in *The Bystander* magazine. During World War I, Lieutenant Bairnsfather assigned to the Royal Warwickshire Regiment was nearly court-martialed after joining with other Allied troops and German soldiers in singing, merriment, and exchanging gifts in what later became known as the (unofficial) 1914 Christmas truce.

William's body is being lifted, thrown through the air...he is numb all over with the taste of vomit in his mouth, but from somewhere within his scrambled brain he comprehends that he has not landed. There is no thud or jarring concussive shock as before, just a rush of blood to his head as he remains upside-down, hearing mumbling, grumbling—in English. It is Chief! William hears his savior saying, "I've come to kill and doing it...damn it, he could have surrendered like these three. This is sanctioned murder. He could have surrendered....damn duty. Who started this war anyway?" William opens one eye a crack to see the German officer lying in the muck at the bottom of the crater. A hole has been blown in his chest. The cavity, where the German officer's heart used to be, slowly fills with muddy water. Looking around Chief's back as he is being carried over his friend's squared shoulder, William watches as the three German soldiers are led single file out of the crater, their hands held high with Chief's .45 caliber pistol pointing the way.

Before falling into unconsciousness, William looks back at the dead officer. Floating next to the body is the object of the soldier's hilarity, an issue of *The Bystander* magazine. It is open to a cartoon of *Old Bill* with a fellow soldier squatting in an artillery crater under bombardment. The caption reads: "Well, if you knows of a better 'ole go to it." Having had a terrible taste of one such hole, William's jaw flaps loosely, as he laughs until the blackness overtakes him.

William opens his eyes. His vision is blurry, but slowly clears. The first thing he focuses on from his medical-station cot is Chief. William tries to grin, but an excruciating pain flashes through his jaw.

"Don't try to smile, private," Major Tydings states, his posture rigid with a knitted brow. "Your jaw is broken." In his hand is the tortoise shell snuffbox given to his ancestor by Admiral Cockburn. "The nurse told me she had to pry this from your hand." Chief shakes his head, dismayed, as he assesses the bruised and swollen face of a boy who he has saved twice, once from the grip of the Chesapeake Bay during winter, and the second from the Germans, "If you tell me you were captured because you stopped to pick this up, when your jaw heals, I'm going to break it again."

Wincing through the pain, and trying to move only his lips, William says, "But it's important...a symbol."

"It's an old trinket, you fool."

Swallowing his saliva, his Adam's apple bouncing as he searches for the reason he unnecessarily placed himself in danger, William asks, "Isn't it why we fight? Isn't it why you keep it in the pocket over your heart... for family... for country?"

Hearing these words of truth spoken by a boy whose main concern is his own needs, chokes the breath out of Chief as this is what he lives by, and if a good-for-nothing, lay-about like William can understand this, then there is more than just hope for mankind—good will conquer evil. Chief shakes off the warm and cuddly feeling, and as Major Tydings, he reminds his private, "Don't for a minute think that because you're injured you'll get off. You were the last man down the mountain. You're buying the drinks and cleaning up after the mules."

The very edges, the tiniest corners of William's mouth curl into a devilish grin at hearing his friend's decree. Chief exits the tent while placing the snuffbox into its appointed pocket and ensuring the button on the flap is secure. William's pain and, surprisingly, an ounce of discretion kept him from saying, "Actually we were both the last ones down the hill."

Major Tydings stands outside the medical station. He surveys a camp preparing for another stab at the enemy. Quickly wiping away a tear, Chief strides toward his tent as he mentally composes a letter to be addressed to the parents of his best friend.

It is customary for the editor of the *Republican* to assign the writing of obituaries to the cub reporter. This informal policy is not because the notice of the passing of one in the community is not worthy of the experienced wordsmith, just the opposite. There is a specific lesson that is being taught, hopefully to be ingrained into the character of the eager scoop hound. That lesson is, news happens to people. It is not an abstract event occurring in a void for the entertainment of the paper's subscribers. The news is usually painful. It is true that a good reporter is objective, but that does not mean unfeeling. Having the newbie overwhelmed by grieving loved ones usually puts the heart back into the journalist who was only seeking the facts.

This obituary is different as it is the first of the Havre de Grace's boys to be lost, to be sacrificed to war. His dreams and hopes forever wrenched from parents who nurtured the child through diapers, scraped knees, math problems, celebrations of birthdays, the sharing of everyday moments, and the discovery of loves found and lost. Death is the destruction of potential, of the contribution to society unfulfilled. There is no measure that can calculate the loss, and yet the editor must put down on paper words that will sum up the young man's life in a way that brings pride to the parents, solace to friends, and strength to other families...and there are so many families whose sons will not be returning. Picking up his pen, the editor stares at the blank page, the nemesis of all writers, and then pauses, as the preposterously colored decoy painted by his son distracts him. His gut twists at the thought of losing his boy because adults cannot solve their problems in a diplomatic way. Placing pen to paper the editor begins:

WE HAVE LOST OUR FIRST SON

August 18, 1918: Joe Davis[110] died—

In mid-sentence a thought other than his focus interrupts the editor's flow: *friends are invited to parties, but no one is invited to the house of mourners. They simply show up to quietly celebrate the one who can no longer attend.* Donning his jacket, more out of formal habit than against the miserable morning, the editor makes no excuses to his arriving staff as he leaves the office to pay his respects to the Davis family, and then recalls the joy-filled face of a euphoric young woman who placed an engagement announcement some months ago. The editor wonders if Florence has been told.

New Year's celebrations have never witnessed a party, the revelers, or the jubilation that is erupting on this, the 11th day of November: ARMISTICE!!!

It is a cessation of hostilities on the Western Front, shouted in a myriad of languages across the beleaguered globe. Deafening explosions of artillery and the screaming of dying men is replaced by the roar of elation, the giddy drunken laughter of survival, the rejoicing of life, and for Nathaniel Joiner, it is as good a reason as any other to toast a good brawl, especially when he had no dogs in the fight. Moving through his 75th year, he is living as a man who caught a leprechaun, and is forcing it to give up its pot of gold a handful at a time. Nathaniel's pockets are replenished with coins with each telling of the same old story. He does not need to embellish the facts, and can retell it to the same unamused gentleman who has reached the bottom of his purse, but his own survival demands he finds what he knows is blood money.

---

110 Davis, Joseph L. (1896-1918). In 1922, the Joseph L. Davis American Legion Post #47 was established in Havre de Grace. Millard E. Tydings (Chief) was the Post's first commander.

Nathaniel's new wool suit is warm against the chilly breeze blowing along the scrubbed and shellacked wooden deck of the *Emma Giles*. Across choppy waters, the chugging, black billowing, smoke-stacked, side-wheeler toot-toots its whistle to encourage its paying partiers. The captain of this elegant and stalwart workhorse of a passenger and cargo transport vessel, sensing a financial opportunity, announced at each port of call along the western and eastern shores that this is a patriotic cruise: food and alcoholic drinks to be served for a price, and dancing under hastily hung bunting that flaps colorful in the wind. The captain mentioned dancing many times, "... to the delightful musical notes of..." whoever could play the ship's piano and any other instrument for the lowest hourly wage. The only concession to a ticket holder is once they purchased passage, they can remain aboard as long as they please, or until the new day, the 12th of November announces its arrival over the Eastern Shore. At that time, the revelers must depart to begin the somber, heart-breaking chore of counting the human cost of the war. [111]

Nathaniel joined the bow-to-stern celebrants at the Havre de Grace wharf. He was enticed aboard by the cheers that incited jubilee, by the mouth-watering aromas of sizzling duck, pork, and beef that reminded him that it was past dinner time, and by his aching, pinched feet that had been squished into a pair of patent-sole leather shoes that came with the suit. The salesman said, "They need to be broken in," though Nathaniel has a sneaking suspicion that he is the butt of some cobbler's joke. Nathaniel figures that sitting at the never-before used mahogany bar on a cruise ship is far preferable to a long walk home.

Nathaniel works his way past the thrumming 25-foot paddle-wheel box as its wheel digs for purchase. Edging between towering shoulders of lively men and women onto the covered fantail, he is coaxed there by the singing of songs accompanied by a pianist, a flutist, a trumpeter, a trombonist, and a snare drummer, but more so by the popping of champagne corks and the clinking of filled-to-the-brim glasses, a one-time exception to the prohibition against the sale and consumption of alcohol aboard this Quaker-owned ship. Nathaniel surveys the ebb and flow of the young and old as he reconnoiters for a place to perch. There are servicemen, veterans that are too young, who are home early with injuries and stories. Surrounding them are adoring young ladies who are entranced, enthralled, and enamored by all the heroes wearing ribbons and medals. There are wrinkled old men who remember too vividly the acrid and putrid smells, and the terrible sounds of their own battles on American soil of years past when brother fought brother, north

---

111 The human cost of World War I is 10 million dead; 20 million wounded. Sadly, WWI was not the war to end all wars.

against south. The arms of these men are held by enduring old women who counted each tear for a son or husband lost. And mingled among the singles and pairs, the tales and memories, are families. Seated at tables are several generations. They are feasting, wrapped in the joy of being together on a party boat paddling in circles on the grandest of bays after a man-made storm that shook the world.

"Excuse me."

Nathaniel turns. A man, equal in age to Nathaniel, carries a tray filled with steaming plates of sliced suckling duck, juicy and hot off the ship's stove.

"Quite a crowd, isn't it?" the slender man with thinning brown hair shouts above the happy melee as he squeezes by Nathaniel.

"Quite a celebration," Nathaniel replies, as a chill, a phantom that has haunted his years pricks his conscience. Backing slowly toward the bar, and without thoughts for a drink or consideration to the vacant seat he sits down on in this standing room only vessel, Nathaniel stares at the back of a man quickly swallowed by the crowd. His was a pleasant face, open, with eyes that sparkled in contented old age, but Nathaniel saw something else, too. Seeping at the corners of his irises, barely masked by joy-filled pupils, is something only a lover would sense, or another who has suffered, endured, and survived the same unspeakable horrors. There are more than the psychological deprivations and physical sufferings; there is the deepest cut that permanently wounds the soul by the realization of the extent of man's cruelty to another. Those exposed share a kinship of never belonging to what was of humanity, and exiling themselves to forever live at the edge of society. The inexplicable something is to be surrounded by a crowd, embraced by family and friends, but always preferring to be alone, feeling that you are no longer worthy of the good things in life. This feeling is not from any overt act that causes shame, but from being touched by an evil so dark and fearful that somehow, if you get too close to others, it will be passed on to infect them.

Nathaniel reaches out to grab hold of the sleeve of a man with a clipboard. He is not a reveler, but a harried employee of the Tolchester fleet, the purser assigned to the *Emma Giles*. His round spectacles are indicative of a man focused on numbers and facts. His expression is a mixture of emotion. His thin lips are tight with worry over the captain's rebellious decision to allow and promote the consumption of alcohol, but his rich brown eyes twinkle because the only consequence so far is a strongbox crammed with cash. The final outcome, the hoped for trading of the owner's morality for money may not end as the captain believes, until then toot-toot the whistle.

"Can you tell me who that old man is?" asks Nathaniel.

The purser first looks down at the little old man in the expensive tailored suit, and then follows Nathaniel's outstretched arm to his dirty fingernail pointing in the direction of a table occupied by three generations of one family. The patriarch holding court is apparently the man of interest. Switching between a studious gaze at the distant table, and squinting at the names he has scribbled on sheets of paper, the purser comes to a decision.

"Ransom, John. Party of five. Boarded in Baltimore to celebrate a wedding anniversary, though I don't know if it's for the older or younger couple, but if I were to choose," the purser, with permanently indented writing fingers from hours of figuring this and summing up that, glances at the affectionate family, and concludes, "I'd say it's the older."

The two items around Nathaniel's neck, secured by an old, leather bootlace, burn his skin. Shrinking in stature, the rare weight of shame and guilt pressing heavily upon Nathaniel's rounded shoulders produce a contradictory smile of relief that reveals dentures that slip with each word, "I'd like to purchase a bottle of your finest champagne."

The purser is about to summon a waiter for this menial task, but the iron grip of resolve upon his arm makes him think better of it, and besides, a bottle of the finest champagne aboard this vessel is mere soda water in a fancy bottle with an exorbitant mark-up—a purser's dream.

It is the two women at the Ransom table who squeal with astonished delight at the man standing behind their father and husband. The mature daughter, Kate, is excited by the thought of toasting her parents' 50th wedding anniversary with champagne, an incredibly kind gesture by the management of this steamboat company to a visiting family from Chicago. Finette, John's wife, sobs uncontrollably from her opal blue eyes, though it is not the champagne, but a memory that has uncorked her tears. Jerking around, John expects an attack, danger of some kind, tragedy fitting the evoked responses from his girls that will ruin a wonderful evening, but what John finds is a skinny, bookish fellow holding what had been lost during his stay in hell. John blinks back his own tears, as with shaking hands, he lifts the two gold rings from around the neck of the bottle. Holding them carefully, fearing that if they are jiggled they will disintegrate in his timeworn palm, or vanish as a cruel hallucination by a malicious god who only allows his children to glimpse happiness.

John searches the face of the man holding the bottle for answers, some explanation for this miracle. With none forthcoming, and with a lump in his throat making speech difficult, John asks, "Where? Who?"

With the clipped precision of a naval man who is all business, and who, without a hint of the painful back-story, the long journeys of men or tokens of strength and shame that destiny or happenstance brought together, the purser repeats the simple words that he was ordered to memorize, "Wishing you a happy anniversary. Sorry for the delay."

Announcing the 12th of November are ducks and geese riding the crest of a storm created by nature. The front is heavy with whipping wind, slashing rain, and black clouds that replaced the night's sky. Nathaniel walks the empty decks of the pitching vessel, impatient at each port as the party boat disgorges hungover passengers. He is fidgety in his desire to return home, to take up his salvaged shotgun, and get at the returning wildfowl. Nathaniel's suit drips wet with cold rain; his feet, broken in with blisters, are irritants of no consequence, as a heady buzz not attributable to alcohol acts as a soothing balm, a warm blanket, a euphoric narcotic against the discomfort and pain. Nathaniel is whole again. His is a life without regrets, living each moment to the fullest and taking advantage of each opportunity that Luck brings his way.

Nathaniel's shoulders are squared as he stands tall.

Luck takes a swing.

The young mate, all of a pimpled 19, who is standing in for the quartermaster of the watch, spins the ship's wheel as he is eager to cross the bay and back to Baltimore. The oversized rudder, five feet in length and breadth, throws the *Emma Giles* broadside to the Arctic wind which is racing down the Chesapeake. Its decks roll, slanting precariously, sending the unoccupied tables and chairs sliding, tumbling across the wet deck. One table, its frilly cloth flapping as a too-short skirt on a teasing woman, heavy with momentum, crashes into Nathaniel to topple and carry him toward the ship's railing and the bay's black water. Caught off guard, and with the wind knocked from his lungs, a cry for help is made impossible. Nathaniel's eyes bulge as he careens toward a wet grave. His new shoes are worthless as the slippery soles are apparently made of grease.

Perfect, thinks Nathaniel. *I make things right and then I die—just perfect.*

From an opening door that releases a gagging stench, identifying it as the overused head, the shipboard commode, an arm reaches out to snatch Nathaniel off the racing table an instant before it crashes into the railing, splintering, and flying overboard.

"Gotcha!"

Nathaniel clings, weak-kneed to John Ransom.[112]

---

112 Ransom, John (1843-1919). John died at age 76, but the haunting words in his Andersonville diary live on.

"Easy there, my good man. We can't have you lost so soon after peace being declared. It wouldn't seem fair."

Righting himself as the side-wheeler steadies itself on its sturdy iron keelsons, Nathaniel says, "Thanks, it's lucky for me you were here."

John studies Nathaniel as if trying to place a familiar book on its correct shelf, "Forgive me, but do we know each other?"

Nathaniel's impulse to blurt, "Of course, Andersonville," is removed by the returning of the gold rings, that unpleasant chapter forever closed, and not worthy of weaving into an adventure as it was real. Nathaniel has made his way through life's ups and downs by telling stories worthy of remuneration, so he says without missing a beat, "Doubtful, unless you've been to the Klondike. Ever climb the golden stairs?"

"Can't say that I have, but it sounds interesting. How about I buy you a drink and you can tell me all about it?"

"How about I buy you that drink and tell you about a gold seeker turned archeologist? He told me he found canvasback fossils; something about the Pleistocene[113] epoch. Imagine that, eating 10,000-year-old duck."

John, not much of a hunter, a retired printer for the Merganthaler Linotype Company by trade, feels a strange kinship to this little man. Wrapping his arm about Nathaniel's broad shoulders, he introduces himself, "I'm John Ransom. Pleased to meet you."

Using his tongue to adjust his dentures, Nathaniel says, "I'm glad we met."

Luck is not upset because its plan for Nathaniel was thwarted. It knows that one day there will be no one and nothing to stand in its way—Luck is patient. Its will shall be done.

Ignoring the ignorance of a myth whose source of power exists only in the minds of men, the Voice, which is the gentlest baritone, soothes the cries of Seth. Left alone, Anna's half-brother shivers from fever as his mother, too weak to rise from her own bed, suffers aching joints, sweats and chills, and coughs that tear chest muscles.

---

113 Pleistocene epoch. A period of time estimated between 10,000 to 1,700,000 years ago when at different times at least 28% of the earth's surface was covered by ice. At present, only 10% is covered by ice, but this is decreasing rapidly.

The storm that blew through the Chesapeake region came in loud and rambunctious, carrying flocks of wildfowl that spread out among its many winding tributaries. It began with pelting rain that stung the exposed skin, and then, as an old man ignored among the youth, it sputtered out, ending with a silent snowfall. The playful ducks and chattering geese hidden within the curtain are the only sounds of life along Buzzards Glory or on the Susquehanna Flats.

The side-wheelers have ceased churning the waters of the bay.

The oyster skipjacks have stopped tonging the beds; they remain moored, abandoned at the wharf. Not a shot is heard from a sinkbox or blind. The decoy rigs are piled on shore.

Every window and door in Havre de Grace is shuttered and locked against the thing, against death that seeps through cracks and crevices and accompanies Anna as she runs panicked through the empty streets, a bundle with its life ebbing is cradled in her arms.

Anna had sat comfortable, contented as she carved and painted next to the blazing stove in the shack, drinking a steaming, extra-sweet cup of she-man coffee, but a growing unease made her restless. "Something is wrong," she said with gnawing concern to Beauty, who would lift an ear now and then, as if listening for distant gunshots that were strangely absent. Anna tried to dismiss the warning voice in her head by thinking that she was simply missing Seth and Olivia. With only the ducks and geese about, not a sign or sound of another human, not even a brief visit from Jim Currier who was late in picking up the strings of ducks that hung from the porch posts, Anna began to feel fear. Its pricklings she beat back with a rational mind that declared her concern was without substance.

Anna did not have enough experience with women's intuition to listen to and heed its early warning and advice. Intuition always speaks true, but as with faith, trust in the unseen is difficult. What finally sent Anna's feet running to Havre de Grace was an unexpected visit from Delbert. He and his pa had returned from what he described as a ghost town, "Never seen it so quiet, as if everyone became eligible for the rapture. Even the country store was closed. My pa was more spooked than upset, happy to leave town, even if we left without shotgun shells."

"Doctor Webster!" Anna cries as she hammers on the door, shaking loose snow from the porch overhang. "Are you home?" No answer comes from inside. No cheery face pulls back the curtains to smile warmly, welcoming all visitors. From behind, giggles float from across the street. Anna turns as triplets, curly-haired seven-year-old dolls wearing matching pink mittens dash from around the corner of a house, dragging a jump rope. Finding a suitable spot in the street, two turn the rope for the third, a rare treat with no traffic, as flakes of snow kick up with each jump and skip of the twirling rope. Together, the triplets sing the latest children's rhyme:

> "I had a little bird,
> Its name was Enza.
> I opened the window,
> And in-flu-enza."

The front door to the triplets' home bangs open as their mother rushes out and into the street to grab their little arms to drag them back into the house. "What did I tell you three?" Their mother's eyes search up and down the street. She casts fright-filled glances at the barren branches of the trees lining the walk, and then scans the gray skies of the overcast day, seeking something and fearful of finding it. "No playing outside."

"Where's Doctor Webster?" Anna calls out.

As if she were invisible until she had spoken, drawing the terrified attention of the triplets' mother, Anna steps off the doctor's porch.

"Stay away!" the mother shouts as she shoves her whining girls through the doorway.

"But where is he? I need his help. My baby brother is sick."

"If he's sick, it's too late."

"Please tell me where he's gone."

"He's gone to bury his wife," the mother's words are spoken in anger, as if it is the doctor's fault that death has come into this town, this "Harbor of Grace."

Anna chokes back tears which prevent the questions she would have screamed in her desperation from being uttered. Instead, they go off in Anna's head as a breech explosion: *How can Mrs. Webster be dead? If Doctor Webster could not save his wife, what hope is there for the town? What hope is there for my brother?*

Seth's face is tinted blue. He gulps as a fresh-caught perch, unable to swallow enough oxygen to cry out.

Only one person had occupied Tavern Bouvard when Anna pushed open the heavy door in an attempt to discover the reason for finding Havre de Grace's streets empty of its citizens when she ran into town. This surreal scene; businesses without customers, sidewalks without pedestrians, and a wharf without docksmen provided the missing substance to confirm Anna's fear and elevated it to a terror, even though she still could not put a name to it. It was Nathaniel Joiner, who Anna failed to recognize at first due to his fine suit, wrinkled though it was, sitting on a stool, slumped over the bar with all the many-shaped liquor bottles lining the counter. Nathaniel was mumbling something about, "Walking through the valley of the shadow of death..."[114] Hearing Anna enter, he turned, glassy-eyed, surprised to see another person.

"Join me, girl. I'm buying all the drinks today," Nathaniel indicating the toppled stack of coins among the bottles.

After stepping off the gangway of the *Emma Giles*, Nathaniel paused to watch it withdraw from the wharf to disappear into the falling snow. His last glimpse was of the Stars and Stripes of our nation's ensign hanging limp from the stern pole, signaling fatigue, exhaustion, not from celebrations of victory, but from one human tragedy, and a sadness at its inability to cope with another. Nathaniel turned to face a town without people, businesses without owners, and a tavern full of drinks but empty of patrons. Nathaniel feared no man, but a world without men to astonish with stories of his adventures would be frightful indeed. He chose to remain within the familiar and drink himself into a stupor.

Anna realized that with Nathaniel drowning in liquor, he would not be able to provide her with answers, coherent or otherwise, and before the tavern door slammed shut on his offer of a commiserating drink, Anna was halfway to Olivia's. Having thrown open the back door to Olivia's home, Anna entered a battlefield of a bedroom. The bed was askew, covers crumpled at the foot, and sheets ripped from the mattress while fighting fever. Olivia was found on the cold floor wedged between the wall and bed. While lifting Olivia's raggedy body back onto the mattress, it was evident to Anna that Olivia neither recognized her, nor did she comprehend or acknowledge her presence as she gazed into the distance, mumbling incoherently. Tucking the covers tightly, hoping they would remain to secure Olivia, Anna turned to the second bedroom where she found her brother. Anna first thought he was sleeping until she touched his forehead and found him to be on fire.

---

114 Psalm 23:4. "Yea, though I walk through the valley of the shadow of death, I will fear no evil: for thou art with me; thy rod and thy staff they comfort me." *Holy Bible*, King James Version, 1987 printing. Public domain.

Angel Hill Cemetery, where Doctor Webster mourns, is too far off to run to for help, and bringing a sick child to a graveyard would be like teasing the devil with sin. Anna runs past the jump rope lying in the middle of Lafayette Street, and then turns up Union toward the old Baker mansion. It is not the ice crystals hanging suspended, crisp and sharp, in the air that prick her eyes to tears, but seeing on every second or third porch, dusted with snow, one, two, and sometimes three winding sheets covering what can only be a man, a woman, or children.

Approaching the hospital, Anna passes the only conveyance moving slowly along the street. The two ageless Negro gravediggers are leading a jumpy mule pulling a cart, its wheels squeaking on greaseless hubs as the axle bends under the strain of so many wrapped bodies—dead weight. The men softly sing a spiritual, the notes quaver across the vocal scales with amazing grace, making it haunting as they proceed in their morbid duties, carrying their charges to the final resting place.

Entering the open double doors of the hospital, a charnel house in the making, Anna finds the hallways crowded with the sick, who lay, covering every inch of the floor. They wait for those farther through death's door on the cots to expire, so they will have a softer place to die.

Anna picks her way through the silent bedlam to the only nurse in sight. The crazy look of desperation on the disheveled matron tells more than a thousand stories of helplessness.

"Please, I need your help," Anna begs of the kneeling nurse.

"Find a place to lie down. I'll get to you if I can," the nurse responds. She is busy trying to clear the airway of a choking patient whose mouth and nose bubble with bloody froth, and who has the deadly hue of cyanosis,[115] a blue so deep that many believe they are being infected with the Black Death[116]— the plague.

"Where are the other nurses? Aren't there any doctors?"

---

115 Cyanosis is a condition where the lungs are unable to supply the blood with adequate oxygen. The blood vessels react by pulling oxygen from the body's extremities which causes the skin to turn bluish-black.

116 Black Death was an epidemic of plague likely both bubonic and pneumonic that ravaged Europe between 1347 and 1351. It originated in China and inner Asia and was transmitted to Europeans when a Kipchak army laying siege to a Genoese trading post in the Crimea, catapulted plague infested corpses into town. Rough

Without turning away from her patient, the nurse says, "The other doctor died last night. And as for the other nurse, this here is Betty."

The mortality of the ravaging flu, the swiftness of its destruction is staggering and beyond Anna's grasp. In a normal season it would claim two or three elderly or sickly babies, but this pandemic is cutting swaths through a community of healthy folk, strong folk who brag of, "Never been sick a day in my life." Anna's instinct to help others, to come to their need is selfishly ignored as she can only think of her brother, the only other living Buchanan, who, with every breath has given Anna joy—a family. Though Anna remembers, too, Olivia's pain at the grave site when her father was buried, she speaks tenderly to the old nurse while placing her hand on her shoulder. "I'm so sorry."

Anna's kind words, simple as they are, break the spell of stalwart despair, giving the nurse freedom to shed tears that have been dammed up in professional demeanor. Her sweet tears, a balm of love for her life-long friend, carries her sister of mercy to that place of peace where we all become children waiting to hear His words: "You have done well. In you, I am proud."

Waiting an eternity, which in a crisis, an emergency, a minute seems to be, Anna allows the nurse to become composed after covering Betty's face, now serene, with a sheet, Anna says, "It's my baby brother. Can you help him?"

"What's his name?" asks the nurse, always remembering her first day in nursing school, 30 years ago, when the scarecrow of an instructor whose voice grated with each syllable she spoke, admonished the class of bright-eyed Florence Nightingales:[117] You are the ones with patience. They are people with names and concerned and frightened loved ones.

"Seth."

Placing her stethoscope under the blanket to listen to the child's heart and lungs, the nurse says, "That's a strapping name," but feeling the heat

---

estimates are that 25 million people died in Europe from the Black Death—more than any war or plagues up to that time.

117 Nightingale, Florence (1820-1910). Known as the Lady of the Lamp for her services to the sick. She was a British nurse who reorganized training programs and reformed hospital conditions. Born into a well-to-do family, Florence found the social life of the upper crust unsatisfying and turned her energies to public service, specifically the welfare of the British Army. In 1907, as the first woman to receive the honor, the king conferred on her the Order of Merit. As a national hero, she could have been buried in Westminster Abbey but by her wish declined. With the greatest reverence, she was borne to the family grave in East Wellow, Hampshire by six sergeants of the British Army.

radiating from Seth's body and hearing the weakened heart and shallow breathing, she fears he will not have the chance to grow big and strong. There is no need to take Seth's temperature and from his lethargic, almost catatonic response to her delicate pinch, the administration of laudanum will make no difference. Medical science can only do so much and those unquantifiable entities: hope, prayer, and love are more for the living than the dead, but how do these three affect the dying? The nurse knows the sad outcome. She should be better prepared after so many deaths to look into the eyes of yet another family member whose hopes ride on the expression she wears when she looks up from their loved one with the answer to the repeated question: "Can you help?"

What the scarecrow instructor never got around to teaching, and what will always haunt this nurse, is when do you take away hope? Is knowing the truth better or worse? If the family is already grieving the loss, how does that affect the dying? Or does it make any difference? Is it God's will or allowance?

Steeling herself, as she looks into the sister's anxious face, the nurse realizes the obvious. There are no parents. They are either too sick to bring the child or have passed, making the words she needs to speak even more tragic, leaving this young woman alone, "It's the fever. I'm very sorry."

The two common responses to a prognosis of death are collapse or anger. These two emotions the nurse is prepared for, but Anna's is neither. The nurse detects an instant of panic that is quickly and remorselessly crushed by denial and determination. This response is admirable, but always seems to end with wailing and a loss of faith in the strength they believed in to get them through and to save their loved one. Anna looks down at her brother's pudgy face. His big eyes are squeezed tight and his tiny hands are balled into fists—the Buchanan spirit to fight. Some things in life are taught: how to lead the duck on the wing when you aim your gun to shoot; how to clean and pair each species drake to hen; how to carve the perfect rig decoy or decorative mantel piece. Some things in life are innate, simply a part of the essence of who your parents are: the will to battle against what is unjust; to appreciate the natural beauty of a thing or creature for its existence alone, and not for how it can be exploited or profited from.

"Can you make him comfortable?" Anna asks, not wanting Seth to suffer.

The nurse's brief experience with this cruel disease is that is its character. The infected will suffer. If there is a saving grace, death is usually swift, where a victim can be healthy for lunch and dead before dinner dessert is served. There is nothing left in the medicine cabinet except for an overdose of morphine, and even though the late doctor reluctantly prescribed its administration, the nurse cannot bring herself to do likewise. Reaching into her pocket, the nurse withdraws a small bottle and empties into her palm several small, chalky pills.

"These are aspirin. Crush them into water and try to feed it to your brother. It should ease his pain some."

Anna accepts the pills, and looking up and down the hallways at the dying and dead, people she knows by name, acquaintance, or a cordial, "Hello," and back to the one nurse who has remained at her station despite the risk to herself and apparent uselessness, Anna softens her expression, and says, "Thank you. I don't know where we'd be without you. You're a godsend." Then, with Seth held to her side, Anna reaches out to embrace the elderly nurse, who allows Anna's strength to flow into her, to know that uselessness does not mean in vain.

Olivia struggles against the bonds that are her double-tucked covers. Drenched in sweat, she shivers from a spiking fever. Despite her eyes showing only white, the pupils having rolled back into her head, her stare is fixed upon her own reflection in the full-length, standing mirror across the small bedroom. What her infected mind sees is not the spunky, red-haired girl be-spotted with freckles, but the flowing, onyx-colored hair of the creamy complexioned friend who she played with as a child, and who lies under a wooden marker with the word *Beloved* carved by hand across it.

Seeing a woman who is more alive, vibrant, in death, than when the two splashed each other in girlish delight while playing in the bay too many summers ago, and the woman who captured Clay's heart, Olivia's shivers are from fear under Jennifer's inspection.

"Have you come for me?" Olivia asks, the words spoken are heard only in her mind, though she believes her lips are moving.

"No," spoken without hate or vengeance, Jennifer says, "I've come for my husband's child."

The shock at hearing this proclamation nearly stops Olivia's heart. A shriek of panic reverberates inside her head, as she tries to come up with some reason, rational, logical, or otherwise to alter Jennifer's statement. "He's only a baby. He has not seen his first birthday. He knows nothing of life. Would you deny him everything?"

"The child has known the most important thing, happiness—love from the day of his conception. As his mother, would you want him to know the pain that comes with life, the suffering and heartbreak that accompanies growing into old age?"

"I want him to experience life, the full measure, and if there is to be pain from loss, it will only be equal to the love of life and for those he shares it with."

"Then knowing the love that we mothers have for our children, your pain will be beyond your belief to survive it."

A terrible, gut wrenching thought jolts Olivia. *It is her fault that her child is being taken from her,* and with a fear-filled hesitancy, Olivia asks, "Is this my punishment? If it is, please, I beg you, I'm sorry for loving Clay. Please Jennifer, forgive me. Don't make my child bear my sin."

Contrasting the dimming light cast through the bedroom window as the gray day wanes to evening, there is a magnificent glow, a radiance illuminating Jennifer's soft, hazy around the edges form.

"My dearest friend, you were always there for me. We walked and ran as children through the streets of Baltimore and the marshes along the bay, and as young women, we kicked up our heels at life's twists and turns, and when I could walk no longer, you sat with me, and then with a willing heart, after I departed, you took up my responsibilities. You have done me no wrong, and therefore you needn't apologize or ask forgiveness of me. No. You are not being punished. It is what it is."

In a lucid corner of Olivia's mind, a place not muddled by infection, she considers the wonderment, that Jennifer has become a messenger, and in her own death she is an angel of sorts, today charged with bringing sad tidings. Desperate, Olivia's heart groans, her spirit calling out, beseeching, "Please, as a mother, you would do anything, sacrifice everything for your child. I beg you, as my friend, to intercede for me."

The reflection of Jennifer in Olivia's mind never leaves the mirror, and though the solidity of this vision is questionable, Olivia feels Jennifer's gentle touch upon her cheek. At the same time, though Jennifer's words are spoken softly, their meaning is ominous and reproachful, "Is it your desire to change the plan that was set down before time began? Is it your belief that you know what is best?"

Anna finds herself sitting in the snow at the base of the Concord Point Lighthouse. The rotating beam a constant, reaching out for miles to warn and guide the lost to safe harbor. Tonight its beacon casts a light of hope, reminding those hiding behind barricaded doors that one, the faithful keeper of the light will never let them down, leaving no one alone in the darkness.

Anna did not consciously choose this spot at the joining of the Susquehanna River and the bay. Her wandering feet were hedging her losing bet, deciding to share the enchanting vista in spite of the tragedy unfolding, the magical essence of the natural beauty, what she adores, with her brother before...

Cradling Seth, Anna crushes the aspirin between her fingers, allowing the dust to sprinkle into his tiny mouth. Then dipping a finger into the snow, she scoops a teaspoon of flakes and dabs them across Seth's blue lips, letting them melt, to mix with the drug, in the hope that some will be swallowed and enter his system.

As Anna gently rocks Seth, she looks around at a world that has been placed on pause with silence commanded of all creatures and the elements.

No wildfowl call out or chatter chipper among themselves.

The dissipating clouds drift away on a night without wind.

The grieving sob into their pillows.

Only one thing disobeys. From somewhere, moving along some street named after a glorious event or esteemed person, approaching from an unknown direction, the squeaking wheel hubs of the grave diggers' cart announces its job of carrying away the dead is not finished. It is a frightful sound, grating at the soul, and tearing down what little hope Anna has built up for her brother's survival. If the squeaking was from some unknown spectral entity without form, it would only be a curiosity for Anna whose life within the marsh is filled with ghosts, phantoms, and things barely seen in the corner of the eye. This chalkboard screech of fingernails has a deadly substance and purpose. What is unknown is whether it merely carries away the vessel after the spirit has departed, or whether it is delivering coded instructions to be decisive to those wavering and straddling the fence between life and death? Is it announcing the time has come to step over into the hereafter because the chariot is arriving?—climb aboard.

Anna is torn between running as fast as she can from the sound, but that would rob both her and Seth of these last few moments of tranquility under the stars that twinkle, reflecting the diamonds held forever in snow crystals and sparkling across the calm water.

The turning hubs squeak again—approaching, coming closer.

Anna shivers with fear and from the cold. The seat of her coverall is soaked through, chilling her. A slap to the face could not have been more startling than the solution that surrounds her to the nurse's diagnosis: "It's the fever."

SNOW.

"Del almost died in the snapper's frozen pond because his temperature was lowered," Anna blurts out as she unwraps the blanket from around Seth. "Yours is too high. God, let this save him." Anna lays Seth's body onto the ground. He is limp as if having already surrendered the fight. Anna pulls snow around and over Seth as if it were summer and she were burying him in the sand. Worrying aloud, Anna asks, "How long to break your fever without killing you?"

Shadows quickly pass over brother and sister. Anna looks up to see a perfect "V." It is a flock of Canada geese nearly a mile long. They are all silent, respectful of the dying, or fearful that if they attract attention that they will also be imperiled. Focusing again on the blue face surrounded by snow, Anna wishes she, her brother, and Olivia could fly. Together they would escape this town of death, believing in error that anywhere but here would be safe.

The squeaking grows louder. It claws into Anna's heart. Anna refuses to look up, fearing that if she catches the eyes of the men and mule, they will hasten toward her with the cart of death. Pushing away the snow, brushing Seth dry and rewrapping him, Anna places her ear against his mouth hoping to hear or feel his breath.

The squeaking is accompanied by footsteps crunching the frozen ground...closer they come.

Turn away. Please, turn away, Anna's heart pleads of the approaching life stealers. Snatching the blanket away, frantic, as she again places Seth back into the snow. Her tears fall hot to melt dimples in the mound she piles onto Seth. Anna begs of him and whoever will listen, "No. No. No. You can't die on me. Fight for your life, Seth. Fight!"

"Here, girl. Let the child go. We'll take care of him." The voice is not from a disembodied ghoul, joy-filled at her misery, but from the black face of the grave digger that is pained with sympathy as he reaches out to pick up the lifeless baby.

The mule snorts a snotty stream, distracting Anna, as the other grave digger attempts to calm the beast that stomps its hooves, turning the cart.

"No!" Anna's scream is both a refusal, her unwillingness to give up Seth, and horror, as hanging limp, exposed from a winding sheet is a small hand. It was covered with care against the cold in a pink mitten. Anna collapses with deep, full body sobs as the meaty, calloused, and scarred black hands from a lifetime at the pick and shovel, lift Seth out of the snow.

"Shush!" The grave digger holding the mule's reins commands. Floating across the town like a tissue on the breeze is the tinkling of a bell, as if Mr. Stewart decided to open his store and the little bell above the door is ringing with a sale. This bell, however, is sounding from Angel Hill Cemetery, ringing with urgency—a call for attention. "Saved by the bell.[118] Seems we've buried one too soon," says the mule handler.

"It was bound to happen," replies the Negro holding Seth. Without reason, other than hope, faith, and love that were liberally sprinkled with aspirin and heaped on with snow, Seth fills his lungs with a full, fresh breath of salty bay air, and cries out. Both grave diggers look at the baby as its blue-tinted skin turns pink. The mule stamps its hooves again as Anna reaches for her brother.

"You got yourself a miracle baby," says the astonished and smiling grave digger. His perfect teeth, framed by a wide grin, are whiter than crushed oyster shells in the blazing summer sun, as he hands Seth back to Anna. His is a smile not worn in many days as Anna hugs and smothers Seth with kisses of joy and relief.

Anna bursts through Olivia's bedroom door. She is out of breath, panting with excitement. Within her arms Anna cradles Seth. He is a baby who has not stopped crying.

Somehow the child already knew his mother was added to the count.

Olivia lies, too quiet in her bed, a mixture of sadness and gratitude is expressed on her freckled face.

---

118 Saved by the bell. In times of mass burials due to plagues or pandemics, bodies were quickly buried without close examinations, due to scarce medical personnel. A string was attached to a bell and tied to the hand of those buried. In the event the person was not dead, he could ring the bell, and then be exhumed.

- 1919 -

Wildfowl of all species enjoyed a holiday while influenza cut its swath of destruction through the human population. For each hunter that remained bedridden or was carried away, never to pick up a shotgun again, a thousand ducks and geese lived through Christmas 1918 and New Year's 1919. For Anna and other hunters who were not afflicted, the misleading abundance of waterfowl gave the impression that the birds were making a resurgence in their numbers. This falsehood bolstered the hunters' belief that bag limits, rest days, and seasons are unnecessary, because nature can take care of itself.

With fewer hunters to saturate the sinkboxes and blinds, and nary a captain to guide a gunning yacht, the remaining wildfowlers' pockets should have been heavy with coin with the duck brokers' purchase of their weighty bounty, but the barrels that transported the bootleg birds to market were mostly empty. The family of man, the cohesiveness of the community may be diminished, shaken, and in some cities and towns decimated, but humanity, the essence, that indefinable willingness to sacrifice for the benefit of others without financial reward, to give, did not dim, but unwavering, shines stronger.

Wildfowlers, including Anna, hunted, numb with grief. The bitter winter cold and perpetually bruised shoulders from the shotguns' mule kicks cannot penetrate the sadness. Mechanically, they hunt because that is what they do, and with each pull of the trigger their broken hearts are being mended, as what follows each kill is a hug of gratitude, tears of relief, and joy for the meat meal. For the families too distant for the hunter to reach within an hour's walk, men like Jim Currier drive their teams throughout the day and into the night to distribute the ducks and geese, swearing, "Of course I can drive asleep at the reins, and that whiteout of a storm—no problem. My horses know where we're going." The few fed the many, reminiscent of when a basket containing loaves of bread and two fish fed thousands.[119]

Umbrella George seemed to be everywhere, encouraging the weary, comforting the grief-stricken, and extolling the blessings that are masked by sadness, fear, and hardships. "The means will always be provided; men and women whose aim is true; merchants giving away shotgun shells and warming their hands and spirits with the flames of pages torn from their credit book; and a constable who helps to pull a wagon out of a ditch while ignoring the cargo of illegal wildfowl destined for families whose provider no longer walks the earth. It's a conspiracy of good will...a miracle that is mankind."

Anna sits in the hogshead blind, one of three barrels at Swan Creek Point. On her right, in a barrel all his own, Seth sleeps in a bundle of winter clothes and a quilt. He has learned to sleep through the gunshot blasts, and when awake, intuitively, as a Buchanan would, he scans the skies, silent, not so much as a gurgle. On Anna's left is Delbert in the pickle barrel. Delbert's only remark when choosing to sit in the stink of brine is, "Nothing's better than a crispy pickle." His company, the constant companionship after Olivia's passing is a quiet strength. Delbert never offers platitudes of consolation simply to fill the empty silences. He allows Anna to work through grief in her own way and in her own time. Delbert's presence meets Anna's needs, and when he does speak, it is not with trepidation that his words will fracture a delicate crystal, that Anna is not. He is "Del" and any change would be unacceptable to Anna and out of character for Delbert.

They are friends.

"Are you going to move to town?" Delbert asks, squinting against the sun that has cracked the horizon over the Eastern Shore.

"It would be easier and it's a nice home," Anna shades her eyes, as specks appear in the distance, flying fast and high.

"Black ducks," Delbert remarks to Anna's scrutiny. "I'm sure with some redecorating; you can make Olivia's house your new home." The specks continue on their path, ignoring Anna's Judas bird and its welcoming calls.

---

119 Mark 6:38-44. Jesus fed 5,000 with five loaves of bread and two fish. *Holy Bible*, King James Version, 1987 printing. Public domain.

"If I do, I'm not ever going to erase everything that was Olivia. She was my second mother and Seth's only one," Anna turns her attention to dots flying from the south beyond Spesutie Island.

"Gadwalls," states Delbert. "I wasn't implying any such thing, but my ma tells me that each woman has to make the house their own."

"I suppose she's right," Anna says, as the dots land out on the Flats somewhere beyond the island. "I don't know if I'm cut out to run the tavern. Helping out occasionally was one thing, but every night, I don't know how Olivia did it. I'm exhausted." Swinging in a long distant arc, as if considering Anna's goose's invitation, a dark gray smudge moves across sparsely patched, light gray clouds, fronting the bluing sky.

"Spoonbills," proclaims Delbert without hesitancy. "Owning a house in town, a business, the marsh property, and selling your *little* decoys, you're now some kind of tycoon."

Anna puzzles over Delbert's identification of each species of duck, if in fact that is what they are, as the "spoonbills" turn away at a distance that prevents Anna from clearly seeing the color patterns or distinguishing flight movements. "I don't feel like a tycoon. I'm overwhelmed with responsibility. I didn't create any of it and am barely hanging on." From the north a string of birds that have flown over Havre de Grace are making a beeline eastward as if late for a dawn appointment.

"The way you received all of it is tragic, and if all you can do is hang on, well, that is succeeding...white-winged scoters...but, if you're not cut out to be a bar maid, quit. Sell the place, but do so for the right reasons, and not because it's too difficult." A small flock rises from the southern end of Spesutie, and then quickly lands again. Anna glimpses only a flash, a tangle of bodies lifting and dropping. "Common goldeneye. You have choices," continues Delbert.

"Just stop right there," huffs Anna, standing in her barrel. Ignoring Delbert's career advice, Anna focuses in on that which hunters, especially friends will tolerate, but contest when detected, and that is the spreading of bull. "My eyesight is as good as yours, Delbert Joiner. Actually it's better as I have two and you only one. I couldn't tell what species any of those birds were, or even if they were ducks or geese, yet you expect me to believe you can?"

Smiling, unperturbed by Anna's accusation that he is pulling her leg, Delbert responds confidently, "Well, I cannot be blamed if the set of your rig and the calls of your goose are not enticing enough to bring in the birds so that I can be proven right or wrong, and, Anastasia Nicole Buchanan, until you rectify your inadequacies, I'd appreciate it if you wouldn't insinuate that I would lie to you, calling my character into question...mallards and pintails." Delbert points through snow-dusted brown foliage camouflaging the hogshead blind toward a smear that are some species of wildfowl traversing the horizon.

Seth, awakened by the banter, giggles.

The resiliency of children and the qualities of friends and hunting partners are matchless.

Anna sits down in her barrel. Seth's giggles tickle her right ear, Delbert's snickers tease her left. Beauty, who had been half-listening, half-napping, nuzzles the back of Anna's neck. Without turning to expose the smile stretching from ear to ear, Anna admits to herself: *yep, they can only be mallards and pintails.*

It is the whinnying of a mare that works its way through the fog of Anna's deep sleep that stimulates sweet memories, recalled in the form of dreams of Olivia riding her horse; that mare now many years gone to the tannery, and Olivia several months asleep in Angel Hill Cemetery. Truths and reality do not affect the unconscious nor control its creations. The dreaming mind is not bound by facts, nor is it limited to earth's confines. The dreamer can be a king or queen, a soaring eagle or shooting star, or a carefree vagabond, and can surround themselves with friends who do not know of the dreamer's existence or family who have departed the earthly realm.

Anna dreams of a skin-warming summer day, wherein Clay sits on the steps of the porch. He is whittling a mallard's head while Jennifer rocks wildly in her chair. Her mother is laughing and clapping her hands as Olivia's mare performs a prancing dance under its rider's gentle persuasion. Clay, with his straight-faced, no-nonsense annoyance at these childish antics, attempts to ignore the show that he watches from the corners of his eyes. This only encourages the two women to exaggerated playfulness.

The three are filled with the life of youth, not a care or worry, certainly pre-Anna and Beauty, yet arriving, rackety-boom, in an automobile whose make and model is unknown, yet to roll off the assembly line, is Anna and her husband. She is heavy with child, beaming, and restraining a spunky retriever that is impatient to leap from the convertible to wreak havoc, yapping tirelessly, to devil this season's tollers.

Squeak-creak.

Jennifer leaps off the weather-worn and cracked wooden plank porch to embrace Anna in a hug that brightens the sun, turning the yellow, pink, and blue petal marsh flowers toward mother and daughter, envy blushing their many faces.

Squeak-creak.

The rocking chair continues to rock. Its runners move back and forth across a loose plank as if the weight of a body is still upon it.

The mare whinnies and snorts, irritated, rattling its harness, and stomping its hooves...extinguishing the brilliant sun.

The world created by the dreamer, Anna's universe held fragile within a bubble of wishes, hopes, and desire is popped as a pin to a carnival balloon as her eyes open with a start.

Squeak-creak.

Beauty snores softly at the foot of Anna's bed. Hers is the only sound to orient Anna in the darkness of the shack. Beauty's nights as watchdog have ceased with age and infirmity.

Squeak-creak.

Adrenaline from fear of the unknown mixes with hope that the noise is William returning safely from war. Anna scrambles out of bed and into unlaced boots. Anna's lavender flannel gown trails behind.

Squeak-creak.

But why hasn't he knocked? Anna reaches for her Winchester. Its blue steel barrel reflects the glow of hot embers at the bottom of the stove. Anna checks Seth who is sleeping soundly on her old cot; and then peeks above the windowsill. Anna spies a soft-brim hat covering the back of a man's head. Smoke from a cigarette rises from between his fingers that drum the armrest. He rocks slowly, comfortably, with familiarity. The rocker's runners move back and forth across a loose plank.

Squeak-creak.

Cautious, Anna unlatches the door, the shotgun's barrel leading the way.

Twisting his head to the scrape of the swollen door against its jam, a three-day beard bristles as whiskers partially conceal his face, he says, "Going hunt'n in your nightgown, are we?"

"Mr. Currier?" Anna lowers the shotgun. "What are you doing here again, this late? You already picked up my ducks."

"Actually, it's this early, round about 3:30 in the morning, I suspect." Harnessed to the wagon that transports the wildfowl to market and the needy are two mares, both dead tired, and annoyed by what they perceive is an unnecessary stop. The wagon is empty and they want to go home to their clean stalls with fresh hay and nourishing oats.

Mr. Currier draws deeply on the cigarette. Its cherry burning brightly as it nears his fingers. He coughs as a man who smokes only occasionally. The smoke, both acrid and sweet, explodes from his lungs. "My wife says it's a nasty habit and I tend to agree with her, but here I am, puffing away while sitting on the porch of a friend who's no longer here to chew the fat with."

"I don't remember..." Anna props the shogun against the door frame and moves to lean against the support post.

"As a younger, wilder man, before I married, when you were sleeping as a tot through the night, I'd somehow find my way to this porch. Your father would sit right there on the step, carving in the dark with his hand-rolled hanging from his lip. I'd complain about this or that, the injustice of laws against hunters, the price of shotgun shells at the country store, a girlfriend nagging me to marry her, and the whole time your father would listen. When I finished, he'd lean back, as if preparing to reveal some insight, a great wisdom passed secretly down through the generations, and then sneak a peak back through the open door to be sure you and your mother were asleep, and say with a sigh after taking a lung full of air, 'God, it's a beautiful night.'"

"My father used the word, 'beautiful'?" Anna slides down the post to sit, unknowingly, like her father, with one foot on the ground, and the other on the first step.

"Yep. He'd say it as an absolute, leaving no room for challenge. I'd have to stop my bitch'n, pardon my language, and look around. Didn't matter if it was a warm summer, a brisk fall, or a storm'n winter night, it was beautiful to him, and still is."

Looking around at the thin layer of snow coating the ground, then out across the peaceful, placid water of the Flats, Anna is about to agree when Mr. Currier continues.

"After a quiet spell, your father would say, 'Jim, seems as choices are confounding you.'"

"Del told me that I've got choices, too."

"Life is about choices...decisions that shape our destiny. Sounds ominous, I know, but it's comforting to know that we are mostly in control. Your mother used the term, 'free will.' I'd of course tease her that there is nothing free about it. It's a costly privilege if we choose incorrectly."

Perplexed as to the purpose of Mr. Currier's early visit, Anna asks, "But why are you here now?"

"I've always made my best decisions from the choices I've had right here. That nagging girlfriend is my wife and I couldn't be happier. Despite the laws and cost of shotgun shells, I hunt, and because I've chosen to ignore certain restrictive laws, I've been able to feed many less fortunate than I, but now it's time for a change."

"What do you mean?"

"My wife misses my company at night, saying, 'I need my manly bedwarmer.' And frankly, I'm tired of dodging the law, always looking over my shoulder. The Grossos want to resume, and my hours at the post office can be increased to full-time, if I want it, and I believe I do. So I'm giving you notice that tonight's run was my last." Mr. Currier[120] pauses, a nervous, uncomfortable tension accompanies his silence, as if he is unsure if it is his place to broach the next subject. "And, as Del said, 'You have choices.'"

Anna believes Mr. Currier is referring to choices regarding residence and business, "I haven't decided if my life should be in town or here."

"I'm not talking about those choices. The boys..." Mr. Currier emphasizes the plural, "are steadily returning from overseas..." Anna is uneasy by the conversation's turn to her personal life, but out of respect remains quiet.

"...and, unlike a priest who one goes to confess secrets, as a postal worker, all secrets are written in ink in the form of *to* and *from*."

Anna is horrified; never giving any thought that each time she dropped a letter in the mailbox or received one from William or Tim, that she was exposing her secret—*Idiot! Idiot! Idiot!*

"They are just friends," Anna's defense lacks conviction.

Mr. Currier holds up his hand, the cigarette nearly out, "I'm not insinuating one thing or another. As a friend of your parents, I wanted to share with you a quality of your father's and that rock'n in this chair, I made good decisions among the choices laid before me." Taking a deep, satisfying breath of air, a mixture of bay salt and marsh iodine, Mr. Currier says, "I think it's time I quit my nasty addiction." Rising from the rocking chair, he flicks the cigarette butt away. It fizzles out, drowned in the melting snow. Climbing onto the seat of the wagon, Mr. Currier takes in the view, satisfied, and states as an absolute, "God, it's a beautiful night." He snaps the reins, giving his mares what they want, permission to go home.

Anna moves to her mother's rocking chair.

Squeak-creak.

Beauty waddles through the doorway to squint one-eyed and sleepy at the shotgun, and then curiously up at her mistress clothed in her nightgown, as if asking, "Did I miss something?"

---

120 Currier, James A. (1886-1969). Jim began working at the Havre de Grace post office around 1918, continuing for 43 years, retiring as postmaster in 1959. Throughout the many ensuing years, Jim continued to hunt, carve decoys including decoratives for the mantle, guide sports, and captained his own gunning yacht.

William is again in the city of his base desires, New York City. However, none of his needs are being met. Today, the harshness of the common folk, who at one time or another are down on their luck, is William's reality. Ignored, he is sitting on a dirty curb in the middle of Wall Street. His nostrils curl against a steaming pile of horse manure and the wandering stream of urine deposited by a dilapidated horse. The offending nag struggles to pull an old, canvas-covered cart under the midday September sun.

The significant difference between William's poverty and those hidden within the fecund tenements is that his ends with a telephone call home for funds to be wired, or at least that is what William believed when he scrambled down the long, bouncing gangway of the troop ship after it docked. Lured aboard the wrong transport by the invitation to easy money at the roving poker game, William chose the long way home, not boarding his designated vessel that would have disembarked him close to home in Baltimore. Finding too late that the game was rigged, and not wanting to confront the smiling *Joes* pocketing his cash, for one, he was outnumbered, and two, his jaw, though mended, was still fragile and would shatter at the slightest impact. William decided that discretion over valor, temporary poverty over pride, should win the day.

William's experience with war had taught him one thing. He did not like pain.

Penniless and hungry, William feels sorry for himself as he sits in his wrinkled and perspiration-stained uniform, clothes that remained unwashed throughout the Atlantic crossing. William scratches the few whiskers, a week's growth. He is perplexed by his father's refusal to send funds. Instead, William was sternly instructed to meet his father in front of the House of Morgan at noon. "I have urgent business with Mr. Remy," his father had said with something of a catch, almost a panic in his voice, "and you might as well attend as the substance of our discussion affects you, too." Then he roared, his old, bellowing self, "And I'm not sending funds for you to fritter away. We'll return home together."

Expecting his father to be chauffeured by Roman to the front of the imposing building, a building faced with polished granite that exudes wealth, permanence and stability, William is caught off guard as his father accosts him from the sidewalk.

"My Lord, William, you're a mess," Frank McQuay stands over his son, imposing, impeccably attired, yet deep circles under puffy and bloodshot eyes indicate exhaustion and worry.

William leaps to his feet, and casting his eyes about, asks, "Where's Roman?"

"Left him at home. Said he didn't feel like driving, so I took the train, besides it's more economical."

William stares in disbelief. His jaw, slightly skewed to the left, dares not ask the questions: *You allowed Roman to beg off a task for which he was instructed? And, when did the word economical enter your vocabulary?*

"You cannot present yourself in that condition to Mr. Remy. You'll have to wait out here until the meeting is over," Frank McQuay turns on the heel of his polished shoe to stride toward the entrance of the House of Morgan. A liveried doorman with a top hat holds the heavy and ornate brass door open for the kings of Wall Street to enter and exit.

"May I have some money? I haven't eaten and it's now lunch time," whines William, as two men rushing out the open door jostle him and his father. They are immigrants, laborers, bearded with dusty caps and soiled overcoats, out of place among wealth, snubbed and ignored as sewer vermin.

"Excuse me!" Frank McQuay shouts to the backs of the men disappearing into the crowd, a conglomeration of businessmen whose only focus is on the deal of a lifetime they are all striving toward.

"Apologies, sir," says the effacing doorman, his hand out, always posturing for a tip. "Obviously workers failing to use the service entrance."

"Obviously," replies Frank McQuay, sarcasm oozing as grease from a broiling goose, as he fumbles in his pockets for change. "Here," Frank McQuay hands his son two coins and dismisses him. "Wait over there and don't get into trouble." Stern-faced and leaving no room for pleadings for more, Frank McQuay walks past the doorman whose open palm remains embarrassingly empty.

With meager means squeezed within his fist, William's nose begins the process of elimination to find his stomach's desire:

Ignore the acrid, choking exhausts of passing automobiles; reject the sickly sweet mounds buzzing with flies; snub the light perfumes and heavy colognes of the fancy dressed; and overlook his own pungent odor to focus on the baked aroma of salted pretzels dripping cheddar cheese. Approaching the sidewalk vendor, a man whose quick eyes keep vigilance for roving police, because the price of a street license, or in lieu of such, a payoff, exceeds his weekly income, William allows his stomach to grumble in anticipation, disregarding thoughts of nutritional value, as it is quantity that it craves.

"Two," William says as he hands over the coins. "Extra cheese, please."

Impatiently waiting and watching as the obese vendor, obviously a heavy user of his own product, double dips the breadbox-sized pretzels in the milk pail of melted cheese, a glossy brochure in a spinning kiosk next to the pretzel cart catches William's attention. Slipping the folded paper out of its slot, William opens the colorful Michelin Tire Company[121] guidebook of World War I battle sites. Blinking, trying to focus, to read what he recently lived, William breaks out in a clammy sweat. The church bells at Trinity church overlooking Wall Street strike noon as a brilliant light engulfs William. A thunderous explosion erases the hustle and bustle of the street, replacing the backfiring automobiles with the waking nightmare of the tack—tack—tack of Vickers machine guns. The swooping pigeons darting here and there seeking crumbs of bread become shrieking star shells searching out flesh; and the hollering vendors hawking their wares are transformed into screaming men shouting for help. The whump-thump against William's back knocks him off his feet and tosses him through the concussive air...his nose bleeding and eardrums punctured by the explosion.

Lying in the offal of the New York street at the bottom of a canyon made from mighty buildings shaken to their foundations, William blinks, as he lifts his head to focus on the pretzel vendor. The weighty man, tossed like a leaf in a sudden gale, is across the street, sprawled on the undercarriage of an overturned automobile. Between the running, and staggering wounded, William clearly sees that the cheese melting down the front of the vendor's apron is red.

The editor of the Havre de Grace *Republican* would prefer to place this bit of news on an inside page, relegating death to a lesser place of importance, as he and his town are tired of the effects of war, disease, and all forms of destruction. Unfortunately, he is precluded from his wants by the prominence of one of the victims. *He was a giant among men,* the editor thinks, *and is due proper respect, to be admired, lauded, and emulated.*

The next morning, the 17th of September, the bold headline will read:

WALL STREET EXPLODES!!!

Terrorists set off a bomb[122] outside the House of Morgan, one of New York City's financial institutions. The violent blast killed 30, injured 100,

---

121 Guidebook. In an effort to promote European travel, hopefully using automobiles riding on Michelin tires, the Michelin Tire Company produced guidebooks of World War I battle sites.

122 On September 16, 1920, a bomb delivered on a wooden wagon pulled by a horse, consisting of 100 pounds of dynamite packed with hundreds of small chunks of iron was detonated on Wall Street. It is the first act of terrorism against New

and caused an estimated two million dollars in damage. The explosion may have cracked the financial walls of New York, but it toppled a pillar of our community.

Frank McQuay, age 54, while attending a meeting of great fiscal importance at the House of Morgan, was one of those killed when pieces of iron blew through the window he was seated next to. He leaves behind a family that includes a son, William, who was injured in the explosion. Reports are that William will recover to take the helm of the always-expanding McQuay agricultural empire. Grieving her husband's loss, the adoring wife, Dorothy Parker McQuay, has sequestered herself, refusing to be comforted even by her loyal and loving servants.

Funeral services will be held this Saturday. The mayor and other dignitaries will speak on the many accomplishments of a man who wrenched productivity from a land that was wild, and seemed to the timid and visionless, as untamable and useless. We are all diminished by the loss of Frank McQuay. May he rest in peace in a place of honor among the great men who reside in Angel Hill Cemetery.

"Rumor has it that you're the man to speak with when it comes to local history," says a hesitant voice barely above a whisper, from one who is sorely out of place in the crowded and rowdy Tavern Bouvard.

Nathaniel Joiner spins on his extra-tall stool to scrutinize the impish man standing next to him. Fifty-ish, with a pale complexion and squinty eyes that gives the impression of a man who rarely steps outside, and who spends his waking hours studying within the tomes of academia. "I never countenance or spread rumor, sir, and as to history, I know nothing, but, for the duration of a tall mug of this establishment's finest brew, I'll tell you of adventures that span this continent." And before the imp can beg off, Nathaniel pounds his fist on the bar that is awash with brown froth and spilt liquor. "Barkeep! Barkeep! Two tall ones, please."

York's financial district. Thirty were killed, 100 were injured, and $2 million in damages were done to the buildings. Marks are still visible on the façade of the J. P. Morgan building. Exhaustive investigation by the Justice Department and Bureau of Investigations (now the F.B.I.) concluded that Mario Buda, a member of Luigi Galleani's anarchist organization, was the driver of the wagon. No one was ever prosecuted for the bombing as Galleani had been deported and Buda returned to Italy after the bombing.

Moving down the bar, pouring mixtures of hard liquor and dark brew, Anna, her hair falling disheveled into her face, slams two heavy mugs onto the bar, "Mr. Joiner, please, I've told you a dozen times to call me Miss Buchanan, or Anna. Olivia was the barkeep. I'm..."

Tumbling, with bare-knuckle fists flying, two best friends whose evening of drink and merriment began five hours ago, pummel each other to punctuate their point of view: the retriever best suited for the Flats is... the Chesapeake...the Labrador. The crowd of hunters, oystermen, and local businessmen immediately take sides, not as to the outcome of the fight, but the rightness of the physical debaters' argument. And, the fight is a temporary diversion from card games, late dinners, and the spinning of yarns.

Under the counter and out of harm's way, Seth, who can sleep through shotgun reports, cries as the two men slam into the facing of the bar, shaking glasses and rattling bottles.

Anna grabs the worn-with-use oak club that has quelled many a brawl.

Nathaniel, fearing the scuffle, that to him appears more of a wrestling match, will scare off his skittish new drinking buddy, grabs the two mugs and breaks them over the heads of the two friends, who crumple, unconscious to the floor.

Order is restored to the chaos that is Tavern Bouvard.

"Now, sir, I didn't catch your name?" Nathaniel gently, but firmly eases the twitchy man onto the stool next to him. Anna replaces the broken mugs, and then looks across the lantern-lit room to where Constable Jenkins is drinking and playing cards with two of his deputies.

Constable Jenkins, seeing Anna's plea for help, shrugs his shoulders, indifferent, as no harm—no foul. It was only a dispute between two drunken friends. *Let 'em lie where they fell* is the constable's thought. If they awake, and are still in a combative mood, he will then haul them off to jail.

Extending his bony hand, the imp says, "I'm George Archer, President of the Historical Society of Harford County."[123]

"President, you say? Well, Mr. Archer, I have to admit that is an impressive title, but I've never heard of you or your society."

Not the least bit put off by Nathaniel's ignorance, or his slept-in and soiled suit with non-matching and shabby hunting boots that are tied with two different kinds of twine, Mr. Archer places several coins on the bar for the harried lass to scoop up and pocket. "Well, that's okay, as we often work without much fanfare to collect and catalogue artifacts and document events in our county."

---

123 The Historical Society of Harford County, Inc. was incorporated in 1885. The society motto is "Preserving Our Past for Your Future." Dr. George W. Archer, society historian, who collected the bulk of its early material, established the society.

Suppressing the urge to laugh, not wanting to offend this man who is buying, Nathaniel says, "Artifacts? All we got are ducks, geese, and oysters. I suppose you can collect 'em, but if you don't eat 'em quick they get to smell'n awful bad."

"Mr. Joiner, you've hit two of the many nails right on their heads, but it seems I've not explained myself adequately. It is the way the birds and oysters are collected, and the changes over time that are important; the types of guns used, the decoys, and the oyster skipjack with its tongs. These make up history."

"You saying my old fowling pieces are valuable?"

"They're historical and in need of preservation."

Nathaniel lifts his mug to gulp the fermented malt drink. Mr. Archer sips his bitter brew, preferring tea, or if it is a special occasion, sherry.

"Guess I shouldn't have tossed them," and to Anna, who is only half listening while trying to sooth Seth, "Fill 'er again?"

Anna looks to Mr. Archer, who reluctantly nods, opening his tiny change purse, and then Mr. Archer adds, "It may be hard to believe, but what we do today, what we may think of as permanent, will eventually all pass away, and, just as you tossed what you perceived as useless or outmoded, and replaced with something newer and more efficient, has an intrinsic value that those who have yet to be born will one day marvel at. Your adventures, the hardships of the individual man, the way each of us makes our living, which extends to our community, our country as a whole, must be preserved, exhibited, and learned from." Having a sensitive constitution, Mr. Archer's stomach rumbles, revolting against the harsh beer.

"Hmm," Nathaniel, thinking, looks for profit, "So if I scrounge up artifacts, how much are you paying?"

"Mr. Joiner, we're a non-profit organization."

"I've never heard of such a thing!"

"All our members volunteer their time and folks donate to our collection."

"I cannot imagine your society will be around for very long if you're counting on the generosity of folk. Times are always tough. It's only if you're lucky like me that you get ahead or can afford to give things away."

"Respectfully, sir, I disagree, but if you'll excuse me, I require the use of the lavatory," Mr. Archer looks to Anna who points to the back door.

Left alone in a room that is wall-to-wall disorderly conduct, Nathaniel studies Anna who stares back with weary eyes, joyless. Anna scrutinizes Nathaniel, and wonders about the sudden economic change; from the man who bought the rounds, to the storyteller of old, who sells his adventures for a pint or two.

"I'm not trying to pry into your personal affairs," Anna hesitates, not wanting to be rude, but curiously concerned, comments, "Seems to the observant that your fortunes have turned for the worse."

Nathaniel sighs, "It's my ship."

"Your ship?"

"My ship of fortune that came in, well, to speak the truth, it sunk, or more precisely, he died. Got himself blown up."

Anna is unsure as to how a no account rogue like Mr. Joiner could be mixed up with a brute like Frank McQuay, assuming Nathaniel is referring to Mr. McQuay, as Anna knows of no other person who has recently died in an explosion. Ignoring that question, Anna asks with a sympathetic tone, "Have you ever considered that your luck may not be all it's cracked up to be?"

Offended, Nathaniel throws his old, creaking shoulders back, spits on the wooden floor, and stares unflinching at Anna, who for an instant fears that he will strike her, and then with a voice that is firm in its conviction, says, "Miss Buchanan, just because it seems I get the tail's side of the flipped coin, you ever see me complaining? No. To admit something ain't as great as it should be, well, in my book that's admitting defeat." Nathaniel scans the dim and smoke-filled room. He is the oldest and healthiest among those in attendance. "Look at me. I'm still here when others have passed. God knows I'm far from perfect; made lots of mistakes, some unpardonable, but I never give up or quit...ship in—ship out."

Anna pours Nathaniel one on-the-house, as she is surprised to hear him admit his deeply held truth, and because something inside her tells her that his revelations have only begun, but may need coaxing, though she doubts any amount of alcohol could cause a man such as Mr. Joiner to say anything against his will.

"You want to know what Mr. McQuay and I had in common?"

Anna slides the mug toward Nathaniel, but doesn't let go; gentle persuasion. She says nothing.

"Nathaniel leans over the bar and lowers his voice, as if what he is about to say is only for the privilege of Anna, "Felipe LeCompte."

Stunned by the implications, Anna releases the mug, to stare gape-mouthed at the little old man as he swallows unimpeded. Then, setting the mug onto the bar, Nathaniel transforms into the adventurer-storyteller, his eyes brightening with euphoric recall, "The moon rode high on that bitter-cold October night, 1916. I was doing my civic duty, wandering the marsh to anonymously assist the local game warden by freeing wildfowl caught in duck traps. I was south of your place when I came upon a poacher and his Negro accomplice. Being unarmed, I kept myself hidden among the tall grasses, waiting to see if they were building or emptying the trap. Then, surprise, surprise, springing with fearless bravery, as a cat onto an elusive mouse, LeCompte leapt from the narrow trail, shouting, 'You're surrounded. Stand where you are. You're under arrest,' but the poor man never stood a chance. The poacher whirled around, and with only a moment's hesitation, shot LeCompte dead."

Anna grabs hold of the edge of the counter to keep from fainting. Her question is not heard as she moves her lips, but clearly understood, anticipated by Nathaniel, "The poacher was...?"

Nathaniel nods, "Yep, the poacher, the man who murdered Game Warden Felipe LeCompte was Frank McQuay."

"But my father was accused."

"That was unfortunate and I would have come forward if he had been convicted, but luckily he wasn't and, after sharing this information with McQuay, he and I came to a financial arraignment. He didn't like it much but he had no choice."

Smiling, smug in his cleverness, Nathaniel slides the empty mug toward Anna, who mechanically refills it. Considering whether she should bash Nathaniel over the head with the bottle, but the emotion that takes control is sadness for all that she and her father suffered because of Frank McQuay's acts. Anna has learned to live with loss, but knows she will never get over, or completely move on, as that place in her heart that her father filled by his presence will always be vacant.

Only partially understanding the source of Anna's misery, Nathaniel states as a question, "You're not happy here, are you?"

Hearing the truth wrapped within a question allows Anna to come clean as this is a night filled with confessions, "No This was Olivia's world. My place is in the marsh, but you, you're happy here, telling your stories."

"Adventures. They're adventures."

Anna scans the room. It is absent the two people that gave the tavern its warmth and character—Olivia and her father. Anna wants to run, to flee from what is now cold, vulgar, and alien, but responsibilities remain, and choices—decisions. Then like the tarnished gears in the old clock on the wall clicking into place for the out-of-tune chime to sound, Anna's thoughts register the solution, opening her eyes to what has always been before her. She thinks, *God, I'm so blind. What an idiot I am. He is perfect.*

"Mr. Joiner, you should own this place."

Chuckling at the absurdity, the obvious joke, Nathaniel says, "Me? A businessman? That's a riot, besides, I've got no money."

"That may be, but what you have is character, defined by necessity, and that's what this place needs," Anna bends down to pick up Seth who settles down in her arms. "Pay me what you can at the end of each month, agreed?" Anna holds out her hand.

Presented with an opportunity of a lifetime, an offer to succeed by his own wit, relying not on Luck but craft, Nathaniel's wrinkled hand trembles as he lifts it to shake Anna's.

The deal is sealed.

Wearing a smile in a decision made, Anna squeezes through the men celebrating the end of another day of surviving what life has thrown at them. Approaching the door, a strong hand, firm in its grasp, grips Anna's arm, stopping her. Constable Jenkins has paused in his dealing of the cards, "The proprietress is leaving early tonight?"

"You are mistaken. Mr. Joiner now owns this establishment."

"Does he now? I suppose this means you'll be returning to your roots; hunting running through the Buchanan blood and all?"

"I will make ends meet for my family through carving and hunting, yes."

"Miss Buchanan, you've had some unfortunate luck, as have many of us, but don't risk any more misery by using the Davenport. One day I will hold it in my hands and it will not go well for you. Think of your brother and the future."

"Constable Jenkins, I know there are eyes and ears everywhere," out of the corners of Anna's eyes, and through the choking smoke hanging heavy in the room, Anna observes Mr. Archer ease back onto the stool, his expression is one of surprise as Nathaniel, standing behind the bar, pours drinks to those moving closer to better hear of an adventure. Anna catches a snippet, "The horror of the golden stairs..."[124] Then she says to the constable, "They may hear things in the night, but they will never see this mysterious gun you speak of, but who knows, one day you may indeed get to hold it."

Seth giggles, as only a child with a family secret will do.

----

124 The Golden Stairs. At the height of the 1898-99 Klondike gold rush, 100,000 set off for the Yukon Territory in northwestern Canada. To reach the gold fields, most stampeders chose to cross the Chilkoot Pass out of Dyea. The Golden Stairs, just below the pass was a steep trail covered with thick ice year round. Those who climbed it had to abandon their pack animals and carry their year's worth of supplies on their backs or pay porters to make the many trips. Step by step their boots made deep cuts in the ice or *stairs* in the endless trail. On April 3, 1898, after an exceptionally heavy snowfall, a series of avalanches struck the Chilkoot Pass trail killing dozens of impatient gold seekers who ignored the Indians' warnings against proceeding.

Venturesome ducks, mallards and canvasbacks, that fly through crisp air over the Buchanan shack in the late Saturday afternoon, lured there by Anna's Judas birds that incessantly call from their enclosure, witness a sight, a playful struggle, a humorous battle for dominance between brother and sister. The measure to be used in distinguishing winner over loser is who laughs loudest and the volume of water dripping from the jocular combatants—it is Seth's bath time.

Hauling three pails of water from the dunking barrel to the porch before the crackling fire beneath heats the water to boiling, Anna filled the new, steel wash tub, added two soap chips, and plopped Seth, naked and squirming into it. This was accomplished only after chasing him back and forth between the shack and bay, where if not for a quick snatch and grab by Anna, Seth would have taken his bath by way of a purposeful belly flop. Despite being saved from the frigid waters, goose bumps the size of cat-eye marbles covered Seth's pink skin, but he was too amused with their game to notice.

Seth sits belly deep in steaming water and popping bubbles, the bubbles not all created by the soap chips, but by toddler flatulence that further delights their maker, and which would smell sweet to a mother, but is a tad sour to a sister regardless of the depth of her love. Seth is making it his mission to drench Anna who washes his every nook and cranny. And not wanting a single family member to feel left out, Seth flings soapy drops as far as the open doorway, where Beauty sleeps exhausted, sprawled across the threshold, the morning hunt depleting her small reserve of energy.

The pile of 68 birds, still colorful in death with plumage that shimmers, reflecting the dancing orange, red, and blue flames, stacked neatly beside the dunking barrel, were 27 more than the grand old retriever was up for. Upon returning to shore, her gray coat matted and dripping chilly, carrying number 41, a fat drake canvasback within her mouth, Beauty placed it dutifully behind the hogshead blind with the others, and let loose air from within her lungs that came out as a wheeze. To Anna, this sighing defeat was a sign, an admittance by Beauty that her time of unending endurance was indeed past. The blindness in one eye causes Beauty to swim an indirect, almost sideways route to the bird that has been *knocked down*. If there is a fleeing cripple, Beauty's painful swollen joints make it impossible to chase the bird through the thick stands of cattails. Watching with a broken heart the distress Beauty suffered, Anna chose her shots with care, allowing the ducks out over the deeper, icy water to pass, and only pulling the trigger when the wildfowl would fall into her lap.

For some hunters, men especially, their working dogs are means to an end, a cog in the machinery that provides food and coin. These animals are penned when not in use, disciplined harshly for mistakes or disobedience, and when their usefulness has ended, they are dispatched with a shot to the back of the head. Hunters such as these see only a utilitarian purpose for their animals, ignorantly missing out on traits that all dogs will express freely and without regard for their master's character—companionship and loyalty. Some say it is love. The all-business hunter who grants himself the liberty of tenderness toward his retriever, within the boundaries of a firm work ethic, is rewarded. His gain is not only an excellent hunt, but affection that in other human to human relationships is difficult for a man to accept and return. No man is accused of being soft when he praises and scratches the ears of his dog.

It is because of their lifetime of affection, companionship, and freely admitted love that Anna rubbed Beauty's head, encouraging her to rest, while Anna climbed out of the fragrant hogshead barrel to retrieve the ducks that fell to her gun the remainder of the morning.

Believing he is victorious in the water wars, Seth holds up his arms to allow Anna to slide on his wool shirt before he jumps into his mini winter coveralls—a matching set to Anna's.

With care and nervous anticipation, Tim, in his pressed uniform, navigates the bank's automobile down the seldom-used drive to the Buchanan home. Having unintentionally kept the vehicle's keys before shipping out in service to his country, and it being a Saturday, Tim was able to *borrow* the vehicle, knowing that he could return it before anyone noticed it was missing. "The perfect plan," Tim says aloud.

Turning from tying Seth's boots, Anna's smile grows to a cheek-aching grin. With eyes sparkling in recognition of the approaching driver, Anna shouts, "Tim!"

Yanking on the emergency brake, Tim leaps from the cab, and extends his arms with the flair of a thespian milking his audience for another encore, "Yes, it is I, returned from battle, damaged but not broken." Half serious, half playful, Tim makes the sign of the cross with his hand, even though he is not a Catholic.

With five quick steps, and an embrace of relief by his safe return, Anna hugs Tim, surprising both by her exuberant affection. "I was so worried." Not wanting to embarrass Tim, Anna quickly releases him, and with a quick once-over inspection to see that he is indeed in one piece, she slugs him in his stomach. "Why did you stop writing?" Anna attempts a serious glare to impart displeasure, but all she can manage is crossed eyes over a cockamamie smirk, "I was worried sick."

Catching his breath after the sucker punch that leaves him bent over and holding his stomach, Tim gapes, with bulging eyes, saying with measured words, "I got shot..."

"Oh my god, Tim, I'm so sorry."

"...in my butt cheek," Tim grins with deviltry.

Believing Tim is joking, Anna slugs him in his shoulder, knocking him off balance, where he raises his arms in surrender. "I'm not kidding. Do you want to see the doctor's suture marks?"

The answer that wants to blurt from Anna's mouth is, "Hell yes!" but with agonizing restraint over her impulse and curiosity, wanting this older young man to know that she has manners, says instead, what to Anna sounds a bit stilted, out of character, and strained, "That wouldn't be proper, but please tell me all about it. Are you in pain?"

"Only when I'm punched in the stomach and shoulder," Tim says, his grin, again devilish, as he feels nothing but the warmth of Anna's welcoming hug.

Anna is about to apologize when Tim's eyes grow wide as he dashes around her to catch Seth who, in his traditional style, is leaping, belly flop, off the porch. His target is the pile of ducks that look so soft.

"Gotcha!"

"Seth!" Anna places her hands on her hips, "I've told you before. No one will buy smashed ducks." And then to Tim, says, "It seems like he has no ears as he never listens to me."

Tim holds up the kicking child, remembering with sadness the words in Anna's letter telling of Olivia's death, "So you're Seth."

"Yes, he's my brother," Anna relieves Tim of his burden and sits on the edge of the porch. "He's a nuisance but he's adorable."

Sitting down gently as his backside is still tender, Tim watches as Anna releases Seth to wobble about, and says, "He's a boy. A blessing and a curse. That's what my folks always say about me, but they'd add to tease me, 'He can chop wood so we'll keep him for a while.'"

"Seth can't chop wood yet, neither can he carve nor hunt, but I've decided to keep him with the hope that one day he'll be useful," Anna laughs as Seth completes his desired journey by falling onto the birds, reclining in a newly formed feathered chair. "How did you get shot in the butt?"

Tim shakes his head, rolling his eyes, "It happened on Armistice Day. We were marching back to camp after a stab at the Germans when word came that the war was over. Boys were jumping up and down, hugging each other, and some even broke down crying. It was a New Yorker; a city boy of course, who hadn't safetied his rifle. He dropped it in the celebration, and bang, shot me in my right cheek."

Anna stifles, not too successfully, giggles of amusement.

"It wasn't funny then," Tim begins to laugh, seeing in his mind's eye how he danced around holding his butt, and cursing the trembling boy.

"That doesn't explain why you're letters stopped."

Looking up as a flock of Canada geese noisily pass high overhead, Tim says softly, "The doctors said it was a mosquito bite[125] that nearly done me in."

Tim's ominous tone left no doubt that he told the truth, but still, Anna is astonished, because each summer, mosquitoes the size of red-wing blackbirds constantly bite those who dwell within the marsh, and nothing more than red, itchy bumps arise. "Your letters spoke of artillery, poison gas, rockets, and grenades exploding all around you; soldiers being cut down by machine gun fire, and some even drowning in trenches if they fell asleep during downpours. You survived all that to almost die from a mosquito?"

"I never saw the blood sucker, but the bite turned septic and it was touch and go. I credit my life to the one nurse at the field hospital who stayed by my side night and day. She read scripture, prayed over me, 'fighting the Angel of Death on my behalf,' she said, as she'd decided it wasn't my time. She was right, but after the delirium passed, I was weeks convalescing." Tim turns, rather boldly, to look into Anna's eyes, saying, "Your letters, the one's that found their way to me were honey on toast."

Embarrassed, Anna blushes, "They were just boring letters telling of the goings on around here."

Tim places his hand atop Anna's, "For a boy far from home, homesick, and ailing, the words carried," Tim stumbles for the appropriate words to express that emotion which language only diminishes, "courage, strength, and..."

The revving of a powerful V-8 engine interrupts Tim as a polished Cadillac[126] with wide, white-wall tires, a Town Limousine, that is chauffeur-driven, comes round the shack to park beside Tim's conveyance.

---

125 England's most famous young poet at the time, Rupert Brooke, was a lieutenant with the British Naval Division at Antwerp. He was inspired to write the patriotic verse: If I should die, think only this of me, that there's some corner of a foreign field that is forever England..." Six months later, Rupert was dead. He died from a mosquito bite that turned septic and gave him blood poisoning.

126 Cadillac Town Limousine, produced in 1918, was a four-door, six-seater with a 90 degree V-8 L head producing 31.25 horsepower. It weighed 4,295 pounds and, when introduced, the crème de la crème of luxury vehicles sold for $4,100 though there were several price increases during the war, partly due to war taxes.

"Oh dear Lord!"

Beauty opens her good eye at Tim's exclamation to access the new arrival.

"Who's that?" asks Anna, as the gloved chauffeur opens the limousine's door for his charge. The chauffeur's movements are smooth, practiced, and efficient as he holds out his arm to steady the cashmere-coated and top-hatted octogenarian until his cane can be stabbed into the soft black soil.

The color drains from Tim's face, leaving him ashen, and though a bead of sweat runs down his forehead, he shivers.

Taking careful steps toward the porch, a curious, quizzical expression of recognition crosses the old man's face. His keen eyes examine the parked automobile. He then scrutinizes Tim, whose expression acknowledges his goose is cooked. And lastly, looking upon the young lady, he realizes that she must be the impetus behind the grand theft. Leaning heavily on the black cane, its carved ivory handle hidden under his grip, the slender, slightly bent man remembers his own impulsive youth. He decides to give the returning soldier the break every lad deserves, at least once. "So, Mr. Ross, it's good to see you safely home, and that you've taken the initiative to test drive the bank's property to ensure it's road-worthy before resuming your duties."

"Uh...umm," the throbbing in Tim's temples prevent him from immediately understanding the words spoken to him.

"Confidence, lad. Ladies prefer confidence in their men, and as I have business with this young lady, I suggest you make your apologies, and return to Boston where I know you will polish to a mirror shine, that horseless carriage."

Stunned by the reprieve, Tim leaps to his feet, and to the amusement of the old man, and Anna's bewilderment, Tim shakes her hand as if they have concluded a business transaction, saying, "Forgive me, but I have to go."

Watching with a measure of envy at youthful infatuation as Tim drives away, the old man reminds himself of the reason for this detour on his way to the Wellwood Club. Extending his bony, liver-spotted hand, he says, "Miss Buchanan?" Anna nods. "My name is Leonard Crightington. I'm the president of the bank that holds the mortgage on this property."

A look of fear crosses Anna's face, "It's paid up! I have the receipts."

Gently, soothing as a grandfather would, he says, "It's okay. You are in good stead with the bank. I have come today to ask your forgiveness on behalf of the bank."

"I don't understand."

"May I sit?"

"Please."

Without a word spoken, the chauffeur produces a leather cushion stuffed plump for his employer to sit on as he eases himself down beside Anna.

"There is no excuse, and I'm not giving one, though it is an explanation for what should never have happened to you. The time leading up to this country entering the war was great in turmoil for financial institutions around the world. I felt it necessary to personally travel to England and Europe to coordinate and oversee financial aid to our allies. Unfortunately, in my absence, department heads came and went, paperwork was neglected and misplaced to the detriment of customers, you included."

Seth leaves his chair of wildfowl to crawl to Anna to be picked up, "Have you lost my payments?"

"No. All payments were properly credited. What was misplaced was your father's bond file and emergency instructions."

Anna settles Seth on her knee, bouncing to keep him occupied, "I don't know anything about bonds."

"They are investments that return an interest to increase your assets. The point is your father, regular as clockwork, bought bonds. His emergency instructions were, in the case of his premature death, that the bonds were to be sold and the proceeds used to pay off the mortgage, and to supply you with an income so that you'd never be destitute."

"You're saying that the bank made a mistake in sending the foreclosure notice?"

"I'm very sorry. Appropriate measures have been put in place so that this never happens again, and I was quite distressed to learn of your father's passing. You probably don't know this, but I hunted with your father long before you were a twinkle in your parents' eyes. He and his retriever, Rebel, I believe his name was, were a team second to none, the best guide and dog to ever work a rig if anyone asks my opinion." Mr. Crightington holds up his cane to reveal its ivory handle that is carved in the shape of a mallard's head. "Your father gave this to me as a present for approving his loan. I've cherished it ever since."

"It's beautiful." Running her fingers along the oily-smooth surface of the bill, and then up and over the head where the feather detail provides a slip-proof grip, Anna marvels once again at her father's skill.

"Nothing can replace your father, but because you've managed to make a living without using the bonds," Mr. Crightington withdraws a folded paper from inside his breast pocket and hands it to Anna, "you're in a financially good position. I've worked up the maturity figures and the bottom line is, you're quite well-off."

Anna scans the paper as Seth grabs a corner, less from curiosity and more from wanting to be involved in all family matters. The cotton rag paper, embossed with the bank's emblem, with neatly drawn lines and figures, represents the balance sheet of her father's life, and tangible evidence of his love for her, his sacrifice and commitment to provide for her needs if he could no longer do so. The many numbers after the dollar sign at the bottom of the page leave her speechless.

"What would you like me to do with the bonds?" asks Mr. Crightington.

"Do you need to know right now?"

"No. Of course not," replies Mr. Crightington, his old joints creaking as he rises to his feet, "You can write me directly with your decision, or," with a conspiratorial wink, "have Mr. Ross drive you in to Boston to meet with me personally. Again, I apologize, and my deepest condolences."

Settling into the back seat of the Cadillac, Mr. Crightington says to his chauffeur, "Beautiful piece of property...good husbandry."

Delbert's stealth within the marsh has allowed him to watch folk, who are unaware of his presence, doing the strangest things. Anna teases him, calling it despicable spying—Delbert calls it innocent observations. From the cover of the trees just outside the clearing in front of the Buchanan home, Delbert struggles to keep hold of the animal wiggling in his hands as he watches with rapt fascination the goings on in front of the shack. If it were not for the tollers constantly honking to call in their brethren he would be able to hear every word spoken between Anna and her unexpected guests, though if the geese were quiet it is likely that his presence would be betrayed by the furry bundle that gives an occasional yap.

Curious about the fuss made over the document that the ancient gentleman gave to Anna, Delbert is about to break from cover, but instinct, that has served him well in the past, urges him to stay put—watch and learn—the show may not be over.

Sitting on the edge of the porch, holding Seth with one arm, and the ledger in her hand, Anna stares, stunned by the columns and numbers, she is confused by the drops of water that sprinkle onto the paper, smearing the ink. Realizing that she is crying, feeling overwhelmed, and at the same time, ashamed that she ever questioned her father's love for her, Anna allows herself a good, heart-felt sob, and surprisingly, laughter from deep in her belly. "I'm such a silly girl," she says to Seth who stares wide-eyed, and unsure of the emotion he should be feeling.

Has something bad happened?

Did I miss a funny?

Has my sister lost her mind?

"What do we do now?" Anna asks as Seth reaches up to wipe the tears from her cheeks. Remembering words that seemed to make sense, Anna sets Seth down so she can climb up into her mother's rocking chair to think about her choices, decisions to be made, and the many possibilities. Anna looks again at the dollar amount at the bottom of the paper. doing the math in her head, her income from the cocktail decoys, the maturing bonds, and what will likely be erratic payments from the bar, the sum can change her life completely. It can allow Anna to remake her world. Then from above a rare sound, a harsh, laughing cackle causes Anna to look up. Flying, coasting on broad wings, a group, an extended family of 12 snow geese, heavy in meat, each in excess of 10 pounds, head in directly toward the shore in front of the shack. Their white feathers gleam, almost painful to Anna's eyes, as they reflect the sun falling in the west. The mighty birds show no fear as they follow the oldest gander, wings flaring, as wide, webbed feet lower to skim, skid, and then splash down in the shallows. Their brashness in landing mere yards from Anna, an easy shot from the porch, and their familial interaction while ignoring her, takes Anna's breath away.

From concealment, two other pairs of eyes watch the small flock. One set wishes he had brought his shotgun, as geese have become a rare treat, and snow geese, rarer still. The second pair of eyes are large and brown. They stare with intensity, a need to possess those mammoth creatures.

Anna turns her head left to right, and then back again to take in the full measure of her surroundings, that which encompasses her world. There is the old, weathered maple tree. It is a confidant, a co-conspirator in secreting and protecting the family treasure, but as its leaves turn fall colors of orange, red, gold, and brown in preparation for winter's shed, it may be relieved of this sinister responsibility. There is the marsh that extends out on each side, its oceans of waving grasses, stands of towering cattails hide secret trails, meandering streams, creatures and critters, and provide sustenance, shelter, and a playground for those who call it home. Farther back are the stands of old growth, of mighty oaks, pines with towering branches that seem to hold up the sky and provide platforms for passing eagles to rest upon. Mingled between these giants are sweet gum and chestnut trees that stretch wide to provide shade on sweltering summer days, and there are the slender birches, hardy in their resistance to the brackish waters of the swamps to provide stability against tidal pulls. And there is the bay itself, muddy brown and black at this time of the year. Regardless of its formal names: Chesapeake Bay, Susquehanna Flats, or Buzzards Glory, it is a mingling of above and below the shimmering, ripple-capped surface where skipjacks tack and jibe in the wind while their hearty crews tong the bottom. Scuttling around the grabbing tongs, blue crabs nibble on the falling detritus that is cascading down from above and snatched from the swirling current. And often heard but never seen is the sneak skiff punt gunner who pursues his skittish quarry. The bay is the heart, the pulsing beat that sustains all life, welcoming, enriching, and offering peace to everyone and everything without reservation or charge.

Scrutinizing the numbers at the bottom of the page with eyes that see clearly and with a broader, proper perspective of worth and value, Anna says to Seth who pokes with a crooked stick at the settling flames under the boiling barrel, "I've always been rich." Seth turns, grinning with a smirk and tilted head that reminds Anna of her father, and leaves no doubt that Seth is inwardly laughing at his big sister, but because of love and the inability to form the words, he refrains from saying, "You've just figured that out?"

The snow geese take flight, scared off by an approaching automobile that backfires through its tail pipe. Anna wonders if Tim is returning. Rattling, metal against metal and sliding on slender tires, the McQuay Buick comes to a smoking halt.

"William?" Anna is surprised by William's arrival today, the day of his father's funeral. Despite the inappropriateness, she is pleased, and suddenly aware that the affects of the explosion have made William even more handsome. The raw cuts and scratches to his face from the flying debris create a rugged air to his soft features. And then there is his auburn hair that today is windblown to devil-may-care perfections. Combined, they transform his flippant smile into a dazzling bewitchment that Anna quickly falls under.

That familiar rush of blood flushes Anna's cheeks as a surge of tingles caused by unchecked hormones cover her flesh with tiny bumps. Anna unconsciously licks her lips and whispers, "William." She tastes each letter as they flow across her tongue. They are sweet as she realizes that in his long absence, she has forgiven his past transgressions.

Adjusting his tailored mourning suit, he meets Anna halfway between the convertible and porch steps. Without a single word of: "Hello," "Glad to be home," or "You're a sight for sore eyes," but with the attitude of ownership and expectation, William embraces Anna, planting an open-mouth kiss that is returned as Anna collapses within his arms with a submitting sigh. In pursuit of his yearnings, his need for sexual relief, William slides his hand between their embrace to roughly squeeze Anna's right breast, hoping that this foreplay will be adequate to stimulate Anna to willingness without reservation or a second's thought. William's promiscuity abroad has taught him new tricks to teach his old dog. Out of courtesy he does not think of

Anna as old, neither would he equate the acts he wants to perform on her as debauchery, though he does require a submissive partner.

Interrupting the excitement growing within his creased trousers, an object falls against William's leg. "What the?" William looks down to see a toddler slumped against him. The child is using William's pant leg to grab hold of to pull himself back up. "Who is this?" William asks as he jerks his leg away from the child.

"That's Seth," Anna bends down to pick up her brother. "I told you about him in my letters."

William flashes back to his horse ride to fetch Doctor Webster, and vaguely, something written about Olivia and the Spanish flu. "Are you taking care of him?" William's displeasure by this small interloper distracting Anna and interfering with his plans is creased in the tight furrows lining his forehead.

"Of course, who else would? He's my brother."

If William's overall plan is to succeed, if he is to have unfettered access to Anna's charms, he will have to assign the care and feeding of this child to Nanna Maude, but until then, he will have to finesse Anna. "Well, you of course. I'm so mixed up at the moment. You could say frazzled. Burying my father this morning, I should be filled with grief, but all I feel is excitement, freedom, finally being my own man, and the first thing I wanted to do was to see you, to share this with you." As an actor drawing in his audience, William lowers his voice, hesitating between each word, "And to be with you after all these months. Anna, we don't have to hide anymore." William's enthusiasm, his infectious bravado returns, "We can be together whenever and wherever we want. We're adults with no parental supervision. We can choose for ourselves." Concluding his winning speech, William gently takes Seth from Anna, places him dismissively on the ground, and leads Anna toward the shack, his grip on her arm is firm, as he never forgets the old adage told to him by a wise man of challenged stature; take the lady, so in the morning she has the excuse that she did not go willingly.

Stepping onto the porch, William is confronted by his nemesis, Beauty, who stands, blocking the doorway. Stalling for time, and thinking of a way around the growling dog, William asks, remembering a question he had for Anna, "Who was that in the fancy car I saw pulling out of your drive?"

For a reason that is unknown to Anna, she deftly slides the ledger paper into her back pocket, and then using the truth to avoid a direct answer, says, "Just an old man asking for directions." Then smiling, her last best defense in Beauty who is unwavering in her protection, and silently agreeing with William that she can choose for herself, pulls back, saying, "That's a marriage bed. I've told you that before."

Frustrated, William confronts Anna, believing he can belittle her and break down her sudden resistance, "It's a lumpy bed with smelly covers," and then softening his tone, "but expecting you'd still be holding to sentimentality, I've asked Pastor Davies to meet us at my home in about an hour. I just thought we could have a pre-nuptial romp...on the floor if you insist."

Anna wants to both slap and hug William. He has insulted her and proposed marriage in the same breath. Anna's hesitation in answering prompts William to expand on what accepting his offer of matrimony would mean. "You'll live like a queen with servants at your beck and call. You'll have a different dress for each day of the week, and my home will now be yours."

"What about your mother? She'll never consent to our marriage."

"My mother is irrelevant. I'm the man of the house now, king of the castle. What I say goes."

Thinking of her own mother, Olivia, and Claire Joiner, each with distinguishing character and passions, Anna says, "I can't imagine any mother being irrelevant."

Knowing too well the many beatings he suffered that his mother ignored, or worse, denied they occurred, William bitterly replies, "Mine has been irrelevant for as long as I can remember, but if she makes a stink, we'll move out. We can leave this place and live in the city." William's mind pictures the basement rooms and the dance hall ladies, a bonus to city living, "You'll never have to hunt ducks or struggle to feed yourself. You can leave all this behind forever."

Anna's answer to William's proposal flashes, sparkling in her rich, burnt umber and sweet root beer eyes an instant before the corners of her lips curl upward.

William yelps with joy, "You'll never be sorry." Though, for himself, seeing that Anna is unflinching about the marriage bed and not budging toward the worn spot on the floor, he reluctantly accepts the fact that his needs will have to wait until after the "I do's." Planting a quick kiss on Anna's lips, William leaps off the porch, saying in his wake, "Be there in one hour." The devilish grin returns to his face. His crooked jaw speaking parting words of romance as he throws the Buick's shifter, grinding the gears, into position to drive off, "Then like every good wife, you'll never say no to me again."

Easing herself into the rocking chair, Anna listens as the Buick's rattle and bang fades into the distance, returning its owner to the other side of the road where at one time she wondered about the symbolic separation between the two sides, the two families, and could the road ever be crossed. The curl at the corner of her lips grows into a full grin as the long, sought-after answer gives her comfort. Anna calls out, "I know you're out there, Del. Come on out."

Emerging from concealment, with not a hint of shame for spying on his lifelong friend, Delbert saunters forward in his comical limping way to present Anna with his offering. "It's a runt, destined for a burlap-sack bath, until I thought of you." Delbert's nonchalant statement belies his tone of pleading for Anna to take on the challenge. Regardless of maturity, he cannot stomach killing for killing sake, or because something appears to be useless. Delbert holds out a golden Labrador retriever. The bundle twists, kicks, and nips to free itself from Delbert's clutches.

"She's gorgeous!" squeals Anna, as she accepts the puppy. It settles down, snuggling within Anna's arms. "She's mine?"

"If you want her. She'll have to be trained."

Anna sets the puppy down next to the rocker where it comes nose to nose with Beauty. The two retrievers, one weak and covered with gray fur, the other standing its ground on wobbling legs, inspect each other, sizing up the past and taking measure of the future.

"Del?"

"Anna?"

"Assuming you've been lurking in the bushes for some time, observing what has been going on here, I have a question for you. Do you want to come with me?"

Surprised at being asked, and teasingly offended, Delbert takes a step backward, almost falling off the porch, and huffs, "I never lurk, but to answer your question with a question, not admitting knowledge of anything gleamed from observations, you want me to accompany you to your wedding?"

The expression of hurt on Anna's face, the lowering of her gaze is momentary, as she replies, "What? Do you think I'm *that* much of an idiot?" Anna pauses for effect, and then says, "Have you seen the geese that are about today? I'm going hunting."

Leaving Delbert to work through his confusion, Anna steps past Beauty to retrieve the two shotguns and her shotgun shell bucket from inside her home. Like a whirlwind, Anna passes Delbert on the porch to release her Judas birds, saying, "Grab Gorgeous and Seth, will you?"

Together, the hunting party heads south, disappearing along the trail that leads to Swan Creek Point and the hogshead blind.

Lying quietly on the porch, Beauty makes no attempt to follow. Her eyes are closed. She becomes aware of Anna's return when the fur behind her ears is rubbed as only Anna knows how to do. Beauty opens her one good eye. The two females, friends, companions, and conspirators, look upon each other's faces, recognizing the changes the years have brought to each. The crisp, fall breeze, skimming across the wide bay ruffles Beauty's sagging fur and tosses loose strands of Anna's hair across a face that exudes confidence.

"You can rest ol' girl," Anna wipes away a tear, knowing that Beauty is relinquishing her responsibilities over the Buchanan family. She will never again accompany Anna to the blinds or out onto the Flats. Anna chokes back the emotion of loss, the inevitable pain. Her only solace is in knowing that like her mother, her father, and Olivia, Beauty will always be with her, in her heart, and a part of her daily life, "You've done your job well. I couldn't be prouder." Hugging Beauty and rubbing her face in Beauty's fur, reminiscent of when both were young and sleeping on the floor, Anna whispers, "Without you, I couldn't have survived, but I'll be okay."

For a time without minutes, the two watch a distant skipjack licking an unseen oyster bed. The sky, darkening with the lateness of the day, filling with gathering clouds that are pushed over the horizon by the rising wind, is filling with the calls and chatter, and the thundering wingbeats of thousands of waterfowl, ducks and geese returning on the approaching weather front. Struggling to her feet, Beauty crosses the threshold to sleep uninterrupted in front of the blazing potbelly stove. Anna does not turn to watch Beauty leave her side, but instead, seeking courage, inhales deeply to fill her lungs with the aroma, the essence of the marsh and bay.

Bang! Bang! Bang!

A smile slowly forms on Anna's lips as the shotgun reports echo across the marsh. Rising, she darts off the porch to catch up. Anna knows that wildfowl wait on no one, and neither will Delbert, who is the embodiment of what is best in all hunting partners.

Epilogue

Rebel, Clay's Chesapeake retriever, did not freeze to death or drown on that winter's night. He drifted south on his island of ice to be found half starved and unconscious along the Eastern Shore, 25 miles south of Spesutie Island. The hunter who found Rebel was returning from visiting relatives who lived along the Sassafras River. Believing that the retriever's owner was dead, or if not, should be, for allowing a fine animal to come to such a state, placed Rebel in the back of his wagon, and then nursed him back to health as they traveled to the hunter's home on Smith Island, which is located near the mouth of the Chesapeake Bay.

Being loyal to his savior, Rebel remained with the hunter, rising to the level of legend status with his retrieving skills. Throughout his long life, Rebel sired many generations of prized ofspring. Each learned a behavioral quirk from Rebel, which in turn they taught to their pups. On nights when ice flowed on the bay and snow filled the sky, they would go to the water's edge to howl, either waiting for a reply that never comes, or to call a warning to stay focused on the task at hand.

William was first embarrassed, and then became angry when Anna did not appear at his home for the impromptu wedding. Waylaid by his inconsolable mother, he was confined to the house until Monday morning. As William was preparing to leave, he was met in his driveway by Constable Jenkins, two deputies, and a smartly-dressed young man who identified himself as a messenger from a bank in New York. Constable Jenkins, in his most business-like demeanor, informed the new head of the household that the bank had concluded foreclosure proceedings, and he was there to evict the occupants of the house. With no savings of his own, and finding that his father's accounts registered zero, he sold several pieces of his mother's jewelry to pay for passage to his mother's cousin's family home in Savannah, Georgia, where Daisy Gordon, Mrs. Juliette Gordon Low's niece took them in.

Returned to her southern roots, Dorothy Parker McQuay was surrounded by Negroes and she believed they all knew she had been responsible for her playmate's death. Paralyzed with fear she remained within her assigned room, allowing admittance only to those of good breeding.

William mistook Daisy Gordon's hospitality as infatuation, and while the two cousins were on a stroll, he attempted to take her in the Biblical way; confident that her screams and pleadings were so that in the morning she would have the excuse that she did not give him her charms willingly, she being a lady.

Fortunately, a local lad named Mr. Lawrence, who was hunting squirrels and within earshot of the assault, came running to Daisy's aid. Mr. Lawrence, in defense of Miss Daisy's honor, thrashed William to within an inch of his life. He then threatened to kill William if he did not leave town immediately. William dragged himself off into the woods, where in the ensuing years, his late-stage syphilis caused insanity, and he became known as the Wild Man of the Woods. Local parents would scare their children into obedience, saying, "If you're not good, the Wild Man of the Woods will get you."

Using as an excuse his concern for Daisy's recovery, Mr. Lawrence began courting her, and after asking permission of Daisy's father, proposed marriage that was happily accepted.

After the eviction was served on the McQuay household, Roman spoke privately with the bank's messenger, who gladly helped Roman to purchase 10 acres at the northernmost corner of the McQuay property. Roman built a modest home for Nanna Maude and himself. Roman never disclosed where he had acquired the money for the purchase and construction, and when Nanna Maude confronted him about it, all Roman would say was, "It's between me and God."

Eight days after Beauty relinquished her responsibilities over the Buchanan family, Anna awoke to find Gorgeous whimpering next to Beauty. From the bedroom doorway, Anna allowed her tears to flow freely. It was apparent that Beauty was sleeping too peacefully in front of the potbelly stove. The stove's embers, as with Beauty's life, had turned gray and gone out. Expecting a visit from Tim, and it being Sunday, a day when town folk would be in church, leaving no witnesses, Anna enlisted Tim in a conspiracy to bury Beauty next to her father at Angel Hill Cemetery. The two ancient Negro grave diggers, sitting in their shed sipping he-man coffee, grinned as they loaned Tim a shovel, secretly knowing that more than one favorite retriever had been buried in family plots.

Tim continued to visit Anna, always admiring her independence, and never once feeling intimidated by her abilities, innate or taught, as some men do when faced with an intelligent and resourceful woman. Anna never violated her marriage bed rule, but occasionally she weakened, not under Tim's force or pleadings, as he would never stoop to these ploys, but because of natural yearnings to be held by a caring man. Delbert, with his stealth, was witness to one of these tender couplings. He sat quietly, chewing on a grass stem, happy for his hunting partner.

In retirement, Judge Jeremiah P. Hathaway, began working with Dr. George W. Archer at the Harford County Historical Society. On Christmas day, the two men reported to Constable Jenkins that there had been a break-in at the Society's museum. Upon investigation, the men discovered that no items had been taken, and in fact, there had been an addition. Held in Constable Jenkins' hands was a mysterious punt gun. Its donor remained anonymous. However, several mornings each winter, following nights when clouds hung low, heavy with snow, and the ice floes crunched against each other on the Flats, when Dr. Archer or Judge Hathaway would unlock the Society's front door, they would find that a window had been jimmied open. The air in the room had the smell of burnt black powder and stacked in front the display of punt guns would be a brace of ducks tied drake to hen. These break-ins were never reported.

The 18th Amendment to the United States Constitution was ratified on January 16, 1919. The prohibition of alcohol took effect one year later. In an attempt to save his business, Nathaniel Joiner built a still deep in the birch swamp. Unlucky for Nathaniel, while constructing the still, he dropped the pressure release valve in the muck and failed to properly clean it. The still exploded, killing Nathaniel.

Luck sighed, because Nathaniel had been an entertaining project, but time was running out. Nathaniel could have died of natural causes. How boring would that be? No adventure in it at all.

Learning of Nathaniel's death, the Grossos offered to take over Tavern Bouvard, paying Anna monthly from the profits. When Anna asked how they would make any money running a bar when alcohol was illegal, they smiled, wiggling their giant mustaches, and with twinkling eyes, Jack Sr. said, "We know people in New York, and Jack Jr. is no longer smuggling ducks."

Doctor Webster, brokenhearted after his wife's passing, tried to battle through his depression by working himself to exhaustion at the Harford County Hospital. One year to the date of Martha's death, a hospital orderly was sent to the Webster's home as the doctor had failed to show for his rounds. Doctor Webster was found deceased in his bed. The orderly contacted Constable Jenkins only after disposing of the empty bottles of laudanum he found on the doctor's dresser.

Doctor Webster's funeral was attended by the entire population of Harford County, most of whom the doctor had helped into the world.

Umbrella George was seen less and less as the years past. When asked about his absences, his reply was, "I've sold Bibles to just about everyone in the state. Now it's up to folk to use them. I'm working my way out west as I hear it's a wild place that is in need of heavenly guidance."

Madison Mitchell returned to Havre de Grace in 1920, receiving his embalmer's license in 1922. In 1924 Madison decided to supplement his income by carving decoys for Samuel Barnes. After Samuel died of pneumonia in 1926, Madison handled the funeral, and then opened his own decoy manufacturing shop behind the funeral parlor on Washington Street.

Realizing that his crush on Anna Buchanan was merely a youthful infatuation, Madison fell in love with and married Helen Maslin. Their marriage lasted until her death in 1973.

Madison Mitchell passed away on January 14, 1993, at age 91. He was laid to rest next to his beloved in Angel Hill Cemetery.

James A. Currier, "Jim" to his friends, continued to work for the post office and eventually became the postmaster. In his off hours, Jim carved decoys, hunted, and guided for sports, acquiring a 35-foot "Sharpie" as a gunning yacht to take the well-heeled and free-spending gentlemen out onto the Flats.

James Currier passed away in 1969. His funeral was handled by his close friend, Madison Mitchell.

After World War I, Millard Tydings returned to Havre de Grace as a war hero. He was awarded the Army Distinguished Service Medal and the Distinguished Service Cross. He married Eleanor Davies Cheesborough Tydings Davies who was the daughter of United States Ambassador to the USSR, Joseph E. Davies. Encouraged to enter politics, Chief, running as a Democrat, was elected to the Maryland State House of Delegates (1920-22), the Maryland State Senate (1922-23), the United States Congress for Maryland's 2nd (1923-27), and United States Senator for Maryland (1927-51). Chief lost his senatorial seat in 1950 to a Republican challenger, John Marshall Butler. John Butler was supported by Senator Joseph McCarthy, who Chief had opposed during the red-baiting era. Chief abhorred Senator McCarthy's witch hunts for communist spies because they ruined careers and reputations on unfounded accusations. Chief died February 9, 1961 and was buried in Angel Hill Cemetery.

The enactment of state and federal laws to curb abusive hunting, and their enforcement by tireless game wardens, helped prevent the ducks and geese from going the way of the passenger pigeon. Unfortunately, the loss of wetlands habitat to development and the use of pesticides, continued the decline of waterfowl and other avian species. In the latter half of the twentieth century, non-profit organizations, working alone and then with hunters, landowners, and state and federal governments, have purchased, set aside, and restored traditional wetlands along the North American flyways, and restricted excessive pesticide use. The goal is to provide safe areas for waterfowl of all species to rest, feed, and produce the next generation.

Hunters, through the purchase of licenses, contribute financially to the efforts of those involved in bringing the wildfowl back to the numbers that Christopher Columbus and the early settlers experienced. Unfortunately, and surprisingly, hunters are declining, being replaced by lovers of wildlife who shoot only with cameras that do not require the purchase of licenses.

To continue the good work of restoration, the author encourages everyone who enjoys nature, in all its wondrous forms, to contribute in the manner that best fits their abilities. Whether it is donating money to a non-profit of their choice, volunteering time, being aware and reducing their own negative impact on nature, or simply picking up a piece of litter that did not make it to the trash bin, every little bit helps.

Worthy Organizations of Interest

International Wildfowl Carvers Association
www.iwfca.com

Ducks Unlimited
www.ducks.org

Havre de Grace Decoy Museum
www.decoymuseum.com

National Audubon Society
www.audubon.org

The Nature Conservancy
www.nature.org

Sierra Club
www.sierraclub.org

Bibliography

Books:

Basile, Kenneth, and Doerzbach, Cynthia. *American Decorative Bird Carving.* Maryland: Ward Foundation, 1981.

Clark, Carolyn M, Editor. Photography by Harp, David W., Essays by Horton, Tom. *Water's Way, Life Along the Chesapeake.* Montgomery, Alabama: Elliot & Clark Publishing, 1992.

Earnest. Adele. *The Art of the Decoy.* New York, New York: Bramhall House, MCMLXV.

Elman, Robert. *The Atlantic Flyway.* Tulsa, Oklahoma: Winchester Press, 1980.

Fleckenstein, Henry A. Jr. *Decoys of the Mid-Atlantic Region.* Atglen, Pennsylvania: Schiffer Publishing, Ltd., 1979.

Goetz, Philip W., Editor-in-Chief with editorial advice of the University of Chicago. *The New Encyclopedia Britannia,* 15th Ed. U.S.A.: Encyclopedia Britannica, Inc., 1990.

Gresham, Grits. *The Complete Wildfowler.* New York, New York: Winchester Press, 1973.

Groom, Winston. *A Storm in Flanders, The Ypres Salient, 1914-1918, Tragedy and Triumph on the Western Front.* New York, New York: Atlantic Monthly Press, 2002.

Harrison, Colin, and Greensmith, Alan. Editorial Consultant Mark Robbins. Editor Edward Bunting. *Birds of the World.* New York, New York: DK Publishing, Inc., 1993.

Holly, David C. *Steamboat on the Chesapeake, Emma Giles* and the Tolchester Line. Centreville, Maryland: Tidewater Publishers, 1987.

Keith, Caroline H. *For Hell and a Brown Mule: The Biography of Senator Millard E. Tydings.* Lanham, Maryland: Madison Books, 1991.

Kimball, David and Jim. *The Market Hunter.* Minneapolis, Minnesota: Dillon Press, 1969.

McGeveran, William A. Jr. Editorial Director. *The World Almanac and Book of Facts 2006.* New York. New York: World Almanac Education Group, Inc., 2006.

McKinney, J. Evans. *Decoys of the Susquehanna Flats and Their Makers.* Ocean City, Maryland: Decoy Magazine, 1978.

Meanley, Brooke. *Waterfowl of the Chesapeake Bay County.* Centreville, Maryland: Tidewater Publishers, 1982.

Ransom, John L. *John Ransom's Andersonville Diary.* Forest Dale, Vermont: Paul S. Eriksson, Publisher, 1986. New York, New York: Berkley Books, published by The Berkley Publishing Group, a member of Penguin Putnam Inc., 1994.

Richardson, Robert H,, General Editor. Contributors: Bull, Roy; Chesser, Grayson; Fleckenstein, Henry; Pratt, Norris E.; Richardson, Robert H.; Rue, Ronald; Vallianl, J. Newman; Williamson, F. Phillips. *Chesapeake Bay Decoys, The Men Who Made and Used Them.* Burtsonsville, Maryland: Decoy Magazine, 1991.

Sullivan, C. John. *Waterfowling on the Chesapeake 1819-1936.* Baltimore, Maryland: The Johns Hopkins University Press, 2003.

Walsh, Harry M. *The Outlaw Gunner.* Centreville, Maryland: Tidewater Publishers, 1971.

Williams, John Page Jr. *Chesapeake Almanac, Following the Bay through the Seasons.* Centreville, Maryland: Tidewater Publishers, 1993.

Magazine Articles:

Armistead, Henry T. *Why Not Spot A Red Knot?* Bariette, Ohio: Bird Watcher's Digest, March/April 2008.

Magoon, Doug. *How Wash Barnes lost his big gun.* Burtonsville, Maryland: Decoy Magazine, September/October 1993.

Pass, Aaron Fraser. *Evolution of the Shotshell, The earliest shotshells received a dubious welcome from, waterfowlers.* Memphis, Tennessee: Ducks Unlimited, July/August 2007.

Quarstein, John V. R. *Madison Mitchell, The Dean of the Havre de Grace Decoy Makers.* Burtonsville, Maryland: Decoy Magazine, January/February 1993.

Sullivan, John C. *Samuel Treadway Barnes, A maker of practical decoys.* Burtonsville, Maryland: Decoy Magazine, March/April 1993.

Sullivan, John C. *The Era of the Sinkbox.* Burtonsville, Maryland: Decoy Magazine, November/December 1995.

Trimble, James L. *R. Madison Mitchell, The Chesapeake's dominant decoy maker.* Burtonsville, Maryland: Decoy Magazine, January/February 2007.

Young, Matt. *Landmark Waterfowl Conservation Laws.* Memphis, Tennessee: Ducks Unlimited, March/April 1995.

Website Articles:

1918.pandemicflu.gov/your-state/Massachusetts.htm (Author Unknown). *The Great Pandemic, The United States in 1918-1919, Massachusetts.* United States Department of Health and Human Services. Retrieved on 9/3/2008.

1918.pandemicflu.gov/your-state/marvland.htm (Author Unknown). *The Great Pandemic, The United States in 1918-1919, Maryland.* United States Department of Health and Human Services. Retrieved on 9/3/2008.

en.wikipedia.org (Author Unknown). *Havre de Grace, Maryland.* Retrieved on 2/29/2008.

en.wikipedia.org/wiki/Agistroden-contortrix (Author Unknown). *Agkistroden contortrix.* Retrieved on 8/27/2007.

en.wikipedia.org/wiki/Canada-goose (Author Unknown). *Canada Goose.* Retrieved on 3/1/2008.

en.wikipedia.org/wiki/Chesapeake-Bay (Author Unknown). *Chesapeake Bay.* 4/18/2008. Retrieved on 4/21/2008.

en.wikipedia.org/wiki/Ladeview-Gusher (Author Unknown). *Lakeview Gusher.* 4/22/2008. Retrieved on 4/21/2008.

en.wikipedia.org/wiki/Taft-California (Author Unknown). *Taft, California.* Retrieved on 5/19/2008.

everglades.fiu.edu/reclaim/bios/bradley.htm Clement, Gail. *Reclaiming the Everglades Biographies: Guy Bradley.* Publication of Archival Library & Museum Materials. Retrieved on 6/17/2008 and provided courtesy of Patti Colby, The Observer. The Observer Group, Inc.

explorenorth.com/library/yafeatures/bl-chilkoot3.htm Lundberg, Murray. *Reliving the Klondike on the Chilkoot Trail.* 1998-2005. Retrieved on 5/19/2008.

library.thinkquest.org/J002229F/sunkenships/titanictheunsinkableship.htm (Author Unknown). *Titanic*. Retrieved on 11/7/2007.

trucks.about.com Wickell, Dale. *A Ford Truck Timeline*. Retrieved on 7/5/2007.

virus.stanford.edu/uda/Billings, Molly. *The Influenza Pandemic of 1918*. June 1997 modified RDS February 2005. Retrieved on 9/3/2008.

www.100megsfree4.com/cadillac/cadl9l0/cadl8s.htm (Author Unknown). *1918 Cadillac*. May 11, 2000; March 8/03. Retrieved on 7/5/2007.

www.4woman.gov/FAQ/stdsyph.html (Author Unknown). *Syphilis*. United States Department of Health & Human Services. Retrieved on 5/19/2008.

www.acepilots.com/wwi/lafayette.html (Author Unknown). *Lafayette Escadrille, American Volunteer Pilots in WWI*. Retrieved on 2/15/2008.

www.antique-pocket-watch.com/Datek-philippe-pocket-watch-html (Author Unknown). *Antique Pocket Watch, The Patek Philippe Pocket Watch*. Retrieved on 9/3/2008.

www.aviationtrivia.info/vonRichthofen.php (Author Unknown). *Aviation Trivia: Manfred von Richthofen (The Red Baron)*. Retrieved on 9/3/2008.

www.beach-net.com/horseshoe/Dayhorsecrab.html (Author Unknown). *Horseshoe Crabs The Ancient Mariners*. Retrieved on 2/15/2008.

www.copperheadsnakesinfo/bite.php (Author Unknown). *Copperhead Snake*. 2006. Retrieved on 8/27/2007.

Manning, Lona. *9/16 Terrorists Bomb Wall Street*. Crime Magazine, an encyclopedia of crime. 1/15/2006. Retrieved on 11/3/2008.

www.encyclopedia.com/doc/lG2-2536601695.html (Author Unknown). *The Klondike Gold Rush*. Gale Group, a Thomson Corporation Co. 1997. Retrieved on 11/3/2008.

www.firstworldwar.com/poetsandprose/baimsfather.htm Duffy, Michael. *Prose & Poetry—Bruce Bairnsfather*. Updated 1/16/2002. Retrieved on 8/2/2008.

www.firstworldwar.com/weaponry/machineguns.htm Duffy, Michael. *Weapons of War: Machine Guns*. Updated 5/3/2003. Retrieved on 8/2/2008.

www.harfordhistory.net/archhshcmar01.htm Magness, Marlene, *Overview of the Collection of the Archives of the Historical Society of Harford County*. 3/29/2001. Retrieved on 11/3/2008.

www.harfordhistory.net/timeline2.htm (Author Unknown). *The Historical Society of Harford County, Inc., Harford County Chronology of Events, 1900 to the Present.* Retrieved on 9/10/2007.

www.harrietquimby.org Giacinta Bradley. *Harriet Quimby.* Retrieved on 9/9/2007.

www.ichef.com/recipe.cfm (Author Unknown). *Snapper Turtle Soup.* Retrieved on 7/4/2007.

www.ideaFinder.com/history/inventors/hoffmann.htm (Author Unknown). *Felix Hoffmann.* Retrieved on 11/7/2007.

www.jhsph.edu/publichealthnews/magazine/archives/MagFall04/prologues/index.html Duffy, Jim. *The Blue Death.* Johns Hopkins Public Health, Fall 2004. Retrieved on 9/3/2008.

www.keynux.com/titanic/facts.htm Sadur, James E. *Titanic: Facts & Figures.* Updated: 12/18/2005. Retrieved on 11/7/2007.

www.mdmunicipal.org (Author Unknown). *Havre de Grace.* Retrieved on 2/29/2008.

www.niehs.nih.gov/kids/lyrics/spangle.htm (Author Unknown). *Star Spangled Banner.* Retrieved on 7/9/2007.

www.nndb.com/people/972/000054810/ (Author Unknown). *Millard E. Tydings.* Soylent Communications, 2008. Retrieved on 6/25/2008.

www.petersen.org (Author Unknown). *1912 Buick Model 35 Touring Car.* 2007 Petersen Automotive Museum. Retrieved 7/5/2007.

www.poodlehistory.org/hawker.htm (Author Unknown). *Lt. Col. Peter Hawker.* Retrieved on 6/25/2008.

www.postalmuseum.si.edu/gold/skagdyea.html (Author Unknown). *Banking on Stampeders, Dyea vs. Skagway.* Retrieved on 11/3/2008.

www.sandhurstjuniors.oral.history.htm (Author Unknown). *Sandhurst Junior School, History.* Retrieved on 8/2/2008.

www.theaerodrome.com/aces/canada/brown3.php (Author Unknown). *Roy Brown—The Aerodrome—Aces and Aircraft of World War I. The Aerodrome, 1997-2008.* Retrieved on 9/3/2008.

www.titanic-passengers.com/harperleitch.html (Author Unknown). *Titanic Passengers. Information regarding Titanic's passengers & crew: Jessie Leitch, John and Nina Harper.* Retrieved on 11/7/2007.

www.tnc.org/infield/species/oldprofiles/leatherback/ (Author Unknown). *Leatherback Turtle. The Nature Conservancy,* 1997. Retrieved on 2/19/2001.

www.traphof.org/inductees/kimble-fred.htm (Author Unknown). *National Trapshooting Hall of Fame: Honored Inductees, Fred Kimble.* Retrieved on 7/5/2007.

www.traphof.org/roadtoyesterday/may2001.htm Baldwin, Dick. *The Road to Yesterday, Fred Kimble.* Trap & Field, May 2001. Retrieved on 7/5/2007.

www.voanews.com Chakarian, Vivian. *Bessie Coleman was the First African-American Female Pilot.* 10/22/05. Retrieved on 12/11/2007.

www.wildbirds.org/apidesay.htm (Author Unknown). *Extinction of the American Passenger Pigeon, The True Story.* Original essay, "PASSENGER PIGEON: Ectopistses Migratorius (Linnaeus)" by Edward Howe Forbush in "Game Birds, Wild-Fowl and Shore Birds." Massachusetts Board of Agriculture. Reprinted in Birds of America. T. Gilbert Pearson, Editor-in-Chief, copyright 1917, by The University Society Inc.; copyright 1936, by Garden City Publishing Company, Inc. pages 39-46. Retrieved on 7/5/2007.

www.yukonalaska.com/communities.carerosshist.html Spotswood, Ken. *The History of Carcross, Yukon Territory. 1998-2007.* Retrieved on 5/19/2008.

www.yukonalaska.com Lundberg, Murray. Yukon & Alaska Genealogy Centre. 1997-2006. Retrieved on 5/19/2008.

Miscellaneous:

1925 Fall Catalog and *1928 Spring Catalog*, L.L. Bean MFGR. Freeport, Maine: L.L. Bean, 1925, 1928. Provided by C. Gardner Land, L.L. Bean, Inc. Corporate Archives, 9-15-95.

Georgano, Nick. RAUCH & LANG. *"The beaulieu encyclopedia of the Automobile."* Brochure courtesy of the Nethercutt Collection: The Cars of San Sylmar, 2007.

Girl Scouts of the U.S.A. (archival research). Historic Information provided courtesy of Yevgeniya Gribov, Archivist, National Historic Preservation Center, Girl Scouts of the U.S.A., 6-24-08; 7-8-08; 7-25-08.

Highlights in Girl Scouting 1912-1991. (Author Unknown). New York, New York: Girl Scouts of the U.S.A. Date of publication unknown. Provided courtesy of Ameeta Kumar, Archives & Records Technician, National Historic Preservation Center, Girl Scouts of the U.S.A., 9-6-95.

Juliette Gordon Low, Founder, Girl Scouts of the U.S.A. Biographical Sketch. (Author Unknown). Media Services, 2/86. Provided courtesy of Ameeta Kumar, Archives & Records Technician, National Historic Preservation Center, Girl Scouts of the U.S.A., 9-6-95.

Shulkin, Cathy. *Girl Scout Movement on the Rise.* Nostalgia Magazine. Date of publication unknown. Provided courtesy of Ameeta Kumar, Archives & Records Technician, National Historic Preservation Center, Girl Scouts of the U.S.A., 9-6-95.

U.S. Fish & Wildlife Services. *Endangered & Threatened Species of the Southeast United States, Reptiles, Leatherback Sea Turtle.* 1991.

Wyatt, Ken. Ransom notes. Jackson, Michigan: Jackson Citizen Patriot (Newspaper), 8-18-2002. Provided courtesy of N. Buckland, Reference Librarian, Jackson District Library. Jackson, Michigan, 6-9-2008.

Made in the USA
Lexington, KY
23 December 2010